THE ODYSSEY OF
JUDICIAL CORRUPTION

BARBARA WASHINGTON FRANKLIN, ESQ.

BOOKS ACADEMY
LEARNING LIFE FROM EVERY PAGE

Books Academy LLC
112 SW H K Dodgen Loop,
Temple, Texas 76504
Hotline: (254) 800-1189

Ordering Information:
Quantity sales. Special discounts are available on quantity purchases by corporations, associations, and others. For details, contact the publisher at the address above.

Printed in the United States of America.

ISBN-13:		
	Softcover	978-1-964929-31-6
	eBook	978-1-964929-32-3
	Hardback	978-1-966567-44-8

Library of Congress Control Number: 2024919442

MEMORIAL DEDICATION

TO MOTHER

This literary work is dedicated to the memory of my beloved mother, "Mother," Eunice Vetta Ross Washington, who went home to be with the Lord in August 2022.

Mother forever encouraged me to spend more time on my writing. She saw this finished work long before I did. Thank You Mother.

TO DADDY

This literary work is also dedicated to the memory of my beloved father, "Daddy," Robert Benjamin Washington, who went home to be with the Lord in April 1977, two months after I arrived in Washington and began work on Capitol Hill as Minority Chief Counsel and Staff Director for the U.S. House Committee on the District of Columbia.

Daddy always taught me that truth crushed to the ground would rise again. I have lived long enough to confirm the truth of Daddy's wisdom. Thank You Daddy.

TO MAMA

Additionally, I dedicate this literary work to my beloved paternal grandmother, "Mama," Rosa Lee Bradley Washington Terry, who went home to be with the Lord in August 1995.

It was Mama who introduced me to the Master at the tender age of approximately 6 years old. She also permitted me to accompany her to prayer meetings and love feasts on Wednesday evenings at the St. Luke A.M.E. Church on Prince Street in Newark, New Jersey. Thank You Mama.

TO ELDER WASHINGTON

I dedicate this literary work to my paternal grandfather," Elder Washington," the Reverend Andrew Washington, a Presiding Elder in the African Methodist Episcopal Church in the State of Georgia, whom I never had the pleasure of knowing, and who was referred to by his formal ministerial title by my parents and grandmother. Elder Washington went home to be with the Lord in the early 1940's. I look forward to meeting Elder Washington in person in Glory. Thank You Elder Washington.

TO HARDY

And lastly, I dedicate this literary work to my beloved husband, Dr. Hardy R. Franklin, who went home to be with the Lord in August 2004. I shall be forever grateful to Hardy for his unstinting and unqualified support of my career as a successful Black female solo trial attorney in Washington, D.C., especially his encouragement and support in our resolve that I maintain my participation in the court litigation that is the subject of this judicial expose'. Thank You Hardy.

BARBARA WASHINGTON FRANKLIN

ACKNOWLEDGEMENTS

The years' long journey involved in the creation and completion of the manuscript that produced this literary work could not have been accomplished without the love, support, prayers and encouragement of the members of my beloved family, especially my daughter, Regan Alexandria Hayes Perry, and her relentless and invaluable encouragement needed to bring this literary project to the finish line; my grandson, brothers, nieces and nephews, their respective families, cousins on both sides of my family, my beloved family through marriage, lifetime family friends and supporters, lifetime girlfriends, spiritual mentors, confidants, professional colleagues and associates, members of my beloved church family and brothers and sisters in Christ.

My eternal gratitude to all of you is beyond measure.

ABOUT THE AUTHOR

Barbara Washington Franklin was born in Blakely, Georgia, the oldest of three children and the only daughter, to Eunice Vetta Ross Washington and Robert Benjamin Washington. Barbara was reared by her parents and paternal grandmother in Newark, New Jersey. She received her elementary and secondary education in the Newark Public School System. Barbara was the Valedictorian of her graduating class at Cleveland Junior High School. She is also an honors graduate of Barringer High School. Barbara accepted Jesus Christ as her Lord and Savior at six years of age, under the mentorship of her paternal grandmother, Rosa Lee Bradley Washington Terry. Barbara was also a child classical pianist and participated with honorable mention in Newark's Annual Griffith Piano Auditions.

During her junior year at Barringer High School, at the suggestion of two of her teachers, Barbara entered an essay contest open to all Newark Public High School Students. The contest was created and sponsored by the Newark Chapter of the United Nations Association . As a contest finalist, Barbara was awarded a 56-Day-Trip-Around-The-World. She traveled on the trip as an American Youth Goodwill Ambassador along with four other Newark High School Students and an adult chaperone. The group visited 18 foreign capitals throughout Europe, the Middle East, Far East and Asia. In preparation for this auspicious trip, Barbara and her fellow youth ambassadors were mentored by former First Lady Eleanor Roosevelt in her New York City Offices.

Barbara is a civil trial attorney in Washington, D.C. She is a member of the New York and District of Columbia Bars. She earned the degree of Juris Doctor from the Rutgers University Law School in Newark. She is also a graduate of Douglass College for Women, a Division of Rutgers University in New Brunswick, New Jersey where she majored in Sociology and Psychology. Prior to her graduation from Rutgers University Law School, she was recruited by the Managing Attorney for the New York City Corporation Counsel, Mr. Ed Mallon, to serve as an attorney in its General Litigation Division. In that capacity, she was tasked with the duty of periodically answering the court calendar in New York Supreme Court on behalf of the City of New York. Barbara also served as an attorney in the trial division of the New York City Corporation Counsel.

Following her career as a Commercial Broadcast Standards Editor with the New York City Headquarters Office of NBC (The National Broadcasting Company), she relocated to Washington, D.C. after being appointed the Minority Chief Counsel and Staff Director for the U.S. House Committee on the District of Columbia. Thereafter, she served as the Assistant City Administrator for Intergovernmental Relations for the District of Columbia. Following her federal and local government service, she fulfilled a childhood dream and launched a solo law practice and office in the Chevy Chase Pavilion in Upper Northwest Washington, D.C.

Prior to her career as an attorney, Barbara served as a Foster Care, Adoption and Hospital Social Worker. She also served as an elementary school teacher in the Newark and Philadelphia Public School Systems. She has served as a Peace Corps member in India and is a world traveler. Barbara is a member of Alpha Kappa Alpha Sorority, Inc. She is the mother of one adult daughter and the grandmother of one adult grandson. Barbara is a lifetime practicing Christian and a published author. Barbara Washington Franklin is a resident of Washington, D.C.

BARBARA WASHINGTON FRANKLIN

For a great door and effectual is opened unto

me, and there are many adversaries.

1 Corinthians 16:9 (KJV)

THE ODYSSEY OF JUDICIAL CORRUPTION

First they ignore you.

Then they laugh at you.

Next they fight you.

Then you win.

Mahatma Gandhi

AUTHOR'S NOTE

This story is, in all respects, completely true. However, pursuant to my literary prerogative as an author, I have chosen to use pseudonyms, with certain exceptions, for all individuals and entities portrayed, profiled or referred to herein.

The allegations that comprise this true story are verified by the Superior Court of the District of Columbia official transcripts of court proceedings and case records; the State of Florida Broward County Circuit Court official transcripts of court proceedings and case records; and my extensive legal files regarding the respective State of Florida and District of Columbia lawsuits that are the subject of this spiritual memoir and expose' of judicial corruption.

All Scripture citations are taken from the King James Version of the Bible and marked KJV.

TABLE OF CONTENTS

PREFACE

"The Odyssey of Judicial Corruption" is the exposure and examination of a polished, sanitized and corrupt D.C. Court System located in Washington, D.C. It is also the true and compelling testimony of my 20-year odyssey of egregious judicial injustice at the hands of a team of corrupt, money-mad, conscience-free and amoral D.C. Court Judges and FBI Agents, and their respective facilitators and handlers. It would be my Christian faith, specifically my precious, intimate, personal, genuine, quiet, deep, abiding, penetrating relationship and amazing, productive and powerful partnership with the Holy Spirit Who is always on time, no matter what, that would ultimately bring me out of the fiery trial of D.C. Judicial and FBI egregious injustice fireproof, unbowed, unbound, unbought and "more than conquered" (Romans 8:37).

The District of Columbia Court System is irretrievably corrupt, ostentatiously amoral and diabolically destructive. The District of Columbia Court System is, above all, an amoral court system situated in the heart of the Nation's Capital in Washington, D.C. The corrupt D.C. Court Judges are more committed to the promotion of their own personal power and self-enrichment on the backs of party litigants involved in multi-million-dollar lawsuits than they are to the fair, equal, and impartial application and administration of the *rule of law.*

The Co-Conspirators, without fear of investigation, punishment or prosecution, designed, organized, executed and orchestrated the historic criminal enterprise whose mission, goal and purpose was to successfully swindle and defraud me and my family out of an estimated $50 million in attorney's fees by means of a common court practice and judicial power known as *absolute judicial discretion. In the hands of a corrupt D.C. Court Judge, absolute judicial discretion becomes his playbook and trump card for fraud, theft, corruption and extortion.*

The ultimate reason that an individual or institution of government reforms its corrupt behavior is because a penalty will have to be paid for such violation of law. Corrupt D.C. Court Judges pay no penalty for their corruption. There is no incentive to uphold the *rule of law* when the opportunity for judicial self-enrichment is presented and offered to a corrupt D.C. Court Judge assigned to the adjudication of a lawsuit involving millions of dollars. Thus, the D.C. Court System flourishes and remains mired in extraordinary, if not exponential, D.C. Judicial and FBI fraud, theft, corruption and extortion that knows no bounds.

And so these corrupt D.C. Court Judges go on their merry way stealing, swindling, and defrauding party litigants at will, just as was audaciously and brutally done to me and my family. The scenes and venues of their crimes of opportunity were open D.C. courtrooms, D.C. courthouse hallways, D.C. Judges' chambers and Washington area hotel suites. In the absence of any D.C. Judicial accountability to anybody whatsoever, fraud, theft, corruption and extortion reign supreme in the District of Columbia Court System, and to the detriment and destruction of law-abiding party litigants, residents and citizens.

Having exhausted all means of a just resolution of my lawsuit and the acquisition of impartial, fair and equal justice from the District of Columbia Court System in Washington, D.C. , I have written this judicial expose' in the spirit of an appeal and petition to the Court of Public Opinion for the redress of justice denied me by a cavalier, compromised, corrupt, untouchable and unaccountable District of

Columbia Court System that audaciously dares to answer to no one for its open and notorious multi-million-dollar rigged adjudication of my lawsuit which is the subject of this expose' of judicial corruption.

In retrospect, it has been the relentless and tenacious demand of my self-respect, more than any other reason, that has compelled and challenged me to pen and publish my testimony of the traumatic, iniquity-permeated, faith-tested season of my life's journey, as I head towards the fulfillment of my destiny in Christ Jesus.

BARBARA WASHINGTON FRANKLIN

Introduction
Backstory

In the 8th grade, I auditioned and was selected to play the role of the defense counsel in a junior high school class play. While performing the part, I decided to become an attorney. I never dreamed that while on a necessary sabbatical to care for Mother and one that morphed into a permanent one, I would craft and create a judicial expose' detailing my nightmarish experience of being swindled and defrauded of an estimated $50 million in attorney's fees, not by so-called white-collar criminals, but by a team of corrupt D.C. Court Judges and FBI Agents in Washington, D.C. and Fort Lauderdale, Florida.

The specific dream planted in my heart as the result of the role I played in the Cleveland Junior High School class play in Newark was to one day have my own law office in order to represent those who had been dealt with unjustly by life in one way or another.

It would be decades later and in the early nineties when I would launch my solo law practice and shortly thereafter open my law office in the Chevy Chase Pavilion in Upper Northwest Washington, D.C., known as Friendship Heights, and only minutes from my home.

The Adversary Appears on Assignment

Fast forward to the summer of 1995. Brianna Jones appeared in the office, having made the required appointment for legal consultation. The appointment lasted for over an hour. She sat for the entire appointment in dark sunglasses. It would be years later, and upon reflection of the nightmarish trauma that my family and I had endured as a result of my refusal to withdraw my legal representation of her, and on the eve of the $34 million settlement of the $100 million lawsuit that I had crafted and filed; and the resulting traumatic and relentless attack the U.S. government, represented by corrupt D.C. Court Judges and FBI Agents, that I realized that Brianna Jones was on assignment by the Adversary. She had reported for duty in my law office. Her mission was to kill, steal and destroy, which is the trademark and modus operandi of the Adversary and those in his camp.

THE ODYSSEY OF JUDICIAL CORRUPTION

My 20-Year Odyssey of D.C. Judicial and FBI Egregious Injustice

In the most simplistic of terms, this judicial expose' is my testimony of the 20-year odyssey of egregious D.C. Judicial and FBI injustice that my family and I experienced, beginning in the summer of 1996. It is the true story of how I was savagely swindled, stripped, defrauded and robbed of an estimated $50 million in attorney's fees earned from my legal representation of Brianna Jones, an indigent and homeless Black female client, suffering with Post Traumatic Stress Disorder (PTSD), Depression and related symptoms.

The Politically Motivated Criminal Prosecution

This historic D.C. Judicial and FBI Criminal Conspiracy and Enterprise was premeditated, organized, executed and orchestrated by a pack of corrupt, money-mad, conscience-free and amoral D.C. Court Judges, in concert and alliance with a pack of corrupt, money-mad, conscience-free and amoral FBI Agents, and their respective facilitators and handlers.

The D.C. Judicial and FBI Conspiracy and Criminal Enterprise, whose mission was to defraud me of an estimated $50 million in attorney's fees, was launched in 1997 with the politically motivated criminal prosecution, conviction, house arrest and supervised probation of my husband, the late Dr. Hardy R. Franklin, then serving as Director of the D.C. Public Library and past President of the American Library Association.

The Historic D.C. Judicial and FBI Criminal Enterprise

The D.C. Judicial and FBI Conspiracy and Criminal Enterprise was launched simultaneously in Washington, D.C. and Fort Lauderdale, Fla. In the spring of 1996. It was thereafter executed and orchestrated in open D.C. courtrooms, D.C. court hallways, Washington area hotel suites and private D.C. Judges' chambers, as verified by sworn testimony, official D.C. court transcripts, case filings and court records.

I should not have to write a book or take my case to the Court of Public Opinion because my allegations of massive judicial fraud, theft and corruption, involving corrupt D.C. Court Judges, are outright rejected and swept under the rug so that the career criminals in black robes can continue to flourish through their illicit dealmaking in their private judges' chambers of corruption and criminality.

When I began to craft the manuscript for this judicial expose', during a prayer time, the Holy Spirit admonished me in 2013, through a message by a well-known pastor, that if I did not have the courage, based on the level of my anointing, to go into the enemy's camp, and take back what was stolen from me, then I would not fulfill my purpose. I believe I have been called for such a time as this. Moreover, I believe I have been called to go within myself, and release my story which touches and inspires the world in a brand-new way.

There is no greater agony on earth than the agony of having been unceremoniously and brutally swindled, defrauded, robbed, and financially and economically raped by a team of corrupt, conscience-free and amoral D.C. Court Judges and FBI Agents. The criminal enterprise team of Co-Conspirators was comprised of predominantly Black male D.C. Court Judges.

The theft of $50 million owed to me in attorney's fees carried out in broad daylight by the above-named government Co-Conspirators was abominable and breathtaking. By any measure, it was a classic 21st Century legal high jacking. The grand swindle was masterfully accomplished and primarily designed, engineered and orchestrated by a team of D.C. Court Judges, FBI Agents, D.C. Prosecutors and at least one D.C. Federal Court Judge who adjudicated the politically motivated criminal prosecution of my husband.

My D.C. Judicial Nightmare

My D.C. Judicial and FBI nightmare began on January 21, 2011, upon my entrance into D.C. Superior Courtroom 517, presided over by D.C. Associate Judge Matthew D. Ekans and thereafter, Judge Ekans' *rigged dismissal* of my lawsuit on January 16, 2015 and thereafter, Judge Ekans' *rigged dismissal with prejudice* of my lawsuit in March 2015.

Through a common D.C. court practice known as *absolute judicial discretion*, my D.C. Superior Court lawsuit, filed in response to the former client's breach of the contingency fee agreement, was adjudicated by the rule of the *gaslighting predilections and pontifications of the Presiding D.C. Court Judge* and not by the legally mandated rule of law that Judge Ekans had sworn to apply and uphold in his sacred role as a D.C. Court Judge.

D.C. Court Judges Are Above the Law

While it is often said that no one is above the law, the District of Columbia Court System, as represented by its judicial officers, proves every day that it is not only above the law, but it is *far above* the law. *In fact, the District of Columbia Court System proves every day that it is the law*. It does so through the depth and breadth of the deep fraud, theft, corruption and extortion that saturates and hamstrings the D.C. Court System. Personality characteristics of corrupt D.C. Judges are identical to those described as the "Noah Generation" in Genesis, Chapter 6, of the Bible. They are cavalier, careless and corrupt.

Found within the pages of this judicial expose' is my personal and unvarnished testimony of how I, a principled, hard-working, law-abiding citizen and Black female solo trial attorney, in partnership with the Holy Spirit, was ruthlessly defrauded, robbed and stripped of an estimated $50 million in earned attorney's fees.

My reason, more than any other, for writing and finishing this manuscript entitled *The Odyssey of Judicial Corruption*, is so the Holy Spirit will allow me to sleep through the night again, instead of waking at 12 and 1 o'clock a.m. and not being able to go back to sleep until several hours later, after partnering with the Holy Spirit on the crafting of the manuscript that preceded this finished literary work.

My Appeal to the Court of Public Opinion

This judicial expose' is intended, in part, as my appeal to the Court of Public Opinion for the redress of the egregious and shameless injustice to which me and my family were subjected to for approximately 20 years, fashioned by the historic D.C. Judicial and FBI Conspiracy and Criminal Enterprise, executed and orchestrated by a team of corrupt, money-mad, conscience-free and amoral D.C. Court Judges and FBI Agents who prided themselves in having escaped all accountability, admonition, investigation, prosecution, indictment, conviction and incarceration where warranted.

Above all, this judicial expose' is the personal and unvarnished testimony of how I was robbed of millions of dollars in attorney's fees by a team and pack of money-mad thieves and thugs consisting of corrupt D.C. Court Judges and FBI Agents. To remain silent and to not tell this story is to be as complicit and guilty of criminal wrongdoing as are the unindicted D.C. Judicial and FBI Co-Conspirators.

Given the uniqueness of this one-of-a-kind judicial expose', and with a focus on the whole truth and transparency, I have chosen to annotate select official D.C. Court transcripts of court proceedings with my pertinent commentary and analysis as the primary literary format for the presentation of the story that is the message of this nonfiction narrative that I have chosen to entitle *The Odyssey of Judicial Corruption.*

Representing the Adversary

The earned attorney's fees were the result of the $34 million settlement of the $100 million lawsuit I had crafted and filed in the Broward County Circuit Court in Fort Lauderdale, Florida on May 30, 1996, the last day of the statute of limitations. The lawsuit was filed pursuant to a contingency fee agreement with Brianna Jones, an indigent and homeless 31-year-old Black female client suffering with Post-Traumatic Stress Disorder (PTSD), depression and related symptoms. PTSD is medically defined as a mental illness.

When Brianna Jones first appeared in my law office in 1994, she told a harrowing story of having been molested and raped at the age of 11 years old by a neighborhood vendor. The level of her rage was so stunning and even frightening, I graciously declined to take her case. I did not charge her a fee for my services for the appointment and legal consultation.

A year or so later, she called the office for a second appointment. She appeared in my law office minus the sunglasses and a lot calmer. I listened for a second time to her story. This time when she was finished, I agreed to take her case on a contingency fee basis, since she alleged that she was estranged from her natural family, was indigent and homeless and currently living with a friend. After all attempts to settle the client's credible claims against the alleged pedophile's estate had been exhausted without success, I crafted and filed a $100 million lawsuit in Broward County Circuit Court in Fort Lauderdale, Florida, the then domicile of the widow and legal representative of the estate.

Team Player

I had been previously warned by Hank Hennessy, Head of the Miami-Dade Office of the FBI, that if I did not withdraw as Plaintiff's Counsel from the $100 million lawsuit I had filed on behalf of Brianna Jones, (and in so doing, voluntarily forfeit the 40% in attorney's fees should settlement of the lawsuit occur), my family (husband) would be attacked, since a search of my background revealed no derogatory information that could be used to blackmail me. The FBI told the client that a search of my background also confirmed that I was not a team player, as was the FBI Special Agent in charge of the Miami-Dade Office of the FBI.

These earned attorney's fees resulted from my legal retainment and representation of an indigent, homeless and mentally ill client, pursuant to a contingency fee agreement, and thereafter the crafting and filing of a $100 million lawsuit on behalf of the client. The lawsuit settled for $34 million without compensation to me in any amount, irrespective of my supererogatory legal representation and services on behalf of the client.

The fact that I was a Black female and a solo practitioner of the law, and not associated with a large law firm, made me a more attractive target for the Co-Conspirator D.C. Court Judges and FBI Agents engaged in the D.C. Judicial and FBI Conspiracy and Criminal Enterprise of Fraud, Theft, Corruption, and Extortion designed and orchestrated to strip me of the millions of dollars owed to me in attorney's fees.

A Pack of Money-Mad D.C. Court Judges

It never dawned on me that corrupt D.C. Court Judges, at least one corrupt D.C. Federal Judge, corrupt D.C. Prosecutors and corrupt FBI Agents would be so avaricious, ruthless, reckless, and resolved in their determination to steal millions of dollars in case settlement proceeds of which a substantial portion was owed to me in attorney's fees.

They did so without any concern or fear of indictment or punishment due to the absolute absence of any requirement that a corrupt D.C. Court Judge account for his rigged court decisions designed and guaranteed to enable him to steal millions of dollars belonging to specific court litigants under the judicial power of *absolute judicial discretion* which translates in lay parlance as: Do what you want; to whom you want; however you want and whenever you want.

If it's millions of dollars that you want, they are yours for the taking. It is the statement of the rule of law in the District of Columbia. The rule of law in the District of Columbia is the rule of the Presiding Judge.

Therefore, D.C. Court Judges are allowed to steal at will. They demonstrate every day that they are above the law. They also demonstrate that they are untouchable by anyone. They demonstrate the classic lawless persona unrestrained and unbound.

It is critical that I point out that I was charged and instructed by both the D.C. Superior Court and the D.C. Court of Appeals to go and search for the money, i.e., the so-called missing millions in case settlement proceeds, and then return to Court for an appropriate revised and newly issued court judgment. That's how the corrupt D.C. Court Chiefs brazenly and shamelessly stomped all over me and my meritorious legal claims and pursuit of justice.

The fraudsters, swindlers, robbers and thieves did not come from the streets of Washington, D.C. or from its area prison systems. No, the criminals sat propped on the court benches of the Nation's Capital, and were required to be addressed as "Your Honor," after you've asked yourself "What Honor"?

My Relationship and Partnership with The Holy Spirit

My survival of the severe economic loss and deep emotional trauma caused by the criminal and protracted judicial nightmare was due ultimately to my intimate relationship and amazing partnership with The Holy Spirit. He brought me out of the fiery trial fireproof and more than conquered. Moreover, He, and He alone, has enabled me to share my story with the watching world that includes other similarly situated survivors. My lifetime relationship and partnership with The Holy Spirit served as a perfect preparation for the odyssey of judicial injustice that is the central story of this judicial expose'.

In the words of author Tonya Stoneman, "A man (woman) makes his (her) mark in the world by surrendering his (her) ambitions to The Holy Spirit and wildly abandoning himself (herself) to God."

I knew that God and I were a majority. I also knew that the Holy Spirit dwelt within me and walked beside me. That is why He is called the *Paraclete*. (John 14: 16-17 KJV) I knew that no weapon formed by the Adversary and his government Co-Conspirator officials against me would be able to prosper. And thus, I was not intimidated by the weapons being formed against me by the D.C. Court Judges, FBI Agents and D.C. Prosecutors.

If I do not tell this story as only I can tell it, then I will have disobeyed a divine instruction for which I shall one day have to answer to my Lord. I no longer fear the diabolical plots and plans of my enemies to destroy me. I do fear God, however. And His Holy Spirit has taught me that the fear of man bringeth a snare. (Proverbs 29:25 KJV) That being the case, under no circumstances will I willingly ensnare myself. I am sure by now dear reader you must be asking what pray tell is the assignment that requires the accompaniment of all of Heaven to carry it through to completion?

Dream Revelations

One of the precious and powerful benefits of being a daughter of the King and being in partnership with the Holy Spirit is that He makes early morning visits, usually in the wee hours of the morning to inspire me, encourage me, warn me and often reveal to me coming events that I can prepare for and that will not take me by surprise, rattle me, or shake my confidence in the work God has called me to do.

My dreams are angel food that feed and nourish me and point me to a divine destiny that lies ahead. A particular dream is given to me with divine creativity, specificity and intentionality. Further, my dream has drawing power that will motivate me to go beyond where I am and show me a road map of things that already exist for me. If I shall walk in faithfulness towards it, I shall arise and enter into it with great assurance, calm and courage. The meditation of my heart is that I stay faithful to what God fed me in the dream. For many years, I have kept a dream journal by my bedside in which I make a practice of recording my dreams upon waking. I review my dream notes as needed or as certain events transpire in my life. I consider my dream journal an invaluable resource for my use.

My dreams during the years of the court adjudication of my lawsuit included dreams of close family members, D.C. Court Judges involved in the massive swindle to rob me of my attorney's fees, and the client. And in addition to my dreams, most of which proved to be prophetic, my close family members and at least one close friend had dreams that were powerful and prophetic and included me as a major figure or included some aspect of my lawsuit as a major event.

Prior to the initial court hearing in February 2010 of my lawsuit before Judge Kate Starr, Judge Starr appeared in my dream entering the center hall of my home. Symbolically, the dream scenes revealed that Judge Starr would adjudicate my case in such fashion and with such appropriate action, that justice would prevail for me and the former client. And that is exactly what happened. The client and I settled the case in one day. In fact, I first saw Judge Starr in my dream before seeing her in the actual courtroom.

I had a number of dreams involving Judge Ekans, the Presiding Judge, to whom my case was transferred for adjudication upon the retirement of Judge Starr. They all served to show me Judge Ekans' real character and personality underneath the black robe. In one dream, Judge Ekans appeared as an alligator. I took careful note of the dream symbol since, for almost 20 years, I had entered the courthouse never failing to remind myself that I would be walking on alligators while in the courthouse.

BARBARA WASHINGTON FRANKLIN

In the wee hours of the morning of March 29, 2013, Good Friday, I had a dream of 4 swine heads. Each head was individually framed. The frames were side by side, two above and two below. The frames were approximately 8 ½ x 11 inches in size. Upon waking from the dream, I had no idea at first as to the correct interpretation of the symbolic pictures of the swine heads. And so, I prayed and asked the Holy Spirit to reveal to me the meaning and accurate interpretation of the dream. Thereafter, the Holy Spirit revealed to me that the 4 swine heads represented the 4 key D.C. Judicial Co-Conspirators involved in the theft of my attorney's fees. They were Senior and Former D.C. Superior Court Chief Judge George P. Skinner, Presiding Judge Matthew D. Ekans, Stakeholder Judge Richard Mandarin and U.S. District Court Judge Carlos Cezar Carballo. The Holy Spirit knew how important it was that I understood the character and personality of each of the men who had designed, organized and executed the massive swindle of the millions of dollars owed to me in attorney's fees. *I was also made aware that the root word for swindle is swine.*

During the midst of the court hearings before Judge Ekans, he repeatedly asked whether I thought the client had been paid. I had no answer. And then in the wee hours of one morning, I awakened from a vivid, unforgettable dream in which appeared my father who had passed in April 1977. This was two months after I had relocated to Washington to work on Capitol Hill. I had been appointed by the late Congressman Stewart B. McKinney of the 4th District of Connecticut to serve as Minority Chief Counsel and Staff Director of the U.S. House Committee on the District of Columbia. This professional opportunity that would forever change the trajectory of my life and that of my family was made possible through the political relationships of my brother, Attorney Robert B. Washington, Jr.

In the dream, my father and the client were arguing in my kitchen over my not being paid the attorney's fees due me from the $100 million Florida lawsuit I had filed on the client's behalf and that had settled for $34 million. Daddy was very angry. I could hear it all in his voice. I could not see Daddy in the dream. I could just hear his voice. I could see the client. And she appeared standing at my kitchen counter and holding by the legs a dead and naked chicken in her hands. That sealed it for me. I knew from the dream symbol of the chicken that the client had been paid or had access to some portion of the settlement proceeds.

THE ODYSSEY OF JUDICIAL CORRUPTION

Two of the most dramatic dreams regarding my case were given to me five days after my case was dismissed by Judge Ekans in January 2015. The two dreams complimented each other. One of the dreams featured my niece in vigorous and victorious combat on my behalf with the Presiding Judge. The dominant symbols in the dreams were clear and unambiguous. The dreams revealed that I would ultimately prevail and experience victory, restoration and restitution of my attorney's fees. Further, the dream symbols confirmed that I would recover all. All that God said. All that God promised.

And finally, in the summer of 2018, my young adult grandson, upon waking, shared with me an unforgettable and massive dream he had. He said he knew he had to tell me because he had never had such a dramatic and graphic dream. The setting of the dream was the backyard of our home. In the dream, my grandson saw himself lying on his back on top of piles of snakes, all slithering on top of each other in an old large metal tub. I quickly came to his rescue, pulled him up and off the snakes, while telling him to remain calm and that I was going to help him.

Our house had been somehow and in some way substantially demolished and my daughter could be seen trying to escape from the house. My grandson and I then noticed that several White teenagers were trying to steal our vehicles off the side street of the house where they were parked. The boys managed to steal one of the vehicles before we could stop them.

In another part of the backyard adjacent to the staircase leading to the back porch, a fierce fight ensued between a large black snake and a large tiger. My grandson said the large snake lounged at the large tiger at least three times or more trying to destroy the tiger, but had not succeeded. And then all of a sudden, the tiger, in one swoop, took the head off the snake. With the large snake decapitated, all the other piles of snakes quickly slithered out of the backyard, into the alley and onto the side street bordering our backyard. At that point, the dream ended, and my grandson woke up.

My grandson said what was most prominent in the dream was my attitude and demeanor while I stood tall in the midst of all the chaos, fighting and destruction that dominated the backyard scene of the dream. My grandson said I remained calm, firm and fearless at all times. He took note that I did not try in any way to escape or run away from the fierce fighting in the backyard.

I told my grandson that the Holy Spirit had given him the dream that was symbolic of all my husband, and I had endured during the nightmare of the 1997 politically motivated criminal prosecution of my husband and the rigged adjudication that ended in the rigged dismissal of my lawsuit against the client in January 2015, all designed and executed by the D.C Judicial and FBI Co-Conspirators profiled herein. However, the Holy Spirit had used my grandson to tell me through his dream that I would ultimately prevail in my never-ceasing pursuit of justice, and one day soon experience victory, promotion, vindication, restoration, restitution and the fullness of my destiny in Jesus' name. Amen.

A Divine Assignment

My assignment is clear and uncomplicated. It is the task of pulling back the curtains on "official Washington", specifically its local and federal court systems, and allowing the American public to see the massive judicial fraud, theft, corruption and extortion that flourishes system wide, with impunity and unabated in the court systems of Washington, D.C., our Nation's Capital.

Given the nature and specifics of the assignment, I am sure you will agree that it would have to be none other than marching orders issued from above that have endowed me with the necessary boldness and fearlessness to speak the truth and tell a story that needs to be told from my experience and perspective.

The other reason for writing this work is that I have been given it as my assignment by the Holy Spirit. And you don't say no to the Holy Spirit—not if you have any sense. I have lived long enough to know that to ignore a divine instruction is death. Not necessarily physical death, but certainly death to one's spirit and soul. And it's not in my DNA to go through life like the walking dead. And when our spirit, mind, will and emotions have died, we go through life dead on the inside, even though we may appear very alive on the outside.

But the corrupt D.C. Court Judges, the corrupt FBI Agents, the corrupt D.C. Prosecutors, and their respective corrupt handlers and facilitators failed to factor in my lifetime faith perspective regarding the government's brutal and relentless 20-year attack on me and my family that has never ended, just periodically paused. Unlike my enemies, I know that faith is a perspective.

And more importantly, the Holy Spirit admonished me that I must maintain the attitude of David in my unwavering pursuit of justice and the restitution of my attorney's fees. The Bible records that when David returned from battle and home to Ziklag, he found that his enemies had destroyed his home and possessions, and had taken all the women and children captive. The Bible further tells us that David inquired of the Lord: "Shall I pursue?" and the Lord answered David: "*Pursue, and you shall, without fail, recover all*" (*1 Samuel 30:8 KVJ*).

The Presence of the Adversary

Judge Ekans' intentional and purposeful mischaracterization of me as a j*udgment creditor* when, in fact, he knew I was a Party Plaintiff attempting to have the settlement agreement breached by the Defendant/Former Client enforced by the Court was clear evidence of the intrusion by Satan into the proceedings, and on its face, evidence of D.C. judicial corruption, demonic influence and persuasion.

At each court hearing, the atmosphere of the courtroom was, without exception, dominated by deception and lies, the inevitable and obvious hallmark that is characteristic of Satan. It is, moreover, the authentic sign of the presence of the Adversary.

Around 12:00 a.m. on February 2, 2015, the Holy Spirit told me to accept the D.C. Court's Order of Judgment for the Defendant and the rigged dismissal of my lawsuit on January 16, 2015 as a part of God's plan and purpose for my life and destiny. According to Romans 8:28, I have been promised that He's causing all things to work together for my good. This explains and is the reason for my peace. This also explains why I shall never give up my pursuit of justice that I have been so brutally and relentlessly denied by the D.C. Judicial and FBI Co-Conspirators responsible for the theft of my attorney's fees.

Metaphorically, while I cannot always eject fear from my car as I journey forward and in the direction of my destiny, I make sure it remains in the back seat, with its hands off the steering wheel. The Holy Spirit forever reminds me of God's promise that *He has not given me a spirit of fear, but of power and of love and of a sound mind (2 Timothy 1:7 KJV).* And finally, the Holy Spirit further reminds me that God is above man, and He always will be.

More importantly, I knew that no D.C. Court Judge, no FBI Agent, no D.C. Prosecutor, no nothing would be able to come against me to harm or hurt me in any way without God first giving the green light. And if God gives the green light to the particular injustice or attack, however protracted or excruciatingly painful, He has promised me, His daughter, that it will serve my ultimate good and His ultimate glory. More importantly, whatever the injustice tailor-made by my Father for me , it would serve God's will, plan and purpose for my life as a child of God. I resolved to forever stand committed to this faith perspective.

It has taken me awhile, but I finally realize that my case has gone just the way it was supposed to go, according to the Sovereign plan and purpose of the Holy Spirit in the fulfillment of my divine destiny. Had it not been for the Lord on my side, and my decision and resolve to trust Him no matter what, I would not have been able to survive the 20-year odyssey of egregious D.C. Judicial and FBI injustice dominated by the illegal and traumatic confiscation of the millions of dollars owed to me in attorney's fees.

During the 20-year nightmare that I prefer to refer to as an odyssey of egregious judicial injustice, God used important prophetic dreams as angel food to guide, instruct me, warn me, as well as encourage and inspire me as I navigated around, above and through the traps, minefields and pitfalls that had been created by the Presiding Judge in conspiracy with his Judicial and FBI Co-Conspirators to accomplish the singular, demonic mission of their D.C. Judicial and FBI Criminal Enterprise which was to strip me of the millions of dollars owed to me in attorney's fees.

Although my journey was traumatic and grievous, God never left me. He kept me and kept me and kept me. The Holy Spirit taught me that though man can take much from me, he will never take the destiny that God has ordained for my life. Therefore, all praise, honor, gratitude and glory goes to my Heavenly Father, the Sovereign Creator, Ruler and Master of the Universe.

The Grand Marshall of D.C. Judicial Corruption Parade

My D.C. Judicial nightmare began on January 21, 2011, upon my entrance into D.C. Courtroom 517, presided over by D.C. Associate Judge Matthew D. Ekans and thereafter, Judge Ekans' *rigged dismissal* of my lawsuit in January 2015 and, thereafter, Judge Ekans' *rigged dismissal with prejudice* of my lawsuit in March 2015.

THE ODYSSEY OF JUDICIAL CORRUPTION

Ekans' use and abuse of his *absolute judicial discretion* was always on steroids. Without any apologies, his courtroom style in adjudicating my case was to preside rogue. And the only law that prevailed in his courtroom was the *Law of the Judge. It was clear that Judge Ekans' focus and goal was on protecting the D.C. Judicial and FBI Co-Conspirators in their criminal enterprise to defraud me of my attorney's fees.*

To Be the Law Is to Be Above the Law

As I observed Ekans during each court hearing, I became convinced that I was not the first party litigant whose case he had rigged for final dismissal, and I wouldn't be the last. That is because as a D.C. Court Judge, Judge Ekans was free of any and all accountability to anyone for his actions on the bench. *To be a D.C. Court Judge is to be the law. And to be the law is to be above the law.*

After the first several court hearings before Judge Ekans, beginning with the first hearing on January 21, 2011, I realized that I was not dealing with a court judge committed to the administration of justice or application of the rule of law. I was dealing with a member of *a team of mobsters on a mission.* And their sole and solitary mission was to defraud me of an estimated $50 million owed to me for my legal representation of Brianna Jones, based on the $34 million settlement of the $100 million lawsuit that I had crafted and filed on her behalf in May 1996.

This was also the first instance in which I had to witness, albeit to my shock and surprise, the virtually exclusive use by a Presiding Judge of the judicial tool of all-encompassing silence by the Court in the face of my allegations of massive judicial fraud, theft, corruption and extortion. More importantly, these allegations were also repeatedly made by the Defendant and former client in open court and under oath. The Presiding Judge, through his demeanor and commentary, let everyone in the courtroom know he could care less. His lips were zipped and sealed.

Absolute Judicial Discretion

Judge Ekans' conduct in such circumstance was far beyond inappropriate based on the facts and circumstances of the case. It was an egregious misuse and abuse of absolute judicial discretion. The core message of *A Judicial Expose'* is that *absolute judicial discretion served as the corrupt D.C. Court Judge's playbook and trump card for fraud, theft, corruption and extortion.* Further, absolute judicial discretion empowered Presiding Judge Ekans to cavalierly and audaciously rig my case for final dismissal, instead of adjudicating my case in accordance with the rule of law and justice, which is the duty of an honest and ethical D.C. Cout Judge.

The D.C. Judicial and FBI conspiracy and criminal enterprise played out in the open courtrooms of D.C. Superior Court in January 2011 when my lawsuit against Brianna Jones for breach of the contingency fee agreement was added to the court docket of D.C. Associate Judge Matthew D. Ekans due to the retirement of D.C. Associate Judge Kate Starr to whom my lawsuit was initially assigned in March 2009. While under the adjudication of D.C. Associate Judge Kate Starr, my lawsuit was amicably and voluntarily settled with Brianna Jones in February 2010. Nevertheless, after 9 months under Judge Ekans' adjudication followed by a premeditated 2 ½ year layover in the D.C. Court of Appeals, my lawsuit was dismissed by Judge Ekans in January 2015, and dismissed with prejudice in March 2015, all in accordance with the goal and purpose of the flourishing criminal enterprise.

Judge Ekans' announcement that if he couldn't enforce the Court's orders, he should hang up his black robe and turn in his gavel was nothing more than gaslighting rhetoric. Judge Ekans never enforced Judge Kate Starr's Order of October 18, 2010 mandating that Brianna Jones produce bank statements and records which Jones testified more than once as having in her possession. The enforcement of such an order would defeat the mission, goal and purpose of the criminal enterprise to swindle me our of the millions of dollars owed to me in attorney's fees.

The Elephant of D.C. Judicial Fraud, Theft, Corruption and Extortion Conspiracy stands in the open courtrooms of D.C. Superior Court every day and corrupt D.C. Court Judges simply remain silent. After all, there are no cameras, videos or audios of the given proceeding, and so who is to know that, based on the *absolute judicial discretion* legally afforded the Presiding Judge, justice is liable to be audaciously trampled, tattered and torn by the very individual who is being handsomely and generously compensated to uphold and enforce the rule of law in Washington, D.C.

From the very beginning, this D.C. Court refused and failed to address the issue of massive D.C. Judicial and FBI fraud that had dominated my case. Instead, the Court chose to give its allegiance to its fellow corrupt judicial colleagues ahead of its sacred duty to dispense the fair and equitable administration of justice owed to me in my right to due process of law in having the issue of D.C. Judicial and FBI fraud, theft, corruption and extortion examined and investigated by the Court through an independent investigation.

I have, at all times, refused to compromise my integrity with the Defendant. I have also, at all times, refused to compromise my integrity with the D.C. Judicial and FBI Co-Conspirators. My professional soul was not for sale. Thus, I was referred to by the FBI Special Agent as not being a "team player."

Judge Ekans' premeditated silence throughout the proceedings (that went on for nine months) on the issue of judicial fraud, theft, corruption and extortion made it clear that his first commitment was to the protection of his colleagues on the D.C. Court Bench identified by me as Co-Conspirators in this massive fraud and corruption scheme based on their conduct specified in my *December 16, 2014* court filing captioned *Plaintiff's Response to the Motion to Intervene*.

However, in my case, faced with the dominant issues of D.C. Judicial fraud, theft, corruption and extortion, that included other D.C. Court Judges, colleagues of the Presiding Judge for over 25 years, Judge Ekans boldly and bluntly, and without shame or excuse, on the record and in open court, proceeded to avail himself of his own brand and bag of tricks,

Having set aside the traditional and typical remedies in such a case, including that of an *independent court investigation*, all designed to "legally' extinguish my claim of D.C. judicial fraud, theft, corruption and extortion and ultimately enable the D.C. Judicial and FBI Co-Conspirators to escape examination or punishment and, more importantly, to do so while maintaining possession and enjoyment of the stolen case settlement proceeds, including my attorney's fees in the tens of millions of dollars.

Another trick used by Judge Ekans was that of repeatedly referring to me as a *judgment creditor* when he knew that I was never a *judgment creditor* for the entire 9 months that the proceedings were adjudicated by him, prior to his issuance to me of the October 2011 "Paper" Money Judgment for $13.6 million, overturned almost 3 years later by the D.C. Court of Appeals in accordance with its key role in the mission of the D.C. Judicial and FBI Criminal Enterprise to defraud me of my attorney's fees.

A further trick used by Judge Ekans against me that enabled furtherance of the criminal enterprise was that of referring to my case as *smoke and mirrors*. In my 30 plus years of being a prominent member of the Bar and my 15 plus years of being a trial attorney, no judge had ever so insulted and disrespected me. Surprisingly, during the March 18, 2011 court hearing, Judge Ekans went so far as to say that he suspected that I was wasting his time, and he didn't have time to waste. *This was a purely gaslighting admonition.*

One of the first tricks used by Judge Ekans from his bag of tricks was that of referring to the officials that Brianna Jones had testified that she had been summoned to meet with periodically as "Phantom People" (August 19, 2011 Court Hearing).

One of the biggest developments in the case in which Judge Ekans showed his hand to help the Co-Conspirators in their plot and plan to crush me was Judge Ekans' repeated refusal to order an investigation of my allegations of D.C. Judicial fraud, theft and corruption. The Court's reason for its denial of my request for an independent investigation? One word: inappropriate. This was nothing but a classic example of egregious abuse of *absolute judicial discretion.*

By Judge Ekans' repeated refusal to address the dominant issues of D.C. judicial and FBI fraud, theft, corruption and extortion in my case, this then allowed the Court to continue to inform me that it was my job to find the money and that I needed to be more aggressive in my pursuit. While I appeared cool and calm on the outside, I was hot and outraged on the inside. Nevertheless, Judge Ekans would never be able to infuriate me to the point that I would stoop to his level in my words, my attitude, my demeanor or my perspective. *I knew who I was and whose I was. He had yet to find out.*

The Court managed to succeed in using its silence as a tool to annihilate my claims of D.C. Judicial and FBI fraud, theft, corruption and extortion. The appropriateness of Judge Ekans' silence on the issue of judicial fraud, theft, corruption and extortion was ratified by the D.C. Court of Appeals when it, too, chose to remain silent on the issues of D.C. judicial fraud, theft, corruption and extortion, and in so doing abdicated its inherent judicial leadership role as an appellate tribunal following its premeditated 2 ½ year review of the adjudication of my lawsuit by Judge Ekans.

Where else in America, other than in the District of Columbia, could an attorney who also happens to be the Plaintiff in a case present evidence and make allegations of massive judicial fraud, theft and corruption before a D.C. Superior Court Judge and the Judge does nothing, and takes no action whatsoever without any fear of having to answer to anybody for such an obvious egregious abuse of absolute judicial discretion, power and authority?

The Court's preference was the rule of the mob. Period. Full stop. And It pursued its preference for the entirety of the adjudication of my lawsuit in the hands of Judge Ekans from January 2011 until January 2015.

THE ODYSSEY OF JUDICIAL CORRUPTION

This Is Animal House

While it is often said that no one is above the law, that might be true on occasion. But it is not "the truth." The District of Columbia Court System proves every day that it is not only above the law, but *it is far above the law. In fact, the District of Columbia Court System proves every day that it is the law*. It does so through the depth and breadth of the deep fraud, theft, corruption and extortion that saturates and hamstrings the D.C. Court System. The systemic D.C. Court fraud, theft, corruption and extortion is illustrated by this judicial expose' and chronicle of my personal pursuit of justice navigated through the odyssey of egregious D.C. Judicial injustice.

My case demonstrates that this Court considers itself sacrosanct, untouchable and above the law. While it tramples the rights of litigants before it by adamantly and repeatedly refusing to apply *the necessary remedy of investigation* of the dominant issues of D.C. Judicial and FBI fraud, theft, corruption and extortion, as well as other appropriate remedies when the issue is massive D.C. Judicial and FBI fraud, theft, corruption and extortion committed by its fellow corrupt colleagues on the court bench.

For 6 years the D.C. Court System had abused its discretion , power and authority through the misuse and abuse of the rules of the Court and sat on my case so as to avoid addressing the issues of massive D.C. Judicial and FBI fraud, theft, corruption and extortion and finally dismissing the case with the judgment for Defendant, at all times a key Co-Conspirator in the massive conspiracy to defraud and strip me of the millions of dollars owed to me in attorney's fees. The D.C. Court has demonstrated over and over again that when faced with allegations of D.C. Judicial and FBI fraud, theft and corruption, it will erect a wall of deafening silence and do nothing more.

Pursuant to the design and orchestration of the judicial conspiracy and criminal enterprise, my case purposefully was allowed to languish in the D.C. Court System for 6 years before *premeditated and final rigged dismissal* because I had the audacity, courage and temerity to request that the court investigate the issues dominant in the case of D.C. Judicial and FBI fraud, theft, corruption and extortion.

BARBARA WASHINGTON FRANKLIN

The D.C. Court System, comprised of the D.C. Superior Court and the D.C. Court of Appeals, without qualification, is an amoral court system located in Washington, D.C. Moreover, the D.C. Court System is a judicial cesspool, culture, snake pit and environment dominated and controlled by a group of corrupt, money-mad, conscience-free and amoral D.C. Court Judges. Further, this team of corrupt D.C. Court Judges is saturated and marinated in premeditated fraud, theft, corruption and extortion, and in partnership with a team of corrupt, money-mad, conscience-free and amoral FBI Agents.

But nothing is more telling and evident of the systemic and flourishing fraud, theft, corruption and extortion that is the audacious and unqualified practice of the D.C. Court System (comprised of the D.C. Superior Court and the D.C. Court of Appeals) than is the reading of the four-page decision of the D.C. Court of Appeals issued in my case in July 2014.

The appellate decision carefully and intentionally avoids any mention of D.C. Judicial and FBI fraud, theft, corruption and extortion, which were the dominant issues in my lawsuit. Moreover, the Court, without shame, but with moral catastrophe that is the handmaiden of *absolute judicial discretion*, instructs Judge Ekans to revise his rigged order of dismissal of my case should I ever recover *the stolen and or missing millions of dollars in case settlement proceeds.*

It is a known fact and commonly understood by D.C. trial attorneys and others that D.C. Court Judges, without exception, have at their disposal an arsenal of unlimited tools and resources to use as remedies and solutions to issues presented to them by party litigants in the adjudication of those issues.

What is scary is that there exists among us a group of individuals, albeit handpicked, who regard themselves as untouchable and above the law and by and large are treated as such by the unsuspecting and naïve community at large. The scary part is that these same individuals are tasked with sitting in judgment on the conduct and behavior of their fellow American citizens, often resulting in incarceration or house arrest, when their own hands are not clean, and when, to paraphrase the late Dr. Martin Luther King, Jr., their own judicial conduct is "washed in interposition and nullification of the truth" necessary for the fair and equal administration of justice.

Nevertheless, at the end of the day and too often, they are mere "career criminals in black robes." Their weapon of choice is not a knife or gun. Rather, it is their writing pen used to sign their dastardly orders and judgments. Their silence is deafening in the face of court testimony, facts and circumstances evidencing within its ranks egregious abuses of *absolute judicial discretion*, fraud, theft, corruption and extortion. It is a silence reminiscent of the silence of the world while six million Jews were slaughtered during World War II. As far as this Court was concerned, it made no difference that silence is complicity.

Evidence of System-Wide and Systemic D.C. Court Corruption

It is not so much what the decision said as to what it did not say. The D.C. Court of Appeals carefully and intentionally avoided any mention of the issues of D.C. Judicial and FBI fraud, theft, corruption and extortion that dominated the case. Having refused to address these issues, it logically followed that it was excused from having to address, as erroneous, Judge Ekans' repeated refusal of my repeated requests for an *independent court investigation* of evidence of D.C. Judicial and FBI fraud, theft, corruption and extortion in connection with the so-called missing $34 million in case settlement proceeds. This is simply evidence of the moral rot that permeates and saturates the D.C. Court System from top to bottom.

These officials, whether they be D.C. Court Judges, FBI Agents, Federal Prosecutors and other government officials, see themselves as untouchable and more importantly, above the law, and therefore arrogantly function accordingly.

The Rule of Law Mandates the Judicial Enforcement of Court Orders

I no longer need to withhold the hard edges of the portrait that must be painted of the critical and corrupt role the D.C. Presiding Judge played in this massive judicial fraud, theft, corruption and extortion conspiracy and criminal enterprise case. I no longer need to be concerned about those who are hacking into my computer and reading the original drafts of my manuscript. I am committed to telling the truth. Period. And it is the truth that is going to uphold me against all the future attacks that are going to come my way both during my finishing of the writing of the final draft of the manuscript, as well as the final publication of it.

Given the final ruling of the Court in favor of Defendant Brianna Jones, an acknowledged Co-Conspirator in this massive D.C. Judicial and FBI fraud and corruption case, and the sum total of the facts and circumstances and evidence in this case, it appears that my pursuit of fairness, equity and justice has had to take a back seat to the judicial fraud and corruption of D.C. Superior Court that has swirled around me for 6 years from the date of my filing suit against Brianna Jones in March 2009.

If nothing else, I hope this judicial expose' will significantly contribute to a serious look at the need for video and audio installations in all the courtrooms in Washington, D.C., whether they are local or federal.

I conclude the work by observing that the D.C. Judicial and FBI Co-Conspirators were able to accomplish the mission of the theft of millions of dollars owed to me in attorney's fees because the Presiding Judge, in his abusive exercise of *absolute judicial discretion*, refused to enforce a legitimate D.C. Court Order which is one of the primary duties of a D.C. Court Judge. Specifically, Judge Ekans intentionally and purposefully refused to enforce the October 18, 2010 Court Order issued by Judge Kate Starr which mandated that Brianna Jones produce and turn over to me copies of Bank of America bank statements of the settlement proceeds in the amount of an estimated $80 million due to accumulated interest according to sworn testimony provided by Brianna Jones at the court hearing adjudicated by Judge Ekans on January 21, 2011, Afternoon Session.

Ultimately, Satan won the battle on January 16, 2015, when Judge Ekans dismissed my case and rendered judgment for the Defendant, Brianna Jones. But the Holy Spirit assured me that the Adversary had not won the war. In my spirit, I knew that even though the fight had been fixed, it was not over. I didn't know how it was going to work out, but I knew the matter was not over by a long shot. More importantly, I knew that God and I were a majority. Further, I knew that God would, in His own way, have the last say. I just didn't know that it would take so long.

"Because Then the Law Does Not Mean Anything"

As early as the court hearing held on February 2, 2011, Judge Ekans understood and was fully cognizant of his primary responsibility, if not ultimate duty, as a D.C. Court Judge, to enforce court orders issued by him or that originated with another D.C. Court Judge. To his credit, Judge Ekans forsook his characteristic judicial engagement in gaslighting from the bench on this important legal issue that called for the judicial administration of the rule of law.

On this point, Judge Ekans' admonishment of Brianna Jones regarding her contempt of Judge Kate Starr's Order and his legal obligation as a D.C. Court judge to enforce such order is powerfully reflected in the official court transcript of the proceeding held on February 2, 2011 and is recorded as follows on page 11 of the transcript:

> **Ms. Jones**: When I signed on the 25th that I will return on -- --
>
> when I signed on the 21st that I would return on the 25th, I knew
>
> there was a chance that the documents I have may not appease
>
> this Court.
>
> **The Court**: You knew there was a chance of that. The Court is not
>
> trying to be appeased. The Court is trying to enforce the judgment
>
> that you entered into after a lawsuit was filed and was settled. If I
>
> don't do that then I need to turn in my gavel and my robe **because**
>
> **then the law does not mean anything.**

Conclusion

The D.C. Court record of my lawsuit verifies that rather than turn in his gavel and robe following his premeditated refusal and failure to enforce Judge Kate Starr's Order of October 18, 2010, Judge Ekans carried out his role as a key D.C. Judicial Co-Conspirator in this historic D.C. Judicial and FBI Conspiracy and Criminal Enterprise through the rigged dismissal of my lawsuit in January 2015 and thereafter, the rigged dismissal of my lawsuit with prejudice in March 2015.

Consequently, in the words of D.C. Court Presiding Judge Ekans, my case stands, above all else, for the reality that in the District of Columbia *"...the law does not mean anything."*

BARBARA WASHINGTON FRANKLIN

SUPERIOR COURT OF THE DISTRICT OF COLUMBIA
CIVIL DIVISION
WASHINGTON, D.C.

THE HONORABLE MATTHEW D. EKANS, ASSOCIATE JUDGE, PRESIDING

THE FOLLOWING IS THE ENTIRE OFFICIAL COURT TRANSCRIPT OF THE
JANUARY 21, 2011 PROCEEDING, *MORNING SESSION*
ANNOTATED BY THE AUTHOR'S PERTINENT COMMENTARY AND ANALYSIS.

JANUARY 21, 2011

P R O C E E D I N G S

COMMENT AND ANALYSIS: #1 *IN MAY 1996, I CRAFTED AND FILED A $100 MILLION LAWSUIT IN BROWARD COUNTY CIRCUIT COURT IN FORT LAUDERDALE, FLORIDA. THE LAWSUIT WAS FILED, PURSUANT TO A CONTINGENCY FEE AGREEMENT AND ON BEHALF OF BRIANNA JONES, A BLACK FEMALE CLIENT WHO WAS INDIGENT, HOMELESS AND SUFFERING WITH POST-TRAUMATIC STRESS DISORDER (PTSD)). THE FLORIDA LAWSUIT SETTLED FOR $34 MILLION IN DECEMBER 1996 WITHOUT PAYMENT TO ME IN ANY AMOUNT FOR MY LEGAL SERVICES AND SUBSTANTIAL OUT-OF-POCKET EXPENSES PROVIDED TO AND ON BEHALF OF BRIANNA JONES.*

IN MARCH 2009, I FILED SUIT AGAINST BRIANNA JONES IN D.C. SUPERIOR COURT IN WASHINGTON, D.C. FOR BREACH OF THE CONTINGENCY FEE AGREEMENT AND FAILURE TO PAY THE ATTORNEY'S FEES IN THE AMOUNT OF 40 PERCENT OF THE $34 MILLION SETTLEMENT AMOUNT, AS PROVIDED BY THE PROVISIONS OF THE CONTINGENCY FEE AGREEMENT.

MY CASE WAS ORIGINALLY ASSIGNED TO D.C. SUPERIOR COURT JUDGE KATE STARR FOR ADJUDICATION AND FINAL DISPOSITION. IN FEBRUARY 2010, BRIANNA JONES AND I REACHED AN AMICABLE SETTLEMENT AGREEMENT REGARDING THE CLAIMS SET FORTH IN MY LAWSUIT. THE WRITTEN SETTLEMENT AGREEMENT SPECIFICALLY STATED THAT BRIANNA JONES AGREED TO TURN OVER TO ME WITHIN A SPECIFIED TIME CERTIFIED AND NOTARIZED COPIES OF THE BANK STATEMENTS OF THE TOTAL CASE SETTLEMENT PROCEEDS IN THE ESTIMATED AMOUNT OF $100 MILLION AND HELD ON DEPOSIT AT BANK OF AMERICA

THEREAFTER, BRIANNA JONES BREACHED THE SETTLEMENT AGREEMENT BY FAILING AND REFUSING TO TURN OVER TO ME THE BANK OF AMERICA BANK STATEMENTS AND RELATED BANK RECORDS.

UPON MOTION, JUDGE KATE STARR, ON OCTOBER 18, 2010, ORDERED BRIANNA JONES TO TURN OVER TO ME THE SPECIFIED BANK OF AMERICA BANK STATEMENTS OR BE TAKEN INTO CUSTODY UPON HER REFUSAL TO DO SO.

IN DECEMBER 2010, JUDGE STARR RETIRED AND MY CASE WAS TRANSFERRED TO THE CALENDAR AND COURT DOCKET OF JUDGE MATTHEW D. EKANS. FROM MY VERY FIRST APPEARANCE BEFORE JUDGE EKANS, I POINTED OUT TO HIM THAT THE NARROW ISSUE BEFORE THE COURT WAS THAT OF DISCLOSURE BY BRIANNA JONES OF THE BANKING INSTITUTION AND PRODUCTION OF BANK STATEMENTS RELATED TO DISBURSEMENT TO ME OF ATTORNEY'S FEES OWED TO ME AS A RESULT OF MY REPRESENTATION AND LEGAL SERVICES PROVIDED TO BRIANNA JONES IN THE $100 MILLION FLORIDA LAWSUIT THAT I HAD CRAFTED AND FILED IN BROWARD COUNTY CIRCUIT COURT, AND THAT HAD SETTLED IN DECEMBER 1996 FOR $34 MILLION WITHOUT DISBURSEMENT TO ME IN ANY AMOUNT.

*NOTHING IN MY OPENING REMARKS OR THEREAFTER WOULD CAUSE JUDGE EKANS TO BEGIN THINKING OF ME OR REFERRING TO ME THEREAFTER AS A **JUDGMENT CREDITOR,** OTHER THAN HIS KEY ROLE AS A JUDICIAL CO-CONSPIRATOR IN THE ONGOING D.C. JUDICIAL AND FBI CRIMINAL ENTERPRISE.*

*IT HAS BEEN REPORTED THAT IN THE 1930'S, A MASS COMMUNICATIONS EXPERT AT YALE UNIVERSITY COINED THE TERM **"THE SLEEPER EFFECT"** OR **"THE BIG LIE."** THE TERM MEANS THAT IF YOU KEEP REPEATING SOMETHING FALSE LONG ENOUGH, IT STICKS AND EVEN THOUGH FALSE, IT BEGINS TO BE REGARDED BY PEOPLE AS THE TRUTH.*

*WHEN JUDGE EKANS FALSELY AND INTENTIONALLY LABELED ME A **JUDGMENT CREDITOR,** HE BEGAN TO APPLY AND PRACTICE **THE SLEEPER EFFECT** AND **THE BIG LIE** REGARDING THE LEGAL THEORY, STATUS AND POSTURE OF MY LAWSUIT.*

*JUDGE EKANS WOULD PROVE TO BE RELENTLESS IN PROMOTING **"THE BIG LIE"** OF MY BEING A **JUDGMENT CREDITOR** RIGHT UP TO AND DURING THE FINAL HEARING OF HIS ADJUDICATION OF MY LAWSUIT, INCLUDING HIS RIGGED DISMISSAL, ON JANUARY 16, 2015.*

*AS PRESIDING JUDGE, EKANS' UNRELENTING AND PERPETUAL PRACTICE OF **THE BIG LIE** OF MY BEING A **JUDGMENT CREDITOR** WOULD CONFIRM, ABOVE ALL, THAT IF IT CONTRIBUTES TO THE ACHIEVEMENT OF HIS GOALS AND MISSION, **THE ADVERSARY** WILL FABRICATE EVIDENCE WHEN AND WHERE NECESSARY.*

BARBARA WASHINGTON FRANKLIN

DEPUTY CLERK:	CALLING THE CASE OF BARBARA WASHINGTON FRANKLIN V. BRIANNA JONES, CIVIL ACTION 4417, 2009. PLEASE COME FORWARD, IDENTIFY YOURSELF FOR THE RECORD.
MS. FRANKLIN:	GOOD MORNING, YOUR HONOR.
THE COURT:	GOOD MORNING.
MS. FRANKLIN:	BARBARA WASHINGTON FRANKLIN, YOUR HONOR.
THE COURT:	GOOD MORNING.
DEPUTY CLERK:	YOUR HONOR, MS. JONES CALLED JUDGE STARR'S CHAMBERS ABOUT 30 MINUTES AGO, AND SAID SHE WAS RUNNING LATE, AND SHE'S NOT HERE.
THE COURT:	MS. FRANKLIN, YOU'VE BEEN HERE FOR SOME TIME. I'M NOT SURE WHAT YOU WANT ME TO DO. I'M JUST INFORMED THAT THE DEFENDANT CALLED JUDGE STARR'S CHAMBERS TO SAY THAT SHE'S RUNNING LATE. THEY PASSED THAT INFORMATION ON TO US.
MS. FRANKLIN:	I'M PREPARED TO GIVE HER, GIVE HER TIME TODAY SINCE I'M DOWN HERE---
THE COURT:	WELL, I WAS GOING TO SAY THE SAME THING.
MS. FRANKLIN:	---AND SHE DID CALL ME A LITTLE BEFORE NINE TO SAY THAT SHE HAD JUST GOTTEN INTO WASHINGTON AND, YOU KNOW, SHE WAS BEHIND TIME AND SHE NEEDED SOME TIME, SO---
THE COURT:	WELL, I THINK THAT WOULD BE GENEROUS AND HOPEFULLY HELPFUL---
MS. FRANKLIN:	YES.
THE COURT:	---IF YOU ARE WILLING TO WAIT AWHILE.
MS. FRANKLIN:	YES. I'M WILLING TO DO THAT, YOUR HONOR.
THE COURT:	I HAVE---
MS. FRANKLIN:	DEPENDING ON YOUR HONOR'S SCHEDULE, I DON'T KNOW---

THE COURT:	WELL, I WAS GOING TO SAY, I HAVE A CASE THAT'S SET FOR 12 O'CLOCK THAT I HAVE TO DO IN A DIFFERENT COURTROOM BECAUSE WE DON'T HAVE A CELLBLOCK ATTACHED TO THIS COURTROOM. IF SHE'S HERE YOU KNOW, IN THE NEXT 15 MINUTES, WE'LL GO AHEAD AND DO THIS, BUT IF NOT, I'M GOING TO HAVE TO RECESS AND GO DOWN TO COURTROOM 302 TO TAKE CARE OF THAT, BUT THAT'S BRIEF. I CAN TAKE CARE OF THAT IN PROBABLY LESS THAN 15 MINUTES. SO, I COULD JUST COME BACK UP HERE---
MS. FRANKLIN:	THEN WE WILL HAVE TO WAIT FOR YOU.
THE COURT:	---YOU KNOW---
MS. FRANKLIN:	BECAUSE SHE, SHE DID ASK ME TO ASK THE COURT FOR A CONTINUANCE, SHE NEEDS ANOTHER---SHE WANTED TO DO MONDAY. I SAID I CAN'T DO THAT. FIRST OF ALL, I DON'T KNOW THE COURT'S SCHEDULE.
THE COURT:	THAT'S WHY---I'LL BE IN TRIAL MONDAY AND THAT'S---
MS. FRANKLIN:	EXACTLY. AND I SAID IT'S MY UNDERSTANDING THAT THESE KIND OF MATTERS, YOUR ORAL EXAM IS ON FRIDAY, AND BASICALLY, YOUR HONOR, THIS IS ABOUT DISCLOSURE OF THE BANKING INSTITUTION LOCATION AND DISBURSEMENT, AND I WOULD ONLY BE WILLING TO CONSENT TO A CONTINUANCE IF, IN FACT, WE CAN GO TO THE BANK THIS AFTERNOON.
THE COURT:	RIGHT, RIGHT.
MS. FRANKLIN:	SO, I PREFER TO JUST WAIT.
THE COURT:	WELL, LET'S SEE WHAT HAPPENS IN THE NEXT 15 MINUTES, BUT PROBABLY AROUND FIVE MINUTES TO NOON, WE'RE GOING TO HAVE TO RECESS---
MS. FRANKLIN:	EXACTLY.
THE COURT:	---AND GO DOWN THERE AND DO THAT OTHER BUSINESS.
MS. FRANKLIN:	THAT'LL BE FINE, AND MAYBE THAT'LL GIVE US AN OPPORTUNITY TO TALK.
THE COURT:	THAT'S GREAT. THAT'S GREAT. I WOULD HATE FOR HER THOUGH TO COME UP AND LOOK IN AND NOT SEE THE JUDGE AND LEAVE.
MS. FRANKLIN:	NO, NO, I WILL STAY, I WILL STAY, YOUR HONOR.
THE COURT:	OKAY.
MS. FRANKLIN:	THANK YOU, YOUR HONOR.
THE COURT:	VERY GOOD.

BARBARA WASHINGTON FRANKLIN

(CASE PASSED.)

DEPUTY CLERK: CALLING THE CASE OF BARBARA WASHINGTON FRANKLIN V. BRIANNA
                  JONES CIVIL ACTION 4417, 2009. PARTIES, PLEASE COME FORWARD AND IDENTIFY
                  YOURSELVES FOR THE RECORD.

MS. FRANKLIN: GOOD AFTERNOON, YOUR HONOR. BARBARA WASHINGTON FRANKLIN,
                  PLAINTIFF PRO SE.

THE COURT: THANK YOU, MA' AM. GOOD AFTERNOON.

MS. JONES: GOOD AFTERNOON, YOUR HONOR. BRIANNA JONES, DEFENDANT PRO SE AT
                  AT THIS TIME.

THE COURT: GOOD AFTERNOON.

MS. JONES: LET ME FIRST OFFER MY PROFOUND APOLOGIES. I DROVE ALL THE WAY FROM

                  SOUTH FLORIDA WITHIN A 24-HOUR OR 36-HOUR PERIOD. I DID MOST OF THE

                  DRIVING. I JUST GOT IN THIS MORNING.

                  COMMENT AND ANALYSIS: #2 BRIANNA JONES, *WITHOUT FINANCIAL MEANS TO
                  TRAVEL TO WASHINGTON TO ATTEND THE HEARING, BORROWED $1,500 FROM ONE
                  OF MY FRIENDS TO RENT A VEHICLE. THIS SAME FRIEND HAD ASSISTED HER
                  FINANCIALLY MANY TIMES IN THE PAST AND WAS NEVER REPAID BY BRIANNA JONES
                  NOR BY THE D.C. JUDICIAL AND FBI CO-CONSPIRATORS.*

THE COURT: WELL, I'M HAPPY THAT YOU WERE ABLE TO MAKE IT AND MAKE IT SAFELY.

MS. JONES: THANK YOU.

THE COURT: HOW DID YOU LEAVE SOUTH FLORIDA?

MS. JONES: BY CAR.

THE COURT: HOW WAS IT SOUTH---

MS. JONES: OH, I LEFT IT FINE. I LEFT---THE WEATHER WAS BEAUTIFUL, WARM AND SUNNY.

THE COURT: GOOD. WE LIKE TO HEAR---WE HERE IN THE COLD WINTRY MID-ATLANTIC, WE LIKE

                  TO HEAR GOOD WEATHER STORIES.

MS. JONES: I ALSO, THOUGH, JUDGE EKANS---IN 1996, AND THIS IS RELEVANT WITH REGARD TO THIS CASE, DR. STELLA EKANS SAW ME AS A PATIENT WITH REGARD TO THIS MATTER. SHE POTENTIALLY WAS GOING TO PROVIDE AN EXPERT WITNESS OPINION AS A RESULT OF THIS MATTER. I DON'T KNOW IF SHE IS RELATED TO YOU. I RECOGNIZE THE LAST NAME, SO I THOUGHT THAT I SHOULD CERTAINLY BRING THAT MATTER HERE TODAY.

> **COMMENT AND ANALYSIS: #3** *HERE BRIANNA JONES CRAFTILY DISGUISES HER SUGGESTION TO JUDGE EKANS THAT HE RECUSE HIMSELF FROM THE CASE BECAUSE OF HIS LEGAL RELATIONSHIP TO DR. STELLA EKANS. SHE ALSO USED HER VEILED RECUSAL REQUEST TO LET EKANS KNOW, RIGHT FROM THE START, THAT SHE WOULD TRY ANYTHING TO DEFEAT MY EFFORTS TO BE COMPENSATED. HER GOAL WAS TYPICAL OF THE SOCIOPATH---TO WIN AT ANY COST, AND IN HER CASE THIS INCLUDED ONGOING PATHOLOGICAL LYING WHILE TESTIFYING AND IN FILED COURT PLEADINGS PREPARED BY THE TEAM OF D.C. JUDICIAL AND FBI CO-CONSPIRATORS.*

THE COURT: YEAH. DR. STELLA EKANS, IF YOU'RE TALKING ABOUT THE SAME PERSON, I THINK YOU'RE TALKING ABOUT---

MS. JONES: GEORGETOWN---

THE COURT: ---IS MY SISTER-IN-LAW.

MS. JONES: YES, YES. WELL, SHE TREATED ME AND---FOR VIRTUAL---FOR THE PERIOD OF TIME AS RELATES TO THE NATURE OF THE CASE, THE ABUSE AS IT LINKS TO THIS SETTLEMENT, AND SHE SAID TO, ALLEGEDLY TO THE PLAINTIFF AT A BELAY (PHONETIC SP.) EVENT THAT THE DAMAGE HAD BEEN QUITE SEVERE, AND I REALLY WASN'T READY OR AFRAID TO BEGIN THE HEALING PROCESS. BUT MY UNDERSTANDING WAS THAT THE COMMENTS WERE VERY LIMITED AND JUST SIMILAR TO THE FACT THAT SHE WAS NO LONGER TREATING ME BECAUSE I WAS NOT READY FOR THAT TYPE OF TREATMENT.

> **COMMENT AND ANALYSIS: #4** *ANOTHER LIE. AT NO TIME DID I DISCUSS BRIANNA JONES' CASE WITH DR. EKANS. AFTER NUMEROUS MEETINGS AND CONVERATIONS WITH BRIANNA JONES, I CAME TO REALIZE HER DEEP EMOTIONAL AND MENTAL INSTABILITY. I, THUS, REQUESTED THAT SHE SUBMIT TO A PSYCHIATRIC CONSULTATION IN SUPPORT OF AND PRIOR TO MY FILING OF THE FLORIDA COMPLAINT IN BROWARD COUNTY CIRCUIT COURT IN MAY 1996. I ARRANGED FOR BRIANNA JONES TO BE EVALUATED BY DR. STELLA EKANS, A PSYCHIATRIST AND ALSO THE SISTER-IN-LAW OF JUDGE EKANS. HOWEVER, ACCORDING TO JONES, DUE TO HER REPEATED CANCELLATION OF SCHEDULED APPOINTMENTS, DR. EKANS DECLINED TO MEET WITH HER FURTHER.*

I THEN SEARCHED AND ARRANGED FOR A SECOND WASHINGTON PSYCHIATRIST, DR. SHEILA MONROE, TO PROVIDE A PSYCHIATRIC EVALUATION OF BRIANNA JONES. THE PSYCHIATRIC EVALUATION WAS INCLUDED AS AN EXHIBIT IN THE FLORIDA LAWSUIT, NOTIFYING THE OPPOSITION, AS WELL AS THE FUTURE D.C. JUDICIAL AND FBI CO-CONSPIRATORS FROM THE VERY BEGINNING, THAT THEY WERE DEALING WITH A MENTALLY IMPAIRED PERSON AS THE PLAINTIFF.

*I WOULD LEARN SOON ENOUGH THAT THE D.C. JUDICIAL, FBI CO-CONSPIRATORS AND THEIR RESPECTIVE FACILITATORS AND HANDLERS COULD CARE LESS ABOUT THE EMOTIONAL AND MENTAL CONDITION AND OVERALL HEALTH OF BRIANNA JONES. **THE UNEQUIVOCAL MISSION OF THE D.C. JUDICIAL AND FBI CRIMINAL ENTERPRISE WAS TO STEAL AND DEFRAUD ME OF THE ESTIMATED $50 MILLION OWED TO ME IN EARNED ATTORNEY'S FEES.***

THE COURT: I THINK THAT THE MATTER IS HERE TODAY AS A RESULT OF THE CASE HAVING REACHED A SETTLEMENT, IS THAT RIGHT?

MS. JONES: YES, YOUR HONOR.

THE COURT: AND THE ISSUE TODAY IS---

MS. FRANKLIN: **THE ISSUE TODAY, YOUR HONOR, IS COMPLIANCE WITH THE SETTLEMENT AGREEMENT---**

THE COURT: RIGHT.

MS. FRANKLIN: ---BY THE DEFENDANT.

THE COURT: **WHAT, IF ANYTHING, DO I HAVE TO DECIDE?** BECAUSE THE CASE IS LISTED AS ORAL EXAMINATION AND, GENERALLY SPEAKING, AT ORAL EXAMINATIONS, THE COURT'S ROLE IS PRETTY LIMITED. IN FACT, I'D SAY THAT IN A HIGH PERCENTAGE OF THE CASES, THE MATTERS ARE WORKED OUT, OUT IN **THE WITNESS ROOMS** OUT THERE WITH SOME OPPORTUNITY FOR THE **JUDGMENT CREDITOR** TO SPEAK WITH THE **JUDGMENT DEBTOR** ABOUT ASSETS. AND IT'S WHEN THERE'S NOT AN OPPORTUNITY OR, GIVEN AN OPPORTUNITY, THERE'S NO SUCCESS IN GETTING RESOLUTION THAT WAY, THAT THE ORAL EXAMINATION THEN COMES INTO COURTROOM AND THE **JUDGMENT CREDITOR** GETS TO EXAMINE THE **JUDGMENT DEBTOR** UNDER OATH. THE COURT'S ROLE IS FAIRLY LIMITED UNLESS IT APPEARS THAT THE COURT NEEDS TO USE ITS AUTHORITY TO GET TRUTHFUL ANSWERS.

COMMENT AND ANALYSIS: **#5** *RIGHT OUT OF THE GATE, JUDGE EKANS DELIBERATELY, INTENTIONALLY, DECEPTIVELY AND PURPOSEFULLY DEFINES, CHARACTERIZES AND MISLABELS ME AS A **JUDGMENT CREDITOR.** THE JUDGE, ALTHOUGH CORRECTED BY ME MORE THAN ONCE DURING THE PROCEEDINGS, HELD BETWEEN JANUARY 2011 AND JANUARY 2015, FOUR LONG YEARS, NEVERTHELESS PERSISTED IN DEFINING AND CATEGORIZING ME AS A **JUDGMENT CREDITOR**. EKANS' MISCHARACTERIZATION OF ME AS A* **JUDGMENT CREDITOR** *WAS NOT MERE JUDICIAL ERROR OR INADVERTENCE. IT WAS CAUSED BY SOMETHING MUCH DEEPER AND FAR MORE SINISTER THAN THAT. INACCURATELY DEFINING ME AS A **JUDGMENT CREDITOR** LAID THE FIRM FOUNDATION FOR EKANS TO AVOID THE COURT'S SERIOUS OBLIGATION TO ORDER AN INVESTIGATION OF THE ISSUE OF THE MASSIVE JUDICIAL AND FBI FRAUD, THEFT, CORRUPTION AND EXTORTION THAT FRAMED THE CASE FROM THE VERY BEGINNING AND THAT BEGGED FOR **COURT INVESTIGATION BY AN INDEPENDENT ENTITY.***

JUDGMENT CREDITORS ARE, BY LAW, RESPONSIBLE FOR THE SEARCH OF ASSETS. *HOWEVER, I WAS NOT A **JUDGMENT CREDITOR**. THIS WAS NOT A JUDGMENT CREDITOR'S RIGHTS CASE. WHEN JUDGE EKANS INSISTED ON ADDRESSING ME AS A **JUDGMENT CREDITOR** RIGHT UP AND UNTIL THE FINAL HEARING IN JANUARY 2015, JUDGE EKANS INTENTIONALLY, PURPOSEFULLY **AND WITH PREMEDITATION RIGGED MY CASE AND LAID THE TRAP FOR FINAL DISMISSAL OF MY LAWSUIT IN JANUARY 2015 WHEN I FAILED TO FIND ANY PORTION OF THE $34 MILLION IN SETTLEMENT PROCEEDS THAT HAD NOW MATURED WITH INTEREST TO APPROXIMATELY $100 MILLION.***

*THE DECEPTIVE MANUEVER AND UNETHICAL COURT STRATEGY AND TACTIC TRAPPED AND LOCKED ME INTO A POSITION OF A BOXER IN THE RING WHOSE FEET AND HANDS HAVE BEEN TIED BY HER OPPONENT, ALBEIT THE OPPONENT NOW INCLUDES THE PRESIDING JUDGE HIMSELF. **I WOULD, ULTIMATELY, NOT PREVAIL BECAUSE THE FIGHT WAS FIXED AND MY LAWSUIT HAD BEEN RIGGED BY JUDGE EKANS FOR FINAL DISMISSAL.***

JUDGE EKANS' INTENTIONAL MISAPPLICATION OF THE JUDGMENT CREDITOR LEGAL THEORY TO MY CASE WAS NOT ONLY A CASE OF JUDICIAL ABUSE OF DISCRETION, IT WAS JUDICIAL CORRUPTION BY ANY STANDARD AND DEFINITION. *NO COURT JUDGE SHOULD BE ALLOWED TO HIDE BEHIND INTENTIONAL MISCHARACTERIZATION AND MISLABELING OF A COURT LITIGANT IN ORDER TO AVOID THE ADOPTION OF APPROPRIATE JUDICIAL REMEDIES THAT A PARTICULAR CASE BEGS FOR, SUCH AS THE NEED OF THE REMEDY OF AN INDEPENDENT INVESTIGATION OF THE MISSING TENS OF MILLIONS OF DOLLARS IN CASE SETTLEMENT PROCEEDS IN MY LAWSUIT.*

NEED I SAY THAT FOR AN EXPERIENCED COURT JUDGE AS WAS JUDGE EKANS, IGNORANCE OR MISAPPLICATION OF THE LAW WAS NO EXCUSE, NOR SHOULD IT HAVE BEEN.

JUDGE EKANS HAD SERVED A TERM APPROACHING 30 YEARS ON THE BENCH AS A D.C. COURT JUDGE. SO HE HAD MANY YEARS OF PRACTICE UNDER HIS BELT OF RIGGING CASES FOR DISMISSAL IF HE CHOSE TO.

MS. FRANKLIN: YOUR HONOR, THE OCTOBER 18TH ORDER THAT JUDGE STARR ISSUED BASICALLY REQUESTED AND REQUIRED MS. JONES TO PROVIDE PLAINTIFF, YOURS TRULY, WITH THE FINANCIAL INFORMATION WITH REGARDS TO THE IDENTITY AND LOCATION OF THE BANK, THE BANKING INSTITUTION THAT HOLDS THE ASSETS, THE SETTLEMENT PROCEEDS, AND ALSO TO PROVIDE CERTIFIED AND NOTARIZED STATEMENTS FROM THE BANK CONFIRMING THE TOTAL AMOUNT OF THE SETTLEMENT PROCEEDS.

THE SETTLEMENT AGREEMENT SPECIFICALLY STATED THAT ALL OF THE SETTLEMENT PROCEEDS WERE TO BE DEPOSITED IN THE ATTORNEY ESCROW ACCOUNT AND THEN THEREAFTER, THE AGREED UPON DISTRIBUTION BETWEEN THE PARTIES BASED UPON THE ATTORNEY RETAINER AGREEMENT. AND BECAUSE I HAVE NOT UNTIL THIS TIME BEEN PROVIDED WITH THAT INFORMATION FROM MS. JONES, I HAVE---- SHE HAS NOT PROVIDED ANY DISCLOSURE AT ALL, I HAVE NO IDEA WHERE THE FUNDS ARE, WHAT BANK IS HOLDING THE FUNDS, THE TOTAL AMOUNT OF THE FUNDS. SHE HAS SIMPLY REFUSED. THE OCTOBER 18TH ORDER GAVE HER UNTIL OCTOBER 25TH TO COMPLY. SINCE THAT ORDER WAS NOT COMPLIED WITH, ON OCTOBER 27TH, I DID FILE A MOTION FOR CONTEMPT---

COMMENT AND ANALYSIS: #6 *I STATED IN PLAIN AND CLEAR ENGLISH THE ASSISTANCE I WAS SEEKING FROM THE COURT. THERE WAS NO EVIDENCE AT ALL OF MY COMING BEFORE THE COURT ARMED WITH A JUDGMENT WHICH WOULD HAVE RIGHTLY CLASSIFIED ME AS A JUDGMENT CREDITOR.*

JUDGE EKANS' ENTRAPMENT OF ME IN THE JUDGMENT CREDITOR RABBIT HOLE UNFAIRLY AND UNJUSTLY DENIED ME MY RIGHT TO BE PAID FOR MY MANY YEARS OF SERVICE TO BRIANNA JONES, AND THE REIMBURSEMENT OF APPROXIMATELY A QUARTER OF A MILLION DOLLARS IN OUT-OF-POCKET EXPENSES RELATED TO MAINTENANCE OF THE CLIENT, HER NEED, AT ONE POINT, FOR ROUND THE CLOCK SECURITY DUE TO CONSTANT THREATS FROM THE OPPOSITION, AS WELL AS THE LONG AND PROTRACTED LITIGATION THAT OCCURRED IN TWO JUDICIAL JURISDICTIONS, NAMELY, BROWARD COUNTY, FLORIDA AND WASHINGTON, D.C.

THE COURT: THAT'S WHAT I'M READING NOW.

MS. FRANKLIN: ---AND THE COURT THEREAFTER GRANTED THE MOTION FOR CONTEMPT BECAUSE THERE WAS ABSOLUTELY NO COMPLIANCE WITH THE ORDER AT ALL. I HAVE NEVER RECEIVED ANY INFORMATION, NO DOCUMENTATION, NOTHING. AND SO, THEREFORE, THE SETTLEMENT AGREEMENT THAT'S ON FILE WITH THE COURT CAN'T POSSIBLY BE ADHERED TO BECAUSE THERE'S BEEN NO INFORMATION PROVIDED TO ME.

THE COURT: MS. JONES, BEFORE I GET INTO THIS, LET ME JUST ASK YOU. YOU BROUGHT UP YOUR

                PRIOR ASSOCIATION WITH DR. EKANS. IS THERE SOMETHING YOU WANT ME TO DO

                ABOUT THAT?

MS. JONES: WELL, I'M JUST SAYING THAT DR. EKANS EXPRESSED TO HER THAT WHAT HAPPENED TO ME AS A RESULT OF THIS CASE AND THE, THE PLAINTIFF'S REPRESENTATION OF ME WAS TOKENISTIC AT BEST. SHE HAS PERPETRATED A FRAUD UPON THE RECORD IN ORDER TO ENRICH HERSELF. AT THE TIME OF ANY SETTLEMENT, SHE WAS NOT THE ATTORNEY. THE BROWARD DISTRICT---THE BROWARD COUNTY COURT. THEY GAVE HER AMPLE OPPORTUNITY TO COME IN AS COUNSEL.

                COMMENT AND ANALYSIS: #7 HERE BRIANNA JONES BEGINS WHAT WILL BE HER *CHARACTERISTIC PATHOLOGICAL LYING AND THE FABRICATION OF THE FACTS. FOR BRIANNA JONES, LYING WAS LIKE BREATHING. IT JUST CAME NATURALLY. AT NO TIME DID I SPEAK WITH DR. STELLA EKANS REGARDING HER EVALUATION OF BRIANNA JONES. I WAS AT ALL TIMES THE ATTORNEY OF RECORD IN THE FLORIDA CASE, HAVING BEEN PROPERLY AND LEGALLY ADMITTED THROUGH A MOTION PRO HAC VICE FILED BY RETAINED FLORIDA CO-COUNSEL.*

                BRIANNA JONES' SETTLEMENT WITH THE RIDGEWAY ESTATE WAS CONDUCTED BEHIND MY BACK AND IN CONCERT WITH THE JUDICIAL AND FBI CO-CONSPIRATORS.

                BRIANNA JONES WAS ADEPT AT TWISTING THE FACTS AND TRUTH. SHE KNEW NO OTHER WAY. SHE WAS ADEPT AT TAKING A KERNAL OF THE TRUTH AND MIXING IT WITH A CUP OF LIES. AND SO, SHE WAS CORRECT IN SAYING THAT FRAUD WAS THE DOMINANT ISSUE IN THE CASE. HOWEVER, SHE INTENTIONALLY FAILED TO POINT TO THE CO-CONSPIRATOR "OFFICIALS" THAT SHE WOULD BE SUMMONED TO MEET WITH PERIODICALLY IN WASHINGTON AREA HOTEL SUITES.

THE COURT: IS IT YOUR---ARE YOU SAYING YOU WANT TO OVERTURN THE SETTLEMENT, IS THAT WHAT YOU---

MS. JONES: I WANT TO MAKE---THE REASON I WENT ALONG WITH REGARD TO THE SETTLEMENT IS THAT I DID NOT WANT TO PUBLICLY DISROBE ATTORNEY FRANKLIN, AND I STILL HAVE INTENTIONS OF COMPENSATING HER. THIS IS NOT A MATTER OF NOT COMPENSATING HER. EVEN IF THE LAW SAYS THAT I DO NOT HAVE TO, I FEEL I AM MORALLY OBLIGATED. BUT TO NOW TAKE THIS AS A RESULT OF A DIFFERENT CASE IN A DIFFERENT ARENA AND PERPETRATE A FRAUD UPON THIS COURT, THIS--- SHE HAS PERPETRATED AN OUTRIGHT LIE. THESE DOCUMENTS FROM THE COURT TELLING HER THAT IF SHE DID NOT COME IN OR OBTAIN FOREIGN COUNSEL WITHIN 30 DAYS, SHE WOULD NOT BE ALLOWED TO PRACTICE. SHE HAS ASSISTED ME OUTSIDE OF THE SCOPE OF REPRESENTATION. AGAIN, HER REPRESENTATION OF ME HAS BEEN TOKENISTIC AT BEST. WE HAD DEVELOPED AN EXTREMELY, VERY CLOSE RELATIONSHIP.

THE COURT: CAN I JUST---I MEAN, IT'S---

MS. FRANKLIN: YOUR HONOR, YOUR HONOR, COULD I JUST SPEAK TO THIS?

THE COURT: WELL, CAN YOU JUST HOLD ON---

MS. FRANKLIN: SURE, YOUR HONOR.

THE COURT: ---BECAUSE WHAT I'M TRYING TO, I GUESS, GET TO IS THAT WE SEEM TO BE WAY

BEYOND THAT.

MS. FRANKLIN: THAT IS CORRECT.

THE COURT: I MEAN, I'M---I DIDN'T GO THROUGH THIS FILE, YOU KNOW, WITH A VIEW OF METICULOUSLY CHECKING EVERY ENTRY BECAUSE IT'S SET DOWN FOR ORAL EXAMINATION. **AN ORAL EXAMINATION** IS A FAIRLY ROUTINE HEARING FOR A COURT. WE SET THEM, TWO OR THREE OR FOUR OF THEM AS NEEDS BE FOR 11 O'CLOCK OR NOON ON FRIDAYS BECAUSE **THEY'RE ROUTINE ATTEMPTS TO ENFORCE OR COLLECT ON *JUDGMENTS*.**

COMMENT AND ANALYSIS: **#8** *JUDGE EKANS REPEATEDLY REFERRED TO THE PROCEEDING ON JANUARY 21, 2011 AS AN ORAL EXAMINATION, BASED ON THE* TERM USED IN JUDGE STARR'S OCTOBER 18, 2010 ORDER. HOWEVER, JUDGE *STARR'S ORDER SPECIFICALLY SET THE ORAL EXAM FOR A VERY NARROW AND SPECIFIC PURPOSE. THE ORDER STATES IN PERTINENT PART: "THE COURT WILL SET THIS FOR ORAL EXAM AT WHICH TIME ALL DOCUMENTS REQUIRED TO BE PRODUCED MUST BE BROUGHT TO COURT."* **THERE'S NOTHING IN THE OCTOBER 18, 2010 ORDER THAT IN ANY WAY REFERS TO ME OR IMPLIES THAT I AM A JUDGMENT CREDITOR.**

MS. JONES: YOUR HONOR, WHAT I WOULD---

THE COURT: BUT, BUT, BUT---

MS. JONES: I'M SORRY.

THE COURT: ---AS I'M GOING THROUGH THESE ENTRIES NOW, IT SEEMS TO ME THAT THE LAST THING THAT HAPPENED HERE IS THAT JUDGE STARR ENTERED AN ORDER OF CONTEMPT AND GAVE YOU UNTIL TODAY TO COME IN WITH RECORDS OR YOU'D BE ARRESTED. THAT'S WHAT I'M READING HERE.

MS. JONES: THE REASON---AND THE IRONY IS THIS. WHEN I WALKED INTO HER OFFICE IN 1994, I ASKED HER TO HAVE THE CHILD RAPIST ARRESTED, AND THE IRONY IS THAT SHE WAS FOUND IN CONTEMPT OF COURT. IT WAS NOT AN ASSAULT AND BATTERY CASE; IT WAS A MAN THAT BRUTALLY RAPED ME FROM THE AGE OF 10 TO 12 AND STALKED ME UNTIL THE AGE OF 16, AND THEN SHE WOULD NOT HAVE HIM ARRESTED. HER RESPONSE WAS I'M NOT IN THE HABIT OF ARRESTING PEOPLE. AND TO THEN FILE THIS CONTEMPT ORDER. I HAVE PROTECTED HER. THE NEW EVIDENCE IS SIMPLY THAT I WANT TO INTRODUCE THAT EVIDENCE BECAUSE THEN THAT HAS A WHOLE LIGHT---THIS WHOLE ENTIRE MATTER A TO---

                COMMENT AND ANALYSIS: #9 *AT NO TIME, IN MY LIFETIME, HAVE I EVER BEEN FOUND IN CONTEMPT BY A COURT OF LAW. ANOTHER BRIANNA JONES LIE.*

THE COURT: LET ME ASK YOU THIS. DID YOU BRING DOCUMENTS THAT YOU WERE ORDERED TO BRING TODAY?

MS. JONES: NO, I DID NOT.

THE COURT: YOU DIDN'T.

MS. JONES: BECAUSE I WANT TO INTRODUCE THE EVIDENCE THAT GOES TO THE VERY HEART OF HER REPRESENTATION OF ME. IT'S BEEN TOKENISTIC AGAIN AND UNETHICAL AT BEST.

MS. FRANKLIN: YOUR HONOR, MAY I PLEASE SAY SOMETHING? THIS IS THE KIND OF RUNNNG COMMENTARY THAT JUDGE STARR WOULD NOT PERMIT. WHEN WE WENT BEFORE | JUDGE STARR, AND YOUR HONOR CAN DISCERN FROM THE RECORD, MS. JONES HAS NEVER RESPONDED TO ANY OF THE FILINGS. SHE HAS NEVER FILED AN ANSWER. JUDGE STARR SET THE MATTER FOR TRACK ONE MEDIATION TRIAL. THE VERY SAME DAY, MS. JONES ASKED ME TO SETTLE THIS MATTER. I CAME BACK TO THE COURTHOUSE AND WE MET DOWN IN THE CAFETERIA. SHE---

COMMENT AND ANALYSIS: #10 BRIANNA JONES *PLEADED WITH ME TO SETTLE MY LAWSUIT ON THE SAME DAY IN FEBRUARY 2010 WHEN JUDGE STARR SET THE MATTER FOR TRACK 1 TRIAL AND MEDIATION.*

MS. JONES: YOUR HONOR, MAY I OBJECT?

MS. FRANKLIN: YOUR HONOR, MAY I CONTINUE, PLEASE?

THE COURT: YOU, YOU, YOU ARE, YOU ARE IN CONTEMPT OF COURT, AND I'M NOT ALTOGETHER CLEAR THAT YOU UNDERSTAND THE PRECARIOUS SITUATION THAT YOU HAVE PLACED YOURSELF IN. I DON'T---I'M NOT SURE WHAT YOU THOUGHT WAS GOING TO HAPPEN TODAY, BUT YOU'VE JUST TOLD ME THAT YOU'VE COME HERE WITHOUT THE DOCUMENTS THAT YOU WERE ORDERED TO BRING, AND THE JUDGE HAS ALREADY ENTERED AN ORDER FINDING YOU IN CONTEMPT. I JUST LEFT A COURTROOM WITH A CELLBLOCK AND I STILL CAN GO BACK DOWN THERE. I'M NOT CLEAR THAT YOU FULLY APPRECIATE THE POSITION THAT YOU'VE PLACED YOURSELF IN.

MS. JONES: YOUR HONOR---

THE COURT: MA' AM, YOU MIGHT WANT TO CONSIDER FOR A MOMENT BEFORE YOU START SPEAKING. NOW, I'M NOT SURE WHAT YOU DIDN'T UNDERSTAND ABOUT THE ORDER. YOU SAID YOU DROVE UP HERE---

MS. JONES: I'VE BEEN IN COMMUNUICATION WITH---

THE COURT: ---FROM FLORIDA, YOU DROVE UP HERE TO DO WHAT?

MS. JONES: I'VE BEEN IN COMMUNICATION BECAUSE I WANT, I WANT THE RECORD TO REVEAL THE TRUTH---

THE COURT: WELL---

MS. JONES: ---WITH REGARD TO---AND I THOUGHT THAT THIS---

THE COURT: ---I'M GOING TO TELL YOU WHAT THE RECORD REVEALS. THE RECORD REVEALS THAT YOU HAVE BEEN ORDERED BY A JUDGE OF THIS COURT TO BRING DOCUMENTS SHOWING WHERE THIS ACCOUNT IS, AND THAT'S WHAT YOU ARE GOING TO DO OR YOU'RE GOING TO SUFFER THE PAINS OF CONTEMPT UNTIL YOU DO.

COMMENT AND ANALYSIS: #11 *BRIANNA JONES DID NOT DENY HAVING THE BANK STATEMENTS ORDERED BY JUDGE STARR TO BE PRODUCED.*

THE ODYSSEY OF JUDICIAL CORRUPTION

MS. JONES: YOUR HONOR, I UNDERSTAND WITH ALL DUE RESPECT, AND I DEFER TO THIS
                 COURT.

THE COURT: I'M TRYING TO GIVE YOU ALL DUE RESPECT---

MS. JONES: I DID SPEAK WITH COUNSEL---

THE COURT: ---BUT I'M TRYING TO COMMUNICATE TO YOU THAT WE'RE NOT HERE FOR---

MS. JONES: I'VE BEEN IN TOUCH WITH HER UNTIL ONCE---AND I WANT TO MAKE THE RECORD
                 CLEAR. THERE WAS SOMEONE THAT---WELL, I'VE BEEN IN, I'VE BEEN IN
                 COMMUNICATION WITH HER ON A DAILY BASIS AND I SPOKE WITH HER ATTORNEY
                 AND HE---AND THE ATTORNEY---

THE COURT: I DON'T THINK YOU'RE COMMUNICATING THE THING THAT YOU'VE BEEN ORDERED TO
                 COMMUNICATE. I'M NOT---I DON'T KNOW WHAT THE SUBJECT OF THE
                 COMMUNICATION IS, BUT---MAYBE YOU DIDN'T---DID YOU GET A COPY OF THIS
                 ORDER?

MS. JONES: YES, I DID.

THE COURT: YOU DON'T NEED TO SEE IT. YOU'VE SEEN IT.

MS. JONES: YES, I HAVE.

THE COURT: IS THERE SOMETHING THAT YOU DIDN'T UNDERSTAND ABOUT IT?

MS. JONES: MY UNDERSTANDING WAS THAT BECAUSE I SETTLED THE CASE UNDER EXTREME
                 DURESS AND TO PROTECT THE PLAINTIFF---

THE COURT: WELL, **RIGHT NOW THE PROTECTION THAT THE PLAINTFF'S LOOKING FOR IS TO
                 ENFORCE THE SETTLEMENT AGREEMENT**. THAT'S THE ONLY PROTECTION THAT
                 SHE'S ASKING FOR. NOW, IF YOU REFUSE TO PROVIDE THIS INFORMATION---

MS. JONES: I'M NOT REFUSING YOUR HONOR. I'M NOT REFUSING.

THE COURT: THEN PROVIDE IT. NOW---

MS. JONES: I DON'T HAVE IT WITH ME.

                 COMMENT AND ANALYSIS: #12 *BRIANNA JONES DOES NOT DENY POSSESSION OF
                 THE BANK STATEMENTS. SHE JUST DENIES HAVING THEM WITH HER AT THIS
                 PARTICULAR HEARING.*

BARBARA WASHINGTON FRANKLIN

THE COURT: I'M WONDERING WHO YOU'RE GOING TO SEND TO GET IT.

MS. JONES: WELL, I DON'T HAVE IT WITH ME AND THIS IS WHAT I'VE GOTTEN FOR PROTECTING

THE PLAINTIFF. NOW, SHE SAID OVER AND OVER AGAIN---

THE COURT: RIGHT, RIGHT, RIGHT. WE'RE NOT---

MS. JONES: ---THAT I WAS---

MS. FRANKLIN: NO---

THE COURT: ---WE'RE NOT, WE'RE NOT GOING INTO THAT.

MS. JONES: I SEE.

THE COURT: WE'RE NOT---THIS IS NOT A FORUM FOR THAT. OCTOBER 18, 2010, ORDER REQUIRED DEFENDANT TO IDENTIFY HER ASSETS AND PROVIDE CONTEMPORANEOUS RECORDS OF SAME TO PLAINTIFF. **BECAUSE DEFENDANT HAS NOT OPPOSED THE MOTION AND IT IS QUITE EVIDENT THAT WHAT WAS ORDERED IN THE OCTOBER 18, 2010, ORDER MUST BE PRODUCED**, THE COURT WILL SET THIS FOR ORAL EXAM AT WHICH TIME ALL DOCUMENTS REQUIRED TO BE PRODUCED MUST, MUST BE BROUGHT TO COURT.

IF DEFENDANT FAILS TO APPEAR ON THE DATE AND TIME, A BODY ATTACHMENT SHALL ISSUE FOR HER. IF SUCH OCCURS, THE U.S. MARSHAL SHALL BE COMMANDED TO BRING THE DEFENDANT TO COURT. ORDERED PLAINTIFF'S MOTION FOR CONTEMPT IS GRANTED IN PART AND ORDERED THAT PLAINTIF'S MOTION TO SUPPLEMENT THE MOTION TO REINSTATE AND COURT ENFORCEMENT OF EXECUTED SETTLEMENT IS GRANTED AND SET FOR ORAL EXAM TODAY. (EMPHASIS ADDED.)

COMMENT AND ANALYSIS: #13 *JUDGE EKANS' SWIFT AND PRECISE ACTIONS COMBINED WITH HIS IMPARTIAL ATTITUDE AND JUDICIAL DEMEANOR TO SEE TO IT THAT THE OCTOBER 18, 2010 ORDER ISSUED BY JUDGE STARR AND UNOPPOSED BY BRIANNA JONES AT ALL TIMES WAS APPRECIATED AND ENCOURAGING. BASED ON MY OBSERVANCE OF EKANS' ACTIONS, ATTITUDE AND DEMEANOR, I HAD NO REASON TO BELIEVE THAT NOT ONLY HAD THE CO-CONSPIRATORS CREPT INTO THE D.C. COURT SYSTEM LONG BEFORE MY CASE WAS FILED IN MARCH 2009, THEY WERE ABOUT TO SHOW ME, IN GRAPHIC AND UNEQUIVOCAL TERMS, THAT NOT ONLY HAD THEY TAKEN OVER THE PROTRACTED LITIGATION OF MY CASE, BUT THEY HAD ALSO DONE SO IN A WAY THAT PRE-DETERMINED JUDGE EKANS' FINAL DISMISSAL OF MY CASE IN JANUARY 2015 AND SUBSEQUENT DISMISSAL WITH PREJUDICE OF MY CASE IN MARCH 2015.*

THE ODYSSEY OF JUDICIAL CORRUPTION

MS. JONES: YOUR HONOR, MAY I BRING, MAY I NOW---BECAUSE I, BECAUSE I---

THE COURT: I'M GOING TO HAVE YOU GET UP HERE ON THE WITNESS STAND, I'M GONG TO PUT YOU UNDER OATH, AND YOU'RE GOING TO ANSWER THE QUESTIONS IDENTIFYING THESE ASSETS, OR I'M GOING TO SEND YOU TO D.C. JAIL. THAT'S ALL THERE IS TO IT.

MS. JONES: THAT'S PERFECTLY FINE, BUT ALSO---

THE COURT: WELL, IT'S FINE OR NOT FINE, BUT THAT'S THE WAY I'M GOING TO ENFORCE THE

ORDER. SO, YOU CAN COME UP HERE ON THE WITNESS STAND.

MS. JONES: CERTAINLY.

DEPUTY CLERK: REMAIN STANDING AND RAISE YOUR RIGHT HAND.

THEREUPON,

BRIANNA JONES,

THE DEFENDANT HEREIN, HAVING BEEN FIRST DULY SWORN BY THE DEPUTY CLERK, WAS EXAMINED AND TESTIFIED AS FOLLOWS:

DEPUTY CLERK: YOU MAY BE SEATED.

THE DEFENDANT: YES, YOUR HONOR.

THE COURT: MS. FRANKLIN?

DIRECT EXAMINATION

BY MS. FRANKLIN:

Q   GOOD AFTERNOON, MS. JONES.

A   GOOD AFTERNOON.

Q   WOULD YOU PLEASE STATE YOUR FULL NAME FOR THE RECORD?

A   IT'S BRIANNA JONES.

Q   WHERE DO YOU CURRENTLY RESIDE?

A   BROWARD COUNTY, FLORIDA.

THE COURT: THE ADDRESS, PLEASE, MA' AM. THE ADDRESS.

THE DEFENDANT: MY ADDRESS IS 4321 MT. TOWSON BOULEVARD SOUTH, UNIT---UNIT D AS IN DAVID, AND I'VE HAD A COUPLE OF ADDRESSES IN THAT SAME FACILITY BECAUSE I'VE HAD PROBLEMS WITH THE UNIT, AND MOSTLY I'VE BEEN IN TRANSIT BACK AND FORTH HERE---

BY MS. FRANKLIN:

Q   AND---I'M SORRY.

A   -- TO FLORIDA. I'M SORRY.

Q   ARE YOU FINISHED? ARE YOU FINISHED WITH REGARD TO---

A   YES.

Q   ---YOUR ADDRESS? I'D LIKE TO DIRECT YOUR ATTENTION TO THE YEAR 2010. DID THERE COME A TIME IN 2010 WHEN YOU WERE SERVED WITH AN ORDER OF THIS COURT DATED OCTOBER 18TH, 2010?

A   YES. YES.

MS. FRANKLIN: YOUR HONOR, MAY I APPROACH?

THE COURT: (NO AUDIBLE RESPONSE.)

BY MS. FRANKLIN:

Q   I'D LIKE TO SHOW YOU WHAT HAS BEEN MARKED AS PLAINTIFF'S EXHIBIT A. DO YOU RECOGNIZE THE DOCUMENT?

A   YES.

Q   WOULD YOU READ THE CAPTION OF THE DOCUMENT, PLEASE?

A   ORDER GRANTING MOTION FOR REINSTATEMENT AND COURT ENFORCEMENT OF EXECUTED SETTLEMENT AGREEMENT AND MOTION TO SUPPLEMENT SAME.

Q   MM-HMM. DOES THAT ORDER DIRECT THAT YOU TAKE CERTAIN ACTION?

A   YES.

Q   DO YOU AGREE THAT YOUR OBLIGATIONS UNDER THE ORDER BEGINS ON THE SECOND PAGE OF THE ORDER? IF YOU'D TURN TO PAGE TWO OF THE ORDER, AND I'D LIKE TO DIRECT YOUR ATTENTION TO THE SECOND PARAGRAPH OF PAGE TWO OF THE ORDER. HAVE YOU FOUND IT?

A   YES.

Q   ALL RIGHT. WOULD YOU PLEASE READ THAT PROVISION OF THE ORDER?

A   **ORDER THAT ON OR BEFORE OCTOBER 25TH, 2010, DEFENDANT SHALL, SHALL DISCLOSE TO PLAINTIFF IN WRITING, CERTIFIED AND NOTARIZED, THE TOTAL AMOUNT, LOCATION, AND WHEREABOUTS OF ALL SETTLEMENT PROCEEDS AND ANY ACCUMULATED INTEREST ON THE PRINCIPAL AMOUNT OF THE SETTLEMENT PROCEEDS CALCULATED FROM APRIL 1997 UNTIL THE DATE OF DISBURSEMENT AT CALENDAR YEAR 2010, HOWEVER AND WHEREVER THE AFORESAID PROCEEDS ARE HELD, LOCATED OR SITUATED---**

Q   OKAY.

A   --AND IT IS FURTHER—

Q   ALL RIGHT. THANK YOU. AND HAVE YOU BEEN ABLE TO COMPLY WITH THAT SPECIFIC, OR THOSE SPECIFIC OBLIGATIONS UNDER THAT PROVISION OF THE ORDER?

A   NO, I HAVE NOT.

Q   HAVE YOU DISCLOSED TO PLAINTIFF IN WRITING, CERTIFIED AND NOTARIZED, THE TOTAL AMOUNT, LOCATION AND WHEREABOUTS OF ALL SETTLEMENT PROCEEDS?

A   NO, I HAVE NOT.

Q   WHERE ARE THE TOTAL AMOUNT OF THE SETTLEMENT PROCEEDS HELD?

A   I HAVE NO IDEA AT THIS POINT, AT THIS POINT AS OF THIS DAY.

Q   HAVE YOU EVER KNOWN THE LOCATION OF THE SETTLEMENT PROCEEDS?

A   I'D LIKE TO THINK I HAD.

BARBARA WASHINGTON FRANKLIN

Q	WHEN WAS THAT?
A	AT VARIOUS TIMES. I'VE BEEN---
Q	WHEN WAS THE LAST TIME?
A	I WOULD SAY I WAS SURE A FEW WEEKS AGO.
Q	WHERE WERE THE PROCEEDS LOCATED A FEW WEEKS AGO?
A	I SHARED THAT WITH YOU, I BELIEVE.
Q	NO, YOU HAVE NEVER SHARED ANY INFORMATION AT ALL.

THE COURT: SHARE IT WITH THE COURT.

A	I WOULD LIKE TO THINK THAT THEY WERE HELD IN VARIOUS ACCOUNTS.

YOUR HONOR, THIS IS GOING INTO A SECURITY ISSUE FOR ME, AND

ATTORNEY---THE PLAINTIFF IS WELL AWARE OF THAT. WE'VE DISCUSSED

IN GREAT DETAIL---

MS. FRANKLIN: EXCUSE ME, I—

COMMENT AND ANALYSIS: #14 *HERE BRIANNA JONES ACKNOWLEDGES THAT THE CO-CONSPIRATORS HAVE KEPT HER INFORMED OF THE LOCATION AND AMOUNT OF THE SETTLEMENT PROCEEDS, AS OF A FEW WEEKS AGO AND THEY WERE BEING HELD IN* **BANK OF AMERICA** *IN MULTIPLE ACCOUNTS.*

THE COURT: A SECURITY ISSUE?

MS. FRANKLIN: IT'S---

THE DEFENDANT: AND SO, TO PUT THAT ON RECORD---

MS. FRANKLIN: YOUR HONOR, I HAVEN'T---I, I---

THE DEFENDANT: I WOULD LIKE TO COMPLY.

MS. FRANKLIN: I'M NOT AWARE OF A SECURITY ISSUE BECAUSE I HAVE NO KNOWLEDGE AS TO WHERE THE PROCEEDS ARE OR WHO'S HOLDING THEM. THAT'S WHY WE'RE HERE.

THE DEFENDANT: YOU---PLAINTIFF HAS RECEIVED--- I CAN---WHAT I'D LIKE TO DO IS PROVIDE THE DOCUMENTS THAT I DO HAVE AT HOME AND I WOULD LIKE TO HAVE COUNSEL WITH ME, BUT I WOULD LIKE TO PROVIDE PLAINTIFF WITH DOCUMENTS THAT I DO HAVE AS IT, AS IT, AS IT RELATES TO THIS CASE. THERE WAS SOME THINGS WITH REGARD---I'M SORRY. I'LL LET THE PLAINTIFF CONTINUE TO ASK THE QUESTIONS.

COMMENT AND ANALYSIS: #15 BRIANNA JONES *REPEATELY TESTIFIED THAT SHE WAS IN POSSESSION OF THE DOCUMENTS IDENTIFIED IN THE OCTOBER 18, 2010 COURT ORDER. NEVERTHELESS, AT NO TIME DURING THE PENDENCY OF THE CASE BEFORE JUDGE EKANS DID HE AFFORD HIMSELF OF THE NUMEROUS JUDICIAL REMEDIES AVAILABLE TO THE COURT TO CAUSE BRIANNA JONES TO PRODUCE THE BANK STATEMENTS AND RELATED DOCUMENTS. THIS WAS EVIDENCE OF JUDGE EKANS' UNEQUIVOCAL PARTICIPATION IN THE CONSPIRACY AND CRIMINAL ENTERPRISE.*

THIS WAS ALSO EVIDENCE OF THE SYSTEMIC CORRUPTION THAT GRIPPED THE D.C. COURT SYSTEM. THUS, THE CASE CONCLUDED WITHOUT BRIANNA JONES EVER PRODUCING THE BANK STATEMENTS, PROVING THAT EVEN THOUGH SHE CONTINUALLY THUMBED HER NOSE AT THE COURT BY FAILING TO PRODUCE THE COURT-ORDERED BANK STATEMENTS, SHE PROVED THAT SHE WOULD BE TREATED BY THE COURT AS A PERSON ABOVE THE LAW.

THIS WAS, MORE IMPORTANTLY, CLEAR EVIDENCE OF RAMPANT AND FLOURISHING D.C. JUDICIAL AND FBI FRAUD, THEFT, CORRUPTION AND EXTORTION.

MS. FRANKLIN: YOUR

THE COURT: NO, YOU, YOU'RE NOT GOING TO CONTINUE ANYTHING UNTIL YOU ANSWER THE LAST QUESTION THAT'S PENDING.

THE DEFENDANT: NO, I'D LIKE TO THINK---

THE COURT: YOU---

THE DEFENDANT: I'D LIKE TO THINK THAT I HAVE KNOWN AND I KNOW, BUT THERE'S AN ISSUE WITH REGARD TO MY SECURITY AND IT'S--- THROUGHOUT THE COURSE OF THIS SITUATION, THE PLAINTIFF HAS ALSO BEEN THREATENED, AND I AM CONCERNED WITH REGARD TO MY SECURITY. AND I WOULD ALSO LIKE TO HAVE COUNSEL PRESENT, BUT I AM WILLING---

BARBARA WASHINGTON FRANKLIN

COMMENT AND ANALYSIS: #16 *PRIOR TO FILING MY LAWSUIT AGAINST BRIANNA JONES, I HAD INCURRED TENS OF THOUSANDS OF DOLLARS IN OUT-OF-POCKET EXPENSES (TAKEN FROM FAMILY SAVINGS AND RETIREMENT ASSETS) RELATED TO PAYMENT OF HER ROUND-THE-CLOCK SECURITY, ALWAYS EXPECTING TO BE FULLY REIMBURSED AT THE TIME OF DISBURSEMENT OF THE CASE SETTLEMENT PROCEEDS.*

BY MS. FRANKLIN:

Q   ARE YOU REFUSING TO ANSWER THE QUESTION WITH REGARD TO THE LOCATION OF THE TOTAL AMOUNT OF THE SETTLEMENT PROCEEDS THAT YOU WERE AWARE OF THREE WEEKS AGO ACCORDING TO YOUR TESTIMONY?

A   I'M NOT REFUSING TO ANSWER. I WOULD LIKE TO PROVIDE YOU WITH ALL OF THESE DOCUMENTS.

Q   WHERE ARE THE PROCEEDS LOCATED?

A   THE LAST I UNDERSTOOD, THEY WERE LOCATED WITH BANK OF AMERICA.

COMMENT AND ANALYSIS: #17 *BANK OF AMERICA, THE FLAGSHIP BANKING INSTITUTION THAT HELD THE SETTLEMENT PROCEEDS IN MULTIPLE ACCOUNTS HAS PLAYED A MAJOR ROLE IN THIS CASE OF HISTORIC D.C. JUDICIAL AND FBI FRAUD, THEFT, CORRUPTION AND EXTORTION CONSPIRACY AND CRIMINAL ENTERPRISE.*

Q   WHERE? WHAT BRANCH?

A   I DON'T---THERE WAS A BRANCH IN DAVEY, FLORIDA, AND OTHER PARTS, BUT IT'S BEEN MY UNDERSTANDING THAT THE FUNDS HAVE BEEN MOVED. THERE WAS ONE FIRM FROM MARYLAND. I DO HAVE COPIES OF THAT, WITH REGARD TO THE LOCATION AND THE TOTAL AMOUNT OF THE ASSETS.

Q   **WERE THE ASSETS EVER LOCATED IN BANK OF AMERICA IN THE WASHINGTON REGION?**

A   **YES, I BELIEVE SO.**

Q   WHEN WAS THE LAST TIME THEY WERE LOCATED IN THE WASHINGTON REGION WITH BANK OF AMERICA?

A   I WOULD THINK, I WOULD THINK THEY WOULD HAVE TO BE MOST RECENTLY.

COMMENT AND ANALYSIS: #18 *THE CO-CONSPIRATORS KEPT BRIANNA JONES INFORMED AS TO THE LOCATION AND MOVEMENT OF THE SETTLEMENT PROCEEDS. THIS IS ALSO EVIDENCE THAT SHE WAS A WILLING CO-CONSPIRATOR IN THIS HISTORIC D.C. JUDICIAL AND FBI FRAUD, THEFT, CORRUPTION AND EXTORTION CONSPIRACY AND CRIMINAL ENTERPRISE. SHE ALSO CONFIRMED THAT BANK OF AMERICA, LOCATED IN THE WASHINGTON REGION, WAS THE HOLDER OF THE FUNDS AND AN ALLEGED ACTIVE CO-CONSPIRATOR.*

Q   WHAT BRANCH OF BANK OF AMERICA IN THE WASHINGTON REGION HAS HELD THE PROCEEDS?

A   I DON'T KNOW.

Q   HAVE YOU EVER MET WITH BANK OFFICERS IN THE WASHINGTON REGION OF BANK OF AMERICA?

A   **I'VE MET WITH BANK OFFICERS.**

COMMENT AND ANALYSIS: #19 BRIANNA JONES' *MEETINGS WITH BANK OFFICERS MADE NO DISCERNABLE IMPACT ON JUDGE EKANS IN HIS JUDICIAL ROLE AND RESPONSIBILITY IN ENFORCEMENT OF JUDGE KATE STARR'S OCTOBER 18, 2010 COURT ORDER, SPECIFICALLY, THE MANDATED PRODUCTION OF BANK STATEMENTS BY BRIANNA JONES.*

Q   IN WHAT BRANCH DID YOU MEET WITH THOSE OFFICERS?

A   **I'VE MET WITH BANK OFFICERS.** I HAVE PROVIDED YOU WITH THIS, THE PLAINTIFF, BARBARA WASHINGTON FRANKLIN, WITH ALL OF THIS INFORMATION---

Q   I HAVE NO---

A   ---OVER AND OVER, WE'VE DISCUSSED THIS.

Q   ---FINANCIAL DATA WHATSOEVER, MS. JONES, OTHERWISE---

BARBARA WASHINGTON FRANKLIN

A	THE DEFENDANT: YOUR HONOR, MAY I SAY SOMETHING?
	BY MS. FRANKLIN:
Q	---WE WOULD NOT BE HERE.
	THE DEFENDANT: MAY I SAY SOMETHING?
	THE COURT: MA'AM, YOU'RE ON THE WITNESS STAND---
	THE DEFENDANT: OKAY. SURE.
	THE COURT: ---TO ANSWER QUESTIONS. BY MS.
	FRANKLIN:
Q	WHAT BRANCH OF---
A	MS. FRANKLIN---
Q	---BANK OF AMERICA IN THE WASHINGTON REGION HAVE YOU MET
	WITH BANK OFFICERS---
A	TO, TO RESPOND TO THAT THEN, AS I DISCUSSED WITH YOU TIME
	AND TIME AGAIN, **IT'S A SAFETY ISSUE**, AS YOU SAID THE
	THING ABOUT YOUR OWN SAFETY.
Q	MS. FRANKLIN: YOUR HONOR---
THE COURT:	EXCUSE ME, EXCUSE ME. TELL JANE TO GET ME A LOCK-UP COURTROOM WITH A UNITED STATES MARSHAL FOR---
THE DEFENDANT:	YOUR HONOR, I DON'T KNOW. I DON'T KNOW, YOUR HONOR. I HAVE---I DON'T KNOW. BARBARA, YOU---I'M SORRY. YOU KNOW I DON'T KNOW. I THOUGHT---
THE COURT:	IF YOU'RE NOT GOING TO ANSWER THESE QUESTIONS, YOU CAN STEP DOWN BECAUSE YOU'RE WASTING EVERYBODY'S TIME.
THE DEFENDANT:	BUT I DON'T KNOW. IT'S LIKE---I'VE GONE THROUGH THIS WITH THESE PEOPLE THAT WAS ACTUALLY TAKEN IN THE FLORIDA SUPREME COURT. YOUR HONOR, I DON'T KNOW. **I'VE SAID OVER AND OVER AGAIN, I'M NOT TRYING NOT TO PAY HER.**

COMMENT AND ANALYSIS: #20 BRIANNA JONES *INDIRECTLY ALLEGES THE ACTIVE AND ONGOING OPERATION OF A FRAUD, THEFT, CORRUPTION AND EXTORTION CONSPIRACY AND CRIMINAL ENTERPRISE HEADLINED BY THE RIDGEWAY ESTATE LAWYERS, (ONE OF WHOM WAS SUSPENDED BY THE FLORIDA BAR FOR HAVING ALLEGEDLY DEFRAUDED CLIENTS OF MILLIONS OF DOLLARS) D.C. COURT JUDGES, FBI AGENTS AND UNKNOWN OTHERS.*

THE COURT: YOU CAN STEP DOWN.

(WITNESS EXCUSED.)

THE COURT: TELL HER THAT WE'LL NEED THE COURT AT 2:30. I'M GOING TO RECESS, TAKE LUNCH, WE'LL MEET AT 2:30 IN COURTROOM 302.

MS. FRANKLIN: ALL RIGHT. THANK YOU, YOUR HONOR.

(PAUSE.)

MS. FRANKLIN: COURTROOM 302, YOUR HONOR?

THE COURT: I'M CHECKING THAT RIGHT NOW.

(PAUSE.)

THE DEFENDANT: YOUR HONOR, MAY I SAY SOMETHING?

THE COURT: OF COURSE.

THE DEFENDANT: I AM PETRIFIED FOR MY LIFE. I'D LIKE TO WAIVE COUNSEL. I'VE SHARED ALL OF THIS WITH ATTORNEY FRANKLIN. SHE EVEN STATED THAT SHE---WE KNOW WHEN WE TALKED ON THE PHONE, THE PHONE ACT STRANGE. I'VE GONE THROUGH THIS FOR SO MANY YEARS. IT'S NOT ABOUT THE MONEY FOR ME. I WOULDN'T HOLD THIS FROM HER. WE'VE HAD A VERY CLOSE RELATIONSHIP.

THE COURT: I THINK ALL YOU REALLY NEED TO DO IS TO ANSWER THE QUESTIONS WHERE THE MONEY IS. IF YOU DID THAT, WE COULD ---THAT WOULD BE A BIG BREAKTHROUGH.

BARBARA WASHINGTON FRANKLIN

THE DEFENDANT: SHE CAME DOWN FOR A SETTLEMENT HEARING AND THERE WAS A CALL TO HER THAT SAID DIGGER MURDER, I'VE HAD MY HOME---I HAVE THREE DIFFERENT UNITS IN THE SAME COMPLEX. I'M JUST SO TIRED OF THIS. YOUR HONOR, IF I COULD JUST FOR, I COULD JUST FOR---YESTERDAY IT WAS---GET CALLS AND TELL HER TO GO TO THIS BRANCH---I'M SO TIRED OF THIS. I AM NOT TRYING TO HOLD THIS FROM YOU, BARBARA. I'M, I'M NOT DOING THIS. IT'S DAILY---I'M TRAVELING. I FEEL LIKE I'M JUST BEING BOUNCED ABOUT. I HAVE ALWAYS SAID THAT IT WAS NOT ABOUT THE ISSUE WITH THE MONEY FOR ME.

COMMENT AND ANALYSIS: BRIANNA JONES' *ASSERTIONS OF BEING THREATENED BY THE CO-CONSPIRATORS IS HEARD BY THE COURT IN THE CONTEXT OF VOLUNTARY MEETINGS WITH CO-CONSPIRATOR BANK OFFICERS AS WELL AS LAW ENFORCEMENT OFFICIALS AND OTHER CO-CONSPIRATORS.*

THE COURT: MS. FRANKLIN, DO YOU HAVE A COPY OF THE SETTLEMENT AGREEMENT?

MS. FRANKLIN: YES.

THE COURT: CAN I SEE IT?

(PAUSE.)

MS. FRANKLIN: COURT'S INDULGENCE.

THE COURT: IS IT IN THIS CASE?

MS. FRANKLIN: IT'S---OH, YES, YES, YOUR HONOR.

THE COURT: IF IT'S IN THIS CASE, I SHOULD HAVE IT.

MS. FRANKLIN: YOUR HONOR, IT'S EXHIBIT A OF THE MOTION FOR REINSTATEMENT AND COURT ENFORCEMENT OF SETTLEMENT AGREEMENT FILED IN JUNE. IT'S ATTACHED AS EXHIBIT A TO THE MOTION.

(PAUSE.)

THE DEFENDANT: YOUR HONOR, THE REASON I DID NOT RESPOND TO THE INITIAL COMPLAINT WAS NOT ANY DISRESPECT TO THE COURT, AND I EXPLAINED THIS TO ATTORNEY FRANKLIN. WE'VE BEEN IN COMMUNICATION ON A CONSISTENT DAILY BASIS. IT WAS SIMPLY BECAUSE WE BOTH KNEW CONSTANTLY, THERE WERE CONSTANT THREATS, AND THAT'S WHY I DID NOT WANT TO PUT THAT ALL ON RECORD.

COMMENT AND ANALYSIS: BRIANNA JONES *HAD REPEATEDLY, AND WITHOUT EXCEPTION, INFORMED ME THAT THE CO-CONSPIRATOR OFFICIALS HAD ALWAYS INSTRUCTED HER THAT THEY WERE TAKING HER PORTION OF THE SETTLEMENT PROCEEDS AND SO, IF SHE DIDN'T FIGHT ME, TO PREVENT ME FROM BEING PAID, AND I MANAGED TO BE COMPENSATED, SHE WOULD BE LEFT WITH NOTHING. SUPPOSEDLY, THIS WAS HER BOTTOM-LINE MOTIVATION FOR HER UTTERLY FALSE, VICIOUS, MALICIOUS ATTACKS AND CHARACTER ASSASSINATION OF ME DURING THE COURT LITIGATION, ON TOP OF HER SOCIOPATHIC, NARCISSISSTIC PERSONALITY.*

MS. FRANKLIN: YOUR HONOR, FIRST OF ALL, WITH REGARD TO THE THREATS, THIS---WE'RE TALKING YEARS AND YEARS AGO; HOWEVER, I HAVE INSTRUCTED MS. JONES OVER AND OVER AGAIN, YOU HAVE AN OBLIGATION TO SHARE TRUTHFULLY WITH THE COURT, YOU CANNOT PIECEMEAL THE COURT. IF YOU'RE BEING THREATENED, IF YOU KNOW WHERE ASSETS ARE AND THEY'RE BEING MOVED, THAT HAS TO BE SHARED WITH THE COURT BECAUSE YOU ARE THE ONE THAT'S UNDER THE ORDER OF THE COURT TO PRODUCE THE DOCUMENTS, AND SHE KNOWS I HAVE TOLD HER THAT.

SHE'S SAYING TO ME NOW, BARBARA, YOU KNOW I'M BEING THREATENED. YOU MUST TELL THE COURT THAT. YOU MUST TELL THE COURT WHO'S

THREATENING YOU AND WHY. BUT YOU CANNOT COME INTO THE COURT ONE ORDER AFTER ANOTHER---THERE ARE TWO ORDERS OUTSTANDING NOW, YOUR HONOR. SHE HASN'T COMPLIED WITH ONE LINE OF---THERE'S JUST NO WAY YOU CANNOT COMPLY WITH A COURT ORDER. AND IF YOU HAVE CRITICAL INFORMATION WHICH WOULD ALLOW THE COURT TO UNDERSTAND YOUR POSITION, THAT HAS TO BE SHARED WITH THE COURT. BUT YOU CAN'T TALK---YOU KNOW, MAKE THESE I BELIEVE SO AND I WOULD LIKE TO THINK SO, THAT'S PLAYING GAMES WITH THE COURT.

THE DEFENDANT: BUT ONE OF THE FEAR---THE FEAR IS, YOUR HONOR, IS THAT I HAVE NO

SUPPORT SYSTEM, AND THIS HAS BEEN SO ONGOING, THAT THERE ARE

THOSE INVOLVED THAT KNOW THIS, AND SO THE ONE SUPPORT SYSTEM I HAD FOR SO MANY YEARS WAS ATTORNEY FRANKLIN. HOURS, DAYS, ALL HOURS OF THE NIGHT, SHARING. ATTORNEY FRANKLIN, THIS IS GOING ON, WOULD YOU- - --

PLEASE, PLEASE, PLEASE MAKE NOTE OF THAT. WHAT SHOULD I DO?
SHOULD I CONTACT THE U.S. ATTORNEY'S OFFICE? SHOULD I BE---WHAT SHOULD
I DO?

AND IT'S CONSTANT MOVING. I'VE HAD NO LIFE. SO, THIS---I'M JUST TIRED. I
WANT THIS OVER. I'M NOT ABLE TO EVEN MAKE USE---IT'S JUST A CHASE.
YOU GO HERE, YOU GO THERE---ATTORNEY FRANKLIN, THIS IS WHAT'S GOING ON
TODAY. IT'S NEVER BEEN ABOUT NOT WANTING TO COMPENSATE HER. EVEN
DESPITE THE RECORD BECAUSE WE HAVE---

COMMENT AND ANALYSIS: BRIANNA JONES *REITERATES THE EXISTENCE OF
THE HISTORIC FBI AND D.C. JUDICIAL FRAUD, THEFT, CORRUPTION AND
EXTORTION CONSPIRACY AND CRIMINAL ENTERPRISE. NOTHING IS MORE
EVIDENT OF HER SOCIOPATHOLOGICAL MINDSET AND PERSONALITY,
DEMONICALLY MANIPULATED, INFLUENCED AND CONTROLLED BY THE COLD-
BLOODED CO- CONSPIRATORS, THAN TO ADMIT THAT I SERVED FOR MANY YEARS
AS HER ONE SUPPORT SYSTEM (AND SAFETY NET), AND YET TO EVENTUALLY
BETRAY THAT SUPPORT BY HER FALSE AND UNSUBSTANTIATED ALLEGATION
REGARDING THE PROVISION OF MY EXTENSIVE LEGAL SERVICES AND
SUBSTANTIAL OUT-OF- POCKET EXPENSES INCURRED ON HER BEHALF, USED TO
MAINTAIN HER VERY SURVIVAL, AND AS NECESSARY TO MAINTAIN THE FLORIDA
COURT CASE LITIGATION.*

MS. FRANKLIN: BUT YOUR HONOR, SHE'S ALREADY---

THE COURT: 211

MS. FRANKLIN: ---SHE'S ALREADY ACKNOWLEDGED---

THE COURT: COURTROOM 211 AT 2:30.

MS. FRANKLIN: THANK YOU, YOUR HONOR.

THE DEFENDANT: THANK YOU, YOUR HONOR. EXCUSE ME, YOUR HONOR. DO I NEED TO HAVE

COUNSEL OR---

THE COURT: YOU CERTAINLY-- PROBABLY WOULD BE HELPFUL WITH A LAWYER, BUT
WHAT WOULD HELP YOU EVEN MORE WOULD BE TO COMPLY WITH THE
COURT'S ORDER. YOU'LL HAVE AN OPPORTUNITY TO DO THAT AT 2:30.

MS. JONES: YOUR HONOR---

THE COURT: THIS HEARING IS RECESSED UNTIL 2:30 IN COURTROOM 211.

MS. JONES: THANK YOU SO MUCH.

THE ODYSSEY OF JUDICIAL CORRUPTION

SUPERIOR COURT OF THE DISTRICT OF COLUMBIA
CIVIL DIVISION
WASHINGTON, D.C.

THE HONORABLE MATTHEW D. EKANS, ASSOCIATE JUDGE, PRESIDING

THE FOLLOWING IS THE ENTIRE OFFICIAL COURT TRANSCRIPT OF THE
JANUARY 21, 2011 PROCEEDING, *AFTERNOON SESSION*
ANNOTATED BY THE AUTHOR'S PERTINENT COMMENTARY AND ANALYSIS.

JANUARY 21, 2011

P R O C E E D I N GS

COMMENT AND ANALYSIS: #1 DURING THE AFTERNOON SESSION OF THE JANUARY 21, 2011 COURT HEARING BEFORE JUDGE EKANS, BRIANNA JONES TESTIFIED TO THE EXISTENCE AND PERPETUATION OF THE HISTORIC D.C. JUDICIAL AND FBI FRAUD, THEFT CORRUPTION AND EXTORTION CONSPIRACY AND CRIMINAL ENTERPRISE CASE SURROUNDING THE $34 MILLION SETTLEMENT PROCEEDS RESULTING FROM THE $100 MILLION FLORIDA LAWSUIT I HAD CRAFTED AND FILED, ON BEHALF OF BRIANNA JONES, IN BROWARD COUNTY CIRCUIT COURT ON THE LAST DAY OF THE STATUTE OF LIMITATIONS IN MAY 1996.

BRIANNA JONES SPECIFICALLY AND REPEATEDLY TESTIFIED THAT THESE SETTLEMENT PROCEEDS WERE BEING HELD BY BANK OF AMERICA. SHE ALSO INFORMED THE COURT, AND HER TESTIMONY IS A PART OF THE OFFICIAL COURT RECORD, THAT "THEY" (I.E., THE TEAM OF D.C. JUDICIAL AND FBI SWINDLERS AND CO-CONSPIRATORS) HAD A PATTERN OF CALLING HER AND SUMMONING HER TO MEET THEM IN VARIOUS WASHINGTON AREA HOTEL SUITES TO DISCUSS THEIR ONGOING CRIMINAL ACTIONS INVOLVING THE THEFT OF THE $34 MILLION SETTLEMENT PROCEEDS THAT INCLUDED MY ATTORNEY'S FEES. THIS DIRECTIVE WAS ALSO USUALLY COUPLED WITH THE INSTRUCTION TO KEEP ME OUT.

SHE ALSO TESTIFIED IN THE COURT THAT SHE HAD, ON AT LEAST ONE OCCASION, BEEN PHYSICALLY ASSAULTED BY THE CO-CONSPIRATORS, CAUSING HER ARM TO BE BRUISED.

WHEN JUDGE EKANS ASKED BRIANNA JONES WHERE THE BANK DOCUMENTS CAME FROM THAT SHE HAD BEEN ORDERED TO BRING TO COURT, BRIANNA JONES ANSWERED IN HER TYPICAL VAGUE FASHION AS FOLLOWS:

"IT'S JUST DOCUMENTS THAT SAY THIS IS WHAT THIS IS WORTH, THIS IS WHAT IS COMING TO YOU. AND DO NOT -- DO NOT HAVE HER INVOLVED (REFERRING TO ME)."

MORE THAN ONCE DURING THE COURT HEARING, BRIANNA JONES IDENTIFIED BANK OF AMERICA AS THE HOLDER OF THE SETTLEMENT PROCEEDS. THIS TESTIMONY BY BRIANNA JONES CONTRIBUTED TO THE ALREADY OVERWHELMING EVIDENCE, WHETHER DIRECT OR CIRCUMSTANCIAL, THAT A D.C. JUDICIAL AND FBI CONSPIRACY AND CRIMINAL ENTERPRISE WAS ALIVE AND FLOURISHING, DESIGNED AND EXECUTED, BUT NOT LIMITED TO D.C. COURT JUDGES, FBI AGENTS, RIDGEWAY ESTATE ATTORNEYS AND, LAST BUT NOT LEAST, BANK OF AMERICA OFFICIALS AND THEIR RESPECTIVE HANDLERS AND FACILITATORS.

FOLLOWING IS THE VERBATIM TRANSCRIPT OF THE AFTERNOON SESSION OF THE COURT HEARING ON JANUARY 21, 2011, COMMENCING AT APPROXIMATELY 2:48 P.M.

THE DEPUTY CLERK: YOUR HONOR, CALLING THE CASE BARBARA WASHINGTON FRANKLIN VERSUS

BRIANNA JONES, CIVIL ACTION 4417, 2009.

PARTIES PLEASE COME FORWARD AND IDENTIFY YOURSELVES FOR THE RECORD.

MS. FRANKLIN: GOOD MORNING, YOUR HONOR, BARBARA WASHINGTON FRANKLIN, PLAINTIFF,

PRO SE.

THE COURT: GOOD AFTERNOON.

MS. JONES: GOOD AFTERNOON, YOUR HONOR, BRIANNA JONES, PRO SE.

THE COURT: GOOD AFTERNOON. MA'AM, HAVE YOU HAD ANY TIME TO THINK ABOUT WHAT

YOU WANT TO DO?

MS. JONES: I AM GOING TO MEET WITH ATTORNEY FRANKLIN AND WE WOULD LIKE TO MEET HERE IN THIS BUILDING, IN THIS EDIFICE, SO WE CAN HAVE THOSE DOCUMENTS AND WHATEVER RECORDS I HAVE CERTIFIED HERE AND THEN SHE CAN TURN THAT OVER. SHE WILL HAVE IT TURNED OVER FOR HER OWN USE AND THEN SHE CAN DO WHATEVER IS NECESSARY. AND WITH REGARD TO THE THREATS AND THE FEARS, THEN SHE TAKES ON THAT ONUS. BUT I JUST WANT IT OUT OF MY HANDS. EVERYTHING I HAVE BEEN DOING AND I HAVE TRIED TO PROTECT HER, SO TO SPEAK. BUT I AM------I HAVE TALKED OVER IT WITH HER. I AM WILLING TO TURN OVER EVERYTHING.

COMMENT AND ANALYSIS: #2 BRIANNA JONES' *PLEDGE AND PROMISE TO PRODUCE THE BANK RECORDS AND RELATED DOCUMENTS SPECIFIED IN JUDGE STARR'S OCTOBER 18, 2010 ORDER WOULD PROVE TO BE, IN FACT, HER GUARANTEED PROMISE TO DO NOTHING. HER GOAL WAS TO TELL THE JUDGE WHAT HE WANTED TO HEAR SO SHE COULD AVOID LOCK-UP. AND THAT IS ALL. AND IT WORKED.*

AFTER ALL, ON JANUARY 21, 2011, SHE HAD ALREADY BEEN IN CONTEMPT OF JUDGE STARR'S ORDER FOR 3 MONTHS AND SO SOMETHING WAS WORKING FOR HER. BY THE TIME THE CASE CONCLUDED 4 YEARS LATER, SHE WOULD HAVE MADE ALL KINDS OF UNFULFILLED PROMISES TO JUDGE EKANS AND NUMEROUS OTHER PEOPLE.

THUS FAR, SHE HAD SUFFERED NO PENALTY NOR BEEN FINED. HER BEHAVIOR WAS SIMPLY INCONTROVERTIBLE EVIDENCE THAT THE BANK STATEMENTS OF THE SETTLEMENT PROCEEDS WERE IN HER PERSONAL POSSESSION AND THAT SHE WOULD CONTINUE TO BUCK JUDGE STARR'S ORDER TO PRODUCE THEM WHILE MAKING A MOCKERY OF THE COURT SYSTEM.

SHE WAS A PATHOLOGICAL LIAR. LIES WERE HER CALLING CARD. SHE KNEW NO OTHER WAY. THIS TESTIMONY BY BRIANNA JONES ESTABLISHED THAT SHE HAD BANK STATEMENTS IN HER POSSESSION THAT SHE COULD PRODUCE AND THAT WOULD SATISFY HER COMPLIANCE WITH THE COURT'S ORDER. HER TESTIMONY ALSO ESTABLISHED THAT SHE VOLUNTARILY AGREED TO ENTER INTO THE SETTLEMENT AGREEMENT THAT SETTLED MY LAWSUIT AND LAST, BUT CERTAINLY NOT LEAST, HER TESTIMONY ESTABLISHED THAT THE FLORIDA LAWSUIT WAS SETTLED AND BY NO MEANS WAS DISMISSED.

DISMISSAL OF THE FLORIDA LAWSUIT WOULD BE ALLEGED 4 YEARS LATER BY THE OPPOSITION AND ON THE EVE OF THE RIGGED DISMISSAL OF MY LAWSUIT BY JUDGE EKANS ON JANUARY 16, 2015. SIGNIFICANTLY, IT SHOULD BE NOTED THAT THIS TESTIMONY WAS PROFFERED BY BRIANNA JONES PRIOR TO THE TIME OF THE OFFICIAL AND JUDICIAL CO-CONSPIRATORS KICKING UP THEIR HEELS, INCLUDING MY PERSONAL WITNESSING THE INFAMOUS COURT HALLWAY SHAKEDOWN AND INTIMIDATION OF BRIANNA JONES, A COURT WITNESS, BY JUDGE GEORGE SKINNER, SENIOR JUDGE AND THE FORMER CHIEF JUDGE OF D.C. SUPERIOR COURT, AND JUDGE SKINNER'S OBSTRUCTION OF JUSTICE.

JUDGE SKINNER HAD BEEN ENABLED AND ASSISTED IN GAINING THIS ACCESS TO BRIANNA JONES WHEN JUDGE EKANS SUDDENLY INVOKED THE "CONTRIVED" COURT RECESS OSTENSIBLY FOR THE PARTIES TO TAKE THE "NEXT FEW MINUTES" TO SEE IF WE COULD REACH A SETTLEMENT. AT THE TIME OF SETTLEMENT OF THE FLORIDA LAWSUIT IN DECEMBER 1996, SENIOR JUDGE SKINNER WAS CHIEF JUDGE OF D.C. SUPERIOR COURT AND THEREFORE, SUPERVISOR OF JUDGE RICHARD MANDARIN, THE D.C. JUDGE WHO ISSUED THE ORDER THAT THE D.C. LOTTERY BOARD PAY THE RIDGEWAY ESTATE OVER $40 MILLION IN LOTTERY PROCEEDS, AND WAS A KEY CO-CONSPIRATOR IN THIS CASE OF HISTORIC FBI AND D.C. JUDICIAL FRAUD, THEFT, CORRUPTION AND EXTORTION CONSPIRACY AND CRIMINAL ENTERPRISE.

CONSEQUENTLY, I WITNESSED THE TAG-TEAM OBSTRUCTION OF JUSTICE ENGAGED IN BY JUDGES SKINNER AND EKANS IN THEIR ACTIONS DESCRIBED ABOVE AND WHAT I HAVE TERMED "THE GODFATHER EPISODE" SINCE THEIR ACTIONS WERE REMINISCENT OF CERTAIN CHARACTERS AND THEIR BRUTAL ACTS OF FRAUD, THEFT, CORRUPTION AND EXTORTION PORTRAYED IN THE CLASSIC MOVIE, "THE GODFATHER," AND THAT OCCURRED DURING THE MARCH 18, 2011 COURT HEARING CONDUCTED BY JUDGE MATTHEW D. EKANS.

AS TO BRIANNA JONES' ALLEGATIONS OF THREATS MADE AGAINST HER AND HER CONSEQUENT ONGOING FEARS, JUDGE EKANS CHOSE EITHER TO REMAIN SILENT, SPEAK OF THEM IN DISMISSIVE TONES OR DISCREDIT THEM ALTOGEHER. FURTHER, THE COURT'S NONCHALANCE REGARDING BOTH PARTIES' ALLEGATIONS OF OFFICIAL CORRUPTION IN THE CASE WOULD SERVE AS UNMISTAKABLE EVIDENCE OF THE COURT FRAUD, THEFT, CORRUPTION AND EXTORTION THAT DOMINATED THE CASE.

THE COURT: WELL, IT'S GOOD TO KNOW THAT YOU UNDERSTAND THAT YOU HAVE TO

COMPLY WITH THE COURT'S ORDER, BUT I HAVE TO KNOW WHEN YOU FEEL

YOU ARE GOING TO DO THAT BECAUSE TODAY IS THE DAY.

MS. JONES: WELL, WE JUST DISCUSSED THE EARLIEST I COULD GET EVERYTHING TOGETHER

AND MEET WITH HER IS TUESDAY OR WEDNESDAY.

THE COURT: I THINK THAT YOU ARE GOING BACK TO WHAT YOU WERE DOING BEFORE THE LUNCH BREAK THIS MORNING, WHICH IS TALKING IN VERY GENERAL AND VAGUE TERMS. AND I DON'T---I DON'T UNDERSTAND GENERALITIES, VAGUENESS. I NEED TO BE VERY SPECIFIC. THE FIRST THING YOU NEED TO DO IS SAY WHERE THE MONEY IS. THAT'S THE FIRST THING YOU NEED TO DO.

MS. JONES: SIR, I DON'T KNOW. I JUST KNOW WHERE I HAVE BEEN TOLD TO GO.

COMMENT AND ANALYSIS: *#3 BRIANNA JONES REPEATEDLY TESTIFIED TO THE CLANDESTINE MEETINGS WITH "OFFICIALS" TO WHICH SHE WAS "SUMMONED" TO ATTEND IN VARIOUS WASHINGTON AREA HOTELS AND OTHER PLACES. SHE ALSO TESTIFIED REPEATEDLY THAT SHE WAS INSTRUCTED TO GO TO VARIOUS BANKS THAT HELD SOME, IF NOT ALL, OF THE SETTLEMENT PROCEEDS.*

FROM THIS VERY BEGINNING OF JUDGE EKANS' HANDLING OF THE CASE, HE MADE IT CLEAR THAT HE WOULD NOT ADDRESS THE ISSUE OF "OFFICIALS" ALLEGEDLY COMPLICIT IN THE FRAUD THAT DOMINATED THE CASE; AND THEIR CLANDESTINE MEETINGS IN AREA HOTELS TO WHICH JONES WAS SUMMONED TO ATTEND AND PARTICIPATE. FURTHER, BRIANNA JONES' ALLEGATIONS OF HAVING BEEN PHYSICALLY ASSAULTED BY THE CO-CONSPIRATORS WOULD BE IGNORED BY THE COURT. MOST OF ALL, JUDGE EKANS MADE IT CLEAR THAT ANY EVIDENCE OF FRAUD IN THE CASE, FBI, JUDICIAL OR OTHERWISE, WOULD BE TREATED AS THE PINK ELEPHANT IN THE CASE AND RELEGATED TO THE CORNER OF THE COURTROOM. ALL PARTIES WERE EXPECTED TO REMAIN MUM ON THE ISSUE OF FRAUD IN HIS COURTROOM AND DID SO.

*FURTHER, JUDGE EKANS WOULD ABUSE HIS JUDICIAL DISCRETION, POWER AND AUTHORITY TO JUSTIFY HIS SILENCE ON THE DOMINANT ISSUE OF FRAUD BY INTENTIONALLY LABELING AND MISCHARACTERIZING ME A **JUDGMENT CREDITOR** WITH THE REQUISITE RESPONSIBILITY OF CONDUCTING MY OWN INVESTIGATION, IF NEED BE, IN THE SEARCH FOR THE MILLIONS OF DOLLARS IN STOLEN SETTLEMENT PROCEEDS, ALLEGEDLY STOLEN BY CO-CONSPIRATOR OFFICIALS, SOME OF WHOM WERE ALLEGED TO HAVE BEEN HIS JUDICIAL COLLEAGUES, WHO BOLDLY MET PERIODICALLY WITH BRIANNA JONES TO DISCUSS THEIR STRATEGY OF ANNIHILATING ME, JONES' SPECIFIC ROLE IN THAT PLANNED DESTRUCTION, AND OF COURSE, THEIR REPEATED REPORTS AS TO WHAT DOLLAR AMOUNT OF THE SETTLEMENT PROCEEDS WAS ON DEPOSIT AT BANK OF AMERICA AND OTHER BANKING INSTITUTIONS.*

THE FACT THAT JUDGE EKANS COULD CONFIDENTLY AND CONSISTENTLY REFUSE TO ADDRESS THE DOMINANT ISSUE OF FBI AND D.C. JUDICIAL FRAUD IN THE CASE SPEAKS VOLUMES AS TO THE SYSTEMIC CORRUPTION THAT DOMINATES THE D.C. COURT SYSTEM, LED BY D.C. COURT JUDGES WHO DAILY ABUSE THEIR POWERS OF AUTHORITY AND DISCRETION, IRREPARABLY PREJUDICING AND HARMING THE LITIGANTS THAT COME BEFORE THEM, AND DO SO IN AN ATMOSPHERE OF NO ACCOUNTABILITY, NO PENALTY, NO PUNISHMENT, NO ADMONISHMENT. NO NOTHING.

BARBARA WASHINGTON FRANKLIN

THE COURT:	LET ME ASK YOU THIS QUESTION---
MS. JONES:	I DO NOT KNOW, YOUR HONOR.
THE COURT:	---WHEN YOU NEED TO PUT SOME GAS IN YOUR CAR, WHERE DO YOU GET THE MONEY FROM?
MS. JONES:	I DON'T HAVE ACCESS TO THE FUNDS.
THE COURT:	I THINK YOU ARE MISUNDERSTANDING ME. WHEN YOU NEED TO PUT GAS IN YOUR CAR, WHERE DO YOU GET THE MONEY FROM? YOU SAID YOU DROVE UP HERE FROM FLORIDA?
MS. JONES:	YES. ATTORNEY FRANKLIN ASSISTED ME. I DON'T HAVE ACCESS TO THE FUNDS.

COMMENT AND ANALYSIS: **#4** *BUT FOR THE OVER A DECADE OF FINANCIAL SUPPORT I PROVIDED TO BRIANNA JONES, SHE MOST PROBABLY WOULD NOT HAVE SURVIVED TO BE ALIVE TODAY. ENCOURAGED AND SUPPORTED BY MY HUSBAND AND FAMILY, I ASSISTED HER WITH BASIC LIVING EXPENSES, INCLUDING EXPENSES FOR FOOD, HOUSING, CLOTHING, TRANSPORTATION AND AT ONE POINT, ROUND-THE-CLOCK SECURITY, WHEN SHE WAS BEING SERIOUSLY THREATENED AND HARRASSED BY PRESUMABLY THE OPPOSITION, FOLLOWING HER EXECUTION OF THE SETTLEMENT AGREEMENTS IN THE FLORIDA LAWSUIT IN DECEMBER 1996.*

NEVERTHELESS, TYPICAL OF HER SOCIOPATHIC NATURE, COMBINED WITH HER OVERALL, MEDICALLY DIAGNOSED IMPAIRED MENTAL STATE, HER PENCHANT FOR PATHOLOGICAL LYING, AND THE INTIMIDATION AND MANIPULATION OF HER BY THE BRUTAL CO-CONSPIRATOR OFFICIALS, SHE WOULD LATER SHOW HER BRAND OF APPRECIATION AND GRATITUDE FOR ALL MY HELP WHICH WENT FAR ABOVE AND BEYOND MY DUTY AS AN ATTORNEY PROVIDING LEGAL SERVICES ON A CONTINGENCY FEE BASIS, BY ATTEMPTING TO DESTROY MY GOOD NAME IN THE COMMUNITY AND MY REPUTATION FOR HONESTY, INTEGRITY AND HIGH MORAL VALUES AND PRINCIPLES, THROUGH A SERIES OF ATTACKS OF VICIOUS AND MALICOUS LIES, CHARACTER ASSASSINATION, AND ALLOWING HER CO-CONSPIRATORS TO USE HER IN EVERY WAY POSSIBLE IN HAVING MY CASE DISMISSED WHICH LEGALLY EXEMPTED HER FROM HER LEGAL OBLIGATION TO COMPENSATE ME FULLY ACCORDING TO THE PROVISIONS OF THE CONTINGENCY FEE AGREEMENT.

MS. FRANKLIN:	YOUR HONOR, CORRECTION OF THE RECORD. IT WAS A FRIEND OF MINE WHO HELPED YOU TO COME TO WASHINGTON SO THAT YOU COULD BE HERE FOR THE HEARING.

64

MS. JONES: YES. I AM STILL WAITING TO COLLECT THE FUNDS, YOUR HONOR.

MS. FRANKLIN: YOUR HONOR, JUST LET ME SAY, WE HAVE HAD NUMEROUS CONVERSATIONS.
                    AND SHE CONTINUALLY TELLS ME SHE IS MEETING WITH BANKERS. AND THAT'S
                    WHY THE LINE OF QUESTIONING THAT I POSED TO HER EARLIER THIS AFTERNOON
                    IS, WHO ARE THESE BANKERS AT BANK OF AMERICA IN THE WASHINGTON
                    REGION? THEY ARE NOT GHOSTS. WHERE IS THE BRANCH YOU GO TO AND MEET
                    WITH THESE BANK OFFICERS?

THE COURT: ALL RIGHT. THAT IS A FAIR QUESTION. ANSWER THAT.

MS. JONES: **I JUST GET CALLS TO MEET IN A HOTEL, TO MEET HERE. AND IT SAYS, KEEPHER
                    OUT OF IT.** AND IF YOU ARE GOING TO COURT---I HAVE A BRUISE NOW WHERE I
                    WAS NOT SUPPOSED TO BE HERE. AND I AM TIRED OF IT. AND I NEVER
                    TERMINATED HER, YOUR HONOR.

                    COMMENT AND ANALYSIS: #5 BRIANNA JONES' *REASON FOR NOT TERMINATING
                    ME WAS THREEFOLD. THE FIRST IS THAT THE CONTINGENCY FEE AGREEMENT
                    PROVIDED THAT EVEN IF I WERE TERMINATED, I WOULD STILL BE ENTITLED TO BE
                    PAID. THE SECOND IS THAT I WAS BRIANNA JONES' LIFELINE FOR HER SURVIVAL.
                    THE THIRD WAS THAT I SERVED AS HER PROTECTION AGAINST THE OPPOSITION
                    SINCE SHE HAD NEITHER FAMILY NOR FRIENDS.*

                    *BRIANNA JONES REITERATES HER BEING SUMMONED TO MEET WITH THE
                    "OFFICIALS" IN HOTELS AND ELSEWHERE. SHE ALSO REITEREATES HER
                    ALLEGATION OF HAVING BEEN PHYSICALLY ASSAULTED BY THE CO-CONSPIRATORS.*

THE COURT: LET ME ASK YOU THIS QUESTION: YOU ARE UNDER A COURT ORDER TO BRING

                    DOCUMENTS WITH YOU TO COURT TODAY. WHY DIDN'T YOU BRING THEM?

MS. JONES: YOUR HONOR, SIMPLY OUT OF FEAR. I WANT ATTORNEY FRANKLIN TO HAVE

                    THIS. WE TALKED ABOUT THIS OVER AND---

                    COMMENT AND ANALYSIS: #6 BRIANNA JONES *ALLEGES THAT THE CO-
                    CONSPIRATORS HAVE EFFECTIVELY INTIMIDATED HER, CAUSING A LEVEL OF FEAR
                    THAT CAUSED HER TO DISOBEY A COURT ORDER. SHE DEMONSTRATED THAT SHE
                    HAD MORE FEAR OF THE CO-CONSPIRATORS THAN SHE HAD FAITH IN THE COURT
                    TO PROTECT HER FROM THE CO-CONSPIRATORS. SHE OBVIOUSLY UNDERSTOOD
                    THAT THE COURT WAS ALLEGEDLY COMPLICIT IN THE CONSPIRACY. SHE
                    INEVITABLY RECALLED HER ALLEGED MEETINGS WITH JUDGES GEORGE SKINNER
                    AND RICHARD MANDARIN IN THEIR RESPECTIVE CHAMBERS ACCOMPANIED BY
                    ABC TELEVISION ANCHOR, BETH HOLLISTER, HER CLOSE FRIEND AND MENTOR.*

THE COURT:	I DON'T WANT TO SEEM IMPATIENT, BUT I DON'T REALLY WANT TO HEAR THAT.
MS. JONES:	I WOULD LIKE TO BE BACK---WE TALKED ABOUT TUESDAY OR WEDNESDAY. I WANT TO PUT EVEYTHING IN HER HANDS, YOUR HONOR. THIS IS NOT ANY SIGN OF DISREPECT TO THE COURT. I JUST DID NOT KNOW WHAT TO DO.
THE COURT:	I DON'T---SPEAKING ON BEHALF OF THIS COURT, I DON'T FEEL DISRESPECT THAT IS NOT AN ISSUE FOR ME. WHAT I DO FEEL IS THAT I CAN'T HAVE A COURT ORDER HANGING OUT THERE THAT I'M NOT PREPARED TO ENFORCE. AND YOU ---**YOU SHOULD BE CLEAR THAT I'M GOING TO ENFORCE THIS ORDER.**
	COMMENT AND ANALYSIS: #7 *AS A MATTER OF FACT, THE COURT RECORD CONFIRMS THAT JUDGE EKANS CONCLUDED THE CASE WITHOUT THE ENFORCEMENT OF JUDGE KATE STARR'S ORDER OF OCTOBER 18, 2010. INSTEAD, HE FASHIONED A SUBSTITUTE REMEDY OF A MONEY JUDGMENT ISSUED TO ME IN THE AMOUNT OF $13.6 MILLION. TWO YEARS LATER, THIS JUDGMENT WAS OVERTURNED BY THE D.C. COURT OF APPEALS.*
MS. JONES:	I'M VERY CLEAR HOW SERIOUS THIS IS. AND WE SPOKE ABOUT IT. I WILL TURN OVER EVERYTHING TO HER. I WILL COME BACK AND MEET WITH HER AND TURN OVER EVERYTHING, YOUR HONOR.
THE COURT:	WHAT IS EVERYTHING?
MS. JONES:	ALL THE DOCUMENTS, EVERYTHING.
THE COURT:	WHAT ARE THE DOCUMENTS?
MS. JONES:	THE DOCUMENTS AS IT RELATES TO PROCEEDS FROM A SETTLEMENT. I DON'T HAVE IT.
THE COURT:	WHAT ARE THE DOCUMENTS?
MS. JONES:	IT'S DOCUMENT OF LOCATIONS OF WHERE---OF WHAT I WAS TOLD TO DO OF---
THE COURT:	WHAT WERE YOU---TELL ME WHAT YOU WERE TOLD TO DO.
MS. JONES:	WE TALKED ABOUT THIS TO NOT HAVE HER INVOLVED AND I WOULD ALWAYS KEEP HER APPRISED.

THE COURT: YOU DON'T UNDERSTAND WHAT I JUST ASKED YOU. WHAT ARE THE DOCUMENTS?

MS. JONES: THE DOCUMENTS THAT RELATE TO THE FINANCIAL STATUS.

THE COURT: WHAT FINANCIAL INSTITUTION HAS ITS NAME ON THE DOCUMENTS?

MS. JONES: **IT JUST HAS DOCUMENTS WHERE---IT JUST HAS ALL OF THE AMOUNTS AND THAT I'M SUPPOSED TO TAKE POSSESSION OF IT.**

               COMMENT AND ANALYSIS: **#8** BRIANNA JONES *REFUSED TO ANSWER THE COURT'S QUESTION. SHE REFUSED TO GIVE THE NAME OF THE BANK, AND SUFFERED NO CONSEQUENCES FROM THE COURT.*

THE COURT: YOU ARE TOYING WITH ME.

MS. JONES: YOUR HONOR, I AM NOT. THIS IS WHAT---

THE COURT: WHERE DO THESE DOCUMENTS COME FROM?

MS. JONES: **I USUALLY GET CALLS TOLD TO MEET THIS PLACE OR THAT PLACE.**

               COMMENT AND ANALYSIS: **#9** *BRIANNA JONES REITERATES THE "OFFICIALS'" REQUIREMENT THAT SHE MEET WITH THEM IN VARIOUS PLACES.*

THE COURT: WHERE DO THE DOCUMENTS COME FROM?

MS. JONES: **IT'S DOCUMENTS THAT SAY THIS IS WHAT THIS IS WORTH, THIS IS WHAT IS COMING TO YOU AND DO NOT ---- DO NOT HAVE HER INVOLVED.** AND I ALWAYS TELL HER. AND SHE HAS GOTTEN THREATS, YOUR HONOR. I DON'T KNOW WHAT ELSE TO DO. WE HAVE TALKED ABOUT THIS -- WELL, DO I GO TO THE AUTHORITIES? I AM NOT HERE. I AM NOT TAKING THIS LIGHTLY. BUT I AM PREPARED---- I UNDERSTAND THE SERIOUSNESS NOW. AND IF THEY HARM ME, FINE, BUT I AM PREPARED TO TURN EVERYTHING OVER TO ATTORNEY FRANKLIN.

               COMMENT AND ANALYSIS: **#10** *THE TESTIMONY CONFIRMS THAT BRIANNA JONES WAS PRIVY TO INFORMATION REGARDING THE AMOUNT AND LOCATION OF THE SETTLEMENT PROCEEDS.*

THE COURT: THE LAST TIME THAT I LET SOMEBODY WALK OUT OF HERE THAT I SHOULD HAVE TAKEN INTO CUSTODY, I HAD TO SEND TWO MARSHALS TO GET THAT PERSON. AND THOSE MARSHALS GOT INJURED GOING TO GET THAT PERSON. AND THAT WEIGHS HEAVILY ON MY MIND. AND I HAVE GOT THIS DEPUTY UNTED STATES MARSHAL SITTING HERE NOW, BECAUSE IT'S NOT CLEAR TO ME THAT I NEED TO LET YOU WALK OUT OF HERE. NOW, YOU NEED TO GIVE ME SOME STRAIGHT ANSWERS SOMETHING THAT LEADS ME TO BELIEVE THAT YOU HAVE GOT SOME SENSE IN YOUR HEAD. NOW, YOU KNEW THAT YOU WERE SUPPOSED TO BRING THESE PAPERS TODAY. AND THESE PAPERS AREN'T SOMETHING TELLING MS. WASHINGTON TO GET OUT OF THE CASE OR WHATEVER. THESE PAPERS ARE: WHERE IS THE MONEY? WHAT BANK DO YOU HAVE THIS MONEY IN? THAT'S THE DOCUMENT I'M TALKING ABOUT.

MS. JONES: I DON'T HAVE ANYTHING IN MY NAME. THERE IS NOTHING IN MY NAME.

COMMENT AND ANALYSIS: **#10** *JUDGE KATE STARR'S OCTOBER 18, 2010 ORDER MANDATED THAT BRIANNA JONES PRODUCE BANK OF AMERICA BANK STATEMENTS AND RELATED DOCUMENTS.*

THE COURT: FINE. THEN WHOMEVER'S NAME IT IS IN, WHERE IS THE MONEY?

MS. JONES: YOUR HONOR, ALL I KNOW IS BANK OF AMERICA.

COMMENT AND ANALYSIS: #11 BRIANNA JONES *CONFIRMS THE SETTLEMENT PROCEEDS ARE BEING HELD IN THE NAMES OF OTHERS. SHE ALSO STATES THAT THE MONEY IS BEING HELD IN BANK OF AMERICA.*

THE COURT: WHICH BRANCH?

MS. JONES: AND I HAVE AN ACCOUNT WITH BANK OF AMERICA.

THE COURT: WHICH BRANCH?

MS. JONES: I HAVE AN ACCOUNT IN FLORIDA. THERE IS NOTHING---

THE COURT: WHERE IN FLORIDA?

MS. JONES: IT'S THE BAY COLONY BRANCH. AND THAT'S IT. BUT THEY GIVE ME

BRANCHES. THEY GAVE ME PLACES IN WASHINGTON, D.C.

THE ODYSSEY OF JUDICIAL CORRUPTION

THE COURT:	WHEN YOU TALK ABOUT "THEY," WHO ARE YOU SPEAKING OF?
MS. JONES:	I GET THESE CALLS AND, YOUR HONOR, YOU SHOULD DO THIS AND THIS IS WHERE---

COMMENT AND ANALYSIS: #12 *BRIANNA JONES REFUSES TO IDENTIFY THE UNKNOWN CO-CONSPIRATOR OFFICIALS WITH WHOM SHE MEETS AND CONSPIRES. AND THE COURT MAKES NO ATTEMPT TO REQUIRE HER TO DO SO. THE COURT IS OBVIOUSLY PROTECTING THE D.C. JUDICIAL AND FBI CO-CONSPIRATORS.*

THE COURT:	FROM WHO?
MS. JONES:	FROM---IT'S COMPLICATED. IT'S---
THE COURT:	WELL, I CAN SIMPLIFY IT. FROM WHO?
MS. JONES:	YOUR HONOR, I AM FRIGHTENED.
THE COURT:	I AM FRIGHTENED, TOO. I WOULD RATHER TURN THE DOCUMENTS OVER TO ATTORNEY FRANKLIN.
THE COURT:	LISTEN TO THIS QUESTION, IT IS GOING TO BE VERY SIMPLE, VERY EASY: WHO? WHO IS THEY?
MS. JONES:	THE PEOPLE THAT WERE INVOLVED IN THE CASE THAT I FILED AGAINST THE ESTATE.
THE COURT:	WHO?
MS. JONES:	THE PEOPLE THAT WERE INVOLVED IN THE CASE I FILED AGAINST THE ESTATE, THE DECEDENTS. THE REPRESENTATIVES OF THE LATE WILLIE LEE RIDGEWAY. THAT IS WHO. IT HAS BEEN GOING ON SINCE 19—

COMMENT AND ANALYSIS: #13 *BRIANNA JONES FINALLY ADMITS THAT BY "THEY" SHE IS REFERRING TO "THE REPRESENTATIVES OF THE LATE WILLIE LEE RIDGEWAY." HOWEVER, SHE STILL SPEAKS IN GENERALITIES AND REFUSES TO IDENTIFY THE CO-CONSPIRATORS BY NAME. SHE ALSO REFUSES TO IDENTIFY THE "OFFICIALS" BY NAME.*

THE COURT:	WHO? WHO?

MS. JONES: JUST THEY SAY THAT THEY REPRESENT HIM. THIS HAS BEEN GOING ON FOR A NUMBER OF YEARS.

MS. FRANKLIN: YOUR HONOR, I BELIEVE THAT SHE IS REFERRING TO THE ATTORNEY REPRESENTING THE ESTATE THAT WAS SUED. I BELIEVE THAT IS WHO SHE IS REFERRING TO.

MS. JONES: THE FLORIDA SUPREME COURT RECENTLY TOOK ACTION. ONE WAS SUSPENDED FOR KEEPING A CLIENT'S SETTLEMENT. AND INCIDENTALLY, ON THE SAME DAY THAT SHE FILED THE CONTEMPT OF COURT ON THAT DATE, THE FLORIDA SUPREME COURT SUSPENDED THAT PARTCULAR ATTORNEY FOR KEEPING A CLIENT'S SETTLEMENT. I DON'T HAVE IT. AND I WOULD NEVER TERMINATE HER, BECAUSE I KNEW THAT THAT WAS A PROTECTION, AS LONG AS I KEPT ATTORNEY FRANKLIN INVOLVED, THEN SOMEBODY WOULD KNOW IF SOMETHING HAPPENED TO ME. AND I CAN'T ---WE---**MY INTENTION WAS ALWAYS TO HONOR THE AGREEMENT.** AND EVEN WHEN THE FLORIDA COURT SAID SHE WASN'T ALLOWED TO PRACTICE, I DID NOT WRITE A TERMINATION LETTER. AT TIMES OUR RELATIONSHIP HAS BEEN ADVERSARIAL, YET FRIENDLY.

COMMENT AND ANALYSIS*: #14 AT NO TIME WAS I EVER DENIED THE OPPORTUNITY TO REPRESENT BRIANNA JONES IN THE FLORIDA COURTS AND THAT IS CONFIRMED BY THE COURT RECORDS OF BOTH THE FLORIDA BROWARD COUNTY CIRCUIT COURT AND THE D.C. SUPERIOR COURT. SHE SIMPLY LIED, CONSISTENT WITH HER TRUEST CHARACTER TRAIT.*

THE COURT: YOU KNOW, THIS INFORMTION IS NOT HELPFUL. IT HAS NOTHING TO DO WITH THE ORDER THAT JUDGE STARR HAS OUTSTANDING REGARDING YOUR OBLIGATION TO THIS COURT TODAY.

MS. JONES: BECAUSE WE NEVER GOT INTO THE DEPTH WITH REGARD TO THE DOCUMENTS AND THAT SORT OF THING. AND WHEN I SETTLED---

THE COURT: YOU KNOW, I DON'T EVEN WANT YOU TALKING TO ME ANYMORE ABOUT "THE DOCUMENTS." I WANT YOU TO BE SPECIFIC ABOUT WHAT YOU ARE TALKING ABOUT.

MS. JONES: OKAY. ONE SAYS THAT IS A DOCUMENT AND THE ESTATE WAS WORTH AT ONE POINT OVER 40 MILLION. I GOT THAT DOCUMENT. AND JUST, BASICALLY, YOU HAVE THIS IN YOUR NAME AND THAT IN YOUR NAME. THAT'S ALL I HAVE, YOUR HONOR. THAT IS IT. BUT I ASSURE YOU, WHATEVER I HAVE, I WILL TURN IT OVER TO ATTORNEY FRANKLIN. I WANT OUT OF THIS. I DON'T HAVE---I HAVE NEVER GOTTEN A DIME FROM THEM. IT HAS BEEN FEAR.

COMMENT AND ANALYSIS: *#15 BRIANNA JONES ACKNOWLEDGED THAT THE CO-CONSPIRATORS PROVIDED HER WITH ONE DOCUMENT EVIDENCING THE ESTATE WAS WORTH OVER $40 MILLION. NEVERTHELESS, AT NO TIME DID JUDGE EKANS EVER ENFORCE JUDGE STARR'S ORDER OF OCTOBER 18, 2010 THAT JONES TURN OVER BANK STATEMENTS TO ME EVIDENCING THE AMOUNT AND LOCATION OF THE SETTLEMENT PROCEEDS.*

MS. FRANKLIN: YOUR HONOR, DURING THE RECESS, I EXPLAINED TO HER THAT IT IS IMPORTANT, IF NOT CRITICAL, THAT WHEN WE GO BACK BEFORE THE COURT, YOU GIVE THE COURT SPECIFIC, DETAILED INFORMATION, BECAUSETHE COURT WILL NOT WANT TO HEAR ANYTHING ELSE. YOU CANNOT STAND BEFORE THE COURT AND CONTINUE TO GENERALIZE IN THE FACE OF A COURT ORDER. IT IS NOT GOING TO HAPPEN. AND---

MS. JONES: THAT'S ALL I---ATTORNEY FRANKLIN, WE HAVE GONE OVER THIS. THIS

IS ALL THAT I HAVE. AND THE REASON THAT I SETTLED WAS BECAUSE IT

WAS FEAR. I DIDN'T WANT TO HAVE TO PUT THINGS ON THE RECORD.

THAT IS THE REASON. I WAS TOLD---

THE COURT: HERE IS WHAT I'M PREPARED TO DO: I THINK IT IS OUR RESPONSIBIITY TO MAKE SURE THAT OUR ORDERS ARE REASONABLE AND THAT WE SHOW PROPER REGARD FOR THE LITIGANTS AND OTHERS WHO COME BEFORE US. I FIND YOU IN CONTEMPT OF THIS COURT'S ORDER. I WILL GIVE YOU UNTIL TUESDAY TO BRING YOURSELF IN COMPLIANCE WITH THE ORDER THAT YOU PRESENT EVIDENCE OF WHERE THIS MONEY IS LOCATED IN ORDER TO SATISFY THE SETTLEMENT AGREEMENT THAT YOU MADE WITH THIS LAWYER.

NOW, IF YOU COME HERE ON TUESDAY WITH A BUNCH OF MEANINGLESS PAPER THAT DOES NOT SATISFY THE INTENT OF THE COURT'S ORDER, THEN I AM GOING TO TAKE THE NEXT STEP.

DO YOU HAVE ANY QUESTIONS ABOUT WHAT IT IS THAT I EXPECT TO SEE TUESDAY?

MS. JONES:	THANK YOU, YOUR HONOR. YOU HAVE MADE YOURSELF EXTREMELY CLEAR.
THE COURT:	THEN I WOULD LIKE TO HEAR FROM YOU WHAT IS THAT I EXPECT TO SEE.
MS. JONES:	*YOU WANT DOCUMENTS THAT HAVE PROOF OF ASSETS AND WHERE THE ASSETS ARE LOCATED AS IT RELATES TO THE SETTLEMENT AGREEMENT WITH ATTORNEY FRANKLIN AND WHERE SHE CAN TAKE POSSESSION OF THOSE ASSETS.*

COMMENT AND ANALYSIS: #16 *BRIANNA JONES ACKNOWLEDGED HAVING DOCUMENTS EVIDENCING PROOF OF ASSETS (I.E., THE SETTLEMENT PROCEEDS) AND WHERE THE ASSETS WERE LOCATED.*

THE COURT:	THAT'S IT.
MS. JONES:	YOUR HONOR, IF SOMETHING HAPPENS TO ME, WOULD YOU MAKE A RECORD OR LET THE COURT KNOW IF SOMETHING HAPPENS TO ME BETWEEN NOW AND THEN, WOULD THIS COURT LOOK INTO THE ESTATE OF WILLIE LEE RIDGEWAY? I HAVE NEVER GOTTEN A DIME. I HAVE BEEN THREATENED OVER AND OVER AGAIN. I HAVE MOVED THREE TIMES IN THE SAME---
THE COURT:	I WANT THIS LADY TO SIGN A NOTICE TO BE BACK HERE.
THE DEPUTY CLERK:	YES, YOUR HONOR.
THE COURT:	HAVE HER SIGN FOR COURTROOM 517.
	I AM GOING TO HAVE---I AM GOING TO CALL THE CASE IN 517 ON TUESDAY---BUT I AM GOING TO CALL IT THERE AND THEN WE'LL RECONVENE IN COURTROOM 302. I HAVE TWO CASES---CRIMINAL CASES FOR SENTENCING ON TUESDAY. AND SO I WILL HAVE DEPUTY MARSHALS IN THAT COURTROOM. SO WE WILL CALL THE CASE IN 302 AND THEN WE WILL—I'LL CALL THE CASE IN 517 AND THEN WE'LL RECONVENE IN 302.
MS. FRANKLIN:	WHAT TIME WILL THE HEARING---
THE COURT:	I AM GOING TO SCHEDULE IT FOR 9:30. AND I EXPECT THAT THE TWO OF YOU WILL MEET OUTSIDE THE COURTROOM BEFORE YOU COME IN SO THAT WE DON'T WASTE THAT TIME SEEING EXACTLY WHAT THE DEFENDANT HAS BROUGHT WITH HER TO COURT.

COMMENT AND ANALYSIS: #17 *HERE AGAIN, THE COURT HOLDS TO HIS INTENTIONALLY AND KNOWINGLY FALSE DEFINITION OF ME AS A* ***JUDGMENT CREDITOR.*** *BRIANNA JONES WAS IN CONTEMPT OF THE COURT'S ORDER TO PRODUCE BANK STATEMENTS. HER FIRST RESPONSIBILITY WAS TO PRODUCE THE DOCUMENTS FOR THE COURT TO SATISFY THE INTENT OF THE ORDER. THUS, IT WAS INAPPROPRIATE FOR THE COURT TO EXPECT US TO CONFER AS* ***JUDGMENT CREDITOR/JUDGMENT DEBTOR*** *OUTSIDE THE COURTROOM AND PRIOR TO THE COURT HEARING.*

MS. FRANKLIN: YOUR HONOR, I JUST HAVE ONE ADDITION BEFORE THE COURT EXCUSES US. AND THAT IS EARLIER THERE WAS TESTIMONY FROM MS. JONES WITH REGARD TO A CONVERSATION I ALLEGEDLY HAD WITH DR. STELLA EKANS YEARS AGO AT A BOULE' EVENT. FOR THE RECORD, I HAVE NO RECOLLECTION OF THAT CONVERSATION. YES, I DID TALK WITH DR. EKANS BECAUSE I RETAINED HER ON BEHALF OF MS. JONES. AND DR. EKANS PROVIDED CONSULTATION. BUT IN TERMS OF---I DON'T EVER RECALL EVER SPEAKING WITH DR. EKANS AT A BOULE' EVENT. AND THAT IS WHAT SHE REFERENCED AND I JUST WANT TO ADD THAT.

COMMENT AND ANALYSIS: #18 *AT NO TIME DID I DISCUSS BRIANNA JONES' CASE CONSULTATION WITH DR. EKANS. ANOTHER GRATUITOUS LIE BY BRIANNA JONES.*

THE COURT: YOU CAN STEP UP HERE, MA'AM. I AM GOING TO HAVE YOU SIGN A NOTICE REGARDING YOUR REQUIREMENT TO RETURN TO COURT ON TUESDAY.

MS. JONES: YOUR HONOR, I---AFTER THOSE DOCUMENTS ARE TURNED OVER, WOULD THIS COURT---IS THERE A WAY THIS COURT CAN PROVIDE ME WITH SOME SORT OF PROTECTION OR---BECAUSE MY PHONES, I CONSTANTLY---IT IS TERRORIZING. AND ATTORNEY FRANKLIN HAS ENDURED THE SAME THING. SHE KNOWS THAT THERE ARE STRANGE SOUNDS ON HER PHONE.

AND I HAVE NEVER NOT WANTED TO TURN THOSE DOCUMENTS OVER. BUT I JUST WOULD LIKE FOR THE COURT TO KNOW IF SOMETHING SHOULD HAPPEN TO ME---BECAUSE I AM NOT IN CONTACT WITH ANY RELATIVE---I WOULD WANT SOMETHING TO BE DONE WITH REGARD TO THIS MATTER.

THE DEPUTY CLERK: FAILURE TO SHOW UP ON JANUARY 25 AT 9:30 IN COURTROOM 517, A BENCH WARRANT WILL BE ISSUED FOR YOUR ARREST. DO YOU UNDERSTAND?

MS. JONES:	YES.
THE DEPUTY CLERK:	ADDRESS AND PHONE NUMBER, PLEASE.
MS. JONES:	INCIDENTLY, YOUR HONOR, WITH REGARD TO THE SAME MATTER, THEY HAD A CASE IN BROWARD COUNTY---
THE COURT:	YOU CAN STEP BACK TO THE MICROPHONE.
MS. JONES:	I'M SORRY. JUST TO MAKE SURE, YOUR HONOR, THAT ATTORNEY FRANKLIN WAS KEPT OUT OF THE PROCESS; THEY HAD A HEARING IN BROWARD COUNTY AND WE RECEIVED A NOTICE TO APPEAR IN THIS JURISDICTION. AND TO KEEP US FROM KNOWING OR BEING A PART OF THAT HEARING, THEY WOULD CHANGE THE DATES AND NOT TELL US ANYTHING.

COMMENT AND ANALYSIS: #19 *HERE BRIANNA JONES IS REFERRING TO THE HEARING SCHEDULED FOR JUNE 22, 1997 BY JUDGE RICHARD MANDARIN, A KEY D.C. JUDICIAL CO-CONSPIRATOR, REGARDING THE STAKEHOLDER ACTION BROUGHT BY THE DISTRICT OF COLUMBIA AND THE D.C. LOTTERY BOARD.*

THE FORMAL NOTICE OF THE HEARING WAS SCHEDULED FOR JUNE 22, 1997. WE LATER LEARNED THAT THE HEARING HAD BEEN HELD, WITHOUT NOTICE TO US, ON MAY 5, 1997 BEFORE JUDGE RICHARD MANDARIN.

PRIOR TO THE JUNE 1997 SCHEDULED HEARING, BRIANNA JONES, UNDER THE ALLEGED MENTORSHIP OF HER CLOSE FRIEND AND CONFIDANT, BETH HOLLISTER, REFUSED TO ALLOW ME TO FILE, ON HER BEHALF, A MOTION TO INTERVENE IN THE STAKEHOLDER ACTION.

SHE STATED THAT IN A MEETING IN HIS CHAMBERS, JUDGE RICHARD MANDARIN ASSURED HER THAT SHE DIDN'T NEED TO INTERVENE IN THE ACTION, NOR DID I NEED TO BE PRESENT AT THE MEETING IN HIS JUDGE'S CHAMBERS. BRIANNA JONES STATED THAT SHE WAS ACCOMPANIED TO THE MEETING BY BETH HOLLISTER, THE WASHINGTON ABC TELEVISION NEWS ANCHOR.

THE COURT:	YOU ARE TALKING ABOUT THEY. I ONCE SAW A SCIENCE FICTION MOVIE CALLED "THEM" AND I THINK---

MS. JONES:	IT WAS JUST DIFFERENT. HE CHANGED ATTORNEYS SEVERAL TIMES. IT WOULD BE---WE WERE AT THE COURTHOUSE ON AUGUST 6TH 1997. AND OUTSIDE OF JUDGE'S CHAMBERS, THE PHONE RANG AND TOLD US TO ACCEPT $5 MILLION AND THAT WAS IT. WE WERE---ON AUGUST 6 IN JUDGE GILBERT MATTHEWS' CHAMBERS. I AM NOT HOLDING ANYTHING BACK. THIS HAS BEEN HOW MY LIFE HAS BEEN SINCE I FILED SUIT.
THE COURT:	I THINK THAT YOU ARE ANTICIPATING WHAT IS GOING TO HAPPEN IF YOU SHOW UP HERE TUESDAY WITH NOTHING.
MS. JONES:	NO, NO. I AM ANTICIPATING WHAT IS GOING TO HAPPEN WHEN I SHOW UP TO DO WHAT I HAVE ALWAYS WANTED TO DO.
THE COURT:	WELL, IF YOU SHOW UP AND DO WHAT YOU HAVE ALWAYS WANTED TO DO, THAT MAY NOT BE THE OUTCOME THAT I EXPECT. THE OUTCOME I EXPECT IS THAT YOU ARE GOING TO COMPLY WITH THAT ORDER THAT JUDGE STARR ISSUED WHERE YOU ARE REQUIRED TO BRING EVIDENCE OF YOUR ASSETS. NOW, IF YOU DO THAT, THEN YOU WILL HAVE SATISFIED THE REQUIREMENT OF THE SUPERIOR COURT OF THE DISTRICT OF COLUMBIA. IF YOU DON'T DO THAT, THEN THE SUPERIOR COURT OF THE DISTRICT OF COLUMBIA WILL ENFORCE ITS ORDER.

COMMENT AND ANALYSIS: #20 *JUDGE EKANS' WARNING TO BRIANNA JONES REGARDING THE COURT'S INTENTION TO ENFORCE JUDGE STARR'S ORDER WOULD TURN OUT TO BE MERE JUDICIAL GASLIGHTING AND RHETORIC, SINCE JUDGE STARR'S ORDER OF OCTOBER 18, 2010 WAS NEVER ENFORCED BY JUDGE EKANS (THE SUPERIOR COURT OF THE DISTRICT OF COLUMBIA), AND WAS NEVER MEANT TO BE ENFORCED DUE TO THE RAGING D.C. JUDICIAL AND FBI CRIMINAL ENTERPRISE WHOSE MISSION WAS TO DEFRAUD ME OF AN ESTIMATED $50 MILLION IN ATTORNEY'S FEES.*

MS. JONES:	VERY WELL, YOUR HONOR.
THE COURT:	ALL RIGHT. I WILL SEE YOU TUESDAY.
MS. JONES:	THANK YOU, YOUR HONOR.
MS. FRANKLIN:	THANK YOU, YOUR HONOR.
THE DEPUTY CLERK:	THIS COURT STANDS ADJOURNED.
	(PROCEEDINGS ADJOURNED.)

BARBARA WASHINGTON FRANKLIN

SUPERIOR COURT OF THE DISRICT OF COLUMBIA
CIVIL DIVISION
WASHINGTON, D.C.

THE HONORABLE MATTHEW D. EKANS, ASSOCIATE JUDGE, PRESIDING

THE FOLLOWING ARE EXCERPTS OF THE OFFICIAL COURT TRANSCRIPT OF THE
JANUARY 25, 2011 PROCEEDING
ANNOTATED BY THE AUTHOR'S PERTINENT COMMENTARY AND ANALYSIS

JANUARY 25, 2011

P R O C E E D I N G S

COMMENT AND ANALYSIS: #A THE PROCEEDING ON JANUARY 25, 2011
WILL FOREVER STAND FOR A CLASSIC ILLUSTRATION AND MASTER
TUTORIAL IN JUDICIAL GASLIGHTING EGREGIOUSLY AND AUDACIOUSLY
ENGAGED IN BY JUDGE EKANS FOR THE DURATION OF HIS 9-MONTH
ADJUDICATION OF MY LAWSUIT. IN SUM AND SUBSTANCE, EKANS'
GASLIGHTING STRATEGY CRITICALLY CONTRIBUTED TO THE
ACHIEVEMENT OF THE MISSION OF THE D.C. JUDICIAL AND FBI FRAUD,
THEFT, CORRUPTION AND EXTORTION CONSPIRACY AND CRIMINAL
ENTERPRISE WHICH WAS TO STEAL, ROB AND DEFRAUD ME OF AN
ESTIMATED $50 MILLION IN ATTORNEY'S FEES RESULTING FROM MY
REPRESENTATION OF BRIANNA JONES, AND THE $34 MILLION
SETTLEMENT OF THE $100 MILLION FLORIDA LAWSUIT FILED ON HER
BEHALF IN THE BROWARD COUNTY CIRCUIT COURT IN FORT
LAUDERDALE, FLA IN MAY 1996.

JUDGE EKANS MADE IT A POINT OF NEVER REFERRING TO THE BANK **OF**
AMERICA BANK STATEMENTS THAT WERE THE SUBJECT OF JUDGE
STARR'S OCTOBER 18, 2010 COURT ORDER. RATHER, IN JUDICIAL
GASLIGHTING FASHION, JUDGE EKANS REFERRED ONLY TO NEUTRAL
ASSETS OF THE DEFENDANT, BRIANNA JONES, AS OPPOSED TO THE
SPECIFIC COURT ORDERED BANK STATEMENTS EVIDENCING THE
AMOUNT OF CASE SETTLEMENT PROCEEDS ON DEPOSIT AT BANK OF
AMERICA.

THE DEPUTY CLERK:	YOUR HONOR, CALLING THE MATTER OF BARBARA WASHINGTON FRANKLIN VERSUS BRIANNA JONES, CIVIL ACTION 4417-2009.
	PARTIES STEP FORWARD AND STATE YOUR NAME FOR THE RECORD PLEASE.
MS. WASHINGTON-FRANKLIN:	GOOD AFTERNOON, YOUR HONOR. BARBARA WASHINGTON FRANKLIN, PLAINTIFF PRO SE.
THE COURT:	GOOD AFTERNOON.
MS. JONES:	GOOD AFTERNOON, YOUR HONOR. BRIANNA JONES, PRO SE AT THIS TIME.
THE COURT:	GOOD AFTERNOON.
	I WAS ADVISED BY MY LAW CLERK THIS MORNING THAT MS. JONES, YOU HAD CALLED TO SAY THAT YOU WERE HAVING TRANSPORTATION ISSUES, AND SO WE'RE HERE NOW RATHER THAN EARLIER, WHICH WAS NOT A PROBLEM FOR ME.
	MS. WASHINGTON-FRANKLIN, I HOPE IT WASN'T A BIG PROBLEM FOR YOU.
MS. WASHINGTON-FRANKLIN:	NO, IT WASN'T.
	COMMENT AND ANALYSIS: #B WHAT WAS A BIG PROBLEM FOR ME WAS HAVING TO ENDURE THE 9-MONTH ADJUDICTION OF MY LAWSUIT IN A D.C. COURT SYSTEM SATURATED AND MARINATED IN THE DEEPEST OF JUDICIAL AND FBI FRAUD, THEFT, CORRUPTION AND EXTORTION, ORCHESTRATED BY CORRUPT D.C. COURT JUDGES WHO WERE ACCOUNTABLE TO NO ONE.
MS. WASHINGTON-FRANKLIN:	NO, IT WASN'T.
MS. JONES:	YOUR HONOR, WHEN I LEFT HERE MAY I SPEAK?
THE COURT:	YES.
MS. JONES:	WHEN I LEFT HERE FRIDAY I DROVE ALL THE WAY BACK TO FLORIDA. I ARRIVED LATE ON SUNDAY EVENING. AND I TOOK A SCHEDULED FLIGHT AT 7:00 A.M. THIS MORNING. I WAS BUMPED ON THAT FLIGHT. AND THE VERY NEXT FLIGHT NON-STOP TO WASHINGTON, D.C. WAS AT 11:55. I APOLOGIZE. IT CERTAINLY WAS NOT MY INTENTION.

77

THE COURT:	LET'S NOT GET OFF ON THE WRONG FOOT. MAYBE YOU DIDN'T HEAR WHAT I SAID. WHAT I SAID WAS THAT WE WERE ADVISED THAT YOU WERE HAVING TRANSPORTATION DIFFICULTIES, AND THAT'S WHY WE'RE HERE NOW INSTEAD OF WHEN I SET IT AT 9:30.
MS. JONES:	I SEE.
THE COURT:	AND THEN I WENT ON TO SAY THAT IT WASN'T A PROBLEM FOR ME.
MS. JONES:	THANK YOU.
THE COURT:	SO I WAS HOPIING TO SIMPLY MAKE THE RECORD AS TO WHY WE'RE STARTING NOW INSTEAD OF AT 9:30 WHICH IS WHEN I SAID WE WOULD HAVE THE CASE.

I'M ALSO ADVISED THAT YOU WERE HERE RIGHT AROUND 3:00 WHICH IS WHEN WE HAD ANTICIPATED YOU WOULD BE HERE AFTER ARRIVING AT REAGAN NATIONAL. BUT I THOUGHT INSTEAD OF COMING DOWN RIGHT AT 3 I'D WAIT A HALF AN HOUR OR SO TO GIVE YOU TWO A CHANCE TO TALK. BECAUSE TIHS IS REALLY ABOUT YOU PRODUCING DOCUMENTS.

COMMENT AND ANALYSIS: #1 HERE AGAIN JUDGE EKANS, WITH CLEAR AND PREMEDITATED CALCULATION, FALSELY, INTENTIONALLY AND PURPOSEFULLY DEFINES HIS ROLE AS PRESIDING JUDGE AS MERELY LIMITED TO THE NARROW TASK OF OVERSEEING BRIANNA JONES "PRODUCING DOCUMENTS."

JUDGE EKANS WAS BEING CHARACTERISTICALLY DECEPTIVE. JUDGE STARR'S OCTOBER 18, 2010 ORDER MANDATED THAT BRIANNA JONES PRODUCE BANK OF AMERICA BANK STATEMENTS OF THE SETTLEMENT PROCEEDS. JUDGE STARR'S ORDER DIDN'T DIRECT BRIANNA JONES TO REVEAL WHERE THE MONEY WAS. NOR DID JUDGE STARR'S ORDER DIRECT BRIANNA JONES TO PRODUCE DOCUMENTS REGARDING HER PERSONAL ASSETS. JUDGE EKANS, IRRESPECTIVE OF MY MANY YEARS AS A TRIAL ATTORNEY, APPARENTLY DECIDED TO PLAY WORD GAMES AFTER MISJUDGING ME BLIND AND STUPID, AND BRIANNA JONES LEGALLY UNEDUCATED AND THUS IGNORANT OF HIS JUDICIAL DEVICES.

MS. JONES:	YOU'RE RIGHT.

THE COURT:

AND I'D SAY THAT IN PROBABLY 95% OF THE CASES PEOPLE WORK THESE MATTERS OUT, OUT THERE IN **THE WITNESS ROOMS.** AND THEY SIMPLY COME IN AND TELL THE JUDGE THERE IS NO NEED FOR A HEARING, WE'VE GOT IT WORKED OUT. BUT THIS CASE HAS OBVIOUSLY HIT THAT 5% WHERE FOR REASONS **WE HAVEN'T BEEN ABLE TO GET THE TWO OF YOU ON THE SAME PAGE WITH YOUR PAPERWORK.** WHAT HAVE YOU BROUGHT TODAY?

COMMENT AND ANALYSIS: #2 EVEN THOUGH JUDGE EKANS DIDN'T USE THE ACTUAL TERMS "**JUDGMENT CREDITOR**" AND "**JUDGMENT DEBTOR**", NEVERTHELESS THE SUM AND SUBSTANCE OF HIS COMMENTS CLEARLY DESCRIBED THE BEHAVIOR OF THE JUDGMENT CREDITOR AND JUDGMENT DEBTOR IN MEETING IN THE **WITNESS ROOMS** TO RESOLVE THEIR LEGAL MATTER.

SIGNIFICANTLY ENOUGH, JUDGE EKANS HAD NO KNOWLEDGE OF THE EXISTENCE OF THESE ROOMS AT THE CLOSE OF THE JANUARY 31, 2011 COURT HEARING WHEN BRIANNA JONES OFFERED TO REVIEW BANK STATEMENTS WITH ME AND EKANS SAID THERE WAS NO PLACE IN THE COURTHOUSE FOR US TO MEET FOR SUCH PURPOSE. DENYING MY REVIEW OF THE BANK STATEMENTS FURTHERED THE MISSION OF THE CRIMINAL ENTERPRISE TO DEFRAUD ME OF THE MILLIONS OF DOLLARS OWED TO ME IN ATTORNEY'S FEES.

HOWEVER, I WAS NOT A **JUDGMENT CREDITOR** AND BRIANNA JONES WAS NOT A **JUDGMENT DEBTOR.** AND JUDGE EKANS WAS WELL AWARE OF THIS FACT.

NEVERTHELESS, JUDGE EKANS WOULD BEAT THE DRUM OF MY BEING A JUDGMENT CREDITOR AND BRIANNA JONES OF BEING A JUDGMENT DEBTOR BECAUSE IT FIT WITHIN THE SCHEME AND STRATEGY OF THE CRIMINAL ENTERPRISE TO DEFRAUD ME *LEGALLY* OF AN ESTIMATED $50 MILLION IN ATTORNEY'S FEES.

WHAT IS SIGNIFICANT REGARDING JUDGE EKANS' KNOWINGLY LABELING ME A *JUDGMENT CREDITOR* AND BRIANNA JONES A JUDGMENT DEBTOR IS THAT HE KNOWS THAT HE SHALL HAVE TO ANSWER TO NO ONE FOR HIS INTENTIONAL AND PURPOSEFUL MISCONDUCT. **THE D.C. COURT SYSTEM CULTURE IS BUTTRESSED ON AN UNSPOKEN RULE THAT NO JUDGE WILL REPORT ON THE MISCONDUCT OF ANOTHER JUDGE, NO MATTER HOW EGREGIOUS OR EVEN CRIMINAL THEIR JUDICIAL MISCONDUCT OR THE EXTENT OF THE RESULTING DAMAGE CAUSED A PARTY LITIGANT SEEKING JUSTICE, FAIRNESS AND EQUALITY UNDER LAW.**

MS. JONES:	YOUR HONOR, IN MY HURRIED STATE ON FRIDAY WITH I SAID I DIDN'T HAVE DOCUMENTS. THE MAIN DOCUMENT, AND **THIS IS AN EXHIBIT, IT'S FROM THE BAR COUNSEL**. AND IT CLEARLY STATES, AND IF I MAY SPEAK OR READ.
	COMMENT AND ANALYSIS: #3 BRIANNA JONES AND I WERE BOTH ABOUT TO LEARN THAT JUDGE EKANS WAS NOT AT ALL INTERESTED IN ANY INFORMATION FROM THE OFFICE OF D.C BAR COUNSEL, THE DISCIPLINARY ARM OF THE D.C. COURT OF APPEALS.
THE COURT:	YOU CAN TELL US WHERE THE BANK IS THAT HAS THE MONEY. NOW IF YOU'RE TALKING ABOUT SOMETHING ELSE, THEN YOU'VE GOT ME CONFUSED. AND I DON'T LIKE TO BE CONFUSED.
	COMMENT AND ANALYSIS: #4 IN FACT, HERE JUDGE EKANS TELLS JONES THAT HER REFERENCE TO BAR COUNSEL HAS CONFUSED HIM. IN OTHER WORDS, JUDGE EKANS WAS A PART OF A CRIMINAL ENTERPRISE WHOSE MISSION WAS TO DEFRAUD ME OF MILLIONS OF DOLLARS IN ATTORNEY'S FEES AND HIS SOLITARY ATTENTION WAS ON THAT MISSION AND THAT MISSION ALONE.
MS. JONES:	**BAR COUNSEL CLEARLY STATES THAT I'M INDEED ENTITLED AFTER THOROUGH AND EXHAUSTIVE INVESTIGATION, I HAVE NOT YET TAKEN POSSESSION OF THE PROCEEDS. AND DISBURSEMENT HAS NOT YET BEEN MADE TO ME.** IT IS CLEAR I DID NOT HAVE THIS WITH ME. I THOUGHT THAT -- -- AND THIS WAS DATED SEPTEMBER 14TH OF 09. ATTORNEY FRANKLIN FILED THE SUIT MARCH 13TH OF 09. I THOUGHT SHE WOULD DO WHAT WAS RIGHT AND DISMISS THE SUIT. SHE HAS IT IN WRITING. THE RECIPIENT OF THIS LETTER FAXED THIS TO ME SO THAT I WOULD HAVE THIS FOR THIS HEARING. I DID NOT IN MY HURRIED STATE, I DID NOT BRING IT WITH ME. THERE ARE OTHER DOCUMENTATIONS THAT WILL SHOW THAT I DO NOT HAVE IT. I'VE CONSISTENTLY EXPRESSED THAT TO THE PLAINTIFF.
	THIS HAS BEEN AN ATTEMPT TO HAVE ME BEREFT OF NOT ONLY RESOURCES, POTENTIAL RESOURCES, BUT ALSO AT THIS POINT NOW MY OWN FREEDOM. I HAVE A WILL HERE THAT'S DATED OCTOBER 26 OF 1996. SHE PREPARED THE WILL. SHE IS THE SOLE BENEFICIARY AS WELL AS THE EXECUTRESS OF THE WILL. THIS IS A SYSTEMATIC ATTEMPT TO CONSTANTLY ULTIMATELY -- --

80

COMMENT AND ANALYSIS: #5 *BRIANNA JONES CLEARLY STATES THAT THE OFFICE OF D.C. BAR COUNSEL, AFTER "THOROUGH AND EXHAUSTIVE INVESTIGATION" HAS DETERMINED THAT SETTLEMENT HAS OCCURRED, THAT JONES IS ENTITLED TO CONSIDERABLE ASSETS, BUT DISBURSEMENT TO HER HAS NOT YET BEEN MADE.* FOUR YEARS LATER IT WOULD BE THIS FINE POINT, I.E., THAT THE SETTLEMENT PROCEEDS HAVE YET TO BE MADE TO HER THAT THE D.C. COURT OF APPEALS, AT ALL TIMES IN COMPLICITY WITH EKANS AND THE OTHER CO-CONSPIRATORS, WOULD LATCH ONTO TO OVERTURN THE FAKE $13.6 MILLION MONEY JUDGMENT ISSUED BY JUDGE EKANS TO ME IN OCTOBER 2011. THIS KIND OF D.C. JUDICIAL CORRUPTION, FRAUD, THEFT AND EXTORTION SUCCEEDS AND FLOURISHES BECAUSE THE CORRUPT D.C. COURT JUDGES SUCH AS JUDGE EKANS ANSWER TO NO ONE. WHEN A MASSIVE CRIMINAL ENTERPRISE IS UNDERWAY IN THE D.C. COURT SYSTEM, IT IS COMPARABLE TO A FAST-MOVING TRAIN THAT REFUSES TO STOP AT ANY STATIONS ALONG THE TRACK UNTIL ITS MISSION OF THE CRIMINAL ENTERPRISE IS ACCOMPLISHED AND ALL D.C. JUDICIAL, FBI, THEIR RESPECTIVE HANDLERS AND FACILITATORS HAVE BEEN SATISFACTORILY COMPENSATED FOR THEIR INDIVIDUAL ROLES PLAYED IN THE DESIGN, ORCHESTRATION AND EXECUTION OF THE CRIMINAL ENTERPRISE.

MS. WASHINGTON-FRANKLIN: YOUR HONOR, I'M GOING TO OBJECT IF YOUR HONOR PLEASE. YOUR HONOR WAS VERY SPECIFIC AT THE LAST HEARING, WHICH WAS THE HEARING FOR THE ORAL EXAM. YOUR HONOR STATED VERY SUCCINCTLY, VERY SPECIICALLY AND VERY CLEARLY THAT MS. JONES WAS TO PRODUCE THE DOCMENTS THAT SHE DID NOT PRODUCE ON FRIDAY, THE 21ST.

THE QUESTION IS, IS SHE GOING TO PRODUCE DOCUMENTS THIS AFTERNOON, YOUR HONOR, OR IS SHE NOT? YOU TOLD HER YOU WANTED TO KNOW WHERE THE MONEY WAS, WHERE IT WAS LOCATED, WHO WAS HOLDING THE FUNDS. IF SHE'S NOT PREPARED TO DO THAT, YOUR HONOR, THIS IS MY SECOND TRIP DOWN HERE TODAY. I JUST AS WELL, YOU KNOW, ASK THE COURT TO BE EXECUSED BECAUSE I DON'T HEAR ANYTHING ABOUT BANK DOCUMENTS. I DON'T HEAR ANYTHING ABOUT LOCATION OF SETTLEMENT PROCEEDS. THAT IS WHY WE ARE HERE THIS AFTERNOON.

MS. JONES: YOUR HONOR, MAY I SPEAK?

***

THE COURT: YOU MUST REMEMBER AND I REALIZE THAT YOU ARE PRO SE, BUT YOU MUST REMEMBER TO TALK TO ME. IF YOU AND MS. FRANKLIN WANT TO TALK TO EACH OTHER I CAN EXCUSE YOU TO GO OUTSIDE IF THAT WOULD BE HELPFUL. BUT YOU'RE NOT HERE TO DISCUSS YOUR ISSUES WITH MS. FRANKLIN. **YOU'RE HERE AS A JUDGMENT DEBTOR**. AND IT SEEMS TO ME THAT YOU DON'T FULLY APPRECIATE THAT.

COMMENT AND ANALYSIS: #6 IF A CORRUPT D.C. COURT JUDGE IS ALLOWED TO USE HIS VIRTUALLY ABSOLUTE POWER TO CHANGE THE FACTS OF A CASE IN ORDER TO ACHIEVE A PARTICULAR OUTCOME, THEN, JUST AS IN A PRO WRESTING MATCH, **THE WHOLE D.C. COURT ADJUDICATION PROCESS IS FAKE, PRE-SCRIPTED AND RIGGED.** MOREOVER, THE COURT PROCESS HAS ABSOLUTELY NOTHING TO DO WITH THE RULE OF LAW, JUSTICE, FAIRNESS OR EQUITY. IT IS SIMPLY FRAUD, THEFT, CORRUPTION AND EXTORTION ---ALL CAPS.

BRIANNA JONES WAS NOT IN COURT AS A JUDGMENT DEBTOR AND JUDGE EKANS KNEW THAT. HE WAS JUST BEHAVING AS A ROGUE COURT JUDGE WHO DID WHATEVER HE WANTED TO DO, AND DARED ANYBODY TO DO ANYTHING ABOUT IT. PERIOD. BUT WHAT I QUICKLY FOUND OUT IN JUDGE EKANS' COURTROOM WAS THAT HE DETERMINED THE FACTS OF YOUR CASE. AND IF YOUR FACTS COMPLICATED THE MISSION OF THE CRIMINAL ENTERPRISE IN ANY WAY, HE SIMPLY CHANGED THE FACTS. AND HOWEVER YOU CORRECTED THE COURT RECORD, YOU AS A PARTY LITIGANT AND EVEN OFFICER OF THE COURT, AS WAS MY STATION, WERE SIMPLY IGNORED. THIS IS THE ABUSE AND MISUSE OF ABSOLUTE JUDICIAL POWER WITHOUT ANY ACCOUNTABILITY WHATSOEVER.

MS. WASHINGTON-FRANKLIN: YOUR HONOR, SHE'S MAKING IT CLEAR TO THE COURT THAT SHE'S NOT GOING TO PRODUCE THE DOCUMENTS. JUDGE STARR ISSUED AN ORDER ON OCTOBER 18TH. SHE WAS SUPPOSED TO HAVE PRODUCED THE DOCUMENTS BY OCTOBER 25TH. SHE DID NOT PRODUCE THE DOCUMENTS. I THEN FILED A MOTION FOR CONTEMPT ON OCTOBER 27TH. SHE STILL DIDN'T PRODUCE THE DOCUMENTS.

YOUR HONOR FOUND HER IN CONTEMPT ON LAST FRIDAY, JANUARY 21ST. IT IS NOW TUESDAY THE 25TH. SHE'S MADE IT CLEAR, YOUR HONOR, THAT SHE IS NOT GOING TO PRODUCE THE DOCUMENTS. SHE IS NOT GOING TO PAY THE ATTORNEY FEES DUE. SHE'S NOT GOING TO DISCLOSE THE WHEREABOUTS OF THE ASSETS.

AND THE ORDER FROM JUDGE STARR THAT YOUR HONOR IS IMPLEMENTING IS VERY CLEAR. WHEN SHE TOOK THE STAND DURIING THE ORAL EXAM I WALKED HER THROUGH UNTIL SHE BECAME EVASIVE AND THE COURT ASKED HER TO STEP DOWN. I WALKED THROUGH THAT OCTOBER 18TH ORDER WHICH SHE UNDERSTOOD AND READ PORTIONS OF IT. SO SHE'S PLAYING GAMES, YOUR HONOR. YOUR HONOR RECOGNIZED THAT LAST FRIDAY. AND SHE COMES INTO COURT WITH THE BOLDNESS TO CONTINUE PLAYING GAMES.

YOUR HONOR HAS ASKED HER TO BE HERE A SPECIFIC TIME TWICE.

LAST FRIDAY SHE WAS ASKED TO BE HERE ON TIME. SHE WALKED IN AFTER 12. WE HAD AN 11:00 HEARING. SHE WAS ASKED TO BE HERE THIS MORNING AT 9:30. SHE WAS BUMPED FROM A FLIGHT. SHE WAS ASKED TO BE HERE THIS MORNING AT 9:30. SHE WAS ASKED TO BE HERE AT 3:00. SHE WALKS IN   I DON'T KNOW WHATEVER TIME.

SO I MEAN, YOUR HONOR, HOW MUCH AM I SUPPOSED TO ENDURE WITH THIS? SHE'S ACTING AS IF THE COURT HAS ABSOLUTELY NO POWER TO HOLD HER IN CONTEMPT AND ALSO FOLLOW THROUGH WITH A FINE OR PENALTY OR WHATEVER.

I MEAN IT'S NOT A ROCKET SCIENCE. DO YOU HAVE THE INFORMATION WITH REGARD TO THE ASSETS, THE SETTLEMENT PROCEEDS, WHERE THEY ARE, WHO'S HOLDING THEM? ON FRIDAY WHEN SHE WAS QUESTIONED DURING THE ORAL EXAM SHE SAID THEY WERE IN BANK OF AMERICA. AND THEN BECAME VERY EVASIVE WHEN I ASKED HER WHICH BRANCH IN THE WASHINGTON REGION.

NOW SHE'S HOLDING UP PAPER WHICH MEANS WHAT I DON'T KNOW.

MS. JONES: BARBARA, IT'S AN ACCOUNT WITH BOTH OUR NAMES ON IT WITH BANK OF AMERICA, A PROFESSIONAL EXECUTIVE ACCOUNT.

YOUR HONOR, MAY I SPEAK?

THE COURT: IF YOU HAVE ANY PAPERS THAT YOU WANT ME TO CONSIDER, YOU CAN HAND THEM UP.

MS. JONES: IF IT PLEASE THE COURT, MAY I SPEAK?

THE COURT: LET ME LOOK AT THESE PAPERS FIRST.

MS. JONES: CERTAINLY. THERE'S SOMETHING ELSE I HAVE AS WELL.

(PAUSE.)

THE COURT:	THIS PAPER, SOMEONE HAS WRITTEN EXHIBIT 1 OVER THE -- --
MS. JONES:	I WROTE THAT, I WROTE THAT.
THE COURT:	WHAT IS THIS SUPPOSED TO BE?
MS. JONES:	THOSE ARE DOCUMENTS THAT WILL SHOW THAT -- --
THE COURT:	THIS IS JUST ONE SINGLE SHEET OF PAPER.
MS.. JONES:	BUT THE OTHER ONES HE SAID THEY CAME UP WRONG, THEY CAME OUT BLACK.
THE COURT:	HE, WHO IS HE?
MS. JONES:	THE GENTLEMAN, LEONARD LIPPMAN (PHONETIC). AND HIS MOTHER-IN-LAW, GLENDA MARCH, THAT WAS ADDRESSED TO HER FROM BAR COUNSEL. BUT I HIGHLIGHTED THAT LINE WHERE IT CLEARLY STATES THAT I WAS IN FACT ENTITLED TO THE PROCEEDS, HAVE NOT YET TAKEN POSSESSION.

COMMENT AND ANALYSIS: #7 BRIANNA JONES' SECOND ATTEMPT TO IMPRESS JUDGE EKANS WITH D.C. BAR COUNSEL'S NOTICE TO ONE OF MY FORMER CLIENTS WHO HAD MADE A LARGE LOAN TO JONES, THAT SHE WAS ENTITLED TO (SETTLEMENT) PROCEEDS, BUT HAD NOT TAKEN POSSESSION, SIMPLY FELL ON EKANS' DEAF EARS.

WHAT JONES WOULD COME TO LEARN AND THAT I HAD RECOGNIZED FROM THE MOMENT OF MY FIRST APPEARANCE BEFORE EKANS ON JANUARY 21, 2011, WAS THAT HE HAD, AT THE END OF THE DAY, NO REAL INTEREST OR CONCERN ABOUT MY BEING PAID THE MILLIONS OF DOLLARS OWED TO ME IN ATTORNEY'S FEES FOR LEGAL SERVICES ON BEHALF OF BRIANNA JONES.

NOTHING IS MORE DANGEROUS IN OUR SOCIETY THAN HAVING TO SUBMIT YOUR VERY LIFE AND WELL-BEING TO A COURT JUDGE WHO KNOWS, AT THE END OF THE DAY, THAT HE DOES NOT HAVE TO ANSWER TO ANYONE FOR HIS MISCONDUCT ON THE COURT BENCH. HE, MOREOVER, KNOWS THAT HE IS ABOVE THE LAW AND PROVED IT OVER AND OVER AGAIN IN MY LAWSUIT FOR ALMOST A YEAR.

MS. WASHINGTON-FRANKLIN: YOUR HONOR, LET ME HELP THE COURT WITH THAT.   SHE IS NOT PROVIDING THE COURT WITH THE COMPLETE LETTER.

THE COURT: NO, IT'S OBVIOUS.

MS. WASHINGTON-FRANKLIN: BECAUSE THE LETTER, YOUR HONOR -- --

MS. JONES: THAT'S ALL I RECEIVED.

MS. WASHINGTON-FRANKLIN; YOUR HONOR, THE LETTER IS A LETTER THAT I WAS COPIED ON BY BAR COUNSEL. DURING MY --- --

THE COURT: DISTRICT OF COLUMBIA BAR COUNSEL.

MS. WASHINGTON-FRANKLIN: CORRECT.

MS. JONES: THAT'S CORRECT.

MS. WASHINGTON-FRANKLIN: DURING MY REPRESENTATION OF MS. JONES FOR MANY YEARS, VARIOUS FRIENDS AND ACQUAINTANCES OF MINE HAVE PROVIDED HER WITH LOANS FOR SUBSTANTIAL AMOUNTS OF MONEY. GLENDA MARCH OF CALIFORNIA WAS ONE OF THOSE ACQUAINTANCES WHO PROVIDED OVER $30,000 IN CASH IN A LOAN TO HER. THE LOAN WAS SUPPOSED TO HAVE BEEN PAID WITHIN THREE YEARS. IT WAS EXTENDED IN 2007. IT WAS NOT PAID. IT WAS CONSTANTLY BEING PROMISED AND IT WAS NOT PAID.

CONSEQUENTLY, MS. MARCH DECIDED TO WRITE THE BAR AND OBVIOUSLY SINCE I WAS THE ATTORNEY THAT PREPARED THE PROMISSORY NOTE AND THIS WAS MY CLIENT, LET'S GO TO THE BAR ON MS. FRANKLIN. THE BAR RESPONDED TO MS. MARCH THAT I HAD DONE ABSOLUTELY NOTHING WRONG. THE MONIES WERE LOANED. I WAS SIMPLY THE ATTORNEY THAT PREPARED THE PROMISSORY NOTE.

THE REASON MS. JONES DOESN'T WANT YOUR HONOR TO SEE THE FULL LETTER IS BECAUSE IT SPELLS OUT HER INDEBTEDNESS TO A LONG LIST OF PEOPLE. AS A MATTER OF FACT, I NOTICE THERE ARE SOME OTHER CREDITORS IN THE COURTROOM WHO EXTENDED EVEN MORE IN TERMS OF THE AMOUNT OF LOANS MADE TO HER.

MS. JONES: MAY I SPEAK, YOUR HONOR?

BARBARA WASHINGTON FRANKLIN

MS. WASHINGTON-FRANKLIN: AND TO GIVE THE COURT A PAGE OF A LETTER IS RATHER INSULTING TO BOOT. BUT ON THE OTHER HAND, YOUR HONOR, ALL OF THIS IS BESIDES THE POINT. AND WHAT MS. JONES WOULD LIKE TO DO IS HAVE THIS COURT GO OFF IN VARIOUS TRIBUTARIES SO THAT SHE WOULD NOT HAVE TO ANSWER THE QUESTION, WHERE ARE THE FUNDS AND WHY HAVE THEY NOT BEEN DISBURSED SO THAT ATTORNEY FEES CAN BE PAID AND ALL THE CREDITORS CAN BE PAID AS WELL.

I OBJECT TO ALL OF THOSE DOCUMENTS SHE'S PROVIDING TO THE COURT BECAUSE THEY HAVE NOTHING TO DO WITH THIS HEARNG WHATSOEVER.

MS. JONES: AND I OBJECT TO YOUR EXPLANATION BECAUSE THAT IS NOT THE TRUTH.

THE COURT: A MINUTE AGO YOU ASKED BEFORE YOU SPEAK. NOW APPARENTLY YOU'RE GOING TO TAKE A DIFFERENT TACT. YOU CAN SIT DOWN.

LET'S ----- FIRST OF ALL I SAY THAT I'VE LOOKED OVER THIS SO-CALLED EXHIBIT 1 WHICH APPARENTLY -- --

MS. JONES: THAT'S ALL HE COULD FAX.

THE COURT: THIS MAY BE A GOOD TIME FOR ME TO SAY THAT I RECOGNIZE THAT YOU'RE PRO SE, PLAINTIFF IS PRO SE, PLAINTIFF IS AN ATTORNEY. AND I RECOGNIZE THAT. BUT THE NUMBER ONE RULE THAT I HAVE IN MY COURTROOM IS THAT ONE PERSON IS IN CHARGE. AND THAT'S ME. AND ANYBODY WHO SPEAKS, SPEAKS TO THE COURT AND WHEN THE COURT ASKS THEM TO SPEAK. IF YOU CAN'T DO THAT THEN WE'RE GOING TO REALLY HAVE A PROBLEM.

EXHIBIT 1, WHICH APPARENTLY IS A PAGE TAKEN FROM A BROADER PAPER DOES NOT HAVE ANY BEARING ON **THE JUDGMENT THAT THE PLAINTIFF HAS OBTAINED AGAINST THE DEFENDANT IN THIS CASE.** AND CERTAINLY HAS NO BEARING ON THE DEFENDANT'S FAILURE UP TO *THIS POINT TO SATISFY THE COURT'S ORDER TO PROVIDE EVIDENCE OF HER ASSETS.* SO WE'LL PUT THAT -- --

COMMENT AND ANALYSIS: #8 JUDGE EKANS INSISTS ON FALSELY DECLARING THAT I HAD OBTAINED A JUDGMENT AGAINST THE DEFENDANT, BRIANNA JONES. EKANS ALSO FALSELY STATES THAT JUDGE STARR'S ORDER DIRECTED BRIANNA JONES TO PROVIDE EVIDENCE OF HER ASSETS. THIS WAS JUST ANOTHER BIG LIE. JUDGE STARR'S ORDER MANDATED THAT BRIANNA JONES PRODUCE COPIES OF THE BANK OF AMERICA BANK STATEMENTS EVIDENCING THE AMOUNT OF SETTLEMENT PROCEEDS ON DEPOSIT AT BANK OF AMERICA. THIS WAS EVIDENCE OF EKANS' DETERMINATION TO GASLIGHT THE FACTS FOR PROMOTION OF THE CRIMINAL ENTERPRISE UNDERWAY. PERIOD.

MS. JONES: I DON'T HAVE THE ASSETS.

THE COURT: YOU REALLY DON'T HAVE ANOTHER TIME TO INTERRUPT ME. YOU REALLY DON'T HAVE ANOTHER TIME TO INTERRUPT ME.

THE SECOND PIECE OF PAPER IS A PHOTOCOPY OF WHAT APPEARS TO BE A VOIDED CHECK, NATIONS BANK WITH BRIANNA JONES AND BARBARA WASHINGTON-FRANKLIN APPARENTLY AS JOINT ACCOUNT HOLDERS.

MS. FRANKLIN, DO YOU KNOW ANYTHING ABOUT THIS?

MS. WASHINGTON-FRANKLIN: YOUR HONOR, I DON'T RECALL THAT PARTICUALR CHECK, BUT YEARS AGO AT ONE POINT IN TIME, YOU KNOW, WE WERE ON AN ACCOUNT, BUT IT WAS NATIONS BANK WHICH IS NO LONGER IN EXISTENCE. SO THAT WOULD HAVE ABSOLUTELY NOTHING TO DO WITH THE MATTERS BEFORE THE COURT TODAY.

THE COURT: ALL RIGHT. THAT'S NOT HELPFUL. THEN THERE'S EXHIBIT 4, WHICH IS A PAPER DATED AUGUST 8, 2000 ON BARBARA WASHINGTON-FRANKLIN'S LETTERHEAD. DEAR MS. WITHERS, THIS IS TO CONFIRM THAT MY CLIENT AND ASSOCIATE BRIANNA JONES IS A RECIPIENT OF FUNDS IN EXCESS OF A MILLION DOLLARS. THESE ASSETS SHOULD BE MORE THAN SUFFICIENT TO ALLOW HER TO COMPENSATE YOUR COMPANY FOR ANY FIDUCIARY RESPONSIBILITIES ASSUMED ON HER BEHALF. DON'T HESITATE TO CONTACT ME. VERY TRULY YOURS, BARBARA WASHINGTON-FRANKLIN.

WHAT DOES THIS HAVE TO DO WITH ANYTHING? NOW YOU CAN SPEAK.

MS. JONES:	WHEN YOU ASKED ME WHERE THE FUNDS ARE I'VE EXPRESSED I DON'T KNOW WHERE THE FUNDS ARE.
THE COURT:	SO THIS IS -- --
MS. WASHINGTON-FRANKLIN:	YOUR HONOR, WHEN SHE SAYS SHE DOESN'T KNOW WHERE THE FUNDS ARE, IF I MAY SPEAK, WHY DID SHE TESTIFY ON FRIDAY THAT HER LAST KNOWLEDGE OF THE FUNDS THREE WEEKS AGO WAS AT BANK OF -- --
THE COURT:	MS. FRANKLIN, CERTAINLY I MEAN I RECOGNIZE YOUR RHETORICAL QUESTION, BUT RIGHT NOW I'M IN THE MIDDLE OF MAKING A DECISION IN THIS CASE. AND -- --
	EXHIBIT 2, LAST WILL AND TESTAMENT OF BRIANNA JONES, WHAT DOES THIS HAVE TO DO WITH ANYTHING?
MS. JONES:	IT'S TO SHOW A PATTERN WITH ATTORNEY FRANKLIN THAT SHE PREPARED IT, SHE'S THE SOLE EXECUTRIX.
THE COURT:	IS IT CLEAR THEN THAT YOU HAVE NO INTENTION OF PRODUCING ANY DOCUMENTS THAT SHOWS WHERE YOUR ASSETS ARE?
MS. JONES:	YOUR HONOR, I DON'T HAVE THOSE DOCUMENTS.
THE COURT:	IS THAT CLEAR?
MS. JONES:	I DON'T HAVE THOSE DOCUMENTS.
THE COURT:	OKAY. ALL RIGHT. THEN I FIND YOU IN CONTEMPT OF THIS COURT. YOU MAY STEP TO THE RIGHT AND YOU SHOULD KNOW THAT YOU CAN GET OUT OF JAIL ANYTIME THAT YOU LET ME KNOW THAT YOU ARE READY TO PRESENT EVIDENCE OF THE WHEREABOUTS OF YOUR ASSETS.
	COMMENT AND ANALYSIS: #9 JUDGE EKANS PERSISTS IN INFORMING BRIANNA JONES THAT HER FREEDOM LIES IN PRESENTING EVIDENCE OF THE WHEREABOUTS OF HER ASSETS. JUDGE STARR'S ORDER SPECIICALLY MANDATED THAT JONES PRODUCE BANK OF AMERICA BANK STATEMENTS. JUDGE EKANS SIMPLY INTENTIONALLY ABUSED HIS POWER IN THE INTERPRETATION OF JUDGE STARR'S ORDER.
MS. JONES:	YOUR HONOR, I HAVE NO CLUE WHATSOEVER. I'LL BE IN I DON'T KNOW WHERE THEY ARE. THIS IS A FRAUD PERPETRATED UPON THE COURT.
THE COURT:	OKAY.
MS.. JONES:	I HAVE NO CLUE WHERE THEY ARE, YOUR HONOR.

THE COURT: I TELL YOU WHAT, WE -- --

MS. JONES: YOUR HONOR, I HAVE NO CLUE WHERE THEY ARE.

THE COURT: WELL, WE'LL WAIT TO HEAR FROM YOU. AND IN THE MEANTIME I'LL SET A STATUS HEARING. WHAT IS TODAY? WE'LL SET A STATUS HEARING FOR MONDAY. AND I'LL BRING YOU UP AND TALK WITH YOU ON MONDAY AND **SEE WHETHER YOU'VE REMEMBERED WHERE ANYTHING IS.**

                      COMMENT AND ANALYSIS: #10 JUDGE EKANS HAD EVERY OPPORTUNITY TO SPECIFICALLY ORDER BRIANNA JONES TO PRODUCE BANK OF AMERICA BANK STATEMENTS BUT HE PURPOSEFULLY REFUSED TO DO SO.

MS. JONES: YOUR HONOR, YOU CAN -- - I DON'T HAVE THEM. I DON'T HAVE THEM.

MS. WASHINGTON-FRANKLIN: EXCUSE ME, YOUR HONOR, WHAT TIME ON MONDAY, 11:00, 9:30?

THE COURT: LET'S SAY 12 NOON, BECAUSE I'LL HAVE TO FIND A COURTROOM WITH A LOCKUP.

MS. WASHINGTON-FRANKLIN: AND IS THAT GOING TO BE IN YOUR COURTROOM 517?

THE COURT: WELL, YOU CAN CHECK WITH US AT 517 TO FIND OUT WHERE THE COURTROOM IS BECAUSE I DON'T HAVE A LOCKUP IN 517. THAT'S WHY I'M DOWN HERE NOW. I HAVE TO FIND A COURTROOM WITH A LOCKUP.

MS. JONES: YOUR HONOR, MAY I SPEAK? AT THE EXECUTION OF THE SETTLEMENT AGREEMENT SHE UNDERSTOOD I DIDN'T HAVE THE FUNDS.

THE COURT: YOU MAY BE MISTAKEN. I'M NOT REALLY CONCERNED ABOUT THE FUNDS THAT YOU KEEP REFERRING TO . I'M CONCERNED ABOUT ANY *ASSETS.*

                      COMMENT AND ANALYSIS: #11 THE OPERATIVE WORDS WERE *BANK STATEMENTS* AND NOT "ASSETS."

MS. JONES: I DON'T HAVE ANY.

THE COURT: **RIGHT NOW SHE HAS A JUDGMENT**. WELL, YOU FLEW UP HERE. YOU MUST HAVE SOME ASSETS SOMEWHERE. **AND ALL I WANT TO KNOW IS WHERE YOUR ASSETS ARE.**

COMMENT AND ANALYSIS: #12 I HAD NO JUDGMENT. AND EKANS WAS FULLY AWARE I HAD NO JUDGMENT. HOWEVER, EKANS' FOCUS AND COMMITMENT WAS TO THE MISSION OF THE CRIMINAL ENTERPRISE AND NOT TO THE SPECIFICS OF JUDGE STARR'S OCTOBER 18, 2010 ORDER.

MS. JONES: I'M TRYING TO FIND -- --

THE COURT: MAYBE YOU JUST NEED TO HEAR, MAYBE YOU NEED TO LISTEN. IF YOU CAN GET THAT IN YOUR HEAD   LOOK, I DON'T HAVE ANY DESIRE TO SEND YOU TO JAIL. BUT YOU HAVE TO UNDERSTAND THAT THERE'S AN ORDER OF THIS COURT FOR YOU TO PRESENT EVIDENCE OF YOUR ASSETS. YOU'VE PRESENTED EVERYTHING BUT THAT.

MS. JONES: I DON'T HAVE ANY.

COMMENT AND ANALYSIS: #13 *JUDGE STARR'S ORDER MANDATED BRIANNA JONES TO PRODUCE BANK STATEMENTS AND NOT EVIDENCE OF HER ASSETS. EKANS ABUSED HIS POWER BY INTENTIONALLY CHANGING THE FACTS OF THE CASE.*

THE COURT: I'VE GIVEN YOU AMPLE OPPORTUNITY. IF WHAT YOU'VE GOT IS TEN CENTS, THEN YOU NEED TO SHOW ME WHERE THE TEN CENTS IS.

MS. JONES: FROM ATTORNEY FRANKLIN AND HER FRIENDS.

COMMENT AND ANALYSIS: #14 BRIANNA JONES FACTUALLY AND TRUTHFULLY ACKNOWLEDGES THE SUPPORT SHE RECEIVED FROM ME AND MY FAMILY; ALL OF WHICH CRITICALLY CONTRIBUTED TO HER PHYSICAL SURVIVAL.

THE COURT: STEP TO THE RIGHT.

MR. REID: GOOD AFTERNOON, JUDGE EKANS.

THE COURT: GOOD AFTERNOON.

MR. REID: MY NAME IS ANTHONY REID, I'M A PRIVATE PROCESS SERVER. MAY I SERVE THE DEFENDANT WITH DOCUMENTS BEFORE SHE IS STEPPED BACK IN A D.C. CASE?

THE COURT: I DO NOT HAVE PEOPLE SERVED WITH PROCESS IN MY COURTROOM. I'M SORRY.

MR. REID: I THOUGHT SHE MIGHT BE COMING OUT THE FRONT DOOR, I WAS WAITING PATIENTLY.

THE ODYSSEY OF JUDICIAL CORRUPTION

THE COURT: WELL, SHE'S NOT, SHE'S GOING OUT THAT DOOR.

MR. REID: CAN I SERVE HER IN THE BACK WITH YOUR PERMISSION PLEASE?

THE COURT: NO, NO. WE CAN'T DO THAT. WE CAN'T DO THAT. WE CAN'T DO IT.

MR. REID: THANK YOU, YOUR HONOR.

THE COURT: SHE'LL BE AT D.C. JAIL.

MR. REID: THANK YOU, YOUR HONOR.

THE COURT: ALL RIGHT.

MS. JONES: YOUR HONOR, CAN I CALL BACK HOME?

THE MARSHAL: NO.

THE COURT: MA' AM, STEP TO THE RIGHT.

(THEREUPON, THE PROCEEDINGS WERE CONCLUDED AT APPROXIMATELY 4:02 P.M.)

BARBARA WASHINGTON FRANKLIN

SUPERIOR COURT OF THE DISTRICT OF COLUMBIA
CIVIL DIVISION
WASHINGTON, D.C.

THE HONORABLE MATTHEW D. EKANS, ASSOCIATE JUDGE, PRESIDING

THE FOLLOWING IS THE ENTIRE OFFICIAL COURT TRANSCRIPT OF THE
JANUARY 31, 2011 PROCEEDING
ANNOTATED BY THE AUTHOR'S PERTINENT COMMENTARY AND ANALYSIS

JANUARY 31, 2011

P R O C E E D I N G S

DEPUTY CLERK: CALLING ON YOUR HONOR'S CALENDAR BARBARA WASHINGTON V. BRIANNA JONES, CIVIL ACTION 4417, 2009, AND IN THE MATTER OF BRIANNA JONES, CCC 120- 11. PLEASE IDENTIFY YOURSELVES FOR THE RECORD.

MS. WASHINGTON: GOOD AFTERNOON, YOUR HONOR, BARBARA WASHINGTON FRANKLIN, YOUR HONOR.

THE COURT: GOOD AFTERNOON.
DID YOU GET THAT SECOND CASE? I THOUGHT YOU MIGHT HAVE MISSED IT. CALL IT FOR HER AGAIN.

THE DEPUTY CLERK: CALLING THE CASE OF BARBARA WASHINGTON FRANKLIN V. BRIANNA JONES, CIVIL ACTION 4417, 2009 AND IN THE MATTER OF BRIANNA JONES. CCC 120-11. PLEASE IDENTIFY YOURSELVES FOR THE RECORD.

MS. JONES: BRIANNA JONES, DEFENDANT, PRO SE AT THIS TIME.

COMMENT AND ANALYSIS: #1 BRIANNA JONES ENTERED THE COURTROOM IN HANDCUFFS.

THE ODYSSEY OF JUDICIAL CORRUPTION

THE COURT: GOOD AFTERNOON.

MS. JONES: GOOD AFTERNOON, YOUR HONOR.

THE COURT: HOW ARE YOU?

MS. JONES: I AM FINE, THANK YOU. YOUR HONOR, I OWE YOU A PROFOUND APOLOGY.

THE COURT: PLEASE LET'S NOT START THAT. YOU DON'T OWE ME ANY APOLOGIES. YOU MIGHT NOTICE I'M NOT OFFERING YOU ANY. THIS IS NOT ABOUT APOLOGIZING. YOU HAVE NOT HURT MY FEELINGS. YOU PROBABLY DO OWE YOURSELF A PROFOUND APOLOGY, BUT THE FACT THAT YOU COME OUT HERE OFFERING ME ONE LEADS ME TO BELIEVE THAT YOU MAY HAVE MISSED THE REAL POINT OF THIS.

                       I HAVE BEEN VERY CONCERNED ABOUT YOU OVER THE LAST SEVERAL DAYS BECAUSE I HAVE SENT A LOT OF PEOPLE TO JAIL AND TO THE PENITENTIARY OVER THE LAST QUARTER OF CENTURY, BUT SELDOM HAVE I EVER HAD TO SEND SOMEONE TO JAIL JUST FOR BEING UNREASONABLY STUBBORN.

MS. JONES: MAY I SPEAK, YOUR HONOR?

THE COURT: NOT YET.

MS. JONES: VERY WELL.

THE COURT: DO YOU HAVE AN UNDERSTANDING OF WHAT IS REQUIRED OF YOU IN THIS MATTER?

MS. JONES: I DID NOT UNTIL THE DEPUTY SAID, DO YOU REALIZE WHY YOU ARE HERE, YOU DID NOT BRING PERSONAL BANKING STATEMENTS. THAT IS WHEN I REALIZED THAT I HAD COMPLETELY GOOFED IN MY FERVENCY TO DEFEND MYSELF WITH REGARD TO THIS MATTER; THAT EVEN THOUGH YOU MADE IT PERFECTLY CLEAR, I WAS LISTENING I JUST SIMPLY DID NOT HEAR AS WELL AS I NEEDED TO.

THE COURT: WE GOT WHAT I CONSIDER IT TO BE A STRANGE TELEPHONE CALL IN CHAMBERS. WHEN WAS THAT, MS. SUNG?

MS. SUNG: IT WAS FRIDAY.

THE COURT: THIS PAST FRIDAY?

MS. SUNG: YES.

THE COURT: THIS IS MY LAW CLERK, MIA SUNG, SPEAKING. MS. SUNG, WHAT WAS THE TELEPHONE CALL?

MS. SUNG: THIS WAS A CALL FROM A TED MINOR, I BELIEVE, OR A TED MINOR, OR A MR. MINOR SAYING THAT HE WAS HEADED TO YOUR BANK TO GET -- --

THE COURT: NOT MY BANK.

MS. SUNG: NOT YOUR BANK, JUDGE, MS. JONES' BANK TO GET DOCUMENTS FOR HER RECORDS FOR THE LAST TWO MONTHS. HOWEVER, HE WAS NOTIFIED BY THE BANK THAT THEY CANNOT GIVE OUT SUCH INFORMATION WITHOUT A SUBPOENA FROM THE COURT.

AND ACTUALLY THIS MORNING, MR. MINOR'S MOTHER CALLED CHAMBERS ASKING ABOUT WHETHER THERE WAS A BAIL POSTED IN THIS CASE. AND WE TOLD HER THAT WE COULD NOT DIVULGE THAT KIND OF INFORMATION, THAT THERE WAS A HEARING TODAY IN THIS MATTER AT NOON.

THE COURT: THERE WAS MORE WASN'T THERE REGARDING SOMEONE WHO WAS DIRECTING MR. MINOR?

MS. SUNG: HE TOLD US THAT HE HAD BEEN CONTACTED BY MS. JONES' ASSISTANT. HE SAID THAT HE HAD BEEN CALLED IN THE MIDDLE OF THE NIGHT ASKING TO HELP OBTAIN BANK RECORDS.

THE COURT: DID MR. MINOR SAY WHERE HE WAS CALLING FROM?

MS. SUNG: HE DID NOT. I DON'T KNOW WHAT THE GEOGRAPHIC LOCATION. BUT I JUST KNOW THAT HE WAS ON HIS WAY TO THE BRANCH OF THE BANK THAT MS. JONES DOES BUSINESS.

THE COURT: WHEN MY CLERK REPORTED THIS, MY CLERK HAS BEEN WITH ME SINCE SEPTEMBERR AND WE HAVE BEEN DOING FIRST-DEGREE MURDER AND RAPE CASES UNTIL JANUARY 2ND. AND SO I TALKED WITH HER ABOUT THE CAUTION THAT WE HAVE TO EXERCISE WHEN WE ARE RECEIVING CALLS FROM THE UNKOWN PUBLIC IN CHAMBERS, AND THAT IS WHY WE PUT THIS ON THE RECORD NOW.

I CHARACTERIZE THE CALL AS STRANGE BECAUSE OF THE CONTENTS OF IT, AND THE FACT OF THE MATTER IS SOMEBODY TRYING TO DO BUSINESS THROUGH THE COURT ON THE TELEPHONE PUTS US IN A, SAY THE LEAST, AN AWKWARD POSITION BECAUSE THESE MATTERS ARE THE SUBJECT OF RECORD, MUST BE ON THE RECORD, LEST SOMEONE SUGGESTS THAT THE COURT IS SOMEHOW ACTING IN THE INTEREST OF ONE PARTY OR ANOTHER, OR BEING SOMETHING OTHER THAN NEUTRAL IN THE CASE.

I THOUGHT THAT IF MR. MINOR, OR YOUR ASSISTANT, MS. JONES, WANTED TO ACT ON YOUR BEHALF THAT THEY SHOULD PROBABLY HAVE SOME POWER OF ATTORNEY OR SOME OTHER LEGAL FORM OF PROOF THAT THEY HAVE AUTHORITY TO ACT ON YOUR BEHALF.

I AM NOT CLEAR WHY THERE IS SUCH CONFUSION OVER THE MATTER OF THIS COURT'S ORDER OR THE NATURE OF THESE PROCEEDINGS. THERE SHOULD NOT BE THAT KIND OF CONFUSION.

BUT, IF YOU HAVE ANY MORE CONFUSION ABOUT IT, THAT IS WHAT WE SHOULD SPEAK ABOUT NOW BECAUSE I'M BOUND AND DETERMINED TO GET THIS STRAIGHT.

MS. JONES: YES, YOUR HONOR.

THE COURT: SO THAT I COULD MOVE ON TO OTHER THINGS.

MS. JONES: YES. I WAS GIVEN, I THINK, ON THURSDAY, A TWO-MINUTE CALL TO MAKE TO TED MINOR.
HE IS A VERY DEAR, AND CLOSE PERSONAL FRIEND OF MINE. I ASKED HIM, I SAID, WOULD YOU GO TO THE BANK, SEE IF YOU CAN GO ONLINE AND GET A COPY OF THE ORDER, PRESENT IT TO THE BANK. OBVIOUSLY THERE WAS A LEVEL OF CONFUSION IN THE TWO-MINUTE CONVERSATION. AND, IF YOU CAN BE PRESENT ON THE 31ST AT TWELVE NOON. SO I THINK IN HIS TRYING TO HELP ME AND EXPEDITE THIS HE WAS IN ERROR, BUT HE CERTAINLY MEANT NO HARM.

THE COURT: NEITHER DO I. BUT IT IS CERTAINLY PRECARIOUS TO PUT THE COURT IN -- --

MS. JONES: WITH REGARD TO POWER OF ATTORNEY THE ONE THAT HAS THE POWER OF ATTORNEY IS THE PLAINTIFF. SHE HAS A VAST POWER OF ATTORNEY.

THE COURT: I GUESS MY UNDESTANDING IS SHE IS TRYING TO AT THIS POINT IN TIME TRYING TO SETTLE HER OWN ACTION AGAINST YOU. I DON'T THINK SHE IS ACTING AS YOUR ATTORNEY IN THIS LAWSUIT. INSTEAD, SHE HAS BROUGHT A LAWSUIT, AS I UNDERSTAND IT, TO COLLECT LEGAL FEES.

MS. JONES: CORRECT, YOUR HONOR.

THE COURT: WHICH IS SOMETHING THAT MOST LAWYERS ARE LOATHE TO HAVE TO DO. BUT, WHATEVER THE MERITS OF THAT PREVIOUS POWER OF ATTORNEY MAY BE THEY REALLY HAVE NO RELEVANCE OR BEARING ON THE FACT THAT **SHE HAS A JUDGMENT THAT ENTITLES HER TO COLLECT MONEY**. **AND, SHE HAS COME TO THE COURT THAT ISSUED THE JUDGMENT TO BE ABLE TO EXECUTE ON THAT JUDGMENT**. AND RIGHT NOW WE ARE LIKE THIRTY MINUTES PAST MIDNIGHT ON THIS. YOU HAVE TO RESPOND TO THE QUESTIONS REGARDING YOUR ASSETS OR YOU WILL CONTINUE TO BE IN CONTEMPT OF THE COURT'S AUTHORITY TO CARRY OUT ITS ORDERS.

MS. JONES: YES, YOUR HONOR.

COMMENT AND ANALYSIS: #2 JUDGE EKANS, WITH CAREFUL PREMEDITATION, DECEPTIVELY, FALSELY, INTENTIONALLY, PURPOSEFULLY AND DELIBERATELY LAYS THE FOUNDATION FOR THE RIGGING OF MY LAWSUIT FOR FINAL DISMISSAL IN JANUARY 2015 AND THE RESULTING LOSS TO ME OF A 40 PERCENT INTEREST AND ATTORNEY FEE IN THE $34 MILLION SETTLEMENT OF THE $100 MILLION LAWSUIT I HAD FILED ON BEHALF OF BRIANNA JONES, BY FALSELY STATING THAT I HAVE A JUDGMENT THAT ENTITLES ME TO COLLECT MONEY, AND THAT I HAVE COME TO THE COURT THAT ISSUED THE JUDGMENT TO BE ABLE TO EXECUTE ON THAT JUDGMENT. JUDGE EKANS KNOWS THAT ALL OF THESE STATEMENTS ARE BLATANTLY UNTRUE AND INCONSISTENT WITH THE FACTS OF MY LAWSUIT.

HOWEVER, BY INTENTIONALLY AND FALSELY CHANGING THE FACTS OF MY LAWSUIT TO DECLARE THAT I HELD A COURT JUDGMENT, JUDGE EKANS, FROM THE VERY OUTSET OF HIS ADJUDICATION OF MY CASE IN JANUARY 2011 IS ABLE TO THEREAFTER REASON, ALBEIT FALSELY, THAT AS *A JUDGMENT CREDITOR* I THEN WOULD BE RESPONSIBLE FOR ANY NECESSARY INVESTIGATION AND SEARCH FOR THE ALLEGED MISSING $34 MILLION IN CASE SETTLEMENT PROCEEDS RESULTING FROM THE $100 MILLION LAWSUIT I HAD CRAFTED AND FILED ON BEHALF OF BRIANNA JONES, AN INDIGENT AND HOMELESS CLIENT SUFFERING WITH PTSD (POST-TRAUMATIC STRESS DISORDER) IN BROWARD COUNTY CIRCUIT COURT ON THE LAST DAY OF THE STATUTE OF LIMITATIONS IN MAY 1996, AND PURSUANT TO A CLIENT CONTINGENCY FEE AGREEMENT.

GIVEN THIS ARTIFICIAL CASE SCENARIO CLEVERLY AND DECEPTIVELY CRAFTED BY JUDGE EKANS, HIS REPEATED DENIAL OF MY REPEATED REQUESTS FOR AN INDEPENDENT INVESTIGATION OF THE DOMINANT ISSUE OF D.C. JUDICIAL AND FBI FRAUD, THEFT, CORRUPTION AND EXTORTION COULD NOW BE SEEN AS APPROPRIATE COURT ACTION WHEN, IN FACT, IT WAS A MAJOR PLANK IN THE HISTORIC D.C. JUDICIAL AND FBI CRIMINAL CONSPIRACY AND ENTERPRISE THAT DEFINED JUDGE EKANS' RIGGED ADJUDICATION OF MY LAWSUIT.

THE COURT: *AND NO MAN, OR NO WOMAN IS ABOVE THE LAW, NOT I, NOT YOU.*

MS. JONES: CORRECT.

COMMENT AND ANALYSIS: #3 WHERE I COME FROM, I.E., NEWARK, NEW JERSEY, JUDGE EKANS WOULD BE SAID TO BE SELLING SERIOUS WOLF TICKETS IN HIS ADMONITION TO JONES THAT NO MAN OR WOMAN IS ABOVE THE LAW. AND TODAY, WE WOULD SAY THAT EKANS WAS MERELY ENGAGING IN CLASSIC JUDICIAL GASIGHTING, OF WHICH HE WAS A MASTER.

THE COURT RECORD CONFIRMS THAT FOR THE ENTIRETY OF THE ADJUDICATION OF MY LAWSUIT, JONES REMAINED A CONTEMNOR AND IN CONTEMPT OF JUDGE KATE STARR'S ORDER OF OCTOBER 18, 2010 DIRECTING HER TO TURN OVER TO ME BANK STATEMENTS OF SETTLEMENT PROCEEDS ON DEPOSIT AT BANK OF AMERICA.

BRIANNA JONES SUFFERED NO ADMONISHMENT, NO PENALTY, NO FINE, NO NOTHING. AND MORE IMPORTANTLY, SHE SERVED AS A CLEAR AND UNMISTAKABLE EXAMPLE THAT THERE ARE CASES, ESPECIALLY WHERE D.C. JUDICIAL CORRRUPTION IS RAMPANT, IN WHICH CERTAIN LITIGANTS ARE TREATED BY THE COURT AS ABOVE THE LAW.

EVEN RAY CHARLES COULD HAVE SEEN THAT JUDGE EKANS TREATED BRIANNA JONES AS IF SHE WERE ABOVE THE LAW AND THE OFFICIAL COURT TRANSCRIPT RECORD VERIFIES IT.

THUS, JUDGE EKANS' ADMONISHMENT TO JONES TURNED OUT BE PURE JUDICIAL RHETORIC, GASLIGHTING AND THE COURT'S MERELY KICKING THE CAN DOWN THE ROAD AND NOTHING MORE.

AT THE END OF THE DAY, THE COURT'S FIRST COMMITMENT WAS TO THE ACCOMPLISHMENT OF THE MISSION OF THE D.C. JUDICIAL AND FBI CRIMINAL ENTERPRISE TO DEFRAUD AND ROB ME OF AN ESTIMATED $50 MILLION IN ATTORNEY'S FEES.

THE COURT: SO, WHAT ARE YOU GOING TO DO?

MS. JONES: I WANT TO DO EVERYTHING YOU HAVE ASKED FOR WITH REGARD TO BANK STATEMENTS, TO GO AND RETRIEVE THOSE AND BRING THOSE TO THIS COURT, AND LET YOU LOOK OVER EVERY STATEMENT, EVERY FINANCIAL DOCUMENT THAT IS IN MY NAME THAT I AM RESPONSIBLE FOR THAT I HAVE. I AM MORE THAN WILLING TO OPEN THEM UP TO YOU, TO THE PLAINTIFF, I HAVE NO PROBLEMS WITH THAT. I CAN GET IT.

COMMENT AND ANALYSIS: #4 JONES UNEQUIVOCALLY ADMITS HAVING IN HER POSSESSION THE BANK *STATEMENTS AND RECORDS THAT WOULD PUT HER IN COMPLIANCE WITH JUDGE STARR'S ORDER TO TURN OVER BANK RECORDS TO ME. HOWEVER, RATHER THAN ENFORCE JUDGE STARR'S ORDER, JONES WAS ALLOWED BY JUDGE EKANS TO ESCAPE COMPLIANCE WITH THE ORDER AND CONCLUDED THE CASE WITH THE ISSUANCE TO ME OF A MONEY JUDGMENT WHICH WAS LATER OVETURNED BY THE D.C. COURT OF APPEALS, THE D.C. APPELLATE TRIBUNAL AT ALL TIMES COMPLICIT IN THIS HISTORIC D.C. JUDICIAL AND FBI FRAUD, THEFT, CORRUPTION AND EXTORTION CONSPIRACY AND CRIMINAL ENTERPRISE.*

MS. FRANKLIN: YOUR HONOR, MAY I ASK A QUESTION. IS MS. JONES REFERRING TO THE SETTLEMENT PROCEEDS THAT ARE THE SUBJECT OF MY LAWSUIT, OR IS SHE JUST REFERRING TO SOME OTHER ACCOUNTS THAT HAVE NO BEARING ON THE SETTLEMENT PROCEEDS, AND THEIR LOCATION OR WHO IS HOLDING POSSESSION OF THEM?

THE COURT: YOU MAY RESPOND.

MS. JONES: **YOUR HONOR, WITH REGARD TO THE SETTLEMENT PROCEEDS I HAVE NOT YET TAKEN POSSESSION OF THEM.** I AM MORE THAN WILLING TO HAVE A FORENSIC AUDITOR OR WHOMEVER GO THROUGH EVERY ONE OF MY RECORDS.

COMMENT AND ANALYSIS: #5 JONES NEVER DENIES HAVING THE BANK STATEMENTS OF THE SETTLEMENT PROCEEDS SPECIFIED IN THE OCTOBER 18, 2010 COURT ORDER ISSUED BY JUDGE KATE STARR. JONES JUST NEVER PRODUCED THEM, AND IN EFFECT, WITH THE COURT'S ALLOWANCE, MANAGED TO PRE-EMPT THE COURT OF ITS POWER AND AUTHORITY, WITH NO FEAR WHATSOEVER OF PUNISHMENT, INCLUDNG FURTHER INCARCERATION.

JONES STATES THAT THE SETTLEMENT PROCEEDS ARE NOT IN HER PHYSICAL POSSESSION. IN JULY 2014, THE D.C. COURT OF APPEALS, AT ALL TIMES COMPLICIT IN THIS HISTORIC MULTI-MILLION DOLLAR SWINDLE, OVERTURNED THE RIGGED $13.6 MILLION JUDGMENT ISSUED TO ME BY JUDGE EKANS IN OCTOBER 2011, STATING THAT BRIANNA JONES NEVER TOOK POSSESSION OF THE SETTLEMENT PROCEEDS OWED TO HER AS A RESULT OF THE $34 MILLION SETTLEMENT OF THE $100 MILLION FLORIDA LAWSUIT.

THE COURT: IS YOUR FEE A PERCENTAGE OF THE SETTLEMENT?

MS. FRANKLIN: YES.

MS. FRANKLIN: YOUR HONOR, I REPRESENTED MS. JONES ON A CONTINGENCY FEE CONTRACT. AND THE CONTRACT PROVIDES THAT I AM ENTITLED TO 40 PERCENT OF ANY SETTLEMENT PROCEEDS, PLUS ANY OUT-OF-POCKET EXPENSES AS WELL. THAT WAS 1996 OCTOBER, THE DATE OF OUR AGREEMENT. THE AGREEMENT WAS ATTACHED TO THE INITIAL COMPLAINT AS PART OF THE COURT RECORD.

I HAVE NOT BEEN ABLE TO COLLECT ANY OF THOSE FEES. I HAVE NOT BEEN ABLE TO BE PROVIDED WITH ANY BANK DOCUMENTS, BANK RECORDS OF THE SETTLEMENT PROCEEDS AT ALL.

SHE HAS REPEATEDLY STATED THAT SHE HAS NOT BEEN PERMITTED TO DISCLOSE THAT INFORMATION TO ME, THAT SHE HAS BEEN THREATENED AND THAT IS WHY SHE HAS NOT DISCLOSED THE INFORMATION TO ME. AND THIS HAS BEEN GOING ON NOW FOR MANY YEARS AND THIS IS WHERE WE ARE TODAY.

THE COURT: THE SETTLEMENT SIGNALS TO ME THAT THERE WAS NOT A TRIAL, BUT THAT THE PARTIES WHO WERE CONTESTING -- -- WHAT WAS THIS? WAS IT A WILL?

MS. FRANKLIN: YOUR HONOR, WE FILED A LAWSUIT AGAINST -- -- BACK IN 1996 AGAINST THE ESTATE OF WILLIE LEE RIDGEWAY, WHO SUBSEQUENTLY   WELL, PASSED.

AND HE HAD MOLESTED MS. JONES WHEN SHE WAS A CHILD. HE WAS ONE OF THE TWO JACKPOT WINNERS OF THE D.C. LOTTERY, SO HE WON 45 PLUS MILLION DOLLARS. AT SOME POINT PRIOR TO HIS PASSING HE INDICATED WHEN HE WAS TOLD ABOUT THE MATTER, HE INDICATED TO HIS ATTORNEYS SETTLE THIS, SETTLE THIS MATTER.

SUBSEQUENT TO THAT AND I'M SKIPPING OVER, BUT JUST TO GIVE THE COURT A SNAPSHOT, THE ATTORNEYS FOR THE ESTATE REFUSED TO HAVE ANY DEALINGS WITH ME. THEY WOULD SCHEDULE MEETINGS WITH ME IN FLORIDA. I WOULD TAKE TIME OFF FROM MY OFFICE AND FLY TO FLORIDA AND THE MEETING WOULD BE CANCELLED.

THE COURT: I DON'T NEED TO GO INTO EVERYTHING, BUT TELL ME HOW DOES FLORIDA COME INTO THIS?

MS. FRANKLIN: HE (WILLIE LEE RIDGEWAY) MOVED TO FLORIDA AND HE BECAME DOMICILED THERE.

THE COURT: I SEE.

MS. FRANKLIN: AND SO THE CASE WAS SETTLED. SHE HAS CONFIRMED THAT OVER AND OVER AND

OVER AGAIN. I'VE NEVER BEEN ABLE TO GET A COPY OF THE SETTLEMENT

AGREEMENT, PERIOD. FOR THE SAME REASON THAT SHE KEEPS SAYING THEY TOLD

ME NOT TO TELL YOU, I CAN'T TELL YOU.

AND APPARENTLY, YOUR HONOR, THE PLAN ON THE PART OF THE ATTORNEYS FOR

THE ESTATE HAS BEEN THAT OF IF WE DON'T DEAL WITH FRANKLIN, SHE WILL GO

AWAY ONE DAY, WE WILL TAKE HER FEES AND GIVE JONES (MENTALLY ILL AND

HOMELESS) WHATEVER WE WANT, AND THAT IS WHAT THEY HAVE DONE ALL THESE

MANY YEARS.

THE COURT: SO YOU HAVE NEVER SEEN A SETTLEMENT AGREEMENT?

MS. FRANKLIN: I'VE NEVER SEEN THE SETTLEMENT AGREEMENT. I INDICATED THAT IN MY
COMPLAINT, WHEN I FILED THE COMPLAINT IN MARCH OF 2009. **I WAS ADMITTED
TO THE FLORIDA COURT BY VIRTUE OF A *PRO HAC VICE MOTION*.** I WAS PERMITTED
TO REPRESENT HER, AND JUDGE ROSENBAUM ISSUED AN ORDER GRANTING MY
ADMISSION. AND HE SAID ONE OF THE REASONS HE GRANTED THE ADMISSION WAS
THAT THERE WAS NEVER AN ANSWER TO THE COMPLAINT. WE FILED THE COMPLAINT,
AND THEY NEVER FILED AN ANSWER. BUT THEY BEGAN AT SOME POINT IN TIME TO
HAVE MEETINGS WITH HER, AND TO COMMUNICATE WITH HER---

THE COURT: THEY BEING?

MS. FRANKLIN: THE ATTORNEYS FOR THE ESTATE.

THE COURT: THE ATTORNEYS FOR THE ESTATE.

COMMENT AND ANALYSIS: *#6 I WAS FULLY CONVINCED THAT ANY COMPLAINTS OR
LEGAL ACTION BY ME IN OBJECTION TO JONES' CONTACTS AND COMMUNICATIONS
WITH OPPOSING COUNSEL, THE PRESUMED MASTERMIND OF THE GRAND FRAUD
AND THEFT, WOULD CAUSE FURTHER ATTACK ON MY HUSBAND WHOM I BELIEVED
WAS BEING VICIOUSLY SUBJECTED TO A POLITICALLY MOTIVATED CRIMINAL
PROSECUTION BECAUSE OF MY REFUSAL TO WITHDRAW FROM THE CASE AND
VOLUNTARILY FORFEIT MY ATTORNEY'S FEES DUE ME FROM THE $34 MILLION
SETTLEMENT OF THE $100 MILLION LAWSUIT I HAD SOLELY CRAFTED AND FILED IN
MAY 1996 IN THE BROWARD COUNTY CIRCUIT COURT IN FORT LAUDERDALE, FLORIDA
ON JONES' BEHALF.*

MS. FRANKLIN: WHICH AT THAT TIME WAS ADAGIO AND MANDEL OF FLORIDA, THAT WAS THE NAME OF THE LAW FIRM. WHEN WE WERE AT ONE OF THE PRIOR HEARINGS BEFORE YOUR HONOR, MS. JONES INDICATED THAT THE NAMED PARTNER, THE NAMED SENIOR PARTNER, SAMUEL ADAGIO, HAD BEEN RECENTLY SUSPENDED BY THE FLORIDA BAR IN OCTOBER. I CHECKED AND THAT WAS TRUE. HE WAS SUSPENDED IN OCTOBER, AND THERE IS A DISBARMENT PROCEEDING PENDING AGAINST HIM.

AND, ACCORDING TO THE VARIOUS PRESS REPORTS, HIS FIRM HAS MADE A PATTERN AND PRACTICE OF SETTLING LARGE CASES AND THEN THE MONIES NEVER GOING TO THE CLIENT AND THIS IS ONE OF THOSE CASES.

AND SO I AM CONCERNED ABOUT HER, YOU KNOW, MS. JONES INDICATING THAT SHE IS WILLING TO TURN OVER EVERYTHING. AND, IF SHE IS TURNING OVER PERSONAL ACCOUNTS, I HAVE NO INTEREST IN THAT, THAT THEY DON'T PERTAIN TO THE SETTLEMENT PROCEEDS.

I NOT ONLY STAND HERE FOR MY INTERESTS AND MY ATTORNEY FEES YOUR HONOR, BUT THERE HAVE BEEN LARGE SUMS IN TERMS OF MONIES BORROWED BY MS. JONES, HUNDREDS OF THOUSANDS OF DOLLARS TO PAY FOR ALL KINDS OF EXPENSES, BUT PARTICULARLY PRIVATE SECURITY AROUND THE CLOCK BECAUSE SHE HAS BEEN THREATENED. I HAVE BEEN THREATENED. I HAVE BEEN FOLLOWED ON MY TRIPS TO FLORIDA.

THE COURT: BY THESE ATTORNEYS.

MS. FRANKLIN: BY THESE ATTORNEYS. I'VE HAD CALLS TO MY HOME IN THE PRESENCE OF MY HUSBAND THREATENING ME IF YOU COME TO THE HEARING TOMORROW THIS IS WHAT WILL HAPPEN TO YOU. SO, WHEN SHE TALKS ABOUT BEING THREATENED, THAT IS REAL BECAUSE I HAVE BEEN THREATENED ALSO.

FOR THE PAST 15 YEARS I HAVE NOT BEEN ABLE TO MAKE A PRIVATE TELEPHONE CALL IN MY HOME. ALL OF MY LINES ARE TAPPED, ALL OF MY LINES ARE OPEN, AND I'M SURE IT HAS TO DO---BECAUSE IT DIDN'T START UNTIL I GOT INVOLVED IN THIS CASE.

THE COURT: THIS MIGHT SOUND SOMEWHAT NAÏVE, BUT HAVE THESE MATTERS BEEN REPORTED TO POLICE AUTHORITIES?

BARBARA WASHINGTON FRANKLIN

MS. FRANKLIN: YOUR HONOR, I'M SO GLAD YOU ASKED THAT QUESTION. RIGHT AFTER WE FILED THE COMPLAINT, MS. JONES HAD BEGUN LIVING IN FLORIDA. SHE TOLD ME SHE WAS BEING THREATENED. I CONTACTED THE FBI IN FLORIDA AND DISCUSSED THE MATTER WITH THE SPECIAL AGENT IN CHARGE OF THE FLORIDA OFFICE. AND I DID NOT HESITATE TO DO THAT BECAUSE I WAS INVOLVED IN A CASE THAT I HAD SETTLED HERE IN WASHINGTON. HE HAD FLOWN UP FROM FLORIDA TO CONDUCT A SETTLEMENT. AND SO I WAS GIVEN HIS CARD, AND HE SAID MS. FRANKLIN, IF YOU EVER NEED ANY HELP, AND I REALLY NEVER EVEN THOUGHT OF CALLING, DON'T HESITATE TO GIVE ME A CALL.

SO WHEN SHE TOLD ME SHE WAS GETTING THESE THREATS, I IMMEDIATELY GOT ON THE PHONE AND CONTACTED THE HEAD OF THE FBI IN THE MIAMI DADE AREA, AND SAID MY CLIENT IS BEING THREATENED. WE FILED THE LAWSUIT; SHE IS BEING THREATENED AND COULD YOU PLEASE LOOK INTO IT.

THE COURT: ......WHAT IS THE EVIDENCE, PROOF THAT THE DEFENDANT IS IN COLLUSION WITH THIS FIRM REGARDING KEEPING YOU AWAY FROM YOUR SETTLEMENT?

MS. FRANKLIN: I AM NOT SAYING THAT SHE IS IN COLLUSION. WHAT I AM SAYING IS SHE MAINTAINS COMMUNICATIONS WITH THEM. AND I DON'T KNOW WHO ACTUALLY SHE IS TALKING TO.

I REFER BACK TO HER COMMENTS HERE BEFORE YOUR HONOR. SHE JUST TALKS ABOUT THEY, THEY DON'T WANT ME TO TALK TO YOU, THEY DON'T WANT ME TO DO THIS, THEY. I DON'T KNOW WHO THESE PEOPLE ARE. SO, I CAN'T REALLY SAY SHE IS IN COLLUSION, BUT I KNOW SHE IS IN COMMUNICATION IS WHAT I AM SAYING. SHE IS IN REGULAR PERIODIC COMMUNICATION BECAUSE SHE INDICATES THAT, SHE INDICATES THAT.

I MEAN WE WERE BEFORE JUDGE STARR A TIME OR TWO, AND MS. JONES IN THE COURTROOM, OPEN COURTROOM, THREATENED, OH, I'M GOING TO TAKE HER TO THE BAR, REFERRING TO ME, I'M GOING TO TAKE HER TO THE BAR. AND AFTER THAT HEARING WHEN WE SAT DOWN IN THE CAFETERIA, WE'RE SETTLING THE CASE, I SAID, OH, BY THE WAY, WHY WOULD YOU SAY THAT IN THE COURTROOM, WHY WOULD YOU PUT THAT ON THE RECORD WHEN I'VE DONE NOTHING BUT HELP YOU, AND THERE'S ABSOLUTELY NO BASIS AT ALL. OH, THEY TOLD ME TO SAY THAT BECAUSE ONCE I SAID THAT YOU WOULD THROW UP YOUR HANDS AND THEN YOU WOULD SAY, OH, YOUR HONOR, I AM FINISHED WITH THIS, I DON'T WANT TO PURSUE THIS ANYMORE. I SAID, WELL, THEY DON'T KNOW ME.

COMMENT AND ANALYSIS: #7 JONES *DID NOT HESITATE TO DIVULGE THE INSTRUCTIONS SHE WAS GIVEN BY THE CO-CONSPIRATORS IN THEIR HOTEL SUITE MEETINGS IN HOW TO LIE AND THREATEN ME IN THE COURTROOM IN HOPES THAT I WOULD EVENTUALLY GIVE UP AND THROW IN THE TOWEL.*

THE COURT: LET ME ASK YOU A QUESTION. WHEN I RELEASE YOU, WHAT ARE YOU GOING TO DO?

MS. JONES: I AM GOING TO GO TO FLORIDA, I AM GOING TO HOPE AND PRAY THAT I AM SAFE. I AM GOING TO GET THOSE RECORDS, AND ALSO---

THE COURT: WHAT RECORDS?

MS. JONES: MY PERSONAL RECORDS.

COMMENT AND ANALYSIS: #8 JONES *ONCE AGAIN LIES AND PROMISES TO RETURN TO COURT WITH THE BANK STATEMENTS. THIS WAS JUST HER TRICK USED TO GIVE THE JUDGE WHAT HE WANTED TO HEAR AT THE MOMENT. SHE HAD NO INTENTION OF BRINGING BANK STATEMENTS TO COURT AND SHE DID NOT. TIME WOULD PROVE THAT JUDGE EKANS REALLY HAD NO INTEREST IN JONES PROVIDING ME WITH BANK STATEMENTS OF THE SETTLEMENT PROCEEEDS, BECAUSE TO DO SO WOULD GIVE ME ACCESS TO THE MILLIONS OF DOLLARS OWED TO ME IN ATTORNEY'S FEES AND THEREBY DEFEAT THE MISSION OF THE D.C. JUDICIAL AND FBI CRMINAL ENTERPRISE TO DEFRAUD ME OF MY ATTORNEY'S FEES.*

THE COURT: DO YOU HAVE A COPY OF THE SETTLEMENT AGREEMENT, NOT THE ONE THAT YOU MADE WITH MS. FRANKLIN. DO YOU HAVE A COPY OF THE SETTLEMENT AGREEMENT REGARDING THE ESTATE OF---WHAT WAS THAT MAN'S RELATIONSHIP TO YOU?

MS.JONES: WILLIE LEE RIDGEWAY.

THE COURT: FIRST, I WANT A YES OR NO. DO YOU HAVE A COPY OF THAT SETTLEMENT OF THAT ESTATE?

MS. JONES: NOT AT PRESENT, **THE BAR COUNSEL HAS ONE.**

THE COURT: DO YOU HAVE A COPY OF THE SETTLEMENT OF THE ESTATE?

MS. JONES: NOT AT PRESENT. MY HOME WAS RANSACKED AND ATTORNEY FRANKLIN CAN CONFIRM THAT. **BAR COUNSEL HAS BEEN ABLE TO CONFIRM THAT THE SETTLEMENT DID IN FACT OCCUR.**

COMMENT AND ANALYSIS: #9 JONES *AGAIN ACKNOWLEDGES HAVING THE COPY OF THE SETTLEMENT AGREEMENT WITH THE RIDGEWAY ESTATE. SHE ALSO CONFIRMS HAVING PROVIDED D.C. BAR COUNSEL WITH A COPY OF THE AGREEMENT WITH THE RIDGEWAY ESTATE.*

MS. FRANKLIN: YOUR HONOR, MAY I SPEAK TO THAT WITH REGARD TO BAR COUNSEL. WHEN WE WERE HERE LAST, YOUR HONOR, SHE GAVE YOUR HONOR SEVERAL VARIOUS DOCUMENTS. ONE WAS I BELIEVE THE LAST PAGE OF A LETTER---

THE COURT: A WILL.

MS. FRANKLIN: ONE WAS A WILL, THE '96 WILL. AND ONE WAS A PAGE OF A LETTER FROM THE OFFICE OF BAR COUNSEL. AND, I SAID AT THE TIME, YOUR HONOR THAT I COULD CLARIFY THE MEANING OF THAT WHICH WAS SOME FORMER CLIENTS OF MINE WHO LOANED HER $32,000 AT A TIME WHEN SHE WAS BEING THREATENED AND NEEDED ROUND-THE-CLOCK SECURITY.

THIS WAS IN 2007, AND THEY WEREN'T PAID AND THEY WERE GETTING VERY FRUSTRATED, AND SO THEY FILED A COMPLAINT AGAINST ME WITH THE OFFICE OF BAR COUNSEL. IT WAS REALLY IN HINDSIGHT A BLESSING IN DISGUISE, BECAUSE BAR COUNSEL DID A THOROUGH INVESTIGATION. WHEN THEY CONTACTED ME, I SUGGESTED THAT THEY SPEAK WITH MS. JONES AND FEEL FREE TO ASK HER WHATEVER QUESTIONS, BECAUSE ALL OF THE MONIES CAME TO ME AND WERE IMMEDIATELY FORWARDED TO HER FOR HER USE AS SPECIFIED.

NEVERTHELESS, IN BAR COUNSEL'S LETTER, AND I HAVE THE LETTER HERE FOR YOUR HONOR, THEY INDICATED THAT THEY HAD---OH, IN TALKING WITH MS. JONES, MS. JONES TOLD THEM WHICH ATTORNEYS TO CONTACT, WHERE THE ATTORNEYS WERE, WHERE THE FUNDS WERE. AND BAR COUNSEL IN THEIR LETTER TO THE COMPLAINING PARTY SAID THAT WE HAVE DONE A THOROUGH INVESTIGATION, THERE'S ABSOLUTELY NO WRONGDOING HERE BY MS. FRANKLIN. HOWEVER, WE HAVE CONFIRMED THAT MS. JONES IS ENTITLED TO A CONSIDERABLE AMOUNT OF MONEY AS A RESULT OF A CIVIL CLAIM. AND, BEFORE THIS HEARING, YOUR HONOR I CONTACTED MARCIA MCMILLAN, WHO WAS A SENIOR STAFF COUNSEL AT THE OFFICE OF BAR COUNSEL, AND CARLA CORLEONE, WHO ISSUED THE FINAL LETTER INDICATING THAT THERE WAS NO WRONGDOING ON MY PART.

THE COURT:	WHAT BAR COUNSEL IS THAT?
MS. FRANKLIN:	D.C.
THE COURT:	DISTRICT OF COLUMBIA.

MS. FRANKLIN: THE OFFICE OF BAR COUNSEL IN D.C. WHAT I AM GETTING AT, YOUR HONOR, AND IS SO VERY CRITICAL HERE, THEY HAVE ALL OF THE INFORMATION, BECAUSE THAT INFORMATION WAS GATHERED AS A RESULT OF THE COMPLAINT FILED. AND I CALLED MARCIA MCMILLAN, TO SEE IF SHE COULD BE AVAILABLE TO THE COURT EVEN BY PHONE TO LET THE COURT KNOW, YEAH, THESE ARE THE FUNDS, THESE ARE THE ATTORNEYS THAT WE SPOKE TO, ET CETERA. BUT OF COURSE, I HAVE NOT RECEIVED A CALL BACK FROM HER.

I HAVE A COPY OF THAT LETTER, YOUR HONOR, AND I WANTED YOUR HONOR TO AT LEAST HAVE THE OPPORTUNITY TO READ THE LETTER. I CERTAINLY DON'T WANT IT IS A PART OF THE FORMAL FILE, BUT I DID WANT TO PROVIDE YOUR HONOR WITH THE FULL LETTER SINCE MS. JONES ONLY GAVE THE COURT A PAGE. IF YOUR HONOR WOULD LIKE TO TAKE A LOOK AT IT, I'M PREPARED TO LET THE COURT HAVE A COPY.

MS. JONES: YOUR HONOR, MAY I SPEAK TO THAT. THE PLAINTIFF'S BAR COUNSEL WITH REGARD TO A LETTER FROM OUR COUNSEL, BESSIE MARCH, HE SENT ME ALL THREE COPIES BUT THEY DID NOT COME OUT. HE SAID, LET ME SEND YOU THE CLEAREST THAT I HAVE AND THAT JUST HAPPENED TO BE THE SECOND PAGE.

THE COURT: BAR COUNSEL'S INVESTIGATIONS, LIKE THIS COURT, ARE MATTERS OF RECORD. SO, IT IS NOT A PROBLEM WITH GETTING A COPY OF IT. IT'S A MATTER OF RECORD.

COMMENT AND ANALYSIS: #10 *I FOUND IT PUZZLING THAT JUDGE EKANS SHOWED VERY LITTLE INTEREST IN D.C. BAR COUNSEL'S INVESTIGATION OF JONES' SETTLEMENT WITH THE RIDGEWAY ESTATE, AND MORE IMPORTANTLY, D.C. BAR COUNSEL'S FINDINGS OF ITS INVESTIGATION. IT IS UNKNOWN AS TO WHETHER JUDGE EKANS EVER REVIEWED BAR COUNSEL'S INVESTIGATION OR SPOKE WITH ANY OF THE D.C. BAR COUNSEL STAFF HANDLING THE MATTER. **THE JUDGE'S DISINTEREST AND INACTION IN REGARD TO BAR COUNSEL'S INVESTIGATION WAS A CLEAR AND EGREGIOUS ABUSE OF SOUND DISCRETION AND SIGNIFICANTLY PREJUDICIAL TO ME. BUT MORE SIGNIFICANTLY, IT WAS CLEAR EVIDENCE OF D.C. JUDICIAL CORRUPTION ON STEROIDS. IT WAS EVIDENCE OF JUDGE EKANS' UNEQUIVOCAL COMPLICITY IN THE CRIMINAL ENTERPRISE THAT WAS RAMPANT IN MY LAWSUIT.***

MS. JONES: I SPOKE WITH MRS. MCMILLAN FOR TWO AND A HALF HOURS.

MS. FRANKLIN: YOUR HONOR, THE POINT I WAS MAKING IS THAT WHAT IS OF CONCERN TO ME IS WHILE MS. JONES WOULD PROVIDE BAR COUNSEL WITH ALL THE SPECIFIC INFORMATION, WHEN THE COURT ASKED VERY SPECIFICALLY, I WANT TO KNOW WHERE THE MONEY IS, I WANT TO KNOW HOW MUCH EVEN IF IT IS TEN CENTS SHE CAN'T REMEMBER, I DON'T KNOW, I DON'T HAVE IT. BUT, WITH THE INVESTIGATION GOING ON WITH BAR COUNSEL, SHE GAVE THEM VERY SPECIFIC INFORMATION, VERY DETAILED INFORMATION. SO, SHE HAS THE INFORMATION. WE ARE RIGHT BACK TO WHERE WE STARTED WHEN WE CAME BEFORE THE COURT.

MS. JONES: YOUR HONOR, THINGS KEEP CHANGING, AND EACH TIME I SPEAK THE THREATS KEEP GETTING WORSE. THAT IS WHY I SPOKE, AS I WAS SAYING BEFORE, I SPOKE WITH ATTORNEY MIKE REDD WITH REGARD TO COMING ON AND COLLECTING ON MY BEHALF.

HE THEN SAID THAT HE WOULD HAVE TO SPEAK WITH HIS CLIENTS WHO ARE THE SIMPSONS, WITH REGARD TO THERE WOULD BE A WAIVER OF A CONFLICT OF INTEREST. AND WE SPOKE IN GREAT DETAIL, AND I EVEN ALSO IN THOSE CONVERSATIONS MADE A GENEROUS OFFER TO THE SIMPSONS. SO I WAS SURPRISED WITH THE SERVICE. AND OBVIOUSLY I FOUND OUT ON THE 25TH THAT HE WAS NOT GOING TO TAKE MY CASE.

AND, SECONDLY WITH REGARD TO THAT MATTER YOU INSTRUCTED THE BAILIFF - - --I'M SORRY -- -- THE PROCESS SERVER NOT TO COME INTO THE D.C. DEPARTMENT OF CORRECTIONS. HE CAME IN, I WOULD NOT ACCEPT SERVICE. HE LEFT IT WITH A SERGEANT.

THE COURT: YOU ARE WRONG. I DID NOT INSTRUCT HIM NOT TO COME TO D.C. DEPARTMENT OF CORRECTIONS. I TOLD HIM HE COULD NOT SERVE SOMEBODY IN MY COURTROOM, AND IN THE MARSHAL'S CELLBLOCK. I DIRECTED HIM TO LOOK INTO SERVICE AT THE JAIL BECAUSE THAT IS WHERE YOU WERE GOING TO BE.

MS. JONES: THAT WAS NOT A PROPER SERVICE BECAUSE THE -- --

THE COURT: THAT IS A LEGAL MATTER. I DON'T KNOW IF YOU CAN MAKE THAT DETERMINATION.

MS. JONES: AND I DID NOT ACCEPT SERVICES AND THE SERGEANT BROUGHT THE DOCUMENTS TO ME. AND, WHEN THEY   WHAT THEY ARE ASKING FOR, IN LIEU OF FIFTY THOUSAND THEY'RE ASKING FOR EIGHT AND A HALF-MILLION DOLLARS I BELIEVE. AND SO I AM CERTAINLY TAKEN ABACK.

AND I MADE A MORE THAN GENEROUS OFFER THAT FAR EXCEEDED THEIR INITIAL INVESTMENT. I DO UNDERSTAND THE WAIT, AND I AM PREPARED TO BE MORE THAN GENEROUS, BUT NOT EIGHT AND A HALF MILLION DOLLARS.

MS. FRANKLIN: YOUR HONOR, MAY I SPEAK. IF SHE IS RELEASED AND BASED UPON WHAT I AM HEARING, IT IS GOING TO CONTINUE. THIS IS GOING TO CONTINUE.

THE COURT: I WILL ADMIT TO HAVING SOME CONCERN ABOUT THAT.

MS. FRANKLIN: I DO BELIEVE THAT AT THIS POINT, YOUR HONOR, THAT UNLESS THOSE WHO HOLD THE PROCEEDS HAVE TO ANSWER TO THIS COURT IT WILL NEVER RESOLVE BECAUSE SHE IS ALWAYS GOING TO HIDE BEHIND OR USE THE EXCUSE, I DON'T HAVE IT, I DON'T HAVE IT. SHE TAKES GREAT DELIGHT IN I DON'T HAVE IT.

YOUR HONOR, THERE ARE CREDITORS TO THE TUNE OF SEVERAL HUNDREDS OF THOUSANDS OF DOLLARS. FOR YEARS THESE PEOPLE HAVE BEEN WAITING TO BE PAID. THEY HAVE NOT BEEN. IN ONE INSTANCE, THIS PARTICULAR CREDITOR CONTACTED JUDGE STARR BY LETTER. THIS PERSON HAS BEEN THREATENED WITH EVICTION FROM HER DWELLING PLACE AT LEAST FOUR OR FIVE TIMES. BY NOW MAYBE SHE'S ALREADY LOST IT, I DON'T KNOW. IT WAS A MATTER OF $20,000, HER LIFE SAVINGS. SHE'S BEEN WAITING SINCE 2007.

SO, THERE ARE PEOPLE OTHER THAN MYSELF WHO ARE SUFFERING WHO NEED TO BE PAID AND THIS SITUATION IS ONGOING. IT JUST GOES ON AND ON AND-ON-AND IT IS VERY UNFAIR TO ME AND IT IS ALSO VERY UNFAIR TO OTHERS WHO BASED ON THEIR TRUST IN ME ALLOWED HER TO BORROW THESE LARGE SUMS OF MONEY.

WHEN YOU ARE LETTING SOMEBODY BORROW THIRTY THOUSAND, FIFTY THOUSAND, TWENTY THOUSAND THOSE ARE LARGE SUMS OF MONEY FOR THE AVERAGE PERSON, YOUR HONOR. THEY CAN'T AFFORD TO WAIT THREE AND FOUR YEARS TO BE REPAID. AND NONE OF THESE PEOPLE, THANK GOD, WE HAVE ONLY HAD ONE INSTANCE WHEN THE CREDITORS HAVE SUED. THERE IS A LONG, LONG LIST OF CREDITORS.

THE COURT: I THINK THAT MY RESPONSIBILITY IS TO TRY TO KEEP IN FOCUS WHAT WE ARE BOUND TO SEE THROUGH IN THIS CASE. I DON'T HAVE THOSE PEOPLE'S CASES BEFORE ME. WHAT I HAVE IS THE CASE AND THE SETTLEMENT THAT YOU MADE.

I NEED SOMETHING FROM THE DEFENDANT TO GIVE ME SOME REASONABLE ASSURANCE THAT WE ARE NOT GOING TO CONTINUE THIS FOLLY BECAUSE IT IS NOT SOMETHING I AM INTERESTED IN CONTINUING.

MS. FRANKLIN:	YOUR HONOR, FOR THE RECORD YOUR HONOR, IT IS ONLY FAIR FOR THE COURT TO UNDERSTAND THAT THESE REFERENCES TO PRO SE REPRESENTATION ARE TOTALLY UNTRUE. I MIGHT NOT HAVE BEEN IN THE COURTROOM AT ALL TIMES IN FLORIDA, BUT I WAS THERE IN TERMS OF MY EXPERTISE, MY KNOWLEDGE THAT I WAS SHARING WITH HER ON A VERY REGULAR, IF NOT DAILY, BASIS RUNNING IN AND OUT OF COURTROOMS, AND MY PROVIDING HER WITH THE NECESSARY RESPONSES.

I HAD A LONG, LONG CALENDAR OF TRIPS TO FLORIDA FOR COURT HEARINGS TO MEET WITH COUNSEL FOR YEARS, FOR YEARS. AND SO TO ALLOW HER TO STAND HERE NOW AND SAY SHE IS PRO SE, PRO SE HOW, BASED ON WHAT KIND OF TRAINING?

MS. JONES:	ON MARCH 21ST -- --
THE COURT:	THE CONCERN THAT I HAVE IS THAT EVERY OPPORTUNITY THAT I GIVE YOU, YOU USE IT TO TAKE US OFF ON A TANGENT. I AM REALLY FOCUSED ON HOW YOU CAN GET YOURSELF OUT OF CONTEMPT OF THE COURT. THAT IS WHAT I AM FOCUSED ON, AND I WOULD APPRECIATE IF YOU WOULD JOIN ME IN THAT FOCUS.
MS. JONES:	YOUR HONOR, MAY I SPEAK PRIVATELY WITH THE PLAINTIFF?
THE COURT:	PRIVATELY?
MS. JONES:	YES, MAY I HAVE A MOMENT WITH THE PLAINTIFF?
THE COURT:	I THINK THAT YOU NEED TO SPEAK TO ME, AND IT DOES NOT NEED TO BE PRIVATE, IT NEEDS TO BE VERY PUBLIC ABOUT WHAT YOU INTEND TO DO TO GET YOURSELF OUT OF CONTEMPT.
MS. JONES:	I INTEND TO GO TO FLORIDA AND HIRE AN ATTORNEY TO COLLECT AND GET INVOLVED IN THE SUPREME COURT ISSUE WITH SAMUEL ADAGIO, OTHERWISE KNOWN AS SAM ADAGIO, AND TO BRING THIS THING TO LIGHT. I'M HOPING THAT THESE PROCEEDINGS BRING ALL OF THIS TO LIGHT. BUT I INTEND NOW TO AGRESSIVELY BRING THIS TO LIGHT SO I CAN PAY MY CREDITORS INCLUDING ATTORNEY FRANKLIN, AND ALSO THE SIMPSONS AND OTHERS. BUT I INTEND, AS SOON AS I RETURN TO FLORIDA TO SIT DOWN AND BRING COUNSEL IN IMMEDIATELY. AND I'VE DONE IT IN THE PAST. BUT, THEY SAID TO ME YOU WON'T TERMINATE HER, ATTORNEY FRANKIN KNOWS THIS IS TRUE. I HAVE AFFIDAVITS WHERE MANY OF THEM SAID WHY IS SHE SITTING THERE PERCHED IN WASHINGTON, D.C., AND YOU ARE RUNNING AROUND IN FLORIDA.

108

COMMENT AND ANALYSIS: #11 *JONES EXPRESSES HER HOPE THAT THE D.C. COURT PROCEEDINGS WOULD BRING THE OFFICIAL AND JUDICIAL FRAUD, THEFT, CORRUPTION AND EXTORTION CONSPIRACY THAT DOMINATED THE CASE TO LIGHT AND THAT SUCH DISCLOSURE WOULD GIVE HER A CERTAIN PROTECTION FROM THE ALLEGED OPPOSITION AND THEIR FACILITATORS AND HANDLERS. NEEDLESS TO SAY, SHE RETURNED TO FLORIDA, DIDN'T RETAIN COUNSEL, AND AS USUAL, RETURNED TO COURT WITHOUT BANK STATEMENTS AND WAS PERMITTED BY THE COURT TO REMAIN IN CONTEMPT OF THE STATED COURT ORDER.*

THE COURT: YOU HEARD HER PLAN, WHAT IS---

MS. FRANKLIN: YOU HONOR, MY RESPONSE TO HER PLAN IS---SHE IS GOING TO FLORIDA TO HIRE AN ATTORNEY.....WHAT HAS THAT GOT TO DO WITH PROVIDING ME WITH THE DOCUMENTS AND BANK RECORDS WITH REGARD TO THE SETTLEMENT PROCEEDS? WHAT HAS THAT GOT TO DO WITH IT?

THE COURT: YOUR POINT IS WELL TAKEN.

MS. FRANKLIN: THIS IS JUST ANOTHER TRIBUTARY THAT SHE HAS, A RABBIT TRAIL SHE IS GOING TO GO OFF ON AND ENJOY EVERY MOMENT OF IT, AND NOBODY IS GOING TO BE PAID, BEGINNING WITH ME.

THE COURT: MS. JONES, I AM GOING TO GIVE YOU SOME MORE TIME TO THINK ABOUT A BETTER PLAN. YOU WERE ABLE I SUPPOSE TO REACH MR. MINOR, SO MAYBE YOU WILL BE ABLE TO REACH SOMEONE. I NEED TO SEE, IF NOTHING ELSE, THAT SETTLEMENT AGREEMENT.

COMMENT AND ANALYSIS: #12 HERE IS A CLASSIC EXAMPLE OF HOW JUDGE EKANS CONTINUED TO TREAT JONES AS IF SHE WERE ABOVE THE LAW. MOREOVER, JONES' CONTEMPT STATUS WAS AT NO TIME AN URGENT MATTER FOR THE COURT, AND THAT WAS CLEAR. THUS MY INTEREST THROUGHOUT THE PROCEEDINGS REMAINED SEVERELY PREJUDICED GIVEN THE COURT'S PARTIALITY AFFORDED JONES.

BRIANNA JONES HAD TESTIFED EARLIER DURING THE COURT HEARING THAT D.C. BAR COUNSEL HAD A COPY OF HER SETTLEMENT AGREEMENT WITH THE RIDGEWAY ESTATE. HOWEVER, JUDGE EKANS PREFERRED TO IGNORE SUCH IMPORTANT TESTIMONY AND EVIDENCE AND CONTINUED TO REQUEST A COPY OF THE SETTLEMENT AGREEMENT FROM JONES. A COPY OF THE SETTLEMENT AGREEMENT BETWEEN JONES AND THE RIDGEWAY ESTATE DID NOT SERVE THE PURPOSES OF THE D.C. JUDICIAL AND FBI CRIMINAL ENTERPRISE.

MS. JONES: YOUR HONOR, IN MY STORAGE THEY WOULD ALWAYS AS A MATTER OFFACT, THIS PAST APRIL I'VE ALWAYS KEPT STORAGE AT THE BEHEST OF THOSE INVOLVED. AND ATTORNEY FRANKLIN SAID SHE WENT IN ONE TIME LOOKING FOR THE AGREEMENTS. THE STORAGES WERE ALWAYS SOMEHOW SOMEONE HAD GOT INTO IT. I FILED THE REPORT IN 2007. ATTORNEY FRANKLIN CONFIRMED THIS WITH THE BROWARD POLICE DEPARTMENT. MY STORAGE HAD BEEN BROKEN INTO. ALL OF IT -- -- NOTHING ELSE WAS TAKEN EXCEPT THE DOCUMENTS, YOUR HONOR.

MS. JONES: BUT I AM PREPARED ALSO TO RETAIN COUNSEL IN THE DISTRICT OF COLUMBIA BECAUSE MY UNDERSTANDING WITH REGARD TO THE LOTTERY BOARD, TO HAVE IT PUT IN MY NAME BECAUSE THEN IT WAS AN ANNUITIZED PRIZE, IN A LUMP-SUM, I AM PREPARED TO BRING ATTORNEYS ON BOTH ENDS, YOUR HONOR. THERE IS NO ONE BACK AT HOME TO HANDLE MY AFFAIRS.

I TAKE THIS MATTER VERY, VERY SERIOUSLY. I AM MORE THAN WILLING TO PROVIDE ATTORNEY FRANKLIN WITH WHAT SHE NEEDS AND WANTS. THAT'S WHY I HAD EXTENSIVE CONVERSATIONS WITH ATTORNEY MIKE REDD WITH REGARD TO COLLECTING THE ASSETS, WHO IS HERE IN THE COURTROOM TODAY.

THE COURT: I WILL BRING THIS CASE BACK IN HERE ON THURSDAY AND WE WILL SEE IF YOU HAVE GOT A CONCRETE PLAN.

MS. JONES: YOUR HONOR, IS THERE ANYTHING ELSE   YOUR HONOR IS THERE SOMETHING I CAN DO IMMEDIATELY. I REALLY JUST WANT TO DO THE RIGHT THING, YOUR HONOR. I WANT TO BE ABLE TO COLLECT   I'M PREPARED TO ALSO GO AND FILE A POLICE REPORT IN BROWARD COUNTY, AND HAVE COUNSEL ACCOMPANY ME THERE. I'M PREPARED TO GET ANSWERS, YOUR HONOR. I DON'T TAKE THIS LIGHTLY.

THE COURT: I THINK THAT YOU PROBABLY DON'T TAKE IT LIGHTLY, BUT I THINK THAT YOU CAN PROBABLY COME UP WITH A BETTER PLAN.

MS. JONES: I DON'T KNOW WHAT ELSE TO COME UP WITH, YOUR HONOR. ALL I KNOW TO DO IS TO GET THE AUTHORITIES ACTIVELY INVOLVED WITH THIS IN TERMS OF MY SECURITY, AND NOW ALSO IN TERMS OF COLLECTION, AND TO IDENTIFY EXACTLY WHERE THE FUNDS ARE. AND, SHE HAS ASKED ME THAT A FEW TIMES IN RECENT YEARS, AND IT HAS BEEN A FEAR, BUT I WOULD RATHER BE FEARFUL AND DECEASED RATHER THAN LIVING IN A PLACE THAT I'VE NEVER EVER   I HAVE NO CONCEPT OF. I GET IT, AND I WOULD MUCH RATHER -- --

MS. FRANKLIN:	YOUR HONOR, I DON'T HEAR TONES OF GOOD FAITH HERE BECAUSE WHY IS THERE ANOTHER ATTORNEY NEEDED TO COLLECT MY FEES. I'M AN ATTORNEY AND I CAN COLLECT MY OWN FEES IF I AM GIVEN THE PROPER INFORMATION UPON WHICH TO DO IT. THERE IS NO ATTORNEY THAT IS NEEDED TO COLLECT MY FEES, AND IF AN ATTORNEY IS NEEDED THEN I CAN TAKE THE RESPONSIBILITY OF RETAINING AN ATTORNEY TO REPRESENT ME, IF NECESSARY.
MS. JONES:	**YOUR HONOR, THAT'S WHY I WANTED TO SPEAK WITH HER PRIVATELY BECAUSE I DO NOT WANT TO PUT HER IN-HARM'S WAY ANY FURTHER.**
MS. FRANKLIN:	IF I NEED SECURITY, YOUR HONOR, OR PROTECTION, I AM MORE THAN CAPABLE OF ARRANGING THAT. I DON'T NEED MS. JONES TO LOOK OUT FOR ME.
THE COURT:	THURSDAY AT NOON.
MS. JONES:	YOUR HONOR, I AM PREPARED TO TURN IT OVER TO ATTORNEY FRANKLIN.
THE COURT:	WHEN, WHEN?
MS. JONES:	WHENEVER SHE WANTS.
THE COURT:	WHEN?
MS. JONES:	RIGHT NOW.
	I AM PREPARED TO SIT DOWN WITH HER. I HAVE RESPONSIBILITIES AT HOME. I'M PREPARED TO SIT DOWN WITH ATTORNEY FRANKLIN. I COULD CARE LESS ABOUT THE MONEY NOW, IT HAS BEEN A BURDEN. I WOULD RATHER SHE HANDLE IT. THE LONGER I STAY HERE, THE MORE I AM IN DANGER. I WOULD RATHER TURN IT OVER TO HER.
THE COURT:	**WELL, I DON'T HAVE A PLACE FOR YOU TO HAVE A CONFERENCE HERE IN THE COURTHOUSE, BUT YOU KNOW HOW TO GET TO THE D.C. JAIL.**

COMMENT AND ANALYSIS: #13 *OF COURSE, BRIANNA JONES AND I COULD HAVE MET IN AN ADJOINING CONFERENCE ROOM WITH THE COURTROOM, IN A WITNESS ROOM, IN JUDGE'S CHAMBERS OR JUDGE'S CONFERENCE ROOM. TO BRAZENLY LIE AND PROHIBIT BRIANNA JONES FROM REVIEWING WITH ME IN THE COURTHOUSE THE BANK OF AMERICA BANK STATEMENTS OF THE SETTLEMENT PROCEEDS MANDATED BY JUDGE STARR'S ORDER WAS AN AUDACIOUS ABUSE OF ABSOLUTE JUDICIAL DISCRETION, UNQUALIFIED EVIDENCE OF THE COURT'S KNOWING AND PREMEDITATED COMPLICITY IN THE CRIMINAL ENTERPRISE AND MORALLY UNCONSCIONABLE.*

MS. FRANKLIN: I WILL FIND A WAY, YOUR HONOR.

THE COURT: YOU CAN MEET WITH HER OVER THERE, AND I WILL BRING THIS CASE BACK HERE ON WEDNESDAY.

MS. JONES: YOUR HONOR, BELIEVE ME, I AM HAVING SEVERE HEALTH ISSUES. CAN WE MEET OUT IN THE HALLWAY?

COMMENT AND ANALYSIS: #14 *BY THE TIME I ARRIVED AT THE D.C. JAIL THE NEXT MORNING, JONES HAD BEEN PLACED ON SUICIDE WATCH. SHE HAD PERHAPS PLAYED THE SICK (SUICIDE) CARD AND IT HAD WORKED. I WAS NOT GIVEN ANY BANK STATEMENTS AND JONES WAS RELEASED TO RETURN TO FLORIDA UNTIL THE NEXT HEARING. FOR ME, IT ALL SPELLED CHRONIC ABUSE OF ABSOLUTE JUDICIAL DISCRETION, ONE UNRESTRAINED AND UNIMPEDED DISCRETIONARY ABUSE AFTER ANOTHER. IT ALSO SPELLED D.C. JUDICIAL AND FBI FRAUD, THEFT, CORRUPTION AND EXTORTION CONSPIRACY AND CRIMINAL ENTERPRISE.*

THE COURT: STEP TO THE RIGHT, PLEASE. FILL OUT A MEDICAL FORM.

MS. FRANKLIN: YOUR HONOR, MAY I BE EXCUSED?

(WHEREUPON THE PROCEEDINGS CONCLUDED AT 1:55 P.M.)

***

THE ODYSSEY OF JUDICIAL CORRUPTION

SUPERIOR COURT OF THE DISTRICT OF COLUMBIA
CIVIL DIVISION
WASHINGTON, D.C.

THE HONORABLE MATTHEW D. EKANS, ASSOCIATE JUDGE, PRESIDING

THE FOLLOWING IS THE ENTIRE OFFICIAL COURT TRANSCRIPT OF THE
FEBRUARY 2, 2011 COURT PROCEEDING
ANNOTATED BY THE AUTHOR'S PERTINENT COMMENTARY AND ANALYSIS

FEBRUARY 2, 2011

P R O C E E D I N G

COMMENT AND ANALYSIS #1: I HAVE ONE PRIMARY REASON, ABOVE ALL OTHERS, FOR INCLUDING IN THIS JUDICIAL EXPOSE' MY ANNOTATION, COMMENTARY AND ANALYSIS OF THE FEBRUARY 2, 2011 COURT TRANSCRIPT.

THAT REASON IS TO VERIFY AND DOCUMENT FOR THE READER JUDGE EKANS' STATEMENT OF HIS DUTY AS A COURT JUDGE, ABOVE ALL OTHERS, WHICH IS THE DUTY TO ENFORCE THE ORDERS OF THE COURT, WHETHER THEY BE ORDERS THAT ORIGINATE WITH HIM OR WITH ANOTHER D.C. COURT JUDGE.

JUDGE EKANS' SPECIFIC WORDS ADDRESSED TO BRIANNA JONES AND SET FORTH BELOW WERE AS FOLLOWS:

> "......THE COURT IS TRYING TO ENFORCE THE JUDGMENT THAT YOU ENTERED INTO AFTER A LAWSUIT WAS FILED AND WAS SETTLED. *IF I DON'T DO THAT THEN I NEED TO TURN IN MY GAVEL AND MY ROBE BECAUSE THEN THE LAW DOES NOT MEAN ANYTHING.*"

DEPUTY CLERK:	YOUR HONOR, CALLING THE CASE OF BARBARA WASHINGTON FRANKLIN V. BRIANNA JONES, CIVIL ACTION 4417-2009 AND IN THE MATTER OF BRIANNA JONES CCC1-2011.
MS. FRANKLIN:	GOOD AFTERNOON, YOUR HONOR, BARBARA WASHINGTON FRANKLIN.
THE COURT:	GOOD AFTERNOON TO YOU. MA' AM, SAY YOUR NAME.
MS. JONES:	GOOD AFTERNOON, YOUR HONOR, BRIANNA JONES.
THE COURT:	GOOD AFTERNOON TO YOU. HOW ARE YOU TODAY?

BARBARA WASHINGTON FRANKLIN

MS. JONES: I AM FINE, THANK YOU.

THE COURT: GOOD, GOOD, WE RECEIVED A PHONE MESSAGE YESTERDAY FROM MS.
WASHINGTON FRANKLIN SAYING THAT SHE HAD COME OVER THERE TO THE JAIL
TO SEE YOU, BUT THAT YOU WERE UNAVAILABLE. SO, I CALLED OVER THERE TO
FIND OUT WHAT WAS GOING ON AND SEEMS AS IF EVERYTHING WAS OKAY. DO
YOU KNOW OTHERWISE?

MS. JONES: I WENT IN, AND I HAD AS WE WERE GOING BACK INTO THE FACILITY WE WERE
WAITING, I HAD CRAMPS IN MY HEART REGION. AND, I SAID SOMETHING TO THE
MEDICAL STAFF AND SAID IT WAS LIKE A CHARLIE HORSE, BUT BECAUSE IT HAD
TAKEN SO LONG TO ATTEND TO ME, IT HAD SOMEWHAT SUBSIDED.

THEY THEN BROUGHT IN A PSYCHIATRIST AND ASKED ALL OF THESE QUESTIONS
AND THEY WANTED TO KNOW HOW I WAS FEELING AND THAT SORT OF THING.
AND, I SAID I FEEL, IT IS THERE'S JUST A LOT OF PRESSURE AND I'M DEALING WITH
A FRAUDULENT COMPLAINT THAT HAS BEEN FILED AGAINST ME AND HOW DO I
DEFEND MYSELF AGAINST THAT. SO THE DOCTOR THEN DECIDED THAT MAYBE I
SHOULD NOT BE WITH THE GENERAL POPULATION.

AS A RESULT, I WAS HELD IN CONFINEMENT FOR THE LAST 24 HOURS. AND, THEY
WOULD HAVE KEPT ME LONGER, BUT I INSISTED THAT I WAS LUCID, ALL MY
FACULTIES WERE IN ORDER AND THAT I WANTED TO BE HERE TODAY.

THE COURT: THAT IS WHAT THEY TOLD ME. I THINK WE NEED TO FIGURE OUT WHAT IS GOING
TO HAPPEN AND THAT IS WHAT I AM WAITING FOR YOU TO TELL ME.

THE PHRASE THAT IS USED BY THE COURT WHEN THE COURT HAS FOUND A PARTY
IN A CIVIL, AS OPPOSED TO CRIMINAL CONTEMPT OF COURT, THE PHRASE IS THAT
YOU HOLD THE KEY TO THE JAIL HOUSE. YOU MAY BE RELEASED AS SOON AS YOU
COMPLY WITH THE LAWFUL ORDER OF THE COURT.

SO MS. BRIANNA JONES, YOU HOLD THE KEY TO THE JAIL HOUSE. NOW WHAT
ARE YOU GOING TO DO?

MS. JONES: I WOULD LIKE TO SPEAK IF IT PLEASE THE COURT. I HAD A LOT OF TIME TO THINK
IN TERMS OF THAT. I HAVE A TENDENCY   YOU SAID I AM STUBBORN, AND I
MIGHT AGREE WITH THAT. BUT, MORE IMPORTANT, I AM KNOWN TO BEING
LOYAL AND LOYAL TO A FAULT. AND I ASKED MYSELF ON MONDAY WHY THE
PLAINTIFF TRIES SO DESPERATELY TO CONTINUE TO HAVE ME INCARCERATED
WHEN I HAVE BEEN HER ADVOCATE FOR ALL THESE YEARS EVEN AT MY OWN
PERIL, AT MY OWN DEMISE.

AND, EVEN AS I STAND HERE NOW I'M SO PETRIFIED TO SPEAK THE UNADULTERATED TRUTH BECAUSE THAT WILL BEAR LIGHT ON THIS ENTIRE SITUATION.

AND WITH REGARD TO THE ATTORNEYS THERE WERE TIMES WHERE I HAVE THE SPECIFIC CASE, BUT AS I'M SAYING THIS YOUR HONOR I DO HAVE EVIDENCE, UNADULTERATED EVIDENCE THAT THERE WERE ISSUES WHERE THE ATTORNEYS WOULD CALL HER, AND I WOULD BE IN THE DISTRICT RACING TO FORT LAUDERDALE.

ONE OF THE INSTANCES IS MARCH 21ST, 1997 AND SHE WOULD TELL ME NO, THEY ARE NOT GETTING ME IN THIS, YOU CAN HANDLE THIS, HERE IS MY CODE, YOU CALL ME, THEY HAVE BEEN TRYING TO REACH HER, BUT I HAD TO HAVE A CODE TO CALL HER.

AND, TO GO THROUGH ALL OF THIS AND I STAND HERE TODAY FACING CONDITIONS I COULD NEVER EVEN HAVE THOUGHT OF, EVEN FATHOMED, AND ALL I WANTED TO DO WAS JUST MAKE SURE THAT THE PLAINTIFF WAS COMPENSATED FAIRLY EVEN WHEN SHE WOULD NOT ALLOW HERSELF TO BE PUT IN THERE. IT WAS JUST AN ISSUE OF EACH DOCUMENT BECOMING INCREASINGLY MORE AND MORE IN TERMS OF HER PERCENTAGE. EVEN WITH THAT I DID NOT HAVE A PROBLEM BECAUSE YOU SEE -- -- AND I SHARED IT WITH ANOTHER ATTORNEY AND THEY ADVISED ME TO STOP PROTECTING AND TO SPEAK UP.

I SHARED WITH BAR COUNSEL JUNE 26 OF '09 AND THEY SENT ME THE NECESSARY DOCUMENTS, AND ONE OF THE- -- MS. MARCIA MCMILLAN SAID, I DON'T THINK YOU HAVE THE COURAGE TO SPEAK UP WITH THIS, BUT I AM GOING TO SEND YOU THE DOCUMENTS ANYWAY.

AND, SO HAVING SAID ALL OF THAT AS I STAND HERE I AM STILL AFRAID. BECAUSE YOU ASK ME, BRIANNA, WHAT ARE WE GOING TO DO MS. JONES. I HAVE TO BRING IN COUNSEL. I HAVE TO BRING IN OUTSIDE COUNSEL TO GO AND ASSIST WITH TAKING CONTROL OF THE ASSETS. ATTORNEY FRANKLIN INSISTED THAT SHE WOULD COME AND TAKE CONTROL OF THE ASSETS.

WHY DIDN'T SHE TAKE CONTROL OF THE ASSETS WHEN I KEPT MAKING HER AWARE OF EVERYTHING THAT WAS GOING ON. WHEN I CALLED HER AND SAID THAT SAM ADAGIO IS IN TROUBLE, HE WAS BEEN SUSPENDED, WHY DIDN'T SHE INSIST? AND NOW ALL OF A SUDDEN SHE WANTS TO TAKE CONTROL.

YOUR HONOR, THIS IS PERVERTING EQUITY. SHE FEELS THAT IF SOMEBODY FILES AGAINST HER WITH BAR COUNSEL, WE DISCUSSED THAT AND DECIDED SO SHE WON'T COME AFTER ME, BUT LET ME FILE IMMEDIATELY AGAINST MS. JONES.

***

MS. JONES: WHAT I HAVE TODAY IS WHAT I WOULD LIKE TO DO IS IF YOU'LL ALLOW ME TO BE RELEASED FOR AT LEAST 48 TO 72 HOURS TO BRING IN COUNSEL SO THAT WE CAN ADDRESS THIS, AND THEY CAN TAKE A HANDLE WITH REGARD TO THE COLLECTION OF THE FUNDS.

I'M NOT HERE ARGUING WHETHER OR NOT ATTORNEY FRANKLIN DESERVES ANY FUNDS. I SIGNED THE COMPLAINT. I STAND BY THAT, YOUR HONOR, BUT I NEED A CHANCE TO BE ABLE TO GO AND BRING IN THE NECESSARY ASSISTANCE TO COLLECT THE PROCEEDS. AND THAT IS ALL I AM ASKING.

BUT I HAVE SUFFERED ENOUGH, IT IS YEAR, AFTER YEAR, AFTER YEAR I'M TAKING IT. AND IT IS LIKE THIS, YOUR HONOR, BUT I DEFER TO YOU.

THE COURT: YOU ARE SAYING THAT IF I LET YOU OUT YOU WILL GO DOWN TO FLORIDA AND HIRE ANOTHER LAWYER?

MS. JONES: YES, AND I'M ALSO HOPING AGAIN, AND I KNOW IT SOUNDS CRAZY, BUT I WILL BE ABLE TO COMFORTABLY, COMFORTABLY, REALLY GO INTO DETAIL WITH MR. MIKE REDD. I AM HOPING HE AND THE SIMPSONS WILL CONSIDER HIS REPRESENTATIONS, BECAUSE I FILLED HIM IN COMPLETELY, AND I FEEL EXTREMELY COMFORTABLE THAT HE IS ALSO ABLE TO GET THE JOB DONE.

THE COURT: WHO?

MS. JONES: MR. MIKE REDD. AND THAT IS IF THE SIMPSONS WILL ALLOW. I JUST FEEL EXTREMELY CONFIDENT -- --

THE COURT: GET WHAT JOB DONE?

MS. JONES: WITH REGARD TO COLLECTING ON THIS.

THE COURT: HE IS THE LAWYER YOU WANT TO RETAIN?

MS. JONES: I SPOKE WITH HIM, BUT THERE IS A CONFLICT OF INTEREST BETWEEN THE SIMPSONS. I'VE NEVER HAD A CHANCE -- --

116

THE COURT:	I THOUGHT HE REPRESENTED THE SIMPSONS?
MS. JONES:	HE DOES.
THE COURT:	WHY WOULD YOU WANT TO HIRE THEIR LAWYER WHEN THEY ARE AFTER YOU –
MS. JONES:	BECAUSE I HAD A CHANCE TO SPEAK WITH HIM IN GREAT DETAIL AND I FELT REALLY AT EASE.
THE COURT:	LET ME TRY THIS AGAIN. YOUR PLAN IS FOR ME TO RELEASE YOU TO GO TO FLORIDA SO THAT YOU CAN RETAIN THE SIMPSONS' LAWYER TO COLLECT THE MONEY?
MS. JONES:	NO, YOUR HONOR. I AM GOING TO RETAIN FIRST AND FOREMOST A VERY LUCRATIVE ATTORNEY IN FLORIDA, AND I'M HOPING THAT ON THE BACK END OF THE DISTRICT IF I NEED COUNSEL THAT MAYBE THE SIMPSONS ALONG WITH MR. REDD WOULD CONSIDER A LIMITED REPRESENTATION OF ME WITH REGARD TO COLLECTING IF ANYTHING NEEDS TO BE DONE ON THIS AND IN THE WASHINGTON D.C. AREA. BUT I AM MORE THAN CONFIDENT IN FLORIDA THAT THERE IS AN ABLE ATTORNEY THAT CAN STEP RIGHT IN.
THE COURT:	ARE YOU GOING TO SAY HERE ON THIS RECORD WHERE THE MONEY IS?
MS. JONES:	DO YOU WANT TO TRY ANOTHER WEEK, A WEEK FROM TODAY.
MS. FRANKLIN:	YOUR HONOR, MAY I SPEAK. I WOULD OBJECT TO HER BEING RELEASED.
THE COURT:	I AM SORRY?
MS. FRANKLIN:	I WOULD OBJECT TO HER BEING RELEASED.
THE COURT:	DID I SAY ANYTHING ABOUT RELEASE?
MS. FRANKLIN:	NO, YOUR HONOR.

***

MS. JONES:	YOUR HONOR, I AM MORE THAN CONFIDENT THAT EVEN IF YOU'LL ALLOW ME TO LEAVE FOR 48 HOURS I COULD BRING IN PROPER FLORIDA COUNSEL THAT CAN IMMEDIATELY IDENTIFY THOSE FUNDS.
THE COURT:	**LET ME ASK YOU A QUESTION. YOU HAVE TOLD ME THAT WHAT IS AT STAKE HERE IS SEVERAL MILLION DOLLARS, I DON'T REMEMBER THE FIGURE, SEVERAL MILLION DOLLARS. AND THAT UNDER THE SETTLEMENT AGREEMENT YOU OWE THE PLAINTIFF 40 PERCENT OF THAT. IS THAT WHAT YOU ARE TELLING ME?**

COMMENT AND ANALYSIS: #2 IT IS THE SECOND MONTH OF THE ADJUDICATION OF MY LAWSUIT BY JUDGE EKANS. HE BELIEVES WHAT IS AT STAKE ARE SEVERAL MILLION DOLLARS.

BY THE TIME THE MARCH 18, 2011 COURT HEARING ROLLED AROUND, PRESUMABLY JUDGE EKANS HAD HAD AN OPPORTUNITY TO UPDATE HIMSELF ON THE SPECIFIC FACTS OF THE CASE AND IS AWARE THAT THE $100 MILLION FLORIDA LAWSUIT CASE SETTLEMENT PROCEEDS HAD BEGUN AT $34 MILLION, BUT GIVEN ACCRUED INTEREST, WERE NOW VALUED AT AN ESTIMATED $100 MILLION.

IT WAS DURING THE MARCH 18, 2011 COURT HEARING THAT JUDGE EKANS WOULD TAG-TEAM WITH FORMER CHIEF JUDGE GEORGE SKINNER TO SHAKE DOWN AND INTIMIDATE BRIANNA JONES IN THE COURT HALLWAY FOLLOWING A CONTRIVED COURT RECESS ORCHESTRATED BY JUDGE EKANS WITHOUT EVEN A SCINTILLA OF SHAME OR FEAR OF QUESTION OR DISCIPLINE.

MS. JONES:	THAT'S CORRECT.
THE COURT:	WHY SHOULD I EXPECT TO SEE YOU BACK UP HERE IN TWO DAYS IF YOU KNOW THAT WHEN YOU COME BACK HERE WITH THIS SAME STUFF THAT YOU HAVE BEEN GIVING ME FOR A WEEK AND A HALF NOW, THAT I'M GOING TO LOCK YOU UP, WHY?
MS. JONES:	WHEN I SIGN, ANYBODY THAT KNOWS ME KNOWS THAT.
THE COURT:	I DON'T KNOW YOU.
MS. JONES:	WHEN I SIGNED ON THE 25TH, THAT I WILL RETURN ON-------WHEN I SIGNED ON THE 21ST THAT I WOULD RETURN ON THE 25TH, I KNEW THERE WAS A CHANCE THAT THE DOCUMENTS I HAVE MAY NOT APPEASE THIS COURT.
THE COURT:	**YOU KNEW THERE WAS A CHANCE OF THAT. THE COURT IS NOT TRYING TO BE APPEASED. THE COURT IS TRYING TO ENFORCE THE JUDGMENT THAT YOU ENTERED INTO AFTER A LAWSUIT WAS FILED AND WAS SETTLED. IF I DON'T DO THAT THEN I NEED TO TURN IN MY GAVEL AND MY ROBE, *BECAUSE THEN THE LAW DOES NOT MEAN ANYTHING.***

COMMENT AND ANALYSIS: #3 THE COURT RECORD VERIFIES THAT JUDGE EKANS NEVER ENFORCED JUDGE STARR'S ORDER OF OCTOBER 18, 2010. RATHER, IN PREMEDITATION OF THE MISSION OF THE D.C. JUDICIAL AND FBI CRIMINAL ENTERPRISE TO SWINDLE ME OF AN ESTIMATED $50 MILLION IN ATTORNEY'S FEES, JUDGE EKANS ISSUED ME A "PAPER" MONEY JUDGMENT FOR $13.6 MILLION WHICH WOULD LATER BE OVERTURNED BY PREMEDITATION BY THE D.C. COURT OF APPEALS IN DEFERENCE TO THE ONGOING D.C. JUDICIAL AND FBI CRIMINAL ENTERPRISE AND CONSPIRACY.

MS. JONES: I UNDERSTAND THAT. IF I DON'T RETURN IN 48 HOURS THAT AS YOU SAID, I HOLD THE KEY. AND ONCE I COME BACK IT COULD BE FOR A LONG TIME TO COME. I CERTAINLY WANT TO COME BACK WITHIN 48 HOURS WITH WHAT YOU ARE ASKING FOR.

MS. FRANKLIN: YOUR HONOR, SHE HAS ACKNOWLEDGED ON THE RECORD AT THE LAST HEARING THAT SHE HAS HEALTH ISSUES. THOSE ISSUES ARE MENTAL HEALTH ISSUES, YOUR HONOR, AND HER WORD MEANS ABSOLUTELY NOTHING.

MS. JONES: I DON'T UNDERSTAND BECAUSE------ YOUR HONOR, MAY I SPEAK?

THE COURT: MS. JONES, I TRUST THAT YOU UNDERSTAND THAT I TAKE NO PLEASURE IN THIS. EVERY TIME I HAVE COME DOWN HERE, I HAVE COME DOWN HERE HOPING THAT I CAN RELEASE YOU, BUT YOU ARE NOT MAKING SENSE.

MS. JONES: ALL I HAVE IS A FRIEND-OF-THE-COURT, YOUR HONOR. I WILL BE SITTING HERE FOR FOREVER BECAUSE UNLESS I BRING IN COUNSEL IN FLORIDA TO HELP ME GO AND PUT A STAKE AND SAY I AM DUE THIS, THIS IS THE ONLY WAY IT CAN BE DONE. IF NOT, I'M JUST SITTING HERE ROTTING AWAY.

IF YOU GIVE ME THE 48 HOURS SOMETHING WILL HAPPEN. I WILL IMMEDIATELY GET TO FLORIDA, GET THE ATTORNEY, HAVE HIM MAKE A CLAIM ON MY BEHALF WITH THE FLORIDA SUPREME COURT AND IDENTIFY WHERE THOSE FUNDS ARE. AND, I WOULD BE GLAD TO HAVE HIM INTERACT WITH ATTORNEY FRANKLIN.

MS. FRANKLIN:	**YOUR HONOR, AS SHE LEFT THE COURTROOM ON MONDAY SHE YELLED OUT, HERE ARE THE DOCUMENTS, YOUR HONOR, I HAVE THE DOCUMENTS, CAN I MEET PRIVATELY WITH ATTORNEY FRANKLIN. AND YOU SAID THERE WAS NO PLACE FOR YOU TO MEET WITH HER HERE, MS. FRANKLIN, CAN YOU GET TO D.C. JAIL. I SAID, YES, YOUR HONOR.**

I WENT OVER YESTERDAY TO MEET WITH HER, THEY TOLD ME I COULD NOT MEET WITH HER BECAUSE SHE WAS ON SUICIDE WATCH. IF THOSE ARE THE DOCMENTS SHE HAD THEN, WHY HASN'T SHE TURNED THEM OVER? SHE BROUGHT THE SAME OR SIMILAR POUCH TO THE COURTROOM ON MONDAY. SHE IS PLAYING GAMES AND SHE IS GOING TO CONTINUE TO PLAY GAMES.

COMMENT AND ANALYSIS: #4 I SPECIFICALLY REMIND JUDGE EKANS THAT AT THE JANUARY 31, 2011 COURT HEARING HE PROHIBITED BRIANNA JONES FROM MEETING WITH ME IN THE COURTHOUSE TO REVIEW BANK OF AMERICA BANK STATEMENTS OF THE SETTLEMENT PROCEEDS.

NOTHING IS MORE EVIDENT OF JUDGE EKANS' DETERMINATION TO KEEP ME FROM HAVING ACCESS TO THE SETTLEMENT PROCEEDS AND ULTIMATELY BEING PAID MY ATTORNEY'S FEES THAN JUDGE EKANS' REFUSAL TO PERMIT ME AND BRIANNA JONES FROM MEETING IN THE COURTHOUSE TO REVIEW THE BANK STATEMENTS OF THE MILLIONS OF DOLLARS IN SETTLEMENT PROCEEDS ON DEPOSIT AT BANK OF AMERICA.

MS. JONES: WITH ALL DUE RESPECT, YOUR HONOR, I NEVER SAID TO HER I HAVE THE DOCUMENTS. I WANTED TO SPEAK -- --

MS. FRANKLIN: YOU SAID TO THE COURT THAT YOU HAD THE DOCUMENTS.

THE COURT: COUNSEL.

MS. FRANKLIN: I AM SORRY, YOUR HONOR.

MS. JONES: I NEVER SAID THAT THIS WAS ABOUT SPEAKING WITH HER SHE SAID WELL THEN I WILL COLLECT. IT WAS ABOUT BRINGING IN COUNSEL TO COLLECT, AND THAT'S WHAT SHE WAS COMING OVER TO SPEAK TO ME ABOUT AND LEADING HER IN THE DIRECTION.

YOUR HONOR, I DON'T HAVE THE DOCUMENTS IN HAND. I DON'T HAVE THEM HERE IN A SAFE DEPOSIT BOX, I DON'T HAVE THEM HERE. I HAVE A FRIEND OF THE COURT WHO WAS APPALLED TO SEE WHAT WAS GOING ON.

WHEN I PROMISE YOU, YOUR HONOR, THIS COURT, IF I AM GIVEN 48 HOURS I WILL RETURN.

THE COURT: TELL ME WHAT THE FLORIDA SUPREME COURT HAS TO DO WITH THIS.

MS. JONES: IT IS BECAUSE WITH THE HEAD OF THE FIRM, SAM ADAGIO, THE FACT THAT THEY HAVE BEEN HIDING ASSETS. AND SO I'VE BEEN GETTING BITS AND PIECES OF INFORMATION. THAT IS HOW I HAVE BEEN KEEPING HER APPRISED. AND, I HAVE ALREADY SPOKEN WITH AN ATTORNEY IN FLORIDA. AND HE SAID, WHEN YOU'RE REALLY READY TO DEAL WITH THIS, THIS IS WHEN SHE FIRST STARTED WITH THE COMPLAINT. HE SAID LET ME KNOW HOW IT GOES. BUT, HE SAID I THINK I CAN COLLECT FOR YOU; I AM VERY MUCH AWARE OF THE FIRM. I KNOW THEY'RE INVOLVED.

MS. FRANKLIN: YOUR HONOR, MAY I SPEAK, PLEASE ON THAT QUESTION. SAM ADAGIO HAS NOTHING TO DO WITH THIS MATTER, OTHER THAN HE IS A SENIOR NAMED PARTNER OF HIS FIRM AND HE WAS RECENTLY SUSPENDED BY THE BAR AND DISBARMENT PROCEEDINGS ARE PENDING. HE HAS NOTHING TO DO WITH PAYMENT OF ATTORNEY FEES IN THIS CASE, AND SHE KNOWS THAT.

WHAT SHE WOULD LIKE TO DO BASED ON HER COMMENTS TO ME IS GET ALL OF THIS MONEY AND GO AFTER HIM. WELL, FINE THAT IS A SEPARATE ISSUE. IT HAS NOTHING TO DO WITH THE PAYMENT OF FEES THAT ARE THE SUBJECT OF THIS COURT HEARING.

MS. JONES: YOUR HONOR, I SIMPLY WANT THIS OVER. I WANT THE SIMPSONS PAID; I WANT ATTORNEY FRANKLIN PAID. I AM SO TIRED OF THIS. I JUST WANT MY LIFE BACK. THIS IS KILLING ME. IF I HAVE 48 HOURS THEN I CAN LET AN ATTORNEY DEAL WITH THIS, AND HAVE ALL THE QUESTIONS.

I DID THE WRONG THING IN ALLOWING ATTORNEY FRANKLIN TO HAVE ME RIP AND RUN, AND NOW I AM SUFFERING THE CONSEQUENCES. I FEEL LIKE THE LAMB THAT WAS LED TO THE SLAUGHTER.

I WOULD GLADLY, YOUR HONOR, MEET WITH THE ATTORNEY IMMEDIATELY, ALL OF THE INFORMATION THAT YOU REQUESTED, IF I AM ALLOWED TO LEAVE, SITTING HERE, NOTHING IS HAPPENING.

BARBARA WASHINGTON FRANKLIN

MS. FRANKLIN: YOUR HONOR, MAY I SPEAK AGAIN. I CAN PREDICT KNOWING HER SO WELL -- -- I DIDN'T KNOW HER IN '96 AS I KNOW HER NOW. SHE WILL LEAVE THIS COURTROOM, IF THE COURT RELEASES HER, SHE WILL PLAY THE SICK CARD. IT MIGHT NOT BE A SUICIDE WATCH, BUT IT WILL BE SOME OTHER ILLNESS. SHE WILL BE IN THE HOSPITAL AND WHO KNOWS FOR HOW LONG. AND THAT WILL ALLOW HER NOT TO COME BACK TO THIS COURT. THAT'S WHAT IT HAS BEEN FOR 15 YEARS. WE HAVE GONE THROUGH THIS SCENARIO FOR 15 YEARS.

MS. JONES: YOUR HONOR, THAT IS NOT THE CASE. THEY WANTED TO KEEP ME, THE DOCTOR AND I INSISTED THAT I WAS FINE, AND THAT I WANTED TO BE AT THIS HEARING BECAUSE I WANTED TO DEAL WITH MY AFFAIRS. IT IS NOT BEING ABLE TO DEAL WITH MY AFFAIRS THAT CAUSES THE ANXIETY, YOUR HONOR. AND SHE TRUSTED ME ENOUGH WITH MY HEALTH TO RIP AND RUN ALL OVER THE WORLD AND ALL OF A SUDDEN NOW IT IS AN ISSUE.

AND I WOULD ASK THE PLAINTIFF WHY WOULD SHE WANT ME INCARCERATED? WHAT IS THIS ABOUT WHEN I'VE BEEN ON HER SIDE ALL OF THESE YEARS? I JUST SIMPLY WANTED TO DO THE RIGHT THING AS IT PLEASES THIS COURT, AND THAT IS TO GO AND BRING IN COUNSEL, YOUR HONOR, AND FINALLY GET THIS THING RESOLVED AND COMPLETED. I JUST NEED TO HAVE COUNSEL. THIS IS MORE THAN I CAN HANDLE. SO I NEED TO BRING IN COUNSEL.

MS. FRANKLIN: YOUR HONOR, IF I MAY SPEAK. THE ORDER THAT YOUR HONOR IS ATTEMPTING SO VALIANTLY TO HAVE HONORED AND UPHELD WAS ISSUED IN OCTOBER BY JUDGE STARR ON OCTOBER 18. MS. JONES WAS GIVEN UNTIL THE 25TH OF OCTOBER. THEREAFTER, SHE WAS ISSUED AN ORDER OF AN ORAL EXAM, AND THAT WAS HELD, NO DOCUMENTS. IT IS NOW JANUARY, FEBRUARY, EXCUSE ME, ONE YEAR AGO THIS COMING FRIDAY WE ENTERED INTO A SETTLEMENT AGREEMENT. I HAVE WAITED FOR ONE YEAR.

IN 15 YEARS I HAVE NEVER BEEN PAID ONE DOLLAR FOR ANYTHING, FROM COURT COSTS, FILING FEES, TRANSPORTATION , ET CETERA, ET CETERA; ABSOLUTELY NOTHING.

SHE ENJOYS THE GAME. THAT IS PART OF THE ILLNESS, SHE ENJOYS THE GAME. SHE ENJOYS THE GAME ESPECIALLY WITH PEOPLE IN AUTHORITY. SHE ENJOYS PLAYING THE GAME WITH THE COURTS AND WITH ATTORNEYS. FOR HER IT IS HER TIME AND SHE WILL GO ON AND ON AND ON. HER WORD MEANS ABSOLUTELY NOTHING, ABSOLUTELY NOTHING.

AND WHAT SHE WOULD LIKE TO DO IS GET OUT FROM UNDER THE JURISDICTION OF THIS COURT. THAT IS HER AIM ABOVE ALL.

MS. JONES: YOUR HONOR, MAY I SPEAK. THESE WORDS ARE HORRIFYING TO HEAR. WHEN SHE SAYS -- --

THE COURT: THIS IS NOT HELPFUL. THIS IS AN ARGUMENT BETWEEN THE TWO OF YOU THAT IS NOT -- --

MS. JONES: CAN I TELL YOU WHAT KIND OF MONEY SHE SPENT, WHEN SHE SAYS SHE SPENT MONEY.

THE COURT: I DON'T SEE WHY THAT WOULD BE HELPFUL. WHEN YOU DO SPEAK IT TENDS TO ENFORCE THE THINGS THAT MS. FRANKLIN IS SAYING TO ME.

THIS IS NOT ABOUT ANY RELATIONSHIP THAT YOU HAVE HAD OTHER THAN THE LEGAL ONE. THIS IS NOT ABOUT GOING BACK INTO THE MERITS OF THE NEGOTIATED FEE THAT YOU MADE WITH YOUR THEN ATTORNEY. THIS IS SIMPLY ABOUT THE FACT THAT THE ATTORNEY BROUGHT A SUIT TO COLLECT A FEE AND YOU ENTERED INTO A SETTLEMENT AGREEING TO SETTLE THE FEE. NOW, WHEN IT IS TIME COME TO PAY YOU HAVE DONE EVERYTHING BUT PAY.

NOW AT THIS POINT IN TIME, IT SEEMS TO ME THAT THE ONLY WAY THAT WE CAN GET YOU TO UNDERSTAND THAT YOU ARE OBLIGED AS ANY OTHER PERSON IN A CONTRACT IS OBLIGED TO FULFILL YOUR OBLIGATIONS, IS TO GIVE YOU THIS INCONVENIENCE UNTIL YOU DECIDE THAT YOU'RE TIRED OF IT, AND YOU ARE READY TO DO WHAT YOU NEED TO DO.

NOW, I WILL TELL YOU WHAT, I AM GOING TO BRING YOU UP NEXT WEEK TO SEE WHERE YOUR HEAD IS ON THIS, BUT IF IT IS CLEAR TO ME NEXT WEEK THAT YOU ARE STILL IN THE SAME PLACE I'M GOING TO CHANGE THIS FROM CIVIL CONTEMPT TO CRIMINAL CONTEMPT WHICH WILL RESULT IN A TRIAL TO DETERMINE IF IN FACT YOU ARE WILLFULLY DISOBEYING THE ORDER OF THE COURT. AND. IF SO THE COURT HAS THE AUTHORITY TO IMPRISON YOU FOR A VERY LONG TIME. I DON'T THINK YOU'RE GETTING IT.

MS. JONES: YOUR HONR, AGAIN I NEED TO GO HOME AND HAVE COUNSEL. I DON'T HAVE ANY WAY OF GETTING -- --

BARBARA WASHINGTON FRANKLIN

THE COURT:	I WOULD LOVE FOR YOU TO HAVE A LAWYER, BECAUSE I BELIEVE THAT A LAWYER WOULD POSSIBLY GET THROUGH TO YOU WHAT I AM UNABLE TO GET THROUGH TO YOU. BUT THIS PERSON RIGHT HERE WAS YOUR LAWYER, AND NOW YOU'RE TELLING ME YOU WANT TO HIRE THE LAWYER OF SOMEBODY WHO IS ALREADY WORKING FOR PEOPLE WHO ARE SUING YOU. IT IS NOT MAKING SENSE. YOU HAVE HAD PEOPLE CALLING MY CHAMBERS WHO ARE INQUIRING ABOUT HOW THEY CAN HELP YOU, WHY DON'T YOU LET THEM KNOW HOW THEY CAN HELP YOU. THEY CAN GET YOU A LAWYER UP HERE.
MS. JONES:	I CAN'T GET ANY PHONE CALLS, YOUR HONOR. I BEG YOU, IF I CAN GO FOR 48 HOURS -- --
THE COURT:	YOU MUST BE THE ONLY PERSON OVER AT THE JAIL WHO CAN'T USE THE PHONE. PEOPLE HAVE PHONE CALLS OVER THERE ALL THE TIME.
MS. JONES:	YOUR HONOR, IF I CAN GO ON HOME AND GET MY AFFAIRS IN ORDER, AND SHUT THINGS DOWN -- --
THE COURT:	THAT IS NOT HAPPENING, THAT'S NOT GOING TO HAPPEN.
MS. JONES:	YOUR HONOR, I AM BEGGING YOU, PLEASE.
THE COURT:	MS. JONES, YOU HAVE TO UNDERSTAND SOMETHING -- --
MS. JONES:	YOU ARE ASKING ME TO BRING IN DOCUMENTS THAT I DON'T HAVE.
THE COURT:	I AM NOT ASKING YOU TO BRING IN DOCUMENTS AT THIS POINT IN TIME. I AM JUST ASKING YOU TO TELL WHERE THE MONEY IS.

COMMENT AND ANALYSIS #5: I DON'T EVER RECALL EVEN ONCE DURING THE 9-MONTH ADJUDICATION OF MY CASE THAT JUDGE EKANS REQUESTED BRIANNA JONES TO TURN OVER TO ME THE BANK STATEMENTS OF THE SETTLEMENT PROCEEDS WHICH WAS THE CLEAR AND UNEQUIVOCAL MANDATE OF JUDGE STARR'S OCTOBER 18, 2010 ORDER.

RATHER, JUDGE EKANS PREFERRED TO SPEAK OF "DOCUMENTS," "ASSETS," AND "TELL WHERE THE MONEY IS." HIS ACTIONS WERE INTENTIONAL, PURPOSEFUL AND CORRUPT.

MS. JONES:	THEY ARE WITH THE ESTATE. THE WIDOW DIED JUNE 9TH OF 2009. THEY ARE WITH THE ESTATE. I HAVE A FRIEND THAT LOOKED IT ALL UP. THEY HAVE IN DIFFERENT ESTATES, IN DIFFERENCT NAMES. THAT'S ALL I KNOW.

MS. JONES: THEY ARE WITH THE ESTATE. THE WIDOW DIED JUNE 9TH OF 2009. THEY ARE WITH THE ESTATE. I HAVE A FRIEND THAT LOOKED IT ALL UP. THEY HAVE IN DIFFERENT ESTATES, IN DIFFERENCT NAMES. THAT'S ALL I KNOW.

THE COURT: THAT FRIEND, HAVE THAT FRIEND BRING THAT INFORMATION HERE.

MS. JONES: I TOLD ATTORNEY FRANKLIN ABOUT IT, I TOLD THE PLAINTIFF ABOUT IT. THAT IS ALL I KNOW. I DO KNOW A LAWYER. HE SAID IF I RETAIN HIM THAT HE COULD GET THE INFORMATION AND HE COULD -- --

THE COURT: THEN THAT IS WHAT YOU NEED TO DO, YOU NEED TO RETAIN THAT LAWYER.

MS. JONES: IF I COULD HAVE 48 HOURS I PROMISE TO COME BACK, YOUR HONOR. I PROMISE. I HAVE A BIRTHDAY ON SATURDAY. I JUST WANT TO BE ABLE TO GET THAT DONE AND COME BACK. I'LL BE HERE AS LONG AS YOU NEED ME TO BE HERE, BUT I PROMISE YOU I WILL GET THAT INFORMATION.

MS. FRANKLIN: YOUR HONOR, SHE HAS FORGOTTEN THAT SHE ALREADY TESTIFIED BEFORE THE COURT THAT THE FUNDS WERE IN BANK OF AMERICA IN THIS REGION, THAT SHE HAD MET WITH THE BANKERS HERE, AND ALL OF A SUDDEN SHE HAS NO RECOLLECTION AS TO WHAT BRANCH.

MS. JONES: BECAUSE THEY MOVED THEM. THE GIRL MADE IT CLEAR TO ME, SHE SAID MS. BRIANNA THEY HAVE MOVED IT. AND SO WE KNOW WE HAVE SOME LEEWAY WHERE THEY ARE, ATTORNEY FRANKLIN.

YOUR HONOR, I PROMISE YOU I'LL COME BACK IN HERE WITH DEFINITIVE INFORMATION BECAUSE I GET IT NOW. I DO NOT WANT TO ROT IN A CELL AGAIN. I WILL COME BACK IN HERE WITH DEFINITIVE INFORMATION FOR THIS COURT.

THE COURT: DO YOU KNOW THAT AT ANY TIME WHILE YOU'RE OVER AT THE JAIL YOU CAN GET WORD TO ME THAT YOU ARE READY TO COOPERATE, DO YOU KNOW THAT?

MS. JONES: YES.

THE COURT: ALL RIGHT. BRING THE CASE UP MONDAY. STEP TO THE RIGHT. MONDAY AT NOON.

MS. FRANKLIN: THANK YOU, YOUR HONOR.

THE COURT: NOW, IF A LIGHT BULB GOES OFF IN YOUR HEAD BEFORE THEN -- --

BARBARA WASHINGTON FRANKLIN

MS. JONES:	I DON'T KNOW ANYTHING. YOU ASK ME ------ YOU ALL MIGHT AS WELL JUST KILL ME. THIS CASE IS KILLING ME. I DON'T KNOW ANYTHING EXCEPT TO GET AN ATTORNEY. I PROMISE YOU, 48 HOURS -- --
THE COURT:	PLEASE COOPERATE WITH THE DEPUTY.
MS. JONES:	CAN SOMEBODY DO SOMETHING. I'M STUCK HERE. I HAVE DONE NOTHING.
THE COURT:	NOW, HE IS TRYING TO BE COOPERATIVE WITH YOU, MA' AM.
MS. JONES:	BUT YOU KEEP PUTTING ME IN JAIL FOR WHAT? ALL I CAN DO IS HIRE A LAWYER, I HAVE NO COUNSEL, NO REPRESENTATION.
DEPUTY MARSHAL:	LET'S GO, MA 'AM. GRAB YOUR PAPERS.
MS. JONES:	AND NOW I AM STUCK HERE AGAIN, AND I AM GOING TO LOSE EVERYTHING IN FLORIDA, ALL THE DOCUMENTS WILL BE GONE. I ASKED FOR 48 HOURS.
MS. FRANKLIN:	YOUR HONOR, MAY I BE EXCUSED?
THE COURT:	YES.

(WHEREUPON THE PROCEEDINGS CONCLUDED AT APPROXIMATELY 12:45 P.M.)

SUPERIOR COURT OF THE DISTRICT OF COLUMBIA
CIVIL DIVISION
WASHINGTON, D.C.

THE HONORABLE MATTHEW D. EKANS, ASSOCIATE JUDGE, PRESIDING

THE FOLLOWING IS THE ENTIRE OFFICIAL COURT TRANSCRIPT OF THE
FEBRUARY 7, 2011 COURT PROCEEDING
ANNOTATED BY THE AUTHOR'S PERTINENT COMMENTARY AND ANALYSIS

FEBRUARY 7, 2011

P R O C E E D I N G

COMMENT AND ANALYSIS: #1 IN DECEMBER 1996, BRIANNA JONES, WHOM I REPRESENTED ON A CONTINGENCY FEE BASIS, INFORMED ME THAT SHE HAD SETTLED FOR $34 MILLION THE $100 MILLION LAWSUIT THAT I HAD PREVIOUSLY CRAFTED AND FILED, AT MY SOLE EXPENSE AND ON HER BEHALF, ON MAY 30, 1996, THE LAST DAY OF THE STATUTE OF LIMITATIONS, IN BROWARD COUNTY CIRCUIT COURT IN FORT LAUDERDALE, FLORIDA.

BRIANNA JONES HAD SETTLED THE LAWSUIT WITHOUT ANY PRIOR NOTICE TO ME, NOR WAS I EVER PAID ATTORNEY'S FEES IN ANY AMOUNT FOR MY SUPEREROGATORY LEGAL SERVICES AND REPRESENTATION OF BRIANNA JONES. NOR WAS I PAID FOR THE NECESSARY AND SUBSTANTIAL OUT-OFPOCKET EXPENSES TO MAINTAIN THE LITIGATION OF THE $100 MILLION LAWSUIT.

PRIOR TO BRIANNA JONES' SETTLEMENT OF THE FLORIDA LAWSUIT WITH THE RIDGEWAY ESTATE, I WAS WARNED BY THE FBI HEAD OF THE MIAMI-DADE OFFICE TO GET OUT OF THE CASE AND VOLUNTARILY FORFEIT THE MILLIONS OF DOLLARS OWED TO ME, PURSUANT TO THE CONTINGENCY FEE RETAINER AGREEMENT.

I WAS FURTHER WARNED THAT IF I DID NOT WITHDRAW MY REPRESENTATION OF BRIANNA JONES, IN RETALIATION TO MY REFUSAL TO WITHDRAW AS LEGAL COUNSEL TO BRIANNA JONES, AND THEREBY FORFEIT THE MILLIONS OF DOLLARS OWED TO ME IN ATTORNEY'S FEES, MY HUSBAND WOULD BE ATTACKED, SINCE A SEARCH OF MY BACKGROUND PRODUCED NO DEROGATORY INFORMATION THAT COULD BE USED BY THE FBI TO BLACKMAIL ME.

FOLLOWING MY REFUSAL TO GET OUT OF THE CASE AND AFTER CONSULTATION WITH MY HUSBAND, ON OR ABOUT JANUARY 1997, A POLITICALLY MOTIVATED CRIMINAL PROSECUTION WAS LAUNCHED AGAINST MY HUSBAND, THEN SERVING AS DIRECTOR OF D.C. PUBLIC LIBRARY AND PAST PRESIDENT OF THE AMERICAN LIBRARY ASSOCIATION.

THEREAFTER, OUR NIGHTMARE, BROUGHT ON BY THE D.C. JUDICIAL AND FBI CO-CONSPIRATORS OF THE CRIMINAL ENTERPRISE BEGAN. MY HUSBAND WAS INDICTED. HIS AFFLICTION WITH MULTIPLE CHRONIC ILLNESSES RENDERED HIM PHYSICALLY UNABLE TO WITHSTAND THE NECESSARY RIGOROUS PREPARATION FOR TRIAL THAT WOULD BE CONDUCTED BY HIS ATTORNEYS. CONSEQUENTLY, HE PLEADED GUILTY TO A CONFLICT-OF-INTEREST FELONY IN CONNECTION WITH HIS ALLEGED MISAPPROPRIATION OF AN ESTIMATED $24,000 IN D.C. LIBRARY FUNDS WHILE PRESIDENT OF THE AMERICAN LIBRARY ASSOCIATION.

THE D.C. JUDICIAL AND FBI CO-CONSPIRATORS HAD DESIGNED AND TIMED THE LAUNCH OF THE POLITICALLY MOTIVATED CRIMINAL PROSECUTION OF MY HUSBAND SO THAT WHILE D.C. COURT JUDGE RICHARD MANDARIN, A KEY D.C. JUDICIAL CO-CONSPIRATOR, WAS BUSY ISSUING HIS COURT ORDER DIRECTING THE $40 PLUS MILLION DOLLARS IN LOTTERY PROCEEDS, STILL OWED TO WILLIE LEE RIDGEWAY, BE PAID TO THE FLORIDA LAW FIRM REPRESENTING THE RIDGEWAY ESTATE, I WAS BUSY ASSISTING MY HUSBAND AND HIS ATTORNEYS WITH HIS LEGAL DEFENSE TO THE CRIMINAL INDICTMENT, IN ADDITION TO MAINTAINING AN ACTIVE CIVIL LAW PRACTICE AS A SOLO TRIAL ATTORNEY IN WASHINGTON, D.C.

THE ODYSSEY OF JUDICIAL CORRUPTION

THE POLITICALLY MOTIVATED CRIMINAL INVESTIGATION, PROSECUTION, FELONY CONVICTION, HOUSE ARREST AND SUPERVISED PROBATION BROUGHT WITH IT ALL THE CHARACTERISTIC HANDPRINTS AND HALLMARKS OF HELL'S KITCHEN AND THE EVIL ONE, THE PRESENCE OF THE ADVERSARY ON STEROIDS, AND THE CASCADE OF ECONOMIC, SOCIAL, MEDICAL, EMOTIONAL PAIN AND SUFFERING AND THE DEEP AND PROTRACTED TRAUMA THAT GOES WITH THE TERRITORY OF A POLITICALLY MOTIVATED CRIMINAL PROSECUTION AND THE SUBSEQUENT GUILTY PLEA TO A FELONY CONVICTION.

OUR LIVES WOULD NEVER BE THE SAME.

MY VALIANT ENDURANCE OF THIS DARKEST PERIOD IN MY LIFE CAN ONLY BE ATTRIBUTED TO MY LIFETIME, INTIMATE RELATIONSHIP WITH THE HOLY SPIRIT; AND MY KNOWLEDGE THAT JUST AS GOD HAD GIVEN SATAN PERMISSION TO ATTACK JOB AND HIS FAMILY, HE HAD SIMILARLY GIVEN SATAN HIS PERMISSION NEEDED TO ATTACK ME AND MY HUSBAND.

INSPITE OF THE RUTHLESSNESS AND RELENTLESSNESS OF THE GOVERNMENT'S ATTACK ON US, AND IN FURTHERANCE AND PROMOTION OF THE D.C. JUDICIAL AND FBI CONSPIRACY AND CRIMINAL ENTERPRISE, ORGANIZED AND EXCUTED FOR THE SOLE PURPOSE OF SWINDLING AND DEFRAUDING ME OUT OF AN ESTIMATED $50 MILLION IN ATTORNEY'S FEES, LIKE JOB, I DECIDED AND RESOLVED THAT *"THOUGH HE SLAY ME, YET WILL I TRUST IN HIM." (JOB: 13:15 KJV)*

I REASONED FROM A FAITH PERSPECTIVE THAT GOD LOVED ME UNCONDITIONALLY AND MOREOVER, WHATEVER FIERY FURNACE GOD ALLOWED THE ADVERSARY TO PUT US IN, GOD CONTROLLED THE THERMOSTAT THAT SET AND REGULATED THE HEAT OF THE FURNACE.

DURING THIS TIME OF DEEPEST HEARTACHE, HARDSHIP, TEST AND TRIAL, I WOULD PERIODICALLY REMIND MYSELF THAT SATAN HAD TO FIRST GET GOD'S PERMISSION BEFORE HE COULD TOUCH JOB AND HIS FAMILY.

MY FAITH AND TIME IN THE WORD OF GOD HAD TAUGHT ME YEARS EARLIER THROUGH PAUL'S TEACHINGS, THAT FOR THE CHILD OF GOD AND DAUGHTER OF THE KING, *"AND WE KNOW THAT GOD IS CAUSING ALL THINGS TO WORK TOGETHER FOR GOOD FOR THOSE WHO LOVE GOD AND ARE THE CALLED ACCORDING TO HIS PURPOSE."* (ROMANS 8:28) THIS VERSE OF SCRIPTURE HAD BEEN MY ANCHOR IN TIMES OF DEEP TRIAL AND TESTING. IT WOULD NOW BE THIS PARTICULAR TEACHING OF PAUL WHICH WOULD KEEP ME GOING WHEN NOTHING ELSE COULD. PAUL'S ADMONITION HAD BROUGHT ME OUT OF FIERY FURNACES AND DEEP PITS TOO MANY TIMES TO REMEMBER OR COUNT. AND PAUL'S ADMONITION WOULD NOT FAIL ME NOW.

THE DEPUTY CLERK: YOUR HONOR, CALLING THE CASE OF BARBARA WASHINGTON FRANKLIN VERSUS BRIANNA JONES, CIVIL ACTION 4417-2009; IN THE MATTER OF BRIANNA JONES CCC-12011.

PLEASE IDENTIFY YOURSELVES FOR THE RECORD.

MS. FRANKLIN: GOOD AFTERNOON, YOUR HONOR. BARBARA WASHINGTON FRANKLIN, YOUR HONOR, PLAINTIFF PRO SE. EXCUSE ME, YOUR HONOR.

MS. JONES: GOOD AFTERNOON, YOUR HONOR, BRIANNA JONES, DEFENDANT PRO SE AT THIS TIME.

THE COURT: GOOD AFTERNOON.

HOW ARE YOU DOING?

MS. JONES: I'M OKAY. THANK YOU.

THE COURT: GOOD. GOOD. YOU-------YOU CONTINUE TO HAVE SUPPORT AT LEAST INSOFAR AS THERE----- THERE'S A PERSON WHO CONTINUES TO CALL MY CHAMBERS ON YOUR BEHALF, WANTING TO KNOW WHAT CAN BE DONE ON YOUR BEHALF.

MS. JONES: WELL, I MADE A CALL TO THOSE INDIVIDUALS ASKING THEM NOT TO CALL YOU. AND SO I WILL TRY TO INITIATE CONTACT AGAIN TO MAKE SURE THAT ---- THAT IT'S FIRM, AND THAT IT'S COMPLETELY UNDERSTOOD NOT TO CALL YOUR CHAMBERS.

THE COURT:	WELL, I MEAN, IT'S------IT'S, YOU KNOW, THE NUMBER IS PUBLIC AND PEOPLE AREN'T PRECLUDED. THERE'S JUST SUCH A LIMITED AMOUNT OF INFORMATION THAT ----- THAT I CAN ACTUALLY GIVE *BECAUSE IT'S NOT CLEAR TO ME WHAT------ CAN BE DONE TO HELP YOU OTHER THAN TO WAIT FOR YOU TO MAKE YOUR MIND UP TO DO WHAT YOU NEED TO DO.*
	COMMENT AND ANALYSIS: #2 BRIANNA JONES IS A DEFENDANT IN CONTEMPT OF JUDGE STARR'S ORDER OF OCTOBER 18, 2010 TO PRODUCE BANK STATEMENTS.
	THEREFORE, IT WAS INAPPROPRIATE FOR JUDGE EKANS TO ASSUME THE JUDICIAL POSTURE OF WAITING FOR BRIANNA JONES TO "MAKE YOUR MIND UP TO DO WHAT YOU NEED TO DO."
MS. JONES:	MY POSITION IS IT'S IT'S STILL THE SAME AS IT HAS BEEN BECAUSE I DON'T KNOW. AND I'VE BEEN FORTHRIGHT AND FORTHCOMING. AND I WOULD HUMBLY ASK THIS COURT TO ALLOW ME TO AT LEAST GET MY AFFAIRS IN ORDER AND BE ABLE TO RETAIN COUNSEL. I WAS I ALSO HAVE A MATTER WITH THE SIMPSONS AND THAT I NEED TO ADDRESS AN ISSUE BECAUSE TIME IS WINDING DOWN, AND SO I'M RUNNING OUT OF TIME WITH REGARD TO THAT.
THE COURT:	I I DON'T KNOW WHAT YOU MEAN.
MS. JONES:	I WAS SERVED, AND SO I HAVE TO ADDRESS THAT AND THE 20 DAYS HAS -----IS ALMOST EXPIRED. SO I NEED TO ADDRESS THAT.
THE COURT:	WELL, I SUPPOSE IF YOU'RE GOING TO ADDRESS THAT IN THE WAY YOU'VE ADDRESSED THIS, THERE'S NO GREAT HURRY.
MS. JONES:	NO, JUDGE.
THE COURT:	I MEAN, YOU ------YOU ENTERED AN AGREEMENT WITH THIS PLAINTIFF WHICH IS A MATTER OF RECORD, AND------- AND YOU'VE STEADFASTLY FAILED TO HONOR THE AGREEMENT.
MS. JONES:	MAY I SPEAK?
THE COURT:	WAS THAT ADDRESSED TO ME?
MS. JONES:	YES, YOUR HONOR.
THE COURT:	I THOUGHT YOU WERE SPEAKING.

MS. JONES:

WITH REGARD TO------IN THE SPIRIT OF FULL DISCLOSURE, I HAD HOPED THAT THE PLAINTIFF WOULD DISCLOSE THAT A FEW ------- AWHILE BACK SHE HAD A SEVERE ANKLE INJURY -- -- A BREAK-------AND THERE WAS A DR. EKANS THAT TREATED HER, AND SHE INTIMATED TO ME NOT ONLY DID HE TREAT HER, BUT THEY WERE----- BECOME CLOSE ASSOCIATES, AND SHE HAD DISCUSSED THE CASE WITH HIM. I HAVE VERIFIABLE EVIDENCE TO THAT FACT, AND I'VE BEEN WAITING FOR HER TO DISCLOSE THAT.

AND, ALSO, IN AUGUST OF 2004, DR. MAX MAXWELL, SR., HER HUSBAND -- --HER DECEASED HUSBAND -- -- HIS MEMORIAL WAS HELD AT THE UNIVERSITY CHAPEL ON WASHINGTON UNIVERSITY CAMPUS HERE IN WASHINGTON, D.C., AND I DON'T KNOW WHAT THE PROTOCOL WAS FOR THAT. BUT HAVING SAID THAT, I WOULD   I JUST DON'T FEEL THAT I CAN GET A FAIR AND EQUITABLE DISPOSITION OF JUSTICE WITH REGARD TO THE FACT THAT SHE'S HAD SUCH CLOSE ASSOCIATIONS.

COMMENT AND ANALYSIS: #3 BRIANNA JONES LIES INCESSANTLY AND SERVES AS A REMINDER THAT, ABOVE ALL, THE ADVERSARY IS A LIAR.

MS. FRANKLIN:

YOUR HONOR, MAY I RESPOND?

THE COURT:

ALL RIGHT.

MS. FRANKLIN:

FIRST OF ALL, I HAVE NEVER HAD A BROKEN ANKLE IN MY LIFE.

SECONDLY, WHATEVER TREATMENT BY DR. EKANS, I DON'T EVER RECALL DISCUSSING WTH HIM, AND MORE IMPORTANTLY, I WOULD NOT DISCUSS ANYTHING WITH DR. EKANS OTHER THAN WHAT I WAS IN HIS OFFICE BEING TREATED FOR.

YOU KNOW, YOUR HONOR, MY HEART GOES OUT ON A NUMBER OF LEVELS, BECAUSE THIS HAS BEEN QUITE AN ORDEAL. AND IN TERMS OF MY WORKING WITH MS. JONES   AND I WAS THINKING ABOUT THIS, THIS MORNING. PART OF WHAT IS NOT A PART OF THE RECORD AND NOT IN THE COURT IS CLEARLY MENTAL HEALTH ISSUES THAT MS. JONES IS STRUGGLING WITH. I HAVE SAID TO HER ON MORE THAN ONE OCCASION, "AFTER THIS IS OVER, IF YOU DON'T USE SOME OF THIS MONEY TO GET HELP, IT'S NOT GOING TO DO YOU ANY GOOD. IF YOU HAD A BROKEN LEG, YOU WOULD GO TO AN ORTHOPEDIC SURGEON. WHEN YOU HAVE EMOTIONAL WOUNDS, YOU WOULD BE VERY WISE TO SEEK THE SUPPORT AND TREATMENT OF GOOD THERAPIST."

THE ODYSSEY OF JUDICIAL CORRUPTION

MS. JONES:	YOUR HONOR, I OBJECT.
THE COURT:	DON'T INTERRUPT.
MS. FRANKLIN:	I -- --I STRUGGLED FOR MANY YEARS WORKING WITH HER, NOT UNDERSTANDING FULLY WHAT I WAS DEALING WITH UNTIL I HAPPENED UPON AN INTERVIEW THAT I WATCHED ON------- I BELIEVE IT WAS BOOK TV AND DR. MARTHA STOUT FROM HARVARD ----- SHE'S A PROFESSOR AT HARVARD -- -- WAS BEING INTERVIEWED ON A BOOK SHE HAD JUST PUBLISHED. I THINK THIS WAS IN 2000 -----SOMETIME AROUND 2005.

AND I WAS JUST COMPLETELY ASTOUNDED BY THE DISCUSSION BECAUSE SO MUCH OF HER DESCRIPTION OF VARIOUS CLIENTS FIT THE DESCRIPTION OF WHAT I WAS DEALING WITH AND HAD BEEN DEALING WITH FOR A NUMBER OF YEARS WITH MS. JONES: THE PATHOLOGICAL LYING; THE LACK OF ANY REMORSE; THE TREATMENT OF OTHERS WITHOUT ANY FEELINGS OF GUILT, WHATSOEVER.

AND I RECOGNIED AT THAT MOMENT IN TIME THAT THESE WERE ISSUES THAT, YOU KNOW, ONE DOES NOT DETECT NORMALLY; THE LACK OF CONSCIENCE -- -- AND THAT'S ABOVE AND BEYOND EVERYTHING ELSE -- -- THE LACK OF CONSCIENCE.

DR. STOUT'S BOOK WAS ENTITLED "THE SOCIOPATH NEXT DOOR." SHE SAID, YOU KNOW, 1 IN 25 AMERICANS HAVE NO CONSCIENCE, LIE PATHOLOGICALLY, NO REMORSE, AND SOMETIMES THEY'RE LIVING RIGHT NEXT DOOR; SOMETIMES IT'S A BOSS; SOMETIMES IT'S A COLLEAGUE; AND SOMETIMES IT'S A CLIENT THAT YOU'RE DEALING WITH. AND THAT PARTICULAR WORK HELPED ME TREMENDOUSLY BECAUSE I WAS ABLE TO SEE VERY CLEARLY.

AND THAT   THOSE CHARACTERISTICS HAVE BEEN DEMONSTRATED REPEATEDLY IN THIS COURTROOM. THAT'S WHY WE CAN'T GET A HANDLE ON THIS. BECAUSE SHE'S OFF IN ANOTHER WORLD COMPLETELY. TOTALLY IN ANOTHER WORLD. AND I'M SYMPATHETIC. I'M VERY SYMPATHETIC. I'M VERY SMPATHETIC. BUT IT'S VERY HARD TO GRASP WHAT SHE'S TALKING ABOUT BECAUSE IT'S -- -- IT'S   SO MUCH IS A FIGMENT OF HER IMAGINATION, AND IN AN ENVIRONMENT AND IN A CONTEXT WHERE SHE'S NOT GETTING THE KIND OF EMOTIONAL HELP AND SUPPORT THAT SHE NEEDS.

AND SO EACH TIME WE COME TO COURT, SHE'S HAD AN OPPORTUNITY TO COME UP WITH SOMETHING ELSE IN HER MIND, YOU KNOW. "IT'S NOT DR. STELLA EKANS THAT I CONSULTED WITH. "NOW IT'S DR. EKANS THAT TREATED ATTORNEY FRANKLIN'S BROKEN ANKLE," AND I'VE NEVER HAD A BROKEN ANKLE IN MY WHOLE LIFE.

AND THIS WILL GO ON, YOUR HONOR, BECAUSE THAT'S THE FIGMENT OF HER   IT'S HER IMAGINATION THAT'S AT WORK HERE. AND IT HAS ABSOLUTELY NOTHING TO DO WITH THE BUSINESS BEFORE THIS COURT, WHICH IS HER BEING IN CONTEMPT OF A COURT ORDER, AND SHE'S BEEN IN CONTEMPT OF THAT ORDER SINCE OCTOBER 25TH.

AND I -- --I   I THOUGHT VERY LONG ABOUT WHETHER I SHOULD EVEN SHARE THIS KIND OF INFORMATION. BUT THE COURT HAS TO UNDERSTAND THE PERSONALITY OR HAVE SOME SENSE OF THE PERSONALITY THAT WE'RE DEALING WITH HERE. AND IT'S GOING TO GO ON LIKE THIS, YOU KNOW. AND DRAGGING OTHER PROFESSIONALS INTO THIS HEARING IS TOTALLY INAPPROPRIATE, BUT IT COMES OUT OF THE PATHOLOGY THAT IS   THAT IS PRESENT HERE. IT COMES OUT OF THAT PATHOLOGY.

I HAVE DEALT WITH HER FOR 15 YEARS, AND I RECOGNIZE SO MUCH SO WHAT SHE'S TALKING ABOUT BECAUSE SHE CAN'T -- -- SHE'S AT A POSITION IN TIME WHERE SHE REALLY CAN'T HELP HERSELF. SHE REALLY CANNOT HELP HERSELF. AND THE HIRING OF OTHER ATTORNEYS AND THE COLLECTION OF FEES, AND YOU HAVE AN ATTORNEY IN THE COURTROOM THAT'S SUING HER ON BEHALF OF HIS CLIENT, AND NOW SHE WANTS TO HIRE HIM TO COLLECT THE FEES. I MEAN, IT'S JUST -- -- IT'S OUT OF TOUCH WITH REALITY.

IT'S JUST TOTALLY OUT OF TOUCH WITH REALITY. AND I DON'T EVER KNOW IF SHE RECALLS HER PRIOR TESTIMONY BEFORE, YOUR HONOR. SHE SAID VERY SPECIFICALLY AT THE ORAL EXAM ON THE 21ST OF JANUARY, SHE   SHE IDENTIFIED THE BANK. SHE TESTIFIED THAT SHE HAD EVEN MET WITH BANKERS AT VARIOUS TIMES. NOW, TODAY, "YOUR HONOR, MY POSITION IS STILL THE SAME. I DON'T KNOW."

IT MAKES NO SENSE. AND, YOUR HONOR, UNLESS WE UNDERSTAND, AS I SAID, THE PERSONALITY THAT WE'RE DEALING WITH HERE, IT MAKES NO SENSE. ANYBODY WITH ANY COMMON SENSE WOULD SAY "WAIT A MINUTE. WHY DID YOU SAY   WHY DID YOU IDENTIFY A BANK AT THE ORAL EXAM BUT YOU JUST COULDN'T REMEMBER THE BRANCH? WHY ARE YOU PLAYING GAMES?"

AND WHAT I'M SAYING TO YOUR HONOR IS, ITS   IT'S BECAUSE OF WHAT SHE STRUGGLES WITH IN TERMS OF HER OWN EMOTIONAL HEALTH AND HER OWN MENTAL HEALTH. AND THAT IS WHY WE SOUGHT OUT DR. EKANS FROM THE VERY BEGINNING, AND THERE WERE OTHER PHYSICIANS AS   AS WELL WHO ACTUALLY WROTE A REPORT FOR US. BUT I -- -- YOU KNOW -- --I'M NOT SURE HOW -- --

HOW WE HANDLE IT, YOUR HONOR, BUT I JUST FELT CONSTRAINED THAT THE COURT HAS -- -- HAS TO UNDERSTAND THAT THAT IS THE BACKGROUND AND THAT IS THE CONTEXT OUT OF WHICH SOME OF HER TESTIMONY IS -- -- IS COMING FROM. AND I DON'T KNOW HOW   AS A RESULT OF THAT HOW VERY RELIABLE THE COURT CAN TAKE HER -- -- HER -- -- THE ALLEGATIONS AND THE STATEMENTS THAT SHE'S   SHE'S MAKING.

I DO KNOW   BECAUSE THIS COURT HAS DEALT SO FORTHRIGHTLY AND PROMPTLY WITH THIS MATTER, I DO KNOW THAT'S A CONCERN TO HER. AND AS I SAID AT THE LAST TIME, SHE DEFINITELY WANTS TO GET OUT FROM UNDER THE JURISDICTION OF THIS COURT. AND SHE WILL SIT OVER AT THE D.C. JAIL -- -- AND EACH AND EVERY TIME SHE COMES BEFORE THE COURT, SHE'S GOING TO HAVE ANOTHER REASON AS TO WHY THIS COURT SHOULD NOT BE HEARING THIS MATTER.

 AND THERE'S ABSOLUTELY NO REASON   AND SHE KNOWS THERE'S NO REASON -- -- THAT THIS COURT SHOULD NOT BE HEARING THIS MATTER. ALL THESE ALLEGATIONS OF THIS DR. EKANS AND THAT DR. EKANS. THIS HAS ABSOLUTELY NOTHING TO DO WITH THIS. BUT THIS IS A PART OF THE CLEVER ASPECT OF TRYING TO PUT RESTRAINTS ON THE COURT OR HAVE THE COURT THINK MAYBE THIS IS NOT SOMETHING I SHOULD BE HEARING.

THANK YOU, YOUR HONOR.

MS. JONES: YOUR HONOR, FIRST I WANT TO SAY THIS IS A HORRIBLE PREVARICATION.

THE COURT:	WELL, WHY DID YOU BRING UP THE ISSUE OF WHETHER OR NOT THE PLAINTIFF HAS HAD AN ANKLE TREATED BY -- --
MS. JONES:	BECAUSE SHE INTIMATED TO ME SHE BROKE HER ANKLE AT ROBBINS.
THE COURT:	OKAY. BUT WHAT---- WHAT IS THE POINT?
MS. JONES:	AND SHE------ AND SHE SPECIFICALLY MENTIONED DR. EKANS OVER AND OVER -- --
THE COURT:	OKAY. BUT WHAT IS THE POINT?
MS. JONES:	I WAITED FOR HER FOR FULL DISCLOSURE WITH REGARD TO HER HONESTY. YOUR HONOR, THIS IS AN ATTEMPT TO NOW SAY MENTAL ISSUES.
	FIRST, FOR THE RECORD, DR. BLACK IN THE -- --IN THE RECORD OF BROWARD COUNTY, SAW ME FOR QUITE SOME TIME AND MADE IT VERY CLEAR THAT I HAD EXCELLENT JUDGMENT AND INSIGHT.
THE COURT:	CAN WE COME BACK TO THIS FIRST MATTER THAT YOU'VE RAISED. YOU'VE RAISED DR. EKANS; YOU'VE RAISED UNIVERSITY CHAPEL. IS IT -- --
	YOU GO AHEAD.
MS. JONES:	I JUST FEEL AS THOUGH AT THIS POINT, YOUR HONOR, THAT THIS ATTORNEY SEEMINGLY HAS SO SUCCINCTLY PERPETRATED THIS FRAUD, YOUR HONOR.
THE COURT:	WHAT FRAUD?
MS. JONES:	THIS FRAUD UPON THE COURT WITH REGARD TO THE WHOLE COMPLAINT.
THE COURT:	IS YOUR SETTLEMENT AGREEMENT A FRAUD?
MS. JONES:	YOUR HONOR, SHE KNEW AT THE TIME OF THE EXECUTION OF THE AGREEMENT I DID NOT HAVE THE FUNDS. I HAVE PHONE RECORDS, YOUR HONOR. I HAVE ALL KINDS OF EVIDENCE THAT SHE -- --
THE COURT:	DID ANYONE -- -- MA' AM. DID ANYONE PUT ANY PRESSURE ON YOU TO ENTER THAT SETTLEMENT AGREEMENT?
MS. JONES:	I DO NOT WANT TO DISCLOSE THE NATURE OF THE RELATIONSHIP. I DID NOT WANT TO PUBLICALLY -- --

COMMENT AND ANALYSIS: #4 HERE BRIANNA JONES BEGINS TO ALLUDE TO AN ILLICIT AND IMMORAL RELATIONSHIP BETWEEN US WHICH WAS FACTUALLY UNTRUE, MORALLY ABHORRENT TO ME, AND AN OBVIOUS FIGMENT OF HER WICKED AND DEMENTED IMAGINATION.

THE COURT: IS THAT NO -- -- IS THAT -- -- IS YOUR ANSWER NO, NO ONE PUT ANY PRESSURE ON YOU TO ENTER A SETTLEMENT AGREEMENT? THAT YOU MADE YOUR MIND UP ON YOUR OWN?

MS. JONES: YES, YOUR HONOR.

THE COURT: OKAY. SO------SO LET'S COME BACK THEN. WHAT IS THE RELEVANCE OF YOU SAYING TODAY THAT MS. FRANKLIN WAS TREATED BY DR. EKANS AND THAT SOMEBODY HAD A FUNERAL AT UNIVERSITY CHAPEL? WHAT --- -- - WHAT ----- WHAT'S THE POINT?

MS. JONES; BECAUSE IT'S -- --I'M ----- I'M STILL IN CUSTODY WITHOUT AN ATTORNEY.

THE COURT: WHY DON'T YOU HAVE AN ATTORNEY?

MS. JONES: BECAUSE I NEED TO BE ABLE TO GET HOME AND END MY AFFAIRS. THE

COURT: WHY DIDN'T YOU BRING AN ATTORNEY WITH YOU? YOU ------- YOU TRAVELED -- --

MS. JONES: BECAUSE I SPOKE WITH HER. I HAVE DOCUMENTED EVIDENCE, YOUR HONOR, WHERE SHE CLEARLY STATED AS----- AS EARLY AS JANUARY. 'WE ARE FORMIDABLE TEAM, BRIANNA. YOU DON'T------ YOU DON'T HAVE TO HAVE AN ATTORNEY."

COMMENT AND ANALYSIS: #5 MORE GRATUITOUS LIES WHICH ARE BRIANNA JONES' CALLING CARDS.

THE COURT: MA' AM -- -- MA' AM, DO YOU UNDERSTAND THAT YOU CAN GET A LAWYER ANY TIME YOU WANT?

MS. JONES: BUT I DID NOT UNDERSTAND THE SERIOUSNESS OF THIS, YOUR HONOR.

THE COURT: NOW, YOU DON'T? HOW LONG HAVE YOU BEEN OVER AT THE JAIL?

MS. JONES: BUT------ SINCE THE 25TH. WHEN I CAME ON THE 21ST, THAT'S WHEN I FULLY UNDERSTOOD.

THE COURT:	YOU UNDERSTAND IT'S SERIOUS NOW?
MS. JONES:	I UNDERSTAND IT THE 21ST OF JANUARY. BUT, YOUR HONOR, I DID NOT, UNDER ANY CIRCUMSTANCE ------SHE ENGAGED ME IN CONVERSATION.
THE COURT:	MS. JONES, YOU'RE DIRECTING YOUR REMARKS IN THE WRONG TO THE WRONG SUBECT MATTER. YOU WANT TO TURN THIS HEARING INTO YOU KNOW, ALLEGAIONS AGAINST MS. FRANKLIN, AND THEN MS. FRANKLIN GETS BAITED, AND SHE TURNS AND MAKES ALLEGATIONS ABOUT YOU. THAT'S NOT WHY WE'RE HERE.
	WE'RE HERE BECAUSE YOU ENTERED AN AGREEMENT TO PAY THE PLAINTIFF MONEY THAT REPRESENTS HER LEGAL FEE, AND YOU HAVE SO FAR STEADFASTLY REFUSED TO DO THAT HAVING THE ABILITY TO DO IT.
MS. JONES:	YOUR HONOR, I HAVE A PLAN, AND THE PLAN IS TO GO BACK TO FLORIDA, DEAL WITH THE -- --
THE COURT:	CAN YOU COME UP WITH A PLAN THAT DOESN'T INVOLVE BACK TO FLORIDA?
MS. JONES:	BECAUSE I HAVE TO HAVE THE ATTORNEYS THAT DEALT WITH ME THERE.
THE COURT:	THEY DON'T KNOW HOW TO GET HERE?
MS. JONES:	YOUR HONOR, I HAVE -- -- I HAVE----- I HAVE MATTERS AND BUSINESS I HAVE TO TEND TO. I HAVE TO SHUT MY HOME DOWN. THERE'S NOBODY THERE TO ASSIST ME.
THE COURT:	WHY DO YOU HAVE TO SHUT YOUR HOME DOWN?
MS. JONES:	BECAUSE I HAVE -- -- EVERYTHING I HAVE IS WITH ME. I CAN'T DO ANYTHING FROM HERE. I ASKED FOR -- --
THE COURT:	EVERY----- EXCUSE ME. EVERYTHING YOU HAVE IS WITH YOU?
MS. JONES:	I -- -- I BROUGHT WITH ME, IN TERMS OF FINANCIALS -- --
THE COURT:	WHY DON'T YOU PRODUCE THOSE? THAT'S WHAT WE'VE ASKED YOU FOR.

MS. JONES:	IN TERMS OF MY ------ IN TERMS OF MY CHECKBOOK AND THAT SORT OF THING?
THE COURT:	YES.
MS. JONES:	AND I NEED TO GO BACK -- --
THE COURT:	WHERE IS THAT?
MS. JONES:	--------------------------------STATEMENT.
	THAT'S WITH -- -- THAT'S WITH THE -- -- THAT'S WITH THE ------ IT'S IN LOCKUP. BUT I HAVE TO DEAL WITH MY AFFAIRS YOUR HONOR -- --
THE COURT:	ITS IN LOCKUP.
MS. JONES:	YES.
THE COURT:	YOU MEAN THE DAY THAT YOU WERE HERE WITH YOUR BAGS, YOU DIDN'T SAY TO ME "HERE, JUDGE EKANS, HERE'S MY FINANCIAL PAPERS; HERE'S MY CHECKBOOK."
	COMMENT AND ANALYSIS: #6 WHILE BRIANNA JONES WAS FULLY AWARE THAT HER CHECKBOOK HAD ABSOLUTELY NOTHING TO DO WITH AN ACCOUNTING OR EVIDENCE OF THE MILLIONS OF DOLLARS IN CASE SETTLEMENT PROCEEDS, **JUDGE EKANS CONTINUED TO GASLIGHT THE ISSUE.**
MS. JONES:	THAT'S ----- THAT'S BEEN WITH ME THE WHOLE TIME.
THE COURT:	WHY DIDN'T YOU GIVE IT TO US?
MS. JONES:	YOUR HONOR, I JUST ----- I'VE BEEN SO CLOSE WITH ATTORNEY FRANKLIN -- --
THE COURT:	IN OTHER WORDS, IF I SEND YOU BACK TO THE JAIL AND BRING YOU BACK HERE TOMORROW, YOU'LL BRING ME YOUR CHECK BOOK?
MS. JONES:	I HAVE MY CHECKBOOK, OF COURSE. I HAVE MY CREDIT CARDS.
THE COURT:	OKAY.
MS. JONES:	I HAVE THOSE THINGS, YOUR HONOR.
THE COURT:	THAT COULD WORK. WE CAN DO THAT.
MS. JONES:	BUT, YOUR HONOR, IF I CAN -- --

THE COURT:	I'LL RECESS THIS HEARING THEN UNTIL TOMORROW.
MS.. JONES:	CAN WE MAKE -- -- BUT WITH ALL DUE RESPECT, CAN WE HAVE THE -- -- THE HEARING EARLY, SO THAT I CAN POSSIBLY BECAUSE TOMORROW I WILL LOSE ALL MY BELONGINGS. IT'S THE LAST DAY, AND THEY WILL DISPOSE OF THEM, IT'S THE 15TH DAY. AND SO THAT'S WHY I WOULD LIKE TO YOUR HONOR, I WANT TO DEAL WITH THIS ISSUE, BUT ALSO I WANT TO SAY FOR THE RECORD, I HAVE NEVER EVER INDULGED IN NARCOTICS. I'M NOT AN ABUSER OF ALCOHOL.
THE COURT:	LISTEN. LISTEN. LISTEN. WHAT IS THE -- --
MS. JONES:	I WANT TO MAKE A POINT -- --
THE COURT:	WHAT IS THE POINT?
MS. JONES:------------------------------	THAT I'VE ALWAYS SAID NO MATTER WHAT HAS HAPPENED TO ME, I WANT TO BE FULLY ALERT, NOT MEDICATED, AND I HAVE A STRONG FAITH BASE.
THE COURT;	OKAY.
MS. JONES:	SO TO COME IN HERE TODAY AND SAY I HAVE MENTAL PROBLEMS, WELL, YOU'VE GOT TO TRUST IN ME TO STAND BEFORE MEN AND WOMEN -- --
THE COURT:	MS. JONES, DO YOU UNDERSTAND THAT THAT IS NOT A CONCERN FOR US IN THIS HEARING?
MS JONES:	VERY WELL. VERY WELL.
THE COURT:	IF -- -- IF YOU WANT TO YOU KNOW, IF YOU WANT TO WRITE MS. FRANKLIN LETTERS AND TELL HER ALL ABOUT THAT, WHY DON'T YOU DO THAT? BUT WE'RE TRYING TO ACCOMPLISH SOMETHING THAT'S VERY FOCUSED, VERY MUCH DIRECTED TOWARDS A SETTLEMENT THAT YOU HAD IN THIS COURTHOUSE TO PAY YOUR LAWYER -- -- A TRIAL LAWYER -- -- A FEE.
	NOW, IF YOU BROUGHT CHECKBOOKS AND OTHER FINANCIAL RECORDS, GOD KNOWS, WHY DIDN'T YOU GIVE THAT TO ME? I -- --
MS. JONES:	THEY TOOK THEM SO FAST FROM ME AND SAID THEY -- --
THE COURT:	OH, PLEASE. PLEASE. PLEASE.
MS. JONES:	I HAVE RECORDS OF ALL OF THEM HERE.

THE COURT:	ALL OF WHAT?
MS. JONES:	ALL -- -- ALL OF MY BELONGINGS INCLUDING THE--------THEY HAVE THE CHECKS, THE NUMBER OF CHECKS AND EVERYTHING. THEY HAVE EVERYTHING HERE IT'S -- --
THE COURT:	LET ME SEE THAT. GIVE IT TO THE MARSHAL.
MS. JONES:	YOUR HONOR, IF I MAY BE RELEASED SO I WON'T LOSE MY BELONGINGS.
THE COURT:	YOU'RE NOT GOING TO LOSE ANY BELONGINGS.
	YEAH. I THINK THIS WILL GET US SOMEWHERE. HERE'S A MASTERCARD, A VISA CARD AND A DEBIT VISA CARD FROM BANK OF AMERICA.

COMMENT AND ANALYSIS: #7 BRIANNA JONES WAS UNDER COURT ORDER OF JUDGE KATE STARR TO PRODUCE BANK STATEMENTS OF THE FLORIDA CASE SETTLEMET PROCEEDS IN EXCESS OF $34 MILLION AND ON DEPOSIT AT BANK OF AMERICA.

BRIANNA JONES' MASTERCARD AND DEBIT VISA CARD HAD NO RELEVANCE TO THE BANK STATEMENTS OF THE SETTLEMENT PROCEEDS.

THIS WAS SIMPLY ANOTHER EXHAUSTING INSTANCE OF JUDGE EKANS REVELING IN ENDLESS JUDICIAL GASLIGHTING AND TO MY OBVIOUS PREJUDICE AND DETRIMENT.

MS. JONES:	AND IF I COULD POSSIBLY MAKE A CALL TO MY BANK, I COULD PROBABLY HAVE THEM FAX OVER THE MOST RECENT BANK STATEMENT.
THE COURT:	IT DIDN'T OCCUR TO YOU TO DO THAT BEFORE?
MS. JONES:	IT OCCURRED TO ME ON THE 25TH WHEN THE MARSHAL SAID, "DO YOU KNOW WHY YOU'RE BEING -- -- YOU'RE BEING ARRESTED? **YOU DIDN'T BRING YOUR BANK STATEMENTS."**

COMMENT AND ANALYSIS: #8 EVEN THE U.S. MARSHAL RECOGNIZES THAT BRIANNA JONES IS BEING JAILED BECAUSE OF HER REPEATED *FAILURE TO PRODUCE BANK STATEMENTS*. NEVERTHELESS, JUDGE EKANS INTENTIONALLY AND PURPOSELFULLY CONTINUES TO REFER TO BRIANNA JONES' FAILURE TO PRODUCE *"FINANCIAL PAPERS."* HOWEVER, NEITHER JUDGE EKANS NOR BRIANNA JONES INTENDS TO REFER TO BANK STATEMENTS OF THE SETTLEMENT PROCEEDS.

MS. FRANKLIN:	YOUR HONOR, MAY I SPEAK?

YOUR HONOR, AT ONE POINT YOU ASKED A QUESTION WITH REGARD TO THE SETTLEMENT AGREEMENT, AND I RECALL THE DEFENDANT SAYING SOMETHING ABOUT IT WASN'T IN STORAGE. IT'S NOT IN HER STORAGE NOW, BUT THAT SHE HAD PROVIDED A COPY TO BAR COUNSEL. IS IT MY UNDERSTANDING THAT SHE DOES NOT HAVE THE SETTLEMENT AGREEMENT? BECAUSE THE SETTLEMENT AGREEMENT IS THE FOUNDATION DOCUMENT WITH REGARD TO PROCEEDS THAT ARE DUE, SETTLEMENT PROCEEDS THAT ARE DUE, AS WELL AS THE WHATEVER ACCUMULATED INTEREST WOULD BE COMPOUNDED ON THE PROCEEDS. AND SHE'S STILL SAYING THAT SHE DOES NOT HAVE THE SETTLEMENT AGREEMENT AT ALL? |
| THE COURT: | IT'S NOT CLEAR TO ME WHAT MS. JONES IS SAYING. |
| MS. JONES: | **THE BAR COUNSEL ----- THE BAR COUNSEL WAS ABLE TO CONFIRM THE SETTLEMENT.**

COMMENT AND ANALYSIS: # 9 JUDGE EKANS' PREMEDITATED SILENCE COMMUNICATES LOUDLY THAT HE HAS NO INTEREST WHATSOEVER IN THE INVOLVEMENT, INVESTIGATION OR FINDINGS OF D.C. BAR COUNSEL WITH REGARD TO THE ISSUE OF BRIANNA JONES' SETTLEMENT AGREEMENT WITH THE FLORIDA ESTATE, OR THE FACT THAT SHE HAS A SUBSTANTIAL AND OUTSTANDING CLAIM AGAINST THE RIDGEWAY ESTATE THAT HAS BEEN CONFIRMED BY THE OFFICE OF D.C. BAR COUNSEL.

YOUR HONOR, IF IT PLEASE THE COURT, MAY I HAVE SOME WATER? |
| THE COURT: | I DON'T HAVE ANY WATER. |
| MS. JONES: | WITH REGARD TO BAR COUNSEL. BAR COUNSEL WAS ABLE TO CONFIRM THE SETTLEMENT. UM, JUST LIKE I THOUGHT I HAD LOST THE COPY OF THE -- --OF THE -- -- WILL. I WAS ABLE TO FIND IT, AND I'M SURE I CAN ---I CAN FIND A COPY OF THE SETTLEMENT AGREEMENT BECAUSE I'VE HAD TO MOVE BECAUSE OF THREATS AND SECURITY CONCERNS. |

AND SO I DID NOT THINK I WOULD FIND A COPY OF THE WILL, BUT I WAS ABLE TO FIND IT. SO I'M SURE I CAN PRODUCE A COPY OF THE SETTLEMENT AGREEMENT. AND, MORE IMPORTANTLY, WHAT THIS DID WAS USE MY CLAIM IN ORDER TO GET THE -- -- THE--- WAS A NEW ADVERTISED PRICE. THEY USED MY CLAIM AND MATTER OF FACT, YOUR HONOR, HE HEARING WAS HERE.

WHILE I WAS IN FLORIDA, THE HEARING WAS HERE AND THE ATTORNEY WAS NOT ON IT. SHE DIDN'T FIND OUT UNTIL LATER ON THAT THEY USED MY CLAIM IN ORDER TO GET THE PAYMENT IN A LUMP SUM PAYMENT.

THE COURT:	WHO IS THE "THEY?" YOU ALWAYS TALK TO ME ABOUT "THEY." WHO IS THEY?
MS. FRANKLIN:	BACK TO THEY.
MS. JONES:	THE ATTORNEYS FOR THE FOR THE DECEDENT. THEY WERE ABLE TO USE THE SCHEDULE FOR MAY THE 6TH, 1997, AND IT WAS GIVEN DOCMENTATION THAT WE WERE TO ATTEND ON JUNE 22ND, 1997. AND I SAID TO THE-TO THE ATTORNEY – I SAID – ATTORNEY OF THE PLAINTIFF. I SAID, "THEY'RE PULLING SOMETHING. THEY HAVE ME, AND THEY'RE FIGHTING ME ALL ALONG IN BROWARD COUNTY, AND YET THEY'RE -- --THEY'RE MAKING A RECORD IN BROWARD, AND THEY'RE COLLECTING IN MY NAME IN THE DISTRICT. AND LOW AND BEHOLD AS THEY WOULD, THEY HAD THE HEARING ON MAY THE 6TH, 1997, WITHOUT INFORMING US.

AND SO IT'S BEEN THAT WAY, YOUR HONOR. GOD KNOWS TO BE IN THAT PLACE, IT'S AN EXPERIENCE I HAVE NEVER EVER HAD. I'VE HEARD STORIES I COULD NEVER EVEN FATHOM. AND SO IF I KNEW AT PRESENT AT THIS MOMENT WHERE THOSE FUNDS ARE, I WOULD GLADLY, IMMEDIATELY, YOUR HONOR. BUT I HAVE AN IDEA OF THE PERSON THAT
-    THAT TELEPHONED HER – HER OFFICE, AND THAT'S THE PERSON THAT I WANT TO HIRE COUNSEL TO SEEK OUT BECAUSE THAT PERSON CALLED HER OFFICE AND ADMITTED WRONGDOING THAT HERE WAS SOMETHING -- THEY WERE MISAPPROPRIATED WITH REGARD TO THE FUNDS.

COMMENT AND ANALYSIS: #10 JUDGE RICHARD MANDARIN, A KEY D.C. JUDICIAL CO-CONSPIRATOR, SCHEDULED THE IMPORTANT COURT HEARING ON JUNE 22, 1997 FOR THE PURPOSE OF ANNOUNCING THE LEGAL REPRESENTATIVES OF THE RIDGEWAY ESTATE AS THE LAWFUL RECIPIENTS OF THE $40 MILLION PLUS LOTTERY PROCEEDS OWED TO WILLIE LEE RIDGEWAY, AND IN RESPONSE TO THE STAKEHOLDER LAWSUIT BROUGHT BY THE DISTRICT OF COLUMBIA AND THE D.C. LOTTERY AGENCY.

JUDGE MANDARIN, THEREAFTER, WITH CONSIDERED PREMEDITATION, AND IN COMMITMENT TO HIS KEY ROLE IN THE D.C. JUDICIAL AND FBI CONSPIRACY AND CRIMINAL ENTERPRISE, AND WITHOUT NOTICE TO ME OR BRIANNA JONES, ACCELERATED AND CHANGED THE DATE OF THE JUNE 22, 1997 COURT HEARING TO MAY 6, 1997. THIS IS AN EXAMPLE OF A CORRUPT D.C. COURT JUDGE'S WIELDING OF *ABSOLUTE JUDICIAL DISCRETION* IN FURTHERANCE OF THE MISSION OF THE D.C JUDICIAL AND FBI CONSPIRACY AND CRIMINAL ENTERPRISE AND HIS OWN PREMEDITATED SELF-ENRICHMENT.

MS. FRANKLIN:

YOUR HONOR, THIS TESTIMONY IS SO BEYOND ANY RHYME OR REASON OF WHY WE'RE HERE, AND THIS IS WHAT HAPPENS EACH TIME. SHE -- -- SHE DIBBLES AND DABS AND BRINGS IN THE MERITS, AND ALL OF IT ALWAYS IS CENTERED ON HER GOAL TO STAY IN CONTEMPT OF THIS COURT'S ORDER. THAT IS HER GOAL. SHE IS MEETING HER GOAL. SHE IS NOT COMING FORTH WITH ANY INFORMATION. SHE'S TESTIFYING, "YES, I DEALT WITH THIS BANK. YES, I MET WITH BANKERS. NOW I HAVE NO KNOWLEDGE. I DON'T KNOW." JUST A GAME.

FROM -- - FROM JANUARY 21ST, HER FIRST APPEARANCE BEFORE YOUR HONOR UNTIL NOW, ONE WORD DESCRIBES HER BEHAVIOR: "GAME." AND SHE WILL CONTINUE. NO LOSS TO HER. MAKE SURE ALL HER THINGS ARE PRESERVED. SHE'LL CONTINUE.

MS. JONES: YOUR HONOR, THAT'S NOT THE CASE. I SUFFER. I BATHE INCESSANTLY. THIS IS THE WORST THING THAT COULD HAPPEN TO ME, SO TO THINK THAT I WOULD HAVE THIS AS A GAME AND TO SHARE PUBLIC FACILITIES, THIS IS ABSOLUTELY -- -- AND TO THINK EACH DAY THAT I -- -- I'M   I'M ENDURING THIS, IF I HAD THE ANSWER FOR YOU, YOU WOULD HAVE HAD IT ON THE 21ST, YOUR HONOR. AND I CERTAINLY WOULDN'T COME BACK INTO TOWN THINKING THAT I HAD THE ANSWER ON THE 25TH, YOUR HONOR. I WOULD ASK YOU THIS DAY, I BESEECH YOU, IF YOU WOULD RELEASE ME THIS DAY SO I CAN AT LEAST ATTEND TO MY AFFAIRS AND RETURN, AND AT LEAST HAVE COUNSEL, AND WE GET ANSWERS *SO THAT THE PLAINTIFF CAN BE PAID AS PER AGREEMENT.*

MS. FRANKLIN: YOUR HONOR, AT THE LAST HEARING SHE BEGGED YOUR HONOR TO RELEASE HER FOR 48 HOURS SO SHE COULD RETAIN COUNSEL TO COLLECT -- -- AND I'M SURE IN HER MIND THAT WAS A TERM OF ART -- -- COLLECT FEES. THAT WAS HER LAST   THAT WAS HER PRIOR REQUEST: "48 HOURS IS ALL I NEED. I CAN GO TO FLORIDA, RETAIN COUNSEL AND COLLECT THE ATTORNEY FEES."

I MEAN -- --

MS. JONES: BECAUSE I CAN GO WHERE   I CAN GET TO WHERE THE HEAD OF THE FIRM -- -- AND I CAN GET ANSWERS. I HAVE FRIENDS IN THE COURT THERE. AND I'LL PROVIDE YOU WITH ALL OF THOSE ANSWERS, ATTORNEY ATTORNEY FRANKLIN.

MS. FRANKLIN: YOUR HONOR , SHE'S NOT TO BE BELIEVED.

MS. JONES: YOUR HONOR, I -- --

MS. FRANKLIN: SHE'S NOT TO BE BELIEVED.

AND IF THERE IS   IF THERE IS KNOWLEDGE WITH REGARD TO WHERE THE FUNDS ARE, WHO IS HOLDING THE FUNDS, THOSE PERSONS OR INDIVIDUALS CAN BE REACHED BY PHONE. THEY CAN BE REACHED BY FAX. YOU DON'T HAVE TO FLY ALL THE WAY TO FLORIDA AND HAVE A FACE-TO-FACE MEETING WITH INDIVIDUALS TO DETERMINE WHERE PROCEEDS ARE.

MS. JONES: YOUR HONOR -- --

MS. FRANKLIN: I MEAN -- --

THE COURT:	EXCUSE ME. EXCUSE ME.
MS. FRANKLIN:	TO EVEN -- --
THE COURT:	EXCUSE ME. EXCUSE ME.
MS. FRANKLIN:	I'M SORRY, YOUR HONOR.
THE COURT:	I'M GOING TO RELEASE YOU, AND HAVE YOU SIGN A NOTICE TO BE IN -- -- BACK HERE IN THE DISTRICT OF COLUMBIA IN THIS COURTHOUSE MONDAY.
MS. JONES:	VERY WELL.
THE COURT:	WE'LL SEE HOW YOU ----- HOW YOU DECIDE TO PROCEED.
MS. JONES:	I EXPECT A LOT OF THINGS WILL BE ACCOMPLISHED.
THE COURT:	WELL, WE'RE GOING TO SEE. I ----- DON'T KNOW. UM, WE'LL SEE.
MS. JONES:	THANK YOU.
THE COURT:	HAVE HER SIGN A NOTICE TO BE IN 517.
MS. JONES:	517.
MS. FRANKLIN:	YOUR HONOR, WHAT TIME ON MONDAY?
THE COURT:	10:00 O'CLOCK. I'VE ALWAYS THOUGHT 10:00 O'CLOCK WAS SUCH A CIVILIZED TIME.
	WHAT WAS YOUR QUESTION, MA' AM?
MS. JONES:	IS THIS NOW A CRIMINAL MATTER?
THE COURT:	IT WILL BE MONDAY.
MS.. JONES:	VERY WELL.
THE COURT:	LET ME BE CLEAR WITH YOU. I'VE KEPT YOU IN JAIL NOW FOR A WEEK AND A HALF -- --
MS. JONES:	THIRTEEN DAYS.

THE COURT:------------------------------WITH THE KEY TO THE JAIL IN YOUR HANDS. THE ONLY THING THAT YOU NEED TO DO TO GET YOURSELF OUT OF CIVIL CONTEMPT OF COURT IS TO PRODUCE FINANCIAL PAPERS IN ACCORDANCE WITH THE SETTLEMENT AGREEMENT THAT YOU MADE AND IN ACCORDANCE WITH THE ORDER THAT JUDGE STARR ISSUED FOR YOU TO BRING TO THE ORAL EXAMINATION. YOU REFUSED TO DO THAT.

SO I'M RELEASING NOW. I'M GIVING YOU AN OPPORTUNITY TO RETURN TO YOUR HOME STATE TO MAKE WHATEVER ARRANGEMENTS YOU NEED TO MAKE TO EITHER SATISFY THE COURT ORDER PURSUANT TO YOUR SETTLEMENT, OR YOU'LL COME BACK HERE AND YOU'LL FACE CRIMINAL CONTEMPT OF COURT.

COMMENT AND ANALYSIS: # 11 JUDGE EKANS INTENTIONALLY AND PURPOSEFULLY MISCONSTRUES AND MISCHARACTERIZES THE MANDATE OF JUDGE STARR'S ORDER. JUDGE STARR'S ORDER MANDATED THAT BRIANNA JONES PRODUCE AND TURN OVER TO ME *"BANK STATEMENTS OF THE SETTLEMENT PROCEEDS"* ON DEPOSIT AT BANK OF AMERICA.

JUDGE EKANS PURPOSEFULLY AND INTENTIONALLY REVISES JUDGE STARR'S ORDER AND STATES THAT IT MANDATES THAT BRIANNA JONES PRODUCE *"FINANCIAL PAPERS."* THIS IS A PART OF THE "BIG LIE" THAT IS REPEATED AND PERPETRATED INTENTIONALLY AND PURPOSEFULLY BY JUDGE EKANS THROUGHOUT HIS ADJUDICATION OF MY LAWSUIT AND IN KEEPING WITH HIS UNEQUIVOCAL COMMITMENT TO THE SUCCESS OF THE D.C. JUDICIAL AND FBI CONSPIRACY AND CRIMINAL ENTERPRISE AND ITS MISSION TO DEFRAUD ME OF STATED ATTORNEY'S FEES.

THE COURT RECORD VERIFIES THAT BRIANNA JONES RETURNED TO COURT FROM FLORIDA AT THE POSTPONED AND RESCHEDULED COURT HEARING ON MARCH 11, 2011. *SHE APPEARED WITHOUT AN ATTORNEY AND WITHOUT THE BANK STATEMENTS MANDATED BY JUDGE STARR'S ORDER. SHE REMAINED IN CONTEMPT OF JUDGE STARR'S ORDER AND SUFFERED NO FURTHER PENALTIES FOR THE REMAINDER OF THE EIGHT MONTHS OF JUDGE EKANS' ADJUDICATION OF MY LAWSUIT.*

MS. JONES: VERY WELL.

THE COURT: NOW, THE SENTENCE FOR A CRIMINAL CONTEMPT IS DIFFERENT FROM CIVIL CONTEMPT. AND WHEN YOU CONSULT WITH YOUR ATTORNEY, YOU MIGHT WANT TO CONSULT ABOUT THAT, BECAUSE THE COMPLEXION OF THIS WILL CHANGE. DO YOU HAVE ANY QUESTIONS?

MS. JONES:	YOU'VE BEEN VERY CLEAR.
THE COURT:	GOOD.
MS. JONES:	AND THIS TIME I COMPLETELY UNDERSTAND.
THE COURT:	WELL, GOOD. STEP TO THE RIGHT.
MS. JONES:	THANK YOU.
THE COURT:	NO, THAT WON'T DO. I DON'T WANT ----- I'M NOT GOING TO WRITE YOU A LETTER. I HAVE TO KNOW WHERE TO SEND THE MARSHALS, SO I DON'T WANT A LETTER P.O. BOX. I WANT AN ADDRESS, A VERIFIABLE ADDRESS.
MS. JONES:	IT'S THE SAME ONE THAT'S ON THE RECORD. IT'S ALSO ON MY CHECKBOOK.
THE COURT:	WELL, I HAVEN'T SEEN YOUR CHECKBOOK.
	ALL RIGHT. RECESS -- --
MS. JONES:	YOUR HONOR, MAY I BE EXCUSED? MAY I BE EXCUSED?
THE COURT:	YES. THANK YOU.
MS. JONES:	THANK YOU.
THE COURT:	SEE YOU MONDAY.
MS. JONES:	THANK YOU.

(PROCEEDINGS ADJOURNED AT APPROXIMATELY 12:51 P.M.)

SUPERIOR COURT OF THE DISTRICT OF COLUMB IA
CIVIL DIVISION
WASHINGTON, D.C.

THE HONORABLE MATTHEW D. EKANS, ASSOCIATE JUDGE, PRESIDING

THE FOLLOWING IS THE ENTIRE OFFICIAL COURT TRANSCRIPT OF THE
FEBRUARY 14, 2011 COURT PROCEEDING
ANNOTATED BY THE AUTHOR'S PERTINENT COMMENTARY AND ANALYSIS

FEBRUARY 14, 2011

P R O C E E D I N G S

THE DEPUTY CLERK:	YOUR HONOR, CALLING THE CASE OF BARBARA WASHINGTON FRANKLIN VERSUS BRIANNA JONES, CIVIL ACTION 4417-2009; AND IN THE MATTER OF BRIANNA JONES CCC1, 2011.
	PARTIES, PLEASE COME FOREWARD AND IDENTIFY YOURSELVES FOR THE RECORD.
MS. FRANKLIN:	GOOD MORNING, YOUR HONOR, BARBARA WASHINGTON FRANKLIN, YOUR HONOR, PLAINTIFF, PRO SE.
MS. JONES:	GOOD MORNING, YOUR HONOR, BRIANNA JONES, DEFENDANT, PRO SE AT THIS TIME.
THE COURT:	WHY?
MS. JONES:	I SPOKE WITH ATTORNEY SARAH TURNER OF THE LAW FIRM RHODES, MEYER & BANNON AND I GOT -- -- I HAVE MY TICKET. I GOT IN ------ I WAS RELEASED ON MONDAY, THE 7TH WELL AFTER ------ CLOSE TO 9:00 P.M. AND SO I COULD NOT GET MY BEARINGS ABOUT ME. I COULD NOT GET MY POSSESSIONS UNTIL TUESDAY.
	I HAVE MY TICKET. I GOT IN LATE TUESDAY. THE FLIGHT WAS DELAYED EXTREMELY LATE SO I DIDN'T GET IN UNTIL THE WEE HOURS OF MONDAY MORNING, ACTUALLY. I STARTED CALLING, I STARTED EXCUSE ME, GOING ON THE INTERNET WITH REGARD TO VARIOUS ATTORNEYS.

I CALLED THE D.C. BAR COUNSEL -- -- BAR ASSOCIATION AND I ALSO CALLED THE FLORIDA BAR ASSOCIATION, I SPOKE WITH A NUMBER OF ATTORNEYS AND THEY KEPT SAYING WE'LL GET BACK WITH YOU, THE TIME WAS   WAS GETTING AHEAD OF ME AND, FINALLY, I HAD SENT OUT A LOT OF FEELERS WITH FRIENDS AND THAT SORT OF THING.

AND MY   MY PASTOR, HIS WIFE HAD WORKED FOR A FIRM AND SHE MADE A CALL IMMEDIAELY ON FRIDAY AND I HAD A CHANCE TO SPEAK TO MRS. YATES BRIEFLY AND SHE INTIMATED THAT HAVE   WE HAVE A MEETING SCHEDULED, DEPENDING UPON IF I SHOULD RETURN   WE HAVE A MEETING SCHEDULED FOR WEDNESDAY AT 10:00 A.M. AND IF NOT, THEN TOMORROW. BUT SHE INTIMATED FOR ME TO IMMEDIATELY ASK FOR A CONTINUANCE BECAUSE SHE'S ONLY LICENSED TO PRACTICE IN THE STATE OF FLORIDA AND THAT WOULD BE WITH REGARD TO COLLECTING THE PROCEEDS.

AND SHE WOULD HAVE TO   SHE SAID SHE NEEDS TIME TO BRING SOMEONE IN TO ASSIST ME IN THE DISTRICT IN THIS MATTER. I HAVE HER NUMBER, IF YOU LIKE. AND WE'RE GOING TO SIT DOWN AND DO A RETAINER ON WEDNESDAY.

I HAD SPOKE WITH HER JUST AS SOON AS I LEFT THE AIRPORT. I WANT TO ALSO APOLOGIZE FOR THE LATENESS OF THE HOUR, MY FLIGHT   I WAS WALKING OUT OF THE AIRPORT AT 9:25 AND INTO A TAXI.

MS. FRANKLIN: YOUR HONOR, MAY I RESPOND, YOUR HONOR?

THE COURT: YES.

MS. FRANKLIN: YOUR HONOR, I USED THE TIME FROM LAST   THE LAST HEARING UNTIL NOW TO THINK ABOUT THIS SITUATION AND, OF COURSE, I CONSIDERED THE FACT THAT MS. JONES WOULD COME IN WITH NOT HAVING A PLAN THAT WAS SUFFICIENT FOR THE COURT TO PASS ON UP OR DOWN, AND GIVEN THAT, YOUR HONOR, AND GIVEN THE FACT THAT I'VE SAID TO THE COURT THAT I THINK IT WOULD BE FUNDAMENTALLY UNFAIR FOR THE COURT TO PERMIT HER TO BRING IN COUNSEL TO COLLECT MY ATTTORNEY FEES. I CAME UP WITH A PROPOSED REMEDY THAT WOULD IT BE POSSIBLE FOR THE COURT TO APPOINT COUNSEL TO COLLECT THE SETTLEMENT PROCEEDS THAT WOULD BE FAIR TO BOTH OF US.

THE COURT WOULD HAVE IMMEDIATE INFORMATION PROVIDED WITH REGARD TO WHAT IS GOING ON HERE, WHAT IS THE STATUS. AND I CAME UP WITH THIS IDEA, YOUR HONOR, BECAUSE I HAVE NO OTHER AGENDA HERE BUT TO HAVE THE SETTLEMENT PROCEEDS COLLECTED AND DISBURSED.

I HAVE NO INTEREST IN HAVING MS. JONES BE LOCKED UP. THAT WAS NEVER MY INTENTION AND IT STILL IS NOT. AND IN THE MOTION FOR CONTEMPT I SIMPLY ASKED THE COURT TO IMPOSE A PENALTY. I NEVER MENTIONED INCARCERATION. AND I HAVE BEEN A POSITIVE FORCE IN HER LIFE ALL OF THESE MANY YEARS, SO I WOULDN'T CHANGE AT THIS POINT BUT I AM DETERMINED TO COLLECT ATTORNEY FEES. I AM DETERMINED TO HAVE CREDITORS PAID. THAT IS MY DETERMINATION AND I THINK IT'S AN HONORABLE ONE. I THINK IT'S FAIR.

WE DID HAVE A CONVERSATION, SHE AND I, OVER THE WEEKEND. SHE CALLED TO RUN THIS WHOLE IDEA ABOUT A FIRM AND I SAID TO HER, FIRST OF ALL, I CAN'T GO AROUND THE COURT'S ORDER AND THERE'S NO PROVSION IN THE ORDER WITH REGARD TO SOME FIRM COMING IN.

AND, SECONDLY, THE FIRM IS GOING TO COME IN BIASED AGAINST ME IN REPRESENTING HER. IT WOULD JUST BE AN UNFAIR SITUATION. SO THAT WAS AN IDEA I CAME UP WITH, I THINK IT MIGHT BE SOMETHING TO ACHIEVE THE END THAT WE'RE TRYING TO REACH HERE AND ALLOW US TO ELIMINATE ALL THIS WASTED COURT TIME IN RUNNING BACK AND FORTH TO COURT.

THE COURT: LET ME BE CLEAR ABOUT SOMETHING THAT MAY HAVE GOTTEN LOST HERE IN THE BACK AND FORTH, *THE REASON I SENT MS. JONES TO JAIL BECAUSE SHE WON'T TELL ANYBODY WHERE THE MONEY IS, THE ISSUE LATER WILL BECOME COLLECTION. THE ISSUE PRESENTLY IS THAT SHE WON'T TELL WHERE THE MONEY IS.*

COMMENT AND ANALYSIS: #1 JUDGE KATE STARR'S ORDER MANDATED THAT BRIANNA JONES PRODUCE BANK RECORDS. JUDGE EKANS HAS INTENTIONALLY, PURPOSELFULLY AND SURREPTITIOUSLY CHANGED THE MANDATE OF JUDGE STARR'S ORDER OF OCTOBER 18, 2010 TO PRODUCE BANK STATEMENTS.

MS. FRANKLIN:	THAT'S CORRECT, YOUR HONOR.
THE COURT:	THAT'S CORRECT. THAT'S CORRECT.
MS. FRANKLIN:	I STAND CORRECTED, YOUR HONOR.
THE COURT:	NOW, LET ME JUST SAY THIS: I -- -- I DON'T TAKE LIGHTLY THE RESPONSIBILITIES OF THE COURT, I TAKE VERY SERIOUSLY. AND I'M AWARE OF OF THE VARIETY OF MEASURES THAT ARE AVAILABLE TO ENFORCE THE COURT'S ORDERS. I DARE SAY THAT OVER THE YEARS IN DIFFERENT SITUATIONS I'VE HAD AN OPPORTUNITY TO USE DIFFERENT COERCIVE METHODS.
	YOU, KNOW, IF MS. JONES WANTS TO ARRANGE TO HAVE A LAWYER FROM FLORIDA COME UP HERE AND REPRESENT HER, THEY'RE NOT A MEMBER OF THE D.C. BAR, THEN WE'RE GOING TO HAVE TO, OBVIOUSLY, CONSIDER THAT BUT AT THE END OF THESE PROCEEDINGS MS. JONES IS GOING TO TELL WHERE THE MONEY *IS OR SHE WILL NOT HAVE HER LIBERTY TO MAKE THESE BACK-AND-FORTH JAUNTS FROM D.C. TO FLORIDA AND SO FORTH.*
	I'M I'M HAPPY TO HAVE YOU HAVE YOUR LAWYER BUT I DON'T WANT ANYBODY COMING UP HERE WITH A MISUNDERSTANDING OF WHAT MY PURPOSE IS AND I SURE DON'T WANT YOU WITH A MISUNDERSTANDING OF WHAT MY PURPOSE IS, DON'T WANT YOU TO THINK THAT I'M PLAYING. YOU MAY BE PLAYING, I DON'T KNOW.
	COMMENT AND ANALYSIS: #2 IN HIS PREFERRED GASLIGHTING FASHION, JUDGE EKANS STATES THAT HIS PURPOSE IS TO HAVE BRIANNA JONES TELL WHERE THE SETTLEMENT PROCEEDS ARE WHEN HIS ACTUAL PURPOSE IS TO MAKE CERTAIN THAT I AM PROHIBITED FROM ANY ACCESS TO THE PORTION OF THE MILLIONS OF DOLLARS IN SETTLEMENT PROCEEDS OWED TO ME IN ATTORNEY'S FEES.
MS. JONES:	NO, I'M NOT PLAYING.
THE COURT:	WELL, I DON'T KNOW. I DON'T KNOW. I'M CERTAINLY NOT TAKING YOU AT YOUR WORD. IT OUGHT TO BE CLEAR -- -- CLOSE YOUR MOUTH IT OUGHT TO BE CLEAR THAT I'M NOT TAKING YOU AT YOUR WORD AT THIS POINT. I HAVE NO REASON TO BELIEVE ANYTHING THAT COMES OUT OF YOUR MOUTH BUT I HOPE THAT YOU HAVE REASON TO BELIEVE WHAT COMES OUT OF MINE.

MS. JONES: YES, YOUR HONOR.

THE COURT: SO YOU GO DOWN AND GET YOU A LAWYER, DO WHAT YOU NEED TO DO BUT IF YOU THINK THAT THIS IS GOING TO END WITHOUT *YOU TELLING WHERE THAT MONEY IS,* YOU MAY BE RIGHT BUT YOU WON'T BE IN ANY POSITION TO DO ANYTHING EXCEPT EAT THREE SQUARES A DAY AND LOOK AROUND AT SOME CELLS.

NOW, YOU SAID YOU'RE MEETING WITH YOUR LAWYER ON WEDNESDAY?

COMMENT AND ANALYSIS #3 HERE JUDGE EKANS SPENDS TIME DOING NOTHING MORE THAN WHAT WAS CALLED SELLING WOLF TICKETS WHEN I WAS GROWING UP IN NEWARK AS A CHILD AND ADOLESCENT.

MS. JONES: YES, AT 10:00 A.M.

THE COURT: OKAY.

MS. JONES: AND SHE REQUESTED -- --

THE COURT: I DON'T CARE TO KNOW WHAT SHE REQUESTED, THAT'S BETWEEN YOU AND HER BUT YOU MAKE SURE THAT SHE KNOWS THAT IF SHE KNOW SHE'S NOT A MEMBER OF THE DISTRICT OF COLUMBIA BAR, THAT SHE'LL BE STANDING BY YOU JUST LIKE ANY OTHER LAY CITIZEN.

MS. JONES: VERY WELL.

THE COURT: AND I'M NOT SURE WHAT GOOD THAT WILL DO. NOW YOU MAY OR MAY NOT BE AWARE THAT WASHINGTON, D.C. IS CITY OF LAWYERS, IT'S HARD TO GO OUT AND WALK 10 FEET WITHOUT PASSNG 15 OF THEM. IF YOU GO DOWN AND FIND YOURSELF ONE DOWN IN FLORIDA, THAT'S FINE. MAKE SURE THEY GOT A LICENSE TO PRACTICE UP HERE.

YOU COULD SHORT CIRCUIT ALL THIS BY TELLING ME NOW WHERE THE MONEY IS. CAN YOU DO IT? CAN YOU DO IT?

COMMENT AND ANALYSIS: #4 MY INSTINCTS TOLD ME THAT BY NOW JUDGE EKANS HAD CONFERRED WITH HIS D.C. JUDICIAL CO-CONSPIRATORS SKINNER AND MANDARIN AND HE IS NOW SIMPLY ENJOYING THIS JUDICIAL GASLIGHTING CHARADE.

MS. JONES:	I DON'T KNOW.
THE COURT:	OKAY. ALL RIGHT. ALL RIGHT. PLEASE BEAR IN MIND WHEN YOU SPEAK TO YOUR LAWYER WHAT I TOLD YOU LAST TIME THAT I'VE TRIED THE CIVIL CONTEMPT, DIDN'T WORK OUT, SO WE'LL BE LOOKING AT THE CRIMINAL CONTEMPT NEXT TIME. JUST MAKE SURE SHE UNDERSTANDS THAT SO SHE CAN READ UP ON THAT, ALL RIGHT.
MS. JONES:	YES, YOUR HONOR.
THE COURT:	ALL RIGHT. WE'LL POSTPONE THIS HEARING A WEEK FROM TODAY, NEXT -- -- WELL, NEXT MONDAY'S A HOLIDAY, LET'S MAKE IT A WEEK FROM WEDNESDAY SINCE YOU'RE MEETING YOUR LAWYER ON WEDNESDAY.
MS. FRANKLIN:	YOUR HONOR, WITH REGARD TO MY PROPOSAL FOR COURT APPOINTED COUNSEL -- --
THE COURT:	I'LL CONSIDER THAT. I'LL CONSIDER THAT BUT I'M---------I'M NOT CLEAR THAT WE GET TO THAT STEP BEFORE WE -- --
MS. FRANKLIN:	EXACTLY.
THE COURT:	-- -- TO WHERE THE MONEY IS.
	COMMENT AND ANALYSIS: #5 ALTHOUGH I FELT CONSTRAINED TO MAKE THE REQUEST, I WAS FULLY AWARE THAT MY REQUEST FOR EKANS TO APPOINT COUNSEL TO ASSIST IN THE RECOVERY OF THE SETTLEMENT PROCEEDS WAS GOING NOWHERE. WHY? BECAUSE SUCH AN APPOINTMENT WOULD BE COUNTER TO THE MISSION OF THE D.C. JUDICIAL AND FBI CONSPIRACY AND CRIMINAL ENTERPRISE
MS. FRANKLIN:	EXACTLY, YOUR HONOR.
THE COURT:	*THAT'S NUMBER ONE. NOW, ONCE SHE GETS HERSELF CLEAR THAT SHE HAS TO TELL WHERE THE MONEY IS, THEN WE'LL FIND OUT WHO GETS THE GO GET YOUR FEE.*

COMMENT AND ANALYSIS: *#6* ALTHOUGH IT WAS JUST FEBRUARY 2011 AND THE BEGINNING OF JUDGE EKANS' ADJUDICATION OF MY CASE, WHICH WOULD NOT END UNTIL JANUARY 2015, I WAS FULLY AWARE THAT JUDGE EKANS' GOAL IN KEEPING WITH THE MISSION OF THE CRIMINAL ENTERPRISE, WAS TO MAKE SURE I DID NOT COLLECT A FEE IN ANY AMOUNT.

MS. FRANKLIN:	THANK YOU, YOUR HONOR.
THE COURT:	BUT FIRST WE'RE GOING TO START WITH WHERE IT IS, ALL RIGHT.
MS. FRANKLIN:	THANK YOU, YOUR HONOR.
MS. JONES:	THANK YOU, YOUR HONOR.
THE COURT:	10:00 O'CLOCK. WE'RE GOING TO HAVE TO SET THIS AT 9:30, I HAVE A HEARING AT 10:00 UNLESS YOU HAVE ANOTHER TIME.
MS. FRANKLIN:	NO, WHAT IS THE DATE, YOUR HONOR, THE DATE.
THE COURT:	IT'S THE 23RD, 10:00 O'CLOCK.
MS. FRANKLIN:	OF FEBRUARY.
THE COURT:	NOW, WE CAN MAKE IT LATER IN THE DAY. MS. JONES HAS HABIT OF CALLING US TO TELL US THAT SHE'S LATE SO WE CAN MAKE IT LATER IN THE DAY SO THAT WE CAN SAVE YOU THE .25 CENTS.
MS. JONES:	THE FLIGHT SCHEDULE IS MUCH MORE CONDUCIVE TO JUST A LITTLE BIT LATER IN THE MID-MORNING.
THE COURT:	REALLY,
MS. JONES:	THANK YOU.
THE COURT:	WELL, I THINK THAT THAT MORNING WE'RE PROBABLY GOING TO HAVE OUR HANDS FULL, IS IT ANYTHING OTHER THAN THE ------- ALL RIGHT, WELL, WE CAN SAY 11:00 O' CLOCK.
MS. FRANKLIN:	11:00 ON THE 23RD, YOUR HONOR, IN COURTROOM 517?
THE COURT:	RIGHT HERE.
MS. FRANKLIN:	THANK YOU, YOUR HONOR.
MS. JONES:	THANK YOU, YOUR HONOR.

BARBARA WASHINGTON FRANKLIN

THE DEPUTY CLERK: I NEED FOR YOU TO SIGN NOTICE.

MS. JONES: I NEED TO SIGN?

THE DEPUTY CLERK: YES. THIS IS YOUR NOTICE TO APPEAR. YOU'RE TO APPEAR BEFORE
FEBRUARY 23RD, 2011, JUDGE EKANS IN COURTROOM 517. FAILURE TO
SHOW UP ON THAT DATE, THERE WILL BE A BENCH WARRANT ISSUED FOR
YOUR ARREST, DO YOU UNDERSTAND?

MS. JONES: YES.

THE DEPUTY CLERK: YOUR SIGNATURE.

(PROCEEDINGS CONCLUDED)

THE ODYSSEY OF JUDICIAL CORRUPTION

SUPERIOR COURT OF THE DISTRICT Of COLUMBIA
CIVIL DIVISION
WASHINGTON, D.C

THE HONORABLE MATTHEW D. EKANS, ASSOCIATE JUDGE, PRESIDING

THE FOLLOWING IS THE ENTIRE OFFICIAL COURT TRANSCRIPT OF THE
FEBRUARY 23, 2011 COURT PROCEEDING
ANNOTATED BY THE AUTHOR'S PERTINENT COMMENTARY AND ANALYSIS

FEBRUARY 23, 2011

P R O C E E D I N G

THE DEPUTY CLERK:	YOUR HONOR, CALLING THE CASE OF BARBARA WASHINGTON FRANKLIN VERSUS BRIANNA JONES, CIVIL ACTION 4417 2009; IN THE MATTER OF BRIANNA JONES, CCC1 2011. PLEASE STATE YOUR NAME FOR THE RECORD.
MS. FRANKLIN:	HI, GOOD AFTERNOON, YOUR HONOR; BARBARA WASHINGTON FRANKLIN, PLAINFIFF, PRO SE, YOUR HONOR.
THE COURT:	I GOT AN E-MAIL WHILE I WAS IN THE MIDDLE OF A HEARING THIS MORNING FROM MY LAW CLERK THAT READS: "JUDGE, JUST GOT OFF THE PHONE WITH MS. JONES. SHE IS STILL IN FLORIDA WITH NO FLIGHT TICKETS PURCHASED. APPARENTLY, SHE HAD SOME ISSUE WITH HER CREDIT CARD AND HAS ONLY NOW GOTTEN CREDIT FOR A CASH PAYMENT ON THE CARD WHICH SHE PAID YESTERDAY. SHE SAYS SHE'S HAPPY TO IMMEDIATELY BOOK A FLIGHT TODAY IF YOU WOULD BE SO KIND AS TO RESCHEDULE THE HEARING FOR TOMORROW MORNING. HOW SHOULD WE PROCEED?"
	SO I THOUGHT I WOULD READ THAT TO YOU AND GET YOUR REACTION BEFORE I DID ANYTHING ELSE.
MS. FRANKLIN:	ARE YOU AVAILABLE, YOUR HONOR?
THE COURT:	TOMORROW?
MS. FRANKLIN:	YES.

THE COURT:	I HAVE SCHEDULED AN ALL-DAY HEARING FOR WELL, I SAY AN ALL-DAY HEARING. STARTING MONDAY, I'M ASSIGNED TO THE LANDLORD/TENANT BRANCH FOR A FULL WEEK, MONDAY THROUGH FRIDAY. THAT'S OVER IN BUILDING B. SO THAT MEANS THAT I'M AWAY FROM I'M AWAY.
MS. FRANKLIN:	FIVE-SEVENTEEN.
THE COURT:	IT'S LIKE BEING IN ANOTHER WORLD. WHEN I RETURN THE FOLLOWING MONDAY, I'M BEGINNING JURY SELECTION FOR A TRIAL THAT IS SCHEDULED FOR THREE FULL WEEKS, PRACTICALLY THE MONTH OF MARCH, FROM THE 7TH THROUGH THE 25TH. TOMORROW, I'M SCHEDULED TO DO THE PRETRIAL MOTIONS, THE MOTIONS IN LIMINE OF WHICH THERE ARE A LOT ON BOTH SIDES. IT'S A MALPRACTICE TRIAL.
	SO WHEN YOU ASK ME IF I'M AVAILABLE TOMORROW, YES AND NO, SORT OF LIKE TODAY.
MS. FRANKLIN:	RIGHT.
THE COURT:	IT WOULD BE SOMETHING THAT WE WOULD FORCE ONTO THE CALENDAR. BUT IF I DON'T DO IT TOMORROW, I CAN'T DO IT AT ALL THE FOLLOWING WEEK BECAUSE I'LL BE IN LANDLORD/TENANT. AND THEN ONCE I COME BACK, THAT TRIAL IS GOING TO BE -- --
MS. FRANKLIN:	YOUR HONOR, WHAT ABOUT YOUR CALENDAR FOR FRIDAY, FOR FRIDAY THIS WEEK?
THE COURT:	YEAH, THAT'S PROBABLY ----- BECAUSE I CAN MAKE IT WORK ON FRIDAY. SO THAT WOULD BE PREFERABLE TO TOMORROW.
	ARE YOU LOOKING AT FRIDAY?
THE DEPUTY CLERK:	YES.
THE COURT:	HOW MANY MATTERS?
THE DEPUTY CLERK:	THERE'RE 17.
THE COURT:	SEVENTEEN?
(PAUSE.)	
THE COURT:	OKAY. FRIDAY'S NOT -- --
MS. FRANKLIN:	FRIDAY'S NOT GOOD?

THE COURT:	FRIDAY'S OUT. FRANKLY, I THINK WE'RE PROBABLY LOOKING AT MARCH THE 11TH IF WE DON'T TRY TO SQUEEZE IT IN TOMORROW. IT'S NOT CLEAR TO ME THAT THERE WOULD BE ANY REAL ADVANTAGE TO HAVING THIS HEARING TOMORROW. WHAT I HAD ANTICIPATED, PERHAPS A LITTLE OVERLY OPTIMISTICALLY WAS THAT SHE WOULD HAVE A LAWYER APPEARING FOR HER. WITHOUT THAT, I'M NOT CLEAR THAT WE'RE GOING TO DO ANYTHING OTHER THAN SAY HELLO.
MS. FRANKLIN:	I SPOKE WITH HER. SHE CALLED YESTERDAY TO INDICATE THAT SHE HAD MET WITH THIS ATTORNEY THAT SHE HAD DESCRIBED TO THE COURT AT THE LAST HEARING. AND SUPPOSEDLY THE ATTORNEY HAS INFORMED HER THAT SHE HAS NOT BEEN ABLE TO GET ANY RETURN CALLS FROM THE VARIOUS PARTIES THAT SHE'S BEEN CALLING, ATTORNEYS SHE'S BEEN CALLING, FORMER JUDGES SHE'S BEEN CALLING. SHE COULDN'T GET ANY CALLS BACK. BUT THAT BASED ON THE INFORMATION THAT SHE HAS BEEN ABLE TO ACQUIRE THUS FAR, SHE WOULD NOT BE ABLE TO HELP HER UNLESS THERE IS AN INVESTIGATION. *THAT SHE THINKS AN INVESTIGATION NEEDS TO BE LAUNCHED.* THAT SHE, IN FACT, TOLD HER TO SAVE HER MONEY BECAUSE SHE HAD ARRANGED FOR A RETAINER.
SO SHE WILL NOT BE COMING IN WITH AN ATTORNEY BASED ON MY CONVERSATION WITH HER YESTERDAY. NOW THAT MIGHT CHANGE BUT SHE'S SAYING THE ATTORNEY SAYS THIS NEEDS TO BE LOOKED INTO BECAUSE, YOU KNOW, YOU MIGHT NOT HAVE THE FUNDS BUT THE FUNDS ARE OUT THERE. AND UNLESS THERE'S AN AUTHORITY THAT'S GOING TO INVESTIGATE, THIS WILL GO ON AND IT'S NOT GOING TO WORK, SO. I MEAN, I'M SHARING BECAUSE THAT'S PART OF WHAT I ANTICIPATED THAT SHE WOULD BE SHARING WITH THE COURT TODAY HAD SHE ARRIVED.
THE COURT:	WELL, SHE HAD CALLED LAST WEEK. YOU KNOW, I DON'T TALK TO HER, BUT SHE'S CALLED MY LAW CLERK AND TOLD HER AT SOME POINT IN TIME THAT SHE HAD THIS LAWYER, BUT AND MY CLERK SORT OF RUNS IN -- -- SHE'S A YOUNG PERSON SHE RUNS AND ASKS ME WHAT TO DO. AND I SAY DON'T DO ANYTHING. TELL THE LAWYER TO ENTER AN APPEARANCE IN THE CASE.

MS. FRANKLIN:	I DID FURTHER STATE, THOUGH, YOUR HONOR THAT FOR THE BENEFIT OF THIS COURT, THAT EVEN THOUGH THIS ATTORNEY THAT YOU'VE CONSULTED WITH HAS TOLD YOU THAT SHE CANNOT HELP YOU AT THIS POINT, COULD SHE PUT THAT INFORMATION IN A LETTER TO THE JUDGE. AT LEAST DO THAT MUCH TO LET THE JUDGE KNOW THAT YOU'RE IN GOOD FAITH WITH TRYING TO RETAIN COUNSEL, AND WHAT THE ATTORNEY HAS FOUND BASED ON HER PRELIMINARY INVESTIGATION. AND SHE SAID SHE WAS TRYING TO GET A LETTER, BUT SHE WASN'T SURE SHE WAS GOING TO BE ABLE TO. I SAID OR LET THE ATTORNEY CONTACT, YOU KNOW, THE COURT WHEN WE'RE IN SESSION BY PHONE AND SHARE THAT WITH THE COURT. AND SHE HAD ALSO MENTIONED THAT SHE HAD CONTACTED SEVERAL FIRMS HERE IN WASHINGTON. AND SHE INCLUDED DICKSTEIN AND SHAPIRO, AND SHE NAMED ONE OR TWO OTHER FIRMS AND THEY DID NOT RETURN HER CALLS. SO SHE HAS NOT RETAINED AN ATTORNEY THAT'S ADMITTED IN D.C.

THE ATTORNEY THAT SHE HAS BEEN DEALING WITH IN FLORIDA, WHOM SHE'S DESCRIBED AS A FEMALE, SHE DID NOT GIVE ME THE ATTORNEY'S NAME NOR HAS SHE GIVEN ME HER NUMBER, IS NOT ADMITTED IN D.C. THIS IS THE PERSON, APPARENTLY, THAT SHE DESCRIBED TO YOUR HONOR AT THE LAST HEARING, SO.

THE COURT: WELL, WHAT I PROPOSE DOING IS COMMUNICATING TO MS. JONES THAT WE WILL CALL THIS CASE ON MARCH THE 11TH AT 1:45 IN THE AFTERNOON. MY PLAN IS TO GO FORWARD WITH WHAT I SAID I WAS GOING TO DO THE LAST TIME. MY HOPE, AND INDEED MY FERVENT PRAYER IS THAT SHE'LL HAVE A LAWYER WITH HER BECAUSE IT'S VERY UNNERVING FOR ME TO MOVE INTO CONTEMPT, MUCH LESS CRIMINAL CONTEMPT WITH THE PARTY WHO'S NOT REPRESENTED BY COUNSEL. AND YET I'M REASONABLY CONFIDENT THAT MS. JONES HAS HAD A LOT OF DEALINGS WITH LAWYERS OVER THE YEARS AND HAS A WAY TO GO ABOUT HIRING A LAWYER IF SHE WANTS TO HIRE ONE.

MS. FRANKLIN: IF PER CHANCE, YOUR HONOR   WELL, MAYBE WE'LL JUST CROSS THAT BRIDGE WHEN WE GET TO IT. I'M THINKING ABOUT MARCH 11TH, BUT WE'LL JUST WAIT.

THE COURT:	YEAH, I MAKE NO DECISIONS UNTIL I ABSOLUTELY HAVE TO.
MS. FRANKLIN:	WE'LL JUST WAIT UNTIL THE 11TH. WHAT I WAS REALLY GETTING AT IF, IN FACT, THAT SHE DOES NOT SHOW ON THE 11TH FOR WHATEVER REASON, BUT I THINK IT'S PROBABLY APPROPRIATE THAT WE WAIT UNTIL THE HEARING.
THE COURT:	I DON'T HAVE I MEAN, I HAVE NO REASON TO THINK THAT MS. JONES WON'T BE HERE.
MS. FRANKLIN:	OKAY.
THE COURT:	I MEAN, I THINK SHE'LL BE HERE. THE FRUSTRATION IS THAT -- --
MS. FRANKLIN:	WILL SHE BE PREPARED.
THE COURT:	SHE JUST COMES AND JUST TO HAVE A CHAT.
MS. FRANKLIN:	EXACTLY.
THE COURT:	I MEAN, SHE SAID I DON'T THINK SHE WOULD'VE CALLED TO SAY THAT SHE'D BE HERE TOMORROW IF SHE DIDN'T PLAN TO COME TOMORROW. SHE SEEMS TO ENJOY WASHINGTON, SO I DON'T THINK THAT'S A PROBLEM.
MS. FRANKLIN:	I THINK SHE ENJOYS COURT AS WELL.
THE COURT:	I DON'T KNOW. IT'S NOT FOR ME TO PREJUDGE. BUT THAT'S WHEN WE'LL SCHEDULE THIS CASE, AND WE'LL INFORM HER MARCH THE 11TH AT 1:45. AND THAT WILL GIVE HER SUFFICIENT TIME TO GET HER TICKETS AND EVERYTHING.
MS. FRANKLIN:	ALL RIGHT, YOUR HONOR.
THE COURT:	THANK YOU VERY MUCH.
MS. FRANKLIN:	THANK YOU, YOUR HONOR.
	(THEREUPON, THE PROCEEDINGS WERE CONCLUDED.)

BARBARA WASHINGTON FRANKLIN

SUPERIOR COURT OF THE DISTRICT OF COLUMBIA
CIVIL DIVISION
WASHINGTON, D.C.

THE HONORABLE MATTHEW D. EKANS, ASSOCIATE JUDGE, PRESIDING

THE FOLLOWING IS THE ENTIRE OFFICIAL COURT TRANSCRIPT OF THE
MARCH 11, 2011 PROCEEDING
ANNOTATED BY THE AUTHOR'S PERTINENT COMMENTARY AND ANALYSIS

MARCH 11, 2011
P R O C E E D I N G S

COMMENT AND ANALYSIS: *#1 THE COURT BEGINS TO BACK PEDDLE. JUDGE EKANS DOESN'T RECALL BRIANNA JONES SAYING SHE KNEW WHERE THE MONEY WAS. I FOUND THIS SHOCKING SINCE THE COURT RECORD WAS EXPLICITLY AND UNEQUIVOCALLY CLEAR WITH REGARD TO THIS SPECIFIC TESTIMONY. LITTLE DID I REALIZE THAT I WAS ON THE THRESHOLD OF ONE OF THE LARGEST D.C. JUDICIAL AND FBI FRAUD, THEFT, CORRUPTION AND EXTORTION CRIMINAL ENTERPRISES IN U.S. COURT SYSTEM HISTORY.*

I INFORMED THE COURT THAT I HAD FILED A MOTION FOR INVESTIGATION ON FEBRUARY 25, 2011. JUDGE EKANS SAID THE COURT DOESN'T NORMALLY CONDUCT INVESTIGATIONS; HE WILL CONSULT WITH HIS JUDICIAL COLLEAGUES.

MY HEART SANK IN RESPONSE TO THIS NOTICE BECAUSE I KNEW IT MEANT THAT JUDGE EKANS WOULD BE CONFERRING WITH TWO OF THE OTHER KEY D.C. JUDICIAL CO-CONSPIRATORS INVOLVED IN THIS MASSIVE FBI AND D.C. JUDICIAL FRAUD, CORRUPTION AND EXTORTION CONSPIRACY AND CRIMINAL ENTERPRISE, NAMELY D.C. COURT JUDGE RICHARD MANDARIN, AND FORMER D.C. SUPERIOR COURT CHIEF JUDGE AND NOW SENIOR JUDGE, GEORGE SKINNER.

THESE JUDICIAL CO-CONSPIRATORS WOULD CERTAINLY ARGUE TO KEEP ME IN MY DEFRAUDED STATE, AND MOST IMPORTANT OF ALL, THEY WOULD DO EVERYTHING IN THEIR POWER TO PERSUADE JUDGE EKANS TO DO WHATEVER WAS NECESSARY, WHILE OSTENSIBLY LEGAL AND PROPER, TO KEEP THEMSELVES AND THE OTHER CO-CONSPIRATORS IN POSSESSION OF THE ILLEGALLY CONFISCATED $100 MILLION IN STOLEN SETTLEMENT PROCEEDS. I RECOGNIZED EARLY ON THAT FAIRNESS, EQUITY AND JUSTICE WOULD TAKE A BACK SEAT TO THE SYSTEMIC D.C. JUDICIAL AND FBI FRAUD, THEFT, CORRUPTION AND EXTORTION THAT STARED ME IN THE FACE. **BRIANNA JONES, DEFENDANT, DID NOT APPEAR IN PERSON AT THE PROCEEDING**.

THE ODYSSEY OF JUDICIAL CORRUPTION

THE DEPUTY CLERK:	YOUR HONOR, CALLING THE MATTER OF BARBARA WASHINGTON FRANKLIN VERSUS BRIANNA JONES, CIVIL ACTION 4417 2009.
MS. FRANKLIN:	GOOD AFTERNOON, YOUR HONOR.
THE DEPUTY CLERK:	CALLING IN THE MATTER OF BRIANNA JONES, 2011 CCC1.
MS. FRANKLIN:	GOOD AFTERNOON, YOUR HONOR; BARBARA WASHINGTON FRANKLIN, YOUR HONOR.
THE COURT:	I THINK YOU PROBABLY ARE AWARE THAT MS. JONES IS NOT HERE, AS IN WASHINGTON, D.C.?
MS. FRANKLIN:	I WASN'T---I'M NOT.
THE COURT:	I RATHER THOUGHT YOU WOULD KNOW THAT. SHE CALLED, AS SHE TENDS TO DO, THIS MORNING EXPLAINING THAT SHE HAD MISSED A SEVEN O'CLOCK FLIGHT, AND THAT SHE WANTED TO ASSURE ME THAT SHE COULD GET HERE LATER, BUT IT WOULD BE LATE IN THE DAY. ASKING MY LAW CLERK TO PLEASE TELL ME NOT TO SEND THE MARSHALS AFTER HER. AND MY LAW CLERK ASKED ME WHAT TO SAY TO HER. AND I DIRECTED MY CLERK TO TELL HER THAT I DON'T---THAT THE COURT DOESN'T DO ITS BUSINESS ON THE TELEPHONE. SHE'S GOTTEN TOO COMFORTABLE CALLING ME. SO, I THOUGHT I'D PUT IT TO YOU AND SEE WHAT YOU WANT TO DO.
MS. FRANKLIN:	SHE CALLED ME THIS MORNING, YOUR HONOR, AS WELL, ASKING IF I WOULD CONSENT TO A CONTNUANCE UNTIL MONDAY. I SAID I COULD NOT DO THAT. FIRST OF ALL, I COULDN'T PRESUME ON THE COURT, AND HAD NO KNOWLEDGE OF THE COURT'S SCHEDULE, THAT WE BARELY GOT IN ON THE COURT'S SCHEDULE TODAY BECAUSE THE COURT IS VERY BUSY.
THE COURT:	I CANNOT BEGIN TO TELL YOU WHAT WE'VE BEEN THROUGH TODAY.
MS. FRANKLIN:	YES. AND I TOOK A LOOK AT THE DOCKET OUT THERE. YOU KNOW THAT THE COURT IS IN TRIAL, IN OTHER COURTS AND HANDLING ALL KINDS OF MATTERS, YOU KNOW, I COULDN'T AGREE TO IT. **I BASICALLY, YOUR HONOR, JUST DECIDED TO FOCUS ON---I FILED A MOTION WITH THE COURT ON THE 25TH ASKING THE COURT TO CONDUCT AN INVESTIGATION, BECAUSE AT THIS POINT I FEEL I'M AT THE MERCY OF THE COURT, AND IF THE COURT DOES NOT LOOK INTO THIS MATTER IT WILL JUST GO ON.**
THE COURT:	I HAVEN'T SEEN IT YET, BUT I'LL TAKE A LOOK AT IT.

COMMENT AND ANALYSIS: #2 *I KNEW FROM MY MANY YEARS OF EXPERIENCE AS A TRIAL ATTORNEY THAT NOW THAT THE COURT HAD JUDICIAL CO-CONSPIRATOR COLLEAGUES AND OTHERS SPEAKING INTO ITS EAR, JUDGE EKANS' DETACHED QUIET DEMEANOR SIGNALED TO ME THAT **MY MOTION FOR AN INDEPENDENT INVESTIGATION HAD ALREADY REACHED D.C. SUPERIOR COURT DEAD ON ARRIVAL. AN INDEPENDENT INVESTIGATION WOULD OPEN THE BARREL OF WORMS THAT IS THE D.C. JUDICIAL AND FBI FRAUD, THEFT, CORRUPTION AND EXTORTION CRIMINAL ENTERPRISE THAT PERMEATED THE COURT'S ADJUDICATION OF MY CASE.** THIS WAS EXACTLY WHY I HAD REFRAINED FROM SEEKING REDRESS IN D.C SUPERIOR COURT YEARS EARLIER. I KNEW FROM EXPERIENCE THAT I WOULD BE FACED WITH THE STEEP MOUNTAIN OF SYSTEMIC D.C. JUDICIAL AND FBI FRAUD, THEFT, CORRUPTION AND EXTORTION THAT WOULD STAND IN MY WAY, EFFECTIVELY BLOCKING MY PATH TO FAIR AND EQUAL JUSTICE, IRRESPECTIVE OF WHAT THE RULE OF LAW DICTATED.*

THE COURT: WELL, YOU KNOW, I NEED SOME GUIDANCE FROM YOU BECAUSE I THINK THAT --I MEAN, I'M PREPARED TO DO WHAT HAS TO BE DONE TO SEE THAT THE ORDER OF THE COURT IS CARRIED OUT. **BUT TO THE EXTENT THAT AN INVESTIGATION NEEDS TO BE DONE AND THAT EVIDENCE NEEDS TO BE PRESENTED, THAT BALL HAS TO BE IN YOUR COURT.** OTHERWISE, I DON'T LOOK LIKE I'M THE NEUTRAL THAT I HAVE TO BE.

COMMENT AND ANALYSIS: #3 *HERE JUDGE EKANS THREW DOWN THE COURT'S GAUNTLET WITH REGARD TO MY REQUEST FOR INVESTIGATION OF THE DOMINANT ISSUE OF D.C. JUDICIAL AND FBI FRAUD, THEFT,CORRUPTION AND EXTORTION THAT DEFINED MY CASE. **JUDGE EKANS WAS SAYING THAT IF AN INVESTIGATION WERE GOING TO BE, IT WOULD BE UP TO ME.** IN OTHER WORDS, EVEN IN THE CASE OF A MASSIVE D.C. JUDICIAL AND FBI FRAUD, THEFT, CORRUPTION AND EXTORTION CONSPIRACY CASE, IT WOULD BE THE RESPONSIBIITY OF THE LITIGANT TO INVESTIGATE SUCH A MATTER. THE COURT'S RESPONSE AS AN EXPERIENCED JURIST WAS EMBARRASSING. IT WAS ALSO A CLASSIC IIUSTRATION OF THE COURT'S EGREGIOUS ABUSE OF ITS ABSOLUTE DISCRETION, POWER AND AUTHORITY FOR THE EXPRESS PURPOSE OF PROTECTING AND MAINTAINING THE STATUS QUO POSITIONS OF THE JUDICIAL AND FBI CO-CONSPIRATORS IN THEIR AUDACIOUS PARTICIPATION IN THIS HISTORIC CRIMINAL ENTERPRISE OF D.C. JUDICIAL AND FBI FRAUD, THEFT, CORRUPTION AND EXTORTION.*

THE COURT: NOW, IF YOU WANT TO---IF YOU HAVE, YOU KNOW, OTHER THAN YOUR OWN TESTIMONY, OF COURSE, IF YOU HAVE ANY OTHER WITNESSES OR EVIDENCE THAT SHOWS HER MEANS. I MEAN, SHE'S OBVIOUSLY---I THINK YOU---I MEAN, I DON'T KNOW THIS PERSON, BUT SHE'S LIVING SOMEWHERE. SHE'S EATING, SHE'S TRAVELING, SHE'S DRESSING. SHE'S DOING ALL THOSE THINGS. **I MEAN, I HAVE JUDGMENT DEBTORS COME IN COURT.** I THINK THE FOCUS THAT WE'VE HAD UP TO THIS POINT IN TIME IS ON A PARTICULAR SUM OF MONEY FROM A PARTICULAR SOURCE. AND WHILE THAT'S WELL AND GOOD, IN TERMS OF SATISFYING A LEGAL FEE, IT DOESN'T STRIKE ME THAT IT MATTERS WHETHER THE SOURCE IS FROM PRIZE WINNINGS OR FROM SOME OTHER SOURCE, AS LONG AS YOU'RE PAID THE MONEY SHE OWES. AND I GUESS THAT IS TRUE FOR OTHER PEOPLE WHO SHE'S INDEBTED TO. SO, I'M NOT SO CONCERNED ABOUT WHETHER IT'S THE PRIZE MONEY. MY CONCERN WOULD BE, YOU KNOW, FIND OUT WHEREVER THE MONEY COMES SHE'S LIVING AND BUYING AIRPLANE TICKETS ON, GO TO WHATEVER DEBTS THAT SHE OWES.

COMMENT AND ANALYSIS: *#4 HERE THE COURT INTENTIONALLY, PURPOSEFULLY AND FALSELY CHARACTERIZES BRIANNA JONES AS A **JUDGMENT DEBTOR**, MAKING ME A **JUDGMENT CREDITOR** WHICH I WAS NOT.*

*THE COURT'S REASONING WITH REGARD TO THE RELATIVE INSIGNIFICANCE OF VIEWING THE SETTLEMENT PROCEEDS (DERIVED FROM LOTTERY WINNINGS) AS THE SOLE AND PRIMARY SOURCE OF ASSETS FROM WHICH BRIANNA JONES WOULD BE OBLIGATED TO PAY THE ATTORNEY'S FEES OWED TO ME WAS SERIOUSLY FLAWED, BUT ALWAYS PURPOSEFUL, INTENTIONAL AND MORE IMPORTANTLY CONSISTENT WITH **THE COURT'S RIGGING OF MY CASE FOR ULTIMATE DISMISSAL.***

BRIANNA JONES LIVED OFF LOANS FROM OTHERS. JUDGE EKANS' VIEW THAT BRIANNA JONES' DEBT TO ME IN THE AMOUNT OF AN ESTIMATED $50 MILLION COULD BE PAID FROM WHATEVER SOURCE MADE NO PRACTICAL NOR ACTUAL SENSE. HOWEVER, IT DID MAKE CRIMINAL ENTERPRISE SENSE. IT WAS ALSO THE BEGINNING OF THE JUDICIAL GASLIGHTING ABUSE THAT I WOULD HAVE TO ENDURE EACH TIME I APPEARED BEFORE JUDGE EKANS.

IT ALSO SHOWED HIS BLATANT ATTEMPT TO PLAY ME FOR A FOOL, NOT WITHSTANDING MY PROMINENCE IN WASHINGTON AS A FORMER CONGRESSIONAL MINORITY CHIEF COUNSEL AND STAFF DIRECTOR OF THE U.S. HOUSE COMMITTEE ON THE DISTRICT OF COLUMBIA AND ASSISTANT D.C. CITY ADMINISTRATOR FOR INTERGOVERNMENTAL RELATIONS.

MS. FRANKLIN: WELL,   YOUR   HONOR, WITH.
(PAUSE)

BARBARA WASHINGTON FRANKLIN

THE COURT:	SHE'S ON THE TELEPHONE. THE DEPUTY CLERK: HELLO, MS. JONES?
MS. JONES:	YES.
THE COURT:	MS. JONES, YOU'VE OBVIOUSLY, YOU'VE REACHED US HERE IN THE COURTROOM. I'M STANDING HERE RIGHT NOW TALKING TO BARBARA WASHINGTON FRANKLIN. THIS IS JUDGE EKANS SPEAKING.
MS. JONES:	GOOD AFTERNOON, YOUR HONOR.
THE COURT:	I WANT YOU TO KNOW, I WANT YOU TO CLEARLY UNDERSTAND THAT I'M NOT DEALING WITH YOU IN THE FUTURE ON THE TELEPHONE. SO, THIS IS SOMETHING THAT WE DO FROM TIME TO TIME TO MAKE ACCOMODATIONS. YOU HAVE TRIED TO MAKE IT A PRACTICE, AND IT'S NOT A PRACTICE THAT I'M GOING TO TOLERATE. SO, IT SEEMS AS IF EVERY TIME RECENTLY THAT WE'VE SET A HEARING YOU'VE FOUND REASON TO CALL TO SAY WHY YOU MISSED AN AIRPLANE, AND TO ASK US NOT TO TAKE ACTION WHICH WOULD NEGATIVELY IMPACT YOU AND YOUR LIBERTY. I WANT YOU TO BE VERY CLEAR THAT I'M NOT AMUSED. AND I ALSO WANT YOU TO BE CLEAR, I'VE JUST SAID TO MS. FRANKLIN THAT THE FOCUS IN THE PAST, AS FAR AS I'M ABLE TO DISCERN, HAS BEEN ON WHERE CERTAIN MONEY IS THAT REPRESENTS PRIZE WINNINGS. **I'M NOT CONCERNED ABOUT WHERE THE SOURCE OF THE MONEY IS THAT YOU'RE GOING TO USE TO PAY THE DEBTS**. AS FAR AS THE COURT IS CONCERNED, WE'RE SIMPLY ENFORCING THE SETTLEMENT AGREEMENT FOR YOU TO PAY A LEGAL FEE. AND IF IT COMES FROM ANY SOURCE FROM WHERE YOUR ASSETS ARE, THAT SATISFIES THE COURT'S ORDER, WHICH IS ALL THAT I'M TRYING TO DO. NOW, THAT MEANS WHEN I SEE YOU IN THIS COURTROOM, NOT WHEN I TALK TO YOU ON THE TELEPHONE, WHEN I SEE YOU IN THIS COURTROOM, WE WANT EVIDENCE OF YOUR ASSETS. HOW YOU PAY YOUR CREDIT CARD BILLS, HOW YOU PAY YOUR LIVING EXPENSES, HOW YOU MANAGE TO LIVE ON YOUR FINANCIAL MEANS, WHATEVER THEY MAY BE. DO YOU UNDERSTAND?

COMMENT AND ANALYSIS: **#5** *JUDGE EKANS INTENTIONALLY RESORTED TO DENIAL AS TO WHO BRIANNA JONES WAS, I.E., AN IMPOVERISHED, HOMELESS AND MEDICALLY DIAGNOSED MENTALLY ILL BLACK WOMAN, SUFFERING WITH POST TRAUMATIC STRESS DISORDER (PTSD), WHICH WOULD PRECLUDE HER ABILITY TO PAY, PURSUANT TO A CLIENT CONTINGENCY FEE AGREEMENT, A LEGAL FEE IN THE AMOUNT OF $50 MILLION OR MORE BASED ON THE VERIFIED $34 MILLION SETTLEMENT OF THE $100 MILLION LAWSUIT I FILED ON HER BEHALF IN THE BROWARD COUNTY CIRCUIT COURT IN FORT LAUDERDALE, FLORIDA IN MAY 1996.*

*MOREOVER, BRIANNA JONES WAS NOT A **JUDGMENT DEBTOR** AS JUDGE EKANS HAD FALSELY AND INTENTIONALLY LABELED HER.*

JUDGE EKANS ABUSED THE EXERCISE OF HIS JUDICIAL DISCRETION IN HIS ADAMANT DETERMINATION TO ADJUDICATE THE CASE AS A JUDGMENT CREDITOR'S RIGHTS CASE BROUGHT AGAINST A JUDGMENT DEBTOR.

HOWEVER, JUDGE EKANS' INSISTENCE ON FRAMING THE CASE AS A JUDGMENT CREDITOR'S RIGHTS CASE ALLOWED HIM TO JUSTIFY HIS REFUSAL AND FAILURE TO ORDER AN INVESTIGATION OF THE DOMINANT ISSUES OF D.C. JUDICIAL AND FBI FRAUD, THEFT, CORRUPTION AND EXTORTION.

JUDGE EKANS' ACTIONS WERE IN ALL RESPECTS PREMEDITATED AND IN CONCERT WITH THE MISSION OF THE CRIMINAL ENTERPRISE TO DISMISS MY LAWSUIT AND DEFRAUD ME OF THE ESTIMATED $50 MILLION OWED TO ME IN ATTORNEY'S FEES.

JUDGE EKANS' UNETHICAL, IF NOT AMORAL, RULINGS AND DECISIONS MADE ME SICK TO MY STOMACH ON MORE THAN ONE OCCASION DURING HIS 9 MONTHS OF ADJUDICATION OF MY LAWSUIT, AND FURTHER, MADE ME SIMPLY WANT TO THROW UP ON THE COURTROOM FLOOR.

MS. JONES: YES, YOUR HONOR.

THE COURT: NOW ALL WE NEED TO TALK ABOUT IS A DATE BECAUSE THE ONLY THING THAT I DO ON THE TELEPHONE IS TO TALK SCHEDULING, AND THAT'S ALL WE'RE TALKING HERE. THESE MATTERS THE COURT TENDS TO TRY TO DO ON FRIDAYS BECAUSE WE'RE IN TRIAL MONDAY THROUGH THURSDAY, AND WE'RE IN TRIAL NOW, AND IT'S A VERY INTENSE CASE SO I WON'T HAVE ANY TIME IN THE AFTERNOON UNTIL FRIDAY OF NEXT WEEK. AND WE DON'T NEED TO PUT THIS IN THE AFTERNOON. WE CAN SCHEDULE THIS FOR 11 O'CLOCK IN THE MORNING, HERE IN COURTROOM 517, AND I WANT YOU TO BE VERY CLEAR THAT IF I GET A TELEPHONE CALL FROM YOU, AS SOON AS I HANG UP, I'M MAKING A PHONE CALL TO THE UNITED STATES MARSHALS' OFFICE DOWNSTAIRS IN THE BASEMENT OF THIS BUILDING.

MS. JONES: I UNDERSTAND.

THE COURT: VERY GOOD. THEN WE'LL SEE YOU NEXT WEEK AT 11 A.M.

YOU HAVE A NICE DAY AND A NICE WEEKEND.

MS. JONES: THANK YOU, YOUR HONOR.

THE COURT: GOOD-

BYE. (PAUSE.)

MS. FRANKLIN: YOUR HONOR, I JUST WANTED TO RESPOND TO YOUR HONOR'S COMMENTS WITH REGARD TO **THE MOTION FOR COURT INVESTIGATION.** I WAS VERY SENSITIVE TO YOUR HONOR'S OBLIGATION AND DUTY TO REMAIN NEUTRAL, THEREFORE, **IN THE MOTION I ASKED THE COURT TO DESIGNATE THE FBI AS CONDUCTING SUCH INVESTIGATION ON BEHALF OF THE COURT,** BECAUSE I RECOGNIZE THAT, YOU KNOW, THE COURT HAS TO BE A NEUTRAL ARBITER.

BUT---

THE COURT: DIDN'T YOU SAY THAT YOU BROUGHT THIS TO THEIR ATTENTION AT SOME

POINT IN TIME? I THOUGHT I HEARD---

MS. FRANKLIN: TO YOUR ATTENTION?

THE COURT: NO. I THOUGHT YOU TOLD ME THAT YOU WENT TO FEDERAL AUTHORITIES---

MS. FRANKLIN: OH, NO, THAT'S WHEN I FIRST GOT INVOLVED 15 YEARS AGO WITH THE CASE AND THREATS WERE BEING MADE TO MS. JONES, AND I WENT TO THE HEAD OF THE FBI AGENCY DOWN IN MIAMI, MIAMI DADE OFFICE.

BUT, YOUR HONOR, WHEN I TOLD HER THIS MORNING THAT I COULDN'T CONSENT FOR THE REASONS I STATED, BECAUSE I DIDN'T KNOW THE COURT'S CALENDAR; THE COURT IS VERY BUSY. SHE MADE IT CLEAR TO ME, WELL, I DON'T KNOW WHERE THE MONEY IS.

AND I SAID WHAT ARE YOU COMING TO COURT FOR? WHY CONTINUE TO WASTE THE COURT'S TIME? YOU KNOW, THIS IS A WASTE OF TIME.

WE'VE BEEN HERE---I THINK THIS IS OUR SEVENTH HEARING, AND YOUR HONOR KEEPS PUTTING IT ON, YOU KNOW. AND YOUR HONOR HAS BEEN FASTIDIOUSLY FAIR AND BALANCED THROUGHOUT.

THE COURT: DIDN'T YOU SAY THAT YOU BROUGHT THIS TO THEIR ATTENTION AT SOME

POINT IN TIME? I THOUGHT I HEARD---

THE COURT: I THINK THE PROBLEM IS, AND I MAY BE WRONG ABOUT THIS, **BUT I THINK THE PROBLEM IS THAT WE KEEP FOCUSING ON ONE SOURCE OF MONEY.** AND I DON'T THAT'S---AND IT MAY BE INTERESTING, BUT WHATEVER THE FEE IS, YOU KNOW, THAT'S THE MONEY THAT SHE OWES AND IT DOESN'T HAVE TO COME FROM THERE. **IT CAN COME FROM SOMEWHERE ELSE.** BUT IT'S CLEAR THAT SHE HAS ASSETS. I MEAN, I---

COMMENT AND ANALYSIS: #6 *JUDGE EKANS PREFERRED TO TALK ABOUT BRIANNA JONES' "ASSETS" RATHER THAN THE "SETTLEMENT PROCEEDS." BRIANNA JONES TESTIFIED REPEATEDLY DURING COURT PROCEEDINGS THAT HER PORTION OF THE CASE SETTLEMENT PROCEEDS WERE NOT IN HER NAME.*

THUS, SHE MADE ADMISSIONS MORE THAN ONCE DURING COURT PROCEEDINGS THAT SETTLEMENT OF THE FLORIDA CASE HAD OCCURRED AND HER PORTION OF THE PROCEEDS WAS BEING HELD IN TRUST BY OTHERS.

MS. FRANKLIN: YOUR HONOR, THE ASSETS, AND I WOULD SAY THIS WITH HER BEING PRESENT, AS WELL, FOR THE PAST 15 YEARS SINCE I HAVE KNOWN HER, SHE HAS LIVED OFF OF THE GENEROSITY AND LARGESS OF ME, MY FAMILY, MY FRIENDS, AND IN LATER YEARS, HER FRIENDS. SHE HAS NOT WORKED IN THE WHOLE 15 THAT I HAVE KNOWN HER. AND WHEN I SUGGESTED TO HER, YOU NEED TO GET A JOB, SHE RESPONDS, **I'M A MILLIONAIREIST** (PHONETIC). I DON'T NEED TO WORK. AND SO, SHE BORROWS MONEY BASED ON THE SETTLEMENT PROCEEDS FROM HER CASE WHICH ARE NEVER DISTRIBUTED AND ARE NEVER DISBURSED.

THAT'S HOW SHE LIVES. SHE IS NOT GAINFULLY EMPLOYED. SHE IS NOT A WORKING PERSON. SHE SAYS WHEN SHE'S TRIED TO GET PUBLIC ASSISTANCE IN THE PAST, HER SOCIAL SECURITY NUMBER COMES UP AND SHOWS THAT SHE HAS SUBSTANTIAL ASSETS AND SO SHE HASN'T BEEN ABLE TO QUALIFY.

SO, THIS IS WHY---

THE COURT: WELL, WE NEED TO HAVE HER ON THE WITNESS STAND TO GET THAT EVIDENCE IN THE RECORD.

MS. FRANKLIN: AND DURING THE ORAL EXAM THAT WE HAD, YOUR HONOR. AND OBVIOUSLY, I HAVE MORE OF A RECOLLECTION OF THESE FACTS THAN YOUR HONOR. **SHE ACKNOWLEDGED THAT BANK OF AMERICA WAS THE INSTITUTION.** SHE ACKNOWLEDGED MEETING WITH BANKERS HERE IN THE REGION. AND WHEN YOUR HONOR SAID---WHEN I ASKED HER WHAT BRANCH, SHE SAID SHE DIDN'T RECALL. AND THAT'S WHEN YOUR HONOR SAID, YOU CAN STEP DOWN BECAUSE YOU'RE WASTING THE COURT'S TIME.

SO, IT'S JUST A GAME, AND I'M CONCERNED---**AND I GUESS THAT MY ULTIMATE, BOTTOM LINE REASON FOR FILING THE MOTION FOR COURT INVESTIGATION** IS BECAUSE I SEE THE COURT'S TIME JUST BEING TAKEN UP WITH, BASICALLY, NO REAL EVIDENCE AND REAL INFORMATION. AND IT'S JUST ONGOING, BECAUSE WE'VE BEEN DOING THIS NOW, YOU KNOW, SINCE JANUARY.

AND I DON'T SEE HER AS BEING AT ALL IN GOOD FAITH, AT ALL. AND I JUST DON'T SEE ANY INFORMATION BEING PROVIDED BY HER. AND, AND THE OTHER REASON I SUGGESTED THE COURT INVESTIGATION IS BECAUSE AT ONE POINT LAST YEAR--- NOT LAST YEAR, 2009 I THINK IT WAS, **THE BAR DID AN INVESTIGATION AND CONFIRMED THAT SHE WAS ENTITLED TO CONSIDERABLE ASSETS.** AND I THNK THE COURT MIGHT RECALL THAT SHE GAVE THE COURT A PAGE OF THAT COMMUNICATION FROM THE BAR. SO THE FUNDS ARE OUT THERE SOMEWHERE. WHERE IS THE QUESTION, AND WHO'S HOLDING THEM AND, YOU KNOW. THAT'S MY DELIMMA.

COMMENT AND ANALYSIS: #7 *IN JANUARY 2009, FOLLOWING THE FILING OF A D.C. BAR COMPLAINT AGAINST ME BY CERTAIN CREDITORS OF BRIANNA JONES, THE D.C. OFFICE OF BAR COUNSEL INVESTIGATED THE MATTER AND FOUND THAT BRIANNA JONES HAD SETTLED THE FLORIDA LAWSUIT AGAINST THE RIDGEWAY ESTATE, AND FURTHER CONFIRMED THAT SHE WAS ENTITLED TO "CONSIDERABLE ASSETS." THE D.C. OFFICE OF BAR COUNSEL IS ACKNOWLEDGED AS AN INVESTIGATIVE ARM OF THE D.C. COURT OF APPEALS.*

THIS IMPORTANT FINDING BY THE D.C. OFFICE OF BAR COUNSEL WAS NOT ADDRESSED BY JUDGE EKANS. NOR WAS THE FINDING ADDRESSED BY THE D.C. COURT OF APPEALS IN ITS DECISION OF JULY 2014.

IN OTHER WORDS, THE D.C. COURT SYSTEM AVOIDED ANY MENTION OF THE FINDING OF THE OFFICE OF BAR COUNSEL, AFTER FULL INVESTIGATION, THAT BRIANNA JONES WAS ENTITLED TO "CONSIDERABLE ASSETS" RESULTING FROM SETTLEMENT OF THE FLORIDA LAWSUIT THAT I BROUGHT ON HER BEHALF IN MAY 1996 IN THE BROWARD COUNTY CIRCUIT COURT IN FORT LAUDERDALE, FLORIDA AND AGAINST THE RIDGEWAY ESTATE.

THE COURT: ALL RIGHT. I'M GOING TO LOOK AT YOUR MOTION. IT'S MY RESPONSIBILITY TO LOOK AT THE MOTION. I DON'T HAVE ANY EXPERIENCE WITH THE COURT ORDERING AN INVESTIGATION. WE SOMETIMES APPOINT MASTERS, SPECIAL MASTERS TO DO AUDITS AND OTHER THINGS OF THAT NATURE. I'LL READ YOUR MOTION. I'LL SEE WHAT SUPPORT THERE IS OUT THERE FOR IT. I'LL EVEN TALK TO MY COLLEAGUES TO SEE IF ANYBODY HAS MORE EXPERIENCE THAN I DO IN SOMETHING LIKE THAT. BUT AS FAR AS MY EXPERIENCE AND THE LAW IS CONCERNED, THE ONLY JUDGES WHO INVESTIGATE ARE IN ITALY OR IN SOUTH AMERICA WHERE THAT'S THE RESPONSIBILITY OF THE JUDGE IN THE JUDICIAL SYSTEM. HERE, WE TEND TO TAKE EVIDENCE AND DECIDE BASED ON INVESTIGATIONS THAT OTHERS HAVE DONE. I DON'T KNOW THE EXTENT TO WHICH YOU MAY ALREADY HAVE HIRED A PRIVATE INVESTIGATOR. I DON'T KNOW.

BUT RIGHT NOW, I'M GOING TO TELL YOU RESPECTFULLY THAT I DON'T KNOW THAT THERE'S ANYTHING ELSE FOR US TO DO PRODUCTIVELY. I'LL READ YOUR MOTION. WE'LL SEE IF THE COURT SHOULD DO WHAT YOU SUGGEST.

COMMENT AND ANALYSIS: #8 *JUDGE EKANS' REMARKS REVEAL HIS VIEW OF THE EXTENT OF HIS RESPONSIBILITY REGARDING A MOTION FOR INVESTIGATION OF ALLEGED D.C. JUDICIAL AND FBI FRAUD, THEFT, CORRUPTION AND EXTORTION. FROM JUDGE EKANS' PERSPECTIVE, HIS RESPONSIBILITY WAS LIMITED TO LOOKING AT THE MOTION, AND THAT IS ALL HE DID PRIOR TO DISMISSING IT.*

THE COURT WAS FULLY AWARE THAT IT COULD NOT WITHSTAND THE INVESTIGATION OF ITS JUDICIAL COLLEAGUES COMPLICIT IN THE MASSIVE D.C. JUDICIAL AND FBI FRAUD, THEFT, CORRUPTION AND EXTORTION CONSPIRACY AND CRIMINAL ENTERPRISE THAT DEFINED MY CASE.

THUS, CORRUPT D.C. SUPERIOR COURT JUDGES COMPLICIT IN FRAUD, THEFT CORRUPTION AND EXTORTION CASES ARE TREATED BY THEIR FELLOW COLLEAGUES, SUCH AS JUDGE EKANS, AS IF THEY ARE ABOVE THE LAW, UNTOUCHABLE, AND EXEMPT FROM ANY AND ALL ACCOUNTABILITY FOR THEIR ABUSE OF JUDICIAL DISCRETION AND ACTS OF OFFICIAL MISCONDUCT, NO MATTER HOW EGREGIOUS OR CRIMINAL IN THEIR IMPORT AND IMPACT.

IN DEFERENCE TO HIS JUDICIAL COLLEAGUES COMPLICIT IN THE MASSIVE JUDICIAL AND FBI FRAUD, THEFT AND CORRUPTION CONSPIRACY AND CRIMINAL ENTERPRISE, JUDGE EKANS ABDICATED HIS RESPONSIBILITY AS A JUDICIAL OFFICER AND COURT JUDGE WHEN HE REFUSED AND FAILED TO ORDER AN INDEPENDENT INVESTIGATION OF THE CASE.

MY LAWSUIT BEGGED FOR AN INVESTIGATION BY AN INDEPENDENT BODY OR ENTITY BASED ON THE SERIOUS ALLEGATIONS OF D.C. JUDICIAL AND FBI FRAUD, THEFT, CORRUPTION AND EXTORTION ARTICULATED IN THE COURT TESTIMONY OF BRIANNA AND ME AND LATER SET FORTH IN FILED COURT PLEADINGS WHICH JUDGE EKANS CHOSE TO SWEEP UNDER THE RUG BY SIMPLY IGNORING THEM AND REMAINING SILENT ON THE ISSUES.

JUDGE EKANS' DECISION TO DENY THE MOTION FOR INVESTIGATION SHOULD NOT HAVE BEEN BASED ON HIS STATED LACK OF EXPERIENCE IN SUCH MATTERS, OR THE RELATIVE INEXPERIENCE OF HIS JUDICIAL COLLEAGUES IN SUCH MATTERS.

JUDGE EKANS' DENIAL OF THE MOTION FOR INVESTIGATION WAS NOTHING MORE THAN AN EGREGIOUS ABUSE OF ABSOLUTE JUDICIAL DISCRETION, POWER AND AUTHORITY THAT FURTHERED THE FLOURISHING OF THE MASSIVE D.C. JUDICIAL AND FBI FRAUD, THEFT, CORRUPTION AND EXTORTION CONSPIRACY AND CRIMINAL ENTERPRISE.

MS. FRANKLIN: AND IF NOT THE INVESTIGATION, YOUR HONOR, I HAD ASKED THE COURT SOMETIME BACK ABOUT THE POSSSIBILITY OF APPOINTING INDEPENDENT COUNSEL APPOINTED BY THE COURT, WHO COULD PROBABLY, VERY WELL DO THE SAME. YOU KNOW, SERVE THE SAME FUNCTION. SO, IF THAT IS AN ALTERNATIVE THAT IS GOING TO ACHIEVE OUR GOAL, THAT WOULD CERTAINLY BE SUFFICIENT AS WELL. SO, I'M NOT COMPLETELY WEDDED TO JUST THE INVESTIGATION. WHAT I'M TRYING TO DO IS COME UP WITH A PLAN OF ACTION THAT IS GOING TO IDENTIFY THE SETTLEMENT PROCEEDS, WHERE THEY'RE BEING HELD, WHO'S HOLDING THEM, ESPECIALLY AFTER SHE'S ALREADY TESTIFIED---

COMMENT AND ANALYSIS: #9 *EVEN THOUGH I CONTINUED TO PLEAD FOR AN INVESTIGATION THROUGH THE APPOINTMENT OF AN INDEPENDENT COUNSEL, I REALIZED THAT MY WORDS, HOWEVER NOBLE, WERE FALLING ON DEAF EARS. JUDGE EKANS HAD MADE UP HIS MIND. THERE WOULD BE NO COURT ORDERED INVESTIGATION ON HIS WATCH---THAT WAS FOR SURE. HIS ACTIONS SPOKE VOLUMES THAT HE WAS FULLY COMMITTED TO THE MISSION OF THE D.C. JUDICIAL AND FBI CRIMINAL ENTERPRISE TO STEAL THE MILLIONS OF DOLLARS OWED TO ME IN ATTORNEY'S FEES. HIS JUDICIAL COLLEAGUES AND CO-CONSPIRATORS, ALSO ALLEGEDLY COMPLICIT IN THE MASSIVE D.C. JUDICIAL AND FBI FRAUD, THEFT, CORRUPTION AND EXTORTION CONSPIRACY AND CRIMINAL ENTERPRISE COULD TAKE A SIGH OF RELIEF.*

MORE THAN ONCE DURING THE PROCEEDINGS I SAID TO MYSELF "SO, THIS IS HOW D.C. JUDICIAL FRAUD, THEFT, CORRUPTION AND EXTORTION OPERATES. THIS IS HOW CORRUPT D.C. COURT JUDGES GET AWAY EVERY DAY WITH STEALING MILLIONS OF DOLLARS FOR THEIR OWN ENRICHMENT AND NEVER HAVING TO ACCOUNT TO THE IRS OR ANYBODY ELSE."

THE COURT: WELL, LET ME ASK YOU THIS QUESTION. YOU'VE KNOWN THIS INDIVIDUAL FOR A LONG TIME?

MS. FRANKLIN: YES, YOUR HONOR.

THE COURT: HOW DO YOU KNOW THAT SHE KNOWS WHERE THE MONEY IS?

COMMENT AND ANALYSIS: #10 BRIANNA JONES *TESTIFIED REPEATEDLY THAT THE SETTLEMENT PROCEEDS WERE ON DEPOSIT AT BANK OF AMERICA. SHE ALSO INFORMED THE COURT OF HER REVIEW OF BANK RECORDS IN HER CLANDESTINE WASHINGTON REGION HOTEL SUITE MEETINGS WITH CO-CONSPIRATOR "OFFICIALS" THAT SHE WAS SUMMONED TO ATTEND IN THE WASHINGTON REGION. EKANS REMAINED SILENT ON THIS TESTIMONY.*

MS. FRANKLIN: WELL, SHE HAS USED SEVERAL OF MY FRIENDS AND BORROWED SUBSTANTIAL SUMS TO TRAVEL, TO---

THE COURT: IT'S CLEAR THAT SHE HAS ASSETS. MY QUESTION IS HOW DO YOU KNOW THAT SHE KNOWS WHERE THE MONEY IS? YOU SEE, SHE'S VERY EMPHATIC WHEN SHE SAYS SHE DOESN'T KNOW WHERE IT IS. HOW DO YOU KNOW THAT SHE DOES KNOW? BECAUSE I CAN'T COMPEL HER TO GIVE MEINFORMATION SHE DOESN'T HAVE. AND THAT'S HER POINT.

COMMENT AND ANALYSIS: #11 BRIANNA JONES *WAS UNDER COURT ORDER BY JUDGE STARR TO PRODUCE BANK OF AMERICA BANK STATEMENTS AND RELATED SETTLEMENT PROCEEDS DOCUMENTS. HOWEVER, FOR SOME REASON, THE COURT PREFERS TO FOCUS ON WHERE THE MONEY IS, A COLLATERAL ISSUE. JUDGE EKANS ALSO PREFERS MIXING APPLES AND ORANGES, AND JUST CALLING IT ALL FRUIT.*

MS. FRANKLIN: BUT YOUR HONOR, SHE HAS REPEATEDLY IN THE SEVEN HEARINGS THAT WE'VE HAD, SHE HAS AT LEAST AT MORE THAN ONE HEARING TESTIFIED UNDER OATH THAT SHE WAS AWARE OF WHERE THE MONEY WAS, AND THAT SHE HAS MET WITH BANKERS.

THE COURT: I HAVE NOT HEARD HER SAY THAT. I HAVE HEARD---

COMMENT AND ANALYSIS: #12 *MY REMARKS ARE INTENDED TO MAKE A RECORD THAT JUDGE EKANS HAS CONVENIENTLY AND BY DESIGN DUMMIED UP ON THE FACT THAT BRIANNA JONES **HAD REPEATEDLY TESTIFIED THAT THE MONEY WAS IN BANK OF AMERICA IN MULTIPLE ACCOUNTS BEARING THE NAMES OF UNKNOWN OTHERS.***

MS. FRANKLIN: YES, YOUR HONOR, AT THE ORAL EXAM, SHE SAID THAT.

THE COURT: WELL, WE'LL HAVE TO GET A RECORD OF THAT BECAUSE I DON'T REMEMBER THAT. WHAT I DO REMEMBER IS HER SAYING THAT PEOPLE GET IN TOUCH WITH HER. PEOPLE GET IN TOUCH WITH HER AND TELL HER WHAT BRANCH TO GO TO OR SO FORTH. THAT'S WHAT I REMEMBER HER SAYING.

COMMENT AND ANALYSIS: #13 *JUDGE EKANS ACKNOWLEDGES BRIANNA JONES' TESTIMONY REGARDING THE EXISTENCE OF A CONSPIRACY AND HER DESCRIPTION OF BEING INSTRUCTED BY CO-CONSPIRATOR "OFFICIALS" AS TO WHAT BRANCH TO GO TO. NEVERTHELESS, JUDGE EKANS DID NOT CONSIDER SUCH INFORMATION SUFFICIENT TO PROMPT HIM TO TAKE ANY ACTION WHATSOEVER. IT IS MY OPINION THAT HIS REFUSAL TO TAKE ANY ACTION WHATSOEVER IS FURTHER EVIDENCE OF SYSTEMIC, MASSIVE D.C. JUDICIAL CORRUPTION UNADDRESSED AND UNRESTRAINED.*

MS. FRANKLIN:

NO, I ASKED HER HAD SHE EVER MET WITH BANKERS, BECAUSE SHE HAD SHARED THAT INFORMATION WITH ME, AND SHE SAID, YES. AND I SAID, IN THE WASHINGTON REGION? SHE SAID, YES. AND I SAID, WHICH BRANCH. AND THAT'S WHEN SHE SAID, I DON'T RECALL. AND YOUR HONOR SAID, STEP DOWN.

SO, YES, SHE HAS TESTIFIED TO THAT, AND THAT WAS THE TESTIMONY GIVEN AT THE ORAL EXAM. AND THEN, AS FAR AS DOCUMENTS REGARDING THE SETTLEMENT PROCEEDS, THE HEARING THAT OCCURRED. AND I'VE FORGOTTEN THE EXACT DATE, BUT THE HEARING THAT OCCURRED THE DAY BEFORE I ATTEMPTED TO VISIT HER AT THE D.C. JAIL, SHE ASKED YOUR HONOR IF SHE COULD MEET WITH ME.

SHE WAS HOLDING A LARGE MANILA ENVELOPE, AND SHE SAID, OH, I HAVE THE DOCUMENTS, YOUR HONOR. COULD I PLEASE GO OVER THEM WITH MS. FRANKLIN. **YOU SAID THERE'S NO PLACE HERE IN THE COURTHOUSE.** MS. FRANKLIN, CAN YOU GO TO THE JAIL? AND I SAID, YES. AND I ATTEMPTED TO VISIT HER IN THE JAIL AND OF COURSE, THEY SAID I COULDN'T BECAUSE SHE WAS ON SUICIDE WATCH.

COMMENT AND ANALYSIS: #14 *I REMIND JUDGE EKANS THAT AT THE HEARING ON JANUARY 31, 2011, BRIANNA JONES OFFERED TO REVIEW WITH ME RIGHT THERE IN THE COURTROOM THE BANK RECORDS SHE HELD IN HER HANDS ENCLOSED IN A LARGE MANILA ENVELOPE. I FURTHER REMIND JUDGE EKANS THAT HE WOULD NOT ALLOW BRIANNA JONES TO DO SO. JUDGE EKANS PROVED BY THIS ACTION THAT HE WAS PROTECTING AND PROMOTING THE ONGOING D.C. JUDICIAL AND FBI CRIMINAL ENTERPRISE. HE ALSO PROVES THAT HE IS AN UNQUALIFIED PARTICIPANT IN THE ONGOING CRIMINAL ENTERPRISE THAT DOMINATES MY LAWSUIT AND WHOSE MISSION IS TO DEFRAUD ME OF AN ESTIMATED $50 MILLION IN ATTORNEY'S FEES.*

JUDGE EKANS' REFUSAL TO ALLOW BRIANNA JONES TO REVIEW BANK DOCUMENTS WITH ME IN THE COURTHOUSE WAS NOTHING BUT AN ACT AND ILLUSTRATION OF IN YOUR FACE, IN THE OPEN COURTROOM AND IN BROAD DAYLIGHT, A CLASSIC ILLUSTRATION OF AN EGREGIOUS ABUSE OF JUDICIAL DISCRETION THAT TRANSLATES INTO D.C. JUDICIAL FRAUD, THEFT AND CORRUPTION.

MS. FRANKLIN: SO, SHE HAS---THAT WAS ONE INSTANCE, AND THEN WE HAVE THE OTHER INSTANCE AT THE ORAL EXAM. SO, MY CONCERN, TOO, YOUR HONOR, IS HAS SHE TAKEN UP THE COURT'S TIME LYING AND NOT BEING TRUTHFUL WITH THE COURT, **AND NOW ALL OF A SUDDEN SHE DOESN'T KNOW. AND, YOU KNOW, A MONTH OR SO AGO SHE KNEW VERY SPECIFICALLY.** THIS IS WHY I SAY IT'S JUST THIS CONSTANT BACK-AND-FORTH, AND HER WORD IS JUST, IT'S JUST NOT RELIABLE.

THE COURT: ALL RIGHT.

MS. FRANKLIN: SO, YOUR HONOR, YOU SAID 11 A.M. ON FRIDAY?

THE COURT: NEXT FRIDAY, NEXT FRIDAY.

MS. FRANKLIN: ALL RIGHT. THANK YOU, YOUR HONOR.

THE COURT: THANK YOU VERY MUCH. HAVE A GOOD DAY AND A GOOD WEEKEND.

MS. FRANKLIN: YOU, TOO, YOUR HONOR.

(THEREUPON, THE PROCEEDINGS WERE CONCLUDED.)

SUPERIOR COURT OF THE DISTRICT OF COLUMBIA
CIVIL DIVISION
WASHINGTON, D.C.

THE HONORABLE MATTHEW D. EKANS, ASSOCIATE JUDGE, PRESIDING

THE FOLLOWING ARE EXCERPTS OF THE OFFICIAL COURT TRANSCRIPT OF THE
MARCH 18, 2011 PROCEEDING
ANNOTATED BY THE AUTHOR'S PERTINENT COMMENTARY AND ANALYSIS

MARCH 18, 2011

P R O C E E D I N G S

THE COURT:	GOOD AFTERNOON.
DEPUTY CLERK:	YOUR HONOR, CALLING THE CASE OF BARBARA WASHINGTON FRANKLIN VERSUS BRIANNA JONES, CIVIL ACTION 4417 AND 2009 IN THE MATTER OF BRIANNA JONES CCC1, 2011.
	PARTIES COME FORWARD AND IDENTIFY YOURSELVES FOR THE RECORD.
MS. FRANKLIN:	GOOD AFTERNOON, YOUR HONOR. BARBARA WASHINGTON FRANKLIN, PLAINTIFF, PRO SE.
MS. JONES:	GOOD AFTERNOON, YOUR HONOR. BRIANNA JONES, DEFENDANT PRO SE HOWEVER, BEING LEGALLY ADVISED BY ATTORNEY MARCUS ROSEN.
THE COURT:	ALL RIGHT. MS. BRIANNA JONES, DID YOU BRING SOME THINGS WITH YOU?
MS. JONES:	YES, I DID, YOUR HONOR.
THE COURT:	WHAT DID YOU BRING?

COMMENT AND ANALYSIS: #1 *IT SHOULD BE NOTED THAT THIS WAS MY 2ND APPEARANCE DURING THE DAY FOR THE HEARING, WHICH HAD BEEN INITIALLY SCHEDULED FOR 10:00 A.M. HOWEVER, BRIANNA JONES HAD CALLED THE JUDGE'S ADMINISTRATIVE ASSISTANT, AND SAID THAT SHE HADN'T BEEN ABLE TO TAKE THE 7:00 A.M. FLIGHT; THAT SHE WOULD INSTEAD BE TAKING THE 11:50 A.M. FLIGHT; THAT SHE HAD SOME PHYSICAL PROBLEMS THAT PREVENTD HER FROM TAKING THE EARLIER FLIGHT, AND THUS WOULD BE AT THE COURTHOUSE AT 3:00 P.M.*

THE HEARING COMMENCED AT APPROXIMATELY 3:59 P.M. AS VERIFIED BY THE OFFICIAL COURT TRANSCRIPT. BRIANNA JONES WAS ALLOWED TO ENTER HER APPEARANCE WITHOUT MAKING ANY APOLOGY TO THE COURT OR PROVIDING AN EXPLANATION FOR HER ARRIVAL IN THE COURTROOM SOME FIVE HOURS AFTER THE HEARING WAS SCHEDULED TO BEGIN.

THIS WAS NOT THE FIRST TIME SHE, IN FACT, HAD DETERMINED WHEN A HEARING WOULD BEGIN. IT WAS A REGULAR OCCURRENCE, AND SHE SUFFERED NO APPROPRIATE PENALTY IMPOSED BY THE COURT OR ADMONISHMENT BY THE COURT OF ANY KIND WHATSOEVER. NOR DID THE JUDGE ADMONISH BRIANNA JONES IN ANY MANNER FOR THE INCONVENIENCE SHE HAD CAUSED ME, IF NOT THE COURT.

HOWEVER, BY THE TIME THE HEARING HAD ENDED, I WOULD HAVE A COMPLETE UNDERSTANDING OF THE JUDGE'S PERMISSIVE ATTITUDE TOWARDS BRIANNA JONES, EVEN THOUGH SHE HAD BEEN IN CONTEMPT OF JUDGE STARR'S OCTOBER 18, 2010 ORDER FOR 3 MONTHS, AND WITH NO OBVIOUS PROSPECT OF HAVING TO ACCOUNT FOR HER PROTRACTED CONTEMPTUOUS CONDUCT OF WILLFULLY REFUSING TO OBEY JUDGE STARR'S ORDER TO TURN OVER BANK OF AMERICA BANK STATEMENTS TO ME.

BRIANNA JONES REPEATEDLY USED "THE SICK CARD" WHEN SHE WAS IN THE MIDST OF DISOBEYING THE COURT'S ORDER TO APPEAR ON TIME FOR A HEARING AND OTHERWISE. IN ONE INSTANCE, HER FAILURE TO APPEAR AT THE HEARING IN AUGUST 2011 WAS ALLEGEDLY BECAUSE SHE WOULD BE IN THE HOSPITAL FOR SURGERY. BY THIS TIME, THE JUDGE HAD ENOUGH EXPERIENCE WITH JONES TO GO FORWARD WITH THE HEARING IN SPITE OF HER WILLFUL FAILURE TO APPEAR.

MS. JONES: I BROUGHT ALL OF MY FINANCIAL STATEMENTS, AND I ALSO HAVE EVIDENCE OF MY IMMINENT MOVE TO THIS REGION.

THE COURT: YOU MAY HAVE NOTICED THAT I DIDN'T RUN DOWN HERE, AS SOON AS THE CLERK NOTIFIED ME THAT YOU WERE HERE AND READY. I HAD HOPED THAT **IF YOU BROUGHT THINGS** THAT YOU WOULD HAVE SAT OUTSIDE THERE---**I WOULD SAY THAT IN EIGHT OUT OF TEN ORAL EXAMINATIONS, WHICH IS HOW THIS STARTED WITH ME,** THE PARTIES MEET OUT IN THE WHAT WE CALL THE WITNESS ROOMS. AND THE **JUDGMENT CREDITOR** WILL BE [GO] OVER THE **JUDGMENT DEBTOR'S** DOCUMENTS, AND THEY'LL COME IN AND MOST OFTEN TELL THE COURT, YOU KNOW, THAT THEY'VE GOT IT ALL WORKED OUT AND THEY'RE SATISFIED. THE COURT SELDOM HAS TO GET INVOLVED, CERTAINLY NOT TO THE EXTENT I'VE HAD TO GET INVOLVED IN THIS MATTER.
SO IF YOU'VE GOT THINGS, I THINK YOU AND MS. FRANKLIN SHOULD SIT OUT THERE AND GO THROUGH YOUR NUMBERS SO THAT SHE CAN DETERMINE HOW SHE'S GOING TO COLLECT HER DEBT.

COMMENT AND ANALYSIS: #2 *JUDGE EKANS, IN HIS OPENING REMARKS, LAID THE FOUNDATION OR MORE PRECISELY, THE "JUDGMENT CREDITOR TRAP" THAT HE HAD SPECIFICALLY CREATED AND DESIGNED FOR ME THROUGH THE EGREGIOUS ABUSE OF HIS VIRTUALLY UNLIMITED POWER OF JUDICIAL DISCRETION. DEFINING ME AS A JUDGMENT CREDITOR WOULD SERVE TO JUSTIFY THE COURT'S RATIONALE FOR REFUSING TO ORDER THE INDEPENDENT INVESTIGATION THAT, AT A BARE MINIMUM, THE CASE CALLED FOR. FURTHER, IT WOULD BE THE RABBIT HOLE, TAILORED AND CONSTRUCTED BY THE COURT TO WHICH I WAS RELEGATED UNTIL THE ULTIMATE RIGGED DISMISSAL OF MY CASE WITH PREJUDICE IN MARCH 2015.*

DURING THE ENTIRE PENDENCY OF MY CASE BEFORE JUDGE EKANS, NO JUDGMENT EXISTED. THE $13.6 MILLION JUDGMENT HE ISSUED ME WAS ISSUED AT THE CONCLUSION OF MY CASE, AND AS A "QUICK-FIX" SUBSTITUTE REMEDY HE AND HIS CO-CONSPIRATOR JUDICIAL COLLEAGUES CREATED IN RESPONSE TO BRIANNA JONES' PERMANENT REFUSAL TO TURN OVER BANK OF AMERICA BANK STATEMENTS, PURSUANT TO JUDGE STARR'S COURT ORDER. HOW IRONIC. PURSUANT TO COURT ORDER.

THE COURT'S FALSE, REPEATED, PERSISTENT LABELING, MISCHARACTERIZATION AND REFFERAL TO ME AS A "JUDGMENT-CREDITOR" THROUGHOUT THE ENTIRETY OF THE PROCEEDINGS AND DURATION OF MY CASE SERVED AS THE COURT'S NECESSARY BUILDING BLOCKS TO RIG MY CASE FOR ITS ULTIMATE AND "FINAL DISMISSAL" ON JANUARY 16, 2015, AND A FURTHER "DISMISSAL WITH PREJUDICE" IN MARCH 2015 OF ALL MY CLAIMS AGAINST BRIANNA JONES, IN RESPONSE TO MY REQUEST THAT THE COURT RECONSIDER THE SERIOUS ALLEGATIONS OF D.C. JUDICIAL AND FBI FRAUD, THEFT, CORRUPTION AND EXTORTION CONSPIRACY AND CRIMINAL ENTERPRISE THAT DOMINATED THE CASE FROM THE VERY BEGINNING.

IN THE END, THROUGH THE EGREGIOUS ABUSE OF JUDICIAL DISCRETION, THE "JUDGMENT CREDITOR TRAP" THAT JUDGE EKANS MADE, LAID AND SPRUNG FOR ME WAS IN DEFERENCE TO THE PROTECTION OF THE D.C. JUDICIAL AND FBI CO-CONSPIRATORS. IT ALSO SERVED TO SHIELD THEM FROM INVESTIGATION, PROSECUTION AND PUNISHMENT. AND MOST SIGNIFICANTLY, IT ALLOWED THEM TO MAINTAIN THEIR CONTINUED ENJOYMENT OF THE MILLIONS OF DOLLARS THAT REPRESENTED MY STOLEN ESTIMATED $50 MILLION IN EARNED ATTORNEY'S FEES. FURTHER, IT SERVED AS THE DEADLIEST OF WEAPONS, THE MOST POISONOUS OF ARROWS, AND THE MOST DESTRUCTIVE OF MISSILES IN EXTINGUISHING ALL MY CLAIMS, HOWEVER MERITORIOUS, AGAINST BRIANNA JONES.

JUDGE EKANS' ACTIONS IN FAVOR OF THE CO-CONSPIRATORS IS A CLASSIC ILLUSTRATION OF WHAT I HAVE TERMED "STEALTH ADVOCACY BY THE COURT" IN A CASE OF MASSIVE, D.C. JUDICIAL AND FBI FRAUD, THEFT, CORRUPTION AND EXTORTION.

MY CASE STANDS FOR, AMONG OTHER THINGS, THE REALITY THAT IN THE DISTRICT OF COLUMBIA, RELIEF FOR D.C. COURT JUDGES, FBI AGENTS, AND OTHER OFFICIALS ENGAGED IN MASSIVE D.C. AND FBI FRAUD, THEFT, CORRUPTION AND EXTORTION IS SPELLED "JUDGMENT CREDITOR."

THE THRESHOLD QUESTION IS HOW DOES A PARTY LITIGANT ADDRESS A PRESIDING COURT JUDGE WHO AUDACIOUSLY, SHAMELESSLY AND INTENTIONALLY CHANGES AND TWISTS THE MAJOR FACTS IN A CASE, REFUSES TO ADOPT APPROPRIATE REMEDIES AND DEFINES THE MAJOR ISSUES AND THE MAJOR ROLES OF THE PARTIES IN THE CASE TO SERVE, NOT THE SEARCH FOR THE TRUTH, NOR THE ENDS OF JUSTICE, BUT RATHER THE SUBORDINATION OF THE TRUTH AND JUSTICE TO THE GRAND SCHEME, MASTER PLAN AND CRIMINAL ENTERPRISE OF THE KEY D.C. JUDICIAL AND FBI CO-CONSPIRATORS, SOME OF WHOM SERVE AS HIS FELLOW COLLEAGUES ON THE BENCH OF D.C. SUPERIOR COURT AND THE D.C. COURT OF APPEALS?

FINALLY, HOW DOES A PARTY LITIGANT ADDRESS A PRESIDING JUDGE WHO, AT THE END OF THE DAY, WHEN ALL THE FACTS AND CIRCUMSTANCES ARE CONSIDERED, AND IN SPITE OF HIS PERIODIC GASLIGHTING MONOLOGUES (ALL OF WHICH RING FALSE) THROUGHOUT THE PROCEEDINGS OF HIS COMMITMENT TO MAKING CERTAIN THAT THE AUTHORITY OF THE COURT IS NOT ABUSED, THE OFFICIAL COURT RECORD REFLECTS, IN ONE INSTANCE AFTER ANOTHER, THAT THE JUDGE HAS MANAGED TO EGREGIOUSLY ABUSE HIS POWER OF DISCRETION, NOT BY HAPPENSTANCE, NOR BY HARMLESS ERROR, NOR BY INADVERTENCE, BUT BY ONE BIASED, PARTIAL, DELIBERATE, INTENTIONAL AND PURPOSEFUL RULING AND DECISION AFTER ANOTHER?

MS. FRANKLIN: YOUR HONOR, MAY I ASK A QUESTION? THE

COURT: YES.

MS. FRANKLIN: **DOES THE DEFENDANT HAVE BANK DOCUMENTS EVIDENCING HER RECEIPT OF SETTLEMENT PROCEEDS THAT ARE THE SUBJECT OF THIS MATTER?**

THE COURT: DO YOU UNDERSTAND WHAT SHE'S ASKING?

MS. JONES: YES, YOUR HONOR.

MS. FRANKLIN: AND FURTHER, EXCUSE ME, YOUR HONOR, DOES SHE HAVE DOCUMENTS WHICH WOULD PUT HER IN COMPLIANCE WITH THIS COURT'S ORDER OF OCTOBER 18, 2010?

MS. JONES: YOUR HONOR, I NEVER HAD DOCUMENTS WITH REGARD TO BANK STATEMENTS TO THE SETTLEMENT. I HAVE NO IDEA WITH REGARD TO THOSE SETTLEMENT PROCEEDS; HOWEVER, YOU REQUESTED I BRING ALL FINANCIAL PERSONAL DOCUMENTS, AND THAT'S WHAT I HAVE DONE.

COMMENT AND ANALYSIS: **#3** *HERE BRIANNA JONES LIES, ONCE AGAIN. SHE HAS COMPLETELY AND CONVENIENTLY FORGOTTEN HER COURT TESTIMONY AT THE HEARING ON* **JANUARY 21, 2011** *IN WHICH SHE ACKNOWLEGED HAVING RECEIPT OF BANK RECORDS EVIDENCING THE AMOUNT OF THE SETTLEMENT PROCEEDS SAID TO BE* **$80 MILLION.**

AND AT THIS POINT, JUDGE EKANS MAKES IT CLEAR THAT WHETHER JONES IS LYING OR TELLING THE TRUTH, IT MAKES NO DIFFERENCE TO THE COURT. AFTER ALL, WHAT HAS TRUTH GOT TO DO WITH IT? MOREOVER, HIS FOCUS IS ON HIS KEY ROLE IN THE MAINTENANCE OF THE FLOURISHING CRIMINAL ENTERPRISE.

THE COURT: OKAY. THAT'S WHAT I---AT LEAST THAT'S WHAT I THOUGHT I ORDERED YOU TO DO.

MS. JONES: THANK YOU.

THE COURT: THESE ARE PAPERS THAT SHOW ME HOW YOU PAY FOR YOUR CLOTHES---

MS. JONES: I THINK---

THE COURT: ---YOUR FOOD, AND WHERE YOU LIVE, AND SO FORTH?

MS. JONES: YES, EVERYTHING.

THE COURT: YEAH, THAT'S WHAT I ASKED FOR. DID YOU BRING---I ASSUME YOU PAY TAXES. MAYBE---I SHOULDN'T MAKE THAT ASSUMPTION, BUT YOU'RE A CITIZEN, SO I ASSUME YOU PAY TAXES EVERY YEAR?

MS. JONES: NO.

THE COURT: YOU DON'T PAY TAXES?

MS. JONES: I GO IN---I'VE GONE IN. I HAVE STATEMENTS FROM THE---I'VE TALKED TO THE INTERNAL REVENUE. I DISCUSSED THIS WITH---

THE COURT: YOU TALKED WITH THEM?

MS. JONES:	SPOKE WITH THEM, I MADE NOTE OF IT.
THE COURT:	I TRY NOT TO TALK TO THEM.
MS. JONES:	I'VE GONE IN ON SEVERAL OCCASIONS.
THE COURT:	CAN YOU JUST---YOU DON'T PAY TAXES?
MS. JONES:	I'M NOT EMPLOYED, AND SO I----
THE COURT:	YOU DON'T HAVE INCOME?
MS. JONES:	YES, I HAVE INCOME---
THE COURT:	WELL, SEE, IRS DOESN'T TALK ABOUT EMPLOYED, THEY DON'T ASK IF YOU'RE EMPLOYED. THEY ASK IF YOU HAVE INCOME.
MS. JONES:	I HAVE THE SOURCE FOR THE SUPPORT.
THE COURT:	THAT'S WHAT SHE'S LOOKING FOR, THE SOURCE.
MS. JONES:	I HAVE THAT INFORMATION HERE.
THE COURT:	WHAT YOU GOT?
MS. JONES:	SHOULD I PASS IT TO YOU?
THE COURT:	TELL ME WHAT YOU HAVE.
MS. JONES:	IT'S A LETTER FROM THE INDIVIDUAL THAT'S THE SOURCE.
THE COURT:	PASS IT TO MS. FRANKLIN. SO YOU'VE GOT A PERSON WHO'S THE SOURCE?
MS. JONES:	THAT'S CORRECT. AND I EXPLAINED THAT TO THE INTERNAL REVENUE ON SEVERAL OCCASIONS.
THE COURT:	WHAT KIND OF A SOURCE IS THAT PERSON?
MS. JONES:	HE'S A DEAR, DEAR FRIEND.
THE COURT:	AND SO---I MEAN, YOU PROBABLY THINK I AM VERY FAMILIAR WITH THIS, BUT I'M NOT. I'VE ALWAYS WORKED, SO MY SOURCE, AT LEAST FOR THE LAST 25 YEARS, HAS BEEN THE FEDERAL GOVERNMENT. BUT YOU'VE GOT A SOURCE THAT'S A DEAR FRIEND. HOW DOES THAT WORK?

MS. JONES:	YOUR HONOR, HE'S BEEN A DEAR FRIEND FOR QUITE SOME TIME. HE UNDERSTANDS WHAT---
THE COURT:	NO, NO, I DON'T WANT TO KNOW YOUR RELATIONSHIP. I WANT TO KNOW HOW IT WORKS.
MS. JONES:	HE OFFERED.
THE COURT:	I'M SORRY?
MS. JONES:	HE SUGGESTED, AND HE SAID, I WILL SUPPORT YOU THROUGH THIS. HE OFFERED.
THE COURT:	DO YOU THINK HE'S WILLING TO SUPPORT MS. FRANKLIN? BECAUSE YOU'RE GOING TO HAVE TO START TURNING OVER YOUR SUPPORT DIRECTLY TO MS. FRANKLIN.
MS. JONES:	YOUR HONOR, IT'S NOT AN ISSUE OF NOT WANTING TO BE EMPLOYED.
THE COURT:	LISTEN, LISTEN, I AM NOT---DON'T MISUNDERSTAND ME. I'M NOT TELLING YOU TO GET A JOB. SHOOT, I THINK IT IS REALLY SPECIAL WHEN YOU CAN HAVE, YOU KNOW, A REASONABLE INCOME WITHOUT WORKING. THAT'S DESIRABLE, SO I'M NOT CRITICIZING. I'M JUST SAYING THAT THAT'S GOING TO HAVE TO FLOW NOW PAST YOU TO THE PERSON YOU OWE.

COMMENT AND ANALYSIS: #4 *THE COURT'S INQUIRY OF BRIANNA JONES REGARDING HER PERSONAL INCOME, WHETHER SHE PAID TAXES, WHO SUPPORTED HER, WAS JUST A COMPLETE WASTE OF TIME, RESULTING IN MY BEING FURTHER STRETCHED BY JUDGE EKANS AND TO THE OBVIOUS SATISFACTION AND RELIEF OF THE D.C. JUDICIAL AND FBI CO-CONSPIRATORS.*

IT HAD ALREADY BEEN ESTABLISHED EARLY ON IN THE CASE, AND BY BRIANNA JONES HERSELF, THAT BRIANNA JONES WAS MENTALLY ILL, PHYSICALLY IMPAIRED AND WITHOUT EMPLOYMENT OR INDEPENDENT MEANS OF SUPPORT. PERIOD.

IT WAS CLEAR THAT SINCE THE LAST HEARING, JUDGE EKANS' ENTIRE ATTITUDE AND DEMEANOR HAD MADE A COMPLETE 360 DEGREE TURN. NOW THE JUDGE WAS ALL BUT CASUAL, EASY, DETACHED, AND EVEN AMUSED AT TIMES.

JUDGE EKANS APPEARED TO ENJOY THE MINDLESS AND INSIGNIFICANT REPARTEE WITH BRIANNA JONES. AT TIMES THEIR DIALOGUE, AND THE OVERALL ATMOSPHERE OF THE COURT, REMINDED ME OF THE ONE OR TWO TIMES I HAD SURFED PAST "FAMILY FEUD" WHILE WATCHING TELEVISION.

JUDGE EKANS LET IT BE KNOWN TO ALL PRESENT THAT HE DIDN'T GIVE A HOOT AS TO THE FACT THAT BRIANNA JONES WAS, EACH TIME SHE CAME BEFORE HIM, IN BOLD, OPEN AND NOTORIOUS CONTEMPT OF JUDGE STARR'S ORDER TO TURN OVER BANK OF AMERICA BANK STATEMENTS TO ME. THIS WAS A CLEAR EXAMPLE OF HOW THE EVIDENCE OF THE D.C. JUDICIAL AND FBI CRIMINAL ENTERPRISE PLAYED OUT IN THE COURTROOM.

IT WAS ONLY REASONABLE AND FAIR TO PRESUME THAT JUDGE EKANS HAD NOW BEEN SUFFICIENTLY BRIEFED AND SCHOOLED BY JUDGES MANDARIN AND SKINNER, BOTH ALLEGED TO HAVE BEEN COMPLICIT IN THIS MASSIVE CULTURE OF COMPLICITY AND CRIMINAL ENTERPRISE OF D.C. JUDICIAL AND FBI FRAUD, THEFT, CORRUPTION AND EXTORTION.

THE COURT: THAT'S FAIR, ISN'T IT? JUST HOW DEAR IS THIS FRIEND? I MEAN---

MS. JONES: HE'S A DEACON AT MY CHURCH.

THE COURT: WELL, THEN IT'S HONEST---MAYBE.

MS. JONES: WE SHARE AN HONORABLE PROFOUND LOVE AND AFFECTION FOR ONE ANOTHER AND RESPECT.

THE COURT: I DON'T WANT TO GET INTO YOUR PERSONAL LIFE, BUT HOW ARE WE GOING TO GET----YOU KNOW, HOW WE GOING TO GET THAT TO MS. FRANKLIN?

DO YOU KNOW WHAT I'M SAYING?

MS. JONES: ABSOLUTELY, YOUR HONOR.

THE COURT: **OKAY. HOW WE GOING TO DO THAT?**

SEE, SHE WANTS A LUMP SUM, BUT I AM NOT REALLY CONCERNED WHETHER SHE GETS A LUMP SUM OR NOT, AS LONG AS YOU'RE SATISFYING YOUR OBLIGATION UNDER THE SETTLEMENT TO PAY HER THE MONEY. THEN I'LL FEEL LIKE WE DID WHAT WE HAD TO DO.

COMMENT AND ANALYSIS: #5 THIS STATEMENT BY EKANS TO BRIANNA JONES THAT I WANTED A LUMP SUM, AND THAT HE REALLY WASN'T CONCERNED WHETHER I GOT A LUMP SUM OR NOT, AS LONG AS SHE WAS "SATISFYING HER OBLIGATION UNDER THE SETTLEMENT TO PAY THE MONEY" WAS AN ILLUSTRATION OF HOW I WAS, AT VARIOUS TIMES, MOCKED, DISRESPECTED, DEMEANED, DISMISSED AND PREJUDICED BY JUDGE EKANS IN OPEN COURT AND ON THE RECORD.

BARBARA WASHINGTON FRANKLIN

THE FACT THAT, AS A TRIAL ATTORNEY, I WAS ALSO AN OFFICER OF THE COURT, DIDN'T COME INTO PLAY AS FAR AS THIS JUDGE WAS CONCERNED. HIS EYE WAS ON THE PRIZE HE WOULD RECEIVE FOR THE CRITICAL ROLE HE PLAYED IN THE ONGOING D.C. JUDICIAL AND FBI CRIMINAL ENTERPRISE WHOSE MISSION WAS TO STRIP AND ROB ME OF AN ESTIMATED $50 MILLION IN ATTORNEY'S FEES.

FURTHER, THIS STATEMENT BY THE COURT WAS NOTHING MORE THAN JUDICIAL TRASH TALK AND ABUSE. MOREOVER, I INTERPRETED THE JUDGE'S STATEMENT TO MEAN THAT HE, BOTTOM LINE, WAS REALLY NOT CONCERNED AS TO WHETHER I WAS PAID ANYTHING AT ALL. HE CONFIRMED MY INTERPRETATION WITH HIS EVENTUAL RIGGED DISMISSAL OF MY CASE FOUR YEARS LATER IN JANUARY 2015.

MS. JONES: I'M WILLING, EVEN NOW----

THE COURT: I'M NOT ASKING WHAT YOU'RE WILLING, SEE, IT'S A COURT ORDER. AT THIS POINT, YOU DON'T HAVE TO BE WILLING AT THIS POINT, YOU DON'T HAVE TO BE WILLING.

MS. JONES: WELL, I HAVE RECEIVED AN OFFER FROM RALPH DELL, A HARVARD-EDUCATED ATTORNEY, AND HE VETTED ME, AND HE SAID YOUR STORY IS SO UNBELIEVABLE, IF THAT'S TRUE, WAS THAT I WANT TO---HE WANTS TO BECOME AN AGENT.

THE COURT: YOU KNOW I THINK THAT THAT SHOULD BE A CONFIDENTIAL COMMUNICATION BETWEEEN YOU AND MR. DELL. I'M NOT REALLY CONCERNED ABOUT THAT. I MEAN, YOU KNOW, IT'S---WHAT AM I GOING TO DO WITH THAT INFORMATION?

MS. JONES: IT'S IN REGARD TO GENERATING INCOME.

THE COURT: WHAT AM I GOING TO DO WITH THAT? HOW CAN I USE THAT INFORMATION? YOU SEE. I DON'T LIKE TO CLUTTER MY MIND WITH INFORMATION I CAN'T USE---

MS. JONES: I SEE.

THE COURT: ---BECAUSE I HAVE SO MUCH INFORMATION THAT I HAVE TO PROCESS THAT I DON'T HAVE ANY SPACE FOR INFORMATION I CAN'T USE. SO, THE ONLY THING THAT WE NEED TO GET DONE HERE, SINCE THAT'S YOUR SOURCE OF INCOME AND SINCE YOU OWE THAT INCOME TO THIS SIDE OF THE TABLE, WE JUST NEED TO WORK THE MECHANICS OUT.

AND SO, INSTEAD OF YOUR DEAR FRIEND THE DEACON, YOU KNOW, PAYING YOU, HE JUST PAYS MS. FRANKLIN. HOW ARE WE GOING TO GET THAT DONE?

MS. JONES:	AS YOU SAID, WE'D HAVE TO ALL SIT DOWN AND WORK OUT THE MECHANICS.
THE COURT:	I'M NOT SITTING DOWN WORKING ON THAT.
MS. JONES:	I HAVE TO SIT DOWN WITH THE PLAINTIFF.
THE COURT:	OKAY. DID YOU WANT TO SHOW HER THE REST OF THOSE PAPERS?
MS. JONES:	ABSOLUTELY.

MS. FRANKLIN: YOUR HONOR, MY COMMENT THAT WITH REGARD TO THE STATEMENT FROM MR. TED MINOR THAT HE HAS PROVIDED SUBSTANTIAL FINANCIAL SUPPORT FOR NEARLY FIVE YEARS TO BRIANNA JONES. THIS IS DATED MARCH 16, 2011.

THIS MATTER HAS BEEN GOING ON FOR APPROXIMATELY 15 YEARS. AND I MIGHT ADD, I'VE HAD FRIENDS IN THE COURTROOM, SOME OF WHOM ARE PRESENT TODAY. DURING THAT PERIOD OF TIME, THEY HAVE PROVIDED TENS OF THOUSANDS OF DOLLARS FOR HER SUPPORT.

THE COURT: **MS. FRANKLIN, I WANT YOU TO UNDERSTAND SOMETHING. I'VE BEEN TRYING TO FIGURE OUT HOW TO EXPLAIN THIS TO YOU, AND THE ONLY THING I CAN THINK TO DO IS JUST BE DIRECT AND BLUNT.**

YOU FILED A PAPER SAYING THAT ONE THING I COULD DO WOULD BE TO BRING THE FBI IN HERE AND HAVE THEM INVESTIGATE. YOU KNOW, I DON'T *SEE THAT AS THE COURT'S RESPONSIBILITY*. I INTEND TO USE THE AUTHORITY THAT I HAVE UNDER THE LAW TO SEE THAT ORDERS THAT WE ISSUE ARE FAIR, ARE WELL CONSIDERED AND ARE LEGAL.

NOW, I'LL SAY IT AGAIN, SINCE IT'S NOT SINKING IN. YOU'VE GOT A SETTLEMENT AGREEMENT THAT CALLS FOR HER TO PAY A SUBSTANTIAL SUM OF MONEY, AND YOU DON'T KNOW WHERE THAT MONEY IS. SHE SAYS SHE DON'T KNOW WHERE THE MONEY IS.

MS. FRANKLIN: YOUR HONOR, MAY---

THE COURT: DON'T INTERRUPT ME.

COMMENT AND ANALYSIS: #6 *THIS DIRECT, BLUNT, UNEQUIVOCAL, PREJUDICIAL AND PROLONGED STATEMENT BY JUDGE EKANS GAVE HIM THE OPPORTUNITY TO CARVE IN STONE HIS ENSHRINED POSITION WITH REGARD TO MY PREVIOUS REPEATED REQUESTS FOR INVESTIGATION BY THE FBI OR A COMPARABLE ENTITY: HE DIDN'T SEE SUCH INVESTIGATION AS THE COURT'S RESPONSIBILITY. HE SAW AN INVESTIGATION OF ALLEGED D.C. JUDICIAL AND FBI FRAUD, THEFT CORRUPTION AND EXTORTION CONSPIRACY AND CRIMINAL ENTERPRISE AS MY RESPONSIBILITY.*

THIS STATEMENT, MORE THAN ANY OTHER, IS EVIDENCE THAT JUDGE EKANS HAD WHOLLY AND COMPLETELY THROWN THE COURT'S SUPPORT, POWER AND AUTHORITY TO MY ADVERSARIES AND HIS JUDICIAL COLLEAGUES, CO-CONSPIRATOR D.C. SUPERIOR COURT JUDGES GEORGE SKINNER AND RICHARD MANDARIN, UNKNOWN FBI AGENTS, AND THEIR RESPECTIVE FACILITATORS AND HANDLERS. I WAS IN MOB COUNTRY. PERIOD.

BUT MOST IMPORTANTLY, JUDGE EKANS WAS MAKING IT CLEAR THAT WHILE "MASSIVE D.C. JUDICIAL AND FBI FRAUD, THEFT, CORRUPTION AND EXTORTION" MIGHT BE THE DOMINANT ISSUES IN THE CASE, HE DIDN'T INTEND TO TOUCH THEM. HE WOULD TREAT THE ISSUE OF D.C. JUDICIAL AND FBI FRAUD, THEFT, CORRUPTION AND EXTORTION IN THE CASE AS "THE PINK ELEPHANT" IN THE COURTROOM THAT HE AND EVERYONE ELSE SAW BUT WERE UNDER COURT ORDER, PROHIBITION AND RESTRAINT NOT TO ADDRESS. THIS WAS D.C. JUDICIAL CORRUPTION. ALL CAPS.

THE COURT: MS. JONES HAS FLOWN HERE FROM SOMEWHERE, I GUESS. I GUESS SHE'S HERE FROM SOMEWHERE. AND SHE DOESN'T STRIKE ME AS A PAUPER. SHE SAYS THAT THE GENEROUS DEACON TAKES CARE OF HER.

I GUESS I SHARE THE NOTION WITH THE IRS THAT INCOME IS MONEY FROM WHATEVER SOURCE DERIVED. AND SO, IF IT'S FROM A LOTTERY OR IF IT'S FROM DIGGING DITCHES, AS I SEE IT, SHE OWES YOU MONEY.

NOW, APPARENTLY, SHE OWES THOSE FOLKS MONEY THROUGH ARRANGEMENTS THAT AT SOME POINT IN TIME YOU HAD SOMETHING TO DO WITH. I DON'T KNOW ANYTHING ABOUT THAT, BUT I UNDERSTAND THAT THERE MAY BE SOME OTHER LAWSUITS TO TRY TO TAKE CARE OF THAT. BUT RIGHT NOW, THE ONLY THING I'M REALLY CONCERNED WITH IS GET MONEY FLOWING FROM THIS TABLE TO THAT TABLE. NOW SHE SAYS SHE WANTS TO SIT DOWN AND WORK OUT WITH YOU HOW THAT'S GOING TO HAPPEN. I SUGGEST YOU TAKE HER UP ON THAT.

MS. FRANKLIN: YOUR HONOR, MAY I SPEAK?

THE COURT: YES, YOU MAY. TRY TO BE HELPFUL. TRY TO BE CONSTRUCTIVE.

MS. FRANKLIN: YES, I WILL, YOUR HONOR.
YOUR HONOR, AT THE LAST HEARING IN WHICH MS. JONES APPEARED BRIEFLY BY PHONE, AS WE WERE ADJOURNING, I MENTIONED THAT, IN FACT, SHE HAD ACKNOWLEDGED DURING THE ORAL EXAM, UNDER OATH, WHERE THE MONEY WAS, WHAT BANK---

COMMENT AND ANALYSIS: #7 *HERE BELOW, EKANS CUT ME OFF. HE INTENDED TO SHUT ME DOWN. HE DIDN'T WANT THE TRUTH OF THE CASE ON THE COURT RECORD. HE KNEW BRIANNA JONES HAD TESTIFIED EARLIER TO HER MEETINGS WITH BANK OF AMERICA OFFICERS AND MOREOVER, SHE HAD ALSO TESTIFIED TO HAVING IN HER POSSESSION BANK STATEMENTS AND RECORDS EVIDENCING THE AMOUNT OF THE SETTLEMENT PROCEEDS ON DEPOSIT WITH THE BANK. HE ALSO KNEW THE HISTORIC FBI AND D.C. JUDICIAL FRAUD, THEFT, CORRUPTION AND EXTORTION CONSPIRACY AND CRIMINAL ENTERPRISE WERE RAGING IN HIS COURTROOM, IN JUDGES' CHAMBERS, COURT HALLWAYS AND IN WASHINGTON AREA HOTEL SUITES WITH BRIANNA JONES IN ATTENDANCE.*

HOWEVER, NOW THAT EKANS WAS PRESIDING OVER MY CASE WITH THE ALLEGED ULTIMATE MISSION OF PROTECTING HIS FELLOW JUDGES, ALLEGED TO BE KEY CO-CONSPIRATORS IN THIS HISTORIC OFFICIAL AND D.C. JUDICIAL FRAUD, THEFT AND CORRUPTION, CONSPIRACY AND CRIMINAL ENTERPRISE, HE HAD A SUITABLE AGENDA TAILORED TO ACHIEVING THAT END. HE WOULD NOW HAVE TO BE SEEN AS A DE FACTO CO-CONSPIRATOR.

WHAT HAPPENED TO THE COURT'S SWORN AND SACRED OBLIGATION TO SEARCH FOR THE TRUTH, AND TO TREAT ALL LITIGANTS FAIRLY, EQUITABLY, JUSTLY, AND TO APPLY THE LAW IMPARTIALLY?

IT HAD OBVIOUSLY BEEN SNUFFED OUT BY THE IMPLACABLE AND INTRANSIGENT GREED AND CORRUPTION FOSTERED BY A CORRUPT COURT SYSTEM WORKING IN TANDEM AND CLOSE COOPERATION WITH A CORRUPT FBI SYSTEM THAT IS PERMITTED TO FLOURISH IN BROAD DAYLIGHT IN OUR NATION'S CAPITAL.

THE COURT: MS. FRANKLIN, WHAT DO YOU WANT ME TO DO? I'M NOT GOING TO GO OUT AND START LOOKING FOR IT, AND I'M NOT GOING TO ORDER ANYBODY ELSE TO DO IT. *IT'S YOUR JUDGMENT.* IT'S YOUR CLAIM. FIND IT. YOU FIND IT. I'LL GIVE YOU A WRIT OF ATTACHMENT, BUT IT'S NOT THE COURT'S RESPONSIBILITY TO GO OUT AND FIND WHERE PEOPLE'S ASSETS ARE. IT'S YOUR RESPONSIBILITY. *YOU GOT THE JUDGMENT. YOU WON THE CASE. YOU FIND IT. I'LL TAKE IT.*

COMMENT AND ANALYSIS: #8 I WAS SHOCKED TO HEAR JUDGE EKANS SAY HE WOULD TAKE THE SETTLEMENT PROCEEDS THAT REPRESENTED MY ATTORNEY'S FEES. HERE AGAIN THE TRUTH HAD COME OUT OF HIS OWN MOUTH. TAKING MY FEES IS EXACTLY WHAT HE AND HIS TEAM OF D.C. JUDICIAL CO-CONSPIRATORS HAD DONE, AND DONE WITH IMPUNITY.

WHAT IS A LITIGANT TO DO WITH A JUDGE WHO INTENTIONALLY AND RUTHLESSLY FABRICATES THE FACTS OF A CASE? ONE OF THE FIRST IMPORTANT LESSONS I LEARNED IN FIRST SEMESTER, FIRST YEAR OF LAW SCHOOL, WAS TO STATE THE FACTS OF A CASE CORRECTLY AND ACCURATELY. IT IS IMPOSSIBLE TO REACH A RIGHT AND JUST CONCLUSION AND JUDGMENT IN A CASE WHERE THE FACTS HAVE BEEN CHANGED OR TWISTED INTENTIONALLY OR OTHERWISE.

JUDGE EKANS WAS FULLY AWARE THAT I HAD NO JUDGMENT. PERIOD. *HOWEVER, REFERRING TO MY NON-EXISTENT "JUDGMENT" ALLOWED HIM TO PLACE THE BURDEN OF COLLECTION OF THE "JUDGMENT" ON ME.*

EKANS WAS THEN HOME FREE TO ASSURE HIS FELLOW CO-CONSPIRATOR D.C. JUDGES NOT TO WORRY; THEY WOULD NOT BE DISGORGING THEIR MILLIONS OF DOLLARS IN STOLEN SETTLEMENT PROCEEDS ANYTIME SOON.

*BY PLACING ME IN THE **JUDGMENT CREDITOR TRAP**, THE CO-CONSPIRATORS WERE FURTHER ASSURED THAT THE MASSIVE D.C. JUDICIAL AND FBI FRAUD, THEFT, CORRUPTION AND EXTORTION CONSPIRACY WAS ALIVE AND WELL, AND FLOURISHING UNDISTURBED AND UNINTERRUPTED IN OUR NATION'S CAPITAL.*

I WAS FULLY AWARE THAT THE COURT SAW ME AS NO MATCH FOR THE GREAT NUMBER OF ADVERSARIES LINED UP AGAINST ME, INCLUDING THE COURT'S MOST RECENT DE FACTO ENLISTMENT INTO THE ARMY OF MY OPPONENTS.

FIRST AND FOREMOST, THE COURT SAW ME AS A BLACK FEMALE ATTORNEY PRACTICING AS A SOLO TRIAL ATTORNEY. FROM THE COURT'S PERSPECTIVE THIS SPELLED EASY PREY FOR THE MANY ALIGNED AGAINST ME ENGAGED IN THIS MOST HISTORIC D.C JUDICIAL AND FBI FRAUD, THEFT, CORRUPTION AND EXTORTION CONSPIRACY AND CRIMINAL ENTERPRISE..

THE COURT ALSO KNEW THAT I WAS A WIDOW, MY HUSBAND HAVING DIED IN 2004 FROM A BROKEN HEART THAT HE SUFFERED, ON TOP OF CHRONIC BOUTS OF DEMENTIA, DIABETES AND A LIFE-THREATENING HEART CONDITION, AFTER BEING TARGETED AND SUBJECTED TO A SELECTIVE AND POLITICALLY MOTIVATED CRIMINAL PROSECUTION BY THE U.S. ATTORNEY'S OFFICE IN THE DISTRICT OF COLUMBIA THAT WAS AT ALL TIMES DESIGNED AND EXECUTED TO FORCE MY WITHDRAWAL AS COUNSEL OF RECORD FROM THE $34 MILLION SETTLEMENT OF THE $100 MILLION FLORIDA LAWSUIT INITIATED AND CRAFTED SOLELY BY ME AND ON BEHALF OF BRIANNA JONES.

BLACK FEMALE ATTORNEYS IN THE NATION'S CAPITAL ARE TRADITIONALLY TREATED AS BLACK FEMALES THROUGHOUT AMERICA, IRRESPECTIVE OF THE NOBILITY OF THEIR RESPECTIVE PROFESSION. BLACK FEMALE ATTORNEYS ARE TREATED IN A SPECIAL, ALBEIT DEGRADED, CATEGORY ALL THEIR OWN. RIGGED DISMISSAL OF COURT CASES INVOLVING BLACK FEMALE ATTORNEYS ARE NOT AN ANOMALY.

TO USE A ROSA PARKS STORY METAPHOR, THEY ARE TOLD TO GO TO THE BACK OF THE BUS, IN ONE WAY OR ANOTHER, 24/7, SIMPLY BECAUSE THEY ARE BLACK FEMALES. AND WHETHER THEY'VE PAID THE REQUIRED FARE OR NOT IS IRRELEVANT. BLACK FEMALES SUFFER WHAT I LIKE TO CALL "ROSA PARKS MOMENTS" EVERY HOUR, EVERY DAY, AND EVERY WEEK IN THE UNITED STATES OF AMERICA.

UNDER NO CIRCUMSTANCES WOULD A WHITE FEMALE ATTORNEY HAVE BEEN ROBBED OF THE FEES DUE HER FROM A $34 MILLION SETTLEMENT OF A COURT CASE THAT HAD BEEN PENDING IN TWO STATE COURTS AND ADJUDICATED BY COURT JUDGES SWORN TO UPHOLD THE LAW.

*THERE IS NO JUDGE IN AMERICA, ON HIS OR HER WORST DAY ON THE BENCH, THAT WOULD HAVE THE TEMERITY OR, MORE ACCURATELY, THE INSANITY, TO TELL A WHITE FEMALE ATTORNEY DEFRAUDED OF MILLIONS OF DOLLARS IN ATTORNEY FEES, "**TO GO OUT AND FIND IT; TO GO AND FIGURE IT OUT, AND WHEN YOU'VE FIGURED IT OUT, COME BACK TO COURT AND LET ME KNOW**" TO QUOTE D.C. COURT JUDGE MATTHEW D. EKANS, THE PRESIDING JUDGE TO WHOM MY CASE WAS TRANSFERRED FOR ADJUDICATION BEGINNING IN JANUARY 2011 DUE TO THE RETIREMENT OF JUDGE KATE STARR TO WHOM MY LAWSUIT HAD BEEN INITIALLY ASSIGNED IN MARCH 2009.*

IT IS BECAUSE I AM A BLACK FEMALE SOLO ATTORNEY THAT THE COURT HAD THE AUDACITY TO DISRESPECT, DEMEAN AND DISMISS ME---ON THE RECORD AND IN OPEN COURT---NOT ONCE, BUT REPEATEDLY AND AS VERIFIED BY THE OFFICIAL COURT TRANSCRIPTS.

THE COURT: NOW, IF IT TURNS OUT THAT THIS WOMAN IS LYING, THEN WE'VE GOT SOMETHING ELSE FOR THAT. BY GOD I'VE SENT ENOUGH PEOPLE TO PENITENTIARIES, IF ANYBODY, ANYBODY WHO THINKS THAT I HAVE ANY HESITATION TO USE EVERY BIT OF THIS COURT'S AUTHORITY, HAS MISSED MY HISTORY AS A JUDGE ON THIS COURT. BUT I ALSO RECOGNIZE THAT THERE ARE WAYS THAT AUTHORITY HAS TO BE USED AND NOT ABUSED. AND I'M NOT GOING **TO SUBECT IT** TO ABUSE IN THIS CASE OR IN ANY OTHER CASE.

COMMENT AND ANALYSIS: #9 *WITH REGARD TO THE COURT'S EXERCISE OF ITS AUTHORITY IN THIS CASE, UNFORTUNATELY, FOR ME, IT MUST BE SUMMED UP IN ONE WORD: "ABUSE."*

THE COURT: **NOW, I APPRECIATE THAT FACT THAT YOU'VE GOT A SUBSTANTIAL INVESTMENT IN SEEING THAT THAT SETTLEMENT AGREEMENT IS CARRIED OUT. YOU KNOW THIS WOMAN FAR BETTER THAN I EVER WILL OR CARE TO. SO, YOU FIND IT; I'LL GIVE YOU THE LEGAL PROCESS TO GET IT.**

IS THAT CLEAR?

COMMENT AND ANALYSIS: #10 *THE COURT RECORD REVEALS THAT THE COURT'S WORDS WERE A FAR CRY FROM THE COURT'S ACTIONS AND ATTITUDES THROUGHOUT THE COURT PROCEEDIINGS. AND WHILE PERHAPS CONSIDERED BY SOME A TIRED PHRASE, IT IS NEVERTHELESS STILL TRUE THAT ACTIONS SPEAK LOUDER THAN WORDS, AND THEY ALWAYS WILL.*

THE COURT: NOW, IF YOU WANT TO SEE HOW YOU CAN WORK OUT HER PAYING SOME---HOW OFTEN DO YOU CALL YOUR FRIEND TO GET YOUR SUBSISTENCE?

MS. JONES: IT'S ON BIWEEKLY BASIS AND---

THE COURT: THEN THERE YOU GO. YOU CAN GET A BIWEEKLY CHECK. HOW MUCH DO YOU GET BI-WEEKLY?

MS. JONES: DEPENDS ON THE EXPENSES.

THE COURT: HOW MUCH DO YOU GET BI-WEEKLY?

MS. JONES: IT COULD BE 800; IT CAN BE A THOUSAND.

THE COURT: HOW MUCH IS IT GOING TO BE TO PAY MS. FRANKLIN?

MS. JONES: WE CAN WORK THAT OUT, WHAT SHE---WHATEVER SHE THINKS---DEEMS IS FAIR

AND APPROPRIATE IN THIS MATTER.

THE COURT: **WELL, SHE THINKS IT'S FAIR TO GET A LUMP SUM OF MILLIONS OF DOLLARS AND YOU KNOW THAT.**

COMMENT AND ANALYSIS: #11 *MY CASE INVOLVED A $34 MILLION CASE SETTLEMENT THAT HAD MATURED TO APPROXIMATELY $100 MILLION OR MORE. WHY WOULD THE COURT TAKE UMBRAGE AT MY EXPECTING THE RECEIPT OF MILLIONS OF DOLLARS IN ATTORNEY'S FEES THAT WERE DUE ME? FOR SOME REASON, AND TO SUBSTANTIAL PREJUDICE AND DAMAGE TO ME, THE COURT SEEMED TO NOT GET BEYOND A "SMALL CLAIMS COURT" MIND-SET IN ADJUDICATING MY CASE.*

THE ODYSSEY OF JUDICIAL CORRUPTION

MS. JONES: WELL, ALSO I'VE GOT AN OFFER WITH REGARD TO A BOOK ON MY LIFE. I HAVE THE TEXT IN MY PURSE.

THE COURT: OH, LORD, HELP ME. I DON'T HAVE THE PATIENCE FOR THIS TODAY.
NOW, WE CAN KEEP THIS CIVIL---

MS. JONES: YES, SIR.

THE COURT:---------------OKAY, OR IT CAN TURN UGLY.

NOW, I SUGGEST YOU GET OUT THERE AND TRY TO WORK SOMETHING OUT "IN *THE NEXT FEW MINUTES.*"

MS. JONES: YES, YOUR HONOR.

THE COURT: GO AHEAD.

MS. JONES: THANK YOU.

(RECESS TAKEN.)

COMMENT AND ANALYSIS: #12 *THE SUDDENLY INVOKED RECESS WAS OSTENSIBLY FOR THE PURPOSE OF SETTLING, "IN THE NEXT FEW MINUTES," IN THE COURT HALLWAY, MY CLAIM TO 40% OF A $34 MILLION SETTLEMENT THAT HAD MATURED TO $100 MILLION OR MORE.*

HOWEVER, IN HINDSIGHT, THE RECESS WAS CONTRIVED AND ORCHESTRATED BY JUDGE MATTHEW EKANS TO FACILITATE HIS JUDICIAL COLLEAGUE, SENIOR JUDGE AND FORMER CHIEF JUDGE GEORGE SKINNER'S PERSONAL ACCESS TO BRIANNA JONES IN ORDER TO SHAKE HER DOWN AND INTIMIDATE HER IN HER CAPACITY AS A COURT WITNESS, AND CHILL HER TESTIMONY WHEN SHE RETURNED TO THE COURTROOM AND THEREAFTER.

MOREOVER, JUDGE SKINNER'S ACCESS TO BRIANNA JONES WAS SPECIFICALLY DESIGNED TO SHUT DOWN JONES' TESTIMONY REGARDING HER CLANDESTINE MEETINGS WITH "OFFICIALS" IN WASHINGTON AREA HOTEL SUITES TO REVIEW BANK STATEMENTS OF THE $100 MILLION IN CASE SETTLEMENT PROCEEDS TO WHICH SHE HAD VOLUNTARILY TESTIFIED IN PRIOR COURT PROCEEDINGS.

THE COURT HALLWAY INTIMIDATION AND SHAKE DOWN OF BRIANNA JONES BY JUDGE GEORGE SKINNER AND THE OPEN AND NOTORIOUS PARTNERSHIP OF CRIMINAL MISCONDUCT ENGAGED IN BY BOTH SENIOR JUDGE AND FORMER CHIEF JUDGE GEORGE SKINNER AND PRESIDING JUDGE MATTHEW EKANS WAS ON ITS FACE JUDICIAL PREMEDITATED OBSTRUCTION OF JUSTICE ENGAGED IN IN OPEN COURT BY TWO SITTING D.C. SUPERIOR COURT JUDGES WHO HAD TAKEN SWORN OATHS TO UPHOLD THE LAW AND THE CONSTITUTION.

A MORE DETAILED ACCOUNT OF THIS APPALLING COURT INCIDENT WHICH I HAVE TERMED "THE GODFATHER EPISODE" IS DOCUMENTED IN "PLAINTIFF'S RESPONSE TO THE MOTION TO INTERVENE" FILED WITH JUDGE EKANS ON DECMBER 16, 2014 IN FRANKLIN VS. JONES. JUDGE EKANS WAS CAREFUL NOT TO MENTION THE EXISTENCE OF THE MOTION AND UNCEREMONIOUSLY SWEPT IT UNDER THE RUG.

AT NO TIME DURING THE COURT PROCEEDINGS DID JUDGE EKANS ADDRESS THIS DOCUMENTED INCIDENT OF THE INTIMIDATION OF A COURT WITNESS BY A SENIOR JUDGE AND FORMER CHIEF JUDGE, BUT INSTEAD JUDGE EKANS USED THE PROCEDURAL TECHNICALITY OF DISMISSAL OF MY LAWSUIT TO SWEEP THIS SERIOUS ALLEGATION OF JUDICIAL CRIMINAL MISCONDUCT UNDER THE PROVERBIAL RUG.

DEPUTY CLERK: YOUR HONOR, RECALLING THE MATTER BARBARA WASHNGTON FRANKLIN VERSUS BRIANNA JONES, CIVIL ACTION 4417 2009, AND IN THE MATTER OF BRIANNA JONES, 2011 CCC1.

COMMENT AND ANALYSIS: # 13 *I RETURNED TO THE COURTROOM AFTER THE RECESS IN SHOCK, TRAUMATIZED AND NUMB ALL OVER. I WAS SHOCKED BY WHAT I HAD WITNESSED MINUTES AGO IN THE HALLWAY. I HAD WITNESSED A SENIOR JUDGE AND FORMER CHIEF JUDGE GEORGE SKINNER COMING WITHIN INCHES OF BRIANNA JONES, A COURT WITNESS, IN ORDER TO SHAKE HER DOWN, INTIMIDATE HER, CHILL HER TESTIMONY AND OBSTRUCT JUSTICE.*

I HAD ALSO WITNESSED THE PRESIDING JUDGE, MATTHEW EKANS, SUDDENLY INVOKE A CONTRIVED RECESS AND DIRECT BOTH PARTIES INTO THE HALLWAY IN ORDER TO ENABLE JUDGE SKINNER TO HAVE PERSONAL ACCESS TO BRIANNA JONES, A COURT WITNESS IN ORDER TO SHAKE HER DOWN AND INTIMIDATE HER. I WONDERED HOW I WOULD MANAGE TO GET THROUGH THE REMAINDER OF THE HEARING.

I NOW REALIZED THAT THE ULTIMATE PURPOSE OF THE COURT HEARING WAS TO GIVE JUDGES GEORGE SKINNER AND MATTHEW EKANS THE OPPORTUNITY TO SHUT DOWN BRIANNA JONES' TESTIMONY AND THEREBY OBSTRUCT JUSTICE BY DEFEATING THE ENTIRETY OF MY MERITORIOUS CLAIMS AGAINST JONES. TO MY SURPRISE, I MANAGED TO REQUEST A CONTINUANCE WHILE THE FUMES OF CORRUPTION CONTINUED TO SUFFICATE ME AND FILL THE AIR OF THE COURTROOM. I WAS IN SHOCK AND TRAUMATIZED BY THE WHOLE INCIDENT.

MS. FRANKLIN: YOUR HONOR, WE'VE TALKED, AND I JUST DECIDED TO ASK THE COURT FOR A STATUS, PRIMARILY TO ASSESS HOW I WANT TO PROCEED FROM THIS POINT ON. SHE DOESN'T HAVE ANY MONEY. HER FRIENDS DON'T HAVE MONEY, AND I'M NOT GOING TO CONTINUE TO WASTE TIME WITH HER GOING THROUGH THAT. IT'S JUST NOT THERE.

AND I---I AM A LITTLE STUNNED, I GUESS, BECAUSE I EVEN BROUGHT THE COURT TRANSCRIPTS IN, AND I MENTIONED IT TO HER AND SHE'S AGREED THAT *BANK OF AMERICA* HAS BEEN INVOLVED. SHE TESTIFIED UNDER OATH TO THAT. *SHE'S MET WITH BANKING OFFICIALS.* SHE'S TOLD ME SINCE YOUR HONOR RECESSED---

THE COURT: MS. FRANKLIN , RESPECTFULLY, I DON'T KNOW WHAT WE'RE DOING RIGHT NOW.

COMMENT AND ANALYSIS: #14 *THE JUDGE DUMMIES UP AND RESORTS TO HIS REPEATED JUDICIAL GASLIGHTING WHEN I ATTEMPT TO POINT OUT EVIDENCE OF THE WHEREABOUTS OF THE SETTLEMENT PROCEEDS, INCLUDING THE MENTION OF THE SPECIFIC BANKING INSTITUTION INVOLVED, I.E., BANK OF AMERICA.*

MS. FRANKLIN: I'M JUST ASKING FOR STATUS, JUST TO GET A CLEAR UNDERSTANDING FROM MY PERSPECTIVE AS TO HOW I WANT TO PROCEED---

THE COURT: OKAY.

MS. FRANKLIN: ---FROM THIS POINT ON, BECAUSE I---I AM NOT JUST SURE.

THE COURT: THAT'S FINE.

COMMENT AND ANALYSIS*: #15* *THE COURT IS PLEASED. THE TWO JUDGES HAVE ACCOMPLISHED THEIR MISSION OF THE COURT HEARING: THE SUCCESSFUL SHAKE DOWN AND INTIMIDATION OF BRIANNA JONES AND THE RESULTING OBSTRUCTION OF JUSTICE. JUDGE EKANS HAS BEEN PRESUMABLY ADEQUATELY BRIEFED BY CO-CONSPIRATOR COURT JUDGES RICHARD MANDARIN AND GEORGE SKINNER, AND HE IS, THEREFORE, FINE WITH MY BEING UNCERTAIN AS TO HOW I WANT TO PROCEED FROM THIS POINT ON. SIGNIFICANTLY, HE OFFERS NO HELP, HAS NO IDEAS. HIS COMMITMENT IS FIRST AND FOREMOST TO HIS JUDICIAL COLLEAGUES WHO WERE COMPLICIT IN THIS HISTORIC D.C. JUDICIAL FRAUD, THEFT, CORRUPTION AND EXTORTION CONSPIRACY AND CRIMINAL ENTERPRISE.*

MS. FRANKLIN: I'M JUST NOT SURE, YOU KNOW, WHAT TO DO OR WHAT DIRECTION. I WILL SAY TO THE COURT THAT, YOU KNOW, SHE'S GIVEN NAMES OF ATTORNEYS THAT SHE'S TALKED---AT LEAST ONE ATTORNEY, AND HE'S TRYING TO INVOLVE OTHER ATTORNEYS TO IDENTIFY THE ASSETS; THAT I HAVE NOT BEEN IN TOUCH WITH ANY OF THESE PEOPLE. I HAVE NOT CONFIRMED ANY OF THIS INFORMATION. AND IT REALLY ISN'T MY DESIRE TO WASTE THE COURT'S TIME COMING EVERY OTHER WEEK OR SO TO THESE HEARINGS. I WAS REALLY TRYING TO---

COMMENT AND ANALYSIS: #16 *I AM STILL TRAUMATIZED AND SHOCKED BY JUDGE SKINNER'S HALLWAY SHAKEDOWN OF BRIANNA JONES, AN EPISODE COMPARABLE TO SCENES FROM THE CLASSIC MOVIE "THE GODFATHER." "THE GODFATHER" INTRODUCES THE VIEWER TO THE LIFE OF AN ITALIAN AMERICAN MOBSTER FAMILY. THE THEME OF THE MOVIE CAN BE SUMMED UP IN ONE LINE FROM THE FILM: "IT WASN'T PERSONAL, JUST BUSINESS." HENCE, MY DESCRIPTION OF THIS INCIDENT AS "THE GODFATHER EPISODE" THAT OCCURRED DURING THE MARCH 18, 2011 COURT PROCEEDINGS BEFORE JUDGE MATTHEW EKANS.*

THE COURT: I'M DONE WITH THAT. I'M DONE WITH THAT.

COMMENT AND ANALYSIS: #17 *NOW THAT THE COURT'S MISSION OF THE SHAKE DOWN AND INTIMIDATION OF BRIANNA JONES AND THE CONSEQUENT OBSTRUCTION OF JUSTICE HAS BEEN ACCOMPLISHED IN BROAD DAYLIGHT BY THE FORMER CHIEF JUDGE AND THE PRESIDING JUDGE WORKING IN CONCERT FROM THE BENCH, JUDGE'S CHAMBERS AND IN THE COURT HALLWAY, THE COURT IS NOW READY TO MOVE ON.*

THE COURT: WHAT I'M PREPARED TO DO IS TO HAVE WHAT I WOULD CALL SUBSTANTIAL---I'VE NEVER HAD A LOT OF MONEY, SO DON'T GO BY ME. BUT YOU KNOW, I'M PREPARED TO HAVE HER PAYING YOU AT LEAST A COUPLE THOUSAND DOLLARS A MONTH. AND I'M FULLY SATISFIED ON MS. JONES' ANSWERS TO THE COURT THAT THAT'S IMMINENTLY DOABLE, BUT IF YOU DON'T WANT TO DO THAT----

COMMENT AND ANALYSIS: #18 *BRIANNA JONES WAS MEDICALLY DIAGNOSED IN 1996 AS MENTALLY IMPAIRED. SHE WAS ALSO PERMANENTLY UNEMPLOYED AND WITHOUT ANY VERIFIABLE SOURCE OF INCOME AND FINANCIAL SUPPORT. MOREOVER, THERE WAS ABSOLUTELY NO EVIDENCE IN THE RECORD THAT BRIANNA JONES WAS FINANCIALLY ABLE TO PAY ANYTHING AT ALL TO ME OR ANYONE ELSE. AND JUDGE EKANS KNEW THAT. HE SIMPLY DELIGHTED IN JUDICIAL GASLIGHTING AND ABUSING HIS POWER OF DISCRETION AND AUTHORITY AND WASTING MY TIME WHICH I WOULD NEVER BE ABLE TO RECAPTURE.*

MS. FRANKLIN: YOUR HONOR, I'M NOT HERE TO TURN DOWN MONEY, BECAUSE I'VE SPENT AND EXPENDED A LOT OF FUNDS OVER THE YEARS WITH REGARD TO THE EXPENSES IN THIS CASE; HOWEVER, I CAN'T GET DOLLAR AMOUNTS FROM HER. I MEAN, IN OTHER WORDS, HOW DOES ONE DO THAT WHEN SHE'S TALKING BOOK DEALS? I AM NOT INTERESTED. DO YOU SEE WHAT I'M SAYING, YOUR HONOR? YOUR HONOR, YOU SENT US OUT TO TALK ABOUT HOW SHE WAS GOING TO PAY ME ON THE JUDGMENT. SHE WANTS TO TALK ABOUT SOMETHING ALTOGETHER......

THE COURT: WELL, I TELL YOU WHAT. WHY DON'T I GRANT YOU THE STAY YOU'RE ASKING FOR AND YOU FIGURE IT OUT. AND WHEN YOU FIGURE SOMETHING OUT, YOU CAN LET ME KNOW. BUT I DON'T HAVE ANY ENERGY TO FOOL AROUND WITH THIS. ALL I CAN DO IS----

COMMENT AND ANALYSIS: #19 I DIDN'T NEED A STAY "TO FIGURE IT OUT." I HAD *FIGURED OUT YEARS EARLIER THAT I WAS DEALING WITH A MASSIVE D.C. JUDICIAL AND FBI FRAUD, THEFT, CORRUPTION AND EXTORTION CONSPIRACY CASE AND CRIMINAL ENTERPRISE. I UNDERSTOOD QUITE WELL WHAT I WAS DEALING WITH. AND I ALSO UNDERSTOOD THE ROLE OF JUDGE EKANS IN THE SCENARIO, NOTWITHSTANDING WHAT CAN ONLY BE TERMED THE COURT'S INSULTING TRASH TALK PASSING FOR JUDICIAL COMMENTARY AND RHETORIC. **THIS HEARING MORE THAN ANY OTHER PROVED THAT CAMERAS IN THE COURT ROOM WOULD HAVE MADE A CRITICAL DIFFERENCE IN THE FINAL OUTCOME OF MY LAWSUIT.***

MS. FRANKLIN: I UNDERSTAND YOUR HONOR. I DO. I UNDERSTAND.

THE COURT: IF YOU KNOW WHERE THE LUMP SUM IS, I'LL GIVE YOU THE LEGAL PROCESS TO GET IT. IF YOU DON'T KNOW WHERE THE LUMP SUM IS, THEN SHE SAYS SHE'S WILLING TO WORK OUT A PAYMENT SCHEDULE, AND THAT'S ALL I CAN MAKE A PERSON DO.

COMMENT AND ANALYSIS: #20 *THIS STATEMENT BY THE COURT, ALBEIT AN OUTRAGEOUS ONE, IS, IN A NUTSHELL, CLEAR EVIDENCE OF THE MASSIVE D.C. JUDICIAL AND FBI FRAUD, THEFT, CORRUPTION AND EXTORTION CRIMINAL ENTERPRISE THAT DOMINATED THE CASE FROM ITS INCEPTION.*

THE COURT IS EMPOWERED BY LAW WITH VIRTUALLY UNLIMITED POWER AND AUTHORITY TO BRING JUSTICE TO A GIVEN SITUATION AND SET OF CIRCUMSTANCES. ALSO AVAILABLE TO IT ARE UNLIMITED RESOURCES AND A WIDE ARRAY OF JUDICIAL REMEDIES. HOWEVER, WHEN THE COURT IS MIRED IN DEEP, SYSTEMIC AND MASSSIVE D.C. JUDICIAL AND FBI FRAUD, THEFT, CORRUPTION AND EXTORTION, IT PLEADS FALSELY AND UNAPOLOGETICALLY, LIMITATION AND POWERLESSNESS, AS JUDGE EKANS DOES HERE.

HERE JUDGE EKANS OFFERS ME THE REVERSE OF THE ACTUAL COURT PROCEDURE. HE SAYS IF I KNOW WHERE THE LUMP SUM IS, HE'LL GIVE ME THE LEGAL PROCESS TO GET IT. THE FACT OF THE MATTER IS THE COURT PROCEDURE IS THAT ONCE A PARTY IS ISSUED A JUDGMENT BY THE COURT, IT IS THE CLERK'S OFFICE, AND NOT THE JUDGE, THAT HANDLES THE LEGAL PROCESS AND PROCEDURE OF EXECUTING ON THE JUDGMENT ISSUED BY THE COURT.

I HAD REPEATEDLY INFORMED THE COURT THAT I HAD BEEN DEFRAUDED OF MY ATTORNEY'S FEES. THUS, MY LACK OF KNOWLEDGE AS TO THE WHEREABOUTS OF THE LUMP SUM SETTLEMENT PROCEEDS WAS IMPLICIT IN THAT ALLEGATION. HERE, AGAIN, JUDGE EKANS JUST ABUSED HIS POWER AND AUTHORITY TO CONTINUE TO WASTE MY TIME, IN HOPES THAT I WOULD EVENTUALLY TURN MY BACK AND WALK AWAY FROM THIS OBVIOUSLY FIXED FIGHT---FIXED IN PART BY HIS JUDICIAL COLLEAGUES, ACTING AS CO-CONSPIRATORS IN THIS CRIMINAL ENTERPRISE OF MASSIVE FBI AND D.C. JUDICIAL FRAUD, THEFT, CORRUPTION AND EXTORTION.

MS. FRANKLIN: SHE'S NOT INDICATED THAT. SHE HAS NOT INDICATED A PAYMENT SCHEDULE.

THE COURT: THAT'S WHAT SHE TOLD ME BEFORE SHE WENT OUT THERE.

MS. JONES: WHEN YOU SAID----

MS. FRANKLIN: A PAYMENT SCHEDULE?

THE COURT: I DIDN'T ASK YOU TO DO THIS IN FRONT OF ME.

MS. FRANKLIN: **YOUR HONOR, THAT'S OKAY. I UNDERSTAND ENGLISH QUITE WELL.**

THE COURT: GOOD.

COMMENT AND ANALYSIS: #21 *HERE I WAS ALSO SAYING, "I KNOW CORRUPTION WHEN I SEE IT, YOUR HONOR." I WAS REMINDED OF JUSTICE POTTER STEWART'S STATEMENT REGARDING DEFINING OBSCENITY: YOU MIGHT NOT BE ABLE TO DEFINE IT BUT YOU KNOW IT WHEN YOU SEE IT.*

MS. FRANKLIN: IF SHE PRESENTED ME WITH A PAYMENT SCHEDULE, I WOULD BE ABLE TO RESPOND TO THAT. SHE HAS NOT PRESENTED ME WITH ANY PAYMENT SCHEDULE WHATSOEVER. AND PERHAPS IF WE GET ANOTHER DATE, IF SHE WANTS TO WHICH I'M SURE SHE---I DOUBT SERIOUSLY THAT'S GOING TO HAPPEN BECAUSE, AS I'VE SAID, WE'VE HAD ENOUGH TIME, YOUR HONOR HAS WAITED ON US, SHE'S NOT PRESENTED ME WITH ONE PAYMENT SCHEDULE AT ALL. AND I'M STILL LISTENING. SHE HAS NOTHING TO SAY.

MS. JONES: YOUR HONOR, I JUST SAID TO HER OUTSIDE, AND SHE SAID I DON'T WANT THAT. ARE YOU KIDDING?

MS. FRANKLIN: I DON'T WANT BOOK DEALS. THAT'S WHAT I SAID.

MS. JONES: WE WERE TALKING SPECIFICALLY ABOUT PAYING IN INCREMENTS, AND YOU ASKED ME AGAIN, WHAT ABOUT THE BANK AND BANK OF AMERICA? I SAID, I STOPPED IN THIS MORNING AND SAW MR. MEHAH (PHONETIC) AND I SAID HAVE YOU HEARD ANYTHING? IS THERE ANY CLUE OF ANY FUNDS?

THE ODYSSEY OF JUDICIAL CORRUPTION

THE COURT: WOULD YOU LIKE TO PRESENT A PLAN, A FORMAL PLAN?

MS. JONES: I'D HAVE TO SIT DOWN AND GO OVER. I'M WILLING---

THE COURT: I JUST ASKED YOU IF YOU'D LIKE TO DO THAT.

MS. JONES: YES.

THE COURT: I DON'T NEED TO KNOW THE DETAILS.

MS. JONES: YES.

THE COURT: HOW MUCH TIME DO YOU NEED IT TO DO?

MS. JONES: A WEEK.

THE COURT: I REALLY HAVE SOMETHING ELSE TO DO NEXT WEEK, SO IF YOU WANT TO TAKE A LITTLE MORE TIME, IT'S FINE WITH ME.

MS. JONES: ARE YOU AMENABLE TO THAT?

MS. FRANKLIN: I'M NOT SURE. AMENABLE TO?

MS. JONES: WORKING OUT A PAYMENT PLAN, A PAYMENT SCHEDULE?

MS. FRANKLIN: YOUR HONOR, I'M AMENABLE, BUT I JUST DON'T KNOW WHAT SHE'S SAYING, BECAUSE WHEN WE GO OUT TO TALK ABOUT IT----

THE COURT: WELL, YOU DON'T HAVE A PROBLEM TALKING, YOU HAVE A PROBLEM COMMUNICATING.

MS. FRANKLIN: RIGHT.

THE COURT: **SO I'M GOING TO ASK YOU TO SEE IF YOU CAN---YOU KNOW, WORK SOMETHING OUT, AND HERE'S WHAT I'M GOING TO PROPOSE. I'M GOING TO PROPOSE THAT YOU FILE A WRITTEN PLAN, PAYMENT PLAN WITH, THE COURT. WE'RE ON THE 18TH. I'LL GIVE YOU TWO WEEKS. OH, YOU'LL LOVE THIS: APRIL FOOL'S DAY. APRIL 1ST, CLOSE OF BUSINESS, I WANT THE PAPERS IN MY CHAMBERS, AND THEN WE WILL JUST SCHEDULE A HEARING ON THOSE PAPERS. WHY DON'T WE HAVE YOU COME IN ON MONDAY. I'LL GIVE YOU MONDAY. YOU'RE GETTING TOO COMFORTABLE WITH FRIDAY. LET'S HAVE YOU COME IN ON THE MONDAY ON THE 4TH OF APRIL, AND WE'LL LOOK AT THE PLAN THAT YOU'VE SUBMITTED AND SEE IF WE CAN APPROVE IT.**

COMMENT AND ANALYSIS: #22 *HOW OUTRAGEOUS IT WAS FOR JUDGE EKANS, THE PRESIDING JUDGE, TO USE THE COURT PROCEEDINGS TO REQUIRE A MENTALLY IMPAIRED, FINANCIALLY BANKRUPT, AND HOMELESS DEFENDANT, TO PRESENT A PAYMENT PLAN AND SCHEDULE TO THE COURT IN SUPPORT OF HER OBLIGATION TO PAY PLAINTIFF $50 MILLION OR MORE IN ATTORNEY'S FEES, ALLEGEDLY STOLEN BY D.C. COURT JUDGES AND FBI AGENTS, PURSUANT TO A CONTINGENCY FEE AGREEMENT WITH THE ATTORNEY, BASED ON THE $34 MILLION COURT CASE SETTLEMENT OF A $100 MILLION LAWSUIT.*

THIS IS A CASE OF EGREGIOUS JUDICIAL ABUSE AND HISTORIC CRIMINAL ENTERPRISE NO MATTER WHAT YOUR PERSPECTIVE. AND JUDGE EKANS, TO MY SURPRISE AND DISMAY, HAD UNEQUIVOCALLY BECOME THE GRAND MARSHALL OF THE PARADE.

NEEDLESS TO SAY, BRIANNA JONES NEVER FILED A WRITTEN PAYMENT PLAN AND SCHEDULE WITH THE COURT, ALTHOUGH GIVEN 2 WEEKS TO DO SO. NOR WAS SHE PENALIZED BY THE COURT IN ANY WAY FOR HER FAILURE TO DO SO.

THE COURT'S SPECIAL TREATMENT OF BRIANNA JONES WAS CAUSED BY THE IMPACT OF THE CO-CONSPIRATORS' INFLUENCE ON THE COURT, AS WELL AS THE OVERALL IMPACT OF THE DEEP, SYSTEMIC AND MASSIVE JUDICIAL AND FBI FRAUD, THEFT, CORRUPTION AND EXTORTION THAT DOMINATED MY CASE AND THE COURT PROCEEDINGS AT ALL TIMES.

MS. FRANKLIN: EXCUSE ME WHAT TIME ON THE 4TH, YOUR HONOR. THE

COURT: WELL, WE USUALLY START OFF ABOUT 9:30.

MS. JONES: CAN WE DO IT A LITTLE LATER SO I CAN GET A FLIGHT IN THAT MORNING, A 7:00 O'CLOCK FLIGHT?

THE COURT: COME IN THE DAY BEFORE.

MS. JONES: BUT THAT'S AN ADDITIONAL EXPENSE.

THE COURT: **LET ME JUST SAY THIS TO YOU: I'VE BEEN VERY INDULGENT WITH YOU. YOU'VE NEVER COME HERE WHEN YOU'RE REQUIRED TO BE HERE, BUT YOU SHOW UP. SO, I'M NOT ALARMED ABOUT THAT, BUT I'M CONCERNED THAT YOU ALWAYS COME ON YOUR TIME. AND YOU'RE NOT THE ONLY ONE WHO'S GOING TO BE INCONVENIENCED BY THIS, SO WHY DON'T YOU COME IN EARLY SO YOU CAN BE ON TIME ON THE 4TH.**

MS. JONES: YES, YOUR HONOR.

THE COURT: THANK YOU FOR BEING SO UNDERSTANDING ABOUT THAT.

COMMENT AND ANALYSIS: #23 *THIS STATEMENT OF ADMISSION BY JUDGE EKANS WITH REGARD TO THE COURT'S SPECIAL AND EXCEPTIONAL TREATMENT OF BRIANNA JONES, A DEFENDANT IN PERMANENT OPEN AND NOTORIOUS CONTEMPT OF THE COURT'S ORDERS DURING THE ENTIRETY OF THE CASE SPEAKS VOLUMES FOR ITSELF.*

THE COURT'S CAPITULATION TO BRIANNA JONES OF ITS POWER AND RESPONSIBILITY TO SCHEDULE THE DATE AND TIME OF COURT HEARINGS WAS AN ABUSIVE ABDICATION BY THE COURT OF ITS JUDICIAL DUTY AND RESPONSIBILITY TO APPLY THE LAW AND TO TREAT ALL PARTIES FAIRLY, EQUITABLY AND JUSTLY BASED ON THE FACTS AND CIRCUMSTANCES OF THE PARTICULAR CASE PENDING BEFORE IT.

MORE IMPORTANTLY, IT IS FURTHER CLEAR AND CONVINCING EVIDENCE OF THE ENTRENCHED AND SYSTEMIC JUDICIAL FRAUD, THEFT, CORRUPTION AND EXTORTION THAT DEFINED THE DOMINANT OPERATION AND STYLE OF THE D.C. COURT SYSTEM IN THE ADJUDICATION OF MY CASE AND IN ABSENCE OF ANY AND ALL ACCOUNTABILITY OF ITS JUDICIAL OFFICERS. **IN OTHER WORDS, THE COURT ANSWERED TO NO ONE.**

THROUGHOUT THE HEARING, THE TRANSCRIPT VERIFIES THAT JUDGE EKANS WAS HAVING FUN MOCKING ME. HE WAS HAVING FUN, ALBEIT SICK FUN, REGARDING MY PERSISTENT, CONCERTED EFFORTS TO ACHIEVE SOME SEMBLANCE OF JUSTICE IN THE MIDST OF THIS PROTRACTED AND CORRUPT LITIGATION NIGHTMARE.

JUDGE EKANS APPEARED TO RELISH THESE MOMENTS OF WHAT WERE FOR HIM THE EXERCISE OF THE VIRTUALLY UNLIMITED POWER AND DISCRETION OVER THE LIVES OF THE LITIGANTS BEFORE HIM.

I KNEW THAT HAD I BEEN AFFORDED THE PRIVILEGE OF A VIDEO AND AUDIO RECORDING OF THIS HEARING, I WOULD HAVE PREVAILED HANDS DOWN, ON THE GROUNDS OF JUDICIAL BIAS AND ABUSE OF A PARTY BY THE PRESIDING JUDGE.

THE COURT: HAVE A NICE WEEKEND.

DEPUTY CLERK: THIS HONORABLE COURT STANDS ADJOURNED.

(PROCEEDINGS ADJOURNED AT 5:04 P.M.)

BARBARA WASHINGTON FRANKLIN

SUPERIOR COURT OF THE DISTRICT OF COLUMBIA
CIVIL DIVISION
WASHINGTON, D.C.

THE HONORABLE MATTHEW D. EKANS, ASSOCIATE JUDGE, PRESIDING

THE FOLLOWING ARE EXCERPTS OF THE OFFICIAL COURT TRANSCRIPT OF THE
APRIL 4, 2011 PROCEEDING
ANNOTATED BY THE AUTHOR'S PERTINENT COMMENTARY AND ANALYSIS

APRIL 4, 2011

PROCEEDINGS

COMMENT AND ANALYSIS: #1 MY ATTENDANCE AT THE APRIL 4, 2011 COURT HEARING WAS PRECEDED BY THE MARCH 18, 2011 COURT HEARING WHICH I WOULD FOREVER REFER TO AS MY IDES OF MARCH. THIS WAS THE HEARING DURING WHICH I WAS MORALLY AND VERBALLY ASSASSINATED AND MY LAWSUIT WAS JUDICIALLY AND PROCEDURALLY EXTINGUISHED BY JUDGE EKANS.

DURING THE MARCH 18, 2011 COURT HEARING, I PERSONALLY WITNESSED JUDGE EKANS COORDINATE AND ORCHESTRATE THE COURT HALLWAY SHAKE DOWN AND INTIMIDATION OF BRIANNA JONES BY SENIOR JUDGE AND FORMER CHIEF JUDGE GEORGE SKINNER.

BECAUSE OF THAT INCIDENT, I WAS NEVER ABLE TO ENTER EKANS' COURTROOM WITHOUT REALIZING THAT I WAS STEPPING INTO THE LION'S DEN. BECAUSE OF THAT INCIDENT, I WOULD NEVER AGAIN BE ABLE TO REGARD JUDGE EKANS AS OTHER THAN WHO HE WAS: AN AUDACIOUS, UNACCOUNTABLE, CORRUPT, CONSCIENCE-FREE AND AMORAL D.C. COURT JUDGE.

JUDGE EKANS' SHAMELESS, ALTHOUGH BRIEF ENTERTAINMENT OF TESTIMONY OF BRIANNA JONES, A HOMELESS AND MENTALLY ILL BLACK WOMAN, REGARDING A PAYMENT PLAN FOR THE PAYMENT OF AN ESTIMATED $50 MILLION IN ATTORNEY'S FEES OWED TO ME IS SIMPLY FURTHER EVIDENCE OF EKANS' PENCHANT FOR JUDICIAL GASLIGHTING AND HIS REPEATED ABUSE OF HIS *ABSOLUTE JUDICIAL DISCRETION.*

THE ODYSSEY OF JUDICIAL CORRUPTION

AT THE END OF THE DAY, I CONCLUDED THAT THE SOLE PURPOSE FOR THE APRIL 4TH 2011 HEARING WAS FOR NO OTHER PURPOSE THAN TO GIVE EKANS THE OPPORTUNITY TO CLOSELY OBSERVE MY DEMEANOR AND BE ASSURED THAT HE DIDN'T HAVE TO WORRY ABOUT MY GOING OUTSIDE OF THE D.C. COURT SYSTEM AND REPORTING WHAT WAS IN ALL RESPECTS THE ONGOING D.C. JUDICIAL AND FBI CRIMINAL ENTERPRISE THAT FLOURISHED WITHIN THE D.C. COURT SYSTEM.

ONCE EKANS WAS SATISFIED THAT HE HAD EVERYTHING UNDER CONTROL, AND THAT I WAS EITHER OBLIVIOUS TO HIS ACTIVE PARTICIPATION IN THE CRIMINAL ENTERPRISE OR THAT I CONSIDERED MYSELF SUFFICIENTLY POWERLESS TO RESIST AND OVERCOME THE OBVIOUS FORCES ALIGNED AGAINST ME, THE PARTIES WERE EXCUSED AND THE HEARING WAS ADJOURNED.

THE DEPUTY CLERK: NOW CALLING THE MATTER OF BARBARA WASHINGTON FRANKLIN VERSUS BRIANNA JONES. THIS IS CIVIL ACTION 4417-2009.

MS. FRANKLIN: GOOD MORNING, YOUR HONOR.

THE COURT: GOOD MORNING.

MS. FRANKLIN: BARBARA WASHINGTON FRANKLIN, YOUR HONOR, PLAINTIFF, PRO SE.

THE COURT: WHEN I WALKED IN CHAMBERS THIS MORNING, MY ADMINISRATIVE ASSISTANT LOOKED AT ME AND SAID, JUDGE, MS. JONES CALLED AND YOU DON'T EVEN WANT TO HEAR ALL THE EXCUSES SHE HAD.

THE COURT: I SAID, YOU'RE RIGHT. I DON'T. I DON'T.

MS. FRANKLIN: I'M SURPRISED. YOUR HONOR.

THE COURT: WELL, APPARENTLY, SHE'S IN BALTIMORE. THAT'S WHAT JANE SAYS, AND THAT SHE'S ON THE WAY. HAVE YOU TALKED TO HER?

MS. FRANKLIN: NO, YOUR HONOR. I HAVE NOT TALKED TO HER SINCE THE LAST HEARING.

THE COURT: OKAY. WELL, SHE CALLED FRIDAY TO SAY THAT SHE WAS HERE. SHE CALLED FRIDAY BEFORE I LEFT FOR THE DAY. AND I TALKED TO HER, AND I'VE TRIED TO DISCOURAGE HER. SHE'S GOTTEN VERY, VERY COMFORTABLE CALLING. AND, YOU KNOW THE TWO WOMEN WHO WORK FOR ME IN CHAMBERS: ONE IS A JUDICIAL ADMINISTRATIVE ASSISTANT; THE OTHER IS THE LAW CLERK. AND BOTH OF THESE PEOPLE ARE JUST   I MEAN, THEY BEND OVER BACKWARDS TO TRY AND HELP FOLKS. AND WHILE WE HAVE TO MAINTAIN, YOU KNOW, I MEAN, IT'S A PUBLIC OFFICE.

BARBARA WASHINGTON FRANKLIN

MS. FRANKLIN:	RIGHT.
THE COURT:	JUDGE IS NOT A PRIVATE POSITION. IT'S A VERY PUBLIC POSITION. AND OF COURSE, OUR PHONE NUMBER AND FAX NUMBER, ALL OF OUR CONTACT INFORMATION IS LISTED, BUT WE TRY TO DISCOURAGE DOING JUDICIAL BUSINESS OVER THE PHONE UNLESS IT'S ON THE RECORD.
MS. FRANKLIN:	EXACTLY.
THE COURT:	AND WE DON'T MAINTAIN THE RECORD IN CHAMBERS UNLESS WE HAVE A COURT REPORTER COME IN CHAMBERS, UNLIKE THE COURTROOM WHERE THERE'S A DIGITAL RECORD THAT'S ON ALL THE TIME. BUT WE DO, OF COURSE, EXPECT PEOPLE TO CONTACT CHAMBERS REGARDING SCHEDULING. AND WE OFTEN INITIATE THOSE CONTACTS, THOSE COMMUNICATIONS TO SCHEDULE MATTERS. AND WE'VE TALKED TO MS. JONES ABOUT THAT. BUT THIS, I GUESS THIS COMES UNDER THE HEADING OF SCHEDULING. SHE CALLS NOW ROUTINELY TO SAY THAT SHE'S LATE, AND WHY SHE'S LATE, AND SO FORTH.
	SO I DON'T REMEMBER THAT TIME SHE'S SUPPOSED TO ARRIVE. DID JANE SAY ANYTHING TO YOU?
MS. FRANKLIN:	YOUR HONOR, IS IT POSSIBLE TO HAVE THIS ON WEDNESDAY OR FRIDAY?
THE COURT:	SURE.
MS. FRANKLIN:	I'M KIND OF -- -- USUALLY I'M FLEXIBLE, BUT TODAY AND TOMORROW -- --
THE COURT:	NO, I MEAN -- -- FRIDAY IS NOT BECAUSE I'LL BE ON LEAVE ON FRIDAY. MY -- --
THE DEPUTY CLERK:	SHE SAID BETWEEN 10 AND 10:30. SHE WAS IN LAUREL WHEN SHE LAST CALLED.
THE COURT:	IN LAUREL?
THE DEPURTY CLERK:	YES.
THE COURT:	ALL RIGHT.
THE DEPUTY CLERK:	THERE MAY BE AN ISSUE WITH PARKING.
THE COURT:	AT ANY RATE, I WON'T BE SITTING ON FRIDAY, BUT YES, WEDNESDAY, THURSDAY. TOMORROW'S NOT GOOD, BUT ANY TIME.
MS. FRANKLIN:	I'M THINKING WEDNESDAY, BECAUSE SINCE SHE'S NOT HERE BETWEEN 10 AND 10:30 AND I DON'T KNOW HOW MUCH MORE SHE'S GOING TO NEED.

THE COURT:	LET ME JUST LOOK AT MY CALENDAR HERE. THIS IS MARCH------ OH, NO, WE'RE NOT IN MARCH ANYMORE ARE WE?
MS. FRANKLIN:	I JUST HAVE SOME, ACTUALLY, SOME DOCTORS APPOINTMENTS WHICH I'VE KEPT, YOU KNOW, RESCHEDULING AND NOW I CAN'T DO IT ANYMORE.
THE COUT:	NO, THAT'S NOT A GOOD IDEA. YOU NEED TO KEEP THOSE.
MS. FRANKLIN:	RIGHT.
THE COURT:	LET'S SEE, WEDNESDAY WE'VE GOT A ----
MS. FRANKLIN;	WEDNESDAY, THE 6TH.
THE COURT:	YEAH, WE'VE GOT A PRETRIAL THAT'S SCHEDULED AT 9:15, AND WE'VE GOT A PRETRIAL SCHEDULED IN THE AFTERNOON, BUT WE COULD HEAR THIS IN THE MORNING AFTER THE PRETRIAL WEDNESDAY.
MS. FRANKLIN:	THAT WOULD BE FINE, YOUR HONOR. SO YOUR HONOR, SHOULD WE SAY 11?
THE COURT:	ELEVEN, TEN, 11.
(PAUSE.)	
MS. FRANKLIN:	YOUR HONOR, SINCE SHE'S SAYING BETWEEN 10 AND 10:30 COULD WE GIVE IT UNTIL 11 TODAY AND THEN IF ----
THE COURT:	SURE. I MEAN, I ----
MS. FRANKLIN: ---------------- AND THEN IF NOT 11, THEN I WOULD ASK THE COURT TO ALLOW US TO DO IT ON WEDNESDAY. I JUST CAN'T ----- TODAY I CAN'T SIT ALL DAY AND WAIT.
THE COURT:	NO, AND THAT WOULD BE VERY UNFAIR. I THINK THAT I'M, YOU KNOW, I'M WORKING IN CHAMBERS TODAY. I'M GETTING READY FOR A BIG HEARING TOMORROW THAT I HAVE, BUT I'M WORKING IN CHAMBERS. I CAN COME DOWN HERE ANYTIME THEY CALL ME.
MS. FRANKLIN:	OKAY. I JUST FEEL THAT TO GIVE HER UNTIL 11 SINCE SHE SAID BETWEEN 10 AND 10:30. THEN IF SHE'S NOT HERE AT 11, THEN I WOULD ASK THE COURT TO ALLOW US TO COME IN ON WEDNESDAY, WEDNESDAY MORNING. IS THAT OKAY, YOUR HONOR?
THE COURT:	THAT'S FINE. IT'S PERFECTLY FINE.
MS. FRANKLIN:	THANK YOU, YOUR HONOR.

BARBARA WASHINGTON FRANKLIN

THE COURT: IF YOU WANT, YOU CAN GO DOWN TO THE FIRE HOOK , GET A CUP OF COFFEE
                    AND JUST COME BACK AT 11. AND I'LL PLAN TO COME DOWN HERE AT 11 AND
                    SEE WHAT HAPPENS.

MS. FRANKLIN: THANK YOU, YOUR HONOR.

THE COURT: OKAY.

                    (THEREUPON, A SHORT RECESS WAS HAD.)

THE DEPUTY CLERK: YOUR HONOR, CALLING THE CASE OF BARBARA WASHINGTON FRANKLIN VERSUS
                    BRIANNA JONES. CIVIL ACTION 4417-2009; AND IN THE MATTER OF BRIANNA
                    JONES, CCC1-2011.

                    PARTIES PLEASE COME FORWARD AND IDENTIFY YOURSELVES FOR THE RECORD.

MS. JONES: THANK YOU. GOOD MORNING, YOUR HONOR, BRIANNA JONES, DEFENDANT,
                    PRO SE AT THIS TIME.

THE COURT: GOOD MORNING.

MS. FRANKLIN: GOOD MORNING, YOUR HONOR; BARBARA WASHINGTON FRANKLIN, PLAINTIFF,
                    PRO SE. MAY I PRESENT, YOUR HONOR?

THE COURT: YES.

MS. FRANKLIN: YOUR HONOR, I'VE HAD A CHANCE TO LOOK AT SOME OF THE TRANSCRIPTS OF
                    SOME OF THESE PROCEEDINGS, AND I JUST THOUGHT I NEEDED TO TIE SOME
                    LOOSE ENDS. FIRST, IT'S VERY IMPORTANT TO ME, AND IN ALL MY MANY YEARS
                    OF PRACTICE I'VE NEVER HAD TO STATE SUCH ON THE RECORD, BUT I HAVE
                    MAINTAINED AN ATTORNEY/CLIENT RELATIONSHIP WITH THE DEFENDANT AT ALL
                    TIMES THAT I'VE KNOWN HER. THAT'S JUST WHO I AM.

                    SECONDLY, YOUR HONOR, ON MARCH 1ST I GOT A VERY STRANGE CALL, AT LEAST
                    STRANGE TO ME, TO MY OFFICE AROUND 6:12 P.M. A MESSAGE WAS LEFT FOR
                    BRIANNA JONES BY AN ANN MARIE, AND SHE GAVE HER COMPANY'S NAME AS
                    RESULTS, INCORPORATED. I RETURNED THE CALL THE NEXT MORNING.

THE COURT: I'M SORRY, WHAT WAS THE NAME OF THE COMPANY?

204

MS. FRANKLIN: RESULTS, INCORPORATED. IT IS A COMPANY LOCATED IN BROWARD COUNTY, FLORIDA. I RETURNED THE CALL THE NEXT MORNING ASKING FOR ANN MARIE, AND I SPOKE WITH A JUDITH, WHO TURNED OUT TO BE THE PRESIDENT OF THE COMPANY. AND I SAID I WAS CALLING BECAUSE I HAD RECEIVED A CALL IN MY OFFICE FOR BRIANNA JONES. AND JUDITH PROCEEDED TO TELL ME THAT THE DEFENDANT HAD GIVEN MY OFFICE AND MY OFFICE NUMBER AS HER PLACE OF EMPLOYMENT. I INFORMED HER THAT THE DEFENDANT HAD NEVER WORKED FOR ME OR FOR MY OFFICE. AND SHE SAID, WELL, IS IT POSSIBLE THAT SHE COULD HAVE WORKED FOR YOU A FEW YEARS AGO. I SAID, NO, IT IS NOT POSSIBLE. SHE HAS NEVER BEEN IN MY EMPLOYMENT. SHE SAID, BECAUSE WE WERE GIVEN THIS INFORMATION IN 2008, AND WE HAVE IT AS A PART OF OUR FILES. HOWEVER, SHE SAID I PROMISE YOU THAT WE WILL REMOVE THAT INFORMATION FROM OUR FILES AND WE APOLOGIZE TO YOU. I HAVE THE TELEPHONE.

AND I'D JUST LIKE TO ASK THE DEFENDANT IN THE FUTURE NOT TO EVER USE MY NAME OR MY OFFICE NUMBER AS HER PLACE OF EMPLOYMENT. BECAUSE AS A MATTER OF FACT, I DON'T HAVE EMPLOYEES. THE MANAGEMENT OFFICE THAT I RENT FROM THEY HIRE ALL EMPLOYEES AND WE USE THEM AS NEEDED. AND I THOUGHT THAT WAS IMPORTANT FOR THE RECORD.

THE OTHER ISSUE, YOUR HONOR, IS YOU ASKED THE DEFENDANT AT ONE POINT TO PROVIDE YOU WITH A CURRENT ADDRESS. SHE HAD GIVEN YOU, APPARENTLY, ON THE RETURN OF SERVICE, A P.O. BOX AND THE COURT SAID, NO, WE WANT AN ADDRESS. ACCORDING TO THE DOCKET, ALL OF THE COURT'S MAIL IS BEING RETURNED TO THE COURT AS BEING UNABLE TO BE FORWARDED. AND I THINK THAT IT'S IMPORTANT THAT THE COURT HAS A CURRENT RESIDENCE OR CURRRENT ADDRESS SO THAT THE COURT'S MAIL IS NOT RETURNED.

AND THEN, YOUR HONOR, WIH REGARD TO, AGAIN, JUST THE BACK-AND-FORTH WITH THE COURT. **AT ONE OF THE HEARINGS YOUR HONOR MENTIONED A JUDGMENT IN THE CASE. AND I JUST WANTED TO POINT OUT TO THE COURT THERE'S NEVER BEEN A JUDGMENT IN THIS CASE.** OF COURSE, THERE WAS A DEFAULT JUDGMENT THAT WAS VACATED ON CONSENT. THE CASE WAS SETTLED, AND WE ENTERED INTO A SETTLEMENT AGREEMENT. AND THEN BASED ON THE SETTLEMENT AGREEMENT, SINCE IT WAS NOT COMPLIED WITH BY THE DEFENDANT, JUDGE STARR THEN ISSUED THE ORDER WHICH, IN EFFECT, CONFIRMS THE AGREEMENT AND ASKS THAT THE DEFENDANT COMPLY. AND, OF COURSE, THAT'S HOW WE HAVE GOTTEN BEFORE YOUR HONOR.

THE COURT:	I SEE.
MS. FRANKLIN:	SO I JUST WANTED TO MENTION THOSE FACTS. AND THEN THE OTHER AND LAST THING, YOUR HONOR, I HAVE, AS YOUR HONOR KNOWS, I THINK THIS IS PROBABLY THE 11TH TIME I'VE BEEN TO COURT. AND I HAVE BEEN SEEKING TO HAVE THE ORDER OF OCTOBER 18, 2010 ENFORCED. AND TO HAVE THE INFORMATION IN THAT ORDER THAT THE DEFENDANT WAS DIRECTED TO PROVIDE TO ME, TO HAVE THAT DONE BY THE DEFENDANT. IF, YOUR HONOR, THE DEFENDANT HAS NO INTENTION TO PROVIDING THAT INFORMATION, AND I HAVE PROVIDED THE COURT WITH THE VERIFICATION THAT SHE DOES HAVE THE INFORMATION, I JUST DON'T SEE THE POINT OF OUR JUST HAVING TO CONTINUE TO COME BACK TO COURT. IF SHE IS NOT GOING TO PROVIDE THE INFORMATION, YOUR HONOR, HOW DO WE PROCEED? WHERE DO WE GO FROM HERE. AND SHE HAS MADE THAT VERY CLEAR. EACH OF THESE HEARINGS, AS I UNDERSTAND IT, I HAVE COME, AND I DON'T BELIEVE THAT I ACTUALLY HAD TO COME, BUT I'VE COME FOR THE PURPOSE OF HAVING HER PROVIDE DOCUMENTS. THAT HASN'T HAPPENED, AND APPARENTLY, THAT IS NOT GOING TO HAPPEN EVEN THOUGH SHE HAS ACKNOWLEDGED ON THE RECORD, UNDER OATH IN OPEN COURT THAT SHE HAS THE INFORMATION THAT THE OCTOBER 18TH ORDER SPECIFIES. THANK YOU, YOUR HONOR.
MS. JONES:	GOOD MORNING, YOUR HONOR. I MEAN, FIRST I WANT TO SAY I APOLOGIZE FOR THE CASUAL ATTIRE. I WAS AT THE AIRPORT. SIR, I HAD TO GET 5 A.M. ON YESTERDAY, FORT LAUDERDALE. I HAD CONFIRMED SEATS. AS A MATTER OF FACT, A COUPLE OF FLIGHTS HAD BEEN PAID FOR.
THE COURT:	WHERE WERE YOU WHEN YOU CALLED ME ON FRIDAY? I WAS TOLD THAT YOU WERE HERE IN D.C.
MS. JONES:	NO, I SAID I WAS GOING TO BE FLYING IN ON FRIDAY. THE ORIGINAL RESERVATION ONLINE WAS FOR FRIDAY, THE 1ST. I WAS GOING TO STAY THROUGH THE 8TH, SO THAT HOPEFULLY I WOULD STAY A WEEK AND THIS WOULD BE RESOLVED. I HAVE ALL OF THE DOCUMENTATION HERE. I HAVE BEEN AT THE AIRPORT--- --

***

THE COURT:	....I'M NOT SURE WHAT DOCUMENTS YOU HAD IN YOUR BRIEFCASE AND SUITCASE THAT WAS LOST. DO YOU WANT TO TELL ME ABOUT THAT?
MS. JONES:	YES.
THE COURT:	THAT WOULD BE THE SUBJECT MATTER THAT WE'RE HERE FOR.

***

MS. JONES: CERTAINLY, YOUR HONOR. I AGREED TO SET UP A PAYMENT PLAN. AND NOW THIS IS CONTINGENT ON SOMEBODY ELSE'S GENEROSITY, BUT AT LEAST $100 A MONTH UNTIL WE COULD LOCATE OR THE FUNDS WERE LOCATED. AGAIN, I STATE, I HAVE NO IDEA WHERE THE ASSETS ARE. AND I BELIEVE THE REASON SHE -- --

THE COURT: DO YOU LIVE ON 100 A MONTH?

MS. JONES: NO, I DO NOT.

THE COURT: WELL, THE DOCUMENTS THAT I WOULD BE INTERESTED IN SEEING ARE THE DOCUMENTS THAT YOU USE TO LIVE ON DAY-TO-DAY, WEEK-TO-WEEK, MONTH-TO-MONTH AND YEAR-TO-YEAR. I WOULD LIKE TO SEE YOUR FINANCIAL RECORDS.

COMMENT AND ANALYSIS: #2 JUDGE EKANS INTENTIONALLY AND PURPOSEFULLY AVOIDED DEMANDING TO SEE THE BANK OF AMERICA BANK STATEMENTS THAT WERE THE SUBJECT OF JUDGE KATE STARR'S ORDER AND NOT THE AMORPHOUS "FINANCIAL RECORDS" WHICH HE, INSTEAD, CHOSE TO REFERENCE.

MS. JONES: THOSE WERE THE -- -- EVERYONE INCLUDING -- --

THE COURT: OKAY. THEN YOU JUST GET COPIES OF THEM.

MS. JONES: I HAD ALL THOSE WITH ME.

THE COURT: WELL, JUST GET THE COPIES BECAUSE NOW THEY'RE LOST, RIGHT?

MS. JONES: WELL, I JUST SPOKE WITH THE AIRLINE. THEY'RE GOING TO TRY AND LOCATE THE BAGGAGE.

THE COURT: WHAT AIRLINE DO YOU USE?

MS. JONES: IT WAS WITH -- -- THIS IS THE FIRST TIME EVER -- --

THE COURT: WHAT AIRLINE DO YOU USE?

MS. JONES: IT WAS THE AIRTRAN. I USUALLY USE US AIRWAYS.

THE COURT: YES.

MS. JONES: AND AIRTRAN, THEY DROPPED ME OFF AT MIDNIGHT LAST NIGHT AT WASHINGTON REAGAN NATIONAL. I HAD TO GO TO BALTIMORE.

THE COURT: OKAY, ALL RIGHT. SO WHEN DO YOU EXPECT TO HEAR BACK FROM THEM?

MS. JONES: I'M GOING AS SOON AS I LEAVE HERE, HOPEFULLY.

THE COURT:	OKAY. BECAUSE WE'RE GOING TO GET BACK HERE, I THINK, ON WEDNESDAY AT 11. I THINK MS. JONES LIKES 11 A LOT BETTER THAN 10. YOU SEEM TO SHOW AN AFFINITY -- --
MS. JONES:	WELL, I'M BOOKED IN TOWN FOR A WEEK, YOUR HONOR.
THE COURT:	-- -- FOR LATER IN THE DAY. I WANT TO BRING TO YOUR ATTENTION THE INCONVENIENCE THAT YOU CAUSE EVERYONE EACH TIME THAT YOU COME LATE. AND IT WOULD BE COMMON COURTESY AND RESPECT IF YOU WOULD BE WHEN EVERYONE ELSE IS HERE.
MS. JONES:	I UNDERSTAND YOUR HONOR.
THE COURT:	SO WHATEVER YOU NEED TO DO, SET YOUR ALARM CLOCK EARLIER, THE AIRPORT EARLIER, COME A DAY EARLY, WHATEVER; WE WOULD EXPECT TO SEE YOU AT 11 A.M. WEDNESDAY.
MS. JONES:	YES, YOUR HONOR.
THE COURT:	THANK YOU. YOU HAVE A GOOD DAY.
MS. FRANKLIN:	YOUR HONOR, MAY I RESPOND?
THE COURT:	RESPOND TO WHAT?
MS. FRANKLIN:	OKAY.
THE COURT:	THERE'S NOTHING TO RESPOND TO. SEE YOU AT 11, WEDNESDAY.
	COMMENT AND ANALYSIS: #3 I WANTED TO REITERATE BRIANNA JONES' OBLIGATION, UNDER JUDGE STARR'S ORDER, TO BRING WITH HER TO THE NEXT HEARING, COPIES OF THE BANK OF AMERICA BANK STATEMENTS.
	NEEDLESS TO SAY, IT WOULD NOT HAVE MADE ANY DIFFERENCE ANYWAY. THE DYE HAD BEEN CAST. MY ATTORNEY'S FEES WOULD NEVER BE POSSESSED BY ME, IF JUDGE EKANS AND THE OTHER CO-CONSPIRATORS HAD ANYTHING TO DO WITH IT. **MY LAWSUIT HAD, FROM THE VERY BEGINNING, BEEN *RIGGED* FOR DISMISSAL, AND THEREAFTER, DISMISSAL WITH PREJUDICE.**
MS. JONES:	THANK YOU, YOUR HONOR.
MS. FRANKLIN:	YOUR HONOR, ARE WE EXCUSED?
THE COURT:	YES. THANK YOU.

MS. FRANKLIN:	THANK YOU.
MS. JONES:	THANK YOU, YOUR HONOR. AND I WILL BE ON TIME AT 11 O'CLOCK WEDNESDAY.
THE COURT:	WELL, YOUR WORDS ARE COMFORTING, BUT I'D RATHER SEE YOUR FACE HERE AT 11.
MS. JONES:	ABSOLUTELY. I'M IN TOWN FOR A WEEK. THANK YOU, YOUR HONOR. YOUR HONOR? EXCUSE ME. MAY I SPEAK JUST WITH REGARD TO THE RESULTS? IT WAS AN OVESIGHT. IT'S PAID IN FULL. I'LL BRING THE DOCUMENT. I'LL HAVE THAT SENT TO HER.

(THEREUPON, THE PROCEEDINGS WERE CONCLUDED.)

BARBARA WASHINGTON FRANKLIN

SUPERIOR COURT OF THE DISTRICT OF COLUMBIA
CIVIL DIVISION
WASHINGTON, D.C.

THE HONORABLE MATTHEW D. EKANS, ASSOCIATE JUDGE, PRESIDING

THE FOLLOWING ARE EXCERPTS OF THE OFFICIAL COURT TRANSCRIPT OF THE
APRIL 6, 2011 PROCEEDING
ANNOTATED BY THE AUTHOR'S PERTINENT COMMENTARY AND ANALYSIS

APRIL 6, 2011

PROCEEDINGS

COMMENT AND ANALYSIS # 1: THE MARCH 18, 2011 COURT HEARING
IMMEDIATELY PRECEDED THE APRIL 6, 2011 PROCEEDING. I HAVE REFERRED TO
THE EVENTS THAT TRANSPIRED DURING THE MARCH 18, 2011 PROCEEDING AS
"THE GODFATHER EPISODE" GIVEN THE SIMILARITY TO MOBSTERS OF THE TAG-
TEAM BEHAVIOR OF THE PRESIDING JUDGE, MATTHEW EKANS, AND FORMER D.C.
SUPERIOR COURT CHIEF JUDGE, GEORGE SKINNER, THEN SERVING AS SENIOR
JUDGE.

IN SHOCK, I HAD EXPERIENCED JUDGE EKANS ANNOUNCE THE *CONTRIVED 15
MINUTE RECESS* AND ORDER ME AND BRIANNA JONES TO GO OUT OF THE
COURTROOM AND INTO THE HALLWAY FOR THE STATED PURPOSE OF SETTLING
MY LAWSUIT.

IN REALITY, JUDGE EKANS ANNOUNCED THE *CONTRIVED RECESS* TO GIVE HIS CO-
CONSPIRATOR COLLEAGUE AND FORMER D.C. SUPERIOR COURT CHIEF JUDGE,
GEORGE SKINNER, ACCESS TO BRIANNA JONES IN ORDER FOR SKINNER TO SHAKE
HER DOWN, INTIMIDATE AND TRAUMATIZE HER AND ULTIMATELY CHILL HER
FURTHER TESTIMONY IN THE COURTROOM. THIS WAS MOBSTER BEHAVIOR 21ST
CENTURY, D.C. COURT SYSTEM STYLE, PLANNED, ORCHESTRATED AND EXECUTED
BY TWO CAVALIERLY CORRUPT, PROMINENT AND VETERAN D.C. COURT JUDGES
WHO WERE ACCOUNTABLE TO NO ONE IN AUTHORITY.

PRESUMABLY, THIS WAS NOT THEIR FIRST MILLION-DOLLAR HEIST AND THEFT OF CASE SETTLEMENT PROCEEDS THAT INCLUDED ATTORNEY'S FEES. HOWEVER, IT WAS PROBABLY THEIR LARGEST. THEY HAD, IN ALL LIKELIHOOD, PARTNERED TOGETHER BEFORE, DURING THEIR RESPECTIVE DECADES-LONG JUDGESHIPS ON D.C. SUPERIOR COURT, AND HAD PRESUMABLY BENEFITED FINANCIALLY FROM THEIR UNSEEN CRIMINAL ENTERPRISES. AND IT CAN ALSO BE PRESUMED THAT MY CASE OF D.C JUDICIAL FRAUD AND THEFT WAS NOT THEIR FIRST, NOR WOULD IT BE THEIR LAST, BASED ON THEIR OBVIOUS JUDICIAL OPPORTUNITY, GREED AND RUTHLESSNESS.

THE EVENTS OF THE MARCH 18, 2011 COURT HEARING CONFIRMED FOR ME, BEYOND A SHADOW OF A DOUBT, THAT JUDGE EKANS WAS A MAJOR PLAYER IN THIS GRAND D.C. JUDICIAL AND FBI CONSPIRACY AND CRIMINAL ENTERPRISE TO STEAL, STRIP AND DEFRAUD ME OF THE ESTIMATED $50 MILLION IN ATTORNEY'S FEES OWED TO ME FROM THE $34 MILLION SETTLEMENT OF THE $100 MILLION LAWSUIT THAT I HAD SINGLE-HANDILY CRAFTED AND PAID FOR FILING IN MAY 1996 IN THE BROWARD COUNTY CIRCUIT COURT LOCATED IN FORT LAUDERDALE, FLA.

FROM THE TIME OF THE MARCH 18, 2011 COURT HEARING, I WAS UNABLE TO REGARD JUDGE EKANS AS ANYTHING OTHER THAN WHAT HE WAS: THE GRAND MARSHALL AND KEY D.C. JUDICIAL CO-CONSPIRATOR IN THIS HISTORIC D.C. JUDICIAL AND FBI CONSPIRACY AND CRIMINAL ENTERPRISE TO STEAL AND DEFRAUD ME OF AN ESTIMATED $50 MILLION IN ATTORNEY'S FEES.

FOLLOWING THE MARCH 18, 2011 COURT HEARING, AND AFTER BEING INSPIRED AND EMPOWERED BY THE HOLY SPIRIT, I RESOLVED TO REMAIN IN THE CASE UNTIL THE OCCASION OF ITS *RIGGED FINAL DISMISSAL* ON JANUARY 16, 2015. FOR ME, THIS WHOLE D.C. JUDCIAL MESS WAS A DIVINE ASSIGNMENT AND I INTENDED TO DO MY PART IN PARTNERSHIP WITH THE HOLY SPIRIT.

THEREAFTER, I WOULD PROCEED, STEP BY STEP, ON THIS UNPRECEDENTED JOURNEY OF MASSIVE D.C. JUDICIAL AND FBI FRAUD, THEFT, CORRUPTION, EXTORTION AND EGREGIOUS JUDICIAL INJUSTICE, ENGINEERED AND ORCHESTRATED IN BROAD DAYLIGHT, OPEN COURTROOMS, PRIVATE JUDGES' CHAMBERS, COURT HALLWAYS, WASHINGTON AREA HOTEL SUITES AND ON THE D.C. SUPERIOR COURT DOCKET PREPARED AND MANNED BY D.C. COURT EMPLOYEES, AND READ AND REVIEWED BY THE UNSUSPECTING PUBLIC AT LARGE.

JUDGE EKANS, AN UNEQUIVOCAL KEY JUDICIAL CO-CONSPIRATOR, NOW WITH MARCHING ORDERS IN HAND, WOULD CAVALIERLY CONDUCT THE APRIL 6, 2011 COURT PROCEEDING AS A *FAMILY FEUD TELEVISION SHOW*, RATHER THAN A COURT PROCEEDING. JUDGE EKANS DIRECTED ME AND BRIANNA JONES TO PARTICIPATE IN THE CHARADE PASSING AS A COURT HEARING. THE EXERCISE IN ABUSIVE JUDICIAL POWER WAS WITNESSED BY A HANDFUL OF OTHER PEOPLE PRESENT IN THE COURTROOM, INCLUDING TWO KNOWN STALKING CREDITORS OF BRIANNA JONES.

IN THE ABSENCE OF CAMERAS IN THE COURTROOM OR A VIDEO RECORDING OF THE PROCEEDING, JUDGE EKANS FELT COMPLETELY COMFORTABLE CONDUCTING THE HEARING FOR WHICH HE WOULD NEVER HAVE TO ANSWER OR ACCOUNT TO ANYONE ABOVE OR BENEATH HIM. HIS ABUSE OF POWER WAS RUTHLESS. HE DID NOT JUST WALK ALL OVER ME AND BRIANNA JONES WITH HIS GASLIGHTING AND SARCASTIC WORDS, HE VERBALLY DEFECATED ALL OVER US, AS VERIFIED AND ILLUSTRATED IN THE ANNOTATED COMMENTARY AND ANALYSIS OF EXCERPTS OF THE PROCEEDING SET FORTH BELOW.

THE DEPUTY CLERK: YOUR HONOR, CALLING THE CASE OF BARBARA WASHINGTON FRANKLIN VERSUS BRIANNA JONES, CIVIL ACTION 4417, AND IN THE MATTER OF BRIANNA JONES, CCC-1-2011.

PLEASE COME FORWARD AND IDENTIFY YOURSELF FOR THE RECORD.

THE COURT: GOOD MORNING.

MS. FRANKLIN: GOOD MORNING, YOUR HONOR. BARBARA WASHINGTON FRANKLIN, ATTORNEY FOR THE PLAINTIFF.

MS. JONES: GOOD MORNING, YOUR HONOR. BRIANNA JONES, PRO SE AT THIS TIME.

COMMENT AND ANALYSIS: #2 FOLLOWING JUDGE EKANS' ENTRANCE INTO THE COURTROOM, TAKING THE BENCH, AND THE OPENING PRELIMINARIES COMPLETED, BRIANNA JONES, STANDING AT THE COUNSEL TABLE TO MY RIGHT, BEGAN RATHER POINTEDLY WAVING PAPERS IN THE AIR, AS IF THEY WERE FIRECRACKERS SHE WAS ABOUT TO FLING IN MY DIRECTION.

JONES' HEAD TURNED TO HER LEFT, AND LOOKING DIRECTLY AT ME, BUT SPEAKING TO THE JUDGE, INFORMED HIM THAT WHAT SHE HELD IN HER HAND WAS A "MOTION TO VACATE THE SETTLEMENT AGREEMENT OF A DEFAULT BY THE INDUCEMENT."

THE ODYSSEY OF JUDICIAL CORRUPTION

THE CO-CONSPIRATORS HAD CONJURED UP A DIABOLICAL LEGAL THEORY AND MOTION FOR JONES TO THREATEN ME WITH IN COURT, HOPING THAT I WOULD BE SO EMBARASSED BY THE FALSE AND UNFOUNDED ALLEGATION IN THE MOTION THAT I HAD PARTICIPATED IN AN IMMORAL RELATIONSHIP WITH JONES, AND SUCH RELATIONSHIP HAD INDUCED JONES INTO SIGNING THE SETTLEMENT AGREEMENT THAT RESULTED IN MY VOLUNTARY DISMISSAL OF MY LAWSUIT AGAINST JONES.

THIS FALSE AND SLANDEROUS ALLEGATION MADE AGAINST ME, DEVISED BY THE CO-CONSPIRATORS, AND GIVEN TO JONES TO FILE IN COURT AS A MOTION TO VACATE THE SETTLEMENT AGREEMENT WAS NO MORE THAN GUTTER SILK DISGUISED AS A COURT PLEADING. FURTHER, IT WAS CLEARLY INTENDED AS A VICIOUS AND MALICIOUS STRIKE AT ME IN HOPES OF DEFEATING MY CLAIM AGAINST JONES FOR THE MILLIONS OF DOLLARS IN ATTORNEY'S FEES THAT THE CO-CONSPIRATOR FBI AGENTS AND D.C. COURT JUDGES HAD STOLEN FROM ME.

THE ALLEGATIONS IN THE CO-CONSPIRATORS' MOTION TO VACATE THE SETTLEMENT AGREEMENT WAS CONSISTENT WITH WHAT JONES HAD REPEATEDLY DESCRIBED TO ME AS TO WHAT OCCURRED IN JONES' "SUMMONED" CLANDESTINE MEETINGS WITH "THE OFFICIALS" IN VARIOUS HOTEL SUITES IN THE WASHINGTON REGION.

THE CLANDESTINE MEETINGS THAT THE "OFFICIALS" REQUIRED BRIANNA JONES TO ATTEND ARE INDICATIVE OF THE DEPTH OF THE GREED, RUTHLESSNESS AND COLDBLOODEDNESS THAT CHARACTERIZED THESE "OFFICIALS" WHO, EVEN THOUGH THEY, AT ALL TIMES, HAD FULL KNOWLEDGE THAT, YEARS EARLIER, BRIANNA JONES HAD BEEN MEDICALLY DIAGNOSED AS MENTALLY IMPAIRED AND SUFFERING WITH POST-TRAUMATIC STRESS DISORDER (PTSD) AND DEPRESSION, NEVERTHELESS ENGAGED IN A LEVEL OF EXPLOITATION, MANIPULATION AND EXTORTION COMMENSURATE WITH THE ILLEGAL CONFISCATION, FRAUD AND THEFT OF THE ESTIMATED $100 MILLION IN CASE SETTLEMENT PROCEEDS.

ACCORDING TO JONES, DURING HER CLANDESTINE MEETINGS WITH "THE OFFICIALS," THE #1 INSTRUCTION THEY GAVE HER WAS THAT WHENEVER SHE APPEARED IN COURT IN MY CASE, SHE MUST "LIE, LIE, LIE" – THAT IS, IF SHE WANTED TO WIN, IF SHE WANTED TO HAVE DISBURSED TO HER ANY PORTION OF THE $100 MILLION IN SETTLEMENT FEES RESULTING FROM THE $34 MILLION-PLUS-INTEREST SETTLEMENT IN DECEMBER 1996 OF HER FLORIDA CASE AGAINST THE WILLIE LEE RIDGEWAY ESTATE.

BRIANNA JONES, BEING THE MEGALOMANIACAL SOCIOPATH THAT SHE IS, REGARDED THIS INSTRUCTION AS PRECIOUS, IF NOT INVIOLATE, BECAUSE WINNING MEANS MORE THAN ANYTHING ELSE TO A SOCIOPATH, AND WILL BE PURSUED AT ALL COSTS.

THE #2 INSTRUCTION GIVEN TO JONES DURING HER CLANDESTINE MEETINGS WITH "THE OFFICIALS" WAS THAT WHENEVER SHE TESTIFIED IN COURT, SHE MUST TESTIFY REPEAEDLY THAT SHE HAD HAD "A RELATIONSHIP" WITH THE ATTORNEY, MEANING ONE THAT WENT BEYOND THE ATTORNEY-CLIENT RELATIONSHIP. EVEN NOW, IT IS DIFFICULT FOR ME TO PEN THESE WORDS BECAUSE THE THOUGHT IS SO REPUGNANT AND ABHORRENT TO ME, WHO I AM, WHO I HAVE ALWAYS BEEN, WHO I WILL ALWAYS BE, AND ALL THAT I STAND FOR.

ONE OF THE IMPORTANT LESSONS THAT I HAVE LEARNED FROM THE EXPERIENCE OF MY CASE IS THAT WHEN CORRUPT D.C. COURT JUDGES AND FBI AGENTS JOIN AS A TEAM TO ENGAGE IN MASSIVE FRAUD, THEFT AND CORRUPTION, THEIR CRIMINAL CONDUCT IS OFTEN PLAYED OUT IN THE PREPARATION OF THE FALSE AND MALICIOUS COURT FILINGS THAT WAS ILLUSTRATED BY THE MOTION TO VACATE THE SETTLEMENT AGREEEMENT PREPARED FOR FILING BY JONES.

THE ESSENTIAL AND CRITICAL INEQUITY AND UNFAIRNESS IN MY CASE WAS THAT I WAS NEVER BEING OPPOSED BY JONES ALONE. MY ACTUAL OPPONENTS WERE, INDEED, NUMEROUS AND COMPRISED OF CORRUPT D.C. SUPERIOR COURT JUDGES, FBI AGENTS, AT LEAST ONE U.S. DISTRICT COURT JUDGE, OTHER GOVERNMENT OFFICIALS AND AT LEAST ONE WELL-KNOWN WASHINGTON MEDIA PERSONALITY.

BEGINNING WITH THE MARCH 18, 2011 HEARING, IF NOT BEFORE, WHEN JONES ENTERED THE COURTROOM, IT BECAME QUITE APPARENT AND QUICKLY UNDERSTOOD BY ALL IN ATTENDANCE, AND MORE IMPORTANTLY, IT WAS UNDERSTOOD BY THE JUDGE THAT JONES APPEARED BACKED BY THE FULL ACCOMPANIMENT OF THE TEAM OF D.C. JUDICIAL CO-CONSPIRATORS, SOME OF WHOM WERE SITTING JUDGES ON THE D.C. SUPERIOR COURT BENCH AS DESCRIBED ELSEWHERE HEREIN AND IN FILED COURT DOCUMENTS.

THUS, THE FIGHT REPRESENTED BY MY LAWSUIT AGAINST JONES WAS FIXED FROM THE VERY BEGINNING AND THE FINAL OUTCOME OF MY CASE HAD BEEN PRE-DETERMINED AND PRE-SCRIPTED BY THE TEAM OF CO-CONSPIRATOR D.C. COURT JUDGES AND FBI AGENTS.

NOW THAT JUDGE EKANS AND I *BOTH* UNDERSTOOD THAT *HE* UNDERSTOOD THAT WHILE MASSIVE D.C. JUDICIAL AND FBI FRAUD AND CORRUPTION MIGHT BE THE DOMINANT ISSUE IN THE CASE, HE HAD MADE IT CLEAR TO ME, AS WELL AS TO ANYONE READING THE TRANSCRIPT OF THE HEARING, THAT HE HAD NO INTENTION OF DOING ANYTHING ABOUT IT. PERIOD.

AND AS FAR AS MY REQUESTS AND MOTIONS FOR INVESTIGATION OF JUDICIAL FRAUD IN THE CASE, THEY WERE JUST THAT --- REQUESTS AND MOTIONS   AND CERTAINLY NOT A SUITABLE TOPIC FOR A COURT OF LAW IN THE DISTRICT OF COLUMBIA, WHERE THE ALLEGATION OF CRIMINAL COMPLICITY OF JUDICIAL OFFICERS IN A CASE OF MASSIVE FRAUD, THEFT, CORRUPTION AND EXTORTION MIGHT BE UNCOVERED AND ESTABLISHED, IF PROMPTLY AND PROPERLY INVESTIGATED.

AT THE MARCH 18, 2011 COURT HEARING, JUDGE EKANS HAD THROWN DOWN THE GAUNTLET, AND BURIED HIS SWORN COMMITMENT TO JUDICIAL IMPARTIALITY AND FAIRNESS IN THE CASE WHEN HE SUDDENLY INVOKED A *CONTRIVED COURT RECESS* OSTENSIBLY FOR GIVING THE PARTIES THE OPPORTUNITY TO GO OUT INTO THE HALLWAY TO SEE IF THEY COULD WORK OUT A SETTLEMENT.

HOWEVER, THE RECESS HAD ALLOWED JUDGE EKANS TO SURREPTITIOUSLY ENALBE FORMER CHIEF JUDGE GEORGE SKINNER TO ENTER THE HALLWAY AT THE SAME TIME IN ORDER TO SHAKE DOWN AND INTIMIDATE THE DEFENDANT, BRIANNA JONES, A COURT WITNESS AND, IN SO DOING, BLATANTLY OBSTRUCT JUSTICE.

JUDGE EKANS' ACTION WAS AN EGREGIOUS ABUSE OF HIS JUDICIAL DISCRETION. HIS ACTION ALSO CAUSED THE D.C. SUPERIOR COURT TO BE COMPLICIT IN THE MASSIVE D.C. JUDICIAL AND FBI FRAUD, THEFT, CORRUPTION AND EXTORTION CONSPIRACY AND CRIMINAL ENTEPRISE THAT DOMINATED THE CASE. JUDGE EKANS WAS NOW ALL IN WITH THE OPPOSITIION AND D.C. CO-CONSPIRATORS.

I KNEW THERE WAS NOTHING FAIR, JUST, EQUITABLE OR IMPARTIAL ABOUT THE COURT PROCEEDINGS THAT I WAS ENGAGED IN. NEVERTHELESS, I DECIDED TO SOLDIER ON.

JUDGE EKANS WOULD USE THE APRIL 6, 2011 PROCEEDING AND THE FIVE OR SIX REMAINING HEARINGS TO BASICALLY TREAD WATER, TRYING TO FIGURE OUT HOW HE WOULD CONTINUE TO PROTECT HIS FELLOW COURT JUDGES COMPLICIT IN THE MASSIVE OFFICIAL D.C. JUDICIAL FRAUD AND CORRUPTION CRIMINAL ENTERPRISE FROM INVESTIGATION, INDICTMEMT, PROSECUTION AND PUNISHMENT, WHILE AT THE SAME TIME ALLOWING ME THE TIME TO REALIZE THAT NOT EVEN A SCINTILLA OF JUSTICE COULD BE RIPPED FROM A COURT SYSTEM SATURATED FOR DECADES IN DEEP, DEMONIC AND PERVASIVE CORRUPTION.

THE PROCEEDING CONTINUED WITH THE COURT'S INQUIRY OF JONES AS TO WHY SHE WAS COMPLETELY AND ECONOMICALLY DEPENDENT, AND HEAR HER ATTRIBUTE HER DEPENDENT STATUS TO THE INJURIES SHE CONTINUED TO SUFFER BECAUSE OF THE CHILDHOOD ABUSE, MOLESTATION AND SEXUAL ASSAULT ALLEGEDLY COMMITTED UPON HER BY WILLIE LEE RIDGEWAY, THE ALLEGED ABUSER AND DEFENDANT IN THE FLORIDA LAWSUIT.

IT WAS DURING THE APRIL 6, 2011 HEARING THAT JUDGE EKANS MADE CLEAR HIS REJECTION OF MY PRIOR SUGGESTION THAT THE COURT APPOINT A FEDERAL AGENT TO INVESTIGATE THE DOMINANT ISSUE OF FRAUD-BY-CORRUPT- D.C. COURT-JUDGES-AND-FBI-AGENTS.

THE COURT:	MISS JONES, DID YOU BRING YOUR PAPERS TODAY?
MS. JONES:	YES, I DID, YOUR HONOR.
THE COURT.	GOOD.
MS. JONES:	MAY I SPEAK?
THE COURT:	I'M SORRY?
MS. JONES:	MAY I SPEAK?
THE COURT:	MAY YOU SPEAK?
MS. JONES:	WITH REGARD TO PLAINTIFF'S COMMENT FROM APRIL THE FOURTH?
THE COURT:	I DON'T WANT TO HEAR ANYTHING ABOUT ANY COMMENTS. DO YOU KNOW WHAT WE'RE DOING?
MS. JONES:	YES.
THE COURT:	HAVE YOU EVER THOUGHT ABOUT WHAT IT IS WE'RE DOING?
MS. JONES:	YES, YOUR HONOR.

THE COURT: OKAY, LET'S STAY FOCUSED ON THAT. WHAT DO YOU HAVE?

MS. JONES: I HAVE A PAYMENT PLAN AND I HAVE THE MOTION HERE TO VACATE THE SETTLEMENT AGREEMENT OF A DEFAULT BY THE INDUCEMENT. AND YOUR HONOR, AS I STAND HERE I'M SO RELUCTANT TO FILE THIS.

COMMENT AND ANALYSIS #3: NOTHING WAS MORE EVIDENT THAT EKANS HAD DECIDED, AFTER PRESUMED CONSULTATION WITH JUDGES SKINNER AND MANDARIN, THE TWO OTHER KEY D.C. JUDICIAL CO-CONSPIRATORS, TO SIMPLY LET THE CLOCK RUN OUT ON MY CASE.

BRIANNA JONES WAS HOMELESS, WITHOUT FINANCIAL RESOURCES IN ANY AMOUNT, PHYSICALLY AND EMOTIONALLY CHALLENGED AND SUFFERING WITH POST-TRAUMATIC STRESS DISORDER (PTSD) AS VERIFIED BY A MEDICAL EXAMINATION THAT WAS INCLUDED IN THE FLORIDA COMPLAINT THAT I HAD CRAFTED AND FILED IN MAY 1996.

NEVERTHELESS, EKANS WOULD HAVE BRIANNA JONES GO THROUGH THE MOTIONS OF COMING UP WITH A PLAN TO PAY ME 40% OF THE $34 MILLION SETTLEMENT AMOUNT.

THERE WASN'T A TIME DURING THE 9 MONTHS THAT EKANS WASTED IN ADJUDICATING MY LAWSUIT THAT I WASN'T REMINDED OF THE BIBLICAL STORY OF THE UNJUST JUDGE DESCRIBED IN CHAPTER 18 OF THE BOOK OF LUKE. THE JUDGE WAS HEARTLESS, COLD, UNFAIR, DIDN'T CARE ABOUT PEOPLE AND WAS SIMPLY A BRUTE IN A BLACK ROBE. IN SUM TOTAL, THIS WAS A JUDGE WHO DIDN'T FEAR MAN NOR GOD. THE BIBLICAL DESCRIPTION OF THE UNJUST JUDGE FIT JUDGE EKANS TO A TEE.

THE COURT: WELL, YOU CAN BE EVEN MORE RELUCTANT BECAUSE YOU'RE NOT GOING TO FILE IT IN HERE. DO YOU KNOW WHERE THE CLERK'S OFFICE IS?

MS. JONES: YES, I'M PREPARED TO FILE IT. AND THAT'S WHY I DIDN'T – I HAVEN'T FILED IT YET.

THE COURT: ALL RIGHT, WELL, WE DON'T NEED TO TALK ABOUT IT SINCE YOU HAVEN'T FILED IT. WE CAN TALK ABOUT WHAT YOU'RE GOING TO DO TO SATISFY THE SETTLEMENT.

BARBARA WASHINGTON FRANKLIN

COMMENT AND ANALYSIS #4: BRIANNA JONES' ATTORNEYS HAD COME UP WITH THE SO-CALLED LEGAL THEORY THAT WOULD PERSUADE EKANS TO OVERTURN THE SETTLEMENT AGREEMENT WE HAD EXECUTED IN RESPONSE TO MY LAWSUIT. THEY CALLED IT FRAUDULENT INDUCEMENT. IN OTHER WORDS, I HAD SOMEHOW INDUCED JONES TO ENTER INTO THE AGREEMENT AGAINST HER WILL AND THEREFORE, THE COURT MUST OVERTURN THE AGREEMENT AND INVALIDATE IT.

MY LEGAL REPRESENTATION OF BRIANNA JONES WAS AT ALL TIMES AND IN ALL RESPECTS LEGAL, PROPER, APPROPRIATE AND, AS MOTHER WOULD SAY, FITTING FOR "A DAUGHTER OF THE KING."

MS. JONES: *I PROPOSE TO PAY THE PLAINTIFF, AS I SAID, A HUNDRED DOLLARS A MONTH BEGINNING ON MAY 1ST, 2011, AND THIS AMOUNT IS BASED ON THE CONTINUED GENEROSITY OF ANOTHER PARTY. DEFENDANT ENTERED INTO ORIGINAL AGREEMENT FEBRUARY THE SECOND OF 2010 WITH PLAINTIFF WITH THE UNDERSTANDING THAT I HAD NOT YET TAKEN POSSESSION OF SETTLEMENT PROCEEDS IN WHICH PLAINTIFF DID NOT REPRESENT ME. HOWEVER, I DID ENTER INTO THE AGREEMENT.*

COMMENT AND ANALYSIS #5: BRIANNA JONES ACKNOWLEDGES THE OCCURRENCE OF HER SETTLEMENT WITH THE RIDGEWAY ESTATE. SHE FURTHER ACKNOWLEDGES THE SETTLEMENT AGREEMENT BETWEEN US. LASTLY, SHE ACKNOWLEDGES THAT SHE HAS NOT TAKEN POSSESSION OF THE SETTLEMENT PROCEEDS.

NEVERTHELESS, SHE CANNOT RESIST THE LIE THAT I DID NOT REPRESENT HER IN THE $100 MILLION FLORIDA LAWSUIT THAT I HAD SOLELY CRAFTED AND FILED AND MOREOVER, UPON WHICH THE $34 MILLION SETTLEMENT WAS BASED.

THE COURT: MISS FRANKLIN, WHAT DO YOU WANT TO DO?

MS. FRANKLIN: WELL, YOUR HONOR, I GUESS IT WAS TWO HEARINGS AGO SHE, IN RESPONSE TO THE COURT'S REQUEST THAT SHE BRING IN DOCUMENTS WITH REGARD TO WHO WAS SUPPORTING HER, SHE PROVIDED, EXCUSE ME, A NOTARIZED LETTER FROM MR. TED MINOR.

THE COURT: I'M SORRY FROM –

MS. FRANKLIN:	MR. TED MINOR, WHO WOULD BE, WHO AGAIN ACCORDING TO HIS LETTER I'M LOOKING AT IT HERE, HE JUST INDICATED HE'S BEEN PROVIDING HER WITH SUBSTANTIAL SUPPORT FOR THE PAST FIVE YEARS.
	HOWEVER, WHAT WAS NOT SHARED WITH THE COURT IS THAT, AND AGAIN I'M PROVIDING INFORMATION THAT THE DEFENDANT HAS PROVIDED TO ME WITH REGARD TO MR. MINOR, I UNDERSTAND HE IS A SCHOOL ADMINISTRATOR IN BROWARD COUNTY, HE LIVES WITH HIS PARENTS, HE HAS BEEN EXPERIENCING FINANCIAL HARDSHIP, IN PART DUE TO AN AUTO ACCIDENT HE HAD RECENTLY IN WHICH HE LOST HIS CAR BUT ALSO HIS WAGES ARE BEING GARNISHEED BY THE IRS.
THE COURT:	HIS WAGES ARE BEING GARNISHED?
MS. FRANKLIN:	YES.
	THIS IS NOT AN INDIVIDUAL WHO I COULD *IN GOOD CONSCIENCE* ACCEPT ANYTHING FROM BECAUSE HE DOESN'T HAVE IT.
	COMMENT AND ANALYSIS: #6 I ACTUALLY FELT UNCOMFORTABLE TALKING ABOUT "GOOD CONSCIENCE" BEFORE EKANS BECAUSE THUS FAR, AND THROUGHOUT THE PROCEEDINGS, HE HAD DEMONSTRATED THAT "JUDICIAL CONSCIENCE" OF ANY KIND WAS NOT A FACTOR IN HIS ADJUDICATION OF MY CASE.
MS. JONES:	MAY I SPEAK, YOUR HONOR? THAT'S NOT THE CASE. HE HAD ASSISTED – HE'S ALWAYS ASSISTED HIS RELATIVE'S SISTER, HE HAD SOME DIFFICULTY, AND HIS FAMILY AND I LED HIM IN THE RIGHT DIRECTION.
THE COURT:	ARE YOU RELATED TO MR. MINOR?
MS. JONES:	NO, HE'S A DEAR, DEAR FREIND.
THE COURT:	MUST BE. HE SUPPORTS YOU?
MS. JONES:	YES.
THE COURT:	WHY DON'T YOU SUPPORT YOURSELF?
MS. JONES:	BECAUSE THERE ARE ISSUES RELATED TO THE ABUSE, AND I'VE BEEN KNOWN, IT'S ON RECORD, AND I'VE HAD FAMILY MEMBERS –
THE COURT:	ISSUES RELATED TO THE ABUSE. HAVE YOU EVER WORKED?
MS. JONES:	SOME.

BARBARA WASHINGTON FRANKLIN

THE COURT:	WHAT KIND OF WORK?
MS. JONES:	USUALLY MANAGEMENT, OFFICE MANAGEMENT. I CAN GO INTO A FIELD AND IMMEDIATELY CAPTURE THE FIELD.
THE COURT:	HOW OLD ARE YOU?
MS. JONES:	I JUST TURNED 47, FEBRUARY THE SECOND.
THE COURT:	HOW LONG HAVE YOU LIVED WITHOUT WORKING?
MS. JONES:	I'VE WORKED SPORADICALLY BUT WHAT HAPPENS IS AS A RESULT OF THE ABUSE – --
THE COURT:	SO PEOPLE – YOU'RE JUST DEPENDENT, YOU'RE TOTALLY DEPENDENT?
MS. JONES:	YES.
THE COURT:	WOW.
MS. JONES:	BUT WHAT HAS HAPPENED, YOUR HONOR ---
THE COURT;	ARE YOU PHYSICALLY SOUND?
MS. JONES:	TO SOME EXTENT. I SUFFER INTERNAL INJURIES BECAUSE OF THE ABUSE TO THIS VERY DAY.
THE COURT:	WHAT KIND OF INJURIES?
MS. JONES:	THERE WAS MASSIVE SCARRING, I'VE HAD SURGERY AUGUST THE 22ND, 1990, JOHNS HOPKINS, I'VE SEEN SEVERAL DOCTORS SINCE THEN I HAD A LARGE MASS, AN 80-POUND MASS. AND IT CONTINUES TO GROW AS LONG AS I REMUNERATE WITH REGARD TO THE RAPE. IT CAUSED SO MUCH DAMAGE THAT EVEN NOW I SUFFER CONSTANTLY WITH THAT.

SECONDLY, I HAVE SEVERE PANIC ATTACKS. I CAN WALK INTO AN OFFICE; I WOULD LOVE TO BE ABLE TO GO INTO A JOB EVERYDAY. AND I'VE BEEN SO EMBARRASSED BECAUSE I HAVE BEEN PROMOTED AND AS SOON AS -- --

COMMENT AND ANALYSIS: #7 EKANS LISTENED PERFUNCTORILY TO JONES AS SHE HIGHLIGHTED HER HEALTH HISTORY ALLEGEDLY CAUSED BY THE PREDATOR'S RAPE. I WAS SURPRISED THAT SHE BROACHED THE SUBJECT OF HER ONGOING MEDICAL ISSUES SINCE IT WAS CLEAR THAT EKANS COULD CARE LESS ABOUT HER HEALTH, MY HEALTH OR ANYONE ELSE'S HEALTH. ALL HE CARED ABOUT WAS GETTING THE MONEY FROM THE SETTLEMENT PROCEEDS FOR HIMSELF AND HIS COLLEAGUES

JUDGE EKANS HAD ONE GOAL IN MIND AS WE SLOSHED THROUGH THIS GARGANTUAN MESS OF A CASE: HOW SOON COULD HE GET HIS SHARE OF THE $34 MILLION SETTLEMENT UPON COMPLETION OF HIS KEY CO-CONSPIRATOR ROLE AS PRESIDING JUDGE IN THIS HISTORIC D.C. JUDICIAL AND FBI CRIMINAL ENTERPRISE THAT SO FAR HE AND HIS CO-CONSPIRATOR COLLEAGUES HAD MANAGED TO KEEP UNDERCOVER, UNDERWRAPS AND IN THE DARK.

THE COURT: YOU MAY HAVE TO GO INTO A JOB.

MS. JONES: I HAVE -- --

THE COURT: IF YOU'VE MADE A SETTLEMENT AGREEMENT AND YOU CAN'T PAY IT OTHER THAN A HUNDRED DOLLARS A MONTH YOU MAY HAVE TO GO INTO A JOB. SEE, I'M GOING TO HAVE TO START THINKING CREATIVE ABOUT HOW TO DEAL WITH THIS MATTER BECAUSE YOU ARE COMING UP WITH WOEFULLY INADEQUATE RESPONSES, AND I'VE TRIED TO BE CIRCUMSPECT IN HOW WE'RE GOING TO DEAL WITH THIS.

COMMENT AND ANALYSIS: #8 THE EVENTS PREVIOUSLY RECITED REGARDING THE MARCH 18, 2011 PROCEEDING VERIFIED THAT JUDGE EKANS HAD ALREADY BEGUN TO THINK CREATIVELY IN HOW TO DEAL WITH MY CASE WHEN HE AND JUDGE SKINNER HAD, WITH PREMEDITATION, INTIMIDATED AND SHAKEN DOWN BRIANNA JONES IN ORDER TO CHILL HER TESTIMONY AS A WITNESS AND FURTHER, HAD ALSO TRAUMATIZED ME IN MY HAVING TO WITNESS THE ACT OF JUDICIAL INTIMIDATION AND PREMEDITATED OBSTRUCTION OF JUSTICE IN THE COURT HALLWAY.

THE COURT: MISS FRANKLIN HAS SUGGESTED THAT I SHOULD APPOINT A FEDERAL AGENT TO INVESTIGATE. I DECLINED THAT SUGGESTION; I THINK IT'S INAPPROPRIATE.

QUITELY FRANKLY, MISS FRANKLIN, I THINK YOU MIGHT BE MORE ASSERTIVE IN YOUR OWN EFFORTS TO HIRE SOMEONE TO DO AN INVESTIGATION.

COMMENT AND ANALYSIS: #9 NOTHING IS MORE EVIDENT OF JUDGE EKANS' ROLE AS A KEY D.C. JUDICIAL CO-CONSPIRATOR THAN HIS REFUSAL TO ORDER AN INVESTIGATION OF THE ALLEGED MISSING (STOLEN) $34 MILLION IN CASE SETTLEMENT PROCEEDS. JUDGE EKANS MADE IT CLEAR THAT HE WOULD NOT ACT IN ANY WAY THAT COULD BE AGAINST THE BEST INTERESTS OF THE D.C. JUDICIAL AND FBI CO-CONSPIRATORS.

IN OTHER WORDS, JUDGE EKANS, KNOWING FULL WELL THAT BOTH PARTIES, THE DEFENDANT, BRIANNA JONES, AND I HAD BOTH REPEATEDLY ALLEGED, IN PROCEEDING AFTER PROCEEDING, THAT THE SETTLEMENT PROCEEDS HAD NOT BEEN DISBURSED TO ME AS PLAINTIFF'S COUNSEL, AND BASED ON THE CONTINGENCY FEE AGREEMENT; AND THAT BRIANNA JONES HAD REPEATEDLY DESCRIBED HAVING BEEN SUMMONED TO MEET WITH CO-CONSPIRATOR "OFFICIALS" IN VARIOUS HOTELS. NEVERTHELESS, JUDGE EKANS WOULD HAVE THE AUDACITY TO TELL ME THAT THE RESPONSIBILITY FOR THE INVESTIGATION OF A MASSIVE D.C. JUDICIAL AND FBI FRAUD, THEFT, CORRUPTION AND EXTORTION CONSPIRACY AND CRIMINAL ENTERPRISE CASE WAS SQUARELY MINE TO PURSUE. OUTRAGEOUS.

AS I SLOSHED THROUGH THE MUCK AND MIRE OF THE REST OF THE COURT HEARING, AND INHALED THE DEEP AND SICKENING FUMES OF D.C. JUDICIAL AND FBI FRAUD, THEFT, CORRUPTION AND EXTORTION THAT DOMINATED THE AIR IN THE COURTROOM, AT LEAST EVERY FIVE MINUTES, I WAS REMINDED OF THE REOCCURING NAUSEA I WAS MANAGING TO HOLD DOWN.

JUDGE EKANS, IN FULL RECOGNITION AND AWARENESS THAT NO JUDGMENT HAD BEEN ISSUED IN THE CASE, BEGAN WHAT I CAN ONLY CHARACTERIZE AS THE *"JUDGMENT CREDITOR HUSTLE, TRAP, DIAGLOGUE AND LABELING PROCESS"* THAT JUDGE EKANS WOULD INTENTIONALLY AND PURPOSEFULLY APPLY TO ME AND THE PURSUIT OF MY CLAIMS PENDING BEFORE THE COURT, EVEN THOUGH FACTUALLY INACURATE AND LEGALLY INAPPLICABLE.

AFTER FILING SUIT AGAINST BRIANNA JONES BECAUSE OF HER BREACH OF THE CONTINGENCY FEE AGREEMENT, WE LATER SETTLED THE LAWSUIT, OR PERHAPS BETTER SAID WE WENT THROUGH THE MOTIONS OF SETTLING THE LAWSUIT BECAUSE, IN FACT, JONES, IN CONSPIRACY WITH THE CO-CONSPIRATORS, WOULD LATER DEMONSTRATE THAT SHE HAD NO INTENTION OF EVER HONORING THE PROVISIONS OF THE SETTLEMENT AGREEMENT WHICH REQUIRED, AMONG OTHER THINGS, THAT SHE TURN OVER TO ME BANK RECORDS INDICATING THE AMOUNT AND LOCATION OF THE CASE SETTLEMENT PROCEEDS THEN VALUED AT AN ESTIMATED $100 MILLION.

WE NOW STOOD BEFORE JUDGE EKANS FOR ONE EXPRESS REASON: I HAD FILED A MOTION ASKING THE COURT TO ENFORCE THE SETTLEMENT AGREEMENT BETWEEN US MADE DURING JUDGE KATE STARR'S *CORRUPTION-FREE* ADJUDICATION OF MY LAWSUIT.

THE ODYSSEY OF JUDICIAL CORRUPTION

JUDGE EKAN'S DEFINITION AND MISCHARACTERIZATION OF ME AS A *JUDGMENT CREDITOR* WAS INACCURATE, HOWEVER CLEVER, AND MORE IMPORTANTLY, AN EGREGIOUS ABUSE OF JUDICIAL DISCRETION AND POWER.

JUDGE EKANS KNEW FULL WELL THAT I WAS NOT A *JUDGMENT CREDITOR*, NOR WAS JONES A *JUDGMENT DEBTOR*. HE KNEW THERE WAS ABSOLUTELY NO EXISTING JUDGMENT IN THE CASE AND THUS, ABSOLUTELY NO LEGAL REASON TO LABEL ME A *JUDGMENT CREDITOR*.

JUDGE EKANS INTENTIONALLY PLACED ME IN **THE JUDGMENT CREDITOR BOX AND LEGAL THEORY** SO THAT HE COULD THEN LEGALLY PLACE THE RESPONSIBILITY OF FINDING THE MONEY ON ME AND FURTHER, PLACING ON ME THE RESPONSIBILITY OF CONDUCTING MY OWN INVESTIGATION AND THE HIRING OF MY OWN INVESTIGATOR. IT WAS ENOUGH TO MAKE ME WANT TO REGURGITATE ALL OVER THE FLOOR OF THE COURTROOM. AGAIN.

THIS, TOO, WAS NOTHING MORE THAN AN OUTRAGEOUS AND CLASSIC EXAMPLE OF JUDGE EKANS' ABUSE OF HIS VIRTUALLY UNLIMITED DISCRETION AND POWER TO DEFINE AND LABEL.

BY STICKING TO HIS INTENTIONALLY FALSE AND ERRONEOUS DEFINITION OF ME AS A *JUDGMENT CREDITOR*, EKANS COULD OSTENSIBLY ABSOLVE HIMSELF OF ANY RESPONSIBILITY OF LAUNCHING AN INVESTIGATION THROUGH THE APPOINTMENT OF A FEDERAL AGENT OR THROUGH ANY OTHER APPROPRIATE MEANS TO ASCERTAIN HOW A $100 MILLION LAWSUIT, CRAFTED AND FILED BY AN ATTORNEY, IS SETTLED FOR $34 MILLION WITH NO DISBURSEMENT IN ANY AMOUNT MADE TO THE ATTORNEY OF RECORD RETAINED AS PLAINTIFF'S COUNSEL.

IF I HAD HAD A CHOICE, I WOULD HAVE RATHER BEEN HELD UP IN A DARK ALLEY BY A PETTY STREET THUG IN HIS PREFERRED DISGUISE, THAN TO HAVE BEEN DEFRAUDED AND STRIPPED OF MY WAGES IN ATTORNEY'S FEES BY A COURT SYSTEM WHICH PERMITS, IN BRIGHTLY LIT COURTROOMS, THE EGREGIOUS ABUSE OF JUDICIAL DISCRETION, POWER AND AUTHORITY, THE MANIPULATION AND MISAPPLICATION OF LEGAL THEORIES, ALL OF WHICH ASSURE THAT THE SYSTEMIC FRAUD, THEFT AND CORRUPTION ENGAGED IN BY D.C. COURT JUDGES IN COLLABORATION WITH FBI AGENTS CAN CONTINUE TO FLOURISH AS A MASSIVE CRIMINAL ENTERPRISE, WITHOUT INTERRUPTION, WITHOUT ACCOUNTABILITY, WITHOUT INVESTIGATION, WITHOUT PROSECUTION, WITHOUT PUNISHMENT, WITHOUT FAIR AND EQUAL JUSTICE.

BUT NOTHING TAKES THE PLACE OF JUDGE EKANS' SPEAKING FOR HIMSELF AS HE SPINS THE FALSE AND FICTITIOUS LEGAL THEORY OF MY BEING A *JUDGMENT CREDITOR* WHO HAS COME INTO COURT, ASKING THE COURT TO GO OUT AND FIND THE JUDGMENT DEBTOR'S ASSETS:

THE COURT:-------------------- WE'VE NOT SEEN A SITUATION LIKE THIS BEFORE. WE'VE HAD ANY NUMBER OF *JUDGMENT CREDITORS* TO BRING THE JUDGMENT DEBTOR IN COURT FOR ORAL EXAMINATION, AND WE'VE GONE SO FAR AS TO HAVE PEOPLE EMPTY THEIR POCKETS OUT AND TURN OVER THEIR AUTOMOBILES BEFORE THEY LEAVE THE COURTHOUSE, BUT IT'S ALWAYS THE SITUATION WHERE THE *JUDGMENT CREDITOR* IS ABLE TO PUT IN FRONT OF THE COURT THE DEBTOR'S FINANCIAL WHEREWITHAL OR LACK OF WHEREWITHAL. *I'VE NOT EXPERIENCED A SITUATION WHERE THE CREDITOR HAS LOOKED TO THE COURT AND SAID YOU GO FIND WHAT THIS PERSON'S ASSETS ARE. SO I DON'T INTERPRET THAT AS OUR ROLE IN THIS MATTER.*

COMMENT AND ANALYSIS: #10 REPEATIING **THE BIG LIE** THAT I WAS A *JUDGMENT CREDITOR* GAVE EKANS A CERTAIN COMFORT IN DENYING MY REQUEST FOR A COURT INVESTIGATION. MOREOVER, IT ENABLED HIM TO DECEPTIVELY ESCAPE HIS ROLE OF ENFORCING JUDGE STARR'S ORDER WHICH MANDATED THAT BRIANNA JONES TURN OVER TO ME THE BANK OF AMERICA BANK STATEMENTS OF THE SETTLEMENT PROCEEDS DEPOSITED THERE. AND SO, CONTRARY TO THE RULE OF LAW THAT HE HAD SWORN TO UPHOLD, EKANS RUTHLESSLY CHANGES THE FACTS OF THE CASE BY FALSELY LABELING ME A *JUDGMENT CREDITOR* WITH THE IMPLIED REQUISITE RESPONSIBILITY OF SEARCHING FOR THE SETTLEMENT PROCEEDS STOLEN BY HIS JUDICIAL CO-CONSPIRATORS AND FBI AGENTS THAT COMPRISED THE TEAM OF THIEVES ORCHESTRATING AND EXECUTING THE D.C. JUDICIAL CRIMINAL ENTERPRISE TO STRIP ME OF THE MILLIONS OF DOLLARS OWED TO ME IN ATTORNEY'S FEES. DURING ONE OF THE COURT HEARINGS, JUDGE EKANS REMARKED THAT HE HAD SERVED ON THE BENCH FOR TWENTY-EIGHT (28) YEARS AND HAD NEVER SEEN ANYTHING SIMILAR TO THIS CASE.

THUS, I WAS NOT DEALING WITH AN INEXPERIENCED JURIST. I WAS, HOWEVER, DEALING WITH A JUDGE WHO WOULD PUT HIMSELF AND HIS COLLEAGUES, COMPLICIT IN THIS CASE OF MASSIVE OFFICIAL AND JUDICIAL FRAUD, THEFT AND CORRUPTION, ABOVE THE INTEGRITY OF THE COURT AND ABOVE THE COURT'S OBLIGATION TO TREAT FAIRLY AND EQUITABLY THE LITIGANTS BEFORE IT, EVEN WHEN BOTH LITIGANTS ALLEGED FRAUD AND CORRUPTION AMONG GOVERNMENT "OFFICIALS."

IN LESS THAN THREE MONTHS OF HAVING HAD MY CASE TRANSFERRED TO HIS CALENDAR, AND FOLLOWING THE RETIREMENT OF JUDGE KATE STARR, JUDGE EKANS WOULD PLAY, AGAIN AND AGAIN, HIS TRUMP CARD OF MISCHARACTERIZING ME AS A *JUDGMENT CREDITOR* WHICH HE KNEW I WAS NOT. SINCE THE MARCH 18, 2011 COURT PROCEEDING, I PERCEIVED JUDGE EKANS TAKING THE BENCH WITH A WHOLE NEW TONE AND ATTITUDE.

NOW JUDGE EKANS WAS OPERATING FROM A WHOLE DIFFERENT CONTEXT. AFTER ALL, TWO OF THE ALLEGED KEY CO-CONSPIRATORS TO THIS MASSIVE FRAUD CONSPIRACY AND CRIMINAL ENTERPRISE CASE WERE HIS COLLEAGUES AND HAD SERVED WITH HIM AS FELLOW JUDGES FOR OVER 25 YEARS ON THE D.C. SUPERIOR COURT BENCH. THEY KNEW EACH OTHER WELL, AND IT WOULD BE REASONABLE TO ASSSUME THAT ALLEGEDLY THESE TWO CO-CONSPIRATOR JUDGES HAD THE COURT'S EAR AND HE HAD THEIRS, GIVEN A CASE INVOLVING SETTLEMENT PROCEEDS OF MORE THAN AN ESTIMATED $100 MILLION.

ONE CAN REASONABLY ASSUME THAT FOR JUDGES ON THE TAKE, MY CASE WAS NOT THEIR FIRST HAUL, BUT IT WAS PROBABLY THEIR LARGEST, AND MIGHT BE THEIR LAST SINCE THEY WERE ALL WELL ELIGIBLE FOR RETIREMENT FROM THE BENCH.

NOW THAT JUDGE EKANS HAD BEEN SUFFICIENTLY AND PRESUMABLY BRIEFED BY FELLOW JUDGES MANDARIN AND SKINNER, AS WELL AS PERHAPS OTHERS, THE COURT ASSUMED A QUIET, EVEN-HANDED COCKINESS AND OVERALL DISMISSIVENESS IN HIS OVERALL JUDICIAL DEMEANOR.

AT ONE POINT DURING THE HEARING, JUDGE EKANS SAID THAT HE HAD NO MORE PATIENCE FOR THE MATTER, AND THIS AFTER A LITTLE MORE THAN 2 MONTHS OF HANDLING THE CASE. THE COURT'S SPECIFIC REMARKS AS SET FORTH IN THE COURT TRANSCRIPT, IN PERTINENT PART, ARE AS FOLLOWS:

THE COURT: ON THE OTHER HAND, I HAVE BEEN DEALING WITH THIS MATTER LONG ENOUGH NOW TO GET SOME CLEARER PICTURE OF **THE DEBTOR** IN THIS CASE OF WHAT HER MOTIVATIONS OR LACK OF MOTIVATIONS APPEAR TO ME TO BE, AND I'VE JUST ABOUT RUN OUT OF PATIENCE, NOT JUST ABOUT, **I DON'T HAVE ANY MORE PATIENCE FOR THIS   THIS MATTER.**

COMMENT AND ANALYSIS: #11 THESE COMMENTS ARE ANOTHER EXAMPLE OF JUDGE EKANS' PENCHANT FOR GASLIGHTING. HE RECEIVED TRANSFER OF THE CASE IN DECEMBER 2010 DUE TO THE RETIREMENT OF JUDGE KATE STARR TO WHOM MY LAWSUIT WAS INITIALLY ASSIGNED. THREE MONTHS LATER HE HAS NO PATIENCE FOR THIS MATTER. NO, THREE MONTHS LATER, HE IS ITCHING TO BE PAID HIS STOLEN SHARE FOR HIS KEY ROLE IN THE RIGGED DISMISSAL OF MY LAWSUIT AND THE THEFT FROM ME OF AN ESTIMATED $50 MILLION IN ATTORNEY'S FEES.

THE CASE HAD BEGUN IN 1996. I HAD SPENT INNUMERABLE HOURS ON THE CASE AND WORKING WITH JONES. I HAD ALSO SPENT APPROXIMATELY A QUARTER OF A MILLION DOLLARS IN MAKING IT POSSIBLE FOR JONES TO SURVIVE WHILE I PURSUED, ON JONES BEHALF, HER CLAIMS AGAINST THE RIDGEWAY ESTATE.

AFTER ENDURING, FOR 15 YEARS, EVERY POSSIBLE METHOD THE OPPOSITION COULD DRUM UP TO KEEP ME FROM BEING PAID, I WOULD HAVE TO LISTEN TO A JUDGE TELL ME AFTER LESS THAN 3 MONTHS IN THE CASE THAT HE NO LONGER HAD ANY PATIENCE WITH THE MATTER.

WHAT I HEARD WITH MY TEN-PLUS-YEARS OF TRIAL ATTORNEY EXPERIENCE WAS THAT THE JUDGE WANTED OUT OF THE CASE, AND THE SOONER THE BETTER. I DIDN'T BLAME HIM. I WANTED OUT, TOO. BUT I ALSO WANTED TO BE PAID FOR SERVICES AND THE GREAT AMOUNT OF OUT-OF-POCKET EXPENSES THAT MY FAMILY AND I HAD INCURRED.

JUDGE EKANS DID NO BOTHER TO HIDE HIS EXASPERATION WITH ME AND MY CASE. IT WAS CLEAR THAT HE NOW REALIZED THAT HE HAD STEPPED INTO A GARGANTUAN MESS OF A CASE THAT COULD BE UNUSUALLY PROBLEMATIC.

JUDGE EKANS NOW SEEMED UNSURE AS TO HOW TO GET A HANDLE ON WHAT HE RECOGNIZED WAS AN ELEPHANT OF A CASE. YET HE APPEARED DETERMINED TO SIDESTEP THE DOMINANT ISSUE OF D.C. JUDICIAL FRAUD, COMBINDED WITH THE COMPLICITY OF HIS FELLOW JUDGES STILL ON THE BENCH, WHO WERE NOW LOOKING TO HIM TO PRESERVE THE INTEGRITY, NOT OF THE COURT, BUT OF THE D.C. JUDICIAL FRAUD, THEFT, CORRUPTION AND EXTORTION CONSPIRACY AND CRIMINAL ENTERPRISE.

THE ODYSSEY OF JUDICIAL CORRUPTION

THE COURT: AND SO WE'RE GOING TO HAVE TO TAKE A DIFFERENT APPROACH, SINCE YOUR APPROACH SEEMS TO BE ONE THAT'S NOT DESIGNED TO GET US ANYWHERE.

MS. JONES: I DO HAVE A PLAN, YOUR HONOR.

THE COURT: APPARENTLY YOU JUST ENJOY COMING DOWN TO THE COURT AND SEEING EVERYBODY. I'M NOT ENTERTAINED.

MS. JONES: YOUR HONOR, I DID SEEK EMPLOYMENT BECAUSE I WAS UNDER --------ALWAYS UNDER THE IMPRESSION THAT I HAVE A SETTLEMENT AGREEMENT.

COMMENT AND ANALYSIS: #12 AGAIN, BRIANNA JONES ACKNOWLEDGES HER COMPLETE UNDERSTANDING THAT SHE HAS ENTERED INTO A SETTLEMENT AGREEMENT REGARDING MY LAWSUIT.

THE COURT: WELL, YOU JUST TOLD ME THAT YOU'RE ABOUT TO FILE A MOTION TO SET ASIDE BASED ON FRAUDULENT INDUCEMENT SO APPARENTLY -- --

MS. JONES: I'M TALKING ABOUT.

THE COURT:----------------------YOU TALK OUT OF BOTH SIDES OF YOUR MOUTH.

MS. JONES: I'M SPEAKING WITH BROWARD COUNTY, THAT WAS ALWAYS THE ISSUE WAS THAT I HAVE THIS SETTLEMENT AGREEMENT.

THE COURT: YOU KNOW WHAT -- --

MS. JONES: **AND ALSO THE PLAINTIFF HAD SUPPORTED ME, I'VE BEEN -- --**

COMMENT AND ANALYSIS: #13 MY FAMILY AND I FINANCIALLY MADE IT POSSIBLE FOR BRIANNA TO SURVIVE. WHEN WE COULD NO LONGER CONTINUE TO SUPPORT HER, GIVEN THE SUBSTANTIAL COSTS OF MY HUSBAND'S LEGAL DEFENSE TO THE POLITICALLY MOTIVATED CRIMINAL PROSECUTION, I TURNED TO FRIENDS AND FORMER LAW CLIENTS TO LEND MONEY TO HER, ALWAYS ASSURED THAT THEY WOULD BE PROMPTLY REIMBURSED UPON PAYMENT BY BRIANNA OR PAYMENT BY ME OUT OF THE ATTORNEY'S FEES OWED TO ME.

DURING THE APRIL 6, 2011 PROCEEDING, I TESTIFIED THAT THOUSANDS OF DOLLARS HAD BEEN SPENT BY ME, MY FAMILY AND FRIENDS ON PROVIDING ROUND-THE-CLOCK SECURITY FOR BRIANNA WHEN SHE WAS RECEIVING DEATH THREATS INTENDED TO FORCE HER TO DROP THE FLORIDA LAWSUIT.

I SPENT A LARGE AMOUNT OF TIME ON THE TELEPHONE MENTORING BRIANNA REGARDING THE FLORIDA LITIGATION AND SUGGESTING HOW TO RESPOND TO THE RELENTLESS ATTACKS FROM THE OPPOSITION. THERE WERE ALSO EXTENSIVE HOTEL BILLS TO BE PAID WHEN SHE HAD NO WHERE ELSE TO GO BUT TO THE STREETS OF FORT LAUDERDALE AFTER SHE HAD OVERSTAYED HER TIME WITH VARIOUS FRIENDS AND ACQUAINTANCES.

WHILE I SPENT AN INORDINATE AMOUNT OF TIME TRAVELING BACK AND FORTH TO FORT LAUDERDALE, SOMETIMES TWO AND THREE TIMES A MONTH, MY LAW PRACTICE IN WASHINGTON SUFFERED IMMENSELY. MY THINKING WAS ALWAYS THAT MY TIME, TRAVEL AND ATTENTION TO BRIANNA'S CASE WOULD BE WORTH IT IN THE END. HOW WRONG I WAS.

I NEVER FACTORED IN THE LOOMING REALITY THAT WHILE THE $100 MILLION FLORIDA LAWSUIT THAT I WOULD FILE ON BRIANNA'S BEHALF MIGHT VERY WELL SETTLE WITH THE RIDGEWAY ESTATE, IT WOULD BE THE D.C. THIEVES AND THUGS REPRESENTED BY CORRUPT AND MONEY-MAD D.C. COURT JUDGES AND THEIR PARTNERS-IN-CRIME, CORRUPT AND MONEY-MAD FBI AGENTS WHO WOULD DECIDE THAT UNDER NO CIRCUMSTANCES OR CONDITIONS WOULD THE ATTORNEY'S FEES DUE ME IN THE AMOUNT OF 40% OF THE SETTLEMENT AMOUNT OF $34 MILLION EVER BE PAID TO ME.

INSTEAD, THESE CORRUPT D.C. COURT JUDGES WOULD USE THE COURT'S PROCESS, POWER AND PROCEDURE TO DESIGN, ORGANIZE AND ORCHESTRATE A CRIMINAL ENTERPRISE WHOSE MISSION WOULD BE TO STRIP ME OF THE ENTIRE AMOUNT OF AN ESTIMATED $50 MILLION DUE ME IN ATTORNEY'S FEES. AND THAT IS EXACTLY WHAT THEY DID, WITHOUT FEAR OF INVESTIGATION, INDICTMENT, PROSECUTION OR PUNISHMENT. IT MATTERED NOT THAT I WENT FAR BEYOND THE CALL OF DUTY AS AN ATTORNEY IN HELPING BRIANNA TO SURVIVE.

THE RIDGEWAY ESTATE WE SUED NEVER FILED AN ANSWER TO THE COMPLAINT. AND I UNDERSTAND THAT JUDGE MICHAEL ROSENBAUM, THE BROWARD COUNTY CIRCUIT COURT PROBATE JUDGE ASSIGNED THE ADJUDICTION OF THE FLORIDA LAWSUIT SAID THAT ONE OF THE REASONS HE ADMITTED ME TO REPRESENT BRIANNA JONES WAS BECAUSE BRIANNA HAD A RIGHT TO BE REPRESENTED BY COUNSEL OF HER CHOICE. IN ADDITION, JUDGE ROSENBAUM ALSO REPORTEDLY SAID THAT WHEN NO ANSWER WAS FILED, HE KNEW THAT THERE WAS SOMETHING TO THIS, AND AGAIN, THAT BRIANNA HAD A RIGHT TO BE REPRESENTED.

THE COURT: APPARENTLY EVERYBODY IN THE AREA HAS SUPPORTED YOU BUT I'M NOT PREPARED FOR THE COURT TO SUPPORT YOU.

MS. JONES: BUT MY PLAN IS TO GO INTO BROWARD – ATTORNEY ADVISED ME TO FILE, GET A JUDGMENT AGAINST THE ESTATE IN BROWARD COUNTY. AND THAT I WOULD -- - -

THE COURT: HOW MANY YEARS HAS IT BEEN?

MS. JONES: IT'S BEEN AT LEAST SINCE ---- THE AGREEMENT WAS ENTERED INTO UNTIL 1997. AND I'VE JUST BEEN ON THIS ROLLER COASTER AND SO -- --

THE COURT: WE'RE ABOUT TO GET OFF THE ROLLER COASTER CAUSE I'M NOT ENJOYING THE RIDE. NOW DO YOU HAVE ANYTHING MORE THAT YOU NEED TO SAY?

MS. JONES: YES, YOUR HONOR.

YOUR HONOR, I NEVER   I DIDN'T RESPOND TO THE ORIGINAL COMPLAINT IN WRITING WITH REGARD TO THE PLAINTIFF BECAUSE I NEVER WANTED TO COME IN HERE AND HAVE TO SHARE ALL OF THIS. **IT HAS ALWAYS AND IT MAINTAINS MY INTENTION TO COMPENSATE THE PLAINTIFF. SHE HAS BEEN MORE THAN AN ATTORNEY.**

COMMENT AND ANALYSIS: #14 BRIANNA JONES STATES HER ABIDING INTENTION TO PAY THE ATTORNEY'S FEES DUE ME.

WHILE I WAS ENCOURAGED BY BRIANNA'S EXPRESSION OF HER FINANCIAL OBLIGATION TO ME, I KNEW THIS WAS A DOWNER TO JUDGE EKANS.

EKANS KNEW THAT IF I WERE PAID, THE PAYMENTS TO HIM AND THE REMAINING CO-CONSPIRATORS WOULD BE JEOPARDIZED, IF NOT ELIMINATED ALTOGETHER.

THE CO-CONSPIRATORS THAT BRIANNA HAD BEEN SUMMONED TO MEET WITH PERIODICALLY IN WASHINGTON AREA HOTEL SUTIES HAD REPEATEDLY TOLD HER THAT THEIR PAYMENT WOULD BE COMING OUT OF HER PORTION OF THE SETTLEMENT PROCEEDS AND HER PAYMENT WOULD COME FROM HER TAKING MY ATTORNEY'S FEES.

MS. JONES: I PHONED HER ON MONDAY EVENING AND I SUGGESTED THAT MY INTENTION WAS TO FILE THE JUDGMENT IN BROWARD COUNTY AND THAT WE DO A NEW AGREEMENT, AND SHE SAID YOU DON'T -- -- I'M NOT DOING ANOTHER AGREEMENT.

I HAVE REFRAINED----- REFRAINED MYSELF FROM DIVULGING SO MUCH IN THIS COURT. THE DEFENDANT WILLFULLY ON MANY OCCASIONS ASSISTED ME AND SAID YOU DON'T NEED TO GET A JOB; YOU HAVE A SETTLEMENT.

BUT I AM -- --I AM NOT------**THIS IS NOT A SITUATION OF NOT WANTING TO COMPENSATE HER, AND I'VE SAID THIS OVER AND OVER AGAIN.**

COMMENT AND ANALYSIS: #15 BRIANNA'S REPEATED ATTESTATIONS OF WANTING TO PAY ME FELL ON EKANS' DEAF EARS. EKANS' BOTTOM LINE INTEREST WAS NOT IN USING THE MYRIAD POWERS OF THE COURT TO GET ME PAID, BUT RATHER IN ASSURING THAT THE 40% OF THE SETTLEMET PROCEEDS OWED TO ME WOULD NEVER BE PAID TO ME, BUT WOULD RATHER REMAIN AVAILABLE FOR STATED DISTRIBUTION TO THE CO-CONSPIRATORS INVOLVED IN THE D.C. JUDICIAL AND FBI FRAUD, THEFT, CORRUPTION AND EXTORTION CONSPIRACY AND CRIMINAL ENTERPRISE.

THE COURT: WHO FILED THE ACTION AGAINST BAR COUNSEL – AGAINST BARBARA FRANKLIN, WHO FILED THAT?

COMMENT AND ANALYSIS: #16 WHEN MY HUSBAND AND I COULD NO LONGER PROVIDE SUBSTANTIAL FINANCIAL SUPPORT TO ASSIST BRIANNA IN HER SURVIVAL, I TURNED TO BESSIE MARCH, A FORMER CLIENT TO ENLIST HER FINANCIAL SUPPORT.

WHEN THE TIME OF PAYMENT OF THE SETTLEMENT PROCEEDS TO BRIANNA AND ME LOOMED FAR INTO THE DISTANCE, BESSIE MARCH'S SON-IN-LAW FILED A BAR COMPLAINT AGAINST ME WITH THE OFFICE OF D.C. BAR COUNSEL, THE DISCIPLINARY ARM OF THE D.C. COURT OF APPEALS.

FOLLOWING ITS INVESTIGATION OF THE MATTER, D.C BAR COUNSEL INFORMED BESSIE MARCH THAT BRIANNA JONES WAS ENTITLED TO A SUBSTANTIAL CLAIM RESULTING FROM A CASE SETTLEMENT.

IN ADDITION, BRIANNA JONES INFORMED BESSIE MARCH THAT SHE RECEIVED THE TOTAL AMOUNT OF THE SUBSTANTIAL LOANS AND THAT NONE OF THE LOAN PROCEEDS HAD BEEN TAKEN OR USED IN ANY WAY BY ME.

MS. JONES: BESSIE, MISS BESSIE MARCH.

THE COURT: WHO IS THAT?

MS. JONES: SHE'S A FRIEND OF BARBARA'S WHO LOANED BARBARA MONEY ON MY BEHALF.

MS. FRANKLIN: EXCUSE ME, THE LOAN WAS NOT TO ME.

MS. JONES: I SAID ON MY BEHALF.

MS. FRANKLIN: THE LOAN WAS NOT TO ME.

MS. JONES: YOU REQUESTED -- --

MS. FRANKLIN: THE LOAN WAS NOT TO ME.

MS. JONES: YOUR HONOR, SHE REQUESTED -- -- I NEVER SPOKEN WITH ANY OF THE INDIVIDAULS THAT WERE SO GENEROUS AND SO KIND TO LOAN HER MONEY ON MY ON BEHALF OF, MRS. MARCH THOUGHT SOMEHOW THE PLAINTIFF HAD SPENT THE MONEY. I CALLED AND MADE IT VERY CLEAR, SHE HAD NOT.

AND IN ANY EVENT THE PLAINTIFF WOULD NOT TAKE PHONE CALLS. I'M STILL IN CONTACT WITH MRS. MARCH THIS VERY DAY, I SPOKE WITH HER SON-IN-LAW THIS MORNING.

SHE FILED, AND AS A RESULT OF THAT INVESTIGATION, THEY THEN CONFIRMED THAT I WAS IN FACT DUE THE SETTLEMENT PROCEEDS. UP UNTIL THE TIME THE PLAINTIFF HAD DONE NOTHING.

COMMENT AND ANALYSIS: #17 THE CO-CONSPIRATORS HAD NO INTENTION OF FINANCIALLY ENABLING BRIANNA TO REPAY HER SUBSTANTIAL LOANS TO MY HUSBAND, MY VARIOUS FRIENDS AND CERTAIN FORMER LAW CLIENTS.

THIS IS AN EXAMPLE OF THE DEPTH OF THE GREED AND BRUTISHNESS THAT CHARACTERIZED THE CORRUPT D.C. COURT JUDGES THAT, IN THEIR DETERMINATION TO STRIP ME OF THE MILLIONS OF DOLLARS OWED TO ME IN ATTORNEY'S FEES, RAISED HELL TO A LEVEL THAT I HAD NEVER EXPERIENCED BEFORE.

MS. JONES: ONCE SHE GOT DOCUMENTATION IN HAND SHE WAS TRYING TO CIRCUMVENT BEING TAKEN INTO COURT HERSELF AND THAT WAS THE MOTIVATION TO FILE A COMPLAINT AGAINST ME ON MARCH 13TH OF 2009.

COMMENT AND ANALYSIS: #18 MY SOLE REASON FOR FILING THE LAWSUIT AGAINST BRIANNA JONES IN MARCH 2009 WAS DUE TO HER BREACH OF THE CONTINGENCY FEE AGREEMENT AND MY DESIRE TO BE COMPENSATED PURSUANT TO THE PROVISIONS OF THE AGREEMENT. I ALSO WANTED TO CLEAR MY CONSCIENCE OF EVER HAVIING IT SAID THAT I WAS COMPLICIT IN THIS HISTORIC D.C. JUDICIAL AND FBI CRIMINAL ENTERPRISE.

THE COURT:	WHY DID YOU ENTER THE FAMILY?
MS. JONES:	BECAUSE I -- --IT WAS ---- IT WAS ALWAYS MY INTENTION TO COMPENSATE HER.
THE COURT:	WHY DID YOU ENTER THE SETTLEMENT?
MS. JONES:	WHY DID I ENTER THE SETTLEMENT? BASED ON THE RELATIONSHIP. BASED ON THE CLOSENESS. BASED ON EVERYTHING WE HAD GONE THROUGH.
THE COURT:	RELATIONSHIP? CLOSENESS?
MS. JONES:	YES.
THE COURT:	DID YOU OWE HER MONEY?
MS. JONES:	UM, I FELT THAT I OWED HER FEES.
THE COURT:	FEES ARE NOT MONEY, IS THAT MONEY? IS THAT MONEY?
MS. JONES:	YOUR HONOR -- --
THE COURT:	IS THAT MONEY, FEES?
MS. FRANKLIN:	YES.
THE COURT:	DID YOU BARTER TO PAY IN SOMETHING OTHER THAN UNITED STATES CURRENCY? I ASKED IF YOU OWED HER MONEY AND YOU SAID, I FELT I OWED HER FEES, I'M ASKING YOU IF THE LEGAL REPRESENTATION WAS TO BE PAID IN BARTER, SOMETHING OTHER THAN UNITED STATES CURRENCY?
MS. JONES:	NO, YOUR HONOR. BUT -- --
THE COURT:	SO YOU OWED HER MONEY?
MS. JONES:	YES.
THE COURT:	FOR THE WORK THAT SHE DID?
MS. JONES:	SHE DIDN'T DO THE WORK, YOUR HONOR.
THE COURT:	WELL, WHY DID YOU MAKE A SETTLEMENT?
MS. JONES:	BECAUSE WE WERE IN A RELATIONSHIP. YOUR HONOR. WE HAD A LONG-TERM RELATIONSHIP, AND -- --
THE COURT:	THE RELATIONSHIP IF YOU'RE TALKING ABOUT A PERSONAL RELATIONSHIP, THE ONLY TIME THAT HAS COME IN COURT, COME BEFORE THE COURT WHERE PEOPLE OWE FOLKS MONEY FOR PERSONAL RELATIONSHIP IS WHERE WE DEAL WITH – WITH PROSTITUTION.

MS. JONES:	THIS IS NOT ----- CERTAINLY NOT THE CASE.
THE COURT:	WELL, THEN – THEN THE RELATIONSHIP THAT I THINK YOU HAVE SUGGESTED YOU OWED HER A FEE FOR MONEY WAS THE LEGAL RELATIONSHIP.
MS. JONES:	YOUR HONOR, BECAUSE SHE -- --
THE COURT:	LEGAL RELATIONSHIP. RIGHT OR WRONG?
MS. JONES:	BUT SHE DID NOT REPRESENT ME IN BROWARD COUNTY. AND I WOULD NOT TERMINATE HER EVEN WHEN OTHER ATTORNEYS SUGGESTED. BECAUSE AND IT WAS BASED ON MY AFFECTION FOR HER -- --
THE COURT:	WELL, THAT'S THAT'S YOUR MOTIVATION. PEOPLE ARE MOTIVATED BY –
MS.. JONES:	THAT'S HERSELF AS WELL, AT LEAST I THOUGHT.
THE COURT:	THE POINT IS THIS, THE POINT IS THIS, DID YOU ENTER INTO A SETTLEMENT AGREEMENT?
MS. JONES:	YES, I DID.
THE COURT:	DID YOU DO SO VOLUNTARILY?
MS. JONES;	AT HER URGING. SHE SUGGESTED -- --
THE COURT:	DO YOU HEAR? CAN YOU HEAR?
THE COURT:	DID YOU DO SO VOLUNTARILY?
MS. JONES:	YES.
THE COURT:	WAS THERE ANY COERCION INVOLVED?
MS. JONES:	BRIANNA, THIS IS A SPIRITUAL THING. WE'RE DESTINED TO BE TOGETHER. AND IF YOU DO IT ANY OTHER WAY IT WON'T WORK. IT WAS CONSTANT, YOUR HONOR. I'M STANDING BEFORE THE COURT TELLING THE ABSOLUTE TRUTH.
THE COURT:	YOU CONSIDER THAT COERCION?
MS. JONES:	IT WAS BRIANNA, WE HAVE A RIGHT TO RIDE OFF INTO THE SUNSET TOGETHER. WE HAVE A RIGHT TO BE TOGETHER.

COMMENT AND ANALYSIS: #19 THIS STATEMENT WAS IN ALL RESPECTS FALSE AND FACTUALLY UNTRUE, BUT RATHER AN OBVIOUS FIGMENT OF BRIANNA'S WICKED IMAGINATION.

THE COURT:	YOU CONSIDER THAT TO BE COERCION?
MS. JONES:	EMOTIONALLY I DO.
THE COURT:	EMOTIONALLY.
MS. JONES:	BUT IT WASN'T AN ISSUE OF NOT WANTING TO PAY HER. SHE WAS ALWAYS GOING TO BE PAID. I HAVE A GREAT LOVE FOR THE PLAINTIFF.
THE COURT:	WELL, YOU KNOW, THAT'S VERY TOUCHING. THE LEGAL RELATIONSHIPS THAT ARE THE SUBJECT OF THIS LAWSUIT ARE THE LEGAL RELATIONSHIP THAT IS THE SUBJECT OF THIS LAWSUIT DOES NOT, AS FAR AS I CAN TELL, INVOLVE ANYTHING OTHER THAN YOUR RETAINING AN ATTORNEY TO HELP YOU TO COLLECT MONEY THAT WAS OWED TO YOU. IS THAT RIGHT?
MS. JONES:	THAT'S CORRECT.
THE COURT:	AND SO, WHEN YOU ENTERED THE LEGAL RELATIONSHIP DID YOU ENTER AN AGREEMENT TO PAY THE ATTORNEY FOR HER TIME?
MS. JONES:	YES, YOUR HONOR.
THE COURT:	WHAT WAS THE ----- WHAT WAS THE NATURE OF THE AGREEMENT?
MS. JONES:	THE ORIGINAL AGREEMENT WAS FOR 33 AND A THIRD.
THE COURT:	THIRTY-THREE AND A THIRD.
MS. JONES:	ON JUNE 12TH, 1995. SHE THEN -- --
THE COURT:	THAT'S A FAIRLY TYPICAL CONTINGENCY FEE IN THIS GEOGRAPHICAL AREA.

***

THE COURT:	WHAT WAS – LET ME ASK YOU THIS, THOUGH, YOU KNOW, I SORT OF GET BITS OF PIECES OF THIS, AND AT SOME POINT IN TIME I GUESS I NEED TO GET A MORE COMPLETE PICTURE.
	WHAT WAS THE RESULT OF YOUR EFFORTS ON HER BEHALF TO COLLECT THE AWARD?
MS. FRANKLIN:	THE RESULTS WERE THIS: A SUIT WAS FILED IN FLORIDA BECAUSE THAT IS WHERE THE DECEDENT -- --
THE COURT:	IS THAT WHEN THE FEE CHANGED FROM 33 AND A THIRD TO 40 PERCENT?

MS. FRANKLIN: I DON'T REMEMBER EXACTLY WHEN THE FEE CHANGED, YOUR HONOR. I WILL SAY THIS, I RECALL IT BEING AT HER REQUEST. I HAD INTERVIEWED APPROXIMATELY 10 OR 15 LAW FIRMS. I CAME TO FLORIDA TO THE FLORIDA COURT BROWARD COUNTY CIRCUIT COURT ON A PRO HAC VICE MOTION FROM JUDGE MICHAEL ROSENBAUM. I HAD RETAINED ONE FIRM, FOR ONE REASON OR ANOTHER THEY DECIDED TO PULL OUT, I WOULD THEN HAVE TO INTERVIEW OTHER FIRMS.

MS. FRANKLIN: AT ONE POINT   I THINK OF THE AFRICAN-AMERICAN ATTORNEY HUGH BANKS THAT WAS ONE OF HIS PARTNERS.

THERE WERE A SERIES OF FIRMS WHO HAD TO COME IN, THIS WAS WORK ON MY PART BECAUSE I'M A D.C. ATTORNEY, I HAVE AN OFFICE HERE, I'M RUNNING BACK AND FORTH TO FLORIDA, JUST CONSTANTLY. AIRLINE FEES, HOTEL FEES, FOR WEEKS AT A TIME.

SO WHEN I STAND HERE AND HEAR HER SAY, OH, SHE DID NOTHING OR IT WAS TOKENISTIC, THIS IS ALL A PART OF HER MIND-SET.

BUT THERE CAME A TIME, AND I HAVE TELEPHONE RECORDS TO THE YING YANG OF BEING ON THE PHONE WITH HER AND SHE'S RUNNING IN AND OUT OF THE FLORIDA COURTROOM BECAUSE I HAVE A D.C. OFFICE, I'M A SOLO PRACTITIONER, I COULDN'T BE AT EACH AND EVERY HEARING.

THE COURT: LET ME JUST BE CLEAR, YOU WERE THERE PRO HAC VICE -- --

MS. FRANKLIN: YES.

THE COURT:-------------------- BUT YOU DID GET LEGAL REPRESENTATION FOR HER?

MS. JONES: NO.

MS. FRANKLIN: PRO HAC VICE, WE HAD CO-COUNSEL. THAT IS THE ONLY WAY I COULD COME IN.

THE COURT: THAT'S WHAT I'M SAYING.

MS. FRANKLIN: YES. YES.

THE COURT: SO THERE WAS AN ENGAGEMENT WITH A FIRM -- --

MS. FRANKLIN: ABSOLUTELY.

THE COURT:----------------------IN BROWARD COUNTY?

MS. FRANKLIN:	MORE THAN ONE FIRM.
THE COURT:	WAS SHE A SIGNATORY ON THE RETAINER AGREEMENT?
MS. FRANKLIN:	ABSOLUTELY, SHE WAS PRIVY TO ALL OF IT. CERTAINLY. SHE HAS ACTUALLY TALKED WITH THE ATTORNEYS IN THE FIRM. I MEAN I HAVE THIS ALL IN MY FILE. SO THIS IS NOT SOMETHING THAT I HAVE TO STAND HERE -- --
MS. JONES:	YOUR HONOR, MAY I SPEAK?
THE COURT:	NO. YOU COULD SIT DOWN.
MS. FRANKLIN:	BUT THERE CAME -- --SO THERE WERE THERE WAS CO-COUNSEL BECAUSE THAT'S THE ONLY WAY I COULD COME IN BEFORE THE COURT, I WOULD HAVE TO COME ON A SPONSORSHIP AND I DID, AND I RETAINED MORE THAN ONE FIRM FOR LONG PERIODS OF TIME.
	BUT THERE CAME A TIME, YOUR HONOR -- --
THE COURT:	THAT'S WHAT I'M TRYING TO UNDERSTAND, DID – DID YOU SIGN A RETAINER WITH THE LOCAL FIRM OR DID SHE -- --
MS. FRANKLIN:	YES.
THE COURT:------------------- SIGN A RETAINER WITH THE LOCAL FIRM?
MS. FRANKLIN:	I RECALL HAVING BOTH SIGNATURES ON THE RETAINER.
	NOW AGAIN WE'RE GOING BACK 15 YEARS, SO, BUT MY FILES ARE COMPLETE AND I CAN ALWAYS PULL THOSE COPIES OF THE RETAINER AGREEMENT BECAUSE I STILL HAVE THEM.
	AND SHE WAS FULLY AWARE BECAUSE I ALWAYS KEPT HER ABREAST OF EVERYTHING.
	BUT THERE CAME A TIME, YOUR HONOR, WHERE SHE STARTED TO MEET WITH OPPOSING COUNSEL. THEY REFUSED TO MEET WITH ME. I WOULD FLY TO FLORIDA, THERE WOULD BE A MEETING SCHEDULED, AFTER I ARRIVED THEY WOULD CANCEL THE MEETING.
THE COURT:	WHO WERE OPPOSING COUNSEL? WHAT WERE THEY OPPOSING?
MS. FRANKLIN:	WHAT WERE THEY OPPOSING? THEY WERE REPRESENTING THE ESTATE THAT WAS DUE.

THE COURT: I SEE.

THEY REPRESENTED THE WIDOW WHO IS THE EXECUTRIX OF THE ESTATE SO THEY REPRESENTED -- --

THE COURT: I SEE.

MS. FRANKLIN: BUT THERE CAME A TIME WHEN SHE BEGAN MEETING WITH THEM AND THEN IT WAS LIKE, OH, WE'RE NOT GOING TO MEET WITH COUNSEL. AND I SAID, BRIANNA, BE VERY CAREFUL WHEN YOU BEGIN TO MEET WITH ATTORNEYS WHO DON'T WANT YOUR REPRESENTATIVE INVOLVED, AND SHE CONTINUED.

AND, YOU KNOW, IT WAS SORT OF LIKE JUST SLIDING ON DOWN THAT HILL WHERE SHE JUST GOT SO WRAPPED UP WITH THEM THAT THEY COMPLETELY STOPPED MEETING WITH ME. AND I FIGURED OUT THAT THE PLAN WAS IF WE DON'T MEET WITH MISS FRANKLIN AND WE GET HER OUT THEN WE DON'T HAVE TO WORRY ABOUT THE PAYMENT OF HER FEES.

THE COURT: OF COURSE THEY WERE IN SERIOUS VIOLATION OF PROFESSIONAL ETHICS FOR DOING THAT. WAS THERE EVER ANY SUGGESTION THAT -- --

MS. FRANKLIN: NO.

THE COURT:----------------------WE REPORT IT TO THE FLORIDA BAR?

MS. FRANKLIN: NO, NO, I DID NOT. NO, I DID NOT.

COMMENT AND ANALYSIS: #20 I WAS NOT COMFORTABLE, NOR DID I THINK IT PRUDENT TO DISCUSS WITH JUDGE EKANS, WHOM I CONSIDERED TO BE A MAJOR PLAYER IN THIS GRAND JUDICIAL AND FBI CRIMINAL ENTERPRISE, THE IMPACT OF MY HUSBAND'S POLITICALLY MOTIVATED CRIMINAL PROSECUTION ON MY RESPONSE OR DECISION NOT TO RESPOND TO ACTIONS OF OPPOSING COUNSEL, HOWEVER UNETHICAL.

MY FOCUS WAS ON THE PROTECTION OF MY HUSBAND FROM THE CORRUPT D.C. JUDICIAL AND FBI OFFICIALS WHO HAD DEMONSTRATED TO ME THE EXTENT THEY WERE WILLING TO GO IN FURTHERANCE OF THE THEFT OF THE ESTIMATED $50 MILLION OWED TO ME IN ATTORNEY'S FEES, THE MISSION OF THE D.C. JUDICIAL AND FBI FRAUD, THEFT, CORRUPTION AND EXTORTION CONSPIRACY AND CRIMINAL ENTERPRISE.

BARBARA WASHINGTON FRANKLIN

***

MS. FRANKLIN: AND AS FAR AS INDUCEMENT, I'LL SAY THIS, YOUR HONOR, THEN I'LL PAUSE. DURING WHAT HAS BEEN TERMED THE SNOWSTORM OF THE CENTURY, THE DEFENDANT CALLED ME TO HER HOTEL IN BALTIMORE. I DUG MY CAR OUT AT MY HOME, TRAVELED ALL THE WAY TO BALTIMORE. SHE HAD A NOTARY, A HOTEL NOTARY, WAITING FOR ME IN THE HOTEL FOR US TO EXECUTE THE AGREEMENT.

NOW IF THAT'S INDUCEMENT, YOU KNOW, THAT'S A NEW ONE FOR ME. THAT WAS PHYSICALLY HOW THE AGREEMENT THAT I HAD PREPARED, AND I HAD SENT HER DRAFTS TO HER HOTEL, FAXED THEM OVER THERE SO SHE COULD LOOK AT IT, AND THEN SHE ASKED, I SAID THE WEATHER IS TOO BAD, MAYBE WE NEED TO PUT THIS OFF. OH, NO, BARBARA, I WANT TO GET THIS DONE, COULD YOU PLEASE COME TO THE HOTEL?

I WENT TO THE HOTEL, SHE HAD THE NOTARY WAITING FOR ME, WE DID THE AGREEMENT DOWN IN ONE OF THE DINING ROOMS, THEN SHE INSISTED ON RIDING BACK IN MY CAR WITH ME TO FILE THE AGREEMENT WITH THE COURT. AND I AGREED TO LET HER RIDE BACK TO THE COURTHOUSE, I SAID, I CANNOT TAKE YOU BACK TO BALTIMORE, BUT THAT WAS THE PHYSICAL CIRCUMSTANCE OF HOW THE AGREEMENT WAS SIGNED, YOUR HONOR.

THE COURT: YOU KNOW, THE AGREEMENT IS ALL WELL AND GOOD AND A MATTER OF RECORD. WHEN THE AGREEMENT WAS ENTERED INTO DID YOU THEN KNOW WHETHER OR NOT THE   THE LOTTERY PROCEEDS HAD BEEN RELEASED TO THE DEFENDANT?

MS. FRANKLIN: NO, I DID NOT KNOW THAT. I DID NOT –

THE COURT: IT SEEMS TO ME THAT WHERE THIS CASE GOT -- --GO WITH THE METAPHOR -- -- --- WHERE THE TRAIN GOT OFF TRACK IS THAT – WHAT WAS THE POINT OF THE SUIT AGAINST THE ESTATE? WHAT WAS -- --

MS. FRANKLIN: AGAINST THE ESTATE OR AGAINST THE DEFENDANT?

THE COURT: AGAINST THE ESTATE.

MS. FRANKLIN: AGAINST THE ESTATE?

THE COURT: YES.

MS. FRANKLIN: THE SUIT AGAINST THE ESTATE WAS BECAUSE OF THE CHILD MOLESTATION BY THE DEFENDANT   BY THE DECEDENT OF THE ESTATE OF THE DEFENDANT. AND HE HAD SAID THERE IS, IT WAS AN ATTORNEY THAT I MET WITH IN RICHMOND, WHO HANDLED THE ESTATE FOR A TIME, ONE OF THE ATTORNEYS, AND INDICATED TO ME THAT THE DECEDENT HAD SAID ON HIS DEATH BED HE WANTED HER PAID, HE WANTED THE CASE SETTLED, HE WAS AWARE, I HAD SENT A SETTLEMENT PROPOSAL TO THE ATTORNEYS HERE IN WASHINGTON BEFORE HE MOVED TO FLORIDA. AND HE WAS AWARE, AND HE SAID, I WANT THIS SETTLED, I WANT HER PAID. AND THAT'S WHAT THE SUIT AGAINST THE ESTATE WAS BASED ON.

THE COURT: OKAY.

MS. FRANKLIN: I HAVEN'T LOOKED AT THE SUIT IN A LONG TIME, BUT THAT'S WHY -- --

THE COURT: THAT'S FINE. YOU SEE, WHAT WE'VE BEEN ENGAGED IN SINCE I'VE BEEN INVOLVED WITH YOU-- --

MS. FRANKLIN: RIGHT.

THE COURT: IS MONIES THAT ARE DUE TO YOU AS AN ATTORNEY FROM A SETTLEMENT THAT -- --THAT THE DEFENDANT MADE WITH YOU BUT YOU'VE SAID TIME ON ANY NUMBER OF OCCASIONS THAT THE SETTLEMENT THAT YOU REACHED IS BASED ON WORK THAT YOU DID TO HELP HER OBTAIN MONEY FROM THE ESTATE.

MS. FRANKLIN;   CORRECT.

THE COURT: ALL RIGHT.

NOW GENERALLY LAWYERS HAVE RETAINER AGREEMENTS THAT HAVE A PAPAGRAPH SAYING THAT YOU HAVE A LIEN -- --

MS. FRANKLIN: THAT'S RIGHT.

THE COURT:-------------------- AGAINST ANY MONEY RECOVERED.

MS. FRANKLIN: FIRST AGREEMENT, THAT'S RIGHT, YOUR HONOR.

THE COURT: RIGHT.

MS. FRANKLIN: AND THAT'S IN THAT AGREEMENT.

COMMENT AND ANALYSIS: 21 JUDGE EKANS QUERIED ME ON WHETHER MY RETAINER AGREEMENT HAD A LIEN PROVISION. HE WENT ON TO SAY THE LAWYER HAS TO ALWAYS KNOW WHERE THE MONEY IS. EVEN IN A CASE OF MASSIVE OFFICIAL AND JUDICIAL FRAUD? RIDICULOUS. BUT FOR THE JUDGE, THAT WAS THE STUMBLING BLOCK HE HAD DECIDED TO TREAT AS THE PINK ELEPHANT IN THE COURTROOM THAT EVERYBODY SAW, BUT WAS UNDER COURT ORDERS TO REMAIN SILENT ABOUT. THE JUDGE HAD MADE IT CLEAR THAT HE WOULD MANAGE AND CONDUCT THE CASE WITHOUT ADDRESSING, TO ANY DEGREE, THE ISSUE OF D.C. JUDICIAL AND FBI FRAUD, THEFT, CORRUPTION AND EXTORTION.

I REALIZED THEN AND THERE THAT WHILE A COURT'S ULTIMATE MISSION IS TO SEEK AND FIND THE TRUTH OF A MATTER, THIS SACRED GOAL WOULD NOT EVER BE ACCOMPLISHED IN MY CASE IN D.C.SUPERIOR COURT BECAUSE EKANS HAD PLACED THE ISSUE OF OFFICIAL AND JUDICIAL FRAUD IN A BOX MARKED "UNTOUCHABLE." THROUGHOUT THE PENDENCY OF THE CASE, THE DOMINANT ISSUE OF FRAUD WAS TREATED AS THE ELEPHANT IN THE COURTROOM THAT NOBODY TALKED ABOUT AND EVERYBODY WAS FORBIDDEN TO ADDRESS IN ANY WAY. IT WAS BECAUSE OF JUDGE EKANS' ADAMANT REFUSAL TO ADDRESS THE ISSUE OF FRAUD AT ANY LEVEL THAT ENSURED THAT THE MASSIVE D.C. JUDICIAL AND FBI FRAUD AND CORRUPTION WOULD CONTINUE TO FLOURISH UNABATED AND UNINTERRUPTED, AND THE D.C. JUDICIAL CO-CONSPIRATORS WOULD REMAIN PROTECTED FROM ANY KIND OF ACCOUNTABILITY OR PROSECUTION AND PUNISHMENT WHERE WARRANTED.

EVEN THOUGH THE COURT REFUSED MY REQUESTS FOR AN INVESTIGATION OF THE D.C. JUDICIAL AND FBI FRAUD THAT DEFINED THE CASE, NEVERTHELESS, JUDGE EKANS, WITHOUT ANY SHAME OR RESERVATION WHATSOEVER, CONTINUED TO ASK ME WHERE THE MONEY WAS. AND, MOREOVER, CONTINUED TO TREAT THE DOMINANT ISSUE OF FRAUD AS THE PINK ELEPHANT IN THE COURTROOM THAT WAS NOT AND MUST NOT BE ADDRESSED.

THE COURT: OKAY. AND SO IN EVERY CASE THAT I'M FAMILIAR WITH, YOU KNOW, MOST OF MY LIFE WAS SPENT IN GOVERNMENT SERVICE, BUT I TOOK OUT TWO AND A HALF YEARS FOR A PRIVATE PRACTICE DOWN HERE ON 5TH STREET, AND ONE OF THE THINGS THAT I LEARNED IN PRIVATE PRACTICE IS THAT YOU GET THE MONEY AND THEN YOU DISTRIBUTE IT TO THE CLIENT AND THE DOCTORS AND WHOEVER ELSE. **AND SO THE LAWYER HAS TO ALWAYS KNOW WHERE THE MONEY IS.**

SO, HERE IT SEEMS LIKE THIS TRAIN GOT OFF TRACK NOT WHEN THIS CASE CAME TO THIS SETTLEMENT THAT YOU DROVE IN SNOW TO BALTIMORE TO GET THE PAPER FROM HER, BUT WHEN THAT MONEY DIDN'T COME TO YOU IN THAT CASE AGAINST THE ESTATE.

SEE, YOU'VE TOLD ME THAT YOU WANT ME TO FIND OUT WHERE THE MONEY IS, I ASK YOU WHERE'S THE MONEY?

COMMENT AND ANALYSIS: #22 JUDGE EKANS' COMMENTARY HERE CAN BE DEFINED AS NOTHING BUT TRASH TALK TO AVOID THE ISSUES OF D.C. JUDICIAL FRAUD AND THEFT, THE DOMINANT ISSUES IN MY LAWSUIT, ABOUT WHICH HE PROHIBITED ALL EVIDENCE FROM BEING INTRODUCED OR TESTIMONY BEING GIVEN.

JUDGE EKANS' SUPREME TASK WAS TO KEEP THE D.C. JUDICIAL AND FBI CRIMINAL ENTERPRISE TRAIN ON TRACK. PERIOD. THUS, WHEN I STATED BELOW THAT IT WAS THE FRAUD THAT UNDERLAY THE WHOLE CASE, HE MATTER-OF-FACTLY IGNORED ME AND RESORTED TO HIS CHARACTERISTIC SILENCE AND DUMMY-UP POSTURE INTENDED TO ACHIEVE PROTECTION OF HIS JUDICIAL AND FBI CO-CONSPIRATORS.

MS. FRANKLIN:	NO, YOUR HONOR, I ACCEPT I ACCEPT YOUR HONOR'S POSITION.
THE COURT:	**BUT WHY DON'T YOU KNOW WHERE THE** MONEY IS?
MS. FRANKLIN:	**BECAUSE OF THE FRAUD THAT UNDERLIES THIS WHOLE LAWSUIT, THIS WHOLE MATTER.**
THE COURT:	WELL, HOW -- -- HOW IS THIS -- --
MS. FRANKLIN:	YOUR HONOR - - - -
THE COURT:------------------	HOW ARE WE SUPPOSED TO ASSIST YOU TO GET MONEY IN THE SETTLEMENT AGREEMENT THAT'S BASED ON MONEY THAT SHE CLAIMS SHE NEVER GOT, AND IN ALL OF MY EXPERIENCE IN THE LAW WOULD HAVE GONE TO YOU IN THE FIRST INSTANCE?
MS. FRANKLIN:	YOUR HONOR, I HAVE NEVER YOUR HONOR, I DON'T DIFFER WITH WHAT YOUR HONOR JUST SAID.
THE COURT:	WELL, WHERE'S THE MONEY?
MS. FRANKLIN:	YOUR HONOR, MAY I JUST RESPOND?
THE COURT:	YES, MA' AM, YOU CAN TELL ME WHERE -- -- WHERE-- --

MS. FRANKLIN: **YOUR HONOR, YOUR HONOR, I HAVE NEVER SAID THAT I COULD EVER VERIFY IT, THAT SHE HAD THE FUNDS. I'VE NEVER SAID THAT.**

WHAT I HAVE BEEN -- -- AND WHAT MY LAWSUIT AND WHAT ALL OF THESE PROCEEDINGS HAVE FOCUSED ON IS THE FACT THAT SHE HAS, UNDER OATH AND IN OPEN COURT, TESTIFIED TO THE FACT THAT SHE HAS ACCESS IN TERMS OF THE INFORMATION REGARDING THE MONEY. WHEN YOU MEET WITH BANKERS, WHEN -- --

THE COURT: OKAY, THAT'S THAT'S ALL WELL AND GOOD BUT THAT HASN'T GOTTEN US ONE INCH CLOSER -- --

MS. FRANKLIN: NO, IT HASN'T.

THE COURT:-------------------- TO RESOLVING THIS. SO I HAVE TO GO BACK TO WHAT CAN HELP US TO RESOLVE THIS AND THAT IS WHAT WAS THE SETTLEMENT? WHAT WAS THE SETTLEMENT WITH THE ESTATE? WAS IT A SETTLEMENT?

COMMENT AND ANALYSIS: #23 IT TOOK EVERTHING IN ME TO MAINTAIN A STRAIGHT FACE WHILE LOOKING INTO THE FACE OF A DIED-IN-THE-WOOL CORRUPT D.C. COURT JUDGE.

FOR THE 9 MONTHS MY CASE REMAINED PENDING BEFORE JUDGE EKANS, I CONSIDERED THE TIME AS BEING NOTHING MORE THAN AN EXTENSIVE TUTORIAL IN THE WORST KIND OF DECEPTION AND JUDICIAL GASLIGHTING PRACTICED BY A D.C. COURT JUDGE WHO HAD SWORN TO UPHOLD THE LAW AND THE CONSTITUTION.

MS. FRANKLIN: YOUR HONOR.

THE COURT: DID IT COME TO JUDGMENT?

MS. FRANKLIN: IT WAS A SETTLEMENT, YOUR HONOR, IT WAS A SETTLEMENT. BUT, YOUR HONOR, CAN I JUST SAY THIS, YOU KNOW WHY I ASKED YOUR HONOR, AND I REFERENCED THE LAW ENFORCEMENT AGENCY TO DO INVESTIGATIONS ON BEHALF OF THE COURT, I WAS REALLY USING A PRIOR EXPERIENCE IN A PROBATE MATTER WHERE A SERIES OF ELDERLY CLIENTS, MY CLIENT HAPPENED TO BE RELATED TO HER AUNT AND UNCLE WERE A PART OF A GROUP OF ELDERLY CLIENTS REPRESENTED BY A D.C. ATTORNEY, HE HAD LITERALLY, YOU KNOW, THROUGH JUST DEFRAUDED ALL OF THEM.

THE COURT: **THAT'S A CRIME.**

COMMENT AND ANALYSIS: #24 WHAT I REALLY WANTED TO SAY WAS "JUST AS WHAT YOU'RE TAKING US THROUGH IS A CRIME."

MS. FRANKLIN: AND WHAT HAPPENED, WHAT HAPPENED WAS ONE OF THE FAMILIES REACHED OUT TO THE FBI AND AS RESULT OF THAT I WAS ALSO IN TOUCH WITH THE FBI WHO WAS ASSIGNED TO THE CASE, AND THE FBI, OF COURSE, REFERRED IT TO THE U.S. ATTORNEY'S OFFICE, THEY WORKED WITH THE U.S. ATTORNEY'S OFFICE AND, OF COURSE, THAT ATTORNEY NOW IS SERVING 10 TO 15 YEARS FOR DEFRAUDING THESE VARIOUS ELDERLY CLIENTS.

SO I THINK I WAS GOING BACK IN TIME TO THAT EXPERIENCE, THAT KNOWLEDGE, OF HOW THE FBI OR SOME OTHER LAW ENFORCEMENT AGENCY COULD LOOK INTO A MATTER WHERE YOU HAVE -- --

THE COURT: **MISS FRANKLIN, YOU SORT OF DOING WHAT MISS JONES DOES. I DON'T KNOW WHAT WE'RE TALKING ABOUT NOW. I KNOW WHAT THE FBI DOES. I HAVE VERY CLOSE FRIENDS WHO HAVE RETIRED FROM THE FBI AFTER 30-YEAR CAREERS, WHO I MAINTAIN CLOSE ASSOCIATION WITH, I KNOW WHAT THE FBI DOES.**

MY CONCERN HERE IS WHETHER OR NOT I'M WASTING TIME WITH YOU, WHICH I DON'T HAVE TIME TO WASTE.

COMMENT AND ANALYSIS #25: JUDGE EKANS' STATEMENT WAS INTERPRETED BY ME AS HIS WAY OF SAYING THAT THE SOONER HE COMPLETED THE RIGGED ADJUDICATION OF MY CASE, THE SOONER THE FLOURISHING CRIMINAL ENTERPRISE WOULD BE ACHIEVED AND HIS PROPORTIONATE SHARE OF THE $34 MILLION SETTLEMENT PIE, AS A KEY D.C. JUDICIAL CO-CONSPIRATOR, WOULD BE DISBURSED TO HIM.

JUDGE EKANS' ABUSE OF HIS POWER OF ABSOLUTE DISCRETION WAS CLEAR AND UNEQUIVOCAL. WHATEVER JUDGMENTS OR ORDERS THE COURT WOULD BE ISSUING IN MY CASE, THE MILLIONS IN SETTLEMENT PROCEEDS STOLEN BY THE CO-CONSPIRATOR "OFFICIALS" WOULD REMAIN JUST THAT: STOLEN. AT THE END OF THE DAY, MY ATTORNEY'S FEES WOULD REMAIN IN THE POCKETS, BANK ACCOUNTS AND POSSIBLY EVEN IN OFF-SHORE BANK ACCOUNTS OF THE D.C. JUDICIAL AND FBI CO-CONSPIRATORS.

AND SO, JUDGE EKANS, IN AN ABUSE OF DISCRETION, WAS FREE TO USE THE LEGAL THEORY OF DEFINING AND LABELING ME AS A JUDGMENT CREDITOR. THIS ABUSIVE ACTION BY JUDGE EKANS FURTHERED THE MAINTENANCE OF THE STATUS QUO OF THE MASSIVE D.C. JUDICIAL AND FBI FRAUD, THEFT AND CORRUPTION CONSPIRACY AND CRIMINAL ENTERPRISE THAT WERE THE DOMINANT ISSUES IN MY CASE AND THAT CONTINUES TO FLOURISH IN BROAD DAYLIGHT IN THE D.C. COURT SYSTEM.

JUDGE EKANS REMAINED PREOCCUPIED WITH HIS REPEATED DENIALS OF MY REPEATED REQUESTS FOR INVESTIGATION OF THE UNDERLYING ISSUE OF FRAUD THAT DOMINATED THE CASE. FURTHER, JUDGE EKANS REVEALED HIS PREOCCUPATION WITH MY REQUESTS FOR INVESTIGATION THROUGHOUT THE HEARING ON APRIL 6, 2011.

JUDGE EKANS OBSCURED THE IN-YOUR-FACE OFFICIAL AND JUDICIAL FRAUD AND CORRUPTION DIMENSION OF THE CASE THAT BEGGED FOR RELIEF AND ADDRESS IN SUBSTANTIAL PART THROUGH HIS PERSISTENT MISAPPLICATION TO ME OF THE INTENTIONALLY FALSE JUDGMENT CREDITOR LEGAL THEORY.

JUDGE EKANS HAD FASHIONED THE CLEVER MANUEVER AND STRATEGY, EXECUTED IN FURTHERANCE OF THE CONSPIRACY AND CRIMINAL ENTERPRISE, THAT EACH TIME THERE WAS A COURT PROCEEDING IN WHICH I WAS PRESENT, JUDGE EKANS WOULD BEAT THE DRUM OF MY BEING A *JUDGMENT CREDITOR* WITH THE RESPONSIBILITY OF SEARCHING FOR THE STOLEN SETTLEMENT PROCEEDS.

THE COURT MADE IT A POINT AND PRACTICE OF NEVER REFERRING TO THE SETTLEMENT PROCEEDS AS STOLEN OR ILLEGALLY CONFISCATED SETTLEMENT PROCEEDS OR ILL-GOTTEN GAINS. THE FACT THAT BOTH PARTIES IN THE CASE HAD ALLEGED OFFICIAL AND JUDICIAL FRAUD AND CORRUPTION, AND THAT THE SETTLEMENT PROCEEDS HAD BEEN STOLEN BY CORRUPT D.C. COURT JUDGES AND FBI AGENTS MADE NO DISCERNIBLE DIFFERENCE TO JUDGE EKANS.

COURT RULINGS DURING THE PENDENCY OF A COURT MATTER, AS WELL AS THE FINAL JUDGMENT IN A CASE, TYPICALLY HINGE ON WHAT IS NOT SAID BY THE PRESIDING JUDGE DURING COURT PROCEEDINGS.

NOTHING IS MORE ILLUSTRATIVE OF THE ADAGE OF *"POWER CORRUPTS AND ABSOLUTE POWER CORRUPTS ABSOLUTELY"* THAN JUDGE EKANS' INTENTIONALLY FALSE REITERATION AT THE FINAL COURT HEARING ON JANUARY 16, 2015 THAT MY LAWSUIT HAD BEEN INITIALLY PRESENTED TO HIM AS A JUDGMENT CREDITOR CASE.

THE ODYSSEY OF JUDICIAL CORRUPTION

MS. FRANKLIN: YOUR HONOR, IF IT'S THE COURT'S FEELING - - --

THE COURT: HERE'S MY QUESTION, NO, HERE'S THE QUESTION: SEE, YOU'VE ASKED THE
                    COURT TO USE THIS PROCESS TO ENFORCE A SETTLEMENT AGREEMENT. I'M
                    ASKING WHAT BECAME OF THE PROCEEDS OF THE SETTLEMENT WITH THE
                    ESTATE? YOU HANDLED THAT, RIGHT?

MS. FRANKLIN: I CAN'T ANSWER THAT, YOUR HONOR.

THE COURT: WHY NOT?

MS. FRANKLIN: I CAN'T ANSWER IT BECAUSE THE FIRM THAT REPRESENTED THE ESTATE WOULD
                    NOT PROVIDE ME WITH THE SETTLEMENT AGREEMENT NOR WOULD THE
                    DEFENDANT PROVIDE ME WITH THE COPY OF THE SETTLEMENT AGREEMENT.
                    AND SHE HAS ACKNOWLEDGED IN THIS COURT AND TO ME MANY TIMES THAT
                    SHE HAD   SHE HAD SIGNED A SETTEMENT AGREEMENT WITH THE OTHER SIDE
                    OR I WOULD NEVER EVEN HAVE CONSIDERED COMING INTO COURT.

THE COURT: LET'S SEE, YOU WENT TO FLORIDA, YOU HIRED A LOCAL LAW FIRM, YOU WERE
                    ADMITTED BEFORE A COURT DOWN THERE PRO HAC VICE, YOU NEGOTIATED -- -
                    - DID YOU NEGOTIATE THE SETTLEMENT?

MS. FRANKLIN: NO, I DID NOT NEGOTIATE, NO, I DID NOT NEGOTIATE IT.

                    COMMENT AND ANALYSIS: #26 I WAS NOT A PARTICIPANT IN THE FRAUDULENT
                    SETTLEMENT OF THE $100 MILLION LAWSUIT UPON WHICH THE $34 MILLION
                    SETTLEMENT WAS BASED.

MS. JONES: **YOUR HONOR, MAY I PLEASE------ MAY IT PLEASE THE COURT, MAY I SPEAK?**

THE COURT: **STAND UP. RAISE YOUR RIGHT HAND. PUT HER UNDER OATH.**

                    (THEREUPON, THE DEFENDANT WAS SWORN).

THE COURT: **SAY YOUR NAME.**

MS. JONES: **BRIANNA JONES.**

THE COURT: **DID YOU NEGOTIATE A SETTLEMENT WITH THE------ WITH THE ESTATE?**

MS. JONES: **YES, YOUR HONOR.**

THE COURT: **DO YOU HAVE A COPY OF THE SETTLEMENT?**

MS. JONES: **THEY BROKE INTO MY STORAGE.**

THE COURT: **DO YOU HAVE A COPY OF THE SETTLEMENT?**

MS. JONES: **I DON'T HAVE A PRESENT COPY BUT I DID REFER -- --**

THE COURT:	I DON'T WANT TO KNOW ABOUT PRESENT. I WANT YOU TO UNDERSTAND SOMETHING.
MS. JONES:	I DON'T HAVE A COPY, YOU HONOR.
THE COURT:	ALL RIGHT. ALL RIGHT.
	WHAT WAS THE AMOUNT OF THE SETTLEMENT?
MS. JONES:	THIRTY-FOUR MILLION DOLLARS.
THE COURT:	WERE YOU ISSUED A CHECK?
MS. JONES:	I WAS NOT ISSUED A CHECK, I WAS TOLD –
THE COURT:	WAS ANYONE ISSUED A CHECK?
MS. JONES:	NOT THAT I KNOW OF, I WAS NOT ISSUED A CHECK, NEITHER WAS THE PLAINTIFF.
THE COURT:	WERE YOU REPRESENTED BY A LAWYER WHEN YOU NEGOTIAED THIS SETTLEMENT?
MS. JONES:	HERE'S THE PRO HOC -- --
THE COURT:	WERE YOU REPRESENTED BY A LAWYER?
MS. JONES:	NO. I WAS PRO SE. IN BROWARD COUNTY. THE JUDGE HAD -------SHE WASN'T ALLOWED TO PRACTICE IN BROWARD COUNTY, AND WHEN I INQUIRED OF THE PLAINTIFF -- --
	COMMENT AND ANALYSIS: #27 I WAS LEGALLY ADMITTED TO THE FLORIDA COURT TO REPRESENT BRIANNA JONES IN BROWARD COUNTY CIRCUIT COURT, PURSUANT TO A COURT ORDER SIGNED BY FLORIDA PROBATE JUDGE MICHAEL ROSENBAUM IN JUNE 1996.
THE COURT:	JUST -- --
MS. JONES:	CERTAINLY.
THE COURT:	------------------LISTEN FOR A MINUTE.
	SO YOU NEGOTIATED A SETTLEMENT FOR 30 SOME MILLION DOLLARS WITHOUT A LAWYER, RIGHT? IS THAT WHAT YOU TOLD ME?

COMMENT AND ANALYSIS: #28 HERE BRIANNA SIMPLY LIES TO JUDGE EKANS. ACCORDING TO BRIANNA JONES, BETH HOLLISTER, A KEY NON-JUDICIAL CO-CONSPIRATOR AND HOLLISTER'S PERSONAL ATTORNEY, A WELL-KNOWN SO-CALLED WASHINGTON SUPERLAWYER, NEGOTIATED, ON BRIANNA'S BEHALF, THE $34 MILLION SETTLEMENT AGREEMENT.

IN FACT, ACCORDING TO BRIANNA, BETH HOLLISTER WOULD HAVE HER ATTORNEY MEET WITH BRIANNA IN HER HOME IN WASHINGTON ON WEEKENDS AND WHILE BRIANNA LIVED THERE FOR SHORT PERIODS OF TIME DURING 1997.

MS. JONES: THAT'S CORRECT.

THE COURT: AND YOU NEVER RECEIVED ANY PROCEEDS FROM THE SETTLEMENT YOU NEGOTIATED?

MS. JONES: I NEVER RECEIVED ANY PROCEEDS. THE PLAINTIFF SAID TO ME -- --

THE COURT: JUST A MINUTE.

MS. JONES: CERTAINLY.

THE COURT: DID YOU HIRE BARBARA WASHINTON FRANKLIN TO COLLECT THE PROCEEDS THAT YOU NEGOTIATED THE SETTLEMENT FOR BUT NEVER RECEIVED?

MS. JONES: I HIRED HER PRIOR TO THE SETTLEMENT.

THE COURT: NO, NO, NO. DID YOU HIRE HER TO COLLECT THOSE PROCEEDS AFTER YOU NEGOTIATED THE SETTLEMENT?

MS. JONES: NO, I DID NOT. SHE WAS----- I NEVER TERMINATED THE ORIGINAL AGREEMENTS. BUT YOUR HONOR ---- CERTAINLY.

(PAUSE).

COMMENT AND ANALYSIS: #29 I AM SURE EKANS WAS DISAPPOINTED TO HEAR JONES ADMIT THAT SHE NEVER TERMINATED THE SETTLEMENT AGREEMENT. THE AGREEMENT INCLUDED A PROVISION WHICH STATED THAT, EVEN IF TERMINATED, I WOULD STILL BE ENTITLED TO FULL COMPENSATION AS PROVIDED BY THE TERMS OF THE AGREEMENT.

THE COURT: ATTORNEY FRANKLIN, YOU'VE TOLD ME THAT YOU BECAME AWARE THAT SHE WAS NEGOTIATING BEHIND YOUR BACK TO RESOLVE THIS MATTER WITH THE ESTATE; IS THAT RIGHT?

MS. FRANKLIN: CORRECT.

THE COURT: DID YOU TAKE ANY STEPS TO PUT THE LAWYERS FOR THE FIRM ON NOTICE THAT YOU WOULD HAVE A LIEN AGAINST ANY SETTLEMENT OR JUDGMENT?

MS. FRANKLIN: NO, I DIDN'T   I DIDN'T PUT THEM ON NOTICE, YOUR HONOR, BECAUSE I'M NOT SURE, THE COURT SAYS BEHIND MY BACK, SHE WAS KEEPING ME   I KNEW SHE WAS MEETING WITH THE ATTORNEYS. AND I HAD DECIDED, AFTER SPENDING SO MUCH TIME AND MONEY FLYING BACK AND FORTH TO FLORIDA, THAT I WASN'T, YOU KNOW I JUST COULDN'T AFFORD TO CONTINUE TO GO BACK AND FORTH DOWN THERE.

THE COURT: SO SHE WAS NOT NEGOTIATING BEHIND YOUR BACK?

MS. FRANKLIN: SHE WAS NOT   SHE WAS NOT—LET ME PUT IT THIS WAY, I KNEW OF HER CONTACT. NOW WHETHER I KNEW EACH AND EVERY TIME SHE MET, WHERE THEY MET, WHO SHE WAS MEETING WITH, I'VE NEVER BEEN GIVEN THAT INFORMATION. SHE WOULD ALWAYS SAY THEY HAVE THREATENED ME THAT IF I SHOULD GIVE YOU A COPY OF THE AGREEMENT, I'VE BEEN THREATENED.

REMEMBER NOW, YOUR HONOR, WE'RE TALKING -- --

THE COURT: SO YOU NEVER GOT A COPY OF THE SETTLEMENT?

MS. FRANKLIN: NO, AND BECAUSE SHE -- --I SAID, BRIANNA -- --

THE COURT: HAVE YOU EVER SEEN IT?

MS. FRANKLIN: NEVER. NEVER. I SAID THAT IN THE COMPLAINT WHEN I FILED THE COMPLAINT, I'VE NEVER SEEN THE SETTLEMENT.

MS.. JONES: YOUR HONOR, SHE CONTACTED THE HEAD OF THE FBI OF MIAMI OFFICE, HANK HENNESSY.

MS. FRANKLIN: CORRECT.

COMMENT AND ANALYSIS: #30 EKANS SEEMED PLEASED THAT I HAD NEVER SEEN THE SETTLEMENT AGREEMENT. THIS CIRCUMSTANCE FIT WITHIN THE DARKNESS AND UNDERCOVER ATMOSPHERE OF THE CRIMINALL ENTERPRISE HE WAS HELPING TO STEER AND MANAGE.

"THE LESS SHE KNOWS THE BETTER" WAS MY PERCEPTION OF EKANS' ATTITUDE. HE ALSO SEEMED NON-PLUSED BY HEARING THAT I HAD CONTACTED THE FBI HEAD IN MIAMI. HE KNEW FBI AGENTS COULD BE AS CORRUPT AS D.C. COURT JUDGES, INCLUDING HIM AND HIS D.C. JUDICIAL COLLEAGUES.

MS. JONES: AND SHE SAID THERE'S A SETTLEMENT FOR 34 MILLION DOLLARS AND SHE SAID -- -- HE SAID, OH, I KNOW SAM ADAGIO, I SIT ON CRIME BOARDS WITH HIM. HE SAID THEY'RE GOING TO HARM HER PROBABLY AFTER SHE GETS 34 MILLION DOLLARS YOU'LL FIND HER IN A CREEK SOMEWHERE.

AND FROM THAT TIME THERE WAS AN AGENT JUDY KIM WHO VISITED ME, SHE SAID, I WANT TO MAKE SURE YOU'RE SAFE, AND FROM THAT TIME ALL HELL BROKE LOOSE WITH REGARD TO THREATS. HER OFFICE, HER PHONE, MY PHONE, THE NEWSPAPER EVERY MORNING, THERE WAS THREATS.

THEY TOLD ME WITH REGARD TO THE SETTLEMENT WE'RE GOING TO SIGN THIS BECAUSE WE'RE GOING TO USE THIS TO GET THE LOTTERY PRIZE, IT'S ANNUITIZED PRIZE, GOING TO GET IT IN A LUMP SUM. THERE WAS A HEARING SCHEDULED FOR JUNE THE 22ND, 1997, THEY THEN NOTIFIED THE PLAINTFF, THEY THEN HAD THE HEARING ON MAY THE 6TH 1997.

COMMENT AND ANALYSIS: #31 JUDGE RICHARD MANDARIN, A KEY D.C. JUDICIAL CO-CONSPIRATOR, AND A DECADES-OLD JUDICIAL COLLEAGUE OF JUDGE EKANS, MET IN HIS CHAMBERS WITH BRIANNA JONES AND BETH HOLLISTER. PRIOR TO THE SECRET MEETING, I HAD REPEATEDLY URGED BRIANNA TO ALLOW ME TO FILE A MOTION TO INTERVENE, ON HER BEHALF, IN THE STAKEHOLDER ACTION FILED BY THE DISTRICT OF COLUMBIA AND THE D.C. OFFICE OF LOTTERY AND GAMING. THE LOTTERY BOARD SOUGHT A COURT ORDER DIRECTING THEM AS TO WHAT CLAIMANT TO PAY WILLIE LEE RIDGEWAY'S 45-MILLION-DOLLAR LOTTERY PRIZE.

ACCORDING TO BRIANNA, JUDGE MANDARIN ASSURED BRIANNA THAT SHE DID NOT NEED TO INTERVENE IN THE STAKEHOLDER LAWSUIT, NOR DID I NEED TO BE PRESENT IN THE MEETING IN CHAMBERS, EVEN THOUGH MANDARIN KNEW THAT I LEGALLY REPRESENTED BRIANNA IN HER CLAIM AGAINST THE RIDGEWAY ESTATE. MANDARIN PROVED TO BE AS CORRUPT AS EKANS IN CARRYING OUT THE MISSION OF THE CRIMINAL ENTERPRISE TO STRIP ME OF THE ESTIMATED $50 MILLION OWED TO ME IN ATTORNEY'S FEES.

MOREOVER, MANDARIN SCHEDULED A COURT HEARING ON THE STAKEHOLDER MATTER FOR JUNE 22, 1997 AND THEN INTENTIONALLY AND, WITHOUT NOTICE TO ME, RESCHEDULED THE HEARING FOR MAY 6, 1997. THIS IS THE SIGNATURE BEHAVIOR OF A CORRUPT D.C. COURT JUDGE. ALL CAPS.

THE COURT:	YOU'VE MADE IT CLEAR THAT YOU DON'T FEEL THAT YOU REALLY OWE MISS FRANKLIN.
MS. JONES:	I DO OWE HER, YOUR HONOR.
THE COURT:	BUT ALL OF THE EXPRESSIONS THAT YOU'VE MADE INDICATE TO ME THAT YOU REALLY DON'T THINK YOU OWE HER ANY MONEY.
MS. JONES:	NO, YOUR HONOR, I WOULD HAVE -- --
THE COURT:	WHICH BEGS THE QUESTION WHY YOU ENTERED THE SETTLEMENT. YOU KNOW, HERE'S THE THING, YOU HAVE WHEN DID THE SETTLEMENT OCCUR, WHAT YEAR WAS IT?
MS. JONES:	IT WAS 1996.
THE COURT:	1996.
MS. JONES:	DECEMBER OF 1996.

COMMENT AND ANALYSIS #32 THE LAST THING EKANS WANTED TO HEAR FROM BRIANNA WAS THAT SHE OWED ME. THIS DECLARATION FROM THE HORSE'S MOUTH DIDN'T FIT INTO EKANS' PRINCIPAL ASSIGNMENT OF RIGGING MY CASE FOR FINAL DISMISSAL.

THE COURT: OKAY. WHAT'S THAT, 15 YEARS, 16 YEARS WHATEVER? AND SO, YOU, ONE DAY OR ANOTHER, MANAGED TO LIVE REALLY WELL. YOU SAID OTHER PEOPLE'S GENEROSITY, I DON'T KNOW, YOU KNOW, BUT YOU'VE MANAGED TO LIVE REALLY WELL.

ON THE OTHER HAND, YOU KNOW, I TRY TO   THE LAW ALWAYS JUDGES PEOPLE ON WHAT'S CALLED THE REASONABLE PERSON STANDARD, AND YOU KNOW, THAT   APPLYING THAT STANDARD HERE I WOULD HAVE TO THINK THAT A PERSON WHO -- --WHO IS OWED THAT SUBSTANTIAL AMOUNT OF MONEY WOULD NOT   NOT KNOW WHERE IT IS OR NOT HAVE TAKEN STEPS TO TAKE POSSESSION OF THAT MONEY.

NOW, DO YOU HAVE THE MONEY?

COMMENT AND ANALYSIS : #33 HERE AGAIN, EKANS INTENTIONALLY REFUSES TO VIEW THE CASE AND ITS FACTS FROM THE PERSPECTIVE OF THE D.C. JUDICIAL AND FBI FRAUD, THEFT AND CORRUPTION THAT DOMINATED THE CASE. HE SIMPLY STAYED IN INTENTIONAL AND PURPOSEFUL DENIAL.

MS. JONES: YOUR HONOR -- --

THE COURT: DO YOU HAVE THE MONEY?

MS. JONES: I ABSOUTELY DO NOT HAVE THE MONEY.

THE COURT: OKAY.

MS. JONES: I HAVE NO KNOWLEDGE.

THE COURT: OKAY, OKAY, ALL RIGHT. SO YOU DON'T HAVE THE MONEY, AND IT'S BEEN 15, 16 YEARS SINCE YOU WERE ENTITLED TO IT. DO YOU EVER INTEND TO GET THE MONEY?

MS. JONES: YES, I WILL BE FILING A JUDGMENT AGAINST THE ESTATE IMMEDIATELY IN BROWARD COUNTY ON THE ADVICE OF FLORIDA COUNSEL.

THE COURT: AND SO 16 YEARS LATER YOU'VE DECIDED TO DO SOMETHING?

COMMENT AND ANALYSIS: #34 BRIANNA'S PLANS ARE CLEARLY IN RESPONSE TO THE LAWSUIT I FILED AGAINST HER.

MS. JONES: BECAUSE IF THIS HADN'T HAVE HAPPENED, ONCE SHE GOT CONFIRMATION FROM BAR COUNSEL -- --

THE COURT: CAN YOU JUST -- -- I MEAN -- --

MS JONES: WELL, THEY HAVE EVEN ENGAGING ME.

THE COURT;   EXCUSE ME, EXCUSE ME. EXCUSE ME. YOU -------THIS IS THE LAST THING YOU CONTACTED MISS FRANKLIN RECENTLY TO TRY AND RENEGOTIATE THE SETTLEMENT?

MS. JONES: ABSOLUTELY, YOUR HONOR.

THE COURT: WHAT DO YOU WANT TO RENEGOTIATE?

MS. JONES: WELL, FIRST OF ALL, HAS TO BE FORMAL REASONABLE.

THE COURT: THAT'S WHAT I'M TALKING ABOUT, WHAT DO YOU THINK IS FORMAL REASONABLE?

MS. JONES: WELL, I PLAN TO BE EXTREMELY GENEROUS WITH THOSE WHO HAVE BEEN SO KIND TO ME.

THE COURT: RIGHT. WITHOUT GIVING ME ALL THE ICING, GIVE ME THE CAKE, WHAT DO YOU THINK IS FORMAL REASONABLE?

MS. JONES: I THINK 10 MILLION IS FAR MORE REASONABLE FOR THE PLAINTIFF.

THE COURT:	WHY?
MS. JONES:	WELL, BECAUSE I THINK JUST ON THE ------SHE JUST ON THE FACT ALONE THAT I NEVER TERMINATED HER. MY INTENTION WAS ALWAYS -- --
THE COURT:	WHY?
MS. JONES:	I'VE NEVER TERMINATED HER, I NEVER FELT TERMINATION.
THE COURT:	WHY DOES THAT MAKE IT MORE REASONABLE?
MS. JONES:	WELL, REASONABLE WITH REGARD TO THE FACT I WAS PRO SE IN THIS. AND SHE HELPED, YOUR HONOR, I CANNOT EVER DENY OR -- --

COMMENT ANALYSIS: #35 IN LIGHT OF THE PROVISIONS OF MY CONTINGENCY FEE AGREEMENT, THIS DIALOGUE BETWEEN EKANS AND JONES TURNED MY STOMACH, CAUSING ME TO WANT TO REGURGITATE ALL OVER THE COURTROOM FLOOR AND ON THE PUBLIC SIDEWALKS, AS I HEADED FOR THE PARKING GARAGE FOLLOWING THE ADJOURNMENT OF THE COURT HEARING.

THE COURT:	HOW CAN YOU HAVE BEEN PRO SE IF -----IF --IF SHE WAS REPRESENTING YOU?
MS. JONES:	IT WAS COMPLICATED, SHE WAS -- --
THE COURT:	IT IS COMPLICATED. BUT IT'S COMPLICATED BECAUSE YOU MAKE IT SO. IT'S FAIRLY UNCOMPLICATED IF YOU DON'T TRY TO COMPLICATE IT.

***

MS. JONES:	I THINK 10 MILLION IS MORE THAN FAIR, YOUR HONOR, THINK WITH ALL THAT WE'VE GONE ON, I HATE TO END THIS WAY, THAT THINGS WOULD BE SAID IN THIS COURT, BUT I WILL ALWAYS HAVE A FONDNESS AND APPRECIATION FOR HER EFFORTS.
THE COURT:	TO BY THE WAY, 10 MILLION AS OPPOSED TO WHAT?
MS JONES:	AS OPPOSED TO 14 PLUS INTEREST NOW I'M THINKING IS DOUBLED WITH THE INTEREST ON IT, THE INTEREST THAT ACCRUED SINCE THAT TIME, BUT I'VE PROMISED OTHERS A SUBSTANTIAL -- --
THE COURT:	YOU'RE JUST TALKING ABOUT LIKE A FLAT 10 MILLION?
MS. JONES:	A FLAT 10 MILLION, I THINK A FLAT 10 MILLION I THINK IS MORE THAN FAIR.
THE COURT:	WHY NOT NINE MILLION?
MS. JONES:	TEN MILLION JUST HIT ME THE RIGHT WAY.

THE COURT: IT IS A NICE ROUND NUMBER. WHY NOT EIGHT? EIGHT'S A NICE ROUND NUMBER.

MS. JONES: TEN MILLION JUST HIT ME THE RIGHT WAY.

THE COURT: IT HAS TWO ROUNDS. WHY NOT FIVE?

MS. JONES: BECAUSE I WANT TO ESTABLISH A FOUNDATION, AND I WANT TO CONTINUE MY EDUCATION. I FEEL LIKE MY LIFE HAS BEEN STOLEN, AND WE'RE INCIDENTALLY HERE ON THE BIRTHDAY OF THE RAPIST, OF THE DECEDENT.

THE COURT: WELL, THAT'S INTERESTING.

NOW, LET'S SAY THAT -- -- LET'S SAY THAT THE PLAINTIFF ACCEDED AND AND -- --AND GAVE UP WHAT WOULD PROBABLY BE ANOTHER MILLION DOLLARS CAUSE AS YOU SAY WITH ALL THE INTEREST ON THAT SUM YOU COULD BE TALKING CONSIDERABLY MORE THAN 10 MILLION. BUT LET'S JUST SAY FOR THE SAKE OF DISCUSSION SHE AGREES TO THE 10 MILLION, WHAT'S YOUR PLAN?

COMMENT AND ANALYSIS: #36 MY STOMACH TURNED AS EKANS HAD THE AUDACITY TO PRESUME THAT I WOULD BE WILLING TO TAKE HIS SUBSTANTIALLY SHAVED-DOWN OFFER HE WAS SUGGESTING THAT BRIANNA JONES MAKE TO ME.

MS. JONES: MY PLAN IS   I DID SPEAK WITH A LAWYER IN BROWARD COUNTY AND SHE SAID, I DON'T UNDERSTAND THIS, FILE A JUDGMENT AGAINST THE ESTATE. HAS NO ONE TOLD YOU THAT YET? AND WHEN YOU'RE DONE WITH THE D.C. SITUATION, THE D.C. -- --

THE COURT: THE ESTATE IS STILL OPEN?

MS. JONES: IT'S CLOSED BUT SHE SAID FILE IT AGAINST THE FIRM AS WELL AS THE ESTATE. I KNOW SOME OF THE ATTORNEYS NO LONGER WORK THERE, OR EMPLOYED THERE, BUT SHE SAID, GO AGAINST THE ESTATE AND ALSO GO AGAINST THE FIRM.

THE COURT: GO AGAINST THE CLOSED ESTATE?

MS. JONES: WELL, IT CAN BE REOPENED, WELL, ACCORDING TO HER IT COULD BE REOPENED. BUT ALSO FILE IT AGAINST THE FIRM.

AND THAT'S THE PLAN, TO GO IN IMMEDIATELY TO ASK --- --

THE COURT: WHAT ABOUT ALL THE INTEREST THAT'S GOING TO ACCRUE BETWEEN NOW AND -- --

MS. JONES:	IF THE INTEREST FROM THE TIME OF THE INITIAL 34 MILLION DOLLARS, IF IT'S UP TO, WE HAVE ONE ESTIMATE 80 MILLION, I WILL DO ANOTHER FIVE, FIFTEEN.
MS. FRANKLIN:	YOUR HONOR. YOUR HONOR, MAY I SAY SOMETHING? YOUR HONOR, THIS TO ME IS YOUR CLASSIC CONTINGENCY FEE CASE. BECAUSE YOU START OUT WITH A CLIENT, THEY HAVE ABSOLUTELY NO MONEY TO PAY FOR ANYTHING. AND SHE HAS NOT EVER PAID FOR ANYTHING HAVING TO DO WITH THE CASE.

I, ON THE OTHER HAND, HAVE NEVER BEEN PAID ANYTHING, NOT EVEN A DOLLAR. AND THE CLIENT IS MORE THAN WILLING TO LET YOU EXPEND ALL THE ENERGY, ALL THE FINANCIAL RESOURCES TO GET THE JOB DONE. NEVER ENVISIONING, SHE NEVER ENVISIONED – HOW DID WE EVEN GET TO 14 MILLION? I'LL TELL YOU WHY, BECAUSE I SAT AT MY DESK IN MY OFFICE, AND CRAFTED THE COMPLAINT WHICH MADE THE DEMAND. THAT'S HOW THEY SETTLED FOR THE 34 MILLION DOLLARS.

COMMENT AND ANALYSIS: #37 I KNEW ALL MY TALK ABOUT THE VAGARIES OF REPRESENTING A CLIENT ON A CONTINGENCY FEE BASIS WAS FALLING ON EKANS' DEAF EARS. HE COULD CARE LESS, AND HAD MADE THAT CLEAR FOR THE ENTIRETY OF HIS ADJUDICATION OF MY LAWSUIT.

MS. JONES:	YOUR HONOR.
MS. FRANKLIN:	AND ---- YOUR HONOR, I DON'T INTERRUPT WHEN SHE'S SPEAKING.
THE COURT:	YOU KNOW WHAT, YOU KNOW WHAT.
MS. JONES:	I'M SORRY.
THE COURT:	ARE YOU ------ IS THIS YOUR WAY OF SAYING THAT YOU WOULDN'T CONSIDER TAKING 10 MILLION DOLLARS?

COMMENT AND ANALYSIS: #38 EKANS SEEMED SURPRISED THAT I WOULDN'T BE WILLING TO JUMP AT A SETTLEMENT OFFER OF $10 MILLION WHEN I WAS OWED SUBSTANTIALLY MORE DUE TO THE PASSAGE OF TIME AND THE ACCRUED INTEREST ON THE INITIAL AMOUNT.

EKANS NEEDED TO GO BACK TO THE HISTORY OF THE CASE AND REALIZE THAT IT WAS I WHO HAD FILED A $100 MILLION LAWSUIT AGAINST THE RIDGEWAY ESTATE TO BEGIN WITH.

MS. FRANKLIN: YOUR HONOR, MAY I SAY THIS? THE REASON I WOULD NOT CONSIDER TAKING 10 MILLION IS BECAUSE SHE IS JUST TALKING. SHE HAS NOT PRODUCED ONE DOCUMENT. ALL OF WHAT SHE'S SAYING TO THE COURT IS JUST TALK, AND SHE ENJOYS IT EVERY TIME WE COME. SHE HAS NOT PROVIDED YOUR HONOR, SHE HAS NOT PROVIDED THE PRIOR COURT, JUDGE STARR, SHE COMES IN WITH WORDS.

THE COURT: WHAT DO YOU WANT ME TO DO? I'VE SENT HER TO JAIL; YOU WANT HER TO GO BACK TO JAIL?

COMMENT AND ANALYSIS; #39 I CONSIDERED JUDGE EKANS' QUESTION TO BE ESSENTIALLY RHETORICAL BECAUSE I CONSIDERED HIS COMMITMENT TO THE CRIMINAL ENTERPRISE AS TAKING PRIORITY OVER ANY WISH THAT I MIGHT HAVE REGARDING DISCIPLINING BRIANNA JONES.

MS. FRANKLIN: YOUR HONOR, WHAT DOES   WHAT DOES, WHAT IS THE RESPONSIBILITY OF A CITIZEN BEFORE A COURT OF LAW WHO HAS BLATANTLY, OPENLY, REPEATEDLY, NOTORIOUSLY DEFIED THE COURT'S ORDERS OVER AND OVER AND OVER AGAIN? DO THEY STILL COME AND GO AS IF NOTHING?

THE COURT: MISS FRANKLIN, MISS FRANKLIN, MISS FRANKLIN, THE COURT DOES NOT NEED TO BE LECTURED ON THIS.

MS. FRANKLIN: YOUR HONOR, FORGIVE ME, I DON'T MEAN THAT, I'M JUST SAYING YOU ASKED ME, YOUR HONOR, AND THAT'S MY FEELING.

THE COURT: I ASKED YOU WHAT YOU WANT ME TO DO.

MS. FRANKLIN: I THINK SHE SHOULD SUFFER THE PENALTY OF BEING TAKEN INTO CUSTODY FOR HER REPEATED FAILURE TO COMPY WITH THIS COURT'S ORDERS BEGINNING ON OCTOBER 18TH, 2010, AND ENDING ON APRIL THE 6TH, 2011. ALMOST SIX   SIX MONTHS SHE HAS NOT COMPLIED WITH ANY OF THIS COURT'S ORDERS. SHE DOESN'T COMPLY WITH WRITTEN ORDERS; SHE DOESN'T COMPLY WITH ORAL ORDERS.

THE LAST ORDER YOU GAVE HER WAS ON MARCH 18TH, SHE DIDN'T EVEN BOTHER TO COME TO THAT -- -- SHE CAME TO THE HEARING. YOU SAID, DO YOU UNDERSTAND? I WANT A PAYMENT PLAN BY CLOSE OF BUSINESS APRIL 1ST.

I DIDN'T EVEN LOOK AT THE DOCKET UNTIL SUNDAY EVENING BECAUSE I KNEW SHE WASN'T GOING TO FILE ANYTHING BECAUSE SHE HASN'T FILED ANYTHING THE COURT HAS ASKED HER FOR. AND I DON'T KNOW OF ANYONE WHO CAN GET AWAY WITH THAT, YOUR HONOR. I COULDN'T GET AWAY WITH IT IN THE COURT.

COMMENT AND ANALYSIS: #40 JUDGE EKANS WASN'T ABOUT TO SEND BRIANNA JONES BACK TO JAIL. A PROLONGED INCARCERATION OF BRIANNA JONES DIDN'T FIT WITHIN THE ULTIMATE GOAL OF THE CRIMINAL ENTERPRISE TO STRIP ME OF ALL OF THE ATTORNEY'S FEES OWED TO ME.

THE COURT: DO YOU THINK SHE HAS THE MONEY?

MS. FRANKLIN: *YOUR HONOR, ALL I HAVE EVER ASKED FOR IS INFORMATION WITH REGARD TO THE BANKING INSTITUTION, THAT'S WHAT THE OCTOBER 18TH ORDER SAID. I'VE NEVER ASKED FOR MONEY I ASKED FOR, AND YOUR HONOR, SHE'S ALREADY TESTIFIED THAT SHE HAS IT. THAT'S ON THE RECORD. I HAVE JUST ASKED FOR INFORMATION.*

MS. JONES: YOUR HONOR.

THE COURT: HOW DID YOU GET UP HERE? AIRPLANE?

MS. JONES: YES.

THE COURT: HOW DID YOU PAY FOR YOU TICKET?

MS. JONES: I HAVE EVERYTHING RIGHT HERE, YOUR HONOR.

THE COURT: WHAT YOU GOT?

MS. JONES: YOUR HONOR, WHEN SHE FOUND OUT WITH BAR COUNSEL THAT THE SETTLEMENT IN FACT EXISTED -- --

THE COURT: YOU'RE ABOUT TO TALK MY COURT REPORTER TO DEATH. WHAT YOU GOT?

MS. JONES: I WANT TO KNOW WHY DID SHE TAKE ACTION -- --

THE COURT: I WANT TO KNOW WHAT YOU HAVE IN THERE.

MS. JONES; CERTAINLY. IT'S IN MY PURSE. BEAR WITH ME, I HAVE IT, YOUR HONOR. THIS IS FROM THE AIRLINE; IT'S ALSO STATING MY LUGGAGE WAS LOST IN THE FLIGHT.

THE COURT: I DON'T WANT TO SEE THAT.

MS. JONES: BUT THIS IS THE AIR, THE TICKET THAT SHOWS -- --

THE COURT: JUST TURN THE PURSE UPSIDE DOWN, LET'S SEE WHAT YOU GOT IN THERE, JUST TURN IT UPSIDE DOWN. TURN IT UPSIDE DOWN, EMPTY IT.

MS. JONES: THE WALLET OR THE----- THIS WHOLE PURSE?

THE COURT: EVERYTHING.

MS. JONES: AND THE REST IS TOILETRIES, THAT SORT OF THING.

THE COURT: STEP BACK. STEP BACK.

THE COURT: **GO OVER THERE AND SEE IF YOU CAN FIND ANYTHING THAT CAN TELL YOU WHERE YOUR MONEY IS. GO AHEAD.**

COMMENT AND ANALYSIS: #41 THIS WAS THE MOST HUMILIATING EXPERIENCE I HAVE EVER ENDURED AS A MEMBER OF THE NEW YORK AND D.C. BARS FOR 35 YEARS AND AS A TRIAL ATTORNEY FOR ALMOST THAT SAME AMOUNT OF TIME.

MS. JONES: THERE'S A COPY OF MY CREDIT REPORT IN THERE AS WELL, AND ALL MY FINANCIAL -- --

THE COURT: I ASSUME YOUR CREDIT IS SHOT. IF YOU'RE LIVING ON THE GENEROSITY OF SOMEBODY WHO'S DISABLED.

MS. FRANKLIN: YOUR HONOR, ALL I SEE IS PERSONAL ----- PERSONAL INFORMATION. I DON'T SEE ANYTHING ABOUT SETTLEMENT PROCEEDS. I DON'T SEE ANYTHING ABOUT----

COMMENT AND ANALYSIS: #42 THROUGHOUT THE COURT PROCEEDING, JUDGE EKANS DEMONSTRATED JUST HOW ABUSIVE HE COULD BE WITHOUT FEAR OF ADMONISHMENT, PUNISHMENT OR ACCOUNTABILITY TO ANYONE.

ADMITTEDLY, SETTING ALL MY CHRISTIAN UPBRINGING ASIDE, I WANTED TO TELL HIM WHAT'S NOT IN THE BIBLE AND NOT IN SCRIPTURE.

THE COURT: MAYBE YOU SHOULD LOOK.

MS. FRANKLIN: I DON'T SEE ANYTHING ABOUT SETTLEMENT PROCEEDS.

THE COURT: YOU KNOW, LET ME TELL YOU SOMETHING.

MS. FRANKLIN: I SEE PERSONAL BANK -- ---

BARBARA WASHINGTON FRANKLIN

THE COURT:	YOU KNOW, I DON'T KNOW WHAT YOUR EXPERIENCE IS WITH THIS BUT WHEN I HAVE **JUDGMENT CREDITORS** COME IN HERE LOOKIING FOR THEIR MONEY THEY'LL TAKE THAT AND GO THROUGH THAT AND TAKE ANYTHING OF ANY VALUE. THAT -- --
	COMMENT AND ANALYSIS: #43 THIS STATEMENT OF JUDGE EKANS, MORE THAN ANY OTHER, SAID THAT JUDGE EKANS, FOR AN UNKNOWN BENEFIT TO BE DERIVED FROM THE D.C. JUDICIAL AND FBI CRIMINAL ENTERPRISE, WAS READY, WILLING AND ABLE TO LOOK ME IN THE FACE AND PERPETUATE *THE BIG LIE* OF MY BEING A *JUDGMENT CREDITOR* AND, IN SO DOING, WOULD ENABLE THE PERPETUATION OF THE D.C. JUDICIAL AND FBI CRIMINAL ENTERPRISE ORGANIZED AND EXECUTED TO SWINDLE AND DEFRAUD ME OF MY ATTORNEY'S FEES.
MS. FRANKLIN:	WELL, YOUR HONOR -- --
THE COURT:	SEE, YOU'RE EITHER SERIOUS OR YOU'RE NOT SERIOUS.
MS. FRANKLIN:	YOUR HONOR, I'M SERIOUS.
THE COURT:	SEE WHAT YOU GOT.
MS. FRANKLIN:	CAN I MAKE COPIES? BANK BOOK. HER CHECKIING ACCOUNT?
THE COURT:	IS THAT WHAT IT IS?
MS. JONES:	YOUR HONOR.
THE COURT:	I DIDN'T ASK YOU TO SAY ANYTHING. IS THAT A CHECKBOOK?
MS. FRANKLIN:	THIS IS A CHECKBOOK.
THE COURT:	WELL, WOULDN'T YOU WANT TO KNOW WHERE THE BANK IS?
MS. FRANKLIN:	YES, MAY I HAVE -- --THEN CAN I HAVE THE OPPORTUNITY TO------ MAY I HAVE A COPY MADE OF THE CHECK OR -- --
THE COURT:	SURE.
MS. FRANKLIN:	BUT THEN AGAIN, YOUR HONOR - --
THE COURT:	JUST TAKE A CHECK, YOU DON'T NEED A COPY, TAKE A CHECK. I MEAN SHE OWES YOU, IF SHE OWES YOU HOW MANY MILLIONS? JUST TAKE A CHECK.

COMMENT AND ANALYSIS: #44 *IT WAS DURING THIS PROCEEDING THAT I REALIZED HOW DIFFERENT JUDGE EKANS' ABUSIVE ACTIONS AND THE TENOR AND ATMOSPHERE OF THE HEARING WOULD HAVE BEEN HAD THERE BEEN CAMERAS IN THE COURTROOM OR A VIDEO RECORDING OF THE PROCEEDING, SIMILAR TO THE VIDEO RECORDING OF THE GEORGE FLOYED MURDER TAKEN BY A COURAGEOUS AND YOUNG BLACK FEMALE BYSTANDER.*

AT THE HEARING, EKANS PROVED HIMSELF TO BE, ABOVE ALL, A BULLY. BULLIES TEND TO BE RESTRAINED BY CAMERAS, AS WELL AS VIDEO RECORDINGS OF THEIR JUDICIAL ABUSE OF POWER, ANTI-SOCIAL AND CRIMINAL ACTIONS AND BEHAVIOR.

MS. FRANKLIN: YOUR HONOR, I DON'T EVEN KNOW HOW MANY MILLIONS BECAUSE I DON'T KNOW WHAT'S ON   I DON'T KNOW WHAT'S ON HAND.

YOUR HONOR, BUT HERE AGAIN, YOUR HONOR, WE'VE ALREADY ESTABLISHED THAT I BROUGHT THIS TO THE COURT'S ATTENTION, THE CHECKBOOK REFLECTS AN ADDRESS WHERE SHE DOESN'T LIVE.

THE COURT: I BET THAT ACCOUNT NUMBER IS TO A BANK.

MS. FRANKLIN: CORRECT.

THE COURT: RIGHT. WHETHER SHE LIVE THERE OR NOT THE BANK LIVE THERE.

COMMENT AND ANALYSIS: #45 HOW PATHETIC.

THE COURT: SEE, IF YOU WANT TO COLLECT MONEY YOU HAVE TO ACT LIKE YOU WANT TO COLLECT MONEY.

MS. FRANKLIN: YOUR HONOR, YOU MADE THAT CLEAR, I UNDERSTAND WHAT I NEED.

THE COURT: *WELL, I WANT IT, BECAUSE YOU WANT TO STAND THERE AND TELL ME ABOUT WHAT SHE'S DEFYING THE COURT, DEFYING THE COURT, YOU KNOW, YOU WANT A JURY? IF SHE OWES YOU THAT -- --*

COMMENT AND ANALYSIS: #46 *THE COURT RECORD VERIFIES THAT AT NO TIME DURING HIS 9-MONTH ADJUDICATION OF MY LAWSUIT DID JUDGE EKANS ENFORCE JUDGE KATE STARR'S ORDER OF OCTOBETR 18, 2010.*

RATHER, HE CAPITULATED TO THE CO-CONSPIRATORS AND THE GOAL OF THE CRIMINAL ENTERPRISE TO DEFRAUD ME OF THE MILLIONS OF DOLLARS OWED TO ME IN ATTORNEY'S FEES.

MS. JONES:	NO, I KNOW YOU'RE NOT KIDDING, YOUR HONOR.
	YOUR HONOR, SHE HAS A CHECKING ACCOUNT, SHE PUTS MONEY INTO IT.
THE COURT:	WELL, THEN YOU'RE NOT GIVING UP ANYTHING THAT SHE DOESN'T ALREADY HAVE.
	BUT I KNOW THIS, THIS COURT WILL NOT BE TOYED WITH.
MS. JONES:	AND I'M VERY SERIOUS, YOUR HONOR. I'M NOT TOYING WITH THIS COURT; I HAVE UTMOST RESPECT FOR THIS COURT.
THE COURT:	THAT'S WHY YOU ALWAYS COME ON TIME, HUH?
MS. JONES:	AND THAT STATES -- --
MS. FRANKLIN:	YOUR HONOR, MY -- --JUST FOR THE RECORD, THOUGH, YOUR HONOR, MY RESPONSE IS NOT BECAUSE I'M NOT SERIOUS, I'M JUST NOT ACCUSTOMED, I'VE NEVER HAD TO DO THIS BEFORE.
THE COURT:	I HAVE, I'VE HAD TO DO IT BEFORE.
MS. FRANKLIN:	IT'S NEW FOR ME, THAT'S THE ONLY REASON I'M HESITANT.
THE COURT:	I TOOK A MAN'S CADILLAC WHEN IT WAS PARKED OUT THERE IN THE GARAGE.
	NOW, THERE'S--- NO, DON'T CLOSE THAT UP.
MS. JONES:	OH, CERTAINLY.
THE COURT:	THERE'S PURSE THERE WITH A DRIVER'S LICENSE IN IT, YOU CHECK THAT ADDRESS ON THAT IDENTIFICATION CARD AGAINST WHAT YOU SAY IS A BAD ADDRESS ON THE CHECK.
	COMMENT AND ANALYSIS: #47 JUDGE EKANS WAS DETERMINED TO FALSELY CLASSIFY AND DEFINE ME AS A ***JUDGMENT CREDITOR*** WITH THE IMPLIED RESPONSIBILITY OF SEARCHING AND FINDING THE STOLEN AND ILLEGALLY CONFISCATED SETTLEMENT PROCEEDS.
MS. JONES:	YOUR HONOR, THAT CREDIT REPORT STATES, IS MOST RECENT, THAT THERE WAS A CHANGE FOR THE POST OFFICE BOX AS OF-- --
THE COURT:	MISS, HAVE I ASKED YOU ANYTHING?
MS.. JONES:	YOUR HONOR, I'D LIKE TO -- --

THE ODYSSEY OF JUDICIAL CORRUPTION

THE COURT: YOU KNOW WHAT?

MS. JONES: I'M SORRY. I'M SORRY.

THE COURT: YOU KNOW WHAT, YOU CAN SIT DOWN BUT YOU MUST BE QUIET. LOOK, THERE'S A PURSE RIGHT THERE WITH I.D. IN IT.

MS. FRANKLIN: RIGHT HERE?

THE COURT: NO, SEE THAT PURSE, THE GUCCI, YEAH, THAT ONE, GO THROUGH THERE AND GET THE I.D. AND FIND OUT WHAT THE OTHER ADDRESSES SHE HAS.

MS. FRANKLIN: **YOUR HONOR, SINCE I, AGAIN I'M NOT A JUDGMENT CREDITOR IN THE NORMAL SENSE OF THE TERM**, IS IT POSSIBLE THAT BASED ON WHAT SHE HAD ADVISED THE COURT, THE SETTLEMENT AGREEMENT, THAT A JUDGMENT COULD BE ISSUED FOR A PORTION OF THAT SETTLEMENT AGREEMENT THAT SHE SIGNED? **BECAUSE I DON'T HAVE ANY JUDGMENT, IT'S NO WAY I CAN ATTACH ANYTHING AT THIS JUNCTURE.**

THE COURT: WHERE IS THE ESTATE? IT'S DOWN IN FLORIDA, RIGHT?

COMMENT AND ANALYSIS: #48 I AM NOT A JUDGMENT CREDITOR. I SAID IT. EKANS HEARD IT, AND THEN DISMISSED IT. IT DID NOT FIT WITHIN THE CONFINES OF THE MISSION OF THE CRIMINAL ENTERPRISE HE WAS COMMITTED TO CHAMPIONING AND CO-EXECUTING AND CO-ORCHESTRATING.

MS. FRANKLIN: THE ESTATE IS CLOSED. SHE'S REALLY -- --SHE'S REFERRING TO SHE'S REFERRING.

THE COURT: IS IT IN FLORIDA? IS IT IN FLORIDA?

MS. FRANKLIN: YES, YOUR HONOR, I'M SORRY.

THE COURT: DID SHE HAVE ANY MONEY, ANY IN REM JURISDICTION IN THIS CITY?

MS. FRANKLIN: **I WOULD HAVE NO WAY OF KNOWING. THERE WOULD HAVE TO BE AN INVESTIGATION. I WOULD HAVE NO WAY OF KNOWING HOW TO ANSWER THAT.**

COMMENT AND ANALYSIS: #49 I REMINDED JUDGE EKANS OF THE NEED FOR AN INVESTIGATION AGAIN. EKANS NEEDED TO KNOW THAT I WASN'T AFRAID TO ASK FOR WHAT WAS NEEDED FOR PURPOSES OF JUSTICE AND THE RULE OF LAW, EVEN THOUGH I KNEW MY REQUEST WAS GOING NOWHERE.

THE COURT: IS THAT AMERICAN EXPRESS? I'D GET THE CREDIT CARD NUMBERS. THAT WILL TELL YOU WHETHER SHE'S GOT SOME MONEY OR NOT BECAUSE THEY LIKE TO GET PAID.

MS. FRANKLIN: NO, YOUR HONOR, IT'S NOT AMERICN EXPRESS. IT'S BANK OF AMERICA.

THE COURT: THAT'S GOOD, THAT WILL GIVE YOU A NUMBER. YOU SEE, IT'S UNTHINKABLE TO ME THAT SOMEBODY WOULD LIVE 16 YEARS HAND TO MOUTH IF THEY'VE GOT THE KIND OF MONEY SHE'S TALKING ABOUT, BUT THIS LADY AIN'T NEVER LOOK POOR TO ME, NOT ONE DAY SHE EVER COME IN HERE, SO I DON'T THINK SHE'S JUST LIVING ON THE GENEROSITY OF OTHERS, I THINK THAT SHE HAS ACCESS AND WHAT YOU NEED TO DO, IF YOU'RE GOING TO BE SERIOUS, IS GET IT.

COMMENT AND ANALYSIS: #50 ALTHOUGH BY THIS TIME I CONSIDERED JUDGE EKANS AS GRAND MARSHAL OF THE CRIMINAL ENTERPRISE AND HAD BEEN GIVEN SPECIFIC MARCHING ORDERS.

MS. JONES: YOUR HONOR, I DO NOT HAVE ACCESS. I'M SORRY.

THE COURT: YOU KNOW WHAT, YOU GOT ONE MORE TIME. MISS, I'M SERIOUS.

MS. JONES: I UNDERSTAND.

(PAUSE.

MS. FRANKLIN: YOUR HONOR, THIS IS THE   FOR THE RECORD YOU ASKED HER TO FILE AND TO BRING INTO COURT, THIS IS A BANK OF AMERICA STATEMENT, AND POA ON THE STATEMENT IS TED MINOR, LAST POSTING WAS 3/15/2011, AND IT'S PAGES FRONT AND BACK I WOULD NEED OBVIOUSLY I CAN'T COPY ALL OF THIS, I WOULD NEED A COPIER BECAUSE THIS IS WHAT YOUR HONOR HAD ASKED HER, THESE ARE THE DOCUMENTS THAT YOUR HONOR HAD ASKED HER TO BRING.

MS. JONES: THOSE ARE COPIES, SO SHE COULD HAVE THOSE, I BROUGHT THEM.

MS. FRANKLIN: OKAY, THAT'S FINE.

THE COURT: THERE YOU GO.

(THEREUPON, THE COURT ENGAGED IN A TELEPHONE CONVERSATION; OFF THE RECORD.

COMMENT AND ANALYSIS: #51 MY INSTINCTS TOLD ME THAT PERHAPS A JUDICIAL CO-CONSPIRATOR WAS CHECKING IN TO SEE HOW THE "FAMILY FEUD" HEARING WAS GOING; EITHER JUDGE MANDARIN OR JUDGE SKINNER CALLING. THE CONTACT WOULD BE SIMILAR TO THE FORMER CHIEF JUDGE'S COURT HALLWAY APPEARANCE DURING THE MARCH 18, 2011 COURT HEARING PRECEDED BY EKANS' THROWING ME AND BRIANNA OUT OF THE COURTROOM AND INTO THE COURT HALLWAY, NOW SERVING AS THE WOLF'S LAIR IN THE PERSON OF SENIOR JUDGE AND FORMER CHIEF JUDGE GEORGE SKINNER.

MS. FRANKLIN:	YOUR HONOR, THIS LAST ONE I WOULD NEED A COPY OF. CAUSE IT'S A FRONT AND BACK.
THE COURT:	WHAT IS IT?
MS. FRANKLIN:	ITS' ---- SHE SAID IT'S A CREDIT REPORT.
THE COURT:	YOU CAN HAVE IT, MY COMPLIMENT.
MS. FRANKLIN:	THANK YOU, YOUR HONOR.
THE COURT:	YOU DON'T WANT IT?
MS. FRANKLIN:	YES, YOUR HONOR, I SAID, THANK YOU, YOUR HONOR.
	YOUR HONOR, AGAIN I APOLOGIZE, JUST NEW EXPERIENCE AND I'M MOVING THROUGH IT.

COMMENT AND ANALYSIS: #52 THE DOCUMENTS PROVIDED BY BRIANNA JONES WERE ALL OF NO VALUE WITH REGARD TO THE WHEREABOUTS OF THE SETTLEMENT PROCEEDS.

JUDGE EKANS WAS WELL AWARE OF THIS WASTE OF PRECIOUS TIME FOR WHICH I WAS NOT BEING COMPENSATED.

AT THE END OF THE DAY, WE BOTH KNEW WHO HAD CONTROL OF THE SETTLEMENT PROCEEDS.

THE COURT:	WELL, YOU KNOW WHAT, THIS IS ONE OF THE UGLIEST THINGS I DO, YOU KNOW, I'VE -- -- PEOPLE ASK ME, OH DO YOU ENJOY YOUR JOB? NO, YOU DON'T UNDERSTAND THE NATURE OF IT. THIS IS NOT WORK THAT A PERSON ENJOYS BUT SOMETIMES I CAN GET SOME SENSE OF SATISFACTION IF I THINK I'M BRINGING A FAIRNESS AND JUSTICE TO OUR LEGAL PROCESS.
	I'VE NOT HAD A REAL GOOD SENSE ABOUT IT IN THIS CASE. I REALLY NOT. THIS HAS BEEN VERY FRUSTRATING FOR ME AS I'M SURE IT HAS BEEN FOR YOU, BOTH OF YOU, BUT YOU KNOW, AT SOME POINT YOU HAVE TO MOVE, YOU CAN'T JUST TREAD WATER, YOU HAVE TO MOVE. AND -- --AND THAT'S USUALLY WHERE THINGS START TO GET UGLY.

BARBARA WASHINGTON FRANKLIN

BUT I HAVE IN MY CAREER AS A JUDICIAL OFFICER SERVED IN THE DISTRICT OF COLUMBIA, I'VE SEEN GROWN MEN CRY WHEN I'VE THROWN THEM AND THEIR FAMILIES OUT ON THE STREET BECAUSE THEY'RE NOT PAYING RENT. I'VE SEEN WOMEN IN TEARS AND JUST WRETCHED BECAUSE I'VE TAKEN THEIR CHILDREN AWAY FROM THEM RIGHT HERE IN THE COURTROOM AND GIVEN THEM TO CHILD WELFARE. I'VE SEEN -- -- I'VE SEEN UGLY, UGLY,UGLY UGLY THINGS, NOT TO MENTION THE FACT THAT I'VE PROBABLY GOT UPWARDS OF THREE OR FOUR HUNDRED MEN AND WOMEN IN PRISONS ALL OVER THIS COUNTRY.

SO THIS CAN BE A VERY UGLY JOB, AND THE ONLY TIME THAT I TAKE ANY SATISFACTION FROM IT IS WHEN I CAN LEAVE AND FEEL THAT I'VE DONE SOMETHING TO TRY AND GIVE THE PUBLIC SOME CONFIDENCE THAT THE COURT SYSTEM IS A SYSTEM THAT STRIVES TO BE FAIR AND TO BRING ABOUT SOME SENSE OF JUSTICE IN OUR COMMUNTY.

AND I DON'T KNOW WHAT'S BETWEEN THE TWO OF YOU, BUT I KNOW THAT SHE'S ENTERED A SETTLEMENT, WHERE SHE'S PROMISED TO PAY YOU MONEY, AND THAT SOMEBODY HAS BEEN REALLY ABUSING MY TIME IN THIS COURT AND I'M SICK OF IT, I'M NOT GOING TO HAVE ANYMORE AND IF WE NEED TO GET REAL UGLY HERE WE'LL JUST GET REAL UGLY.

NOW, YOU SHOULD HAVE ENOUGH INFORMATION TO DO YOUR INVESTIGATION AND FIND OUT IF THERE'S ANY MONEY, WHERE IT IS, AND HOW YOU CAN SEIZE IT.

MS. FRANKLIN:	YOUR HONOR, I'M I'M PREPARED TO DO WHAT I NEED TO DO.
THE COURT:	GOOD. GOOD. WE'LL SET THIS CASE OVER FOR A STATUS HEARING IN ABOUT 30, 45 DAYS AND SEE WHAT YOU GOT.
MS. FRANKLIN:	THANK YOU, YOUR HONOR.
MS. JONES:	YOUR HONOR, I HAVE OTHER DOCUMENTS SHE'S WELCOME TO HAVE.
THE COURT:	WELL, GIVE THEM TO HER.

I'M GOING TO OFFER YOU A DATE FOR A STATUS HEARING OF FRIDAY THE 17TH OF JUNE, YOU COME IN HERE AT 11 O'CLOCK IN THE MORNING AND LET ME KNOW WHAT PROGRESS YOU'VE MADE, AND IF YOU WANT TO FILE A SUIT DOWN IN FLORIDA ,YOU GO AHEAD AND FILE IT, IF YOU WANT TO HIRE AN INVESTIGATOR TO FOLLOW UP ON THAT INFORMATION YOU GO AHEAD AND DO THAT.

COMMENT AND ANALYSIS: #53 *JUDGE EKANS KNEW THAT WITHOUT A COURT JUDGMENT I WOULD NOT BE ABLE TO SEARCH FOR THE SETTLEMENT PROCEEDS. NEVERTHELESS, HE SENT ME ON WHAT WAS NOTHING MORE THAN A WILD-GOOSE CHASE TO SEARCH FOR THE SETTLEMENT PROCEEDS IN ABSENCE OF A COURT JUDGMENT. HE REMAINED COMMITTED TO THE MISSION OF THE HISTORIC D.C. JUDICIAL AND FBI CONSPIRACY AND CRIMINAL ENTERPRISE THAT CONTINUED TO FLOURISH UNIMPEDED BY ANYONE AND BY ANY AUTHORITY.*

AGAIN, I WAS REMINDED OF SAINT LUKE'S DESCRIPTION OF THE UNJUST JUDGE.

MS. FRANKLIN:	JUNE 17TH, AT 11, YOUR HONOR?
THE COURT:	AT 11, JUNE 17TH AT 11.
	ALL RIGHT, THESE PARTIES ARE EXCUSED.
MS. FRANKLIN:	THANK YOU, YOUR HONOR.
MS. JONES:	THANK YOU, YOUR HONOR.
THE COURT:	THANK YOU VERY MUCH.

(THEREUPON, THE PROCEEDINGS WERE ADJOURNED AT 12:40 P.M.)

BARBARA WASHINGTON FRANKLIN

SUPERIOR COURT OF THE DISTRICT OF COLUMBIA
CIVIL DIVISION
WASHINGTON, D.C.

THE HONORABLE MATTHEW D. EKANS, ASSOCIATE JUDGE, PRESIDING

THE FOLLOWING ARE EXCERPTS OF THE OFFICIAL COURT TRANSCRIPT OF THE
JUNE 17, 2011 PROCEEDING
ANNOTATED BY THE AUTHOR'S PERTINENT COMMENTARY AND ANALYSIS

JUNE 17, 2011

P R O C E E D I N G S

COMMENT AND ANALYSIS: #1 THE JUNE 17, 2011 COURT HEARING WOULD
PROVE TO BE A TUTORIAL AND MASTER CLASS IN THE BUILDING BLOCKS OF D.C.
JUDICIAL FRAUD, THEFT, CORRUPTION AND EXTORTION –UNAPOLOGETIC AND
UNREDACTED. JUDGE EKANS WOULD PROVE TO BE THE MASTER TEACHER OF
THE CLASS AS EVIDENCED BY HIS UNRELENTING, TOTAL, INTENTIONAL AND
PURPOSEFUL SILENCE AND REFUSAL TO ADDRESS MY LAWSUIT'S DOMINANT
ISSUES OF D.C. JUDICIAL AND FBI FRAUD, THEFT, CORRUPTION AND EXTORTION.
IN EKANS' CLASS, I WOULD LEARN THAT THESE ISSUES ARE PROHIBITED ISSUES
AND WILL NOT, UNDER ANY CIRCUMSTANCES, BE ADDRESSED BY D.C. COURT
JUDGES. PERIOD.

THIS PRACTICE FALLS WITHIN **THE UNSPOKEN RULE THAT NO D.C. COURT JUDGE
WILL REPORT ON THE MISCONDUCT OF ANOTHER JUDGE, NO MATTER HOW
EGREGIOUS THE JUDGE'S BEHAVIOR**. THIS UNLAWFUL PRACTICE, ANAETHEMA
TO THE RULE OF LAW, IS DECEPTIVELY CALLED *MAINTAINING THE INTEGRITY OF
THE COURT* AND IS USED TO DULL AND ANESTHETIZE THE SENSES OF PARTY
LITIGANTS AND THE UNSUSPECTING GENERAL PUBLIC. IN THAT REGARD, *THE
CORRUPT D.C. COURT JUDGES PROVE EVERY DAY THAT THEY ARE ABOVE THE LAW
BECAUSE THEY ARE THE LAW.*

THE ODYSSEY OF JUDICIAL CORRUPTION

DURING THE HEARING, I IDENTIFIED BY NAME, POSITION AND AFFILIATION BETH HOLLISTER, WASHINGTON ABC TELEVISION NEWS ANCHOR AND KEY CO-CONSPIRATOR OF THE HISTORIC CONSPIRACY AND CRIMINAL ENTERPRISE, SCHEME AND SWINDLE TO DEFRAUD ME OF AN ESTIMTED $50 MILLION IN ATTORNEY'S FEES. I ALSO IDENTIFIED CERTAIN OF BETH HOLLISTER'S HIGH-PROFILE WASHINGTON FRIENDS THAT SHE ENLISTED TO ASSIST HER IN THE MASSIVE SCHEME TO DEFRAUD ME OF MY ATTORNEY'S FEES. THESE KNOWN INDIVIDUALS THUS BECAME CO-CONSPIRATORS IN THE MASSIVE SWINDLE.

JUDGE EKANS' TOTAL SILENCE WITH REGARD TO MY TESTIMONY OF THE ROLE OF BETH HOLLISTER AND OTHER CO-CONSPIRATORS WAS SIMPLY EVIDENCE OF HIS ALL-IN COMPLICITY IN THE CRIMINAL ENTERPRISE AND HIS COMMITMENT TO HIS FELLOW CO-CONSPIRATOR D.C. JUDICIAL COLLEAGUES.

FOR MOST OF THE HEARING, EKANS KEPT HIS HEAD BOWED. HE WAS ALSO CAREFUL NOT TO MENTION HOLLISTER'S NAME OR QUESTION ME WITH REGARD TO HOLLISTER'S ROLE IN THE CRIMINAL ENTERPRISE.

JUDGE EKANS' SEALED LIPS FOR THE BULK OF THE HEARING CONFIRMED THAT I WAS DEALING, NOT WITH A COURT OF LAW, BUT RATHER WITH A KANGAROO COURT RIGHT IN THE HEART OF THE NATION'S CAPITAL.

IT WAS CLEAR THAT EKANS SAW HIMSELF AS ON THE SIDE OF BETH HOLLISTER, A KEY CO-CONSPIRATOR, AND SAW ME AS A POWERLESS PARTY LITIGANT IN THIS UNIQUE SCENARIO OF A D.C. JUDICIAL AND FBI CRIMINAL ENTERPRISE. HIS ROLE WAS TO PROTECT HER AS HE HAD PROTECTED THE OTHER CO-CONSPIRATORS OF THE CRIMINAL ENTERPRISE. AND THAT HE DID TO THE LETTER.

AFTER ALL, THERE WERE NO CAMERAS IN THE COURTROOM, NO VIDEO RECORDINGS OF THE PROCEEDING, AND NO ONE WOULD EVER BOTHER TO READ THE COURT TRANSCRIPT OF HIS INTENTIONAL AND ABUSIVE INACTION PERMITTED BY *ABSOLUTE JUDICIAL DISCRETION* IN THE HANDS OF A CORRUPT D.C. COURT JUDGE, EVIDENCING HIS OBVIOUS ACTIVE COMPLICITY IN THE HISTORIC CRIMINAL ENTERPRISE UNDERWAY IN COURTROOM 517 OF D.C. SUPERIOR COURT, ADJOINING COURT HALLWAYS, PRIVATE D.C. COURT JUDGES' CHAMBERS AND UNDISCLOSED WASHINGTON AREA HOTEL SUITES WHERE BRIANNA JONES HAD BEEN SUMMONED TO MEET MORE THAN ONCE WITH CO-CONSPIRATOR "OFFICIALS."

BARBARA WASHINGTON FRANKLIN

THE CLERK:	BARBARA WASHINGTON FRANKLIN VERSUS BRIANNA JONES, 2009 CA 4417 AND IN THE MATTER OF BRIANNA JONES, 2011 CCC 1. PARTIES, PLEASE COME FORWARD AND STATE YOUR NAMES FOR THE RECORD.
MS. FRANKLIN:	GOOD AFTERNOON, YOUR HONOR. BARBARA WASHINGTON FRANKLIN, YOUR HONOR.
MS. JONES:	GOOD AFTERNOON -- --
MS. FRANKLIN:	APPEARING PRO SE, YOUR HONOR. SORRY.
MS. JONES:	GOOD AFTERNOON, YOUR HONOR. BRIANNA JONES, PRO SE AT THIS TIME.
THE COURT:	I DON'T KNOW WHAT WE'RE GOING TO DO BUT I CAN TELL YOU THAT I HAVEN'T HAD A BREAK SINCE 9:30. SO, IF WE'RE GOING TO DO ANYTHING MORE THAN JUST GREET EACH OTHER AND WISH EACH OTHER WELL IN OUR FUTURE LIVES, I'M PROBABLY GOING TO HAVE TO PUT THIS OFF UNTIL LATER IN THE DAY WHEN I CAN REFRESH MYSELF SOMEWHAT. LET ME HEAR FROM YOU, MS. FRANKLIN. WHAT DO YOU WANT TO DO?
MS. FRANKLIN:	REALLY, YOUR HONOR, YOU ASKED ME TO DO A SEARCH OF ASSETS AND COME INTO THE COURT WITH WHATEVER INFORMATION I COULD.
THE COURT:	RIGHT.
MS. FRANKLIN:	AND I JUST PUT MY FINDINGS IN A WRITTEN STATEMENT WHICH I WAS GOING TO ASK YOUR HONOR'S INDULGENCE TO JUST READ INTO THE RECORD. IT'S ALL OF TWO MINUTES, THREE MINUTES. I CAN SUMMARIZE OR GIVE YOU SOME OF THE HIGHLIGHTS. IN OTHER WORDS, YOUR HONOR, I'D -- --
THE COURT:	HIGHLIGHTS OR LOWLIGHTS? IF THEY'RE HIGHLIGHTS WE COULD PROBABLY MOVE FORWARD.
MS. FRANKLIN:	WELL, I THINK THEY'RE HIGHLIGHTS, YOUR HONOR.
THE COURT:	OKAY.
MS. FRANKLIN:	I MEAN, AS I SAID, YOUR HONOR, I HAD ---- YEAH. I'D PREFER TO READ INTO THE RECORD BUT GIVEN -- --
THE COURT:	NO, GO AHEAD.
MS. FRANKLIN:	--- GIVEN YOUR HONOR'S -- --
THE COURT:	GO AHEAD.
MS. FRANKLIN:	IS IT ALL RIGHT?
THE COURT:	YEAH, GO AHEAD.

MS. FRANKLIN: ALL RIGHT, BECAUSE I'M ALSO SENSITIVE TO YOUR HONOR'S NEED TO TAKE A BREAK. AT THE LAST COURT HEARING ON APRIL 4TH, 2011 YOUR HONOR ASKED ME TO SEE WHAT INFORMATION I COULD FIND WITH REGARD TO LOCATING THE SETTLEMENT PROCEEDS THAT ARE THE SUBJECT OF THESE PROCEEDINGS. IN CARRYING OUT THE COURT'S DIRECTIVE, I CONTACTED A LOCAL INVESTIGATIVE FIRM TO CONDUCT ON MY BEHALF A SEARCH OF THE DEFENDANT'S ASSETS.

THE FIRM, WASHINGTON PROCESS SERVICES, INFORMED ME THAT, IN THE **ABSENCE OF A COURT JUDGMENT ON MY BEHALF**, THEY WOULD NOT BE ABLE TO PERFORM THE REQUESTED SEARCH OF DEFENDANT'S ASSETS. WASHINGTON PROCESS FURTHER INFORMED ME THAT THE FINANCIAL MODERNIZATION ACT OF 2000, A D.C. LAW, PROHIBITS THE SEARCH OF ANOTHER'S ASSETS IN ABSENCE OF A COURT JUDGMENT. MOREOVER, I WAS INFORMED THAT THE PENALTY FOR THE VIOLATION OF THIS LAW IS $10,000 PER INFRACTION. THIS INFORMATION WAS ALSO PROVIDED TO ME IN WRITING IN THEIR LETTER DATED MAY 2ND, 2011, AND I DO HAVE A COPY FOR THE COURT, IF NECESSARY. THEREFORE, IN THE ABSENCE OF A COURT JUDGMENT, I HAVE BEEN PRECLUDED FROM MAKING A SEARCH OF THE DEFENDANT'S ASSETS.

COMMENT AND ANALYSIS: #2 JUDGE EKANS, TRUE TO HIS CHARACTERISTIC JUDICIAL RUTHLESSNESS AND ABUSIVENESS, HAD SENT ME ON A FOOL'S ERRAND. HE KNEW FULL WELL THAT IN ABSENCE OF A COURT JUDGMENT, I WAS LEGALLY PRECLUDED AND PROHIBITED FROM SEARCHING FOR THE ASSETS OF BRIANNA JONES. EKANS' ACTION DEMONSTRATED THAT, IN ABSENCE OF THE RULE OF LAW AND JUDICIAL INTEGRITY OR ANY SENSE OF BASIC HUMAN DECENCY AND MORALITY, HE WOULD DO WHATEVER WAS WITHIN HIS CONTROL TO KEEP THE CRIMINAL ENTERPRISE ON TRACK. MOREOVER, HE WAS WELL ARMED WITH HIS *ABSOLUTE POWER OF JUDICIAL DISCRETION*.

***

MS. FRANKLIN: MY LAST STEP IN LOCATING THE SETTLEMENT PROCEEDS WAS TO GO BACK AND CAREFULLY READ AND REVIEW IN GREAT DETAIL AND WITH GREAT THOROUGHNESS THE ENTIRE CONTENTS OF MY EXTENSIVE 17-YEAR-OLD PLEADINGS, CASE NOTES, COURT ORDERS, AND CORRESPONDENCE FILE. AT THE LAST COURT HEARING, YOUR HONOR WILL RECALL THE DEFENDANT WAS SWORN IN AND ANSWERED QUESTIONS POSED BY THE COURT REGARDING THE SETTLEMENT AGREEMENT. THE DEFENDANT SPECIFICALLY TESTIFIED UNDER OATH AND IN OPEN COURT THAT SHE SETTLED THE CASE FOR $34 MILLION, THAT SHE WAS NOT REPRESENTED BY A LAWYER, AND THAT SHE WAS PRO SE.

BARBARA WASHINGTON FRANKLIN

MS. FRANKLIN: YOUR HONOR THEN ASKED, SO YOU NEGOTIATED A SETTLEMENT FOR SOME $30 MILLION WITHOUT A LAWYER, RIGHT? IS THAT WHAT YOU TOLD ME? THE DEFENDANT ANSWERED, THAT'S CORRECT. WELL, DEFENDANT'S RESPONSE WITH REGARD TO THE NEGOTIATION OF THE SETTLEMENT AGREEMENT IS IN CONTRADICTION TO THE FACTUAL INFORMATION SET FORTH IN MY EXTENSIVE FILE REGARDING THE FACTS OF THE CASE AND MORE SPECIFICALLY, THE CIRCUMSTANTIAL EVIDENCE REGARDING THE NEGOTIATION OF THE SETTLEMENT AGREEMENTS. **MY CASE FILES REVEAL THAT THE DEFENDANT REPEATEDLY INFORMED ME THAT THE SETTLEMENT AGREEMENTS IN THIS CASE WERE NEGOTIATED AND SETTLED BY THE DEFENDANT'S CLOSE PERSONAL FRIEND, MS. BETH HOLLISTER, THE WASHINGTON NEWS ANCHOR OF ABC CHANNEL 7 NEWS, AND MS. HOLLISTER'S ATTORNEYS, INCLUDING ATTORNEY RICK ROBINSON.** (REFERRED TO BY THE MEDIA AS A WASHINGTON SUPERLAWYER)

MS. HOLLISTER'S UNWELCOME, UNWANTED, AND UNNEEDED INTERFERENCE AND INVOLVEMENT IN THE CASE BEGAN SHORTLY AFTER I FILED THE CIVIL ACTION ON BEHALF OF THE DEFENDANT IN BROWARD COUNTY CIRCUIT COURT IN FORT LAUDERDALE IN MAY OF 1996. AFTER DEFENDANT'S ATTEMPTS TO OBTAIN FINANCIAL SUPPORT FROM FAMILY MEMBERS FAILED, DEFENDANT CONTACTED ME AND SAID THAT MS. HOLLISTER WAS OFFERING TO PAY ME $10,000 TO BE USED FOR THE NECESSARY EXPENSES TO PURSUE AND MAINTAIN THE LITIGATION. I REFUSED MS. HOLLISTER'S OFFER WHICH REQUIRED THAT MS. HOLLISTER PAY THE $10,000 TO ME DIRECTLY.

I TOLD DEFENDANT THAT I WOULD NOT ANSWER TO TWO MASTERS, MEANING DEFENDANT AND MS. HOLLISTER. HOWEVER, I SUGGESTED THAT DEFENDANT HAVE MS. HOLLISTER PAY HER AND THEN DEFENDANT PAY ME. DEFENDANT SAID THAT SUCH AN ARRANGEMENT WAS NOT ACCEPTABLE TO MS. HOLLISTER AND SO NO MONEY WAS PAID TO ME. THROUGHOUT THE PENDENCY OF THIS 14, 16-YEAR CASE THE DEFENDANT HAS MADE NO FINANCIAL CONTRIBUTION TO THE MAINTENANCE OF THE CASE WHATSOEVER NOR HAVE I EVER BEEN PAID A DIME FOR MY SERVICES AND MY OUT-OF-POCKET EXPENSES. SOMETIME LATER DEFENDANT INFORMED ME THAT MS. HOLLISTER WANTED ME OFF THE CASE. DEFENDANT ALSO SAID THAT MS. HOLLISTER WAS THREATENING TO TAKE ME TO THE BAR IF I REMAINED ON THE CASE AND I RECALL RESPONDING, "FOR WHAT? I HAVE NO RELATIONSHIP WITH HER."

THE ODYSSEY OF JUDICIAL CORRUPTION

MS. FRANKLIN: DEFENDANT SAID THAT MS. HOLLISTER BOASTED AND BRAGGED ABOOUT HER FRIENDS ON THE BENCH OF D.C. SUPERIOR COURT THAT WOULD ALLOW HER TO PREVAIL NO MATTER WHAT I DID. I IGNORED THESE ATTEMPTS TO INTIMIDATE ME BECAUSE OF MY REFUSAL TO GET OUT OF THE CASE AND MOVED FORWARD WITH THE CASE. HOWEVER, NOT EVER HAVING FACED SUCH A SITUATION AS THIS BEFORE, I SOUGHT THE LEGAL ADVICE AND COUNSEL OF MY BROTHER, ATTORNEY BRADLEY ROSS WASHINGTON, JR. HE ADVISED ME THAT THE SITUATION I HAD DESCRIBED WAS ONE OF ECONOMIC INTERFERENCE BY MS. HOLLISTER. HE RECOMMENDED THAT I SEND HER A LETTER TO THAT EFFECT.

WITH REGARD TO MS. HOLLISTER'S ROLE IN THIS CASE, MY CASE FILES ALSO REVEAL THAT ACCORDING TO DEFENDANT, MS. HOLLISTER MADE A TRIP TO THE COURTHOUSE IN FORT LAUDERDALE IMMEDIATELY FOLLOWING MY FILING OF THE CIVIL ACTION IN MAY 1996 IN ORDER TO GET A COPY OF THE COMPLAINT. FURTHER, ACCORDING TO THE DEFENDANT, MS. HOLLISTER THEREAFTER MADE NUMEROUS TRIPS TO FLORIDA TO CONFER WITH DEFENDANT ABOUT THE STATUS OF THE CASE. DEFENDANT ALSO INFORMED ME THAT SHE ON OCCASION TRAVELED TO WASHINGTON WITH MS. HOLLISTER IN HER PRIVATELY CHARTERED PLANE.

ACCORDING TO MY CASE FILES, DEFENDANT ALSO INFORMED ME THAT MS. HOLLISTER COACHED, COUNSELED, AND DIRECTED DEFENDANT NOT TO MEET WITH ME IN MY OFFICE NOR TO CALL ME AT MY HOME OR OFFICE. DEFENDANT INFORMED ME THAT WHILE A GUEST IN MS. HOLLISTER'S HOME, MS. HOLLISTER HAD HER CONFER WITH HER ATTORNEYS, INCLUDING ATTORNEY RICK ROBINSON REGARDING THE CASE. SHE ALSO INFORMED ME THAT MS. HOLLISTER ENGAGED IN THE NEGOTIATION OF THE SETTLEMENT AGREEMENT WITH THE ATTORNEY FOR THE ESTATE, JEFFREY BRETT WINSLOW, A PARTNER OF THE LAW FIRM OF ADAGIO & MANDEL. DEFENDANT ALSO STATED THAT MS. HOLLISTER ARRANGED FOR DEFENDANT TO MEET HER FRIEND, DR. WILLARD MANCHESTER (PHONETIC SP.), IN MS. HOLLISTER'S HOME.

FROM 1995 UNTIL 1998, DR. MANCHESTER WAS THE CHAIRMAN OF THE FIRST D.C. FINANCIAL CONTROL BOARD. THE D.C. FINANCIAL CONTROL BOARD MAINTAINED BUDGET AUTHORITY OVER THE D.C. LOTTERY. THE D.C. LOTTERY HELD THE LARGEST ASSET OF THE ESTATE IN THE AMOUNT OF $40 MILLION. THE LUMP SUM AMOUNT WAS ULTIMATELY PAID BY THE D.C. LOTTERY TO THE ESTATE PURSUANT TO A D.C. COURT ORDER ISSUED BY JUDGE RICHARD MANDARIN ON MAY 5TH, 1997.

MS. FRANKLIN: ON OR ABOUT FEBRUARY 22ND, 1999, THE DEFENDANT ADVISED ME THAT SHE WAS IN NEGOTIATION WITH MS. HOLLISTER'S PAYMENT FOR NEGOTIATING THE SETTLEMENT AGREEMENT. MY CASE NOTES INDICATE THAT THIS WAS ON THE EVE OF MS. HOLLISTER'S ASSUMPTION OF HER ON-AIR POSITION WITH CHANNEL 7 NEWS. MS. HOLLISTER WAS SCHEDULED TO BEGIN HER CONTRACT ON MONDAY, FEBRUARY 22ND 1999 ON THE 11:00 P.M. NEWS AND WANTED TO RESOLVE THE ISSUE OF HER PAYMENT WITH THE DEFENDANT PRIOR TO THAT TIME. *MY REASON FOR NOT TAKING ACTION AGAINST MS. HOLLISTER AND HER ATTORNEYS AND THE ATTORNEYS FOR THE ESTATE WAS BECAUSE I WAS OVERWHELMED AND TRAUMATIZED BY MY HUSBAND'S DECLINING, RAPIDLY DECLINGING HEALTH, EXCUSE ME, AND HIS EVENTUAL DEMISE.*

LASTLY, THE DEFENDANT INFORMED ME THAT MS. HOLLISTER TOOK A DEEP SIGH OF RELIEF AFTER READING MY LAWSUIT FILED AGAINST DEFENDANT IN MARCH 2009. MS. HOLLISTER KNEW THAT I COULD HAVE EASILY AND HONESTLY INCLUDED HER IN THE ALLEGATIONS OF THE COMPLAINT OR INCLUDED HER AS A CO-DEFENDANT.

MS. JONES: YOUR HONOR, MAY I SPEAK?

MS. FRANKLIN: YOUR HONOR, I'M GOING TO TAKE THE OPPORTUNITY TO STOP AT THIS POINT BECAUSE I SAID TWO TO THREE MINUTES AND I'M GOING BEYOND THAT. BUT IT WOULD TAKE ANOTHER TWO TO THREE MINUTES FOR ME TO FINISH. BUT, YOUR HONOR, WITHOUT THIS INFORMATION PROVIDED TO YOU WE'RE JUST GOING AROUND THE MOUNTAIN AND I'M FULLY AWARE THAT THE COURT HAS BEEN AWARE ALL ALONG THAT THERE ARE GAPS OF INFORMATION.

WHAT I'M GETTING AT, YOUR HONOR, IS THAT GIVEN THE FACT THAT THE FLORIDA BAR HAS NOW LAUNCHED AN INVESTIGAION OF THIS MATTER THAT'S ONGOING, BUT WHAT I WOULD LIKE TO DO IS TO SUBPOENA INTO COURT THOSE INDIVIDUALS WHO WERE EITHER INSTRUMENTAL IN THE PREPARATION AND NEGOTIATION OF THE SETTLEMENT AGREEMENTS, AS WELL AS THOSE INDIVIDUALS WHO WOULD KNOW OF THE CURRENT WHEREABOUTS OF THE MONEY. SO, I'M REFERRING NOW TO BANK OF AMERICA BECAUSE THE DEFENDANT HAS TESTIFIED OVER AND OVER AGAIN THAT SHE'S MET WITH BANK OF AMERICA OFFICIALS. IF ANYONE SHOULD HAVE COPIES OF THE SETTLEMENT AGREEMENT, IT OUGHT TO BE MS. HOLLISTER AND/OR RICK ROBINSON OR OTHERS.

COMMENT AND ANALYSIS: #3 *MY TESTIMONY HERE WAS TO LET JUDGE EKANS KNOW THAT I WAS NOT OPPOSED TO EXPANDING THE HEARING TO CALLING OTHER WITNESSES IN SUPPORT OF THE ALLEGATIONS SET FORTH IN MY LAWSUIT.*

AND YET, UNDERNEATH IT ALL, I KNEW THE DECISION TO DISMISS MY CASE AND THEREAFTER, DISMISS MY CASE WITH PREJUDICE SHOULD I FILE FOR RECONSIDERATION OF THE JUDGMENT TO DISMISS HAD ALREADY BEEN MADE WHICH IS EXACTLY WHAT HAPPENED.

IN OTHER WORDS, THE DYE TO DEFRAUD, ROB AND STRIP ME OF MY FEES HAD BEEN CAST BY THE TEAM OF D.C. COURT JUDGES AND FBI AGENTS FROM THE MOMENT SUPERIOR COURT CHIEF JUDGE SKINNER, A KEY JUDICIAL CO-CONSPIRATOR WEIGHED IN ON THE DECISION TO TRANSFER THE ADJUDICATION OF MY LAWSUIT TO EKANS IN DECEMBER 2010 OR SOLELY MADE THE DECISION HIMSELF, NECESSITED BY THE RETIREMANT OF JUDGE KATE STARR.

JUDGE SKINNER'S LEGENDARY ABUSE OF POWER WOULD BE DEMONSTRATED LATER DURING HIS MARCH 18, 2011 COURT HALLWAY INTIMIDATION AND SHAKEDOWN OF BRIANNA JONES, A COURT WITNESS, AND HIS OBSTRUCTION OF THE MARCH 18, 2011 COURT PROCEEDING, AIDED AND ABETTED AT ALL TIMES BY JUDGE EKANS, THE PRESIDING JUDGE.

MS. FRANKLIN: ANY OFFICIAL AT THE D.C. LOTTERY BOARD OUGHT TO BE ABLE TO PULL THE RECORDS TO DETERMINE EXACTLY WHO WAS PAID SINCE THE COURT ORDER SIGNED BY JUDGE MANDARIN DIRECTED THAT THE LOTTERY BOARD PAY THE LUMP SUM TO THE ESTATE. AND THE MANAGING ATTORNEY, MR. RON MEYER, WOULD BE ANOTHER INDIVIDUAL DEPENDING UPON THE INFORMATION PROVIDED BY THE FLORIDA BAR INVESTIGATION, BUT CERTAINLY HE WOULD BE ANOTHER INDIVIDUAL.

BECAUSE HE'S MANAGING ATTORNEY OF THE FIRM, HE OUGHT TO KNOW WHETHER THERE WAS A SETTLEMENT, WAS MONEY PAID, TO WHOM WAS IT PAID, OR ARE WE JUST WASTING EVERYBODY'S TIME BECAUSE THERE NEVER WAS A SETTLEMENT? BECAUSE I WAS THERE FROM THE BEGINNING, YOUR HONOR, INCLUDING WHEN I FILED THE COMPLAINT, I HAVE NEVER SEEN A SETTLEMENT AGREEMENT. I HAVE NEVER   AND I HAVE DEMANDED IT, I HAVE ASKED FOR IT. I BROUGHT HER INTO COURT. WE'VE BEEN HERE OVER TWO YEARS. THERE HAS NEVER BEEN A SETTLEMENT AGREEMENT THAT I CAN SPEAK TO AND I WOULD NEVER BEGIN TO SPEAK TO IT. AND SO THAT'S WHERE I AM WITH IT, YOUR HONOR, AND THAT'S   THAT'S BASICALLY WHAT I WANTED TO SHARE WITH THE COURT THIS AFTERNOON.

MS. FRANKLIN: I HAVE TRIED TO FIND OUT WHERE THE MONEY IS AND IT TOOK ME ABOUT THREE WEEKS TO GO THROUGH MY 17-YEAR-OLD FILE. IN FACT, THE FILE IS IN AN OFF-SITE STORAGE BUT I FELT I OWED IT TO THE PARTIES, BUT MORE IMPORTANTLY, I OWED IT TO THE COURT BECAUSE MANY TIMES I HAVE COME INTO THIS COURTROOM AND MS. JONES HAS MADE ALL KIND OF STATEMENTS AND I'VE STOOD HERE LIKE A POTTED PLANT, NOT BECAUSE I DIDN'T WANT TO SAY SOMETHING BUT I WANTED TO BE ACCURATE AND I KNEW THAT I HAD NOT LOOKED AT RECORDS, THERE'S NO WAY -- - I HAD NO REMEMBRANCE WHATSOEVER THAT MS. HOLLISTER WAS INVOLVED.

MY WHOLE FOCUS HAS BEEN LET'S GET THIS DONE. WE SETTLED THIS , THERE'S A COURT ORDER, BUT THIS IS THE KIND OF INFORMATION THAT WOULD HAVE COME OUT AT TRIAL. AND WHEN YOUR HONOR POSED THE QUESTION TO THE DEFENDANT SOME TIME BACK, WHY DIDN'T YOU GO TO TRIAL WITH THIS, SHE SAYS, OH THERE'S SO MUCH I WOULD HAVE HAD TO DIVULGE. WELL, THIS IS A PART OF WHAT WOULD HAVE BEEN DIVULGED -- --

MS. JONES: YOUR HONOR, MAY I SPEAK?

MS. FRANKLIN: ---------------- WHICH I HAVE REFRAINED FROM DOING BECAUSE I'M NOT INTERESTED IN BRINGING IN OTHER PEOPLE. THERE IS NOT ANOTHER SOUL THAT'S MENTIONED IN MY COMPLAINT. I HAVE NOT TRIED TO BRING IN ANY THIRD PARTIES. I'VE TRIED TO KEEP THIS BETWEEN THE TWO OF US BUT SINCE SHE HAS BUCKED THE COURT, SHE'S STILL IN CONTEMPT, SHE WILL NOT PROVIDE ANY INFORMATION TO THE COURT. SHE WILL NOT PRODUCE ANY DOCUMENTS. SHE'S FORCED MY HANDS.

I HAVE TO COME INTO COURT AND SAY, YOUR HONOR, CAN WE GO AROUND THIS DEFENDANT TO THESE INDIVIDUALS THAT HAVE PARTICIPATED IN THIS WHOLE CASE AND GET THIS DONE? -- --

MS. FRANKLIN: --------------- **THERE IS NO JUDGMENT IN THIS CASE. THAT'S WHY WASHINGTON PROCESS CAN'T SEARCH ASSETS.**

                 COMMENT AND ANALYSIS: #4 *THERE, I HAD SAID IT. IF THERE IS NO JUDGMENT IN THIS CASE, THEN THERE CAN BE NO JUDGMENT CREDITOR IN THIS CASE. HAD I PERSUADED JUDGE EKANS ON THIS MAJOR FACT OF MY CASE? OF COURSE NOT. HE HAD A HIGHER TASK TO PERFORM. AND THAT WAS TO KEEP THE MISSION OF THE CRIMINAL ENTERPRISE IN GEAR.*

THE COURT: WELL, WE'RE GOING TO -- --

MS. FRANKLIN:	**THERE IS NO JUDGMENT IN THIS CASE.**
	COMMENT AND ANALYSIS: #5 EVEN THOUGH EKANS HEARD ME THE FIRST TIME, NEVERTHELESS, I WOULD REPEAT: **"THERE IS NO JUDGMENT IN THIS CASE."**
	BUT THE LESSON THAT I WOULD LEARN FOR ALL TIME WAS THAT WHEN YOU'RE LITIGATING A CASE IN A CORRUPT COURT SYSTEM WHERE THE UNSPOKEN RULE OF LAW IS THAT NO JUDGE WILL REPORT ON THE MISCONDUCT, AND EVEN CRIMINAL BEHAVIOR OF ANOTHER JUDGE, THE PRESIDING JUDGE CAN, AT WILL, IGNORE THE FACTS, DISREGARD THE FACTS AND EVEN CHANGE THE FACTS, AND THERE IS NOTHING YOU CAN DO WITHIN A CORRUPT COURT SYSTEM TO SET THINGS RIGHT.
	I LEARNED THAT WHEN A HANDFUL OF CORRUPT D.C. COURT JUDGES COMMIT TO ROBBING YOU, ONE OF THE WAYS IN WHICH THEY DO IT IS TO CHANGE THE FACTS OF THE CASE. AND A JUDICIAL SCHEME OF FRAUD AND THEFT THAT IS JUST AS CRIMINAL AS CHANGING THE FACTS OF A CASE IS THE PRESIDING JUDGE'S WILLFUL AND INTENTIONAL REFUSAL TO ADDRESS THE DOMINANT ISSUE OF D.C. JUDICIAL FRAUD WHICH JUDGE EKANS ENFORCED IN MY CASE.
	IT IS, AFTER ALL IS SAID AND DONE, JUDICIAL DISCRETION RUN AMUCK, ABUSED, TATTERED, TRAMPLED UPON AND STOMPED ON BY EKANS INTO OBLIVION AS FAR AS EKANS WAS CONCERNED.
THE COURT:	WE'RE GOING TO GET THERE BECAUSE THAT WAS, OF ALL THE THINGS THAT YOU SAID TO ME IN THE STATEMENT, THE ONE THING THAT I THOUGHT WAS IMPORTANT WAS YOUR EFFORT TO EMPLOY THIS OUTFIT WHICH CAN GET TO THE BOTTOM OF THIS WAS DEFEATED BY THE FACT THAT YOU HAVE A SETTLEMENT RATHER THAN A JUDGMENT, BUT SETTLEMENTS ARE CONTRACTS BETWEEN PARTIES AND WHEN THERE IS A BREACH THEY CAN BE TURNED INTO JUDGMENTS. SO, WHAT YOU NEED TO DO IS FILE A MOTION TO TURN THE SETTLEMENT INTO A JUDGMENT.

COMMENT AND ANALYSIS: #6 GIVEN MY PERCEPTION OF JUDGE EKANS' AS THE GRAND MARSHALL OF THE D.C. JUDICIAL AND FBI CRIMINAL ENTERPRISE; AND MOREOVER, GIVEN THE IMPORTANT INFORMATION THAT THE HOLY SPIRIT HAD GIVEN ME IN MORE THAN ONE DREAM REGARDING THE CO-CONSPIRATOR D.C. COURT JUDGES, I KNEW EKANS' SUGGESTION THAT I FILE A MOTION TO TURN THE SETTLEMENT INTO A MOTION COULD NOT POSSIBLY BE IN MY FAVOR OR TO MY BENEFIT. I KNEW, ALSO, THAT I WAS OUTNUMBERED BY POWERFUL, MONEY-MAD, CONSCIENCE-FREE AND AMORAL D.C. COURT JUDGES WHO HAD ALREADY SHOWN ME THE DEPTH OF THEIR DIABOLICAL DETERMINATION TO STRIP ME OF MY ATTORNEY'S FEES THROUGH THE POLITICALLY MOTIVATED CRIMINAL PROSECUTION OF MY HUSBAND.

MOREOVER, I WAS BECOMING INCREASINGLY AWARE OF THE MOUNTING BUILDUP OF TRAUMA IN MY SOUL AND SPIRIT.

AND GIVEN THOSE FACTS, I AGREED TO FILE THE MOTION TO CONVERT THE SETTLEMENT AGREEMENT INTO A COURT JUDGMENT. THREE YEARS LATER, THE D.C. COURT OF APPEALS, AT ALL TIMES COMPLICIT IN THE CRIMINAL ENTERPRISE TO DEFRAUD ME OF THE ESTIMATED $50 MILLION IN ATTORNEY'S FEES WOULD, IN CONSPIRACY WITH JUDGE EKANS AND THE OTHER KNOWN AND UNKNOWN CO-CONSPIRATORS, OVERTURN THE JUDGMENT.

THE COURT: ARE YOU GOIING TO FILE THE MOTION TO ENFORCE THE SETTLEMENT?

MS. FRANKLIN: YES, YOUR HONOR.

COMMENT AND ANALYSIS: #7 *IN THE END, JUDGE EKANS COMMITTED THE ULTIMATE SWINDLE IN HIS INTENTIONAL AND PURPOSEFUL FAILURE AND REFUSAL TO HAVE BRIANNA JONES TURN OVER THE BANK OF AMERICA BANK STATEMENTS TO ME AS SHE WAS MANDATED TO PRODUCE IN JUDGE KATE STARR'S ORDER OF OCTOBER 18, 2010.*

INSTEAD, HE CHOSE TO ISSUE A MONEY JUDGMENT WHICH HE WAS ASSURED WOULD BE OVERTURNED THEREAFTER, AND IN DUE COURSE, A PERIOD OF ALMOST 3 YEARS, BY THE D.C. COURT OF APPEALS, AT ALL TIMES AND IN ALL WAYS, COMPLICIT IN THIS HISTORIC D.C. JUDICIAL AND F.B.I. CRIMINAL ENTERPRISE, AND IN KEEPING WITH THE PRIMARY MISSION OF THE CRIMINAL ENTERPRISE TO DEFRAUD ME OF AN ESTIMATED $50 MILLION IN ATTORNEY'S FEES.

THE COURT: NOW, ONE OF THE THINGS THAT I'D LIKE TO KNOW NOW BEFORE WE GET BACK INTO ANOTHER ROUND OF THIS THAT LEADS US AROUND IN A CIRCLE, DO YOU HAVE THE SETTLEMENT AGREEMENT?

MS. FRANKLIN: NEVER HAD IT. I'M SORRY, THE SETTLEMENT, I'M SORRY, YOUR HONOR? WHICH
                  -- -- YOU'RE TALKING ABOUT THE SETTLEMENT AGREEMENT BETWEEN -- --

THE COURT: THE SETTLEMENT -- --

MS. FRANKLIN: -------------- BETWEEN THE TWO OF US?

THE COURT: THE SETTLEMENT BETWEEN THE TWO OF YOU.

MS. FRANKLIN: YES, YOUR HONOR.

THE COURT: DO YOU HAVE THAT?

MS. FRANKLIN: YES.

THE COURT: YOU HAVE A COPY OF IT?

MS. FRANKLIN: YES.

THE COURT: IT'S PROPERLY SIGNED AND EXECUTED?

MS. FRANKLIN: ABSOLUTELY.

THE COURT: OKAY.

MS. FRANKLIN: THE COURT ORDER OF OCTOBER 18TH IS, IN FACT, THE SETTLEMENT AGREEMENT.
                  IN OTHER WORDS, THE COURT TOOK THE SETTLEMENT AGREEMENT AND JUST
                  PUT IT IN A COURT ORDER.

THE COURT: WHAT'S THE DATE?

MS. FRANKLIN: OCTOBER 18TH, JUDGE STARR'S ORDER OF 2010. AND THE SETTLEMENT
                  AGREEMENT IS ALSO ATTACHED TO THE DISMISSAL OF THE CASE IN FEBRUARY
                  2010.

MS. JONES: YOUR HONOR, MAY I -- --

MS. FRANKLIN: SO, THE AGREEMENT -- --EXCUSE ME ---- THE SETTLEMENT AGREEMENT IS A PART
                  OF THE COURT RECORD, THE ENTIRE SETTLEMENT AGREEMENT, FEBRUARY 4TH,
                  2010 I BELIEVE.

THE COURT: OKAY, I SEE. YES, I MEAN, IF YOU FILE -- --

MS. FRANKLIN: SO, SO, SO -- --

THE COURT:------------------- IF YOU FILE A MOTION TO TURN THE SETTLEMENT INTO A JUDGMENT, THAT'LL
                  HAPPEN AND YOU'LL BE IN BUSINESS.

MS. FRANKLIN: OKAY.

MS. JONES:	YOUR HONOR, MAY I SPEAK?
MS. FRANKLIN:	YOUR HONOR, I WOULD LIKE TO SAY, HOWEVER, THE DEFENDANT HAS SAID REPEATEDLY THAT SHE WELCOMES A JUDGMENT BEING ISSUED BECAUSE SHE INTENDS TO FILE BANKRUPTCY AND HAVE IT DISCHARGED.
THE COURT:	WELL, IF SHE DOES THAT THEN SHE'LL HAVE TO GO ------ YOU DON'T JUST FILE BANKRUPTCY, YOU HAVE TO GO IN FRONT OF A BANKRUPTCY JUDGE -- --
MS. FRANKLIN:	RIGHT.
THE COURT:	-- -- AND PUT ALL YOUR ASSETS OUT. SO, THAT -- --
MS. FRANKLKIN:	OKAY.
THE COURT:	-- -- THAT WOULDN'T NECESSARILY BE A BAD OUTCOME -- --
THE COURT:	BUT WHEN SHE FILES HER MOTION TO CONVERT THE SETTLEMENT TO A JUDGMENT, YOU CAN FILE WHATEVER YOU THINK IS APPROPRIATE.
MS. JONES:	MAY I DO AN AMENDED COMPLAINT, BECAUSE SOME FACTS NEED TO BE ON RECORD?
THE COURT:	MS. JONES, YOU HAVE AMAZING ACCESS TO ALL SORTS OF PEOPLE, SO I'M SURE YOU CAN TALK TO SOMEBODY WHO CAN GIVE YOU APPROPRIATE LEGAL ADVICE. ALL RIGHT, NOW, WE'LL I HATE TO SAY THIS BUT WE'LL NEED ANOTHER STATUS HEARING IN THIS MATTER. IT'S TAKING A WHILE BUT I THINK WE'RE GOING TO START SEEING SOME PROGRESS IN THIS BECAUSE I DO BELIEVE THAT OUTFIT THAT YOU MENTIONED -- --
MS. FRANLIN:	THEY WERE READY TO GO.
THE COURT:	YES, AND THEY'LL GET -- --
MS. FRANKLIN:	THEY WERE READY TO GO.
THE COURT:	--------------------THEY'LL GET TO THE BOTTOM OF THIS.
MS. FRANKLIN:	YEAH, THEY WERE READY TO GO.
THE COURT:	AND IF, YOU KNOW, IF THE CASE CHANGES FROM THIS COURT TO A BANKRUPTCY COURT THAT'S NOT NECESSARILY A BAD THING BECAUSE THE WHOLE IDEA IS TO FIND OUT WHERE THE ASSETS ARE -- --

THE COURT: EXCUSE ME -- --

THE COURT: YOU SAID THE 19TH IS MY LAST DAY?

DEPUTY CLERK: YES, YOUR HONOR.

THE COURT: OKAY, I'M GOING TO SET IT RIGHT NOW FOR AUGUST 19TH, AND WHAT I'M BELIEVING, HOPING, IS THAT YOU'LL HAVE YOUR MOTION FILED. MS. JONES WILL HAVE HER OPPOSITION FILED, AND I'LL EITHER HAVE RULED OR I WILL RULE ON THAT DAY.

MS. FRANKLIN: VERY WELL, YOUR HONOR. YOU HONOR, WHAT TIME ON THE   THE 19TH, YOUR HONOR?

THE COURT: YEAH, I THINK I ALREADY SET SOMETHING FOR 11:00 BUT LET ME JUST PUT IT DOWN AT 11:00 AND HOPEFULLY GET TO IT RIGHT AROUND THAT TIME. CERTAINLY BEFORE 1:30.

MS. JONES: YOUR HONOR, MAY I SPEAK? IS THAT A PERMANENT JUDGMENT OR THAT'S -- -- IS THAT A FINAL JUDGMENT?

THE COURT: AS OPPOSED TO WHAT?

MS. JONES: I'M GOING TO ----- I'M GOING TO FILE – I'M GOING TO FILE.

THE COURT: WELL, DO WHATEVER YOU NEED TO DO, MS. JONES. HAVE A GOOD DAY.

MS. JONES: THANK YOU, YOUR HONOR.

MS. FRANKLIN: THANK YOU, YOUR HONOR. ENJOY YOUR LUNCH.

THE COURT: THANK YOU.

DEPUTY CLERK: THIS HONORABLE COURT STANDS IN RECESS.

(THEREUPON, THE HEARING WAS CONCLUDED.)

BARBARA WASHINGTON FRANKLIN

SUPERIOR COURT OF THE DISTRICT OF COLUMBIA
CIVIL DIVISION
WASHINGTON, D.C.

THE HONORABLE MATTHEW D. EKANS, ASSOCIATE JUDGE, PRESIDING

THE FOLLOWING IS THE ENTIRE OFFICIAL COURT TRANSCRIPT OF THE
AUGUST 19, 2011 PROCEEDING
ANNOTATED BY THE AUTHOR'S PERTINENT COMMENTARY AND ANALYSIS

AUGUST 19, 2011

PROCEEDINGS

COMMENT AND ANAYLSIS: #1 BUT FOR MY LIFETIME, INTIMATE, PERSONAL, GENUINE, QUIET, DEEP, ABIDING, PENETRATING RELATIONSHIP WITH JESUS CHRIST, THE FATHER, AND HIS HOLY SPIRIT, I WOULD NOT HAVE BEEN ABLE TO REMAIN CALM, CONFIDENT, SECURE AND ACCURATELY RESPOND TO THE DETAILED AND INTENSE INTERROGATION BY THE COURT THAT LASTED FOR SUBSTANTIALLY OVER AN HOUR, KNOWING THAT I WAS LOOKING INTO THE FACE OF A CORRUPT, CONSCIENCE-FREE AND AMORAL D.C. COURT JUDGE WHO WAS ESSENTIALLY ON A FACT-FINDING MISSION, NOT FOR THE TRUTH OR FOR JUSTICE OR IN RECOGNITION AND DEFERENCE TO THE RULE OF LAW, BUT FOR THE USE, PURPOSES AND MISSION OF THE D.C. JUDICIAL AND FBI CRIMINAL ENTERPRISE THAT EFFECTIVELY CIRCUMSCRIBED AND HAMSTRUNG MY LAWSUIT IN ALL WAYS AND AT EVERY LEVEL. MOREOVER, I KEPT UPPER MOST IN MY MIND THAT I WAS DEALING WITH A COURT JUDGE WHO SPECIALIZD IN SOPHISTICATED TRICKERY AND WAS A MASTER GASLIGHTER.

HOWEVER, WHAT THE ADVERSARY IS UNAWARE OF IS THAT FOR THE BELIEVER AND FOLLOWER OF CHRIST, ALL ADVERSITY BECOMES A BRIDGE TO A DEEPER RELATIONSHIP WITH GOD, BECAUSE GOD USES IT TO TEACH US WISDOM AND KNOWLEDGE WE WOULDN'T LEARN ANY OTHER WAY.

I NEVER APPEARED BEFORE THE COURT WITHOUT REALIZING THAT I WAS NOT SO MUCH ENTERING A COURTROOM AS I WAS A CLASSROOM. WHEN I HAD LEARNED THE LESSON OF THE PARTICULAR PROCEEDING, GOD WOULD RELEASE AND PROMOTE ME TO MOVE TO THE NEXT PROCEEDING AND ITS CLASSROOM.

THE ODYSSEY OF JUDICIAL CORRUPTION

WHILE JUDGE EKANS HAD CONTROL OF THE *RIGGED* OUTCOME OF THE CASE, THE HOLY SPIRIT HAD CONTROL AS TO HOW HE WOULD USE EKANS' ACTIONS TO MOVE ME TOWARDS THE FULNESS OF MY DESTINY. IN THE END, WHAT GOD PURPOSED OVERALL WOULD COME TO PASS. I WOULD REMAIN FASTENED TO THAT ETERNAL TRUTH AND UNMOVED BY THE D.C JUDICIAL AND FBI FORCES ALIGNED AGAINST ME.

JUDGE EKANS WAS A CRITICAL AND KEY JUDICIAL CO-CONSPIRATOR OF THIS MASSIVE CRIMINAL ENTERPRISE BASED ON HIS OVERT AND COVERT ACTIONS DEMONSTRATED DURING THE ENTIRETY OF THE ADJUDICATION OF MY LAWSUIT, DOCUMENTED AND VERIFIED THROUGHOUT THIS NARRATIVE NONFICTION WORK BY MEANS OF EXCERPTS OF OFFICIAL COURT TRANSCRIPTS.

I HAVE MY PARENTS, ROBERT BENJAMIN WASHINGTON AND EUNICE VETTA ROSS WASHINGTON AND MY GRANDPARENTS, ROSA LEE BRADLEY WASHINGTON TERRY AND A.M.E. PRESIDING ELDER AND REVEREND ANDREW WASHINGTON, TO THANK FOR MY LIFETIME MEMBERSHIP, NOT IN TRIPLE A (AAA), AMERICAN AUTOMOBILE ASSOCIATION, BUT IN TRIPLE G (GGG), GOD THE FATHER, GOD THE SON AND GOD THE HOLY SPIRIT.

TIMES WITHOUT NUMBER, WHAT GOT ME THROUGH EACH AND EVERY COURT HEARING BEFORE JUDGE EKANS WAS TO SEE MYSELF AS A WRESTLER IN A PRO WRESTLING MATCH. EVERYBODY KNOWS THE WHOLE THING IS FAKE AND RIGGED FOR A PARTICULAR OUTCOME.

IT'S BEEN PRE-SCRIPTED! THEY HAVE ALREADY DECIDED WHO THE WINNER IS GOING TO BE! THE SELECTION OF THE WINNER OF THE MATCH HAS BEEN PRE-DECIDED, PRE-DESTINED, PRE-DETERMINED AND PRE-SELECTED.

IT'S ALL DECIDED BEFORE THE MATCH STARTS! OTHER WRESTLERS COMING OUT RIGHT IN THE NICK OF TIME-- --ALL THAT'S SCRIPTED! WRESTLER AGAINST THE ROPES, BEATEN TO A PULP, THEN SUDDENLY REVIVED WITH INCREDIBLE, EXTRAORDINARY ENERGY! FAKE! IT HAS BEEN SAID THAT THE SPONSORS OF THE MATCH EVEN PAY ADDITIONALLY IF THE WRESTLER BLEEDS! IF, AS A WRESTLER IN THE MATCH YOU BLEED, THEY PAY YOU MORE BECAUSE YOU'VE MADE THE MATCH APPEAR REAL, AUTHENTIC AND NOT THE ACTUAL FAKE THAT IT IS.

SO BOTTOM LINE, THE WHOLE THING HAS BEEN SCRIPTED!

IN THE CASE OF MY LAWSUIT, IN THE MIDST OF MY CASE BEING TRANSFERRED TO JUDGE EKANS UPON THE RETIREMENT OF JUDGE STARR, THE DECISION WAS MADE BY THE TEAM OF CORRUPT D.C. COURT JUDGES AND FBI AGENTS TO DISMISS MY LAWSUIT FOLLOWING A 3 YEAR LAYOVER IN THE D.C. COURT OF APPEALS. THE ULTIMATE GOAL OF THE JUDICIAL AND FBI CRIMINAL ENTERPRISE WAS TO DEFRAUD ME OF AN ESTIMATED $50 MILLION IN ATTORNEY'S FEES, RESULTING FROM THE $34 MILLION SETTLEMENT OF THE $100 MILLION LAWSUIT THAT I HAD CRAFTED AND FILED ON BEHALF OF THE FORMER CLIENT, BRIANNA JONES.

THE ENDLESS HEARINGS BEFORE EKANS? FAKE! THE $13.6 MILLION MONEY JUDGMENT ISSUED BY EKANS TO ME AT THE CONCLUSION OF MY CASE IN OCTOBER 2011? FAKE! THE D.C. APPELLATE REVIEW THAT OMITTED REVIEW OF MY LAWSUIT'S DOMINANT ISSUES OF D.C. JUDICIAL AND FBI FRAUD, THEFT, CORRUPTION AND EXTORTION? FAKE!

HOWEVER, **WHAT WAS NOT FAKE** AND CLEARLY FELL OUTSIDE THE PRO WRESTLING METAPHOR WAS **THE SHAKEDOWN AND INTIMIDATION OF BRIANNA JONES BY THE SENIOR JUDGE AND FORMER CHIEF JUDGE, GEORGE SKINNER, DURING THE MARCH 18, 2011 COURT HEARING, COORDINATED AND ORCHESTRATED BY JUDGE EKANS BY MEANS OF A CONTRIVED COURT RECESS.**

WHAT WAS NOT FAKE WAS EKANS FALSELY, INTENTIONALLY AND PURPOSEFULLY LABELING ME A **JUDGMENT CREDITOR RESPONSIBLE FOR THE RECOVERY OF THE STOLEN SETTLEMENT PROCEEDS** FOR THE DURATION OF THE 9-MONTH ADJUDICATION OF MY CASE. AT THE FINAL HEARING OF MY LAWSUIT ON JANUARY 16, 2015, EKANS BOLDLY CLOSED MY CASE BY *AGAIN* FALSELY STATING THAT MY CASE HAD BEEN INITIALLY PRESENTED TO HIM AS A JUDGMENT CREDITOR CASE. **THAT IS A CLASSIC ILLUSTRATION OF THE ABUSE OF ABSOLUTE JUDICIAL DISCRETION AT ITS BEST.**

WHAT WAS NOT FAKE WAS EKANS' REFUSAL TO ALLOW BRIANNA JONES TO REVIEW BANK OF AMERICA BANK STATEMENTS WITH ME DURING THE JANUARY 31, 2011 COURT HEARING, FALSELY CLAIMING THAT THERE WAS NOWHERE IN THE COURTHOUSE FOR US TO MEET. EKANS HAD COMPLETELY FORGOTTEN THAT HE HAD SUGGESTED, DURING THE JANUARY 21, 2011 HEARING, THAT WE COULD MEET IN ONE OF THE WITNESS ROOMS ADJACENT TO THE COURTROOM TO REVIEW BRIANNA'S DOCUMENTS OF HER FINANCIAL ASSETS. **THIS WILL ALWAYS REMAIN A CLASSIC EXAMPLE OF THE ABUSE OF ABSOLUTE JUDICIAL. DISCRETION ON STEROIDS**

WHAT WAS NOT FAKE WAS THE ISSUANCE OF THE *RIGGED* DECISION BY THE D.C. COURT OF APPEALS WHICH OVERTURNED THE FAKE $13.6 MILLION MONEY JUDGMENT EKANS HAD ISSUED TO ME AT THE CONCLUSION OF MY LAWSUIT IN OCTOBER 2011.

NOW, HOWEVER, **EKANS' COMMITMENT TO THE D.C. JUDICIAL AND FBI CRIMINAL ENTERPRISE** AND ITS CONSEQUENT DEMANDS REQUIRED THAT EKANS DO EVERYTHING WITHIN HIS POWER AND AUTHORITY TO PROHIBIT MY ACCESS TO THE SETTLEMENT PROCEEDS ON DEPOSIT AT BANK OF AMERICA AND THAT INCLUDED THE ESTIMATED $50 MILLION IN ATTORNEY'S FEES OWED TO ME.

THE FINAL OUTCOME OF MY CASE HAD ALREADY BEEN DECIDED UPON JUDGE KATE STARR'S RETIREMENT AND SUBSEQUENT TRANSFER OF THE CASE TO JUDGE EKANS' DOCKET, UNDER THE AUSPICES OF THE CRIMINAL ENTERPRISE.

THERE WERE TIMES DURING THE COURT HEARINGS THAT I FELT AS IF I WERE DANIEL IN THE LIONS' DEN. I KNEW EKANS WAS ON ASSIGNMENT AS A D.C. JUDICIAL CO-CONSPIRATOR TO TEAR ME TO PIECES. HOWEVER, INSTEAD HE JUST STALKED ME DURING HEARINGS WITH HIS CONSTANT RHETORICAL QUESTIONS, CATEGORICAL COMMENTS, AIMLESS MIND GAMES AND ENDLESS GASLIGHTING PONTIFICATIONS. IN THE END, I KNEW JUDGE EKANS WAS BEING HELD IN CHECK BY THE OFFICIAL TRANSCRIPT OF THE HEARING BEING MADE BY THE COURT STENOGRAPHER. BUT MORE IMPORTANTLY, **JUDGE EKANS WAS BEING HELD IN CHECK BY THE EVER-PRESENT HOLY SPIRIT** WHO WAS ALWAYS ON DUTY TO PROTECT ME FROM THE JAWS OF THE ADVERSARY, HOWEVER, AND BY WHOMEVER THEY APPEARED.

THE DEPUTY CLERK: YOUR HONOR, CALLING THE CASE OF BARBARA WASHINGTON FRANKLIN VERSUS BRIANNA JONES, 2009-CA-4417. AND IN THE MATTER OF BRIANNA JONES, 2011-CCC-1.

PLEASE STATE YOUR NAME FOR THE RECORD.

MS. FRANKLIN: GOOD MORNING, YOUR HONOR. BARBARA WASHINGTON FRANKLIN, PRO SE.

THE COURT: UM-- --

MS. FRANKLIN : PLAINTIFF.

THE COURT: MS. FRANKLIN, AS I SAID TO YOU BEFORE I TOOK THAT BREAK -- --

MS. FRANKLIN: UM-HMM.

THE COURT -------------------- MS. JONES HAS CALLED, FRANKLY, NUMEROUS TIMES BETWEEN YESTERDAY AFTERNOON AND CONTINUING UP TO THIS MORNING.

MS. FRANKLIN: UM-HMM.

THE COURT: AND MY CHAMBERS STAFF WHICH CONSISTS OF MY ADMINISTRATIVE ASSISTANT AND MY LAW CLERK, BOTH -- -- I THINK THEY WENT TO GET A PRE-LUNCH -- -- LUNCH, I'M NOT SURE WHAT THEY DID, BUT THEY'RE NOT UP THERE, THEY'RE THE ONES WHO'VE TALKED WITH HER.   BUT -- -- BUT, UH ---------- MY UNDERSTANDING OF WHAT SHE SAID IS THAT SHE IS, I GUESS, PREPARING FOR SURGERY. I THINK SHE SAID SHE'S BEEN QUITE ILL. -- --

MS. FRANKLIN: HMM.

THE COURT:--------------------AND PREPARING FOR SURGERY AND IS GOING INTO JOHNS HOPKINS. THAT SHE WON'T BE HERE TODAY, BUT WOULD BE SENDING US MEDICAL -- --

MS. FRANKLIN: DOCUMENTATION -- --

THE COURT: YEAH. TO SHOW THAT, YOU KNOW, THAT IT'S ------THAT THAT'S WHY SHE'S NOT HERE. SO ON AND SO FORTH. SO -- NOW, YOU KNOW THERE'RE TWO MOTIONS PENDING. YOURS TO ENTER JUDGMENT ON THE SETTLEMENT AGREEMENT.

MS. FRANKLIN: UM-HMM.

COMMENT AND ANALYSIS: #2 ONCE AGAIN, BRIANNA JONES HAD PLAYED THE *SICK CARD* AND GOTTEN AWAY WITH IT. JUDGE EKANS DID NOT REQUIRE BRIANNA JONES TO PRODUCE A DOCTOR'S CERTIFICATE OR ANY OTHER VERIFICATION OF HER ALLEGED SURGERY AND ILLNESS. EKANS DID NOT SEE HER BEHAVIOR AS INTERFERRING WITH THE OPERATION OF THE D.C. JUDICIAL CRIMINAL ENTERPRISE UNDERWAY.

THE COURT: AND THEN, HERE'S HER MOTION TO SET ASIDE THE SETTLEMENT. I TRUST YOU DID GET A COPY OF THAT?

MS. FRANKLIN: YES, I DID.

THE COURT: SO, HOW DO YOU WANT TO PROCEED?

COMMENT AND ANALYSIS: #3 I HAD NO INTENTION OF PROCEEDING. THE TEAM OF D.C. JUDICIAL AND FBI CO-CONSPIRATORS, IN FURTHERANCE OF THE ONGOING CRIMINAL ENTERPRISE, HAD PREPARED FOR BRIANNA JONES' SIGNATURE, A MOTION TO SET ASIDE THE MONEY JUDGMENT THAT I CONSIDERED BEYOND TRASH AND SUITABLE FOR THE GUTTER. I THUS LEFT IT TO EKANS, AN UNQUALIFIED KEY CO-CONSPIRATOR, TO RULE AS HE SAW FIT.

MS. FRANKLIN: WOULD THE MOTION TO -- --WELL, IN TERMS OF HER MOTION, AND I'VE RESPONDED TO THAT PREVIOUSLY, YOU KNOW, I'M JUST -- -- I HAD TO CATEGORICALLY – CATEGORICALLY DENY EVERYTHING IN THAT MOTION, AND I REALLY DON'T CARE TO PROCEED FURTHER WITH REGARD TO ANSWERING YOUR HONOR BECAUSE I INTERPRET IT, FOR ME, AS GOING DOWN INTO THE GUTTER WITH THE DEFENDANT, AND I'M NOT GOING TO DO THAT.

I WAS NOTIFIED ABOUT TWO WEEKS AGO BY LEXIS NEXIS, AHH, BY WAY OF A CONGRATULATORY LETTER CONGRATULATING ME FOR HAVING BEEN A MEMBER OF THE BAR FOR THIRTY-FIVE YEARS. AND, THAT WHOLE MOTION THAT SHE FILED CAME TO MIND, AGAIN. I SAID THAT'S WHY I DID NOT ANSWER.

I'VE BEEN A MEMBER OF THE BAR FOR THIRTY-FIVE YEARS. I DIDN'T EVEN REALIZE. TIME GOES BY.

THE COURT: INDEED IT DOES.

MS. FRANKLIN: AND, I NEVER HAD THAT KIND OF CHARGE OR ACCUSATION IN TERMS OF MY TAKING ADVANTAGE OF SOMEBODY BECAUSE OF SOME IMMORAL, PERVERTED RELATIONSHIP, SEXUAL OR WHATEVER. AND -- -- AND I JUST-- --I CAN'T PUT ANYTHING IN WRITING WITH REGARDS TO THAT.

WITH REGARD TO MY MOTION FOR JUDGMENT, YOUR HONOR ASKED ME AT THE JUNE 17TH HEARING TO FILE A MOTION FOR JUDGMENT. AND I DID SO   AND I DID SO, YOUR HONOR. BASICALLY, FOR ME, IT WAS A CHALLENGE TO PREPARE THE MOTION BECAUSE I'M WITIHOUT ANY FINANCIAL DOCUMENTS. THE COURT IS WITHOUT ANY FINANCIAL DOCUMENTS. AND, SO, WHAT I DID IN THE MOTION WAS SIMPLY INDICATE THAT WE HAD SETTLED THE CASE, UM, ON THE 3RD OF FEBRUARY IN 2010. ALL VOLUNTARY.

THERE WAS NEVER A MENTION OF ANY DOLLAR AMOUNT, THOUGH. IT WAS ALL BASED ON THE RETAINER AGREEMENT, AND THAT WAS A FORTY PERCENT BECAUSE IT WAS A CONTINGENCY FEE AGREEMENT. I'VE SAID NUMEROUS TIMES IN COURT THAT I'VE NEVER BEEN PAID ANY MONEY, WHATSOEVER, FOR ANY OF MY SERVICES OVER THIS FOURTEEN TO SEVENTEEN YEAR PERIOD. AND, UM, THAT SHE HAS REPEATEDLY AFFIRMED THAT THE CASE SETTLED FOR THIRTY-FOUR MILLION DOLLARS. AND I'VE ALWAYS USED THAT FIGURE, I USED IT, ALSO, IN THE INITIAL COMPLAINT, AND THEN I ADDED COMPOUNDED INTEREST.

NOW   BUT HERE, AGAIN, I CAN'T SAY WHAT THE TOTAL AMOUNT IS FROM 1997 WHEN SHE SETTLED THE CASE IT WAS THIRTY-FOUR MILLION. I DID HAVE THE OPPORTUNITY OF JUST HAVING A BRIEF CONSUL   TELEPHONE CONSULTATION WITH MY ACCOUNTANT AND I SAID, YOU KNOW, IF I ASK THE COURT FOR AN ESTIMATED   ONE   HUNDRED-MILLION   DOLLAR   JUDGMENT   IS   THAT UNREASONABLE? HE SAID, ABSOLUTELY NOT. I CAN GIVE YOU THE FIGURES FOR THAT.   BUT I DECLINED BECAUSE I DIDN'T WANT TO BRING IN ANY EXPERT TESTIMONY BECAUSE I DIDN'T THINK IT WAS APPROPRIATE.

COMMENT AND ANALYSIS: #4 *THE ABSENCE OF RELEVANT FINANCIAL RECORDS IN ORDER TO DETERMINE THE SETTLEMENT AMOUNT WAS SOLELY DUE TO JUDGE EKANS' INTENTIONAL FAILURE AND REFUSAL TO ENFORCE JUDGE STARR'S OCTOBER 18, 2010 ORDER MANDATING THAT BRIANNA JONES PRODUCE BANK OF AMERICA BANK STATEMENTS.*

MS. FRANKLIN: AND, SO, IN MY INITIAL COMPLAINT THAT I FILED WITH THIS COURT I DID ATTACH AS AN EXHIBIT, I THINK IT WAS EXHIIT B, IT WAS A COPY OF THE MARCH 14TH, 2007, LETTER FROM ME TO JUDGE MICHAEL ROSENBAUM IN THE BROWARD COUNTY CIRCUIT COURT WHICH PROVIDED, AT THE COURT'S REQUEST, ACCORDING TO THE DEFENDANT, THAT I PROVIDE THE COURT WITH MY ATTORNEY ESCROW BANKING ACCOUNT NEEDED FOR THE DEPOSIT OF EIGHTY-THREE MILLION, FIVE HUNDRED-THOUSAND DOLLARS. AND THAT WAS IN 2007. SO I, ALSO, USE THAT FIGURE.

COMMENT AND ANALYSIS: #5 MY CITATION OF MY MARCH 14TH 2007 LETTER TO JUDGE MICHAEL ROSENBAUM, PROBATE JUDGE OF THE BROWARD COUNTY CIRCUIT COURT, WAS TO STATE TO EKANS THAT MY CASE WAS FAR MORE THAN **"SMOKE AND MIRRORS"** WHICH HE HAD CAVALIERLY TERMED IT JUST AS HE HAD FALSELY AND CAVALIERLY LABLED ME A **JUDGMENT CREDITOR**. HE COULD CARE LESS ABOUT FACTS. HE PROVED TO BE A STAUNCH ABUSER OF THE SACRED POWER ENTRUSTED TO HIM, AS HE BOLDLY MARCHED FORWARD TO FILL HIS POCKETS AND THOSE OF HIS CORRUPT JUDICIAL COLLEAGUES WITH PORTIONS OF THE MILLIONS OF DOLLARS IN CASE SETTLEMENT PROCEEDS RESULTING FROM THE $34 MILLION SETTLEMENT OF THE $100 MILLION LAWSUIT.

MS. FRANKLIN: IN 2007 SUPPOSEDLY IT WAS EIGHTY- --EIGHTY-THREE MILLION, YOU KNOW, FIVE HUNDRED THOUSAND. AND, SO, I WAS USING THAT, ALSO, AS SORT OF LIKE A BASELINE WHEN I SAID AN ESTIMATED ONE HUNDRED-MILLION DOLLAR JUDGMENT.

MS. FRANKLIN: BUT I'M -- -- I'M NOT TIED TO ANY AMOUNT, YOUR HONOR, BECAUSE I'M -- -- THAT'S WHY I'M BEFORE THE COURT. I YOU KNOW, IF THE COURT SAYS, WELL, THAT'S JUST WAY OUT OF LINE OR I THINK YOU SHOULD JUST USE YOUR HALF OF WHATEVER, I'LL GO WITH WHATEVER THE COURT THINKS IS THE BEST COURSE.

COMMENT AND ANALYSIS: #6 I CHALLENGED JUDGE EKANS TO RISE TO THE SACREDNESS OF HIS POSITION AS A COURT JUDGE AND COME OFF THE CORRUPT, CONSCIENCE-FREE AND AMORAL PLATFORM FROM WHICH HE OPERATED, WITHOUT APOLOGY OR REMORSE. AND YET, I KNEW HIS VIEW OF THE BEST COURSE WAS THAT I GET ABSOLUTELY NOTHING. AND THAT IS EXACTLY WHAT HAPPENED BASED ON HIS KEY CO-CONSPIRATOR ROLE AND THE DICTATES OF THE CRIMINAL ENTERPRISE THAT GRIPPED AND DOMINATED MY LAWSUIT.

MS. FRANKLIN: I WAS JUST, AS I SAID, CHALLENGED BY HAVING TO PROVIDE A JUDGMENT TO THE COURT WITHOUT HAVING ANY FINANCIAL RECORDS, AND THE COURT NOT HAVING ANY FINANCIAL RECORDS, AND THAT'S WHY, YOU KNOW, SHE'S IN CONTEMPT BECAUSE SHE HAS REFUSED AT ALL TIMES TO PROVIDE THE COURT WITH THOSE RECORDS.

COMMENT AND ANALYSIS: #7 HERE AGAIN I WAS PUTTING FRONT AND CENTER JUDGE EKANS' CRITICAL COMPLICITY IN THE CRIMINAL ENTERPRISE BY INTENTIONALLY REFUSING TO ENFORCE JUDGE STARR'S ORDER AND ALLOWING BRIANNA JONES TO REMAIN IN CONTEMPT AND DISOBEDIENCE OF JUDGE STARR'S ORDER.

MS. FRANKLIN: I, ALSO, MENTIONED THAT IN MY MOTION ON PAGE 3, I MENTION THAT FACT THAT, UM – THERE HAD BEEN A DEFAULT JUDGMENT ENTERED BY JUDGE STARR AND THIS IS IN PARAGRAPH 9 ON PAGE 3, AND ALSO, PARAGRAH 8 – STARTING AT PARAGRAPH 8 ON PAGE 3 OF THE MOTION. AND JUDGE STARR HAD ENTERED A DEFAULT JUDGMENT BECAUSE THE DEFENDANT NEVER FILED AN ANSWER TO THE COMPLAINT. AND, SO, SHE JUST ENTERED A DEFAULT JUDGMENT.

COMMENT AND ANALYSIS: #8 *WHEN BRIANNA JONES FAILED TO FILE AN ANSWER, JUDGE STARR DID NOT HESITATE, ON HER OWN INITIATIVE AND WITHOUT DELAY, TO ENTER A DEFAULT JUDGMEMT AGAINST BRIANNA JONES.*

JUDGE EKANS, IN CONTRAST, PERMITTED BRIANNA JONES TO REMAIN IN CONTEMPT OF JUDGE STARR'S ORDER FOR APPROXIMATELY A YEAR.

MS. FRANKLIN: AND THE DEFENDANT'S POSITION WAS ALWAYS THAT I HAD RECEIVED A FIFTY MILLION DOLLAR JUDGMENT. WELL, HERE, AGAIN, WE NEVER HAD ANY FIGURES. BUT WHAT I PUT THIS INFORMATION IN MY MOTION FOR WAS TO SAY TO THE COURT EVEN WHEN WE WERE BEFORE JUDGE STARR IN 2009/2010 SHE TALKED ABOUT MY HAVING RECEIVED A FIFTY MILLION DOLLAR JUDGMENT, YOU KNOW, REFERRING TO THE DEFAULT JUDGMENT WHICH WOULD LEAD ONE TO CONCLUDE REASONABLY THAT THEN THE *TOTAL AMOUNT WAS SOMEWHERE AROUND A HUNDRED MILLION. AND THEN, THE FORTY PERCENT, YOU KNOW, PLUS TEN PERCENT BONUS AT THAT TIME WOULD HAVE BEEN FIFTY MILLION DOLLARS.*

I WAIVED THE BONUS, ALSO. SHE HAD   SHE HAD INITIALLY OFFERED THAT -- -- THAT WAS PREPARED, BY THE WAY, BY ANOTHER ATTORNEY. I DID NOT PREPARE THE BONUS AGREEMENT. NEVER ASKED FOR A BONUS AGREEMENT. I'VE NEVER ASKED A CLIENT IN MY THIRTY-FIVE YEARS OF BEING AN ATTORNEY FOR A BONUS ON ANY AMOUNT.

MS. FRANKLIN:　AND I DID STATE TO THE COURT PREVIOUSLY THAT THE SETTLEMENT AGREEMENT, YOU KNOW, OF FEBRUARY 3, 2010, WAS AT ALL TIMES INITIATED BY THE DEFENDANT. IT WAS VOLUNTARY. I MENTIONED TO THE COURT THAT, YOU KNOW, THIS HAD BEEN ACCOMPLISHED DURING THE SNOWSTORM OF THE CENTURY WHERE THE DEFENDANT ASKED ME TO COME TO HER HOTEL IN BALTIMORE. AND I WENT OVER THERE. SHE HAD A NOTARY WAITING FOR ME TO NOTARIZE THE AGREEMENT. AND IT WAS UNDER THOSE CIRCUMSTANCES.

SHE, THEN, INSISTED ON RIDING BACK IN MY CAR TO THE COURT TO BE PRESENT WHEN I FILED IT. SO, I MEAN, THIS IS VERY MUCH INTENTIONAL ON HER PART AND VOLUNTARY. AND I STATED, ALSO, THAT I WOULD　SHE COULD RIDE WITH ME, BUT I CERTAINLY WOULDN'T BE GOING BACK, YOU KNOW, TAKING HER BACK TO BALTIMORE. BUT SHE CAME TO THE COURT AND WE FILED IT. SHE WAS PRESENT. SHE RECEIVED A STAMPED COPY. SO, IT WAS UNDER THOSE CIRCUMSTANCES THAT THE AGREEMENT THAT WE MADE WAS FILED WITH THE COURT.

COMMENT AND ANALYSIS: #9 THE SETTLEMENT AGREEMENT BETWEEN ME AND BRIANNA WAS IN ALL RESPECTS VOLUNTARY.

MS. FRANKLIN:　AND, THEN WHEN THE COURT, AFTER I FILED THE REQUEST FOR A COURT INVESTIGATION AND THE COURT DIRECTED ME TO SEARCH FOR ASSETS, I, THEN, TOOK THE COURT'S DIRECTIVE. CONTACTED A LOCAL FIRM, WASHINGTON PROCESS SERVICES, TO SEARCH FOR ASSETS.

MS. FRANKLIN:　*WASHINGTON PROCESS SERVICES, JIMMY RAINES, THE PRESIDENT OF THE COMPANY, NOTIFIED　INFORMED ME THAT THE DISTRICT LAW, IT'S CALLED THE FINANCIAL MODERNIZATION ACT OF 2000. IT'S A D.C. LAW, PROHIBITS DISTRICT RESIDENTS AND/OR THEIR AGENTS FROM SEARCHING FOR FINANCIAL RECORDS OF AN INDIVIDUAL AND/OR ENTITY IN THE ABSENCE OF A FORMAL COURT JUDGMENT. THAT AS MUCH AS THEY WOULD LIKE TO HELP ME, I WOULD HAVE TO HAVE A COURT JUDGMENT ISSUED ON MY BEHALF AS A DISTRICT RESIDENT IN ORDER FOR THEM TO SEARCH.*

COMMENT AND ANALYSIS: #10 *THIS WAS MY WAY OF SAYING TO EKANS, "YOU SENT ME ON A WILD GOOSE CHASE TO SEARCH FOR THE FINANCIAL ASSETS OF BRIANNA JONES WHEN YOU KNEW A COURT JUDGMENT WAS A CONDITION PRECEDENT TO SEARCHING FOR THE ASSETS OF ANOTHER." EKANS' UNETHICAL ACTIONS WERE JUST FURTHER CONCRETE EVIDENCE OF HIS KNOWING, VOLUNTARY AND PREMEDITATED PARTICIPATION IN THE D.C. JUDICIAL AND FBI CRIMINAL ENTERPRISE WHOSE MISSION WAS TO DEFRAUD ME OF AN ESTIMATED $50 MILLION IN ATTORNEY'S FEES.*

MS. FRANKLIN: AND SO, GIVEN THAT INFORMATION THAT WAS IT FOR ME, I STOPPED. I HAVE NOT ASKED ANYBODY. I HAVEN'T USED ANYBODY'S SOCIAL SECURITY NUMBER. NOTHING. I SAID, WELL, THEN, I'LL JUST HOLD IT RIGHT THERE UNTIL I GET FURTHER DIRECTIVE FROM THE COURT. AND THEN, A COPY OF JIMMY RAINES FROM WASHINTON PROCESS, HIS   HIS LETTER'S ATTACHED AS EXHIBIT D.

COMMENT AND ANALYSIS: #11 *JUDGE EKANS REMAINED STONE FACED AS I LET HIM KNOW I WAS VERY AWARE OF HIS CO-CONSPIRATOR ROLE IN THE CRIMINAL ENTERPRISE.*

MS. FRANKLIN: AND, THE DEFENDANT, YOU KNOW, HAS AT ALL TIMES FAILED TO HONOR THE AGREEMENT, THE SETTLEMENT AGREEMENT, PROVIDED AMONG OTHER THINGS THAT SHE PROVIDE ME WITH ALL OF THE INFORMATION, FINANCIAL INFORMATION. *SHE'S ALREADY TESTIFIED IN THIS COURT, MORE THAN ONCE, THAT SHE MET WITH BANK OF AMERICA OFFICIALS IN THE WASHINGTON REGION. AND, SO, SHE HAS INFORMATION, SHE'S JUST REFUSED   SHE'S JUST REFUSED TO   TO DISCLOSE IT.*

AND, SHE HAS NOT RESPONDED TO THIS -- -- SHE'S NOT RESPONDED TO THIS -- - - SHE HAS NOT REPONDED TO THIS MOTION.

THE COURT: WELL, HER -- -- RESPONSE ----- I GUESS, I MEAN, EXCUSE ME.

MS. FRANKLIN: YES.

THE COURT: SHE WOULD SAY THAT HER RESPONSE IS HER MOTION TO SET ASIDE THE SETTLEMENT AGREEMENT.

COMMENT AND ANALYSIS: #12 *EKANS MADE NO COMMENT ABOUT INTENTIONALLY MISLEADING ME IN MY SEARCH FOR THE DEFENDANT'S ASSETS WITHOUT A JUDGMENT. IT WAS A FURTHER DEMONSTRATION OF HIS CHARCTERISTIC RUTHLESSNESS, GREED AND COMMITMENT TO THE SUCCESS OF THE CRIMINAL ENTERPRISE, OF WHICH HE WAS A KEY D.C. JUDICIAL CO-CONSPIRATOR.*

MS. FRANKLIN: OKAY. WITH REGARD TO ------ WITH REGARD TO THE MOTION TO SET ASIDE THE SETTLEMENT AGREEMENT, YOU HONOR, UM -- --

THE COURT: LET -- -- LET ME -- --

MS. FRANKLIN: AND I DON'T -- -- I DON'T EVEN HAVE THAT. I'LL BE HONEST WITH YOU, I COULDN'T EVEN FIND THE COPY, AND THAT'S PROBABLY BECAUSE I DON'T REALLY WANT TO DEAL WITH IT, AGAIN.

BUT WHEN I TAKE -- -- WHEN I   WHEN I MADE A PRESENTATION BEFORE THE COURT AT THE JUNE 17TH HEARING, THAT WAS SOMEWHAT FROM MY VANTAGE POINT OF VIEW A RESPONSE TO HER MOTION TO SET ASIDE, BECAUSE I WAS SAYING TO THE COURT A NUMBER OF THINGS. AND THE ONE QUESTION I HAVEN'T RAISED WITH THE COURT, AND I THINK THIS IS CRITICAL, *A DEFENDANT WHO IS IN CRIMINAL CONTEMPT OF THE COURT'S ORDERS, DOES THIS DEFENDANT HAVE STANDING TO FILE MOTIONS WITH THE COURT, AND ASKING THE COURT FOR AN ORDER ON HER BEHALF WHEN, IN FACT, SHE HAS BEEN IN CONTINUAL CONTEMPT OF THIS COURT'S ORDERS? AND IS NOW IN CRIMINAL CONTEMPT.*

COMMENT AND ANALYSIS: #13 EKANS NEVER ANSWERED MY QUESTION WHICH WAS INTENDED TO HAMMER HOME THE POINT THAT EKANS WAS ALLOWING BRIANNA JONES TO REMAIN IN CONTEMPT OF JUDGE STARR'S ORDER SO THAT THE MISSION OF THE CRIMINAL ENTERPRISE BE SERVED, AND WHATEVER BOUNTY HE HAD BEEN PROMISED BE UNDISTURBED.

MS. FRANKLIN: AND COME OCTOBER 25TH OF THIS YEAR SHE WILL HAVE BEEN IN CONTEMPT FOR A YEAR. SHE WILL HAVE BEEN IN CRIMINAL CONTEMPT FOR A YEAR. AND, YOUR HONOR HAS, YOU KNOW, JUST DONE EVERYTHING POSSIBLE, BENT OVER BACKWARDS, GIVING HER AN OPPORTUNITY TO GET AN ATTORNEY. SHE COMES IN, YOU KNOW, I'M GONNA GET AN ATTORNEY, THEY'RE GONNA COLLECT FEES, I'M GONNA TAKE THESE ATTORNEYS TO THE BAR. JUST CONSTANT PROMISES, PROMISES AND NOTHING.

COMMENT AND ANALYSIS: #14 *ALLOWING A DEFENDANT TO REMAIN IN CONTEMPT OF A COURT ORDER FOR ALMOST A YEAR MEANS THAT A CORRUPT D.C. COURT JUDGE ENGAGED IN FRAUD, THEFT, CORRUPTION AND EXTORTION CAN, AT WILL, DISREGARD A COURT ORDER, REFUSE TO ENFORCE A COURT ORDER AND IGNORE A COURT ORDER, IF IT IS, AS IN MY CASE, IN FURTHERANCE OF THE ONGOING CRIMINAL ENTERPRISE IN WHICH THE PRESIDING JUDGE IS PLAYING A MAJOR AND CRITICAL ROLE.*

MS. FRANKLIN: SO, I JUST THINK THAT THE MOTION TO VACATE ON HER PART IS JUST A -- -- NOTHING PUT A PLOY, BECAUSE SHE'S RUN OUT OF STRATEGIES. AND I, ALSO, THINK IT WAS FILED BECAUSE THIS WAS SUPPOSED TO CAUSE ME TO, I GUESS, BE SO EMBARRASSED I WAS SUPPOSED TO JUST BACK-OFF. BUT I DON'T HAVE ANYTHING TO BE EMBARRASSED ABOUT, OR TO HIDE OR ANYTHING.

SO, I MEAN, I JUST -- -- AND I -- -- AS I SAID, I REFUSE   YOUR HONOR KNOWS FROM THIS WHOLE COURT RECORD THAT I HAVE NOT HESITATED TO RESPOND IN WRITNG THROUGHOUT THE PENDENCY OF THIS LITIGATION, INCLUDING THE MOTION TO HAVE HER HELD IN CONTEMPT OF COURT FOR HER FAILURE TO ABIDE BY JUDGE STARR'S ORDER.

BUT, IN THIS INSTANCE, AS I SAID, I HAD TO GIVE -- I WAITED LONG AND HARD AND I JUST   I SAID THIS WOULD BE FOR ME, AFTER ALL THESE MANY, MANY YEARS OF COMING BEFORE THE COURT AND BEING A MEMBER OF THE BAR, THIS WOULD BE FOR ME A STEP INTO THE GUTTER WITH HER AND I'M NOT DOING IT -   I'M NOT GOING THERE.

I'LL HAVE TO JUST ------ I'LL HAVE TO JUST TAKE MY CHANCES THAT THE COURT WILL MAKE ITS DECISION ON WHAT HAS ALREADY BEEN SAID, AND DOCUMENTS THAT HAVE ALREADY BEEN PROVIDED. I WOULD NOT ------ I'M JUST NOT GOING TO GO IN THAT DIRECTION. IN WRITING, AT LEAST. AND SO THAT'S ------ THAT WAS MY POSITION, AND THAT REMAINS MY POSITION, ACTUALLY.

COMMENT AND ANALYSIS: #15 HOW MANY WAYS AND HOW MANY WORDS WOULD IT TAKE TO CONVINCE JUDGE EKANS THAT HE WAS THE PROBLEM?

THE COURT: I *KNOW THAT THE DEFENDANT HAS AFFIRMED SEVERAL TIMES ON THE RECORD BEFORE THIS JUDGE THAT SHE DID ENTER INTO THIS SETTLEMENT AGREEMENT. AND THE FACT THAT SHE'S FILED A MOTION TO VACATE IT I THINK CONFIRMS THAT IT'S CLEAR THAT THERE IS A SETTLEMENT AGREEMENT.*

COMMENT AND ANALYSIS: #16 JUDGE EKANS WAS A *MASTER MAGICIAN*, IF NOT *A JUJITSU JOCKEY* IN HIS LEGAL DEFINITIONS AS WE MOVED THROUGH THE ADJUDICATION OF MY LAWSUIT. BY THE TIME WE REACHED THE NOVEMBER 2014 COURT HEARING AND ON THE BRINK OF THE *RIGGED* DISMISSAL OF MY LAWSUIT IN JANUARY 2015, JUDGE EKANS WOULD HAVE ACCUSED ME OF ENGINEERING A FRAUD UPON THE COURT, SAID THERE WAS NEVER A SETTLEMENT AGREEMENT AND THAT HE HAD HAD NO BASIS IN THE FIRST PLACE FOR ISSUING ME A MONEY JUDGMENT AT THE CONCLUSION OF MY LAWSUIT IN OCTOBER 2011. *POWER REALLY DOES CORRUPT. AND ABSOLUTE POWER REALLY DOES CORRUPT ABSOLUTELY.*

THE COURT: BUT WHEN I WENT BACK THROUGH THE RECORD DID SHE EVER – AT ONE
                    TIME THERE WAS A DISPUTE BETWEEN THE TWO OF YOU BECAUSE SHE
                    WOULDN'T -- -- SHE WOULDN'T GIVE YOU A COPY OF THE SIGNED AGREEMENT.
                    DID YOU EVER GET A COPY OF IT?

MS. FRANKLIN: OF THE SETTLEMENT AGREEMENT?

THE COURT: THE SIGNED----- THAT SHE HAD SIGNED?

MS. FRANKLIN: OH, YOUR HONOR, THE SIGNED AGREEMENT OCCURRED AT HER HOTEL -- --

THE COURT: NO, I HEARD YOU SAY THAT, BUT -- --BUT -- --

MS. FRANKLIN: YES. BECAUSE I MADE------ BECAUSE IT'S A PART OF THE DISMISSAL. WE CAME
                    TO COURT AND I DISMISSED THE CASE, AND ATTACHED A COPY OF THE SIGNED
                    AGREEMENT.

THE COURT: LET'S SEE IF I CAN -- --

MS. FRANKLIN: YES. IT'S A PART OF THE COURT RECORD.

                    WHEN WE DISMISSED, I BELIEVE IT WAS A JOINT DISMISSAL, AND -- --

THE COURT: WAS THAT IN '09-- -- OR '10 OR '10?

MS. FRANKLIN: THAT WAS IN '10. THAT WAS LIKE FEBRUARY 4TH, I BELIEVE. BECAUSE I HAD FILED
                    A PRAECIPE. IT'S LIKE A PRECIPE ON FEBRUARY 3RD, AND THEN I FILED, I THINK
                    ON THE 4TH AN AMENDED PRAECIPE. AND IF YOU SEE AMENDED PRAECIPE
                    FERUARY 4TH, 2010, THE SIGNED AGREEMENT, NOTARIZED SIGNED AGREEMENT,
                    IS ATTACHED.

                    (PAUSE.)

MS. FRANKLIN: UNFORTUNATELY, YOUR HONOR, I DON'T HAVE COPIES WITH ME TODAY. SO -- --

THE COURT: I CAN PULL IT UP IF IT'S ALL SCANNED IN HERE.

MS. FRANKLIN: OH, IT'S IN THERE. IT'S -- --

                    (PAUSE.)

THE COURT: SEE, THE FIRST TIME YOU FILED A MOTION TO ENFORCE THE SETTLEMENT
                    AGREEMENT WAS JANUARY 6TH OF 2010. SHE FILED AN OPPOSITION TO THAT ON
                    FEBRUARY THE 1ST, 2010.

                    (PAUSE.)

MS. FRANKLIN: AND THAT WAS A ONE-PAGE FILING AND -- --

THE COURT: RIGHT.

MS. FRANKLIN: ---------------- I THINK IT WAS FOR, YOU KNOW, UNJUST ENRICHMENT BY THE ATTORNEY.

THE COURT: AND HERE'S THE PRAECIPE OF DISMISSAL, THAT'S WHAT YOU'RE TALKING ABOUT?

MS. FRANKLIN: THAT IS RIGHT.

THE COURT: AND HERE'S THE AMENDED PRAECIPE.

MS. FRANKLIN: CORRECT.

                  (PAUSE.)

THE COURT: YEAH, I -- --

MS. FRANKLIN: DO YOU SEE IT, YOUR HONOR?

THE COURT: I DO. BUT, WHEN -----THERE WAS A PRAECIPE FILED ON THE 2ND OF FEBRUARY, AND ANOTHER ONE FILED ON THE 3RD, THE AMENDED ONE -- --

MS. FRANKLIN: UM-HMM.

THE COURT: -- -- ON THE 3RD, AND SHE DIDN'T SIGN EITHER   EITHER AGREEMENT. SHE DIDN'T SIGN THE AGREEMENT THAT WAS FILED WITH EITHER OF THE PRAECIPE. YOUR SIGNATURE, THERE'S A NOTARY HERE, BUT SHE DIDN'T SIGN EITHER ONE OF THEM.

MS. FRANKLIN   WELL, YOUR HONOR -- --

THE COURT: SHE SIGNED   SHE SIGNED THE DISMISSAL.

MS. FRANKLIN: NO, SHE SIGNED THE AGREEMENT, ALSO. I HAVE IT -- --I MEAN, I'VE BEEN BRINGING IT TO COURT EVERY TIME AND, OF COURSE, TODAY I DON'T HAVE IT WITH ME BECAUSE   AND I HAVE IT. I MEAN, SHE SIGNED IT.

THE COURT: I'M NOT DISPUTING YOU, BUT I GUESS I'M CURIOUS WHY -- --

MS. FRANKLIN: YOU'RE SAYING IT'S NOT IN THE FILE?

THE COURT: WHY THE ONE THAT WAS FILED WITH THE PRAECIPE OF DISMISSAL ISN'T SIGNED BY HER. BECAUSE THE PRAECIPE IS SIGNED BY HER. THE DISMISSAL – YOU KNOW, SHE NOBODY DOUBTS THAT SHE IS SAGACIOUS.

MS. FRANKLIN: WELL, IT WAS------ YOUR HONOR, FIRST OF ALL, YOU KNOW, AS AN OFFICER OF THE COURT I WOULD NOT FILE A DISMISSAL, ATTACH -- --

THE COURT: I HAVE NO DOUBT ABOUT THAT. WHAT I HAVE TO DO IS BE AS SURE AS I CAN BE -- --

MS. FRANKLIN: EXACTLY.

THE COURT: -- -- THAT MY ORDERS ARE LAWFUL. AND IF I'M GOING TO CONVERT A SETTLEMENT AGREEMENT, I.E., A CONTRACT, INTO A JUDGMENT BECAUSE IT'S BEEN BREACHED BY ONE OF THE SETTLEMENT PARTIES, I HAVE TO BE CLEAR THAT IT IS A LEGALLY ENFORCEABE CONTRACT.

COMMENT AND ANALYSIS: #17 BY THIS TIME IN THE HEARING, I WAS THOROUGHLY CONVINCED THAT THE DYE HAD BEEN CAST AND THAT THE ISSUANCE OF A MONEY JUDGMENT TO ME WOULD AMOUNT TO NOTHING MORE THAN "SMOKE AND MIRRORS" TO BORROW EKANS' DISCRIPTION OF MY LAWSUIT DURING THE PROCEEDINGS. I WOULD RECEIVE A PIECE OF PAPER THAT WOULD, IN MY VIEW, REPRESENT NOTHING MORE THAN A REMINDER THAT CORRUPT D.C. COURT JUDGES AND FBI AGENTS HAD GOTTEN AWAY WITH STEALING MILLIONS OF DOLLARS OWED TO ME IN ATTORNEY'S FEES. THEY HAD DONE SO IN OPEN COURT AND IN BROAD DAYLIGHT. THEY HAD DONE SO WITHOUT FEAR OF ADMONITION, PROSECUTION OR PUNISHMENT. *THEY WOULD HAVE PROVEN THAT; INDEED, THEY ARE ABOVE THE LAW BECAUSE THEY ARE THE LAW.*

MS. FRANKLIN YOUR HONOR, I HAVE THE -- --

THE COURT: WHY -- -- WHY WAS THE ----- WHY WAS THE AMENDED PRAECIPE FILED THE DAY AFTER THE FIRST PRAECIPE FILED?

MS. FRANKLIN: WHAT HAPPENED WAS, UM, JUDGE STARR'S LAW CLERK SAID THAT THE SETTLEMENT AGREEMENT HAD THE WRONG DATE ON THE FIRST PAGE. AND THAT IN OTHER WORDS WE WOULD HAVE TO CONFORM THE CORRECT DATE ON THE FIRST PAGE WITH THE ACTUAL DATE OF THE NOTARIZED SIGNATURES. IF I RECALL THAT'S WHAT HAPPENED. THE LAW CLERK THE LAW CLERK CALLED AND THAT'S WHY I CAME BACK WITH AN AMENDED -- --

THE COURT:	I DON'T UNDERSTAND HOW ANYONE COULD HAVE MISSED THE FACT SHE DIDN'T SIGN THE AGREEMENT.
MS. FRANKLIN:	YOUR HONOR, MAY I GET----- MAY I PROVIDE YOU WITH A COPY?
THE COURT:	YES.

(PAUSE.)

THE COURT: I SEE WHAT HAPPENED. I SEE. YOU---- YOU SIGNED IT AT DIFFERENT TIMES. YOU SIGNED YOURS -- --

MS. FRANKLIN: RIGHT.

THE COURT:--------------------SHE SIGNED AT A DIFFERENT TIME BEFORE A NOTARY IN MARYLAND.

MS. FRANKLIN: IN BALTIMORE. BECAUSE I HAD TO GO TO HER HOTEL. SHE WASN'T IN D.C. THE NOTARY THAT I USE IS IN MY OFFICE BUILDING. AND, THEN, SHE HAD A HOTEL NOTARY THAT SHE HAD ARRANGED TO   FOR HER SIGNATURE.

(PAUSE.)

THE COURT: **WELL, I'M SATISFIED ON THIS RECORD THAT THIS IS A LEGALLY ENFORCEABLE CONTRACT. SO, I'M GONNA CHANGE IT INTO A JUDGMENT.**

(PAUSE.)

COMMENT AND ANALYSIS: #18 CHANGING MY SETTLEMENT AGREEMENT INTO A JUDGMENT WAS MORE FOR JUDGE EKANS' BENEFIT AND THE BENEFIT OF HIS CO-CONSPIRATORS. **THE ISSUANCE TO ME OF A MONEY JUDGMENT GAVE EKANS THE OFF-RAMP HE NEEDED TO ESCAPE THE ENFORCEMENT OF JUDGE STARR'S ORDER FOR THE PRODUCTION OF BANK STATEMENTS BY BRIANNA JONES.**

THE COURT: NOW, REGARDING THE AMOUNT OF THE JUDGMENT, YOU'VE------ ONCE AGAIN YOU'VE PUT YOUR FINGER ON THE PULSE OF -- --

MS. FRANKLIN: EXACTLY.

THE COURT: -- -- GREATEST CONCERN. TYPICALLY, WE HAVE JUDGMENTS THAT REPRESENT LIQUIDATED DAMAGES OR WE HAVE JUDGMENTS THAT HAVE BEEN PROVEN THROUGH MORE TRADITIONAL   MORE TRADITIONAL METHODS.

WHAT WE'RE CONFRONTED WITH HERE IS NO PROOF OTHER THAN VERBAL TESTIMONY-- --

MS. FRANKLIN: RIGHT.

COMMENT AND ANALYSIS: #19 THE GASLIGHTING ENGAGED IN HERE BY EKANS IS SICKENING. HE HAD A DUTY TO ENFORCE A COURT ORDER WHICH HE INTENTIONALLY AVOIDED FOR HIS BENEFIT AND THAT OF THE OTHER D.C. JUDICIAL BENEFICIARIES OF THE D.C. JUDICIAL AND FBI CRIMINAL ENTERPRISE.

EKANS SHOULD HAVE BEEN ADDRESSING HIS RESPONSIBILITY TO ENFORCE JUDGE STARR'S ORDER. INSTEAD, HE HID BEHIND HIS REQUIREMENTS FOR CONVERTING A COURT SETTLEMENT INTO A JUDGMENT.

THERE SHOULD NEVER HAVE BEEN A DISCUSSION OF THE REQUISITE PROOF NEEDED FOR THE ISSUANCE OF A MONEY JUDGMENT. THIS WAS EKANS' JUDICIAL TRICK AND TOOL HE USED TO AVOID HIS JUDICIAL OBLIGATION TO ENFORCE THE ORDER OF A PRIOR JUDGE WHO WAS NOT A PARTICIPANT OF THE CRIMINAL ENTERPRISE.

THE COURT: ----THAT----THAT THIS AMOUNT OF   WELL, I WON'T SAY THIS AMOUNT, THAT -----THAT AN AMOUNT OF MONEY PASSED THROUGH TESTIMENTARY ESTATE TO MS. JONES. AND THAT THE------ I MEAN, AS I UNDERSTAND IT, THIS WAS IN THE NATURE OF A LOTTERY TICKET ----

MS. FRANKLIN: YES.

THE COURT:--------------------THAT SHE HAD TO, THEN, CLAIM?

MS. FRANKLIN: NO. SHE ---- SINCE WE WERE HERE LAST, YOU HONOR, I CONTACTED THE D.C. LOTTERY BOARD. BECAUSE WHAT HAPPENED WAS SHE----JUST TO REFRESH THE COURT'S RECOLLECTION, WE ---- SHE CAME TO ME SAYING SHE HAD BEEN MOLESTED WHEN SHE WAS TEN OR ELEVEN AND RAPED BY WILLIE LEE RIDGEWAY.

THE COURT: THAT PART I REMEMBER.

BARBARA WASHINGTON FRANKLIN

MS. FRANKLIN: WILLIE LEE RIDGEWAY WAS ONE OF TWO WINNERS OF THE NINETY MILLION DOLLAR JACKPOT IN THE DISTRICT WHEN IT WAS NINETY MILLION DOLLARS. SO, HE GOT FORTY-FIVE AND THIS OTHER GENTLEMAN GOT FORTY-FIVE.

SHE -- -- THIS WAS BACK, YOU KNOW, 1993, WHATEVER, AND SHE------DECEMBER 1993. HE DIED IN 1995 AT HOWARD UNIVERSITY, SEPTEMBER 1995. SHE'S WATCHING T.V ----- AND THIS HAPPENED WHEN SHE WAS TEN OR ELEVEN AND ALL. BUT NOW SHE'S IN HER 30'S, MID 30'S, OR WHATEVER. SHE'S WATCHING T.V. AND ALL OF A SUDDEN SHE SEES THIS NEWS ABOUT THIS MAN. SHE SAYS, OH, MY GOODNESS, THAT'S THE MAN WHO RAPED ME. THAT'S THE MAN WHO MOLESTED ME, BLAH, BLAH, BLAH. SAW ALL THESE DIFFERENT ATTORNEYS. ULTIMATELY CAME TO MY OFFICE.

FIRST TIME SHE CAME TO MY OFFICE 1995 OR SO I SAID, I'M SORRY, I DECLINE. THE LEVEL AND DEGREE OF YOUR ANGER WOULD MAKE IT IMPOSSIBLE FOR ME TO WORK SUCCESSFULLY WITH YOU, AND I DID NOT TAKE HER CASE. ABOUT A YEAR OR SO LATER SHE CAME BACK TO ME AND WE TALKED AND I AGREED TO TAKE THE CASE.

SO, WHEN I CONTACTED MINNIE PEARSON WHO'S REPRESENTING WILLIE LEE RIDGEWAY AT THE TIME OVER AT, YOU KNOW, PEARSON, MANNING AND HENRY, AND I SENT THEM A SETTLEMENT PROPOSAL. SOLID. NOTHING. NEXT THING I KNOW HE HAS MOVED TO FLORIDA, BROWARD COUNTY. AND, SINCE THEY REFUSED TO ENTER INTO ANY KIND OF SETTLEMENT DISCUSSIONS ABOUT IT AFTER I TOLD THEM THE BACKGROUND AND ALL THAT IN A LETTER, I THEN FILED SUIT ON HER BEHALF, IN MS. JONES' BEHALF, IN BROWARD COUNTY CIRCUIT COURT.

AFTER HAVING RETAINED COUNSEL, ET CETERA, ET CETERA, GOT A PRO HAC VICE MOTION IN PROBATE DIVISION FROM JUDGE MICHAEL ROSENBAUM AND ALL OF THAT. AND, AT SOME POINT WILLIE LEE RIDGEWAY TOLD HIS ATTORNEYS ON HIS DEATH BED, SUPPOSEDLY, AND I MET WITH AT LEAST ONE LAWYER IN RICHMOND, VIRGINIA, IN HIS OFFICE, HE SAID, SETTLE THIS WITH THIS WOMAN. JUST SETTLE IT. I DON'T WANT   DO WHATEVER NEEDS TO BE DONE.

MS. FRANKLIN: WELL, THE LAWYERS HAD A DIFFERENT IDEA AND THEY DIDN'T WANT TO SETTLE. AND, SO, WHEN HE DIED AFTER HAVING RECEIVED TWO PAYMENTS FROM THE LOTTERY BOARD, THE   HIS ESTATE NOTIFIED THE LOTTERY BOARD. THEY WERE CLAIMING THE BALANCE. AND ACCORDING TO THE MULTISTATE REGULATIONS OR WHATEVER, A GAMING REGULATION, ONCE A PERSON PASSES HIS ESTATE CAN DEMAND THE ENTIRE AMOUNT.

IN HIS CASE, BECAUSE IT WAS A FORTY-FIVE MILLION DOLLAR JACKPOT WINNING THAT HE WON, HE WAS ENTITLED TO OVER   IT WAS, LIKE, FORTY PLUS ONE OR WHATEVER, MILLION DOLLARS. AND, SO, THE LAWYERS FOR HIS ESTATE IN 1997 - MARCH OF 1997, SETTLED MS. JONES' CASE FOR THE THIRTY-FOUR MILLION, SAYING TO THE LOTTERY BOARD WE NEED THE TOTAL AMOUNT PAID TO THE ESTATE AS SOON AS POSSIBLE BECAUSE WE HAVE THIS THIRTY-FOUR MILLION DOLLAR CLAIM THAT NEEDS TO BE PAID. THIS IS THE LARGEST CLAIM AGAINST THIS GENTLEMAN.

COMMENT AND ANALYSIS: #20 IN MARCH 1997, THE TEAM OF CO-CONSPIRATORS, INCLUDING THE D.C. PROSECUTOR, THE U.S. DISTRICT COURT JUDGE FOR THE DISTRICT OF COLUMBIA WHO SENTENCED MY HUSBAND, THE CORRUPT D.C. COURT JUDGES AND FBI AGENTS HAD UNLEASHED THE POLITICALLY MOTIVATED CRIMINAL PROSECUTION OF MY HUSBAND, IN PART, IN RETALIATION TO MY REFUSAL TO WITHDRAW MY REPRESENTATION OF BRIANNA JONES AND VOLUNTARILY FORFEIT THE ESTIMATED $50 MILLION IN ATTORNEY'S FEES OWED TO ME WHICH WOULD THEREAFTER BE MADE AVAILABLE FOR THEFT AND CONFISCATION BY THE D.C. JUDICIAL AND FBI CO-CONSPIRATORS.

THIS WOULD PROVE TO BE THE MOST DIFFICULT, STRESSFUL AND TRAUMATIC TIME OF MY LIFE. BUT NEVERTHELESS, I NEVER SECOND-GUESSED GOD NOR DOUBTED HIS SOVEREIGNTY. IN FACT, WHEN I LOOKED BACK ON THIS PART OF MY JOURNEY, I REALIZED THAT MY FAITH IN GOD HAD GROWN EXPONENTIALLY.

MS. FRANKLIN: SO, MS. JONES HAD MET WITH THE LOTTERY BOARD. THEY HAD MET WITH THE LOTTERY BOARD. AND, SO, AS A RESULT, THE LOTTERY BOARD FILED A STAKEHOLDER ACTION WITH THE DISTRICT AND SAID LISTEN, TELL US TO WHOM SHALL WE PAY. WE HAVE HIS MONEY. IT IS   IT'S HERE, WE HAVE IT, BUT WE NEED TO KNOW, BECAUSE WE HAVE THIS CLAIMANT, WE HAVE THIS OTHER CLAIMANT.

MS. FRANKLIN: AND THEY WENT BEFORE   JUDGE MANDARIN WAS THE JUDGE. AND AT THAT TIME -- -- THIS IS WHEN, YOU KNOW, THE BEHIND-MY-BACK STUFF STARTED. BECAUSE I SAID TO HER, LISTEN, WE NEED TO GO IN AND INTERVENE BEFORE THE COURT, BUT YOU NEED TO GIVE ME COPIES OF THE SETTLEMENT AGREEMENT. I WILL NOT FILE AN INTERVENTION MOTION WITHOUT HAVING COPIES OF THE SETTLEMENT AGREEMENT. SO SHE WOUDN'T DO THAT, AND SO I NEVER FILED ON HER BEHALF. BECAUSE THE ESTATE WAS THE ONLY CLAIMANT BEFORE THE COURT, JUDGE MANDARIN GRANTED SUMMARY JUDGMENT TO THE ATTORNEYS FOR THE ESTATE.

COMMENT AND ANALYSIS: #21 JUDGE RICHARD MANDARIN WAS A KEY D.C. JUDICIAL CO-CONSPIRATOR. IN RESPONSE TO THE STAKEHOLDER ACTION BROUGHT BY THE D.C. LOTTERY BOARD AND THE D.C. GOVERNMENT IN 1997, HE ISSUED THE COURT ORDER THAT THE D.C. LOTTERY BOARD PAY THE REMAINDER OF THE $40-PLUS MILLION IN LOTTERY WINNINGS OWED TO WILLIE LEE RIDGEWAY TO THE LEGAL REPRESENTATIVES OF THE ESTATE OF WILLIE LEE RIDGEWAY, THE LAW FIRM OF ADAGIO AND MANDEL OF FORT LAUDERDALE, FLA., LED BY ATTORNEY AND FIRM PARTNER, JEFFREY BRETT WINSLOW. THESE FUNDS WERE, THEREAFTER, TRANSFERRED TO AN ACCOUNT AT NATIONSBANK (BANK OF AMERICA) MANAGED BY ADAGIO & MANDEL, LEGAL REPRESENTATIVES OF THE RIDGEWAY ESTATE.

JUDGE MANDARIN MET IN HIS JUDGE'S CHAMBERS WITH JONES, ACCOMPANIED BY BETH HOLLISTER, FOR THE SPECIFIC PURPOSE OF DISSUADING AND EFFECTIVELY PREVENTING JONES FROM INTERVENING IN THE STAKEHOLDER LAWSUIT FILED BY D.C. CORPORATION COUNSEL ON BEHALF OF THE D.C. LOTTERY BOARD AND PRIOR TO HIS ISSUANCE OF THE MAY 1997 ORDER PREVIOUSLY REFERENCED.

JUDGE MANDARIN WAS FULLY AWARE THAT JONES WAS REPRESENTED BY ME. HOWEVER, MANDARIN INTENTIONALLY AND PURPOSEFULLY MADE CERTAIN THAT I WAS NOT NOTIFIED OF THE MEETING IN HIS CHAMBERS. PREVIOUSLY, I HAD APPEARED ON JONES' BEHALF AT A STATUS HEARING IN MANDARIN'S COURTROOM. REPORTEDLY, ADAGIO & MANDEL HAD ARGUED TO MANDARIN THAT THE $40 MILLION PAYMENT TO THE ESTATE BY THE D.C. LOTTERY BOARD WOULD BE USED TO PAY THE $34 MILLION SETTLEMENT WITH JONES.

THE ODYSSEY OF JUDICIAL CORRUPTION

ACCORDING TO BRIANNA JONES, JUDGE RICHARD MANDARIN HAD GRANTED THE RIDGEWAY ESTATE'S MOTION THAT THE REMAINING LOTTTERY PAYMENTS OWED TO DECEDENT RIDGEWAY IN THE AMOUNT OF OVER $40 MILLION SHOULD BE PAID TO THE ESTATE. THE ESTATE'S MOTION WAS IN RESPONSE TO THE STAKEHOLDER SUIT THAT HAD BEEN FILED WITH THE COURT AND ASSIGNED TO MANDARIN BY THE THEN CO-CONSPIRATOR D.C. SUPERIOR COURT CHIEF JUDGE, GEORGE SKINNER. FOR THIS REASON, I ALWAYS REFERRED TO JUDGE MANDARIN AS THE "STAKEHOLDER JUDGE" WHEN CRAFTING THE MANUSCRIPT FOR THIS WORK.

I COULDN'T BELIEVE MY EARS. JONES, ALTHOUGH REPRESENTED BY ME AS HER COUNSEL, WAS MEETING WITH JUDGES IN D.C. SUPERIOR COURT! I COULDN'T RESIST THE THOUGHT THAT PERHAPS BETH HOLLISTER HAD BEEN RIGHT AFTER ALL. SHE HAD LONG AGO INFORMED JONES THAT SHE HAD FRIENDS ON THE D.C. COURT BENCH, AND THAT NO MATTER WHAT I DID, I WOULD NOT PREVAIL. HOLLISTER WOULD PROVE THAT THESE WERE COURT JUDGES WHO, FOR A PIECE OF THE FINANCIAL PIE OF THE $34 MILLION SETTLEMENT, WOULD READILY ABUSE THEIR JUDICIAL POWER OF DISCRETION AND GLADLY DEFEAT THE PURSUIT OF MY ATTORNEY'S FEES, AND THE FAIR AND EQUAL JUSTICE THAT I WAS ENTITLED TO UNDER THE LAW. THESE WERE CORRUPT, CONSCIENCE-FREE AND AMORAL D.C. COURT JUDGES WHO COULD CARE LESS ABOUT THE SO-CALLED RULE OF LAW OR FAIR AND EQUAL JUSTICE.

BUT IN REASONING THE MATTER OUT, I HAD TO CONSIDER THAT JUDGE MANDARIN HAD, WITH THE STROKE OF HIS PEN, WRITTEN AN ORDER THAT DIRECTED THE D.C. LOTTERY BOARD TO PAY OVER $40 MILLION DOLLARS TO THE ESTATE ATTORNEYS' ESCROW ACCOUNT. IF BRIANNA JONES HAD TOLD ME THE TRUTH, IT'S MORE THAN REASONABLE TO CONCLUDE THAT MANDARIN HAD ASSURED JONES IN THEIR FACE-TO-FACE MEETING IN HIS CHAMBERS THAT IT WASN'T NECESSARY FOR HER (WHILE IGNORING MY ROLE AS HER COUNSEL) TO INTERPLEAD AS A RIGHTFUL CLAIMANT IN THE STAKEHOLDER SUIT FILED BY THE DISTRICT OF COLUMBIA AND THE D.C LOTTERY BOARD.

THE INTERPLEADER MOTION THAT I WOULD HAVE FILED ON BEHALF OF BRIANNA JONES WOULD HAVE ESSENTIALLY REQUESTED THAT THE COURT DIRECT THE D.C. LOTTERY BOARD TO PAY TO BRIANNA JONES THE $34 MILLION DOLLARS, PURSUANT TO THE TWO SETTLEMENT AGREEMENTS, OR IN THE ALTERNATIVE, AN ORDER THAT THE D.C. LOTTERY BOARD PAY TO THE ATTORNEYS FOR THE RIDGEWAY ESTATE THE OVER $40 MILLION DOLLARS DUE TO THE ESTATE, SPECIFYING THAT OF THE TOTAL AMOUNT, THE ESTATE BE DIRECTED TO PAY THE CIVIL CLAIM OF BRIANNA JONES OF $34 MILLION.

BUT SUCH AN ORDER WOULD HAVE FLOWN IN THE FACE OF THE OVERALL OPERATION OF THE MASSIVE FRAUD AND CORRUPTION AND SWINDLE OF THE MILLIONS OF DOLLARS OWED TO ME IN ATTORNEY'S FEES. THE DECISION HAD ALREADY BEEN MADE TO DEFRAUD ME OF MY ATTORNEY'S FEES, AMOUNTING TO 40% OF THE $34 MILLION CASE SETTLEMENT. THE DECISION HAD BEEN MADE BY THE DECISION MAKERS, A.K.A. THE D.C. JUDICIAL CO-CONSPIRATORS, THAT I WASN'T GOING TO GET A DIME. PERIOD. AND THAT THERE WAS NOTHING I COULD DO ABOUT IT.

TO FILE SUCH A MOTION WOULD HIGHTLIGHT ME AS THE ATTORNEY OF RECORD IN LINE TO RECEIVE THE MILLIONS OF DOLLARS IN ATTORNEY'S FEES PURSUANT TO THE CONTINGENCY FEE AGREEMENT BETWEEN ME AND BRIANNA JONES. I WAS AGAIN REMINDED OF BETH HOLLISTER'S STATEMENT TO BRIANNA JONES THAT SHE HAD FRIENDS ON THE BENCH AT D.C. SUPERIOR COURT WHO WOULD SEE TO IT THAT MY LAWSUIT WOULD NOT ONLY NOT GO ANYWHERE, BUT WOULD ULTIMATELY BE DISMISSED BY THE PRESIDING JUDGE. HOLLISTER'S PROPHECY PROVED TO BE ALL TOO ACCURATE.

IT STANDS TO REASON THAT THE ESTATE WOULD BE MORE THAN WILLING TO PAY MANDARIN HIS CUT FOR ORDERING THAT THE ENTIRE LOTTERY PROCEEDS OWED TO WILLIE LEE RIDGEWAY BE PAID TO THE ESTATE'S ATTORNEYS ON BEHALF OF THE ESTATE.

THE CONFIRMATION THAT MANDARIN WAS IN SOME FASHION COMPENSATED BY THE ESTATE AND ITS LAWYERS WAS REVEALED TO ME IN THE SUMMER OF 1997, FOLLOWING THE $34 MILLION SETTLEMENT OF THE $100 MILLION FLORIDA LAWSUIT THAT I HAD CRAFTED AND FILED ON BEHALF OF BRIANNA JONES IN THE BROWARD COUNTY CIRCUIT COURT IN FORT LAUDERDALE, FLA.

I HAD REPRESENTED A CLIENT IN A CONTESTED DIVORCE ACTION. THE FINAL HEARING AT WHICH THE DIVORCE WAS SCHEDULED TO BE GRANTED WAS SCHEDULED IN A SMALL COURTROOM ON THE FIRST FLOOR OF THE COURTHOUSE. MANDARIN WAS THE PRESIDING JUDGE ASSIGNED TO HEAR THE CASE AND ULTIMATELY RENDER A JUDGMENT OF DIVORCE.

WHILE WE WAITED FOR MANDARIN TO ENTER THE SMALL COURTROOM, THE COURTROOM CLERK APOLOGIZED FOR THE JUDGE'S DELAY. HE ALSO VOLUNTEERED THAT THE JUDGE HAD BEEN AWAY ON VACATION, BUT HAD DECIDED TO CUT HIS VACATION SHORT AND RETURN TO WORK.

RED FLAGS WENT UP IN MY MIND. WHAT JUDGE CUTS HIS OR HER VACATION SHORT TO RETURN TO PUZZLE PALACE, THE NAME GIVEN TO D.C. SUPERIOR COURT BY TRIAL ATTORNEYS? MANDARIN HAD LIED TO HIS COURTROOM CLERK AND STAFF. HE HAD CUT HIS VACATION SHORT AND RETURNED TO COURT TO CONDUCT MY HEARING AND TO LOOK ME OVER. THAT WAS THE SIMPLE TRUTH OF THE MATTER.

WITHOUT MISSING A BEAT, I SAID TO THE COURTROOM CLERK, "OH, WHERE DID THE JUDGE GO?' LOOKING DIRECTLY AT ME, THE COURTROOM CLERK ANSWERED, "FORT LAUDERDALE." BINGO! THERE WAS MY ANSWER. MANDARIN EITHER WENT TO COLLECT HIS PAYOFF OR HE WENT TO SERVE AS THE BAG MAN FOR ALL THE D.C. COURT JUDGES AND/OR FBI AGENTS INVOLVED IN THE SWINDLE AND THEFT OF MY ATTORNEY'S FEES.

I RESOLVED THEN AND THERE THAT I WOULD NEVER GIVE UP THE PURSUIT OF THE JUSTICE DUE ME IN THE FORM OF THE MILLIONS OF DOLLARS THAT HAD BEEN STRIPPED FROM ME BY THE TEAM OF CORRUPT D.C. COURT JUDGES AND FBI AGENTS. I ALSO RESOLVED THAT I WOULD HAVE TO BEGIN TO CONSCIOUSLY SEE THE D.C. JUDGES INVOLVED IN THIS MASSIVE SWINDLE FOR WHAT THEY WERE---STREET THUGS AND MOBSTERS IN BLACK ROBES, OPERATING WITH ABSOLUTELY NO RESTRAINT OR FEAR OF QUESTION, INVESTIGATION, PROSECUTION, INDICTMENT, ARREST, PUNISHMENT OR PRISON.

IT WAS THE OPPORTUNITY OF CASES SUCH AS MINE THAT JUSTIFIED THEIR STAYING ON THE BENCH AS GOVERNMENT EMPLOYEES AND EARNING FAR LESS THAN THEY WOULD AS LAWYERS IN THE PRIVATE SECTOR. MY CASE REPRESENTED THE OPPORTUNITY OF TAKING MILLIONS UNDER THE TABLE WITHOUT BEING SEEN OR SUSPECTED. IT WAS ALL A MATTER OF ISSUING THE RIGHT ORDER TO THE RIGHT PARTY, STANDING BACK AND WATCHING THE VICTIM BEING DEFRAUDED, THE VICTIM'S CHARACTER BEING ASSASSINATED ON THE PUBLIC COURT RECORD AND, WORST OF ALL, THE VICTIM'S FAMILY BEING CRIMINALLY PROSECUTED, INDICTED AND SUBJECED TO HOUSE ARREST OSTENSIBLY FOR THE ALLEGED THEFT OF AN ESTIMATED $24,000 IN GOVERNMENT FUNDS, BUT IN REALITY, FOR THE MILLIONS OF DOLLARS IN ATTORNEY'S FEES BEING STOLEN BY D.C. COURT JUDGES AND FBI AGENTS.

WHAT ALLOWED ME TO STAY THE COURSE THROUGH THE YEARS OF MY HUSBAND'S POLITICALLY MOTIVATED CRIMINAL PROSECUTION, ILLNESS AND DEATH, AND THE MANY YEARS OF PRACTICING LAW AS A SOLO TRIAL ATTORNEY, AND MAINTAIN AN EQUILIBRIUM THAT EVEN I DIDN'T KNOW THAT I WAS CAPABLE OF, WAS THAT I ALWAYS SAW GOD AT THE CENTER OF THE CAULDRON OF MY HELLISH EXPERIENCE.

I KNEW THAT PHYSICALLY I WAS OUTNUMBERED BY THOSE ON THE TAKE. BUT SPIRITUALLY I KNEW THAT GOD AND I WERE NOT ONLY A MAJORITY, BUT AN UNSTOPPABLE TEAM. I ALSO KNEW THAT I HAD THE VICTORY, EVEN THOUGH IT HAD YET TO MANIFEST ON THE PHYSICAL PLANE.

THE SATANIC STRONGHOLDS OF GREED, CORRUPTION, DECEPTION AND BETRAYAL WERE MILITANTLY ALIGNED AGAINST ME. I WAS NOT SO FOOLISH TO THINK I COULD OVERCOME THEM. I COULD NOT. BUT I WAS WISE ENOUGH TO KNOW WHO COULD---AND THAT WAS JESUS. I ALSO KNEW THAT I WAS NOT IN THIS BATTLE BY MYSELF. THE HOLY SPIRIT WAS WAY UP AHEAD OF ME. AND MY CHALLENGE WAS TO HAVE THE COURAGE TO FOLLOW HIS LEADING, NO MATTER HOW TOUGH, HOW TIGHT OR HOW HOT IT GOT. I KNEW THAT ONE DAY I WOULD EMERGE OUT OF THE FURNACE UNSINGED AND WITHOUT EVEN THE SMELL OF SMOKE ON ME. I LEANED ON THAT PROMISE DAY AND NIGHT.

MANDARIN HAD ISSUED THE ORDER DIRECTING THE D.C. LOTTERY BOARD TO PAY TO THE FLORIDA LAW FIRM REPRESENTING THE ESTATE OVER $40 MILLION. THUS, THERE IS NO WAY HE WAS NOT GOING TO BE COMPENSATED FOR HIS SERVICES, IN CASH, BY THE FIRM. AND I FURTHER BELIEVE THAT MANDARIN'S TRIP TO FORT LAUDERDALE IN THE SUMMER OF 1997 WAS FOR THE PURPOSE OF COLLECTING HIS BOUNTY AND PAY-OFFS FOR HIS JUDICIAL COLLEAGUES AND CO-CONSPIRATORS.

MANDARIN'S COMPENSATION FROM THE SWINDLE WOULD HAVE BEEN GREAT, GIVEN THE SIGNIFICANCE OF HIS ROLE IN THE FRAUD, THEFT, CORRUPTION AND EXTORTION CONSPIRACY AND CRIMINAL ENTERPRISE. MANDARIN'S PAYOFF WOULD ALSO HAVE TO BE GREAT GIVEN THE SWINDLERS' PLAN TO SEE TO IT THAT I NEVER RECEIVED SO MUCH AS A CENT FROM THE $34 MILLION SETTLEMENT. WHAT JUDGE RETURNS EARLY FROM A VACATION IN FORT LAUDERDALE JUST TO HEAR A DIVORCE MATTER THAT IS ESSENTIALLY UNCONTESTED? MANDARIN OBVIOUSLY THOUGHT I WAS ASLEEP WHEN I HAD MY EYES OPEN THE ENTIRE TIME OF THE SWINDLE'S OPERATION.

MS. FRANKLIN: AND, SO, I   SINCE WE WERE HERE LAST I CONTACTED THE LOTTERY BOARD BY LETTER SAYING WOULD YOU PLEASE TELL ME TO WHOM THE FORTY-PLUS MILLION WAS PAID, WHEN IT WAS PAID, AND SO FORTH AND SO ON. THEY GOT RIGHT BACK TO ME WITHIN A DAY OR TWO AND SAID WE'RE GONNA GIVE YOU - - -- WE'RE GONNA TREAT YOUR LETTER AS A FOIA REQUEST AND GIVE YOU THE WHOLE FILE.

SO, I HAVE THE WHOLE LOTTERY BOARD FILE THAT THE FORTY-PLUS MILLION WAS PAID TO THE ESTATE, THE ATTORNEYS REPRESENTING THE ESTATE. I HAVE THE LETTERS BACK AND FORTH BETWEEN NATIONS BANK. I HAVE THE ROUTING NUMBER. ESTATE BANK NUMBER. THEY SENT ME EVERYTHING. MORE THAN I COULD HAVE ASKED FOR. WASN'T ASKING FOR THAT, BUT THEY SAID THAT'S HOW WE'RE GONNA TREAT THIS.

SO, WE KNOW THAT THE MONIES WENT TO THE ATTORNEYS FOR THE ESTATE OF WILLIE LIEE RIDGEWAY. OUT OF THAT FORTY-PLUS MILLION, THEY WERE SUPPOSED TO PAY MS. JONES' CLAIM OF THIRTY-FOUR. BUT, AS IT TURNS OUT, LOOKING BACK, YOUR HONOR, SHE WAS USED, AND I WAS USED AS A STRAW. THIS WAS JUST THEIR WAY OF GETTING THAT MONEY AND THEY NEVER   I CAN HONESTLY SAY THAT NOW BECAUSE THIS IS MY STRONGEST SENSE. THEY NEVER INTENDED TO PAY HER. NEVER   NEVER INTENDED FOR ME TO BE PAID. BUT USED MY LAWSUIT AND USED THAT CLAIM TO TAKE THE FORTY-PLUS MILLION AND THAT MONEY HAS NEVER   HAS NEVER BEEN PAID OUT. AND, SO, THAT'S - THAT'S THE LONG AND SHORT OF IT.

MS. FRANKLIN: SO, I HAVE, AS I SAID, IN TERMS OF SUBPOENAING BANK RECORDS, I MEAN, I HAVE NOW THE CORRESPONDENCE FROM BANK OF ------ NATIONS BANK AT THAT TIME, NATIONS BANK BETWEEN THE ------ ADAGIO AND MANDEL, THE FIRM THAT REPRESENTED THE ESTATE, YOU KNOW, IN TERMS OF ACCOUNT NUMBERS AND ALL OF THAT, AND SO FORTH AND SO ON.

SO, THERE WAS NEVER AN ISSUE   THERE'S NO ISSUE AS TO MONIES BEING PAID TO THE LAW FIRM. AND THE ONLY ISSUE IS WHY HASN'T THAT MONEY BEEN PAID TO THIS CLAIMANT? BECAUSE YOU SETTLED WITH HER. YOU USED   YOU USED HER CLAIM TO SAY THAT THIS   ALL OF THIS SHOULD BE PAID. AND, THE REASON THAT THE LOTTERY BOARD FILED THE STAKEHOLDER ACTION WAS BECAUSE BOTH MS. JONES AND THE ESTATE WENT TO D.C. LOTTERY. SHE MET WITH D.C. LOTTERY AT LEAST TWICE SAYING, YOU KNOW, I SHOULD GET THIRTY- FOUR MILLON BECAUSE I HAD SETTLED IT WITH   AND THEY JUST WENT INTO COURT AND   BECAUSE SHE WOULDN'T GO BEFORE THE COURT.

NOW, WHY WOULDN'T SHE ALLOW ME TO FILE A MOTION, OR WHY WOULDN'T SHE GO BEFORE THE COURT, THAT'S A GOOD QUESTION. I DON'T KNOW. BUT I KNOW SHE CONTACTED THE LOTTERY BOARD.

COMMENT AND ANALYSIS: #22 BRIANNA JONES, ACCOMPANIED BY BETH HOLLISTER, HER CONSPIRACY COACH AND MENTOR AND A KEY CO-CONSPIRATOR, MET IN THE CHAMBERS OF JUDGE RICHARD MANDARIN ACCORDING TO BRIANNA JONES. JUDGE MANDARIN, A KEY D.C. JUDICIAL CO-CONSPIRATOR, ASSURED JONES THAT SHE DIDN'T NEED TO FILE A MOTION TO INTERVENE IN THE STAKEHOLDER ACTION. MANDARIN FURTHER INFORMED BRIANNA JONES THAT NOR DID I NEED TO BE PRESENT IN THE MEETING IN HIS CHAMBERS WITH HER AND HOLLISTER, EVEN THOUGH JUDGE MANDARIN WAS FULLY AWARE THAT I REPRESENTED BRIANNA JONES IN THE $100 MILLION FLORIDA LAWSUIT AGAINST THE RIDGEWAY ESTATE.

IT WAS CLEAR TO ME THAT JUDGES EKANS AND MANDARIN WERE NOW ON THE SAME TEAM OF D.C. JUDICIAL CO-CONSPIRATORS IN THIS HISTORIC D.C. JUDICIAL AND FBI CRIMINAL ENTERPRISE.

ON APRIL 4, 1997, AS LEGAL COUNSEL FOR BRIANNA JONES, I ATTENDED A SCHEDULED STATUS HEARING BEFORE D.C. COURT JUDGE RICHARD MANDARIN. THE DISTRICT OF COLUMBIA HAD FILED A STAKEHOLDER ACTION REQUESTING THAT THE COURT DETERMINE AND IDENTIFY THE LAWFUL RECIPIENT AND PAYEE OF THE REMAINDER OF THE $40-PLUS MILLION LOTTERY PROCEEDS OWED TO THE ESTATE OF WILLIE LEE RIDGEWAY. THE DISTRICT OF COLUMBIA FURTHER REQUESTED THAT THE COURT ORDER THAT THE D.C. LOTTERY BOARD PAY THE $40-PLUS MILLION THEN ON DEPOSIT IN NATIONSBANK (BANK OF AMERICA) TO THE LEGAL REPRESENTATIVES OF THE ESTATE, THE LAW FIRM OF ADAGIO AND MANDEL OF FORT LAUDERDALE, FLA.

ACCORDING TO MY HANDWRITTEN NOTES OF THE HEARING, JUDGE MANDARIN STATED THAT AN ANSWER BY THE RIDGEWAY ESTATE IN THE FORM OF A MOTION FOR SUMMARY JUDGMENT HAD BEEN FILED. JUDGE MANDARIN ALSO STATED THAT NO OPPOSITION WAS IN THE FILE. AND AS A KEY JUDICIAL CO-CONSPIRATOR, HE MADE SURE NO OPPOSITION WOULD BE FILED. HE DID SO BY MEETING WITH BRIANNA JONES AND BETH HOLLISTER IN HIS CHAMBERS WHEN HE ASSURED BRIANNA JONES SHE DID NOT NEED TO FILE AN OPPOSITION OF ANY KIND, NOR DID I NEED TO BE PRESENT IN THE MEETING AS HER LEGAL REPRESENTATIVE.

FURTHER, ACCORDING TO MY HANDWRITTEN NOTES OF THE HEARING, MILES LETT, ASSISTANT CORPORATION COUNSEL, IDENTIFIED HIMSELF AS REPRESENTING THE D.C. LOTTERY BOARD AND THE DISTRICT OF COLUMBIA IN THE STAKEHOLDER ACTION. HE ARGUED THE MATTER WAS NOT APPROPRIATE FOR TRACK 1,2 OR 3. HE FURTHER STATED IT WOULD BE INAPPROPRIATE TO PLACE THE FUNDS IN COURT. HE ALSO ARGUED THAT "SUMMARY JUDGMENT DOESN'T GET US THERE."

WHEN JUDGE MANDARIN ASKED, "HOW DO YOU WANT TO PROCEED?" IT WAS AGREED BY ALL PARTIES PRESENT THAT 10 CALENDAR DAYS WOULD BE PERMITTED FOR ALL INTERESTED PARTIES TO FILE. JUDGE MANDARIN SAID HE COULDN'T TELL THE OTHER SIDE WHAT TO FILE. HOWEVER, ACCORDING TO BRIANNA JONES, HE TOLD HER NOT TO FILE ANYTHING. *IT DOESN'T GET MORE CORRUPT THAN THAT.*

ASSISTANT CORPORATION COUNSEL LETT REQUESTED THAT INTERESTED PERSONS BE ALLOWED TEN BUSINESS DAYS TO FILE.

ATTORNEY MANNING OF PEARSON, MANNING AND HENRY, D.C. COUNSEL FOR THE RIDGEWAY ESTATE, ARGUED THAT THEIR PLEADINGS WERE SUFFICIENT AND THEREFORE, THE MATTER SHOULD BE RESCHEDULED AND SET FOR STATUS.

ATTORNEY O'BRIEN, REPRESENTING AN INTERESTED PARTY FROM THE STATE OF MARYLAND, SAID THE INTERESTED PERSON FILED AND THE MATTER WAS DISMISSED. HOWEVER, DELAY IS NECESSARY TO LET THE COURT DETERMINE HIS APPOINTMENT. THEREFORE, THAT LEAVES ONLY ONE CLAIMANT, I.E. THE RIDGEWAY ESTATE.

JUDGE MANDARIN THEN SAID THE MATTER SHOULD BE CONTINUED FOR 60 DAYS PLUS, I.E., JUNE 20, 1997 AT 10:30 A.M. IN COURTROOM 320.

HOWEVER, IN KEEPING WITH HIS KEY JUDICIAL CO-CONSPIRATOR ROLE, JUDGE MANDARIN HELD THIS HEARING A MONTH EARLIER IN MAY 1997, WITHOUT NOTICE TO EITHER ME OR BRIANNA JONES. JUDGE MANDARIN ORDERED THE D.C. LOTTERY BOARD TO PAY TO THE LEGAL REPRESENTATIVES OF THE RIDGEWAY ESTATE $40-PLUS MILLION, THE REMAINDER OF THE $45 MILLION D.C. JACKPOT WINNINGS OWED TO THE DECEASED WILLIE LEE RIDGEWAY.

BARBARA WASHINGTON FRANKLIN

MY FIRST CONTACT WITH RICHARD MANDARIN WAS DURING MY BRIEF STINT AS A CITY OFFICIAL. AT THE TIME, BACK IN 1979, I WAS SERVING AS ASSISTANT CITY ADMINISTRATOR FOR INTERGOVERNMENTAL RELATIONS. MANDARIN WAS WORKING AS AN ATTORNEY IN THE OFFICE OF THE D.C. CORPORATION COUNSEL. OUR RESPECTIVE OFFICES WERE LOCATED IN THE DISTRICT BUILDING THAT HOUSED THE MAYOR'S OFFICE AND THE OFFICES OF THE MEMBERS OF THE CITY COUNCIL. WE EACH KNEW WHO EACH OTHER WAS IN TERMS OF OUR RESPECTIVE POSITIONS, BUT THAT WAS ABOUT IT.

IT WAS ON OR ABOUT THE LATE 1990'S WHEN MANDARIN CAME INTO FULL VIEW FOR ME AS A PRESIDING D.C. SUPERIOR COURT JUDGE. I CAN STILL REMEMBER THE STATUS HEARING THAT I ATTENDED FOR A VERY HOTLY CONTESTED CHILD CUSTODY MATTER. THE MATTER WAS SCHEDULED BEFORE JUDGE HERNANDEZ, BUT TO MY SURPRISE, AND WITHOUT ANY PRIOR NOTICE TO ME OR MY CLIENT, I WAS INFORMED THAT I SHOULD PROCEED TO COURTROOM WHATEVER AND THAT JUDGE MANDARIN WOULD BE HEARING THE CASE, AND NOT JUDGE HERNANDEZ WHO HAD BEEN INITIALLY ASSIGNED THE ADJUDICATION OF MY CLIENT'S CASE.

ALL MY INTUITIVE ANTENNAE WENT UP BECAUSE BY THIS TIME I WAS AWARE THAT MANDARIN HAD BEEN THE JUDGE THAT HANDLED THE STAKEHOLDER SUIT FILED IN EARLY 1997 BY THE DISTRICT OF COLUMBIA. MANDARIN HAD GRANTED THE MOTION FILED BY THE ATTORNEYS FOR THE RIDGEWAY ESTATE WHICH ASKED THE COURT TO ORDER THE D.C. LOTTERY BOARD TO PAY THE ESTATE $40 MILLION PLUS, THE REMAINDER OF THE LOTTERY PROCEEDS OWED TO THE ESTATE OF WILLIE LEE RIDGEWAY THAT COULD NOW LEGALLY BE PAID IN A TOTAL LUMP SUM TO THE ESTATE.

WHILE THE OUTSTANDING ISSUE SET FOR HEARING WAS A CONTESTED ONE, AT THE END OF THE HEARING, MANDARIN HAD MADE SURE MY CLIENT AND I PREVAILED. OF COURSE, MANDARIN MADE SURE TO CITE THE APPLICABLE LAW AND STATUTES TO SUPPORT HIS RULING IN MY CLIENT'S FAVOR.

THE COURT HEARING WAS ADJOURNED. THE PARTIES WERE EXCUSED. I SAUNTERED OUT OF THE COURTROOM, PLEASED AT THE OUTCOME FOR MY CLIENT, BUT VERY CONCERNED ABOUT WHAT I FELT WAS *RATIFIED CORRUPTION* THAT HAD TRANSPIRED IN THE COURTROOM THAT WAS INVISIBLE TO THE NAKED EYE, BUT THAT I FELT IN THE DEEP RECESSES OF MY GUT. WHOEVER SAID THE STOMACH DOESN'T LIE KNEW WHAT THEY WERE TALKING ABOUT.

THE ODYSSEY OF JUDICIAL CORRUPTION

IT WAS CLEAR TO ME, AND BASED ON WHAT MY INTUITION HAD INFORMED ME, THAT MANDARIN HAD ARRANGED WITH JUDGE HERNANDEZ (WHOM I HAD EXPERIENCED IN A PRIOR CASE AS AN ALTOGETHER CORRUPT D.C. COURT JUDGE) TO HAVE MY CASE REFERRED TO HIM TO GIVE HIM THE OPPORTUNITY TO LOOK ME OVER, FACE-TO-FACE, AND TO SEE IF HE COULD DETERMINE BY HIS EXAMINATION OF MY OUTWARD DEMEANOR IF I HAD ANY CLUE AS TO HIS INVOLVEMENT IN ONE OF THE LARGEST MASSIVE JUDICIAL SWINDLES EVER.

I ATTRIBUTE MY ABILITY TO MAINTAIN A FLAT APPEARANCE BEFORE MANDARIN TO THE PROTECTION OF THE HOLY SPIRIT WHO SAW TO IT THAT I WAS COVERED IN THE BLOOD OF JESUS, MAKING IT IMPOSSIBLE FOR MANDARIN TO SEE ANYTHING IN MY FACIAL EXPRESSION OR BODY LANGUAGE BUT A TRIAL ATTORNEY APPROPRIATELY PURSUING HER CLIENT'S CASE WITH PROPER ZEAL AND PASSION. LITTLE DID MANDARIN KNOW THAT MY LORD HAD MADE ME WISER THAN THE ADVERSARY.

AFTER MY ATTENDANCE AT THE APRIL 1997 COURT HEARING BEFORE MANDARIN, I NOTICED THAT FOR NO APPARENT REASON, MORE THAN ONE OF MY CASES WAS TRANSFERRED TO MANDARIN FROM THE PRESIDING JUDGE INITIALLY ASSIGNED ADJUDICATION FOR THE PARTICULAR CASE. I QUICKLY REALIZED THAT THIS ALLOWED MANDARIN, A D.C. JUDICIAL PREDATOR/CO-CONSPIRATOR/SWINDLER AND RINGLEADER OF THEFT AND FRAUD, TO SATISFY HIMSELF THAT I KNEW NOTHING OF THE ROLE HE WAS PLAYING IN THE HISTORIC D.C. JUDICIAL AND FBI MASSIVE CRIMINAL ENTERPRISE WHOSE MISSION WAS TO DEFRAUD ME OF THE MULTI-MILLION DOLLAR ATTORNEY'S FEES DUE ME.

IN THE SUMMER OF 1997, WHEN I APPEARED BEFORE MANDARIN REPRESENTING AVA SINCLAIR IN HER DIVORCE HEARING, THE COURTROOM CLERK UNWITTINGLY INFORMED ME THAT JUDGE MANDARIN WAS RETURNING EARLY FROM VACATION IN FORT LAUDERDALE. NO JUDGE RETURNS EARLY FROM VACATION TO D.C. SUPERIOR COURT TO HEAR AN UNCONTESTED COURT MATTER.

THERE WAS NO DOUBT IN MY MIND THAT MANDARIN HAD GONE TO FORT LAUDERDALE TO PICK UP HIS PAYOFF FROM THE FIRM AND PERHAPS THE PAYOFF OF THE OTHER D.C. COURT JUDGES AS WELL.

I HAD APPEARED BEFORE MANDARIN ON BEHALF OF RENATA RESTAINO AND HER SON, PHILIP, IN A NASTY CUSTORY BATTLE. ONCE AGAIN, I HAD NOTICED HOW I WAS BEING CAREFULLY AND CLANDESTINELY EXAMINED AND SCRUTINIZED BY MANDARIN TO ASSURE HIM AND KEEP HIS COMFORT LEVEL IN CONFIRMING FOR HIMSELF AND HIS CO-CONSPIRATORS THAT I HAD NO CLUE AS TO THE DEPTH OF THE CORRUPTION THAT ENCIRCLED ME EACH TIME I HAD TO APPEAR IN D.C. SUPERIOR COURT ON BEHALF OF A CLIENT.

ACCORDING TO BRIANNA JONES, MYRON MYRODSKY, A YOUNGER ASSOCIATE AT ADAGIO AND MANDEL, HAD HAD A TELEPHONE CONVERSATION WITH JUDGE MANDARIN, PRESUMABLY AN EX-PARTE COMMUNICATION, AND HAD PREVAILED UPON MANDARIN TO ORDER THAT THE ENTIRE $40 MILLION PLUS LOTTERY WINNINGS BE PAID TO ADAGIO AND MANDEL ON BEHALF OF THE RIDGEWAY ESTATE, IN PART TO PAY BRIANNA JONES' $34 MILLION CLAIM.

AFTER I FILED MY LAWSUIT AGAINST BRIANNA JONES, SHE WOULD BOAST TO ME OF HOW SHE WAS BEING NOTIFIED PROMPTLY EACH TIME I FILED A MOTION IN THE CASE. SHE DID NOT HAVE TO BE NOTIFIED BY MAIL SEVERAL DAYS LATER. OF COURSE, THIS WAS BEFORE THE AGE OF ELECTRONIC FILING OF COURT PLEADINGS.

WHEN I THINK BACK ON MY SEVERAL APPEARANCES BEFORE MANDARIN, AND THE CLOSE SCRUTINY AND PIERCING GAZE HE ALWAYS GAVE ME, I NOW REALIZE THAT WHAT HE WAS DOING WAS HIS OWN PERSONAL SURVEILLANCE OF ME. JUDGE MANDARIN USED THE COURTROOM FOR HIS PLATFORM OF JUDICIAL CORRUPTION.

AFTER ALL, WHERE ELSE COULD HE EXERCISE PERSONAL SURVEILLANCE OF ME? HE WOULD HAVE NO OTHER OPPORTUNITY TO HAVE SUCH UP CLOSE AND PERSONAL ACCESS TO ME.

I ALSO TOOK NOTE THAT I ALWAYS PREVAILED ON BEHALF OF MY CLIENT WHEN I WAS APPEARING BEFORE MANDARIN. THAT MADE SENSE. HE WAS AN ACTIVE PARTICIPANT IN AIDING AND ENABLING THOSE WHO WERE ROBBING ME OF MILLIONS OF DOLLARS. WHY WOULDN'T HE MAKE SURE I RECEIVE THE RELATIVE CRUMBS FROM MY CLIENTS IN TERMS OF THE LEGAL FEES I WAS CHARGING THEM, AND THE USUAL DELAY OF A WEEK OR MORE IN BEING PAID BY CLIENTS OF LIMITED FINANCIAL MEANS?

WHAT OFTEN KEPT ME DEPRESSED AND MY EMOTIONS ANESTHETIZED WAS THAT I HAD TO FACE THE FACT THAT I WAS INVOLVED IN THE DEEPEST OF D.C. JUDICIAL AND FBI CORRUPTION. IN MY EARS, I PERIODICALLY HEARD THE HOLY SPIRIT WHISPER, *"WOE TO UNJUST JUDGES AND TO THOSE WHO ISSUE UNFAIR LAWS, SAYS THE LORD."* (ISAIAH 10:1)

NOTWITHSTANDING THE SERIOUS ALLEGATIONS OF HIS COMPLICITY IN THIS MASSIVE D.C. JUDICIAL AND FBI FRAUD, THEFT, CORRUPTION AND EXTORTION CONSPIRACY AND CRIMINAL ENTERPRISE, JUDGE RICHARD MANDARIN CONTINUES TO SERVE WITHOUT ACCOUNTABILITY AND WITH IMPUNITY AS A SENIOR JUDGE ON THE BENCH OF THE D.C. SUPERIOR COURT, ALONG WITH JUDGE MATTHEW EKANS.

THE COURT: WHAT DO YOU -- -- I MEAN, BASED ON WHAT YOU'VE JUST TOLD ME, THAT CONFIRMS WHAT SHE'S BEEN SAYING CONSISTENTLY WHICH IS THAT SHE WAS NEVER GIVEN ANY MONEY. YOU SEEM TO AGREE THAT SHE WAS NEVER GIVEN ANY MONEY.

MS. FRANKLIN: NO. THAT'S   THAT'S NOT WHAT I'M SAYING.

THE COURT: I THINK   I THINK YOU JUST TOLD ME THAT BOTH OF YOU WERE DUPED, AND THAT THIS FIRM -- --

MS. FRANKLIN: YES.

THE COURT: ---- --- NEVER INTENDED TO GIVE HER -- --

COMMENT AND ANALYSIS: #23 JUDGE EKANS WANTED ME TO TESTIFY THAT NO MONIES WERE EVER PAID TO BRIANNA JONES PURSUANT TO HER SETTLEMENT AGREEMENT WITH THE RIDGEWAY ESTATE. SUCH TESTIMONY ON MY PART WOULD HAVE JUSTIFIED THE *RIGGED DISMISSAL* OF MY LAWSUIT THAT WAS THE MAJOR PLANK AND STRATEGY IN THE SUCCESSFUL ACHIEVEMENT OF THE MISSION OF THE D.C. JUDICIAL AND FBI CRIMINAL ENTERPRISE. IT IS NOT EASY TO TESTIFY BEFORE A COURT JUDGE WHOM YOU CONSIDER TO BE A KEY CO-CONSPIRATOR IN STRIPPING YOU OF MILLIONS OF DOLLARS IN ATTORNEY'S FEES. BUT NEVERTHELESS, I SOMEHOW MANAGED TO CARRY ON AND RESOLVED TO NEVER GIVE UP MY FIGHT FOR JUSTICE AND THE RESTITUTION, WITH INTEREST, OF THE ATTORNEY'S FEES OWED TO ME.

MS. FRANKLIN: THAT'S WHAT I'M SAYING. BUT I'M NOT SAYING ---- *I'M SAYING THAT SHE WAS NOT FORMALLY GIVEN SETTLEMENT PROCEEDS.* I DON'T BELIEVE SHE'S EVER RECEIVED MONIES, WHETHER IT BE MONIES UNDER THE TABLE OR WHATEVER, BECAUSE SHE   AS I SAID WHEN I FIRST CAME BEFORE YOUR HONOR, SHE HAS HAD COMMUNICATIONS -- -- SHE'S BEEN IN TOUCH WITH THE   COUNSEL FOR THIS ESTATE AND THE ATTORNEYS THAT REPRESENT THE ESTATE. SHE'S BEEN IN CONSTANT COMMUNICATION WITH THESE PEOPLE ALL ALONG.

COMMENT AND ANALYSIS: #24 *BRIANNA JONES HAD TESTIFIED TO BEING PERIODICALLY SUMMONED TO MEET IN WASHINGTON AREA HOTEL SUITES WITH "OFFICIALS." SHE HAD ALSO COMMUNICATED TO ME BETH HOLLISTER'S OFFER AND DESIRE TO PAY ME $10,000.00 TOWARDS THE EXPENSES OF HER LAWSUIT. THIS EVIDENCE WAS INCLUDED IN MY TESTIMONY DURING THE JUNE 17TH 2011 PROCEEDING BEFORE JUDGE EKANS AND TO NO AVAIL.*

HOWEVER, JUDGE EKANS HAD PURPOSEFULLY FAILED AND REFUSED TO ENFORCE JUDGE STARR'S ORDER MANDATING THAT BRIANNA JONES PRODUCE BANK OF AMERICA BANK STATEMENTS.

MS. FRANKLIN: AND THE -- -- AND I -- -- YOU KNOW, I'VE ALREADY GONE INTO THE   SOME OF THE CIRCUMSTANCES REGARDING THE SETTLEMENT AGREEMENTS AND HOW THEY CAME ABOUT AND WHAT   AND THEY HAVE ALWAYS MADE IT A POINT, KNOWING FULL WELL THAT I WAS THE ATTORNEY OF RECORD, IF YOU LOOK AT THE BROWARD COUNTY CIRCUIT COURT RECORD MY NAME IS ALL OVER THAT. IT WAS ALL KINDS OF FILINGS, CO-COUNSEL, TRIPS BACK AND FORTH CONSTANTLY TO FLORIDA, CANCELLED THE MEETING, AS SOON AS I WOULD ARRIVE, I WOULD GET A NOTICE AT MY HOTEL THE MEETING'S BEEN CANCELLED, MR. SO-AND-SO HAS A   BOTTOM LINE IS I HAVE NEVER HAD A FACE-TO-FACE MEETING WITH THE MAJOR PARTNERS. I HAVE NEVER MET WITH ANY OF THE MAJOR PARTNERS.

HAVE I   HAVE I TALKED WITH SOME OF THE OTHER ATTORNEYS FOR THE FIRM AND BEEN IN COMMUNCATION WITH THEM, YES, I HAVE. IT WAS JONATHAN MILLER, CAITLIN MEYER (PHONECTIC), A NUMBER OF OTHER ATTORNEYS. I HAVE EVEN HAD ON ONE OCCASION   UM, JUDGE ANNE MESSIAH ALLOWED ME TO HAVE A ---------TO APPEAR BEFORE HER COURT BY PHONE WHERE I SAT IN MY OFFICE AND I ACTUALLY   SHE SAID I'M GONNA SAVE YOU A TRIP. I KNOW YOU COME BACK AND FORTH DOWN HERE, I'VE HEARD ABOUT THAT, SO I'M GONNA SAVE YOU A TRIP. AND I ACTUALLY APPEARED BEFORE HER.

I DON'T RECALL THE EXACT MOTION, BUT ANYWAY ----- SO, WHAT I'M SAYING IS SETTLEMENT PROCEEDS, I DON'T BELIEVE SHE HAS ------ *I DON'T KNOW. THAT'S THE BOTTOM LINE. I DON'T KNOW.* I DON'T BELIEVE SHE HAS, BUT I BELIEVE SHE'S RECEIVED ------- SHE HAS ACCESS TO FUNDS ON SOME LEVEL. WHETHER SHE'S RECEIVED SETTLEMENT PROCEEDS, I REALLY ------ *MY ANSWER IS I REALLY DON'T KNOW.*

I DON'T BELIEVE SHE HAS, BUT THEN, AGAIN, SHE HAS LIED CONSISTENTLY, SO SHE COULD HAVE. BUT I CERTAINLY HAVE NOT RECEIVED ANY SETTLEMENT PROCEEDS.

(PAUSE.)

COMMENT AND ANALYSIS: #25 *THIS WAS A CASE OF MASSIVE D.C. JUDICIAL AND FBI FRAUD, THEFT, CORRUPTION AND EXTORTION. THEREFORE, IT WAS NOT STRANGE OR UNCOMMON NOT TO KNOW WHETHER BRIANNA JONES HAD ACTUALLY RECEIVED FUNDS FROM THE RIDGEWAY ESTATE OR NOT.*

*I WAS ALSO MINDFUL OF THE FACT THAT EKANS HAD MADE IT A POINT OF REFUSING TO ADDRESS THE INVESTIGATION AND FINDINGS OF **THE D.C. OFFICE OF BAR COUNSEL** WHICH STATED THAT BRIANNA JONES WAS ENTITLED TO CONSIDERABLE ASSETS FROM THE SETTLEMENT OF THE FLORIDA LAWSUIT I HAD FILED ON BEHALF OF BRIANNA JONES AGAINST THE RIDGEWAY ESTATE; AND THAT PROCEEDS HAD YET TO BE DISPERSED TO BRIANNA JONES. CLEARLY, **D.C. BAR COUNSEL'S FINDINGS DID NOT FIT WITHIN THE ULTIMATE GOAL OF THE CRIMINAL ENTERPRISE** WHICH WAS TO DEFRAUD ME OF AN ESTIMATED $50 MILLION IN ATTORNEY'S FEES.*

I NEVER ONCE DOUBTED THAT EKANS AND MYRON DAEMON, CHIEF OF THE D.C. COURT OF APPEALS, AS WELL AS OTHER D.C. JUDGES, HAD PUT THEIR HEADS TOGETHER AND DECIDED LONG BEFORE MY CASE WAS DISMISSED IN JANUARY 2015, THAT THE COURT REASONING AND RATIONALE FOR DISMISSAL WOULD BE THE FACT THAT BRIANNA JONES HAD NEVER RECEIVED IN HAND ANY OF THE SETTLEMENT PROCEEDS. THIS WAS NOT JUST THREADING THE NEEDLE; THIS WAS BURYING THE BONES.

THE COURT: AND YOU'VE NEVER SEEN THE SETTLEMENT AGREEMENT.

COMMENT AND ANALYSIS: #26 MY INTUITION TOLD ME THAT EKANS WAS PLEASED THAT I HAD NEVER SEEN THE SETTLEMENT AGREEMENT. IN FACT, HE WAS COMFORTED BY THE THOUGHT, IN LIGHT OF HIS KEY ROLE AS A D.C JUDICIAL CO-CONSPIRATOR IN THE CRIMINAL ENTERPRISE.

MS. FRANKLIN:	SHE HAD MADE THAT A POINT. SHE'S MADE IT A POINT OF NEVER WHEN YOUR HONOR ASKED HER ABOUT IT I THINK AT ONE OF THE HEARINGS THE LAST TIME OR TWO IT'S SOMEBODY BROKE INTO MY STORAGE. *BUT SHE'S NEVER DENIED HAVING THEM. SHE'S NEVER DENIED THAT THEY EXIST, BUT SHE REFUSES TO PRODUCE.*

AND I THINK SHE'S REFUSED TO PRODUCE IS BECAUSE IT WOULD IT WOULD INVOLVE, YOU KNOW, IT WOULD DISCLOSE INFORMATION THAT THESE PEOPLE DON'T WANT DISCLOSED. BECAUSE IF THERE WERE SETTLEMENT AGREEMENTS, I SHOULD HAVE BEEN AT THE SETTLEMENT TABLE. AND MY NAME SHOULD BE ON THOSE SETTLEMENT AGREEMENTS AS THE ATTORNEY. AND, SO, IT WOULD -- -- IT WOULD DO – YOU KNOW, IT WOULD DISCLOSE INFORMATION THAT THEY DON'T WANT DISCLOSED.

MS. FRANKLIN:	BUT, AS I SAID, THE LOTTERY BOARD CAME INTO THIS COURT WITH A STAKEHOLDER ACTION BECAUSE SHE HAD GONE TO THEM, AND THE ESTATE HAD GONE TO THEM. AND, SO, THE LOTTERY BOARD AND, BY THE WAY, AT ONE POINT WELL, YOU KNOW, MY BROTHER WHO HAPPENS TO BE AN ATTORNEY GAVE US A LOT OF, AT THE VERY BEGINNING, A LOT OF HIS TIME AND EFFORT, AND HE WAS, ALSO, IN TOUCH WITH THE LOTTERY BOARD. SO, THE LOTTERY BOARD, YOU KNOW, WAS FULLY AWARE OF THIS OF HER CLAIM.

THEY WERE FULLY AWARE, AND THAT WAS PART OF WHY THE LOTTERY BOARD FILED THE SUIT IN D.C. SUPERIOR COURT AND SAID WE NEED TO HAVE THE COURT TELL US WHO WE SHOULD PAY.

(PAUSE.)	
	COMMENT AND ANALYSIS: #27 THE COURT RECORD AND OFFICIAL TRANSCRIPTS OF PROCEEDINGS VERIFY UNEQUIVOCALLY THAT JUDGE EKANS, COMMITTED TO THE GOAL AND MISSION OF THE CRIMINAL ENTERPRISE, PERMITTED BRIANNA JONES TO AVOID PRODUCING THE SETTLEMENT AGREEMENTS AND THE BANK OF AMERICA BANK STATEMENTS.
THE COURT:	I'M TRYING TO WRAP MY HEAD AROUND WHAT -- -- WHAT FIGURE THE SETTLEMENT ACTUALLY INVOLVED IN LIGHT OF WHAT SEEMS TO BE AN UNDISPUTED FACT THAT -- --
MS. FRANKLIN:	YOUR HONOR, COULD I JUST CHIME IN HERE A MINUTE?
THE COURT:	YES.

MS. FRANKLIN: YOU KNOW, EVEN WHEN I SUED ON MS. JONES'S BEHALF, YOU KNOW, THE REASON I   IT WAS A THIRTY-FOUR MILLION DOLLAR SETTLEMENT IS BECAUSE WE SUED FOR A HUNDRED MILLION. SO, THEY USED THE THIRTY-FOUR MILLION BECAUSE IT WAS BASED ON A HUNDRED MILLION THAT WAS INITIALLY DEMANDED. AND I KNOW THAT AMOUNT   I KNOW THAT AMOUNT, YOU KNOW, IS A LARGE AMOUNT. AND I HAD BEEN THINKING, EVEN BEFORE THIS HEARING, WHAT -- -- GIVEN THE LACK OF INFORMATION, WHAT IS   WHAT IS - - -- HOW DO YOU WORD THIS? WHAT SHOULD BE ASKED FOR? SHOULD IT JUST SIMPLY BE WHATEVER'S -- -- YOU KNOW, SHOULD IT BE THE SETTLEMENT AMOUNT, PLUS COMPOUNDED INTEREST? I MEAN, I'M NOT REALLY TRYING TO PUT A FIGURE ON IT. I'M JUST TRYING TO DO WHAT YOU USUALLY HAVE IN JUDGMENTS.

MS. FRANKLIN: THAT'S WHY THIS   AS I SAID, THIS WAS A CHALLENGE FOR ME BECAUSE I'M NOT TRYING TO PUT ANY PARTICULAR FIGURE IN THERE. I'M REALLY NOT. I JUST DIDN'T KNOW HOW TO WORD IT, YOUR HONOR. I STILL AM NOT SURE HOW YOU WORD SOMETHING LIKE THIS WHEN YOU HAVE NO VERIFICATION. YOU HAVE NO DOCUMENTATION IN TERMS OF THE AMOUNT. SHOULD WE JUST STICK WITH THE RETAINER AGREEMENT LANGUAGE, WHICH IS FORTY PERCENT OF THE SETTLEMENT AMOUNT? BECAUSE, I MEAN, NOW THAT'S SOMETHING THAT CERTAINLY CAN BE   I THINK I CAN HOLD TO.

BECAUSE THAT'S -- -- THAT'S, YOU KNOW - -- BUT THE AGREEMENT   THE AGREEMENT WAS THAT THE ENTIRE SETTLEMENT AMOUNT WOULD BE PAID INTO THE ESCROW ACCOUNT. AND THEN, I WOULD THEREAFTER, DISBURSE TO HER. BECAUSE THAT'S WHAT'S NORMALLY DONE WHEN YOU HAVE A CONTINGENCY FEE CASE.

THE COURT: YOU'RE ABSOLUTELY RIGHT. THE PROBLEM WITH THAT, HOWEVER, IS YOUR UNDERSTANDING AND BELIEF THAT AN AMOUNT WAS, A LUMP SUM AMOUNT WAS   HAS NEVER BEEN PAID TO MS. JONES. I MEAN, YOU AND I BOTH HAVE BEEN WORKING ON AN ASSUMPTION, FACTUAL ASSUMPTION, THAT SHE IS GETTING SOME FINANCIAL PAYMENTS REGULARLY -- --

MS. FRANKLIN: RIGHT.

THE COURT:---------------------- BECAUSE SHE CLEARLY IS NOT IMPOVERISHED. AND, YET IT IS – IT IS, UM, IT IS SOMEWHAT TROUBLING FOR ME IN TERMS OF USING THE COURT'S AUTHORITY TO ENTER A JUDGMENT THAT CAN, YOU KNOW, THAT THERE SEEMS TO BE NO EVIDENCE THAT THIS LAW FIRM EVER ACTUALLY SETTLED THE CASE WITH MS. JONES. THAT SEEMS TO BE THE GAP HERE IN PROOF. *THAT THERE'S A SUGGESTION OF SETTLEMENT, BUT NO EVIDENCE OF A SETTLEMENT.*

COMMENT AND ANALYSIS: #28 ANOTHER INSTANCE OF JUDICIAL GASLIGHTING ENGAGED IN BY JUDGE EKANS FOR THE DURATION OF THE NINE-MONTH ADJUDICATION OF MY LAWSUIT.

MS. FRANKLIN: RIGHT.

THE COURT: THAT'S -- -- THAT'S ABOUT AS WEIRD AS IT GETS. THE CASE - -- I'M SORRY, DID YOU SAY THAT YOU ACTUALLY FILED A CASE IN THE BROWARD COUNTY CIRCUIT COURT?

COMMENT AND ANALYSIS: #29 JUDGE EKANS WAS A MASTER AT JUDICIAL GASLIGHTING USED TO FURTHER THE MISSION OF THE HISTORIC D.C. JUDICIAL AND FBI CRIMINAL ENTERPRISE.

MS. FRANKLIN: OH, YES. THAT WAS WHAT THE SETTLEMET WAS BASED ON.

THE COURT: RIGHT. BUT HOW WAS THAT CASE CLOSED? HOW DID THAT CASE END?

MS. FRANKLIN: THE CASE ENDED BY MARCH 1997, SHE ENTERED INTO A SETTLEMENT WITH THEM. THAT'S HOW IT ENDED.

THE COURT: I MEAN, IS THERE A DOCKET ENTRY THAT SHOWS THAT CASE ENDED BY A -- --

MS. FRANKLIN: THERE IS -- -- NOT FOR THE THIRTY-FOUR MILLION. I THINK IT   I'D HAVE TO GO BACK AND LOOK AT THE FILE, I THINK IT'S SOMETHING LIKE TWENTY-ONE MILLION DOLLARS, WHICH IS -- -- THAT'S -- -- THAT'S – *THERE WERE TWO SETTLEMENT AGREEMENTS.* ONE SETTLEMENT AGREEMENT WAS FOR, LIKE, TWENTY-ONE, AND THE OTHER WAS FOR THIRTEEN. SO, THERE WERE TWO *SETTLEMENT AGREEMETS.* ONE SETTLEMENT AGREEMENT WAS ENTERED INTO DECEMBER 1996, AND THE OTHER SETTLEMENT AGREEMENT WAS ENTERED INTO MARCH 1997.

THE COURT: WHEN YOU'RE REFERRING TO SETTLEMENT AGREEMENTS, ARE YOU REFERRING TO DOCUMENTS, OR -- --

MS. FRANKLIN: YES, I'M REFERRING TO DOCUMENTS -- -- THE

COURT: ------------------------SOMETHING YOU SAW?

MS. FRANKLIN: SOMETHING THAT I HAVE NEVER SEEN. SOMETHING THAT SHE HAS REFUSED TO PROVIDE ME COPIES OF.

THE COURT: OKAY. BUT HOW DO YOU KNOW THAT THE DOCUMENTS EXIST, OTHER THAN HER WORD, BECAUSE -- --

MS. FRANKLIN: EXACTLY.

THECOURT: --------------------WE HAVE COME TO HAVE A SIGNIFICANT DISTRUST OF HER WORD.

MS. FRANKLIN: THAT'S TRUE.

THE COURT: SO, OTHER THAN THAT, HOW DO WE KNOW ----- I MEAN, MS. JONES SAYS A LOT OF THINGS.

MS. FRANKLIN: YES, SHE DOES.

THE COURT: SO, HOW DO WE -- --WHAT -- --HOW DO WE KNOW HER -- --

MS. FRANKLIN: I ONLY HAVE HER ----- I ONLY HAVE HER WORD, YOUR HONOR. I ONLY HAVE HER WORD.

THE COURT: I GUESS WHAT I'M ASKING IS-- -- I MEAN, IN COURTS ----- COURTS OF RECORD ARE COURTS OF RECORD FOR A REASON.

MS. FRANKLIN: RIGHT.

THE COURT: THEY'RE COURTS OF RECORDS SO THAT THERE EXIST FOR ALL TO SEE THAT CASES BEGIN, HAVE A MIDDLE AND END. AND IF THAT CASE ENDED, THERE SHOULD BE SOMETHING ON THAT COURT DOCKET TO SAY SETTLED AND DISMISSED, OR WHATEVER, BUT SOMETHING THAT BROUGHT THAT CASE TO A CONCLUSION SO THAT THE COURT CAN GET IT OFF ITS DOCKET.

I MEAN, THERE HAS TO BE SOMETHING THAT EXISTS TO SAY HOW THAT CASE CONCLUDED, OTHER THAN MS. JONES' WORD, WHICH DOESN'T STAND FOR A LOT HERE.

COMMENT AND ANALYSIS: #30 AS A KEY JUDICIAL CO-CONSPIRATOR AND PARTICIPANT IN THE BEHIND-THE-SCENES OPERATION OF THE CRIMINAL ENTERPRISE, JUDGE EKANS WAS ONCE AGAIN SENDING ME ON A WILD GOOSE CHASE. HOWEVER, THIS TIME I WOULD NOT GIVE ONE MINUTE OF MY TIME TO THE DECEPTION.

THE COURT: THE OTHER THINGS THAT YOU HAVE YOU HAVE SOLID PROOF OF; YOUR INFORMATION THAT THE LOTTERY BOARD ACTUALLY PAID OUT, SO SO, YES, THERE WAS MONEY PAID TO THIS FIRM. BUT WHAT YOU SAID TO ME TODAY IS THAT YOUR SUSPICION IS THAT THAT FIRM THAT GOT THAT MONEY NEVER INTENDED TO PAY MS. JONES OR YOU.

MS. FRANKLIN: ABSOLUTELY.

THE COURT: AND SO -- --

MS. FRANKLIN: I WOULD HAVE TO CONCLUDE THAT BECAUSE THAT IS WHY I'M NEVER ABLE TO SAY TO YOUR HONOR THAT I HAVE HAD SETTLEMENT DISCUSSIONS AND/OR MEETINGS WITH THESE LAWYERS.

THE COURT: NOW, THIS IS CONSISTENT WITH WHAT MS. JONES HAS SAID, WHICH IS THAT
                    SHE'S NEVER RECEIVED A SETTLEMENT. SO, WHAT -- -- WHAT   YOU KNOW, I
                    THINK THAT WHAT WE'RE WORKING WITH IS YOUR SUSPICION PROBABLY
                    SUPPORTED BY CERTAINLY YOUR DEALINGS WITH MS. JONES THAT SHE DID NOT
                    WANT YOU TO BE A PART OF HOW SHE CONCLUDED THAT CASE. SO, YOU KNOW,
                    SHE'S HIDING THE BALL, BUT WE DON'T -- --WE DON'T HAVE   THE PAPER TRAIL
                    ENDS, APPARENTLY, WITH THE LOTTERY BOARD PAYING THE MONEY OUT TO THIS
                    LAW FIRM. IS THAT RIGHT?

MS. FRANKLIN: NO, I WOULD HAVE TO GO BACK AND LOOK   AND LOOK AT THE FILE. YOUR
                    HONOR, IN TERMS OF THE END AS FAR AS HER CLAIM, AND THE ACTUAL LAWSUIT
                    THAT I HAD FILED.

THE COURT: I THINK THAT'S AN IMPORTANT PIECE.

MS. FRANKLIN: BUT, YOUR HONOR, AGAIN, THE REASON WE'RE AT THE POINT WHERE YOUR
                    HONOR ASKED ME TO FILE A MOTION FOR JUDGMENT IS BECAUSE SHE HAS
                    BUCKED THE COURT IN TERMS OF ITS ORDER.

                    COMMENT AND ANALYSIS: #31 *I ONCE AGAIN REMINDED EKANS THAT IF HE
                    HAD DONE THE JOB THAT HE WAS SWORN AND BEING PAID TO DO, HE WOULD
                    HAVE ENFORCED JUDGE STARR'S ORDER, REQUIRED BRIANNA JONES TO COMPLY
                    WITH THE ORDER, AND THE ISSUANCE OF A COURT JUDGMENT WOULD NOT BE
                    AT ALL NECESSARY OR APPROPRIATE.*

THE COURT: WELL, YOU HAVE TO   YOU HAVE TO UNDERSTAND SOMETHING, I THINK I'M IN
                    CONTROL OF THAT. I KNOW THAT YOU HAVE, YOU KNOW, THAT YOU HAVE DONE
                    EVERYTHING YOU CAN TO LET THE LAW TAKE ITS COURSE. AND I THINK THAT,
                    YOU KNOW, TO THE EXTENT THAT, YOU KNOW, THAT THAT IS THE WAY TO KEEP
                    THINGS CIVIL, THAT THAT IS TO BE COMMENDED.

                    BUT IN TERMS OF THIS COURT VINDICATING ITS AUTHORITY, I'M NOT
                    CONCERNED WITH THAT. I THINK THAT I KNOW HOW TO DO THAT.

                    WHAT I'M MORE CONCERNED WITH IS THAT ORDERS AND JUDGMENTS THAT I
                    SIGN MY NAME TO ARE SUPPORTED BY FACTS AND LAW.

COMMENT AND ANALYSIS: #32 JUDGE EKANS ABUSED HIS POWER AND AUTHORITY BY CHANGING MAJOR FACTS IN MY CASE IN ORDER TO RIG MY CASE FOR DISMISSAL IN SATISFACTION OF THE ONGOING CRIMINAL ENTERPRISE. MY POINT WAS THAT EKANS WAS PERMITTING JONES TO UNDERMINE THE COURT FOR PURPOSES OF THE ONGOING CRIMINAL ENTERPRISE WHICH WAS TO STRIP ME OF THE MILLIONS OF DOLLARS IN ATTORNEY'S FEES OWED TO ME AS THE RESULT OF THE CONTINGENCY FEE AGREEMENT WITH BRIANNA JONES AND THE SETTLEMENT OF THE $100 MILLION LAWSUIT THAT I HAD CRAFTED AND FILED ON HER BEHALF.

MS. FRANKLIN: WELL, RIGHT NOW, WE JUST HAVE HER TESTIMONY.

COMMENT AND ANALYSIS: #33 *I COULD NOT HAVE DISAGREED MORE WITH JUDGE EKANS. NO, WHAT WE HAD WAS HIS AND FORMER CHIEF JUDGE SKINNER'S INTIMIDATION AND SHAKEDOWN OF BRIANNA JONES DURING THE MARCH 18, 2011 HEARING. WHAT WE HAD WAS EKANS' REFUSAL TO PERMIT BRIANNA JONES TO REVIEW THE BANK STATEMENTS WITH ME DURING THE JANUARY 31, 2011 COURT HEARING. WHAT WE HAD WAS EKANS INTENTIONALLY CHANGING THE FACTS OF MY LAWSUIT BY FALSELY DEFINING ME AS A JUDGMENT CREDITOR RESPONSIBLE FOR THE SEARCH AND RECOVERY OF THE STOLEN SETTLEMENT PROCEEDS. WHAT WE HAD WAS EKANS' ADAMANT REFUSAL TO ADDRESS MY LAWSUIT'S DOMINANT ISSUES OF D.C. JUDICIAL AND FBI FRAUD, THEFT, CORRUPTION AND EXTORTION. WHAT WE HAD WAS EKANS' REFUSAL TO ENFORCE JUDGE STARR'S ORDER. WHAT WE HAD WAS EKANS' MAKING SURE I GAINED NO ACCESS TO THE SETTLEMENT PROCEEDS ON HIS WATCH AS AN ALL TOO COMPROMISED PRESIDING JUDGE.*

THE COURT: RIGHT NOW WE HAVE TESTIMONY OF SOMEONE WHO-- --

MS. FRANKLIN: WE HAVE JUST HER TESTIMONY, YOUR HONOR. THAT'S ALL WE HAVE.

THE COURT: YEAH, OF SOMEONE WHOSE TESTIMONY DOESN'T HOLD -------CARRY A LOT OF WEIGHT.

MS. FRANKLIN: SHE HAS -- -- SHE HAS UNDERMINED THIS COURT'S, UM -- --

THE COURT: MS. FRANKLIN, LET'S NOT FOCUS ON THAT, HER UNDERMINING THE COURT.

COMMENT AND ANALYSIS: #34 MY POINT WAS THAT EKANS WAS PERMITTING JONES TO UNDERMINE THE COURT FOR PURPOSES OF THE ONGOING CRIMINAL ENTERPRISE AND THAT OBVIOUSLY IRRITATED HIM. HIS COMMENT SAID HE HEARD ME LOUDLY AND CLEARLY.

MS. FRANKLIN: SHE'S UNDERMINED ME. SHE'S UNDERMINED MY ABILITY -- --

THE COURT: THAT'S -- -- THAT'S -- --

MS. FRANKLIN: -- -- TO PROVIDE THE COURT WITH WHAT THE COURT NEEDS -- --

THE COURT: WELL, NOT REALLY. NOT REALLY. SHE   SHE CERTAINLY HAS DONE EVERYTHING SHE CAN TO DO THAT. BUT I   I BELIEVE THAT IT SHOULDN'T BE TOO DIFFICULT TO GET THE DOCKET ENTRY. I MEAN, YOU KNOW, IF WE WERE IN NEW ORLEANS WE PROBABLY BE IN TROUBLE BECAUSE THEY LOST A LOT OF RECORDS DOWN THERE IN NEW ORLEANS AFTER KATRINA. BUT, AS FAR AS I KNOW, BROWARD COUNTY , YOU KNOW, HASN'T HAD THAT KIND OF PROBLEM.

AND I THINK IT WOULD BE IMPORTANT TO SEE HOW THAT CASE RESOLVED. BECAUSE WHAT WE ARE LOOKING AT NOW IS THE WORD OF A WOMAN WHO I DON'T HAVE A LOT OF FAITH IN. AND, YOU KNOW, TO THE EXTENT   I'M GONNA -- -- I'M GONNA TAKE ONE STEP BEYOND AND SAY SOMETHING I PROBABLY SHOULDN'T SAY. BUT IT SEEMS TO ME THAT MS. JONES HAS   HAS- - -- SEEMS TO GET A LOT OF SATISFACTION   AND I GUESS THIS SORT OF SLIDES INTO YOUR POINT.

BUT I -- -- YOU THINK   I THINK THAT YOU THINK THAT SHE IS CONTINUING TO BE CONTUMACIOUS WITH THE COURT. THE WAY THAT I VIEW THIS IS THAT SHE'S SORT OF HAVING FUN.

MS. FRANKLIN: YEAH.

THE COURT: IT SEEMS TO ME THAT THIS IS -- --

MS. FRANKLIN: YOUR HONOR -- --

THE COURT: -- -- I WON'T SAY A GAME, BUT -- --

MS. FRANKLIN: YOUR HONOR, I'M IN AGREEMENT. I SAID   I SAID LONG AGO, YOUR HONOR, I SAID FOR HER IT'S A GAME. IT'S JUST A GAME.

COMMENT AND ANALYSIS: #35 EKANS ACKNOWLEDGED THAT, WITH HIS ALLOWANCE, BRIANNA JONES WAS HAVING FUN *AT MY EXPENSE* AND UNDER HIS WATCH. HE COULD CARE LESS ABOUT THE LOSS TO ME AND MY FAMILY.

THE COURT: WELL, YOU KNOW, BUT ON THE OTHER HAND, I DON'T KNOW HOW YOU FEEL ABOUT THIS, BUT I, YOU KNOW, I CAN   *AFTER TWENTY-SIX YEARS* I CAN JUST ABOUT REMEMBER EVERY TIME I'VE HAD TO SEND SOMEBODY TO JAIL OR PRISON, AND I DON'T TAKE IT LIGHTLY. AND WHEN I THOUGHT THAT SHE WAS SIMPLY BEING CONTUMACIOUS, I DIDN'T HESITATE TO DO THAT. SINCE THEN I HAVE HAD TO HAVE SERIOUS CONCERNS ABOUT, YOU KNOW, ABOUT THIS WOMAN'S -- -- I MEAN, I DON'T   I DON'T KNOW FROM COURT HEARING TO COURT HEARING WHERE SHE'S COMING FROM.

COMMENT AND ANALYSIS: #36 *EKANS WAS PRESSURED AND CONSTRAINED TO ORDER BRIANNA JONES JAILED BRIEFLY BECAUSE OF THE MANDATE OF JUDGE KATE STARR'S ORDER. THEREAFTER, DURING THE JANUARY 31, 2011 COURT HEARING, BRIANNA JONES OFFERED TO REVIEW BANK STATEMENTS OF THE SETTLEMENT PROCEEDS WITH ME THAT SHE STATED WERE IN A YELLOW MANILA ENVELOPE SHE HELD UP IN HER HANDS FOR JUDGE EKANS TO SEE.*

EKANS RESPONDED THAT THERE WAS NO PLACE IN THE COURTHOUSE FOR US TO MEET AND THEREAFTER RETURNED HER TO THE D.C. JAIL. HE THEREAFTER DIRECTED ME TO MEET WITH HER THE NEXT MORNING AT THE D.C. JAILHOUSE. WHEN I ARRIVED AT THE FACILITY, I WAS INFORMED BRIANNA JONES WAS ON SUICIDE WATCH. THESE CASE FACTS ARE VERIFIED IN THE OFFICIAL COURT TRANSCRIPT OF THE JANUARY 31, 2011 HEARING AND ALSO SET FORTH IN THIS JUDICIAL EXPOSE'. JUDGE EKANS WAS OBVIOUSLY DETERMINED TO PROHIBIT MY ACCESS TO THE SETTLEMENT PROCEEDS IN FURTHERANCE OF THE ONGOING CRIMINAL ENTERPRISE IN WHICH HE PLAYED A CRITICAL AND KEY ROLE.

THE COURT: *THIS LATEST THING WITH THIS MEDICAL ISSUE THAT SHE SAYS IS GOING TO RESULT IN SURGERY, WHERE SHE SWEARS SHE'S GOING TO GIVE US PROOF OF, I MEAN, I DON'T KNOW WHAT'S GOING ON WITH THAT.*

COMMENT AND ANALYSIS: #37 JUDGE EKANS NEVER BOTHERED TO REQUIRE BRIANNA JONES TO PRODUCE A MEDICAL CERTIFICATION OF HER SURGERY WHICH WAS SIMILAR TO HIS NOT REQUIRING BRIANNA JONES TO PRODUCE THE BANK STATEMENTS ORDERED BY JUDGE STARR.

THE COURT: BUT WHAT I DO KNOW IS THAT I CAN PUT MY TRUST, AND THIS IS WHAT WE DO, WE PUT OUR TRUST IN COURT RECORDS. IF I CAN HAVE A RECORD THAT SHOWS THAT SHE ACTUALLY SETTLED THIS CASE FOR A SUM OF MONEY, THEN IT'S CLEAR THAT A PART OF THAT MONEY BELONGS TO YOU AS THE PERSON WHO FILED THAT CASE AND -- -- YOU KNOW, WHETHER YOU   WHETHER YOU DESERVE FORTY PERCENT OR SOME OTHER PERCENT, YOU KNOW, THAT'S SOMETHING I THINK WE CAN WORK OUT.

WHAT I'M MORE CONCERNED WITH IS WHETHER THERE WAS AN ACTUAL RESOLUTION OF THAT CASE THAT RESULTED IN A SETTLEMENT. *SUPPOSE IT TURNS OUT THAT THAT CASE WAS SIMPLY ABANDONED.* I MEAN, YOU TELL ME THAT SHE WAS WATCHING T.V. ONE DAY AND SEES THAT THIS MAN, YOU KNOW, WHO HAS WON THE LOTTERY WAS THE SAME MAN THAT SEXUALLY ABUSED HER WHEN SHE WAS A CHILD, AND THAT THE MAN, YOU KNOW, ON HIS DEATH BED OUT OF SOMETHING SAID, YOU KNOW, I ORDER YOU TO SETTLE THE CASE. THAT- - -- THAT IS   YOU DON'T RUN INTO THOSE STORIES EVERY DAY.

COMMENT AND ANALYSIS: #38 HERE EKANS PURPOSELY IGNORES THE FRAUD, THEFT AND CORRUPTION THAT CIRCUMSCRIBED THE CASE. THE SPECIFIC CONTENTS OF THE COURT RECORDS OR THE ABSENCE OF THE SPECIFIC CONTENTS OF THE COURT RECORDS ARE DETERMINED BY THE DEPTH AND BREADTH OF THE ONGOING CRIMINAL ENTERPRISE AFOOT.

EKANS' SUGGESTION THAT THE CASE WAS SIMPLY ABANDONED IS ANOTHER EXAMPLE OF HIS *PENCHANT FOR JUDICIAL GASLIGHTING.*

MS. FRANKLIN: THIS IS FROM AN ATTORNEY, YOUR HONOR. THIS IS NOT FROM HER. THIS IS FROM THE ATTORNEY THAT REPRESENTED -- -- HIS NAME IS TALMADGE CHURCHILL IN RICHMOND, VIRGINIA. I MET WITH HIM IN HIS OFFICE AND THAT WAS FROM TALMADGE CHURCHILL.

THE COURT: WELL -- --

MS. FRANKLIN: I DON'T KNOW   AND IT DIDN'T COME FROM HER. AND I'M JUST TAKING THIS LAWYER'S STATEMENT. BUT, YOUR HONOR, I DID HAVE -- --

THE COURT: BUT IT'S THE SAME   BUT IT'S THE SAME LAWYER AND FIRM THAT YOU'RE TELLING ME HAD NO INTENTION OF EVER PAYING -- --

MS. FRANKLIN: NO, NO, NO -- --

THE COURT:--------------------THE MONEY.

MS. FRANKLIN: ----------------THAT'S ADAGIO AND MANDEL IN BROWARD COUNTY CIRCUIT FLORIDA. THE LAWYER THAT REPRESENTED MR. RIDGEWAY WAS IN RICHMOND, VIRGINIA. TALMADGE CHURCHILL. THE ADAGIO AND MANDEL IS IN FORT LAUDERDALE - -- MIAMI.

THE COURT: WELL, WHAT'S THE CONNECTION BETWEEN THAT FIRM AND THE FIRM THAT -- -- I MEAN, THAT FIRM REPRESENTED RIDGEWAY WHILE HE WAS STILL LIVING?

MS. FRANKLIN: YES.

THE COURT:	AND TOLD WHO TO GO AHEAD AND SETTLE THE CASE? WHO DID THEY TELL TO GO AHEAD AND SETTLE?
MS. FRANKLIN:	HE SAID HE ASKED HIS -- -- THE ATTORNEYS INVOLVED AT THAT TIME, AND TALMADEGE CHURCHILL WAS ONE OF THOSE.
THE COURT	OKAY.
MS. FRANKLIN:	BUT MR. RIDGEWAY WAS ALIVE THEN.
THE COURT:	OKAY.
MS. FRANKLIN:	WHEN ADAGIO AND MANDEL CAME IN, THAT WAS AFTER HE HAD PASSED, AND HE HAD ----- HE HAD MOVED TO BROWARD COUNTY.
THE COURT:	OKAY. BUT, WHO------WHAT FIRM HAD THE DIRECTION TO SETTLE THE CASE?
MS. FRANKLIN:	THIS WAS MR. TALMADEGE'S FIRM.
THE COURT:	THE FIRM IN?
MS. FRANKLIN:	RICHMOND.
THE COURT:	AND DID THEY ACTUALLY SETTLE THE CASE? DID THAT FIRM SETTLE THE CASE?
MS. FRANKLIN;	NO. NO, IT WASN'T SETTLED.
THE COURT:	RIGHT.
MS. FRANKLIN:	THAT'S WHY ----- THAT'S WHY I FILED THE LAWSUIT IN FLORIDA.
THE COURT:	OKAY. SO, NOW -- --
MS. FRANKLIN:	SO, NOW, WE HAVE ADAGIO AND MANDEL.
THE COURT:	SO,----- YEAH. SO, NOW ALL WE HAVE, THOUGH, IS THE WORD OF THAT LAWYER DOWN THERE THAT HE ----- THAT THE MAN SAID YOU CAN SETTLE, BUT THEN HE DIES. AND , SO, WHO'S THE PR OF THE ESTATE?
MS. FRANKLIN:	AT THE TIME IT WAS THE WIDOW. WAS MRS. RIDGEWAY. SHE WAS THE PERSONAL REPRESENTATIVE.
THE COURT:	AND, SO, YOUR BELIEF IS THAT THE PERSONAL REPRESENTATIVE, THE WIDOW OF RIDGEWAY, SAID GIVE THIS WOMAN THIRTY-FOUR MILLION DOLLARS, OR TWENTY-ONE MILLION, OR SOME OTHER -- -- SIXTEEN MILLION? THAT'S -- --
MS.. FRANKLIN:	NO. I'M NOT SURE SHE EVER WADE-IN, IN TERMS OF MY KNOWLEDGE AS FAR AS WHAT -- --

THE COURT:	BUT, THAT'S WHO WOULD HAVE THE AUTHORITY. THAT'S THE ONLY PERSON WHO WOULD HAVE THE AUTHORITY TO DO THAT.

COMMENT AND ANALYSIS: #39 HERE EKANS DUMMIES UP AND PRETENDS NOT TO KNOW THAT WHEN D.C. JUDICIAL AND FBI FRAUD, THEFT, CORRUPTION AND EXTORTION CONTROL, DIFFERENT RULES NECESSARILY APPLY.

MS. FRANLIN;	WELL, THE ATTORNEYS FOR THE ESTATE THE ATTORNEYS -- --
THE COURT:	WHY WOULDN'T HAVE THE -- --
MS. FRANKLIN:	----------------FOR THE ESTATE.
THE COURT:	-- -- AUTHORITY TO SETTLE THE CASE. ONLY THE PR WOULD HAVE THE AUTHORITY TO SETTLE THE CASE.
MS. FRANKLIN:	WELL, I AGREE, YOUR HONOR.
THE COURT:	YEAH.
MS. FRANKLIN:	I AGREE. HOWEVER, THAT'S NOT ALL-- --
THE COURT:	AND IF THE ATTORNEYS----- IF THE ATTORNEYS ACTED AGAINST HER INTEREST OR HER DIRECTION, THEN THEY WOULD CERTAINLY COME UNDER ------ I THINK IF THEY WERE ----- MS. JONES ONE OF THE EARLIER HEARINGS BEFORE ME WHERE SHE SAID THAT THEY HAD BEEN EITHER DISBARRED, OR THE PRINCIPAL IN THE FIRM HAD BEEN DISBARRED DOWN THERE.
MS. FRANKLIN:	YEAH, ADAGIO WAS SUSPENDED.
THE COURT:	BUT AN ATTORNEY CAN'T OVERRIDE THE CLIENT'S DIRECTION IN TERMS OF SETTLING AN ESTATE. THEY HAVE TO DO WHAT THE PR SAYS.

COMMENT AND ANALYSIS: #40 UNETHICAL ATTORNEYS ARE NO DIFFERENT FROM UNETHICAL JUDGES. THEY DISREGARD THE RULE OF LAW EVERY DAY AND AT THE DROP OF A HAT IF IT SUITS THEIR PURPOSES AND FILLS THEIR POCKETS WITH OTHER PEOPLE'S MONEY. IN THAT REGARD, THEY ARE NO DIFFERENT FROM UNETHICAL COURT JUDGES. UNETHICAL ATTORNEYS OVERRULE THEIR CLIENT'S DIRECTIONS EVERY DAY AND EKANS KNEW THAT. *HE SIMPLY COULDN'T AVOID HIS ADDICITION TO JUDICIAL GASLIGHTING.*

MS. FRANKLIN:	YOUR HONOR, IN ALL -- -- IN ALL GOOD CONCIENCE, I CANNOT STAND HERE WITHOUT SAYING, YOUR HONOR, THE LAW WAS NOT ALWAYS COMPLIED WITH IN THIS CASE BY THESE ATTORNEYS. AND THAT IS WHY MR. ADAGIO WAS SUSPENDED BECAUSE HE HAD THE SAME PATTERN OF PRACTICE TO OTHER CASES, MILLIONS OF DOLLARS TAKEN FROM CLIENTS. ULTIMATELY PAID THEM, BUT NEVERTHELESS, THAT'S ANOTHER STORY.

COMMENT AND ANALYSIS: #41 JUDGE EKANS' REMARKS ARE SIMPLY EVIDENCE OF HIS REFUSAL TO ADDRESS MY LAWSUIT'S DOMINANT ISSUES OF D.C. JUDICIAL AND FBI FRAUD, THEFT, CORRUPTION AND EXTORTION.

THE COURT: WHAT I'M -- -- WHAT I'M TRYING NOT TO DO—WHAT I AM   YOU USED THE TERM BENDING OVER BACKWARDS EARLIER. WHAT I'M TRYING NOT TO DO IS TO ALLOW THIS COURT TO BE USED BY MS. JONES.

COMMENT AND ANALYSIS: #42 *WHILE JUDGE EKANS WAS COMMITTED TO NOT LETTING THE COURT BE USED BY BRIANNA JONES, HE WAS ALL-IN AND COMPLETELY COMMITTED TO COORDINATING AND ORCHESTRATING THE PREMEDITATED JUDICIAL OBSTRUCTION OF JUSTICE ENGAGED IN BY CHIEF JUDGE GEORGE SKINNER, HIS JUDICIAL COLLEAGUE, SENIOR JUDGE AND FORMER CHIEF JUDGE IN THE COURT HALLWAY INTIMIDATION AND SHAKEDOWN OF BRIANNA JONES DURING THE MARCH 18, 2011 HEARING PERSONALLY WITNESSED BY ME AND VERIFIED BY MY ANNOTATION OF THE OFFICIAL COURT TRANSCRIPT AND INCLUDED IN COURT FILINGS.*

MS. FRANKLIN: EXACTLY.

THE COURT: NOW, IF -- --IF--- YOU KNOW, THE PATTERN OF BEHAVIOR HAS INDICATED SOMEONE WHO ACTS IN AN UNPREDICTABLE   WELL, IN FASHIONS THAT ARE VERY UNUSUAL TO SAY THE LEAST.

MS. FRANKLIN: RIGHT.

THE COURT: AND SHE SEEMS TO HAVE, BASED ON SOME OF THE ALLEGATIONS SHE'S MADE AGAINST YOU, SHE SEEMS TO HAVE YOU IN HER SIGHTS AS SOMEBODY WHO SHE'S TRYING TO DO SOMETHING. I'M NOT INCLINED TO ALLOW HER TO USE THE COURT TO TRY TO DO THAT.

COMMENT AND ANALYSIS: #43 MORE THAN BRIANNA JONES, IT WAS THE CORRUPT D.C. COURT JUDGES AND FBI AGENTS THAT DESIGNED, EXECUTED AND ORCHESTRATED THE CRIMINAL ENTERPRISE LAUNCHED AND BUTTRESSED ON THE POLITICALLY MOTIVATED CRIMINAL PROSECUTION OF MY HUSBAND THAT DEFRAUDED ME OF AN ESTIMATED $50 MILLION IN ATTORNEY'S FEES THAT DID ME AND MY FAMILY THE MOST DAMAGE.

THE COURT: I, ALSO, RECOGNIZE YOU HAVE -- -- THAT YOU HAVE OBVIOUSLY LEGAL DOCUMENTS SHOWING THAT YOU REPRESENTED THIS WOMAN IN THIS AFFAIR, AND THAT YOU HAD A CLAIM FOR RECOVERY. BUT, AS YOU KNOW, AND YOU SAID IT TIME AND AGAIN, THE CONTINGENCY FEE IS BASED ON THERE BEING A RECOVERY. WHAT WE DON'T HAVE HERE IS ANY INDICATION THAT THERE WAS EVER A RECOVERY.

COMMENT AND ANALYSIS: #44 *JUDGE EKANS REFUSED TO ENFORCE JUDGE STARR'S ORDER DIRECTING BRIANNA JONES TO PRODUCE BANK STATEMENTS OF THE TOTAL AMOUNT OF SETTLEMENT PROCEEDS ON DEPOSIT AT BANK OF AMERICA. THEREIN WAS THE RECOVERY AND EKANS AND HIS CO-CONSPIRATOR JUDGES KNEW THAT.*

THE COURT: I THINK THAT THE STARTING POINT FOR THAT, AT LEAST IN TERMS OF PROOF SINCE WE CAN'T GET FROM MS. JONES, EVEN AFTER JAILING HER FOR A WEEK OR TEN DAYS, THAT   THAT THERE'S ANYTHING OTHER THAN THESE *PHANTOM PEOPLE* WHO GET IN TOUCH WITH HER FROM TIME-TO-TIME TO GIVE HER RESOURCES.

COMMENT AND ANALYSIS: #45 *AT NO TIME DID BRIANNA JONES OR ANYONE ELSE TESTIFY TO PEOPLE GETTING IN TOUCH WITH BRIANNA JONES TO GIVE HER MONEY. JUDGE EKANS WAS INADVERTENTLY DISCLOSING HIS KNOWLEDGE OF BEHIND-THE-SCENES ACTIVITIES PROVIDED BY HIS JUDICIAL AND FBI CO-CONSPIRATORS INVOLVED IN THE CRIMINAL ENTERPRISE. THE TRUTH HAS A FUNNY WAY OF COMING OUT, EVEN WHEN YOU DON'T WANT IT TO. THE TRUTH IS JUST THAT POWERFUL AND PROPHETIC.*

THE COURT: THERE MUST BE A RECORD IN THAT COURT IN BROWARD COUNTY TO SHOW HOW THE CASE RESOLVED. AND CASES THAT RESOLVED THROUGH SETTLEMENTS, THEY DON'T NECESSARILY PUT THE DOLLAR FIGURE OUT. I SETTLED A HUGE CASE TWO WEEKS AGO, BUT THERE'S NOTHING THAT WILL EVER BE IN OUR RECORDS TO SHOW HOW MUCH THAT CASE SETTLED FOR.

MS. FRANKLIN: RIGHT.

THE COURT: BUT IT WAS A HUGE CASE. AND THE RECORD SHOWS THAT THE CASE WAS CLOSED BECAUSE IT WAS SETTLED AND DISMISSED. AND I WOULD EXPECT THAT THE STATE OF FLORIDA WOULD HAVE THE SAME KIND OF RECORD KEEPING IN ITS COURT SYSTEM.

AND, SO, THERE'S AN INDICATION THAT THE CASE WAS SETTLED, THEN I THINK WE CAN AT LEAST HAVE SOME ASSURANCE THAT THIS IS NOT SIMPLY MS. JONES DRAGGING OUT, YOU KNOW, HER   *AS THE O'JAYS SAY, HER HOOKS ON YOU.*

COMMENT AND ANALYSIS: #46 BY THIS TIME I HAD HAD ALL THAT I COULD TAKE OF EKANS' UNVARNISHED, UNADULTERATED, UNAPOLOGETIC, CORRUPT, CONSCIENCE-FREE AND AMORAL JUDICIAL GASLIGHTING ABUSE.

MS. FRANKLIN: YOUR HONOR, I APPRECIATE YOUR HONEST

THE COURT: WELL -- --

MS. FRANKLIN: I APPRECIATE YOUR HONEST VIEW. AND, AS I -- --

THE COURT: YOU GOTTA BE FRUSTRATED.

> **COMMENT AND ANALYSIS: #47** MOTHER, THROUGH HER WISE COUNSEL AND ADMONITIONS, TAUGHT US MANY WORDS, PHRASES, AND LESSONS THAT WOULD EMPOWER US TO STAND AGAINST THE WILES OF THE DEVIL. ONE OF MOTHER'S FAVORITE ADMONITIONS SHE RECOMMENDED THAT WE EMPLOY WHEN IN WARFARE WITH THE ADVERSARY, AND ONE THAT I REPEATEDLY MEDITATED ON DURING HEARINGS BEFORE EKANS, WAS "DON'T LET THEM SEE YOU SWEAT." THANK YOU MOTHER THAT JUDGE EKANS NOR ANY OF HIS CO-CONSPIRATOR COLLEAGUES WOULD EVER BE ABLE TO SAY THAT THEY SAW ME SWEAT. AND THEY NEVER WILL.

MS. FRANKLIN: ----SAID, YOUR HONOR, IT'S NOT -- -I HAVE NO INTENTIONS, NEVER HAD ANY INTENTIONS, OF HAVING THIS COURT MISUSED.

THE COURT: WELL, I DON'T -- -- I'M NOT TRYING TO SUGGEST -- -- --

MS. FRANKLIN: I'M JUST IN A DIFFICULT SITUATION. IT'S JUST-- --

THE COURT: IT'S A VERY UNUSUAL CASE, I'LL SAY THAT. IT'S A VERY UNUSUAL CASE.

MS. FRANKLIN: DIFFICULT FOR ME.

THE COURT: IN THE ANNALS OF CASES YOU SORT OF GET TO A POINT WHERE YOU SAY, WELL, I THINK I'VE SEEN IT ALL. BUT THEN, YOU COME DOWN HERE, AGAIN, AND YOU REALIZE THAT YOU HAVEN'T SEEN IT ALL, YET.

     BUT MS. FRANKLIN, ONCE AGAIN, IT RESULTS IN FRUSTRATION FOR YOU. AND IT LOOKS LIKE MS. JONES IS WINING, AGAIN. BECAUSE OBVIOUSLY WHAT SHE WANTED WAS TO PUT THIS OFF. BUT I AM NOT INCLINED TO DO   TO BRING THIS TO A JUDGMENT UNTIL YOU CAN GIVE ME SOMETHING TO SHOW THAT THERE ACTUALLY WAS A SETTLEMENT. SOMETHING. IF THE SETTLEMENT DOESN'T EXIST IN WRITING, THEN THERE MUST BE A RECORD THAT IT WAS -- -- THAT IT WAS ENTERED INTO.

> **COMMENT AND ANALYSIS: #48** I WAS FULLY PERSUADED THAT GIVEN THE FLOURISHING CRIMINAL ENTERPRISE UNDERWAY, NO MATTER WHAT I PROIVIDED THE COURT, THE FINAL OUTCOME OF MY LAWSUIT WAS *RIGGED FOR DISMISSAL* AND HAD BEEN SO FROM THE MOMENT I ENTERED EKANS' COURTROOM 517 ON JANUARY 21, 2011.

BARBARA WASHINGTON FRANKLIN

THE COURT: IF YOU CAN DO THAT, I THINK I'VE ASKED YOU TO DO ALL THAT I CAN POSSIBLY ASK YOU TO HUMANLY DO.

MS. FRANKLIN: YOU KNOW, YOUR HONOR, I'M WILLING TO DO THAT. SO-- --

THE COURT: WELL   GIVE THAT BACK TO HER. NOW, YOU KNOW, MS. JONES WAS TALKING ABOUT TWO MONTHS FOR HER RECOVERY. I DON'T   I DON'T NECESSARILY KNOW IF ANY OF THAT HAS ANY TRUTH TO IT. BUT I CAN TELL YOU IN TERMS OF MY CALENDAR THAT IT'S VERY BUSY AFTER THE HOLIDAY. LET ME SEE IF I CAN FIND SOMETHING IN SEPTEMBER.

(PAUSE.)

MS. FRANKLIN: YOUR HONOR, SINCE YOU'VE ASKED ME TO PROVIDE YOU WITH SOME EVIDENCE THAT IT SETTLED IF I CAN IN TERMS OF COURT DOCUMENTS, FLORIDA COURT DOCUMENTS, IS THAT INFORMAION THAT YOU WOULD PREFER TO HAVE ME PRESENT TO YOU AT A HEARING?

THE COURT: NOT NECESSARILY. YOU CAN ----- YOU CAN JUST GET IT TO MY CHAMBERS.

MS. FRANKLIN: OKAY.

THE COURT: BUT I'M GONNA PUT ANOTHER DATE ON THIS CASE BECAUSE UNTIL I ACTUALLY ISSUE THE JUDGMENT I'M GONNA STILL CONSIDER AN OPEN MATTER. SO, I'M GONNA PUT IT DOWN FOR -- --

MS. FRANKLIN: THE -- --

THE COURT: GO AHEAD.

MS. FRANKLIN: NO, THE REASON I'M ASKING, YOUR HONOR, IS I DON'T THINK IT'S FAIR TO ME THAT SHE SHOULD BE VIEWING THIS AS IF SHE'S IN CONTROL OF YOUR HONOR ISSUING A JUDGMENT DEPENDING UPON WHEN SHE'S WELL ENOUGH TO COME BACK TO COURT.

THE COURT: NO, NO, NO -- -- THAT   IF I GET THESE PAPERS OR WHATEVER YOU HAVE AND I'M SATISFIED BEFORE THEN, THEN THIS DATE IS MERELY A CONTROL DATE. WE HAVE TO SET CONTROL DATES, IF I ISSUED THE JUDGMENT TODAY -- --

MS. FRANKLIN: OKAY.

THE COURT:--------------------THEN WE WOULDN'T HAVE TO SET THE DATE. BUT SINCE I'M NOT ISSUING IT TODAY WE NEED TO PUT A DATE IN THE -- -

MS. FRANKLIN: CORRECT.

328

THE COURT:	-- -- ENTRY TO SHOW -- --
MS. FRANKLIN:	I APPRECIATE THAT. YOU HONOR, A QUESTION. IF I ------ IF, IN FACT, THE DOCKET, THE BROWARD COUNTY CIRCUIT DOCKET INDICATES SETTLEMENT, WHICH I RECALL IT DID, BUT I------ AGAIN, THAT'S MY RECOLLECTION. I HAVEN'T LOOKED AT IT IN YEARS. IS-------WOULD THAT BE APPROPRAITE TO PROVIDE TO THE COURT?
THE COURT:	SURE.
MS. FRANKLIN:	NOT NECESSARILY AN AMOUNT?
THE COURT:	THE CASE NUMBER -- --
MS. FRANKLIN:	MIGHT NOT INCLUDE AN AMOUNT.
THE COURT:	I WOULD NOT -- -- FRANKLY, I WOULD NOT EXPECT THE DOCKET ENTRY TO INCLUDE AN AMOUNT.
MS. FRANKLIN:	OKAY.
THE COURT:	I WOULD BE SURPRISED IF IT DID.
MS. FRANKLIN:	ALL RIGHT, YOU HONOR. I GOT YOU.
THE COURT:	ALL RIGHT. PUT IT DOWN FOR THE 14TH OF OCTOBER, AT 11:00 A.M.
(PAUSE.)	
THE COURT:	IF IT SHOULD SHOW THAT THERE WAS A SETTLEMENT THAT WAS SEALED, THEN IT WOULD BE MOST -- -- MOST HELPFUL TO ME TO HAVE A CASE NUMBER. BECAUSE THEN, I COULD COMMUNICATE WITH THE-- --
MS. FRANKLIN:	ABSOLUTELY. ABSOLUTELY. HM-HMM.
THE COURT:	BUT, NO, YOU DON'T I WOULDN'T EXPECT YOU TO WAIT UNTIL TWO MONTHS TO GET THAT TO ME.
MS. FRANKLIN:	OKAY. AND I -- -- EVEN THOUGH WE HAVEN'T MENTIONED IT, I'M SURE THE COURT IS AWARE THAT I DID, BASED ON MY CONTACT WITH CHAMBERS I SPOKE TO YOUR HONOR'S LAW CLERK, AND I DID FILE A FOLLOW-UP MEMORANDUM IN SUPPORT OF THE MOTION AND AFFIDAVIT FOR JUDGMENT JUST, YOU KNOW, RAISING THAT ADDRESSING THE ISSUE OF HER PLANS TO FILE BANKRUPTCY IF, IN FACT, THE JUDGMENT IS ISSUED. BUT I DID CONFER WITH TINA ON THAT BEFORE I FILED IT.

BARBARA WASHINGTON FRANKLIN

THE COURT: VERY WELL.

MS. FRANKLIN: OKAY.

THE COURT: ALL RIGHT. WELL. THANK YOU AND HAVE A GOOD DAY.

MS. FRANKLIN: ALL RIGHT, YOUR HONOR. THANK YOU, YOUR HONOR. YOU, TOO. AND HAVE A
                  GREAT VACATION. I CERTAINLY AM HOPING TO HAVE ONE.

                       (THEREUPON, THE PROCEEDINGS WERE CONCLUDED.)

THE ODYSSEY OF JUDICIAL CORRUPTION

SUPERIOR COURT OF THE DISTRICT OF COLUMBIA
CIVIL DIVISION
WASHINGTON, D.C.

THE HONORABLE MATTHEW D. EKANS, ASSOCIATE JUDGE, PRESIDING

THE FOLLOWING ARE EXCERPTS OF THE OFFICIAL COURT TRANSCRIPT OF THE
OCTOBER 14, 2011 PROCEEDING
ANNOTATED BY THE AUTHOR'S PERTINENT COMMENTARY AND ANALYSIS

OCTOBER 14, 2011

P R O C E E D I N G S

COMMENT AND ANALYSIS: #1 DAYS BEFORE THE HEARING, MY INTUITION INFORMED ME THAT BRIANNA JONES WOULD BE A "NO SHOW" AND MOREOVER, THAT SHE WOULD SUFFER NO PENALTIES, NO ADMONITION, NO NOTHING. IN FACT, JUDGE EKANS WOULD BEND OVER BACKWARDS IN TREATING HER WITH KID GLOVES. AND THAT IS EXACTLY WHAT HAPPENED.

AFTER ALL, BRIANNA JONES WAS AN IMPORTANT PLAYER AND PARTNER IN THE D.C. JUDICIAL AND FBI CRIMINAL ENTERPRISE, AND WOULD BE TREATED ACCORDINGLY BY THE ALL TOO COMPROMISED AND COMPLICIT JUDGE EKANS.

WHEN THE HEARING OPENED, JUDGE EKANS APPEARED CALM AND RELAXED IN WAYS I HAD NOT NOTICED BEFORE. PERHAPS IT HAD TO DO WITH THE FACT THAT HE WAS ALMOST AT THE END OF HIS "NIGHTMARE CASE" AND WOULD NO LONGER HAVE TO PLAY HIS KEY ROLE AS THE GRAND MARSHAL OF THE D.C. JUDICIAL AND FBI CRIMINAL ENTERPRISE; ORGANIZED, ORCHESTRATED AND EXECUTED TO STRIP ME OF THE MILLIONS OF DOLLARS OWED TO ME IN ATTORNEY'S FEES FOR THE PAST 15 YEARS.

JUST AS I HAD PREDICTED WHEN THE HEARING BEGAN, JUDGE EKANS INFORMED ME THAT JONES WOULD NOT BE ATTENDING THE HEARING IN PERSON BUT BY TELEPHONE. ACCORDING TO EKANS, BRIANNA JONES WAS ILL, HEMORRHAGING AND UNABLE TO APPEAR IN PERSON.

NEITHER DID BRIANNA JONES ATTEND THE PRIOR HEARING ON AUGUST 19, 2011. THE SICK CARD SHE USED AT THAT TIME WAS THAT SHE WAS ON HER WAY TO JOHNS HOPKINS FOR SURGERY AND WOULD THEREAFTER PROVIDE THE COURT WITH MEDICAL DOCUMENTATION OF HER ILLNESS. OF COURSE, SHE NEVER PROVIDED THE COURT WITH ANYTHING, NOR DID JUDGE EKANS ASK FOR ANYTHING. HE HAD, BY HIS LAISSEZ-FAIRE ATTITUDE AND INACTION IN RESPONSE TO JONES' VARIOUS BEHAVIOR THROUGHOUT THE ADJUDICATION OF MY LAWSUIT, GIVEN BRIANNA JONES SILENT PERMISSION TO PLAY HIM LIKE A FIDDLE. HOWEVER, IT ALL SERVED THE MISSION OF THE CRIMINAL ENTERPRISE.

HOW MANY TIMES DID I HAVE TO REMIND MYSELF THAT BRIANNA JONES AND JUDGE EKANS WERE ON THE SAME TEAM OF SWINDLERS?

JUDGE EKANS HAD THE AUDACITY AND SHAMELESSNESS TO REFER TO HIS ADJUDICATION OF MY LAWSUIT AS A "NIGHTMARE."

WHAT CAN BE CONSIDERED MORE OF A "NIGHTMARE" THAN TO HAVE TO ACKNOWLEDGE THAT THE PRESIDING JUDGE AND YOUR FORMER CLIENT ARE BOTH ON THE SAME TEAM OF SWINDLERS AND CORRUPT D.C. COURT JUDGES AND FBI AGENTS TO DEFRAUD YOU OF THE MILLIONS OF DOLLARS YOU'VE EARNED BY WAY OF A $100 MILLION LAWSUIT YOU CRAFTED AND FILED AND THAT SETTLED FOR $34 MILLION WITHOUT ANY PAYMENT WHATSOEVER TO YOU AS PLAINTIFF'S COUNSEL?

THANK GOD I WAS NOT DECEIVED BY JUDGE EKANS AND HIS BLACK ROBE AND HIS GASLIGHTING PONTIFICATIONS. HE WAS NONE OTHER THAN A COMMITTED CO-CONSPIRATOR IN THIS HISTORIC D.C. JUDICIAL AND FBI CRIMINAL ENTERPRISE WHOSE MISSION WAS TO DEFRAUD ME OF MILLIONS OF DOLLARS IN ATTORNEY'S FEES.

HOWEVER, WHAT I ALWAYS FOUND DISAPPOINTING WAS THAT EKANS NOR HIS CO-CONSPIRATORS FEARED PROSECUTION, INDICTMENT OR INCARCERATION FOR THEIR CRIMINAL BEHAVIOR. IN OTHER WORDS, THERE WAS ENOUGH MONEY FROM MY SWINDLED ATTORNEY'S FEES TO PAY FOR THE BACKING AND COOPERATION OF THE AUTHORITIES TO LOOK THE OTHER WAY WITH REGARD TO THE FLOURISHING CRIMINAL ENTERPRISE. *AND SO GIVEN EKANS' ROLE AS A KEY D.C. JUDICIAL CO-CONSPIRATOR, I WOULD NEVERTHELESS TESTIFY AND MAKE A COURT RECORD OF THE FINDINGS OF D.C. BAR COUNSEL REGARDING BRIANNA JONES' SETTLEMENT WITH THE RIDGEWAY ESTATE. THE D.C. BAR COUNSEL'S FINDINGS ALSO INCLUDED ITS SPECIFIC FINDING THAT JONES WAS ENTITLED TO CONSIDERABLE ASSETS THAT HAD NOT YET BEEN DISBURSED TO HER.*

NEVERTHELESS, I WOULD PERIODICALLY REMIND MYSELF THAT WHEN THE FATE OF YOUR CASE IS IN THE HANDS OF A CORRUPT, CONSCIENCE-FREE AND AMORAL D.C. COURT JUDGE WHO REPRESENTS A CORRUPT D.C. COURT SYSTEM, IT DOESN'T MATTER WHAT YOUR EVIDENCE PROVES, VERIFIES, CONFIRMS OR DEMONSTRATES. NOR DOES IT MATTER WHAT QUESTIONS YOUR EVIDENCE ANSWERS. *YOU STILL SHALL NOT PREVAIL.* I HAD COME TO TERMS WITH THE FACT THAT, FOR ALL INTENTS AND PURPOSES, I WAS A PRO WRESTLER IN A PRO WRESTLING MATCH. FROM THE VERY BEGINNING, THE DISMISSAL OF MY CASE WAS PRE-SCRIPTED, PRE-DETERMINED, AND PRE-DESTINED. FOR ME TO PREVAIL WOULD CAUSE THE MISSION OF THE CRIMINAL ENTERPRISE TO BE DEFEATED. MOREOVER, THE CO-CONSPIRATORS, BEGINNING WITH JUDGE EKANS, WOULD LOSE THEIR PORTION OF THE STOLEN ATTORNEY'S FEES TO BE USED TO FILL THEIR POCKETS AND THE POCKETS OF THEIR FAMILIES, FRIENDS AND COLLEAGUES.

THE MOST DIFFICULT ASPECT OF THE ADJUDICATION OF MY CASE WAS NOT SO MUCH THE WASTED TIME IN RUNNING BACK AND FORTH TO COURT DURING A 9-MONTH PERIOD, OR THE NUMEROUS HEARINGS EKANS USED TO BUILD THE BLOCKS TO ROB ME OF MY FEES, BUT RATHER MY HAVING TO ANSWER TO AN UNMISTAKABLY CORRUPT, CONSCIENCE-FREE AND AMORAL JUDGE THAT ANSWERED TO NO ONE, INCLUDING HIS FELLOW JUDGES. THERE WASN'T A TIME DURING EKANS' ADJUDICATION OF MY CASE THAT EACH TIME I ADDRESSED HIM BY THE REQUIRED "YOUR HONOR," IT WAS FOLLOWED SILENTLY IN MY HEAD AS "WHAT HONOR?" THEREAFTER, I WOULD FIGHT THE SICKNESS WELLING UP IN MY STOMACH. AND THEN I WOULD PRAY NOT TO THROW UP ON THE COURTROOM COUNSEL TABLE.

THE DEPUTY CLERK: YOUR HONOR, CALLING THE CASE OF BARBARA WASHINGTON FRANKLIN VERSUS BRIANNA JONES, 2009-4417, AND IN THE MATTER OF BRIANNA JONES 2011-CCC1. COME FORWARD AND IDENTIFY YOURSELVES FOR THE RECORD.

MS. FRANKLIN: GOOD MORNING, YOUR HONOR. BARBARA WASHINGTON FRANKLIN, YOUR HONOR.

THE COURT: GOOD MORNING.

MS. FRANKLIN: PLAINTIFF.

(PAUSE.)

THE COURT: HAVE YOU TALKED TO MS. JONES?

MS. FRANKLIN: YOUR HONOR, I HAVE NOT TALKED TO HER SINCE APRIL.

***

MS. FRANKLIN: WELL, WHEN WE WERE HERE LAST YOU ASKED ME TO PROVIDE THE COURT WITH SOME FURTHER EVIDENCE OF -- --

THE COURT: OF THE SETTLEMENT.

MS. FRANKLIN: ----------------THE SETTLEMENT.

THE COURT: YES, BECAUSE -- --

MS. FRANKLIN: AND I, I'M SORRY.

THE COURT: BECAUSE THERE HAS TO BE THERE HAS TO BE SOME DOCUMENT. PEOPLE DON'T DO THIS KIND OF SETTLEMENT BY WORD OF MOUTH. THERE HAS TO BE A DOCUMENT SOMEWHERE.

COMMENT AND ANALYSIS: #2 HERE JUDGE EKANS RESORTS TO HIS PATTERN AND PRACTICE OF JUDICIAL GASLIGHTING IN THE MIDST OF A HISTORIC D.C. JUDICIAL AND FBI CRIMINAL ENTERPRISE.

MS. FRANKLIN: I PROVIDED YOUR LAW CLERK, WHO IS NEW TO ME, AND I TAKE IT SHE'S IN THE COURTROOM NOW, LEE, SO WE'RE JUST MEETING FACE-TO-FACE. I PROVIDED HER WITH A LETTER INDICATING THAT THAT ISSUE HAD COME UP AT A HEARING, AND **THE D.C. BAR COUNSEL** HAD DONE A THOROUGH INVESTIGATION, AND I HAVE A COPY OF THEIR LETTER SAYING THAT WE HAVE DETERMINED THAT SHE IS ENTITLED TO A CONSIDERABLE AMOUNT IN TERMS OF A CLAIM THAT SHE HAD FILED. HOWEVER, THE FUNDS HAVE NOT BEEN DISPERSED AS YET. NOW THAT WAS IN 2009. THAT WAS AS A RESULT OF THEIR INVESTIGATION, AND THAT THEIR INVESTIGATION I KNOW WAS EIGHT OR NINE MONTHS. IT MIGHT HAVE EVEN BEEN A YEAR BUT I MEAN, THAT TO ME, I MEAN I DON'T KNOW HOW MUCH MORE EVIDENCE IN TERMS OF AN ARM OF THE COURT SAYING, YES WE'VE DETERMINED THERE WAS A SETTLEMENT, BUT DISBURSEMENT HAS NOT BEEN MADE TO HER, AND SHE HAS INDICATED TO US THAT SHE INTENDS TO PAY THE COMPLAINANTS BECAUSE THEY WERE COMPLAINING, FILED A COMPLAINT AGAINST ME BECAUSE SHE HAD BORROWED FROM THEM, AND THEY WANTED YOU TO KNOW -- --

THE COURT: DID THEY SAY WHAT EVIDENCE THEY HAD FOUND OF THE SETTLEMENT?

MS. FRANKLIN: THEY DID NOT. THEY DID NOT. THEY DID NOT AND I TALKED WITH MARCIA MCMILLAN BRIEFLY, AND SHE, SHE JUST INDICATED THAT THEY DID A NORMAL, WHAT IS THEIR NORMAL PROCEDURE, AND SHE DIDN'T GO INTO, YOU KNOW, WHO SHE TALKED TO AND THAT KIND OF THING, BUT SHE SAID WE DID USE THE FLORIDA RECORDS, THE DOCKET AND I GOT AN UPDATED PROGRESS, YOU KNOW, DOCKET -- --

THE CLERK: JUDGE.

MS. FRANKLIN: HOWEVER -- --

THE COURT: GIVE ME ONE SECOND.

(PAUSE.)

THE COURT: SHE ALWAYS CALLS BACK TO FIND OUT WHAT'S GOING ON. WELL, MS. JONES IS ON THE PHONE WITH MY ADMINISTRATIVE ASSISTANT EVEN AS WE SPEAK.

***

THE COURT: HELLO.

MS. JONES: YES, GOOD AFTERNOON, YOU HONOR.

THE COURT: GOOD MORNING, HOW ARE YOU?

MS. JONES: I'M FAIR. THANK YOU FOR ASKING.

THE COURT: WELL, YOU SOUND LIKE YOU'RE FAIR. HOW DO I SOUND? FAIR.

MS. JONES: I HOPE YOU SOUND WELL.

THE COURT: I'M FAIR. I'M FAIR. I HAD A FITFUL NIGHT BUT THAT'S WHAT HAPPENS FROM TIME TO TIME. YOU COULDN'T COME OVER TODAY?

MS. JONES: NO, SIR.

THE COURT   WELL, WE'RE HERE AND ATTORNEY FRANKLIN IS HERE. WOULD YOU LIKE TO SAY HELLO?

MS. JONES: YES. GOOD MORNING, ATTORNEY FRANKLIN HOW ARE YOU?

MS. FRANKLIN: GOOD MORNING.

THE COURT :   WHAT IS YOUR PLAN, MS. JONES? ***

MS. JONES: NO, I PLAN TO STAY IN THE REGION UNTIL THE NEXT HEARING. SO, I'M HOPING THE HEARING WILL BE IN A WEEK OR SO?

THE COURT: YES. WE TRY TO WORK WITH YOUR SCHEDULE. I THINK THE REASON THAT WE'RE HERE TODAY IS BECAUSE YOU DIDN'T COME LAST TIME.

COMMENT AND ANALYSIS: #3 JUDGE EKANS WENT OUT OF HIS WAY TO HANDLE BRIANNA JONES WITH KID GLOVES DESPITE THE FACT THAT SHE REMAINED IN CONTEMPT OF JUDGE STARR'S ORDER FOR THE ENTIRETY OF THE LITIGATION OF MY LAWSUIT.

***

THE COURT:	MS. JONES.
MS. JONES:	YES.
THE COURT:	YOU HAVE ME, YOU HAVE MY BACK AGAINST A WALL. DO YOU REMEMBER WHAT HAPPENED LAST TIME WHEN YOU HAD MY BACK UP AGAINST THE WALL?
MS. JONES:	I MOST CERTAINLY DO, YOUR HONOR.
THE COURT:	WELL, MY BACK IS AGAINST THE WALL. YOU'RE NOT PLAYING FAIR.
MS. JONES:	I'M SORRY I COULDN'T HEAR YOU.
THE COURT:	YOU'RE NOT PLAYING FAIR.
MS. JONES:	WELL, THAT'S CERTAINLY NOT MY INTENTION, YOUR HONOR.
THE COURT:	WELL, YOU HAVE PUT THE COURT IN A VERY UNTENABLE POSITION. YOU HAVE US LOOKING VERY FOOLISH, MS. JONES.
MS. JONES:	WELL, I APOLOGIZE TO THE COURT BECAUSE -- --
THE COURT:	MY FEELINGS AREN'T HURT, BUT *PEOPLE ARE STARTING TO DOUBT WHETHER THE COURT CAN ACTUALLY ENFORCE ITS ORDERS.* THAT'S NOT GOOD.

COMMENT AND ANALYSIS: #4 I FULLY RECOGNIZE THAT I WAS CAUGHT IN THE MIDST OF A D.C. JUDICIAL AND FBI CRIMINAL ENTERPRISE AND OTHERS PRESENT IN THE COURTROOM HAD RING SIDE SEATS TO THE PROGRESS OF THE EVENT PLAYING OUT IN THE COURTROOM.

JUDGE EKANS HAD MADE IT CLEAR FOR 9 MONTHS OF HEARINGS THAT HE HAD NO INTENTION OF ENFORCING JUDGE KATE STARR'S ORDER OF OCTOBER 18, 2010.

MS. JONES:	THAT'S CERTAINLY NOT MY INTENTION, YOUR HONOR.
THE COURT:	IT'S NOT YOUR INTENTION BUT IT'S WHAT'S HAPPENING. WHILE INTENT IS RELEVANT, THE RESULT IS WHAT WE HAVE TO BE CONCERNED WITH. WHILE YOU MIGHT NOT HAVE INTENDED IT YOU'VE ACCOMPLISHED IT SEVERAL TIMES NOW. WE HAVE TO, WE HAVE TO DO SOMETHING TO GET YOUR ATTENTION AGAIN, MS. JONES.
MS. JONES:	WELL, I CAN ASSURE YOU, YOU HAVE MY ATTENTION.

THE COURT: I'M NOT ASSURED.

MS. JONES: WELL, I PLAN TO BE, IF THE HEARING CAN BE RESCHEDULED THIS WEEK -- -- THE

COURT: IT IS SCHEDULED THIS WEEK. IT'S SCHEDULED NOW AND YOU'RE IN LAUREL. IF YOU CAN GET TO LAUREL, YOU CAN GET TO WASHINGTON, D.C.

MS. JONES: BUT IT'S THE PERSONAL NATURE IN WHICH I'M SUFFERING WITH, YOUR HONOR.

THE COURT: WELL, I DON'T UNDERSTAND. IS THERE, ARE YOU AT THE HOSPITAL IN LAUREL?

(PAUSE.)

MS. JONES: I HOPE A FEW DAYS WILL TAKE CARE OF THE NATURE OF THIS SITUATION.

THE COURT: THE ONLY QUESTION IS WHERE ARE YOU GOING TO SPEND THAT FEW DAYS?

MS. JONES: I'M GOING TO STAY AT THE HOTEL AND JUST STAY QUIET UNTIL THE VERY NEXT HEARING.

THE COURT: DO YOU KNOW THAT THE WARRANTS FROM THIS COURT ARE SERVED BY FEDERAL MARSHALS ALL OVER THE UNITED STATES AND ITS TERRITORY?

MS. JONES: YES, I'M VERY MUCH AWARE, YOUR HONOR.

THE COURT: AND EVEN IN LAUREL.

MS. JONES: WHAT CAN I DO TO GET YOU TO COME TO COURT?

MS. JONES: YOUR HONOR, I AM HEMORRHAGING PROFUSELY.

THE COURT: AS IF YOU HAD BEEN SHOT. WHAT CAN I DO TO GET YOU TO COME TO COURT?

MS. JONES: YOUR HONOR, I DEFER TO YOU.

THE COURT: WELL, THAT'S PROBABLY GOOD BECAUSE I HAVE DEFERRED TO YOU AND THAT HASN'T WORKED.

MS. JONES: WELL, IS IT POSSIBLE WE CAN RESCHEDULE FOR MONDAY?

THE COURT: SURE, THAT'S POSSIBLE. DO YOU THINK YOU CAN BE HERE MONDAY?

MS. JONES: YES.

THE COURT: YOU MIGHT BE HEMORRHAGING.

MS. JONES: IT'S A TIME ISSUE, YOUR HONOR.

THE COURT:	WELL, THAT'S RIGHT. IT IS A TIME ISSUE. WE SET THE TIME AND YOU BREAK IT.
MS. FRANKLIN:	YOUR HONOR, WILL SHE BE BRINGING DOCUMENTS SET FORTH IN THE OCTOBER 18TH ORDER?
THE COURT:	**MS. FRANKLIN IS ASKING WHETHER YOU WILL COME TO COURT WITH THE DOCUMENTS THAT WE HAVE TRIED TO GET FOR THE LAST HALF A YEAR.**
MS. FRANKLIN:	YEAR, YOUR HONOR.

COMMENT AND ANALYSIS: #5 BUT FOR THE FLOURISHING D.C. JUDICIAL AND FBI CRIMINAL ENTERPRISE, THIS WOULD BE A RATHER PATHETIC STATEMENT FROM A COURT PRESIDING JUDGE WHO HAS AT HIS DISPOSAL A PANOPLY OF COURT REMEDIES AND PENALTIES FOR COURT LITIGANTS WHO CHOOSE TO DISOBEY COURT ORDERS AND REMAIN IN CONTEMPT OF THE COURT'S PROCESS.

MS. JONES:	WHAT DOCUMENT WOULD THOSE BE? I HAVE PROVIDED THE COURT WITH THE DOCUMENTS THAT THE COURT REQUESTED. ANY OTHER DOCUMENTS I WOULD NOT HAVE. I HAVE SAID THIS OVER AND OVER AGAIN. I DON'T HAVE WHEREABOUTS OF WHERE THE RESOURCES OR THE FUNDS ARE.
MS. FRANKLIN:	OH, MY GOD.

***

MS. FRANKLIN:	....WHEN I WENT BEFORE STARR, THE VERY FIRST HEARING, I SAID, YOUR HONOR, I WANT CLOSURE. I WANT CLOSURE BECAUSE IF IT HAD BEEN ABOUT THE MONEY, MANY YEARS I COULD HAVE DONE OTHER THINGS. I WANT CLOSURE, BUT I WANT A RIGHT CLOSURE. I WANT IT BE DONE IN A RIGHT FASHION, AND I WANT TO BE PAID PROPERLY, AND I DON'T THINK THAT NEVER HAVING GIVEN HER THE IMPRESSION THAT I WAS PROVIDING PRO BONO SERVICES, THAT I SHOULD NOW JUST FORGET ABOUT ALL THE TIME, AND ENERGY, AND MONEY, AND RESOURCES, AND FRIEND SUPPORT.

IT'S NOT FAIR, IT'S JUST ABSOLUTELY NOT FAIR, AND I KNEW THIS MORNING SHE WASN'T, MY SPIRIT SAID TO ME, INTUITION, SHE'S NOT GOING TO SHOW. I WONDER WHAT CREATIVE EXCUSE SHE'S GOING TO USE TODAY BECAUSE THAT'S WHAT WE'RE FACED WITH, WITH HER. AND THAT'S JUST THE WAY IT'S GOING TO BE, SO, BUT I JUST DON'T THINK IT'S FAIR TO ME THOUGH, YOUR HONOR, THAT SHE SHOULD BE PERMITTED TO JUST CONTINUE TO MAKE UP WHAT I CALL MADE UP MERITS.

SHE SHOULDN'T BE ALLOWED TO GO INTO ANY OF THE MERITS OF THIS CASE. ***THIS IS A DEFENDANT WHO HAS, WITHOUT ANY, ANY EMBARRASSMENT OR SHAME REMAINS IN JUST ABSOLUTELY NOTORIOUS OPEN CONTEMPT OF THE COURT.***

THE COURT: MS. FRANKLIN, I UNDERSTAND HOW -- --

MS. FRANKLIN: FORGIVE ME BECAUSE I'M FULL. I GUESS THAT'S WHAT IT IS, I'M FULL, BECAUSE YOUR HONOR I'VE BEEN COMING DOWN HERE, MARCH 2012 WILL BE THREE YEARS, AND I JUST -- --

THE COURT: MS. FRANKLIN, I UNDERSTAND YOUR FRUSTRATION, AND I HAVE TRIED TO USE THE COURT'S AUTHORITY TO ASSIST YOU IN ENFORCEING A SETTLEMENT FOR YOUR FEE, BUT I HAVE TO SAY THIS TO YOU. NOW, THERE WAS A MAN IN HERE A LITTLE BIT BEFORE YOU ARRIVED TODAY WHO HAS MUCH SMALLER DEBT HE'S TRYING TO COLLECT, BUT IT'S APPROACHING $300,000, AND HE DOESN'T, I MEAN HE'S GOT A PERSON WHO IS JUST AS SLIPPERY AS CAN BE, BUT HE'S GOING ABOUT IT A BIT DIFFERENT. **I MEAN HE'S GOT A PRIVATE INVESTIGATOR AND HE'S DOING THE WORK. YOU HAVE INSTEAD LOOKED FOR THE COURT TO DO -- --**

MS. FRANKLIN: NO. NO, YOUR HONOR.

THE COURT: YES.

MS. FRANKLIN: WE REVISED THAT.

     COMMENT AND ANALYSIS: #6 HERE JUDGE EKANS ASSUMES HIS PREFERRED DEFAULT POSITION OF JUDICIAL GASLIGHTING. I HAD NO JUDGMENT AND HE KNEW IT. I HAD NO INTENTION OF HIRING A PRIVATE INVESTIGATOR. JUDGE EKANS' RESPONSIBILITY WAS TO ENFORCE JUDGE STARR'S ORDER WHICH MANDATED THAT BRIANNA JONES PRODUCE BANK STATEMENTS AND RELATED BANK DOCUMENTS. JUDGE EKANS' REFUSAL AND FAILURE TO HAVE BRIANNA JONES PRODUCE BANK STATEMENTS WAS SIMPLY UNEQUIVOCAL EVIDENCE OF HIS KEY ROLE AND COMPLICITY IN THE D.C. JUDICIAL AND FBI CRIMINAL ENTERPRISE ORGANIZED AND EXECUTED TO DEFRUAD ME OF MILLIONS OF DOLLARS OWED TO ME IN ATTORNEY'S FEES.

THE COURT: WELL, YOU HAVE CONSISTENTLY ARGUED, ATTORNEY FRANKLIN THAT MS. JONES IS THUMBING HER NOSE AT THE COURT. I DON'T THINK MS. JONES IS THUMBING HER NOSE AT THE COURT. I DO THINK THAT SHE IS BEING LESS THAN HONEST WTH THE COURT, BUT I HAVE NOT, NO ONE HAS PUT BEFORE THIS COURT, EITHER MYSELF OR STARR, **PROOF THAT MONEY EVER PASSED FROM THAT ESTATE TO MS. JONES.**

MS. FRANKLIN: RIGHT.

COMMENT AND ANALYSIS: #7 HERE JUDGE EKANS TELEGRAPHS THE REASON THE D.C. COURT OF APPEALS WILL USE ALL MOST 3 YEARS LATER TO OVERTURN EKANS' RIGGED MONEY JUDGMENT ISSUED TO ME IN OCTOBER 2011 AT THE CONCLUSION OF HIS ADJUDICATION OF MY LAWSUIT.

THE COURT: I THINK THAT'S AN IMPORTANT STEP. I THINK THAT WHETHER IT'S FROM THE DOCKET, OR THE ACTION IN FLORIDA, OR WHETHER IT'S FROM SOME OTHER SOURCE THAT THERE HAS TO EXIST HARD EVIDENCE THAT EITHER CASH MONEY, OR STOCKS, OR SOME OTHER FORM OF CAPITAL IS IN HER POSSESSION. YOU KNOW SHE CAME UP WITH SOME ANSWER MONTHS AGO ABOUT HAVING **PEOPLE CONTACTING HER WHENEVER SHE NEEDED RESOURCES** OR WHATEVER. I DON'T KNOW. I MEAN PEOPLE DO A LOT OF STRANGE THINGS IN THE WORLD, BUT-- --

COMMENT AND ANALYSIS: #8 AT NO TIME DID BRIANNA JONES EVER TESTIFY THAT PEOPLE CONTACTED HER WHENEVER SHE NEEDED RESOURCES. JUDGE EKANS OBVIOUSLY GAINED THIS INFORMATION FROM UNKNOWN CO-CONSPIRATORS, THEIR HANDLERS AND FACILITATORS.

MS. FRANKLIN: I WAS REALLY THINKING, YOUR HONOR, THAT THE BAR'S INVESTIGATION WOULD BE MORE THAN ADEQUATE FOR THE COURT.

THE COURT: THE BAR'S INVESTIGATION IS A WHOLE DIFFERENT THING BECAUSE THEY, I MEAN I, I'M SURE I DON'T KNOW IT THE WAY YOU KNOW IT, BUT THEY'RE LOOKING TO SEE IF THERE WAS ATTORNEY MISCONDUCT, AND THEY WEREN'T LOOKING, AS FAR AS I KNOW, THEY WEREN'T LOOKING TO SEE WHAT THE BASIS OF THE SETTLEMENT WAS, OR HOW THE SETTLEMENT TRANSPIRED.

COMMENT AND ANALYSIS: #9 JUDGE EKANS DID NOT HIDE THE FACT THAT HE HAD NO INTEREST IN THE FINDINGS OF THE INVESTIGATION THAT HAD BEEN CONDUCTED BY THE OFFICE OF THE D.C. BAR COUNSEL REGARDING ITS VERIFICATION OF THE EXISTENCE OF THE SETTLEMENT OF THE $100 MILLION FLORIDA LAWSUIT. MOREOVER, JUDGE EKANS MADE NO ATTEMPT TO INQUIRE ON HIS OWN INITIATIVE OF THE DETAILS OF THE FINDINGS OF THE INVESTIGATION CONDUCTED BY THE OFFICE OF D.C. BAR COUNSEL.

MS. FRANKLIN: OH, NO, IN THIS INSTANCE THEY DID BECAUSE THEY ONCE THEY IMMMEDIATELY CONCLUDED THAT THERE WAS NO ATTORNEY MISCONDUCT, THEY WERE TRYING TO DETERMINE WHETHER MS. JONES HAD FUNDS, OR WAS ENTITLED TO RECEIVE FUNDS TO PAY THESE PEOPLE, AND THAT'S WHY THEIR INVESTIGATION WENT IN THAT DIRECTION, AND SO THAT'S WHAT THEIR, AND THAT'S WHAT THEIR FINDS, YOU KNOW, THAT'S WHAT THEIR FINDINGS DEMONSTRATE THAT IN FACT SHE WAS ENTITLED, THERE WAS A SETTLEMENT AND THAT THEY DETERMINED THAT DISBURSEMENT. THIS WAS 2009.

THE COURT: I 'LL SEE IF I CAN FIND OUT EXACTLY WHAT EVIDENCE THEY CAME UPON.

COMMENT AND ANALYSIS: #10 HEARING NOTHING FURTHER FROM JUDGE EKANS, IT WILL BE ASSUMED THAT JUDGE EKANS NEVER MADE ANY ATTEMPTS TO DETERMINE THE EVIDENCE HELD BY THE OFFICE OF D.C. BAR COUNSEL REGARDING BRIANNA JONES' SETTLEMENT OF THE FLORIDA LAWSUIT WITH THE WILLIE LEE RIDGEWAY ESTATE.

MS. FRANKLIN: THEY DID, YOU KNOW, AND I, YOU KNOW AND AS I SAID -- --

THE COURT: THEY MADE A REFERENCE TO IT IN THIS MEMORANDUM, BUT THERE IS NOTHING ATTACHED TO IT. THERE IS NOTHING TO SEE.

COMMENT AND ANALYSIS: #11 JUDGE EKANS WAS NOT INTERESTED IN THE OPINION OF THE D.C. OFFICE OF BAR COUNSEL. HIS OVERALL DISINTERESTED ATTITUDE WAS SIMPLY FURTHER EVIDENCE OF HIS COMPLICITY IN THE CRIMINAL ENTERPRISE.

MS. FRANKLIN: NO, BECAUSE IT WAS GOING OUT TO THE, GOING OUT TO THE COMPLAINANT, RIGHT. THERE WAS NOTHING ATTACHED TO IT, BUT I MEAN THAT'S WHY IT WENT IN THAT DIRECTION. SO, IT WAS A LITTLE DIFFERENT IN TERMS OF THEIR NORMAL INVESTIGATION BECAUSE IT WAS SO CLEAR CUT THAT THIS WAS AN INSTANCE WHERE, YOU KNOW, I JUST INTRODUCED THE COMPLAINANTS TO THE DEFENDANT AND -- --

THE COURT: WELL, I WILL SAY TO YOU THAT MS. JONES IS CERTAINLY UNIQUE, NO ONE CAN DISPUTE THAT, BUT SHE IS NOT UNIQUELY WEALTHY. THERE ARE MANY, MANY, MANY WEALTHY PEOPLE IN THIS COUNTRY, AND MANY OF THEM DO A LOT OF DIFFERENT THINGS TO HIDE THEIR ASSETS, BUT THE FACT THAT THEY HAVE ASSETS IS NOT SOMETHING THAT'S HERE.

COMMENT AND ANALYSIS: #12 JUDGE EKANS INTENTIONALLY FOCUSED ON BRIANNA JONES' ASSETS AS OPPOSED TO THE BANK STATEMENTS OF THE SETTLEMENT PROCEEDS ON DEPOSIT AT BANK OF AMERICA AS SPECIFIED IN JUDGE STARR'S ORDER.

BARBARA WASHINGTON FRANKLIN

MS. FRANKLIN: BUT, YOUR HONOR, BUT MY QUESTION IS, AM I GOING TO HAVE TO BE INVOLVED WITH HER MEDICAL SITUATION?

THE COURT: I DON'T SEE WHY. I MEAN I DON'T KNOW WHY YOU WOULD HAVE TO BE INVOLVED WITH THAT. I THINK THAT, AND I NEED TO, I NEED TO GIVE SOME MORE THOUGHT TO THIS, **BUT I'M AT A POINT NOW WHERE THIS CASE COULD VERY WELL HANG AROUND MY NECK LIKE AN ALBATROSS IF I DON'T DO SOMETHING.**

COMMENT AND ANALYSIS: #13 JUDGE EKANS WAS A KEY CO-CONSPIRATOR IN THE CRIMINAL ENTERPRISE TO DEFRAUD ME OF AN ESTIMATED $50 MILLION IN ATTORNEY'S FEES. IF ANYTHING HUNG AROUND HIS NECK, IT SHOULD HAVE BEEN THAT FACT.

MS. FRANKLIN: YOUR HONOR, WITH REGARD TO THE INVESTIGATOR, I HAVE THAT, AND THAT'S IN THE COURT RECORD. JOHN MEISTER, JOHN MEISTER OF WASHINGTON PROCESS. HE'S WAITING FOR ME TO COME BACK WITH A JUDGMENT BECAUSE WHEN YOUR HONOR TOLD ME TO SEARCH, I THEN CAME BACK TO THE COURT AND SAID, D.C. LAW TIES MY HANDS. SO, I'M NOT BEING A SLOUCH IN TERMS OF SEARCHING, BUT I CAN'T BY LAW DO ANYTHING BECAUSE I CAN'T GET A REPUTABLE FIRM TO HELP ME, YOU KNOW.

COMMENT AND ANALYSIS: #14 I REMIND JUDGE EKANS THAT HE HAD INTENTIONALLY SENT ME ON A WILD GOOSE CHASE TO SEARCH FOR ASSETS WHEN HE KNEW THAT D.C. LAW REQUIRED THAT THE CONDITION PRECEDENT FOR SEARCHING FOR ANOTHER'S ASSETS IS A COURT JUDGMENT WHICH I DIDN'T HAVE. THIS WAS FURTHER EVIDENCE THAT JUDGE EKANS' FOCUS WAS ON THE SUCCESS OF THE CRIMINAL ENTERPRISE UNDERWAY.

THE COURT: WE'LL SEE IF WE CAN RESOLVE THAT ON MONDAY.

MS. FRANKLIN: OKAY, YOUR HONOR.

THE COURT: WE'LL SEE IF WE CAN RESOLVE THAT ON MONDAY.

MS. FRANKLIN: AT 10:00, YOUR HONOR?

THE COURT: AT 10 O'CLOCK.

MS. FRANKLIN: ALL RIGHT. THANK YOU, YOUR HONOR.

THE COURT: THANK YOU.

(THEREUPON THE HEARING WAS CONCLUDED.)

THE ODYSSEY OF JUDICIAL CORRUPTION

SUPERIOR COURT OF THE DISTRICT OF COLUMBIA
CIVIL DIVISION
WASHINGTON, D.C.

THE HONORABLE MATTHEW D. EKANS, ASSOCIATE JUDGE, PRESIDING

THE FOLLOWING ARE EXCERPTS OF THE OFFICIAL COURT TRANSCRIPT OF THE
OCTOBER 17, 2011 PROCEEDING
ANNOTATED BY THE AUTHOR'S PERTINENT COMMENTARY AND ANALYSIS

OCTOBER 17, 2011

PROCEEDINGS

COMMENT AND ANALYSIS: #1 IT WAS NOT JUST HIS WORDS, BUT HIS OVERALL DEMEANOR AND ATTITUDE THAT HIS WORDS CONVEYED THAT TRUMPETED D.C. JUDICIAL FRAUD, THEFT, CORRUPTION AND EXTORTION DURING JUDGE EKANS' 9-MONTH ADJUDICATION OF MY LAWSUIT AGAINST THE FORMER CLIENT. IT WAS OFTEN WHAT JUDGE EKANS DIDN'T SAY AND, BY LAW, WAS OBLIGATED TO SAY, THAT SCREAMED AT ME ALL OVER HIS COURTROOM.

 I HAD VIRTUALLY SPILLED MY GUTS OF NOT JUST THE FACTS OF MY CASE, BUT MORE IMPORTANTLY, THE TRUTH OF MY CASE. IT WAS IMPORTANT THAT AN OFFICIAL RECORD BE MADE OF BOTH. AND YET MY GUT ASSURED ME THAT THE LAST THING JUDGE EKANS WANTED TO HEAR FROM ME WAS THE TRUTH. IN FACT, I WOULD QUICKLY LEARN THAT THE ROLE AND IMPORTANCE OF THE TRUTH IN EKANS' COURTROOM WAS COMPLETELY OVERRATED. NOTHING SEEMED TO IRRITATE HIM MORE THAN WHEN I WOULD DECLARE THE TRUTH OF A PARTICULAR CIRCUMSTANCE OR EVENT. EKANS MADE IT CLEAR THAT HE JUST DIDN'T HAVE TIME FOR THE TRUTH OR ANY EVIDENCE PROFFERED AS THE TRUTH REGARDING MY LAWSUIT.

THIS WAS THE FINAL HEARING OF HIS 9-MONTH- RIGGED- ADJUDICATION-OF-MY-CASE. THE SUCCESSFUL CRIMINAL ENTERPRISE WOULD GUARANTEE THE ILLEGAL CONFISCATION OF THE TENS OF MILLIONS OF DOLLARS IN SETTLEMENT PROCEEDS AND ATTORNEY'S FEES TO BE APPORTIONED TO THE D.C. JUDICIAL AND FBI CO-CONSPIRATORS BASED ON THE SIGNIFICANCE OF THEIR RESPECTIVE ROLES IN THE EXECUTION OF THE CRIMINAL ENTERPRISE WHOSE MISSION WAS TO DEFRAUD ME OF THE MILLIONS OF DOLLARS OWED TO ME IN ATTORNEY'S FEES.

BARBARA WASHINGTON FRANKLIN

GIVEN HIS MARCHING ORDERS CRAFTED BY THE D.C. JUDICIAL AND FBI CO-CONSPIRATORS THAT MADE UP THE TEAM OF THIEVES, THUGS AND MOBSTERS ORCHESTRATING THIS HISTORIC JUDICIAL AND FBI CRIMINAL CONSPIRACY AND ENTERPRISE, JUDGE EKANS WOULD CONCLUDE THE HEARING WITH THE ISSUANCE TO ME OF A $13.6 MILLION MONEY JUDGMENT IN LIEU OF THE BANK OF AMERICA BANK STATEMENTS OF THE SETTLEMENT PROCEEDS AS ORDERED BY JUDGE KATE STARR. HE WAS COMFORTED BY KNOWING THAT THEREAFTER, THE DEFENDANT, BRIANNA JONES, PURSUANT TO INSTRUCTION FROM THE CO-CONSPIRATORS, WOULD APPEAL EKANS' ISSUANCE OF THE MONEY JUDGMENT.

THE D.C. COURT OF APPEALS, COMPLICIT AT ALL TIMES IN THE CONSPIRACY AND CRIMINAL ENTERPRISE TO DEFRAUD ME OF THE TENS OF MILLIONS OF DOLLARS OWED TO ME IN ATTORNEY'S FEES, WOULD INTENTIONALLY AND PURPOSEFULLY SIT ON THE APPEAL FOR ALMOST 3 YEARS AND THEREAFTER, UPON BEING INFORMED OF MY INQUIRY TO TAKE OUT AN ADVOCACY ADVERTISEMENT IN THE WASHINGTON POST, IMMEDIATELY ISSUE A JUDGMENT ON JULY 14, 2014, OVERTURNING THE "PAPER" MONEY JUDGMENT ISSUED BY JUDGE EKANS IN OCTOBER 2011.

MOREOVER, THE D.C. COURT OF APPEALS TOOK DEMONIC PLEASURE BY INCLUDING THE CRYPTIC CAVEAT IN ITS OPINION THAT SHOULD I (THE SURVIVOR OF THE CRIMINAL ENTERPRISE) EVER FIND THE STOLEN PROCEEDS, JUDGE EKANS WOULD BE FREE TO REVISE AND ISSUE A NEW JUDGMENT ACCORDINGLY. THIS IS NOTHING MORE THAN EVIDENCE OF CLEAR, OBVIOUS AND NAUSEATING JUDICIAL CORRUPTION IN THE D.C. COURT SYSTEM AT ITS HIGHEST LEVEL, ITS COURT OF APPEALS.

MOREOVER, IT IS EVIDENCE THAT THE D.C. COURT SYSTEM IS BANKRUPT OF MORAL AND ETHICAL PRINICIPLES THAT DEFINE A VIABLE SOCIAL, ECONOMIC AND POLITICAL DEMOCRACY AND CONSEQUENTLY, AFTER SNUFFING OUT THEIR FREEDOMS OF LIBERTY AND JUSTICE, INTENDS TO CRUSH THE SPIRITS, SOULS AND CREATIVITY OF THE CITIZENS BOUND BY ITS DRACONIAN DECISIONS THAT THRIVE UNCHECKED, UNEXAMINED AND OUTRAGEOUSLY PASS FOR THE RULE OF LAW.

THE DEPUTY CLERK: YOUR HONOR, CALLING THE CASE OF BARBARA WASHINGTON FRANKLIN VS. BRIANNA JONES, 2009 CA 4417; AND IN THE MATTER OF BRIANNA JONES, 2011 CCC 1.

PARTIES, PLEASE COME FORWARD AND IDENTIFY YOURSELVES FOR THE RECORD.

(PAUSE.)

MS. JONES: GOOD MORNING, YOUR HONOR, BRIANNA - - --

THE COURT: GOOD MORNING.

MS. JONES:--------------------BRIANNA JONES, PRO SE, AT THIS TIME. I MUST SAY, YOU HONOR, EVEN UNDER THESE EXTREME DIFFICULT CIRCUMSTANCES, IT IS REALLY GOOD TO SEE YOU AGAIN.

THE COURT: AND LIKEWISE. I WAS -- --YOU----- I WAS JUST ABOUT TO SAY THE SAME THING.

MS. JONES: THANK YOU.

THE COURT: MS. FRANKLIN -- --

MS. FRANKLIN: GOOD MORNING, YOUR HONOR. BARBARA WASHINGTON FRANKLIN, YOUR HONOR.

THE COURT: GOOD MORNING.

MS. FRANKLIN: GOOD SEEING YOU AGAIN, YOUR HONOR. PLAINTIFF.

THE COURT: WELL, YOU'VE SEEN ME A LOT MORE, SO IT MAY NOT BE AS EXCITING FOR YOU.

> **COMMENT AND ANALYSIS: #2** NO NORMAL HUMAN BEING CAN FEEL EXCITEMENT IN THE HANDS OF A CORRUPT, CONSCIENCE-FREE AND AMORAL D.C. COURT JUDGE IN THE PERSON OF JUDGE MATTHEW EKANS.
>
> WHAT I FELT WAS TREMENDOUS RELIEF THAT AFTER NINE LONG MONTHS OF THE WORST KIND OF FIERY TRIALS, I WAS ABOUT TO BE SET FREE, SINCE THIS WAS THE FINAL HEARING BEFORE JUDGE EKANS.

MS. JONES: YOUR HONOR, MAY I SPEAK? SOME NEW INFORMATION CAME TO LIGHT ON FRIDAY EVENING. AND I WANT TO APOLOGIZE, BECAUSE I CALLED THE PLAINTIFF; I GOT REALLY EXCITED. AND I THINK THIS IS THE SMOKING GUN TO THE ENTIRE CASE AS IT RELATED TO THE ESTATE OF THE LATE WILLIE LEE RIDGEWAY (PHONETIC). THE -- -- THE PLAINTIFF DID NOT RESPOND, BUT I WAS -- --

MS. FRANKLIN: YOUR HONOR, I JUST HAVE TO, FOR THE RECORD. I HAVE AN OFFICE. I HAVE LIVE STAFF THAT ANSWERS MY TELEPHONE. I HAVE RECEIVED NO MESSAGES OR CALLS FROM MS. JONES SINCE WE WERE HERE LAST ON FRIDAY.

(PAUSE.)

BARBARA WASHINGTON FRANKLIN

MS. JONES:	YOUR HONOR, I CALLED HER HOME SEVERAL TIMES, AS WELL AS HER CELL PHONE BECAUSE THAT'S -- --
MS. FRANKLIN:	MY HOME IS NOT MY OFFICE.
MS. JONES:	WELL, THAT'S IN THE NORM; SO I UNDERSTAND THAT'S CHANGED.
THE COURT:	I -- --
MS. FRANKLIN:	WELL, IT'S NOT THE NORM ANYMORE.
THE COURT:	I WOULD REALLY HOPE THAT YOU WOULD NOT USE THIS FORUM TO COME IN AND START A -- --
MS. JONES:	I UNDERSTAND.
THE COURT:--------------- A PERSONAL ARGUMENT.
MS. JONES:	THE -- --THE ----- THE IMPORTANT ASPECT IS THAT IN SKOWERING THE COURHOUSE IN 1994-95, TRYING TO LOCATE -- --
THE COURT:	WHERE ----- WHERE?

***

MS. JONES:	AND SO, THAT GOES TO THE HEART OF -- -- I HAVE NOT ----- I HAVE NEVER NOR HAVE I ASSIGNED ANYONE TO TAKE POSSESSION OF ANY FUNDS FROM ME OTHER THAN THE PLAINTIFF.
THE COURT:	IT SORT OF BEGS THE QUESTION OF WHY YOU WOULD HAVE ENTERED INTO A SETTLEMENT AGREEMENT IN THIS ACTION. THIS -- THIS ACTION ----- THE ONLY THING THAT'S REALLY BEFORE ME IS A LAWSUIT THAT BARBARA WASHINGTON FRANKLIN FILED AGAINST BRIANNA JONES FOR -- --
MS. JONES:	BECAUSE THERE WAS A -- --
THE COURT:	-- -- HOLD -- -- HOLD -- -- FOR AN ATTORNEY FEE. AND WHILE THAT CASE WAS PROCEEDING, YOU ENTERED INTO A SETTLEMENT -- --
MS. JONES:	IT WAS -- -- IT WAS THE MOST -- --
THE COURT:--------------- THAT SAID THAT YOU WOULD PAY HER MILLIONS AND MILLIONS OF DOLLARS.
MS. JONES:	BECAUSE I WANTED HER TO KNOW -- --

THE COURT: AND THAT WAS ENTERED INTO THE RECORD. AND THEN THE PREVIOUS JUDGE LEFT THIS CALENDAR, AND I TOOK IT KNOWING THAT THERE WOULD BE A COUPLE OF THINGS ON THERE THAT WOULD NOT BE EASY.

MS. JONES: BUT YOUR HONOR, THAT WAS THE MOST -- --

THE COURT: THEN   THEN THIS HAS BECOME MY NIGHTMARE. THIS HAS BECOME THE ONLY CASE IN 25 YEARS THAT I CAN'T GET A LEGAL GRASP OF, BECAUSE YOU'VE SIGNED A SETTLEMENT TO PAY THIS ATTORNEY WHO YOU TELL ME YOU HIRED TO REPRESENT YOU.

COMMENT AND ANALYSIS: #3 JUDGE EKANS, MORE THAN ANY OTHER INDIVIDUAL THAT I'VE EVER ENCOUNTERED IN MY LIFETIME, PUT THE "N" IN THE NIGHTMARE THAT MY CASE BECAME FOR ME.

AS A COURT JUDGE, IT WAS IMPOSSIBLE FOR EKANS TO GET A LEGAL GRASP OF MY CASE WHEN HE, ALONG WITH HIS JUDICIAL COLLEAGUES, CONSPIRED TO TREAD IN CRIMINAL WATERS AS OPPOSED TO LEGAL PROCESS AND THE RULE OF LAW IN ORDER TO FULFILL THE MISSION OF THE CRIMINAL ENTERPRISE TO STRIP ME OF THE ATTORNEY'S FEES OWED TO ME IN THE ESTIMATED AMOUNT OF $50 MILLION.

WHEN JUDGE EKANS TOOK MY CASE IN JANUARY 2011, IT WAS WITH THE CLEAR UNDERSTANDING THAT HE WOULD RIG ITS ADJUDICATION IN SUCH A WAY THAT I WOULD NEVER RECEIVE A DIME OF THE $34 MILLION SETTLEMENT. THE D.C. SUPERIOR COURT RECORDS VERIFY THAT EKANS COMPLETED HIS CO-CONSPIRATOR ASSIGNMENT TO THE LETTER. I NEVER RECEIVED A DIME. IN SOME CIRCLES, DECIDING THE END FROM THE BEGINNING IS CALLED *REVERSE ENGINEERING.*

THE COUPLE OF THINGS THAT WERE NOT EASY FOR JUDGE EKANS IN HIS ASSIGNMENT TO DEFRAUD ME OF THE $50 MILLION OWED TO ME IN ATTORNEY'S FEES WERE MY STEADFAST RESISTANCE TO HIS RUTHLESS GASLIGHTING OF THE FACTS, EVIDENCE AND CIRCUMSTANCES OF MY CASE AND HIS INTENTIONAL, PURPOSEFUL AND SHAMELESS DISREGARD OF THE FINDINGS OF THE D.C. OFFICE OF BAR COUNSEL REGARDING ITS INVESTIGATION AND ITS CONCLUSION THAT BRIANNA JONES WAS ENTITLED TO CONSIDERABLE ASSETS RESULTING FROM MY FILING OF THE $100 MILLION LAWSUIT AND THE SUBSEQUENT $34 MILLION SETTLEMENT OF THE LAWSUIT.

MS. JONES: BUT WE -- --

THE COURT: BUT THEN SOMEHOW DECIDED THAT YOU WOULD ENTER INTO A SETTLEMENT OF YOUR OWN CASE WITHOUT HER. AND   AND NOW, SHE'S SUED YOU FOR HER FEE.

BARBARA WASHINGTON FRANKLIN

MS. JONES:	YOUR HONOR, SHE WAS -- --
THE COURT:	AND YOU -- --
MS. JONES:	----------------APPRISED ALL ALONG.
THE COURT:	AND YOU ENTERED INTO A SETTLEMENT INSTEAD OF SAYING -- --
MS. JONES:	BUT YOUR HONOR -- --
THE COURT:	**-- -- INSTEAD OF SAYING THAT YOU DIDN'T RECEIVE ANY MONEY -- --**

COMMENT AND ANALYSIS: #4 JUDGE EKANS WAS A MAJOR PLAYER AND KEY D.C. JUDICIAL CO-CONSPIRATOR IN THE CRIMINAL ENTERPRISE TO DEFRAUD ME OF AN ESTIMATED $50 MILLION IN ATTORNEY'S FEES RESULTING FROM THE DECEMBER 1996 SETTLEMENT OF THE $100 MILLION LAWSUIT THAT I SOLELY CRAFTED AND FILED AT MY SOLE EXPENSE IN BROWARD COUNTY CIRCUIT COURT LOCATED IN FORT LAUDERDALE, FLORIDA IN MAY 1996.

MS. JONES:	I SAID IT IN JUDGE STARR'S COURT -- --
THE COURT:	DON'T TALK OVER ME, PLEASE.
MS. JONES:	I'M SORRY, SIR. I'M SORRY.
THE COURT:	IT'S----- IT'S DIFFICULT ENOUGH FOR ME TO TRY TO KEEP MY FOCUS IN THIS CASE WITHOUT YOU INTERRUPTING ME WITH -- -- WITH -- --
MS. JONES:	I PROFOUNDLY APOLOGIZE.
THE COURT:	-- -- WITH -- --WITH MATTERS THAT ARE NOT -- -- THAT ARE NOT ------ THAT DO NOT PERTAIN TO WHAT I'M TRYING TO RESOLVE.

I -- -- I DON'T KNOW WHAT LED YOU TO ENTER INTO A SETTLEMENT IN YOUR LAWSUIT WITH THAT ESTATE. I DON'T KNOW WHAT LED THEM TO ENTER INTO A SETTLEMENT WITH YOU, FOR THAT MATTER. **WHAT I'M CONCERNED WITH IS THE SETTLEMENT YOU ENTERED WITH THE WOMAN STANDING TO YOUR LEFT. TO BE QUITE HONEST, I HAVEN'T BEEN ABLE TO FIND ANY EVIDENCE THAT YOU EVER RECEIVED ANY MONEY. SHE HASN'T BEEN ABLE TO FIND ANY EVIDENCE THAT YOU EVER RECEIVED ANY MONEY. AND AS FAR AS I KNOW, THIS IS ALL A SMOKE AND MIRRORS.**

COMMENT AND ANALYSIS: #5 BECAUSE OF MY PARTNERSHIP WITH THE HOLY SPIRIT THROUGHOUT THE PENDENCY OF MY LAWSUIT AND THE HELP HE HAD GIVEN ME WTH MY "CASE FROM HELL," TO QUOTE MY ACCOUNTANT, I ACCURATELY

INTERPRETED JUDGE EKANS' COMMENTS DURING THE HEARING AS SIGNALING THAT THE MONEY JUDGMENT THAT HE WOULD ISSUE ME WOULD BE OVERTURNED 3 YEARS LATER IN JULY 2014 BY THE D.C. COURT OF APPEALS ON THE FLIMSY GROUNDS THAT BRIANNA JONES NEVER RECEIVED ANY PORTION OF THE $34 MILLION IN SETTLEMENT PROCEEDS. IT DID NOT MATTER THAT JUDGE STARR'S OCTOBER 18, 2010 ORDER HAD DIRECTED BRIANNA TO TURN OVER BANK OF AMERICA BANK STATEMENTS REGARDIING SETTLEMENT PROCEEDS.

NOR DID IT MATTER TO THE D.C. COURT OF APPEALS, AT ALL TIMES COMPLICIT IN THE CRIMINAL CONSPIRACY TO DEFRAUD ME OF MY ATTORNEY'S FEES, THAT JUDGE EKANS HAD INTENTIONALLY AND PURPOSEFULLY REFUSED TO ENFORCE EITHER THE SPIRIT OR THE LETTER OF JUDGE STARR'S ORDER. HE KNEW THAT ENFORCEMENT OF JUDGE STARR'S ORDER WOULD DEPRIVE HIM AND HIS CO-CONSPIRATOR COLLEAGURS THE ONCE-IN-A-LIFETIME JUDICIAL OPPORTUNITY TO STEAL WITH IMPUNITY THE ESTIMATED $50 MILLION OWED TO ME IN ATTORNEY'S FEES AND THEREBY ENRICH THEMSELVES, THEIR RESPECTIVE FAMILIES, FRIENDS AND COLLEAGUES.

WHEN YOU ARE A TRIAL ATTORNEY YOU MUST HEAR WHAT THE PRESIDING JUDGE SAYS, WHAT IS MEANT BY WHAT IS SAID, WHAT IS NOT MEANT BY WHAT IS SAID, WHAT IS NOT SAID, WHAT IS NOT MEANT BY WHAT IS NOT SAID AND WHAT WAS MANDATED BY THE RULE OF LAW TO BE SAID BUT WAS NOT SAID.

AND WHEN YOUR ETERNAL STATUS AS DAUGHTER OF THE KING PRECEDES YOUR TEMPORARY STATUS AS PLAINTIFF IN YOUR OWN LAWSUIT OR AS TRIAL ATTORNEY ON BEHALF OF ANOTHER, YOU MUST LISTEN ATTENTIVELY TO THE STILL AND QUIET PROMPTINGS OF THE HOLY SPIRIT GIVEN DURING THE DAY AS WELL AS THE DREAM REVELATIONS HE BRINGS AFTER MIDNIGHT, BUT USUALLY BEFORE DAYBREAK, POINTING YOU IN THE DIRECTION OF YOUR DESTINY AND HIS DIVINE WILL, PLAN AND PURPOSE FOR YOUR LIFE.

THE COURT: BUT WHAT IS PLAIN IS THAT THE TWO OF YOU HAVE BROUGHT THIS MATTER TO THIS COURT, AND YOU'VE ENTERED INTO A LEGAL CONTRACT THAT THE PLAINTIFF IS TRYING TO ENFORCE THROUGH THE COURT. THE ONLY WAY THAT I KNOW TO ENFORCE IT IS TO ENTER A JUDGMENT AND LET HER PROCEED ON THE JUDGMENT. AND WE'VE GOT A   A MOVING TARGET FOR A FIGURE. I TOLD MY LAW CLERK TO PREPARE A JUDGMENT ORDER, AND SHE SAID IN WHAT AMOUNT, YOUR HONOR? I SAID, I DON'T KNOW. EVEN   **EVEN THAT IS SMOKE AND MIRRORS.** IT STARTS OUT AT 33 MILLION. IT -- --

MS. JONES: THIRTY-FOUR.

THE COURT: -- -- MAGICALLY -- -- WELL, ACTUALLY IT STARTED OUT AT WHAT, 18 -- --

MS. JONES: IT WAS -- --IT WAS TWO AT THE TIME -- -- IT WAS FIRST 18.5 -- --

THE COURT: CAN YOU BE QUIET?

MS. JONES: OH, SORRY, I THOUGHT YOU WERE ASKING ME THE QUESTION.

THE COURT: I WASN'T ASKING YOU ANYTHING.

MS. JONES: I APOLOGIZE.

THE COURT: YOU'LL---- YOU'LL KNOW WHEN I ASK YOU SOMETHING.

MS. JONES: ABSOLUTELY.

THE COURT: IT STARTS OUT, ACCCORDING TO YOU, AT $18,000. AND THEN YOU GET THIS WHAT I WILL CALL A MYSTERIOUS PHONE CALL, ACCORDING TO YOU, FROM THE WIDOW'S ATTORNEY, SAYING, THAT'S NOT ENOUGH, WE WANT TO GIVE YOU MORE. WHOEVER HEARD OF THAT? BUT THAT'S WHAT YOU SAID. AND SO, THE AMOUNT GOES UP TO 30 SOME THOUSAND. THEN YOU GO BEFORE JUDGE STARR ON THIS LAWSUIT THAT'S BEFORE ME AND THE FIGURE 100,000 COMES UP; BECAUSE THROUGH SOME MATHEMATICAL GYMNASTICS, ATTORNEY FRANKLIN'S SETTLEMENT CONTRACT WITH YOU CALLED FOR 40 PERCENT AND A TEN PERCENT BONUS. **AND SO, SHE'S LOOKING FOR $50 MILLION.**

COMMENT AND ANALYSIS: #6 NOTHING WAS MORE EVIDENT OF THE DEPTH AND DEMONSTRATION OF JUDICIAL FRAUD, THEFT AND CORRUPTION PRACTICED, PROMULGATED AND PROMOTED BY JUDGE EKANS THAN HIS EGREGIOUS ABUSE OF JUDICIAL DISCRETION BY CHANGING THE FACTS OF THE CASE.

HE PERSISTED IN FALSELY AND INTENTIONALLY CALLING ME A **JUDGMENT CREDITOR** THROUGHOUT THE RIGGING OF DISMISSAL OF MY LAWSUIT. HE WOULD NOW FALSELY DEFINE MY CASE AS **SMOKE AND MIRRORS** AND DO SO WITHOUT FEAR OF ADMONITION, DISCIPLINE OR PUNISHMENT.

THE COURT: AND I -- --I   I MUST SAY THAT ALL OF THIS SORT OF LEAVES ME JUST VERY, VERY DOUBTFUL THAT **THIS IS ANYTHING OTHER THAN A LOT OF BOLOGNA**. I HAVEN'T SEEN ANY EVIDENE OF A LAWSUIT INVOLVING YOU AGAINST AN ESTATE. I HAVEN'T SEEN EVIDENCE OF THAT. I HAVEN'T SEEN ANYTHING APPROACHING A SETTLEMENT DOCUMENT, WHICH YOU SAY WAS PLACED IN SOME LOCKBOX AND DISAPPEARED.

I'VE BEEN PRESENTED WITH AN EXCERPT FROM A BAR COUNSEL OPINION ABSOLVING FRANKLIN OF ANY WRONGDOING; BUT -- --BUT WITH ------BUT WITH A - - --A REFERENCE, WHICH I COULD ONLY SAY WAS SOMETHING THAT WAS VERY LOOSELY STATED GRAMMATICALLY, TO----- REFERENCE TO A SETTLEMENT THAT YOU WERE ENTITLED TO. I ------I'VE NEVER HEARD ANY JUDICIAL AUTHORITY SPEAK OF ANYBODY BEING ENTITLED TO A SETTLEMENT. SETTLEMENTS AREN'T ------ DON'T COME BY ----- BY WAY OF ENTITLEMENT. SETTLEMENTS ARE NEGOTIATED THROUGH CONTESTED ADVERSARIAL ACTIONS. NOBODY'S ENTITLED TO A SETTLEMENT. THAT - --- THAT'S TERMINOLOGY THAT NEWSPAPAERS USE, MEDIA PEOPLE, WHO AREN'T WELL VERSED IN – IN LAW. WHO IN THE WORLD'S ENTITLED TO A SETTLEMENT? SETTLEMENTS COME ABOUT THROUGH NEGOTIATIONS WHEN PEOPLE COMPROMISE THEIR ACTIONS, BECAUSE THEY'RE WILLING TO GIVE UP SOMETHING TO GET PEACE OF MIND. THAT'S NOT AN ENTITLEMENT. **AND SO, I'M NOT PREPARED TO RELY ON THIS EXCERPT FROM BAR COUNSEL.**

NOW, IF -- -- IF ANYBODY HAS A DOCKET ENTRY FROM BROWARD COUNTY, OR WHEREVER THIS ACTION WAS, THAT SHOWS THAT THIS – THAT CASE DOWN THERE ENDED IN A MONETARY SETTLEMENT, THEN I THINK WE'VE GOT SOMETHING THAT WE CAN MOVE ON. BUT THIS -- -- THIS THAT'S BEEN GOING ON HERE IN MY COURTROOM IS AN EMBARRASSMENT FOR ME, QUITE FRANKLY, AND I'M READY TO PUT AN END TO IT. WHAT?

COMMENT AND ANALYSIS: #7 JUDGE EKANS IS UNABLE TO HIDE HIS INABILITY TO THINK IN TERMS OF AN ESTIMATED $50 MILLION THAT HAS BEEN EARNED AND IS OWED TO A BLACK FEMALE SOLO TRIAL ATTORNEY WHO HAD THE REQUISITE LEGAL TRAINING, SKILL, VISION, TENACITY, MOXIE AND WHEREWITHAL TO CRAFT AND FILE A $100 MILLION LAWSUIT THAT THEREAFTER SETTLED FOR **$34** MILLION.

HE HAD SAT ON THE D.C. COURT BENCH FOR 25 YEARS AND NOW SAW THE LAWSUIT I FILED ON BEHALF OF A HOMELESS AND MENTALLY ILL BLACK FEMALE AND ITS SUBSEQUENT MULTI-MILLION DOLLAR SETTLEMENT AS HIS OPPORTUNITY TO BECOME FILTHY RICH AND AT MY EXPENSE.

LITTLE DID JUDGE EKANS KNOW THAT YEARS AGO I HAD RESOLVED TO FIGHT FOR MY FEES UNTIL THERE WAS NO FIGHT LEFT IN ME, AND MOREOVER, I HAD RESOLVED TO TAKE MY FIGHT TO THE COURT OF PUBLIC OPINION FOR THE REDRESS OF THE EGREGIOUS INJUSTICE THAT I HAD BEEN SUBJECTED TO BY EKANS AND HIS CORRUPT CALVARY OF D.C. COURT JUDGES AND FBI AGENTS.

MS. JONES: MAY I SPEAK, YOUR HONOR?

THE COURT: WHAT?

MS. JONES: THAT'S BEEN THE WHOLE PROBLEM. THEY HAD -- -- THEY ENGAGED ME -------I DIDN'T SPEAK -- -- NOT THE ATTORNEY FOR THE PLAINTIFF, BUT A REPRESENTATIVE. THEY ENGAGED ME. I WAS TOLD -- --

COMMENT AND ANALYSIS: #8 JUDGE EKANS DID NOT WANT TO HEAR OR BE INFORMED, FOR THAT MATTER, BY BRIANNA REGARDING ANY ASPECT OF THE ONGOING D.C. JUDICIAL AND FBI CRIMINAL ENTERPRISE. EKANS' OVERALL ATTITUDE FOR THE DURATION OF THE ADJUDICATION OF MY LAWSUIT WAS THAT HE WAS DONE WITH THAT. WHEN A CORRUPT D.C. COURT JUDGE IS NOT HELD ACCOUNTABLE FOR HIS CRIMES OF OPPORTUNITY, HIS EGREGIOUS ABUSE OF JUDICIAL DISCRETION INCREASES AND EXPANDS EXPONENTIALLY.

JUDGE EKANS, PLEASED THAT HE HAS NOW COMPLETED HIS ASSIGNMENT TO RIG MY CASE TO ITS FINAL DISMISSAL, BOLDLY REFERS TO MY LAWSUIT, IRRESPECIVE OF THE MOUNTAINS OF FACTS, EVIDENCE AND THE FINDINGS FROM THE INVESTIGATION OF THE D.C. BAR COUNSEL, AS **"ANYTHING OTHER THAN A LOT OF BOLONA."** UNDER EKANS' JURISDICTION, MY CASE HAS NOW MOVED FROM **"SMOKE AND MIRRORS"** TO **"ANYTHING OTHER THAN A LOT OF BOLOGNA."** BOTH DESCRIPTIONS WERE FACTUALLY FALSE AND SATURATED IN D.C. JUDICIAL FRAUD, THEFT, CORRUPTION AND EXTORTION.

JUDGE EKANS IS RELENTLES IN HIS REFUSAL TO ACKNOWLEDGE IN ANY WAY THE DOMINANT ISSUES IN MY LAWSUIT OF D.C. JUDICIAL AND FBI FRAUD, THEFT, CORRUPTION AND EXTORTION. EKANS' KICKING TO THE CURB THE D.C. OFFICE OF BAR COUNSEL AND ITS INVESTIGATION OF THE FLORIDA LAWSUIT AND BRIANNA JONES' CLAIM IS NO MORE THAN STARK EVIDENCE OF JUST HOW FAR EKANS WAS PREPARED TO GO TO KEEP HIS CRITICAL AND PIVOTAL PARTICIPATION IN THE CRIMINAL ENTERPRISE ON TRACK.

THE COURT: YOU KNOW WHAT THE WHOLE PROBLEM HAS BEEN? THE WHOLE PROBLEM HAS BEEN THAT I CAN NEVER KEEP YOU FOCUSED ON WHAT WE'RE TALKING ABOUT HERE IN THE COURTROOM WHEN -- --WHEN   WHEN WE'RE HERE. I ASKED YOU MONTHS AGO TO BRING FINANCIAL RECORDS THAT WOULD, AT LEAST, LET THE PLAINTIFF SEE, BECAUSE YOU ENTERED A SETTLEMENT WITH HER THAT WOULD AT LEAST LET HER SEE WHERE YOUR ASSETS ARE. WHAT IS IT THAT ALLOWS YOU TO – TO TRAVEL BACK AND FORTH, TO LIVE, TO SUBSIST, THOSE TYPES OF THINGS; A LOT OF – MUCH – MUCH OF WHICH WOULD PROBABLY BE EXEMPT FROM ANY ORDER OF JUDGMENT, BECAUSE YOU'RE ENTITLED TO   TO SUBSISTENCE. BUT YOU HAVE STEADFASTTLY REFUSED, EVEN THROUGH – EVEN THROUGH WHATEVER IT WAS, TEN OR 12 DAYS IN JAIL, **YOU'VE STEADFASTLY REFUSED TO BRING FINANCIAL PAPERS**. NOW -- --

COMMENT AND ANALYSIS: #9 HERE JUDGE EKANS PLEADS HELPLESSNESS IN HIS INABILITY TO HAVE BRIANNA JONES PRODUCE FINANCIAL DOCUMENTS, I.E., BANK OF AMERICA BANK STATEMENTS AS DESCRIBED IN THE OCTOBER 18, 2010 COURT ORDER ISSUED BY JUDGE STARR. ALL OTHER FINANCIAL RECORDS WERE IRRELEVANT AND JUDGE EKANS KNEW THAT. HE SIMPLY BLATANTLY ABUSED HIS JUDICIAL DISCRETION, WHICH WAS HIS COMMON PRACTICE IN THE *RIGGED ADJUDICATION OF MY LAWSUIT.*

MS. JONES:	I PROVIDED THOSE, YOUR HONOR.
MS. FRANKLIN:	YOUR HONOR -- --
THE COURT:	I'M SORRY?
MS. JONES:	I PROVIDED EVERYTHING, EVEN MY CREDIT REPORT.
THE COURT:	I DON'T THINK YOU PROVIDED EVERYTHING, BECCAUSE I -- - I DON'T KNOW THAT YOU'VE EVER PROVIDED A BANK ACCOUNT.
MS. JONES:	YES, EVERY -- - MONTHS OF -- -- OF EXPENDITURES. I PROVIDED SEVERAL DOCUMENTS. THEY WERE WITH ME THE DAY I WAS ARRESTED. I'VE GAVE ALL OF THAT TO HER ON THE 17TH OF JUNE.
THE COURT:	WHAT ABOUT TAX RETURNS?
MS. JONES:	I DON'T FILE TAXES BECAUSE------------------ I'M NOT GAINFULLY EMPLOYED. SO, I DON'T – AND I -- -- AND I DID SPEAK WITH HER. I WENT TO A TAX -- --
THE COURT:	I'M NOT SURE -- --
MS. JONES:---------------------ACCOUNTANT.	
THE COURT:	-- -- YOU UNDERSTAND THAT -- -- THAT ------THE IRS CONSIDERS INCOME MONEY FROM WHATEVER SOURCE DERIVED. SO, YOU DON'T HAVE TO BE GAINFLLY EMPLOYED TO BE REQUIRED TO FILE TAXES.
MS. JONES:	I'M -- -- YOUR HONOR, I MADE NOT. I I EVEN CALLED THE IRS; I SPOKE TO THEM ON SEVERAL OCCASIONS. I EXPLAINED MY SITUATION. THEY SAID, YOU DO NOT HAVE TO FILE TAXES. I DISCUSSED THAT WITH THE PLAINTIFF. AND SHE SAID, BRIANNA, THEY DON'T PLAY, MAKE SURE YOU COVER YOURSELF.
THE COURT:	WELL -- --
MS. FRANKLIN:	YOUR HONOR -- --
THE COURT:	IT -- --
MS. FRANKLIN:	YOUR HONOR -- --

THE COURT:	THE -- -- THE ONLY WAY THAT SHE WOULD NOT WELL, FIRST OF ALL, I DON'T BELIEVE THAT. BUT SECONDLY, THE ONLY WAY THAT YOU, OR ANYONE, WOULD BE ABSOLVED FROM FILING TAXES WOULD BE IF YOU'RE IN POVERTY; AND YOU ARE, OBVIOUSLY, NOT IN POVERTY. WHATEVER INVESTMENTS YOU HAVE, YOUR INCOMES ARE EITHER INTEREST OR DIVIDENDS AND AND YOU HAVE TO FILE TAXES.
MS. JONES:	THERE ARE NO INVESTMENTS, YOUR HONOR.
THE COURT:	WELL -- --
MS. JONES:	THIS IS THE UNDULTERATED TRUTH.
MS. FRANKLIN:	YOUR HONOR, MAY I MAY I JUST SPEAK FOR A MOMENT?
THE COURT:	YES, OF COURSE.
MS. FRANKLIN:	**YOUR HONOR, YOU -- --YOU'VE YOU'VE PROBABLY ALREADY, BY VIRTUE OF -- -- OF YOUR EARLIER COMMENTS, PERHAPS PREEMPT -- -- PRE PREMPTED MY PLAN TO INTRODUCE CERTAIN EXHIBITS INTO THE COURT THIS MORNING. ONE WAS GOING TO BE THE LETTER FROM BAR COUNSEL OF SEPTEMBER WHERE THEY DID STATE THAT SHE WAS ENTITLED TO A CONSIDEABLE ESTATE. AND I WAS GOING TO ASK THE COURT TO JUST TAKE THE FULL LETTER, UNREDACTED, BUT FOR IN-CAMERA USE BY THE COURT.**
THE COURT:	**BUT -- -- BUT BARBARA, WHAT DOES THAT MEAN? WHAT DOES IT MEAN?**
	COMMENT AND ANALYSIS: #10 HERE, JUDGE EKANS DUMMIES UP AS TO THE SIGNIFICANCE OF THE LETTER OF D.C. BAR COUNSEL CONFIRMING THE FINDINGS OF ITS INVESTIGATION AND FINDINGS THAT BRIANNA JONES IS ENTITLED TO CONSIDERABLE ASSETS.
	NOW THAT WE ARE MINUTES FROM THE ADJOURNMENT OF MY LAWSUIT, I AM NOW "BARBARA" AS OPPOSED TO MS. FRANKLIN OR ATTORNEY FRANKLIN.
MS. FRANKLIN:	HOLD -- -- HOLD -- --
THE COURT:	I MEAN, WHO -- -- WHO SAYS -- --
MS. FRANKLIN:	YOUR HONOR, I I
THE COURT:	WHO SIGNED THAT?
MS. FRANKLIN:	YOUR -- --
THE COURT:	WHO SIGNED IT?
MS. FRANKLIN:	WHO SIGNED LETTER?

THE COURT: YEAH.

MS. FRANKLIN: MARCIA MCMILLAN -- --

THE COURT: WHO -- --

MS. FRANKLIN: ----------------ASSISTANT BAR COUNSEL.

THE COURT: WHO IS THAT?

MS. FRANKLIN: MARCIA MCMILLAN, WHO'S -- --

THE COURT: WHAT -- --

MS. FRANKLIN: ----------------ASSISTANT BAR COUNSEL.

THE COURT: SHE'S ASSISTANT BAR COUNSEL?

MS. FRANKLIN: YES, YOUR HONOR.

> **COMMENT AND ANALYSIS: #11** AT NO TIME DID JUDGE EKANS REACH OUT TO
> BAR COUNSEL WITH AN INQUIRY REGARDING ITS INVESTIGATION AND FINDINGS.
> HE HAD NO INTEREST IN FINDING THE TRUTH. HIS INTEREST WAS IN DISMISSING
> MY CASE AND COMPLETING HIS ROLE IN THE CRIMINAL ENTERPRISE TO DEFRAUD
> ME OF MY ATTORNEY'S FEES.

MS. JONES: AND I SPOKE WITH THEM, YOUR HONOR, AND GAVE THEM -- --

MS. FRANKLIN;   YOUR -- -- YEAH -- --

MS. JONES:--------------------ALL THE INFORMATION.

MS. FRANKLIN: EXCUSE ME. YOUR HONOR -- -- I'M NOT FINISHED. YOUR HONOR, I   THE REASON
                       I WAS GOING TO ASK THAT IT BE   AND I'VE NEVER ASKED THE COURT TO LET ME
                       INTRODUCE IT FOR IN-CAMERA USE ONLY -- -- BECAUSE I   I KNOW THE COURT'S
                       FRUSTRATION, UNDERSTANDABLY. AND I THOUGHT IT WOULD BE SOMETHING
                       TO ALLOW THE COURT TO KNOW THAT THERE HAS BEEN SOME LEGAL ARM OF
                       THE COURT, IN THIS INSTANCE, THE COURT OF APPEALS. AND ACCORDING TO
                       THEIR FINDINGS, DID A THOROUGH INVESTIGATION OF THE UNDERLYING
                       FLORIDA SUIT. AND BY THE WAY, YOUR HONOR, THERE WAS A LAWSUIT. I FILED
                       A LAWSUIT ON HER BEHALF IN BROWARD COUNTY AND THAT'S THROUGHOUT,
                       YOU KNOW, THE -- -- THE -- -- THE   THE DOCKET.

THE COURT: THE LAWSUIT AGAINST THE ESTATE?

MS. FRANKLIN: THE LAWSUIT AGAINST THE ESTATE. IT WAS NEVER   THERE WAS NEVER AN ANSWER FILED TO THE LAWSUIT. BUT THE LAWSUIT WAS A BONA FIDE LAWSUIT. I WAS ADMITTED PROPERLY, PRO HAC VICE. I HAD AT LEAST TWO FIRMS AS CO-COUNSEL, I HAD CO-COUNSEL AGREEMENTS. ALL OF THIS, VERY LEGITIMATE. ALL IN MY FILES. ALL RIGHT, YOUR HONOR. AND SO, WHAT I'M HEARING THIS MORNING, THOUGH, REALLY DISTURBING TO ME; BECAUSE THE ONE THING I SAID TO JUDGE STARR WHEN I FIRST APPEARED BEFORE HER WAS THAT, YOUR HONOR, I WANT CLOSURE. BUT I WANT CLOSURE IN A RIGHT AND PROPER WAY, BECAUSE THIS HAS GONE ON SO LONG. I CERTAINLY CAN'T BE ONE THAT WOULD STAND HERE SAY THAT, YOU KNOW, THIS IS, THIS GREEDY ATTORNEY, BECAUSE I'VE NEVER BEEN PAID FOR ANYTHING, YOUR HONOR, EVER, NOT EVEN A DOLLAR.

MS. JONES: YOUR HONOR, SHE WAS NOT ADMITTED IN BROWARD COUNTY.

COMMENT AND ANALYSIS: #12 I WAS AT ALL TIMES ADMITTED TO PRACTICE LAW IN BROWARD COUNTY CIRCUIT COURT FOR THE PURPOSE OF REPRESENTING BRIANNA JONES IN THE $100 MILLION LAWSUIT I FILED ON HER BEHALF AGAINST THE RIDGEWAY ESTATE.

MS. FRANKLIN: EXCUSE ME. YOU HONOR, I DID NOT INTERRUPT HER, MAY I FINISH.

MS. JONES: I'M SORRY, BUT SHE WAS NOT ADMITTED IN BROWARD COUNTY.

COMMENT AND ANALYSIS: #13 THIS IS NOTHING MORE THAN GRATUITOUS EVIDENCE THAT BRIANNA JONES IS A GRATUITOUS LIAR.

THE COURT: WHY -- -- WHY DON'T YOU SIT DOWN. IT'S -- -- IT'S HARDER TO INTERRUPT PEOPLE WHEN YOU'RE SITTING.

MS. JONES: YES, SIR.

MS. FRANKLIN: YOUR HONOR, I HAVE NEVER -- -- I HAVE BEEN PAID FOR   FOR ANY OF MY EFFORTS   TRAVEL BACK AND FORTH TO FLORIDA, HOTEL BILLS, AIRLINE BILLS, TIME, TIME, TIME. JUST SUPERIOR COURT ALONE, I'VE BEEN COMING DOWN HERE SINCE 2009; COME MARCH, IT WILL BE THREE YEARS. SO, IT'S MY   YOU KNOW, WE ALL ARE FAMILIAR WITH THAT TERM THAT, YOU KNOW, TIME IS MONEY; THAT'S TRUE. BUT FOR ME, TIME IS MY LIFE, BECAUSE I'M NOT GETTING ANY MONEY. BUT I AM GIVING MY TIME THAT I WON'T WILL NEVER BE ABLE TO GET BACK AGAIN. SO, FOR ME, THIS IS ALL-VERY SERIOUS. AND TO HAVE HER COME IN AT THIS JUNCTURE, YOUR HONOR, AFTER YOUR HONOR IS NOW THE SECOND JUDGE HANDLING A MATTER THAT SHE HAS EXPLICITLY STATED, UNDER OATH, REPEATEDLY IN THIS COURT ROOM, THAT SHE SETTLED, THAT SHE KNOWS

WHERE THE FUNDS ARE, THAT SHE'S MET WITH OFFICERS OF BANK OF AMERICA. AND I WOULD -- -- AGAIN, I WAS GOING TO ASK THE COURT IF I COULD INTRODUCE INTO EVIDENCE THE JANUSRY 21ST, 2011 TRANSCRIPT OF THE ORAL EXAM WHERE SHE DOESN'T HESITATE TO SAY, OVER AND OVER AGAIN, WHEN I QUESTIONED HER ON THE STAND. SO, IF, IN FACT, NOW SHE'S COMING IN WITH ANOTHER STORY, THIS IS SERIOUS. BECAUSE THIS -- -- THIS HAS ALL OF THE SOUNDS OF FRAUD. IT HAS ALL OF THE SOUNDS OF FRAUD. AND I START WITH MYSELF, ALONG WITH OTHERS, WHO HAVE ASSISTED HER BASED ON   SHE HAD NEVER ONCE SAID -- -- NEVER ONCE SAID THERE WAS ANY QUESTION WHATSOEVER ABOUT THE SETTLEMENT AGREEMENT. AS A MATTER OF FACT, YOUR HONOR, SHE REITERATED IT TO YOU BY PHONE ON FRIDAY. OH, I GOT TWO SETTLEMENT AGREEMENTS. SHE HAD -- --SHE DID THE SAME THING   SHE NEVER ONCE TOLD JUDGE STARR THAT SHE HAD NEVER BEEN PAID, NEVER ONCE. SHE HAD EVERY OPPORTUNITY TO DO SO, AND JUDGE STARR EVEN SCHEDULED THE MATTER FOR TRIAL. SHE SAID A TRIAL WASN'T NECESSARY AND WE SETTLED -- -- SHE ASKED ME TO SETTLE AND WE SETTLED THE MATTER. SO -- --

MS. JONES:	YOUR HONOR, THAT IS NOT TRUE.
MS. FRANKLIN:	-- -- WHAT I'M HEARING NOW -- --
MS. JONES:	I'M SORRY, THAT'S NOT TRUE.
MS. FRANKLIN:	WHAT I'M HEARING NOW, YOUR HONOR, IS THIS IS A SERIOUS MATTER, NOW. THIS IS THE -- --IF **IF YOUR HONOR FEELS THAT THIS IS BOLOGNA**, I CERTAINLY HAVE NOT GIVEN ALL OF MY TIME AND ENERGY AND I AND AS I TOLD YOUR HONOR – AND AGAIN, IT'S PROBABLY GONG TO SOUND VERY SELF-SERVING AND YOUR HONOR PROBABLY MIGHT EVEN GET TIRED OF ME SAYING IT, BUT, ***YOU KNOW, SOMETIMES YOU'VE GOT TO TOOT YOUR OWN HORN. OCTOBER 6TH, I CELEBRATED 35 YARS OF BEING A MEMBER OF THE BAR, NEW YORK AND THEN D.C. AND I HAVE NEVER BEEN IN A SITUATION LIKE THIS***. I NEVER HAD TO COME INTO THE COURTROOM AND ENDURE THE KIND OF VILE ACCUSATIONS I'VE HAD TO ENDURE. BUT I'M NOT GOING TO GO OFF ON THAT, YOUR HONOR. ALL I'M SAYING IS THIS, TO ME, SOUNDS -- -- I WOULD I CAME IN THIS MORNING TO ASK THAT THE COURT ALLOW ME TO INTRODUCE THESE EXHIBITS IN THE RECORD. AND THAT BECAUSE THIS COURT HAS REPEATEDLY AND ON NUMEROUS OCCASIONS GIVEN THIS DEFENDANT TIME AND TIME AND TIME AGAIN TO COME IN WITH DOCUMENTS; NOT PERSONAL RECORDS, NOBODY'S INTERESTED IN HER PERSONAL RECORDS. THE DOCUMENTS THAT ARE SPECIFIED IN THE OCTOBER 18TH ORDER , AND SHE HAS REFUSED TO DO SO.

AND YOUR HONOR HAS ALLOWED HER TO STAY OUT OF JAIL; BECAUSE ON ONE OCCASION SHE TOLD YOUR HONOR: I'M GOING TO GET AN ATTORNEY; I'M GOING TO FLORIDA; I NEED TIME TO   TO GET MY AFFAIRS IN ORDER; I'M GOING TO HIRE AN ATTORNEY TO COLLECT -- -- COLLECT THE FEES; I'M GOING TO FILE A JUDGMENT AGAINST THE   THE ESTATE; I'M GOING TO GO AFTER SAM ADAGIO WITH THE SUPREME COURT OF FLORIDA. SHE HASN'T DONE ANYTHING. SHE HASN'T DONE ANYTHING. SHE JUST USED IT AS A STALL. SHE USED IT JUST AS A BLUFF, JUST AS SHE USED FRIDAY. SHE COULD HAVE BEEN HERE FRIDAY. I'M SURE. ONE MINUTE YOU'RE DYING, YOU'RE HEMORRHAGING; THE NEXT DAY, YOU KNOW, YOUR'RE READY TO, YOU --------YOU KNOW, FIGHT ME, BECAUSE THAT'S WHAT THIS IS ALL ABOUT.

AND -- --I MEAN, YOUR HONOR, IT -- -- IT   THIS IS SERIOUS. WHAT SHE IS SAYING BECAUSE FIRST OF ALL, I DON'T BELIEVE ANY OF IT. I DON'T BELIEVE ANY OF IT, BECAUSE THERE WAS A LAWSUIT FILED. *THIS IS NOT SMOKE AND MIRRORS WHEN IT COMES TO FILING A LAWSUIT*, BECAUSE I   I SERVED THE ESTATE PROPERLY AND THAT'S ALL ON THE FLORIDA RECORD. AND MARCIA MCMILLAN AND CATHERINE CORLEONE (PHONETIC) OF THE OFFICE OF D.C. BAR COUNSEL, I TALKED WITH BOTH OF THEM.

AND AS A MATTER OF FACT, WHEN I WAS CONTACTED WHEN THE COMPLAINT WAS FILED AGAINST ME BY   BY FORMER CLIENTS OF MINE THAT HAD BEEN VERY GENEROUS, TENS OF THOUSANDS OF DOLLARS THAT THEY LET THIS DEFENDANT BORROW; AND THE COMPLAINT WAS BROUGHT AGAINST ME BECAUSE THEY WERE FRUSTRATED AND THEY WANTED TO BE PAID. I TOLD MARCIA MCMILLAN -- -- BUT MORE SPECIFICALLY CATHERINE CORLEONE -- -- ACTUALLY, IT WASN'T MARCIA MCMILLAN   FEEL FREE TO CALL MS. JONES. I
DON'T HAVE A PROBLEM WITH IT, FEEL FREE.

I DID A FAVOR FOR HER. SHE NEEDED AROUND-THE-CLOCK SECURITY, AT THE TIME AND I WAS TRYING TO   TO BENEFIT BOTH SIDES. I WAS THE BROKER. I THOUGHT MY FRIENDS COULD BENEFIT, BECAUSE SHE WAS MAKING A GENEROUS OFFER. AND I KNEW SHE NEEDED SOME HELP, BECAUSE SHE'S ALREADY STATED REPEATEDLY THAT SHE DOES NOT WORK. SHE HAS NO FORM OF INCOME WHATSOEVER.

AND SO, THAT'S HOW THE BAR GOT INTO IT; AND THE BAR TOOK ABOUT NINE MONTHS, BECAUSE I THINK THEY STARTED IN JANUARY OF '09 AND -- -- AND -- -- AND THEY COMPLETED THEIR INVESTIGATION IN 2009. SO, ACTUALLY, YOUR HONOR, WHEN I WAS COPIED ON THEIR FINDINGS IN THE LETTER FOR MRS. MARCH, I WAS SOMEWHAT ELATED; BECAUSE THAT LANGUAGE IN THEIR LETTER, TO ME, MEANT OKAY, IF NOTHING ELSE, WE'RE NOT DEALING WITH A HOCUS POCUS, SMOKE AND MIRRORS. THIS IS THE D.C. BAR THAT HAS DONE AN INVESTIGATION WITH THEIR STAFF. AND, OBVIOUSLY, I'M NOT PRIVY TO ALL THE PEOPLE THEY TALKED TO AND HOW THEY MADE THE DETERMINATION; BUT THEY DETERMINED, THIS LADY IS ENTITLED TO A CONSIDERABLE SETTLEMENT. THIS IS NOT A SITUATION WHEREBY SHE'S NEGOTIATING AND SHE HAS TO GO THROUGH IT.

THE COURT: BUT WHAT DOES THAT MEAN? WHEN   WHEN DID YOU EVER COME ACROSS - - --

MS.. FRANKLIN: ENTITLED TO A CONSIDERABLE SETTLEMENT?

THE COURT: YEAH.

MS. FRANKLIN: **ACCORDING TO THEIR LETTER, IT WAS -- -- DISBURSEMENT HAS NOT BEEN MADE. THAT'S WHAT IT MEANT TO ME, AND THAT'S WHAT THEY SAID IN THE LETTER. THEY JUST SAID, DISBURSEMENT HAS YET TO BE MADE; THAT'S WHAT THE LETTER SAID, AND THAT'S WHAT -- -- THAT'S HOW -- -- THAT'S HOW I INTERPRETED IT. THAT WE'VE CONFIRMED THAT IT'S THERE; SHE'S ENTITLED, BUT -- --**

THE COURT: DOES IT SAY -- --

MS. FRANKLIN: -- -- SHE HAS NOT RECEIVED - --

THE COURT: DOES IT SAY THAT?

MS. FRANKLIN: YES, IT DOES.

THE COURT: MAY -- -- MAYBE IT -- --

MS. FRANKLIN: YOUR HONOR, MAY I GIVE YOU -- --

THE COURT: YES, THAT -- --

MS. FRANKLIN: -- -- GIVE YOU -- --

THE COURT: THAT WOULD BE HELPFUL.

MS. JONES:	YOUR HONOR, THEY USED MY CLAIM TO GET THE MONEY IN A------- IN A LUMP SUM. IT WAS AN ANNUITIZED PRIZE IN 1993. AND SO, THAT'S WHY THEY CAME BACK AND IT'S BEEN LIKE A HAMSTER ON A WHEEL ALL THESE -- --
THE COURT:	GIVE IT HERE.
MS. FRANKLIN:	OH, EXCUSE ME, YOUR HONOR.
MS. JONES:	-- -- YEARS WAITING TO BE COMPENSATED. THAT'S BEEN -- --
MS. FRANKLIN:	YOUR HONOR -- --
MS. JONES:	-- -- THE PROBLEM. BUT -- --
MS. FRANKLIN:	EXCUSE ME, YOUR HONOR ----- YOUR HONOR, IT'S THE SECOND PARAGRAPH OF PAGE TWO.
MS. JONES:	NOVEMBER THE 19TH, 1996, JUDGE ANNE MESSIAH (PHONETIC) DID NOT ALLOW HER TO PRACTICE. SHE PRACTICED IN THE PROBATE. IT WAS THEN TRANSFERRED TO THE CIVIL. SO, SHE AGREED, YOU DO THE GRUNT WORK -- --
THE COURT:	I -- -- I CAN'T ----- I CAN'T READ AND LISTEN.
MS. JONES:	I'M SORRY, SIR.
(PAUSE.)	
THE COURT:	IS THIS A COPY FOR THE COURT, OR DO YOU -- -- DO YOU -- --
MS. FRANKLN:	I -- -- I-- --
THE COURT:--------------------SHALL I MAKE A COPY?	
MS. FRANKLIN:	NO, NO, NO, I ----- I MADE A COPY FOR THE COURT.
	COMMENT AND ANALYSIS: #14 WHILE I PROVIDED JUDGE EKANS WITH A COPY OF BAR COUNSEL'S LETTER, I WAS FULLY AWARE THAT HE WOULD THEREAFTER TREAT IT AS NOTHING MORE THAN TRASH THAT WAS SURE TO BE DISCARDED OR TRASHED THEREAFTER. WE WERE BOTH SIMPLY GOING THROUGH THE MOTIONS.
THE COURT:	THIS IS A COPY, VERY GOOD.

MS. FRANKLIN: BUT----- BUT I WAS REQUESTING, YOUR HONOR, IF IT'S APPROPRIATE, THAT IT BE USED IN-CAMERA, BECAUSE IT'S -- -- I DIDN'T REDACT ANY PORTION OF IT ------- I MEAN, I - --IF THE COURT CHOOSES NOT TO, IT'S OKAY, BECAUSE ----- I MEAN, IT CERTAINLY EXONERATES ME 100 PERCENT. BUT I'VE NEVER, YOU KNOW, PROVIDED THE COURT WITH THAT IN A CASE BEFORE.

MS. JONES: YOUR HONOR, MAY I -- --

MS. FRANKLIN: BUT – BUT -- --

MS. JONES: -- -- TO THE COURT -- --

MS. FRANKLIN: BUT YOUR HONOR, THE -- -- BUT YOUR HONOR, AS I SAID FRIDAY I MEAN, I KNEW WE WERE NOT -- --I KNEW THERE WOULD BE AN ISSUE ON FRIDAY. BECAUSE WHERE WE ARE WITH THIS, EVERY OPPORTUNITY IS GOING TO BE TAKEN BY THIS DEFENDANT TO STAY OUT OF JAIL. **SHE IS IN VIOLATION OF THE ORDER OF OCTOBER 18TH, 2010. SHE'S BEEN IN VIOLATION CONTINUOUSLY.** THIS COURT HAS GIVEN HER REPEATED OPPORTUNITIES TO BRING IN DOCUMENTS, BANKING DOCMENTS AGAIN. AND I HAVE A COPY OF THE TRANSCRIPT FOR THE COURT. IN THE JANUARY 21ST TRANSCRIPT OF THAT ORAL EXAM, SHE ACKNOWLEDGES THAT SHE KNOWS WHERE THE ASSETS ARE. SHE -- - - SHE ACKNOWLEDGES THAT SHE'S MET WITH BANK OFFICERS IN THE WASHINGTON REGION. SHE ACKNOWLEDGES THAT THE MONEY -- --

MS. JONES: THAT'S NOT THE CASE.

MS. FRANKLIN: -- -- IS NOT IN HER NAME, HOWEVER. AND YOUR HONOR, THIS THIS IS – I MEAN, HOW CAN ONE IGNORE THIS KIND OF TESTIMONY UNDER OATH? OTHERWISE, SHE HAS -- --SHE HAS SHE HAS PERJURED HERSELF AND TAKEN YEARS WITH THIS CASE IF, IN FACT, THIS IS ALL UNTRUE. BUT I I PROPOSE AND - MY POSITION THIS MORNING, YOUR HONOR, KNOWING HER AS I KNOW HER, THIS IS JUST ANOTHER STAY-OUT-OF-JAIL PLOY. AND IF THE COURT GOES FOR IT, SHE'LL GO RIGHT HOPPING RIGHT ON OUT OF HERE. THAT SHE WILL DO ANYTHING I SAID ON FRIDAY, AND SHE ACKNOWLEDGED, WHY WOULD HER SIBLINGS SUE A PERSON WHO DOESN'T WORK.

MS. JONES: MY SIBLINGS HAVE NEVER SUED ME.

MS. FRANKLIN: WHY -- --

MS. JONES: YOU WAS THE ONE THAT PUT -- --

MS. FRANKLIN: EXCUSE -- --

MS. JONES: YOUR HONOR-----------TO SIGN OVER EVERYTHING TO HER, YOUR HONOR.

BARBARA WASHINGTON FRANKLIN

THE COURT:	LET -- -- LET ME ASK YOU A QUESTION. HAVE ------HAVE YOU EVER EXPERIENCED A PROCEEDING BEFORE THIS JUDGE WHEN I DID NOT LET YOU SPEAK WHEN IT WAS YOUR TURN?
MS. JONES:	NO, SIR.
THE COURT:	HAVE YOU?
MS. JONES:	NO, SIR.
THE COURT:	THEN WHY ARE YOU GOING TO BE DISCOURTEOUS LIKE YOU'RE BEING TODAY?
MS. JONES:	I APOLOGIZE. YOUR HONOR, MAY I SPEAK WHEN SHE'S DONE.
THE COURT:	THAT WOULD BE YOUR TURN.
MS. JONES:	OKAY, THANK YOU.
THE COURT:	ALL RIGHT.

***

MS. FRANKLIN:	*I ALSO SAID, AND SHE DID NOT DENY IT SHE ACKNOWLEDGED THAT SHE OFFERED ME A MILLION DOLLARS LAST FALL. WHERE IS SHE GETTING THIS MONEY? AND I WAS SUPPOSED TO TAKE THE MILLION AND PAY HER CREDITORS, AND I REFUSED TO ACCEPT IT; BECAUSE ONE, IT'S IN VIOLATION OF THE SETTLEMENT AGREEMENT.*

AND THE PROMISSORY NOTES -- -- I HAVE TWO PROMISSORY NOTES, HERE BY -- - - BY FRIENDS AND ASSOCIATES WHO'VE LET HER HAVE THESE SUBSTANTIAL SUMS. AND I WAS   AGAIN, I WAS GOING TO ASK THAT I BE PERMITTED TO INTRODUCE THEM INTO THE RECORD, BECAUSE THE PAYMENT OF THOSE SUMS - - -- I WAS TRYING TO PROTECT ALL PARTIES. SO, WHEN I PREPARED THE PROMISSORY NOTE, I ATTACHED AN ATTORNEY CERTIFICATION SAYING THAT ONCE I RECEIVED THE SETTLEMENT PROCEEDS, THE REPAYMENT OF THE NOTE WOULD COME OUT OF THE SETTLEMENT PROCEEDS. I DID NOT WANT TO PUT HER IN A POSITION WHERE ANYBODY COULD COME AFTER HER OR WOULD COME AFTER HER JUST BECAUSE THEY WANTED TO BE PAID, BECAUSE SHE HADN'T PAID THEM ON TIME, BECAUSE WE KNOW HOW LAWSUITS CAN GO.

MS. FRANKLIN: AND SO, THAT'S WHY THESE PROMISSORY NOTES ARE TIED TO THE ESCROW ACCOUNT, BECAUSE THEY SAY THAT HER REPAYMENT WILL BE OUT OF THE SETTLEMENT PROCEEDS THAT ARE TO BE DEPOSITED INTO THE ESCROW ACCOUNT. SO, NOW YOU HAVE   YOU KNOW, YOU HAVE A LONG LIST OF PEOPLE OUT HERE, INCLUDING THE SIMPSONS WHO ARE PRESENT IN THE COURTROOM; THEY'RE TIED UP. BECAUSE IF I'M NOT PAID AND NO MONEY IS GOING INTO MY ESCROW ACCOUNT, DOES THAT MEAN THEY'RE OUT $50,000 IN THEIR -- -IN-- --IN THEIR CASE? SHE'S COLLECTED AND BORROWED TENS OF THOUSANDS OF DOLLARS WITH PEOPLE, ALL ON THE BASIS OF THIS LAWSUIT AND THE SETTLEMENT PROCEEDS TO BE PAID INTO MY ESCROW ACCOUNT.

AND AS I SAID, YOUR HONOR, ALL THESE DIFFERENT APPROACHES TO YOU, THIS IS ALL NEW; BECAUSE THE TIME TO BRING IN ALL THIS INFORMATION THAT SHE'S BRINGING NOW, THE PROPER TIME WOULD HAVE BEEN BEFORE JUDGE STARR. WE COULD HAVE SHUT THIS DOWN THREE YEARS AGO. WE COULD HAVE SHUT IT DOWN THREE YEARS AGO, YOUR HONOR. BECAUSE AS I SAID, NOBODY CAN POINT TO ME AND SAY, WELL, YOU'RE IN IT BECAUSE YOU'RE GETTING PAID. NO, I'M NOT; I'M JUST GIVING MY TIME, WHICH IS VALUABLE.

NEVER SAID A WORD TO JUDGE STARR, NEVER SAID A WORD. JUDGE STARR GAVE HER EVERY OPPORTUNITY. SHE COULD SPEAK WHEN SHE WANTED TO. SHE ALSO, AT LEAST ON ONE OCCASION, CAME IN BY PHONE. **SHE NEVER SAID TO JUDGE STARR, YOUR HONOR, I DON'T HAVE THE MONEY. I HAVEN'T   I NO, I WANT TO SETTLE. I DON'T WANT TO GO TO TRIAL, I WANT TO SETTLE. AND BY THE WAY   AND I'M SURE YOUR HONOR, YOU KNOW, CAN SEE IT ON THE DOCKET -- -- AT ONE POINT BECAUSE SHE DIDN'T ANSWER THE COMPLAINT** BECAUSE SHE DOESN'T ANSWER ANYTHING. SHE HAS NOT EVEN OPPOSED THIS ORDER FOR CONTEMPT OR THE ORDER OF OCTOBER 18TH. THERE'S NO OPPOSITION FILED TO ANY OF THOSE ORDERS. AND SO, BECAUSE SHE DIDN'T ANSWER, OF COURSE, AT ONE POINT IN TIME, A DEFAULT JUDGMENT HAD BEEN ENTERED IN THE RECORD JUST BECAUSE OF HER FAILURE TO ANSWER. AND I AGREED TO VACATE THAT, BECAUSE SHE SAID SHE WOULD SETTLE THE CASE.

MS. FRANKLIN: SO, YOUR HONOR, I'M – I'M – I'M THINKING ABOUT WHAT YOU SAID ABOUT BAR COUNSEL, BECAUSE THEY – THEY GAVE ME HOPE. THAT LETTER GAVE ME HOPE; BECAUSE I   I COULD NOT BELIEVE THAT IF, IN FACT, THEY FOUND THAT ALL THIS WAS SMOKE AND MIRRORS AND THERE LOOK   THERE IS NOTHING THERE AND SOMEBODY'S BEING TAKEN ADVANTAGE OF. THAT'S NOT WHAT THEY SAID. AND THEY NEVER INDICATED THAT TO ME. AND AS I SAID, I TALKED TO CATHERINE CORLEONE, AN ASSISTANT BAR COUNSEL OR STAFF AND MARCIA MCMILLAN ABOUT IT. AND, YOU KNOW, THEY WERE -- --THEY WERE   NO, WE'VE – WE'VE CHECKED AND DONE OUR INVESTIGATION AND, YOU KNOW, MS. JONES JUST HASN'T RECEIVED THE FUNDS AS YET. THAT WAS 2009.

SO, I -- -- I JUST -- -- YOUR HONOR, THE OTHER IMAGE THAT WILL BE   PROBABLY IN MY MIND FOR MANY YEARS TO COME OR MANY MONTHS, IS THAT *ON JANUARY 31ST WHEN SHE WAS HERE AND HAD BEEN LOCKED UP, AND CAME IN WITH A POUCH AND REFUSED TO PRODUCE THE DOCUMENTS OF THE OCTOBER 18TH ORDER,* AND WHEN YOUR HONOR SAID, AFTER LISTENING BACK AND FORTH, TO STEP BACK AND SHE KNEW THEN THAT SHE WAS GOING BACK TO THE CELL, **SHE SAID, OH, YOUR HONOR, I HAVE THEM RIGHT HERE. THAT'S ALL IN THE RECORD. I HAVE THEM RIGHT HERE. I JUST WANT TO MEET WITH ATTORNEY FRANKLIN RIGHT NOW. CAN I MEET WITH HER NOW? JUST GAMES. AND YOU SAID, NO, YOU CANNOT MEET WITH HER. THERE'S NO PROVISION FOR YOU TO MEET WITH HER NOW. MS. FRANKLIN, CAN YOU GO TO THE JAIL IN THE MORNING?**

COMMENT AND ANALYSIS: #15 *I MADE A POINT IN MY TESTIMONY OF REMINDING JUDGE EKANS THAT HE HAD INTENTIONALLY AND PURPOSEFULLY REFUSED TO ALLOW ME AND BRIANNA TO MEET IN THE COURTHOUSE IN ORDER FOR ME TO EXAMINE AND REVIEW THE BANK STATEMENTS OF THE SETTLEMENT PROCEEDS ON DEPOSIT AT BANK OF AMERICA.*

THIS WAS THE ACTION OF A CORRUPT D.C. COURT JUDGE COMMITTED TO THE MISSION OF THE CRIMINAL ENTERPRISE TO DEFRAUD ME OF THE ESTIMATED $50 MILLION IN ATTORNEY'S FEES.

MS. FRANKLIN: I GO TO THE JAIL IN THE MORNING, WHAT HAPPENED? I GO THERE, THE SECURITY TELLS ME I CAN'T SEE HER. WHY NOT? OH, SHE'S ON SUICIDE WATCH. I CALLED -- - I DON'T KNOW IF IT'S JANE OR, I CAN'T REMEMBER ------ ONE OF YOUR LAW CLERKS------ONE OF YOUR LAW CLERKS, AND I SAID, I'M ON MY WAY FROM THE JAIL. I HAVEN'T BEEN ABLE TO SEE MS. JONES. OH, WHY NOT? SHE'S ON SUICIDE WATCH.

MS. FRANKLIN: THE NEXT DAY, SHE COMES RIGHT INTO COURT AND YOU SAID. OH, WE CONTACTED THE JAIL AND THEY SAID EVERYTHING WAS FINE. WHAT HAPPENED? OH. GAMES. THIS IS OUTRAGEOUS CONDUCT ON HER BEHALF, BECAUSE SHE IS DAMAGING AND IMPACTING THE LIVES OF PEOPLE. WE'RE NOT HERE FOR GAMES. I'M NOT HERE TO TAKE ADVANTAGE OF THE COURT AND NEITHER ARE MY FRIENDS AND FAMILY. WE WANT THIS THING OVER. *WE WANT IT DONE. BUT WE WANT IT DONE IN A RIGHT AND PROPER WAY.*

AND I DON'T WANT IT DONE, OBVIOUSLY, IN A WAY THAT I'VE BEEN DEFRAUDED OF MY TIME AND ENERGY AND MONIES AND YEARS OF SUPPORTING HER. NOT JUST SUPPORTING HER OR HELPING HER FINANCIALLY; BUT WHEN SHE CAME INTO MY OFFICE IN 1994, I DIDN'T TAKE THE CASE. I INTERVIEWED HER AND I SAID, LISTEN, YOU'VE GOT TOO MUCH ANGER. WE CAN   I COULD NOT WORK SUCCESSFULLY WITH YOU. I DIDN'T TAKE THE CASE. SHE CAME BACK A YEAR LATER AND SAT IN MY OFFICE IN SUNGLASSES . SHE COULDN'T EVEN FACE THE WORLD. AND AFTER WORKING WITH ME AND I'M MENTORING HER AND HELPING HER IN EVERY WAY THAT I COULD, TREATING HER AS A FAMILY MEMBER; NOW SHE'S STRONG ENOUGH AND SHE FEELS THAT, OH, I CAN EITHER BE A LAWYER OR I CAN, YOU KNOW, I CAN FIGHT THIS   I CAN FIGHT THIS LAWYER NOW. I CAN TAKE   I CAN TAKE HER FEES. I CAN TAKE HER FEES.

AND IF ANYBODY COULD CONFIRM FOR ME THAT THERE IS NOTHING THERE, I'D BE THE FIRST ONE TO SAY, THIS IS   I HAVE TO LET THIS GO. BUT SHE HAS ALLOWED ME AND EVERYONE ELSE INVOLVED IN THIS MATTER   AND AS I SAID. **BAR COUNSEL JUST, YOU KNOW, STANDS IN A BIG LIGHT, BECAUSE I   I REALLY DID RELY ON THEIR INVESTIGATION**. AND WHILE THEY'RE NOT AT LIBERTY TO DISCUSS WITH ME THE INS AND OUTS OF THE INVESTIGATION, HAVING DEALT WITH THEM BEFORE I TRUSTED THAT THEY HAD DONE WHAT THEY SAID THEY HAD DONE. THEY HAD MADE A THOROUGH INVESTIGATION, AND THAT'S WHY I HAVE, YOU KNOW, BROUGHT THEM BEFORE THE COURT EACH AND EVERY TIME. BECAUSE I'M SAYING, YOU KNOW, WHAT I MIGHT BE SAYING, OBVIOULSLY, I'M THE PLAINTIFF AND IT COULD BE SEEN AS SELF-SERVING.

BUT BAR COUNSEL IS A -- -- A NEUTRAL ARBITER AND A NEUTRAL INVESTIGATOR. AND I JUST FELT THAT, IF THERE WAS ANY EVIDENCE WHATSOEVER THAT THERE IS NOTHING HERE, THIS IS BOGUS, THIS IS SMOKE AND MIRRORS; CERTAINLY, THEY WOULD HAVE DISCOVERED THAT IN THEIR INVESTIGATION. AND THAT'S NOT WHAT THEY HAVE INDICATED AT ALL.

THE COURT: WELL, I'M GOING TO   I'M GOING TO FIND OUT WHY THEY INDICATED WHAT THEY INDICATED.

COMMENT AND ANALYSIS: #16 I KNEW EKANS WASN'T GOING TO FIND OUT ANYTHING. HE WAS SIMPLY BLOWING SMOKE TO GET TO THE FINAL DISMISSAL OF MY LAWSUIT. I KNEW THAT NOTHING I SAID AND NO MATTER HOW LONG IT TOOK FOR ME TO SAY IT, IT ALL MEANT NOTHING TO JUDGE EKANS. HIS EYE WAS ON THE SUCCESS OF THE CRIMINAL ENTERPRISE AND HIS PAYMENT FOR THE CRITICAL ROLE HE HAD PLAYED IN THAT SUCCESS.

MS. FRANKLIN: OKAY.

THE COURT: THANK YOU MA' AM.

MS. FRANKLIN: THANK YOU, YOUR HONOR.

THE COURT: YES, MA' AM.

THE COURT: OKAY. ALL RIGHT. -- -- ALL RIGHT. -- -- THANK YOU -- -- THANK YOU ------- THANK YOU. I   I'M PERSUADED, HAVING HEARD THIS STATEMENT BY MS. JONES, THAT THERE IS NO BASIS, IN FACT OR THE LAW, FOR THE COURT TO FIND THAT THIS SETTLEMENT WAS ANYTHING OTHER THAN A VOLUNTARY SETTLEMENT THAT SHE ENTERED INTO. YOUR MOTIVATIONS MAY HAVE BEEN THIS OR THAT, BUT THAT DOES NOT DISTURB THE FACT THAT YOU MADE A VOLUNTARY DECISION TO ENTER INTO THE SETTLEMENT. AND SO THE COURT'S GOING TO DENY YOUR MOTION TO SET THE SETTLEMENT ASIDE.

NOW, THAT LEAVES THE QUESTION OF THE AMOUNT OF THE JUDGMENT. AND IT -- -- IT'S -- -- IT'S A MOVING TARGET, BUT I THINK THAT THE   THAT THE ONE CONFIDENCE THAT I CAN HAVE IS ON THE ASSERTIONS BY MS. JONES THAT THE AMOUNT WAS 18 PLUS 15?

THE LAW CLERK: I THINK IT CAME OUT TO ABOUT THAT, I'LL HAVE TO CHECK THE DOCUMENTS.

THE COURT: SO, WE'RE GOING TO ENTER ------ ENTER AMOUNT PLUS STATUTORY INTEREST OF I THINK IT'S 34, 000. WE'LL HAVE TO CHECK AND MAKE SURE THAT I'VE GOT THE RIGHT AMOUNT.

MS. JONES: THAT'S MILLIONS, YOUR HONOR. I'M SORRY.

THE COURT: I'M SORRY, 34 MILLION; I DIDN'T MEAN THOUSAND. I THANK YOU FOR YOUR CORRECTION. AND I THANK YOU ALL. THE JUDGMENT WILL BE PREPARED THIS WEEK AND WILL BE MAILED OUT.

MS. FRANKLIN: AND IT -- -- IT IS IN WHAT AMOUNT, YOUR HONOR? EXCUSE ME, YOUR HONOR, IN WHAT AMOUNT?

(PAUSE.)

MS. JONES: YOUR HONOR, MAY I SPEAK, FOR THE RECORD ALSO -- --

THE COURT: SO -- --

MS. JONES:--------------------VERY BRIEFLY?

THE COURT: SO, WHAT WE'VE DETERMINED IS THAT THAT AMOUNT THE 14 MILLION, WAS THE AMOUNT THAT WAS TO BE PAID INTO YOUR ESCROW ACCOUNT; AND THEN YOUR FEE WAS, I BELIEVE, 40 PERCENT PLUS A TEN PERCENT BONUS AND YOU WERE TO PAY THE OTHER LOANS OUT OF THAT AMOUNT.

MS. FRANKLIN: RIGHT. THE TEN   TEN PERCENT BONUS, YOUR HONOR, I HAD WAIVED IN THE SETTLEMENT AGREEMENT. SO, I'M JUST REALLY ENTITLED TO THE -- --

THE COURT: FORTY PERCENT.

MS. FRANKLIN: RIGHT.

THE COURT: WELL -- --

MS. FRANKLIN: BUT MY QUESTION GOES TO THE INTEREST -- --

THE COURT: WELL, THE INTEREST -- --

MS. FRANKLIN: -- -- SINCE THIS -- --

THE COURT: -- -- WILL BE -- --

MS. FRANKLIN: NO, NO, I DIDN'T MEAN THAT. FROM THE -- -- IS THE INTEREST BEING CALCULATED FROM THE TIME OF SETTLEMENT. IN OTHER WORDS, FROM THE TIME OF THE $14 MILLION -- --

THE COURT: UHN-UHN.

MS. FRANKLIN: - - WHICH WAS LIKE -- --

THE COURT: UHN-UHN.

MS. FRANKLIN: ----------------THAT WOULD 1997?

THE COURT: UHN.

MS. FRANKLIN: IT WOULD NOT BE INTEREST FROM THE TIME THE COURT IS ISSUING THE JUDGMENT, WOULD IT?

(PAUSE.)

THE COURT: I'M GOING TO HAVE TO CONSIDER THAT.

MS. FRANKLIN: OKAY. AND THE OTHER -- -- THE OTHER-- --

(PAUSE.)

THE COURT:	I'M GOING TO HAVE TO CONSIDER THAT. RIGHT NOW, I'M THINKING, AND MY LAWYER SEEMS TO AGREE, THAT IT WOULD BE FROM THE TIME OF THE SETTLEMENT SINCE THAT'S WHEN THIS -- -- THIS JUDGMENT DATES TO THE SETTLEMENT.
MS. FRANKLIN:	CORRECT, YOUR HONOR.
THE COURT:	BUT WE'RE GOING TO HAVE TO -- --
MS. FRANKLIN:	OKAY- --
THE COURT:	IT MAY SOUND UNUSUAL, DIFFERENT FROM ANY OTHER CASE. IF THE CASE IS CLOSED BECAUSE A JUDGMENT HAS BEEN ISSUED, THEN IT'S CLOSED. BUT IF THERE'S A REASON TO REOPEN A CLOSED CASE, THEN WE'LL CONSIDER THAT AND REOPEN IT. BUT TYPICALLY, ONCE THIS COURT HAS ISSUED A JUDGMENT, AN APPEAL CAN BE TAKEN. PEOPLE LEVY ON THE JUDGMENT; IF THERE'S A PROBLEM LEVYING ON THE JUDGMENT, THEN YOU COME BACK TO THE COURT FOR WHATEVER RELIEF IS NECESSARY. BUT TYPICALLY, THE CLERK'S OFFICE ASSISTS WITH THAT. AND I THINK THAT THE JUDGMENT -- -- **I THINK THAT WE HAVE -- -- HAVE ALREADY CONCLUDED THAT THE JUDGMENT IS THE WAY TO BRING THIS TO A CONCLUSION, BECAUSE THEN YOU HAVE THE LEGAL MEANS TO ENFORCE THE JUDGMENT.**
	WHAT IS IT, MA' AM?
MS. JONES:	WHAT I WANT TO SAY, YOUR HONOR, IS WILL WITH THE JUDGMENT, WILL THAT HELP LOCATE THE ASSETS?
THE COURT:	WELL, I GUESS WE'LL FIND OUT, WON'T WE? ALL RIGHT. THAT'S THE JUDGMENT OF THE COURT. COURT'S IN RECESS.
	COMMENT AND ANALYSIS: #17 JUDGE EKANS KNEW FULL WELL THAT THE MONEY JUDGMENT TO BE ISSUED TO ME WOULD SERVE AS A MONEY JUDGMENT IN NAME ONLY. IT WAS ACTUALLY NOTHING MORE THAN A PIECE OF PAPER TO BE USED FOR DOCKET PURPOSES TO REMOVE MY LAWSUIT FROM HIS CALENDAR AND UPON THE CO-CONSPIRATORS' INSTRUCTIONS, SEND IT ON TO THE D.C. COURT OF APPEALS FOR A 3 YEAR LAYOVER DESIGNED TO PROMOTE AND ENSURE THE SUCCESS OF THE CRIMINAL ENTERPRISE OF WHICH HE WAS A KEY BENEFICIARY.
MS. JONES:	THANK YOU, YOUR HONOR.
MS. FRANKLIN:	THANK YOU, YOUR HONOR.

(THEREUPON, THE PROCEEDINGS WERE CONCLUDED.)

SUPERIOR COURT OF THE DISTRICT OF COLUMBIA
CIVIL DIVISION
WASHINGTON, D.C.

THE HONORABLE MATTHEW D. EKANS, ASSOCIATE JUDGE, PRESIDING

THE FOLLOWING ARE VERBATIM EXCERPTS OF THE OFFICIAL COURT TRANSCRIPT OF THE
NOVEMBER 19, 2014 PROCEEDING
ANNOTATED BY THE AUTHOR'S PERTINENT COMMENTARY AND ANALYSIS

NOVEMBER 19, 2014

PROCEEDINGS

COMMENT AND ANALYSIS: #1 AT THE CONCLUSION OF HIS RIGGED ADJUDICATION OF MY LAWSUIT ON OCTOBER 17, 2011, JUDGE EKANS ISSUED ME A $13.6 MILLION MONEY JUDGMENT IN LIEU OF ENFORCEMENT OF JUDGE KATE STARR'S ORDER OF OCTOBER 18, 2010 WHICH MANDATED THAT BRIANNA JONES PRODUCE THE BANK STATEMENTS AND RECORDS OF THE CASE SETTLEMENT PROCEEDS ON DEPOSIT AT BANK OF AMERICA.

IN MORE THAN ONE DREAM, THE HOLY SPIRIT HAD SHOWN ME THAT ON MORE THAN ONE OCCASION, JUDGE EKANS AND MYRON DAEMON, CHIEF JUDGE OF THE D.C. COURT OF APPEALS, HAD CONSULTED WITH EACH OTHER REGARDING MY CASE. DURING THEIR CONVERSATIONS, THEY HAD COME UP WITH A STRATEGY CONSISTENT WITH THE ULTIMATE GOAL OF THE D.C. JUDICIAL AND FBI CONSPIRACY AND CRIMINAL ENTERPRISE TO STRIP ME OF ALL ATTORNEY'S FEES OWED TO ME AMOUNTING TO AN ESTIMATED $50 MILLION.

THE STRATEGY WAS AS FOLLOWS: AT THE CONCLUSION OF MY CASE, JUDGE EKANS WOULD ISSUE ME A "PAPER" MONEY JUDGMENT. BRIANNA JONES, THEN REPRESENTED BY ATTORNEY SIMEON RAND, WOULD FILE A MOTION TO OVERTURN THE JUDGMENT. JUDGE EKANS WOULD THEN DENY THE MOTION AND BRIANNA JONES WOULD FILE AN APPEAL, SEEKING TO OVERTURN THE JUDGMENT. THE COURT OF APPEALS WOULD THEN SIT ON THE APPEAL FOR ALMOST 3 YEARS.

FOLLOWING MY CONTACT WITH THE WASHINGTON POST IN MAY 2014 REGARDING MY INTEREST IN TAKING OUT AN ADVOCACY ADVERTISEMENT DUE TO THE EXCESSIVE TIME OF THE PENDING APPEAL, THE D.C. COURT OF APPEALS ISSUED ITS DECISION, WITHIN WEEKS THEREAFTER, OVERTURNING THE RIGGED $13.6 MILLION MONEY JUDGMENT, WITH THE CAVEAT THAT IF I SHOULD EVER FIND THE STOLEN SETTLEMENT PROCEEDS, JUDGE EKANS COULD ISSUE A NEW JUDGMENT.

THIS DESCRIBED SCENARIO IS WHAT I CALL COLD-BLOODED, THUGGISH D.C. COURT SYSTEM FRAUD, THEFT, CORRUPTION AND EXTORTION 21ST CENTURY STYLE.

JUDGE EKANS' STRATEGY OF ISSUING A MONEY JUDGMENT WOULD ALLOW ROOM FOR THE OVERTURN OF THE MONEY JUDGMENT BY THE COMPLICIT D.C. COURT OF APPEALS ALMOST 3 YEARS LATER IN JULY 2014. JUDGE EKANS PROVED THAT BRIANNA JONES DID NOT HAVE TO COMPLY WITH A COURT ORDER AND MOREOVER, HE WOULD REFUSE TO ENFORCE THE COURT ORDER, EVEN THOUGH THAT IS ONE OF THE PRIMARY RESPONSIBILITIES OF A COURT JUDGE IN ANY AMERICAN JUDICIAL JURISDICTION, INCULDING WASHINGTON, D.C., THE NATION'S CAPITAL.

AT THE HEARING ON JULY 31, 2011, JUDGE EKANS SAID IF HE COULDN'T ENFORCE A COURT ORDER, HE WOULD NEED TO HAND IN HIS ROBE AND GAVEL. WELL, THE COURT RECORD VERIFIES THAT HE NEVER ENFORCED JUDGE KATE STARR'S ORDER OF OCTOBER 18, 2010 AND THE LAST TIME I CHECKED ON THE THRESHOLD OF THE YEAR 2024, THIRTEEN YEARS LATER, HE HAD NOT TURNED IN HIS BLACK ROBE NOR HIS COURT GAVEL. JUST MORE JUDICIAL GASLIGHTING.

ON THANKSGIVING MORNING IN NOVEMBER 2011, ATTORNEY SIMEON RAND, THEN RETAINED BY BRIANNA JONES, SERVED ME BY EMAIL WITH A DEFAMATORY MOTION TO OVERTURN JUDGE EKANS' RIGGED $13.6 MILLION MONEY JUDGMENT ISSUED TO ME. THE MOTION WAS SO EGREGIOUSLY DEFAMATORY THAT I PROMPTLY FILED A FORMAL COMPLAINT WITH D.C. BAR COUNSEL AGAINST MR. RAND. THIS WAS THE FIRST TIME I HAD FOUND IT NECESSARY TO TAKE SUCH ACTION AGAINST A FELLOW MEMBER OF THE BAR DURING MY THEN OVER 15 YEARS AS A TRIAL ATTORNEY.

DEPUTY CLERK:	YOUR HONOR, NOW CALLING THE MATTER OF BARBARA WASHINGTON FRANKLIN VERSUS BRIANNA JONES, 2009 CA 4417.
	PARTIES, PLEASE STEP FORWARD AND STATE YOUR NAME FOR THE RECORD.
THE COURT:	COUNSELS.
MR. DUNN:	MAY IT PLEASE THE COURT, KEVIN DUNN FOR THE PROPOSED INTERVENERS, DONALD AND DORETHA SIMPSON. AND THEY ARE SEATED IN THE FRONT ROW TO MY RIGHT, YOUR HONOR.
THE COURT:	GOOD MORNING TO YOU.
MR. RAND:	GOOD MORNING, YOUR HONOR. SIMEON RAND FOR DEFENDANT BRIANNA JONES.

THE COURT: GOOD MORNING.

THE LAW CLERK: YOUR HONOR, IT LOOKS LIKE THERE WERE TWO PRECIPES ON BEHALF OF MS. WASHINGTON FRANKLIN. I DON'T KNOW IF YOU WANT US TO –

THE COURT: WHAT TIME DID WE SCHEDULE IT FOR?

THE LAW CLERK: 10:30, YOUR HONOR, TO MY KNOWLEDGE. WE HAVEN'T HEARD FROM EITHER ATTORNEY.

THE COURT: YOU HAVE TWO PRECIPES ENTERING APPEARANCES?

THE LAW CLERK: THE LAST TWO DOCKET ENTRIES ARE PRECIPES ENTERING APPEARANCES, YES.

THE COURT: I DON'T KNOW IF THE – IS THERE – CAN WE CALL INFORMATION AND SEE IF THERE IS STILL A SECURITY LINE OUT THERE ?

THE LAW CLERK: SURE.

THE COURT: PRECIPE TO ENTER APPEARANCES RAMSEY R-A-M-S-E-Y ON BEHALF OF BARBARA WASHINGTON FRANKLIN; PRECIPE TO ENTER APPEARANCE OF BENJAMIN JASON, J-A-S-O-N ON BEHALF OF BARBARA WASHINGTON FRANKLIN. BOTH OF THOSE APPEARANCES WERE ENTERED ON THE 29TH OF OCTOBER.

                       COMMENT AND ANALYSIS: #2 PRIOR TO THE COURT HEARING, BENJAMIN JASON AND PAUL RAMSEY INFORMED ME THAT THEY HAD BEEN INFORMED BY AN UNDISCLOSED SOURCE THAT THERE HAD NOT BEEN A SETTLEMENT IN MY CASE. THEREFORE, FOLLOWING THE COURT HEARING ON NOVEMBER 19, 2014, THEY INTENDED TO WITHDRAW THEIR REPRESENTATION ON MY BEHALF.

                       I DID NOT OBJECT. THEY HAD BEEN ENERGETIC, EXCITED AND PREPARED TO COLLECT, ON MY BEHALF, THE MILLIONS OF DOLLARS OWED TO ME IN ATTORNEY'S FEES, OF WHICH THEY WOULD RECEIVE A SUBSTANTIAL AMOUNT IN ATTORNEY'S FEES BASED ON OUR AGREEMENT.

                       THEY WERE NOT PREPARED TO MOUNT A CAMPAIGN ON MY BEHALF, BASED ON ISSUES OF MASSIVE D.C. JUDICIAL AND FBI FRAUD, THEFT, CORRUPTION AND EXTORTION. WHILE I WAS DISAPPOINTED, I WAS NOT SURPRISED, NOR DID I DESPAIR. I CONSIDERED THE PROPOSED WITHDRAWAL OF THEIR REPRESENTATION AS A PART OF WHAT GOES WITH THE TERRITORY OF D.C JUDICIAL AND FBI FRAUD, THEFT, CORRUPTION AND EXTORTION.

MR. DUNN: I THINK THEY ARE FROM THE SAME FIRM, YOUR HONOR; IS THAT CORRECT?

THE LAW CLERK: THEY ARE, YOUR HONOR.

THE COURT:	THEY ARE. HAVE YOU BEEN IN TOUCH WITH EITHER— EITHER OF YOU GENTLEMEN?
MR. RAND:	NO, YOUR HONOR.
MR. DUNN:	NO, YOUR HONOR. WE SERVED THEM ELECTRONICALLY WITH OUR MOTION TO INTERVENE IN THE EXHIBITS.
THE COURT:	I SEE.
THE LAW CLERK:	I WAS ABLE TO REACH SECURITY AND IT HAS ADVISED US THE LINE IS STILL QUITE LONG.
THE COURT:	STILL A LINE. SO WHY DON'T WE STAND DOWN FOR FIVE OR SO – FREQUENTLY PEOPLE WILL CALL THE COURTROOM IF THEY ARE STUCK, BUT LET'S DO THEM THE COURTESY OF GIVING THEM ANOTHER FIVE MINUTES OR SO.
THE LAW CLERK:	DO YOU WANT US TO CALL THE FIRM TO SEE IF THEY ARE –
THE COURT:	THAT IS A VERY GOOD QUESTION. YES.

***

THE LAW CLERK:	YOUR HONOR, I HAVE ONE OF THE SECRETARIES FOR THE FIRM IS TRYING TO SEE IF SHE CAN REACH THEM TO SEE IF THEY ARE IN THE SECURITY LINE.
	YOUR HONOR, THEY ARE NOT ABLE TO REACH THEM ON THEIR CELL PHONES.
THE COURT:	WELL, YOU KNOW LET'S JUST TAKE NOTE THAT IT IS ABOUT 16 MINUTES UNTIL 11:00, WE HAD SET THIS MATTER FOR 10:30. COUNSEL FOR MS. JONES IS PRESENT, COUNSEL FOR THE – COUNSEL FOR THE MOVANTS TO INTERVENE IS PRESENT. NOW WE HAVE NOT HEARD FROM COUNSEL FOR MS. WASHINGTON FRANKLIN. *I NOTE THAT MS. WASHINGTON FRANKLIN HERSELF IS NOT PRESENT. SHE NEVER FAILED TO MISS A HEARING BEFORE THIS MATTER GOT IN THE APPELLATE POSTURE.*
	COMMENT AND ANALYSIS: #3 THE MORNING OF THE COURT HEARING, MY FAMILY AND I WERE IN THE MIDST OF TRAVELING OUT OF TOWN TO ATTEND THE FUNERAL AND BURIAL SERVICES OF A CLOSE FAMILY MEMBER. THE RIGGED APPELLATE POSTURE OF A RIGGED COURT HEARING HAD ABSOLUTELY NOTHING TO DO WITH MY LACK OF APPEARANCE FROM THIS HEARING.

THE COURT:	WE ALSO NOTE MS. JONES IS NOT PRESENT. SHE FREQUENTLY WAS NOT PRESENT AT LEAST ON THE SCHEDULED DAY AND FREQUENTLY WAS NOT PRESENT AT LEAST ON THE SCHEDULED DAY AND TIME. ALTHOUGH LO AND BEHOLD, I BELIEVE SHE IS WALKING THROUGH THE DOORS RIGHT NOW.
	THAT IS YOUR CLIENT, ISN'T IT?
MR. RAND:	YES, YOUR HONOR.
MS. JONES:	GOOD MORNING YOUR HONOR.
	I HAVE A PARKING TICKET. I HAVE BEEN HERE A WHILE. I HAVE BEEN IN LINE.
THE COURT:	I HEARD THAT THERE WAS AN UNUSUALLY LONG SECURITY LINE. I AM SORRY YOU HAD TO STAND IN THAT LINE SO LONG. *DID YOU SEE MS. WASHINGTON FRANKLIN IN THE LINE?*
MS. JONES:	NO, I DID NOT.
THE COURT:	WELL, IT IS I MEAN, IT IS CLEAR THAT PEOPLE ARE ENCOUNTERING SOME DIFFICULTY GETTING HERE SO –
THE LAW CLERK:	WHEN I WALKED IN, I NOTICED THE FRONT ENTRANCE, ONLY ONE OF THE SECURITY SIDES WAS LETTING PEOPLE THROUGH.
THE COURT:	I DON'T KNOW. IT IS HARD FOR A PERSON IN MY POSITION TO BE UPSET WITH SECURITY FOR DOING THEIR JOB. SO I REALIZE THE IMPOSITION ON PEOPLE TRYING TO GET IN THE BUILDING, BUT I ALSO APPRECIATE THE FACT THAT THERE IS SOME VERY BAD STORIES WE HEAR FROM ROUND THE COUNTRY WITH COURTS THAT DON'T TAKE PROPER SECURITY.
	MAYBE WE CAN TRY TO MOVE AHEAD. I DON'T KNOW – I DON'T KNOW WHETHER THE EFFICACY OF TRYING TO DO FACT FINDING WITHOUT MS. WASHINGTON AND HER ATTORNEY BEING PRESENT, BUT MAYBE WE CAN MAKE SOME PROGRESS ON THE MOTION TO INTERVENE.
	I AM WILLING TO HEAR OTHER VIEWS – OTHER SUGGESTIONS FOR MOVING FORWARD. I AM REALLY NOT ENAMORED OF THE IDEA OF JUST SORT OF SITTING HERE AND WRINGING OUR HANDS BECAUSE WE ARE HERE. AND I THINK THAT WE SHOULD LOOK TO SEE IF THERE IS SOMETHING WE CAN DO TO MOVE FORWARD.

***

MR. DUNN:	THERE WAS AN APPEAL FILED. THE APPEAL WAS AFFIRMED. THERE IS NO SETTLEMENT, THERE IS NO MONEY, THERE IS NO RECOVERY. THE ENTIRE REPRESENTATIONS TO THIS COURT BY MS. FRANKLIN AND WITH MS. JONES PARTICIPATING HAS BEEN AN ATTEMPT TO GET DOCUMENTS FROM THIS COURT OSTENSIBLY TO IMPLEMENT MS. FRANKLIN'S CONTINGENT FEE AGREEMENT WITH MS. JONES THAT WOULD TAPER OVER AND ATTEMPT TO GIVE SOME LEGITIMACY TO THIS NONEXISTENT SETTLEMENT IN FLORIDA.

NOW THERE ARE OTHER LOAN VICTIMS IN ADDITION TO THE SIMPSONS. IN THE PROCEEDINGS BETWEEN THE SIMPSONS AND MS. JONES IN THIS COURT, EVIDENCE EMERGED THAT MS. FRANKLIN HAD BROKERED LOANS TO THREE OTHER PERSONS IN ADDITION TO THE SIMPSONS. MS. JONES TESTIFIED IN THAT CASE THAT SHE RECEIVED HUNDREDS OF THOUSANDS OF DOLLARS THROUGH MS. FRANKLIN BASED ON THIS OSTENSIBLE SETTLEMENT OR CASE In FLORIDA, WHICH TURNS OUT TO BE A COMPLETE FRAUD AND COMPLETELY NONEXISTENT.

COMMENT AND ANALYSIS: #4 THE COURT RECORD CONFIRMS THAT THERE WAS A SETTLEMENT AGREEMENT AS TESTIFIED TO UNDER OATH BY BRIANNA JONES DURING THE APRIL 6, 2011 COURT HEARING.

MOREOVER, IF, IN FACT, I HAD COMMITTED A FRAUD UPON THE COURT, JUDGE EKANS HAD THE REQUISITE RESPONSIBILITY TO ADDRESS THE ISSUE IN A PROPER FASHION. HE DID NOT DO SO BECAUSE HE KNEW THAT THE MASSIVE FRAUD HAD BEEN COMMTTED BY THE TEAM OF CORRUPT D.C. CO-CONSPIRATOR COURT JUDGES OF WHICH HE WAS A MEMBER AND IN FACT GRAND MARSHALL OF THE D.C. JUDICIAL AND FBI CORRUPTION PARADE.

MOREOVER, WHY WAS THERE NEVER THE ISSUE RAISED BY EKANS OF THE REPEATED PERJURED TESTIMONY OF BRIANNA JONES REGARDING THE SETTLEMENT OF THE CASE?

MR. DUNN:	NOW, WE HAVE ASKED FOR LEAVE TO FILE UNDER RULE 24C, OUR COMPLAINT AND FRAUD AGAINST MS. FRANKLIN AND MS. JONES THAT WOULD BE PART OF THIS CASE, BUT WE ALSO WANT TO UNDERSCORE TO THE COURT THAT THE COURT HAS BEEN ENLISTED BY MS. FRANKLIN IN AN ATTEMPT TO GET DOCUMENTS THAT CONTRIBUTE TO A FRAUD. THERE WAS NEVER ANY SETTLEMENT. **AND, YOUR HONOR, AT ONE TIME IN THE PROCEEDINGS BEFORE YOU, YOU SAID THIS MATTER APPEARS TO BE JUST "SMOKE AND MIRRORS" AND YOU WERE CORRECT.**

COMMENT AND ANALYSIS: #5 JUDGE EKANS, CONSISTENT WITH HIS ROLE AS A KEY D.C. JUDICIAL CO-CONSPIRATOR IN THE MASSIVE CRIMINAL ENTERPRISE TO DEFRAUD ME OF THE MILLIONS OF DOLLARS OWED TO ME IN ATTORNEY'S FEES CAVALIERLY, AND IN KEEPING WITH HIS CO-CONSPIRATOR ROLE FALSELY, INTENTIONALLY AND PURPOSEFULLY DEFINED MY CASE AS "SMOKE AND MIRRORS" DURING THE AUGUST 19, 2011 COURT HEARING. HE HAD DONE SO EVEN IN THE ABSENCE OF IMPORTANT WITNESS TESTIMONY YET TO BE GIVEN BY THE DEFENDANT, BRIANNA JONES.

IT IS ALSO SIGNIFICANT THAT AT NO TIME DID JUDGE EKANS SHOW ANY INTEREST IN REVIEWING THE CERTIFIED COPIES OF FLORIDA COURT RECORDS REFERRED TO BY MR. DUNN. HE DIDN'T NEED TO. HE KNEW THE CRITICAL ROLE HE HAD PLAYED IN THIS D.C. JUDICIAL CRIMINAL ENTERPRISE, ALONG WITH HIS JUDICIAL COLLEAGUES.

SIMILARLY, EKANS SHOWED NO INTEREST WHATSOEVER IN THE FINDINGS OF THE D.C. BAR COUNSEL WHOSE INVESTIGATION DETERMINED THAT THERE WAS AN EXISTING SETTLEMENT AGREEMENT BETWEEN BRIANNA JONES AND THE RIDGEWAY ESTATE, THAT BRIANNA JONES WAS ENTITLED TO A SUBSTANTIAL CLAIM TO BE PAID TO HER BY THE ESTATE AND THAT SHE WAS AWAITING DISBURSEMENT OF THE SPECIFIED SETTLEMENT PROCEEDS.

***

COMMENT AND ANALYSIS: # 6 WHILE I NEVER ASKED FOR A MONEY JUDGMENT, BUT REPEATEDLY ASKED THAT THE BANK STATEMENTS BE DELIVERED TO ME, BY THE TIME OCTOBER 2011 ROLLED AROUND, I WAS TIRED OF BEING IN THE GRIP OF A CORRUPT, CONSCIENCE-FREE AND AMORAL D.C. COURT JUDGE WHO, AFTER NINE LONG AND EXCRUCIATING MONTHS, I NOW REGARDED AS NO MORE THAN *A COILED SNAKE DRESSED IN A BLACK ROBE*, IN ADDITION TO HIS OTHER PERSONAL CHARACTERISTICS THAT PERFECTLY SUITED HIM FOR HIS ROLE OF GRAND MARSHALL OF THE MASSIVE D.C. JUDICIAL AND FBI CRIMINAL ENTERPRISE THAT SUCCEEDED, UNHAMPERED, IN DEFRAUDING ME AND MY FAMILY OF AN ESTIMATED $50 MILLION IN ATTORNEY'S FEES THAT I HAD HONESTLY EARNED AND THAT ARE STILL OWED TO ME.

IF THE ISSUANCE OF A MONEY JUDGMENT WOULD SET ME FREE OF EKANS AND HIS MANDATED PRESENCE IN MY PERSONAL LIFE, THEN I WOULD AGREE TO IT. ESCAPE FROM UNDER EKANS' JURISDICTION MEANT MORE TO ME THAN THE MILLIONS OF DOLLARS OWED TO ME IN ATTORNEY'S FEES.

AT THE END OF THE DAY, MY SOUL, SPIRIT, MIND AND BODY YEARNED TO BE FREE OF THE SUFFICATING FUMES OF D.C. JUDICIAL FRAUD, THEFT, CORRUPTION AND EXTORTION THAT PERMEATED AND SATURATED EKANS' COURTROOM.

TIME AND TIME AGAIN DURING THE 9 MONTHS OF EKANS' ADJUDICATION OF MY CASE, MY MIND WOULD FLASH BACK TO THE EASE, PEACE, RESPECT, GRACE, HONOR AND OVERALL JUDICIAL INTEGRITY DEMONSTRATED AT ALL TIMES BY JUDGE KATE STARR. RATHER THAN WANTING TO SHED TEARS, I WOULD WANT TO THROW UP ALL OVER THE COURTROOM FLOOR IN THE COURT ATMOSPHERE THAT WREAKED WITH SUFFICATING FUMES OF THEFT, FRAUD, CORRUPTION, EXTORTION, THE RUTHLESS BREACH OF THE RULE OF LAW, AND THE DEMONIC INFLUENCE AND DEFECATION THAT PERMEATED AND SATURATED EVERY NOOK AND CRANNY OF EKANS' COURTROOM.

THE COURT: ARE YOU COUNSEL?

MR. RAMSEY: I AM, YOUR HONOR. BRIAN RAMSEY FOR MS. FRANKLIN. AND I APOLOGIZE.

THE LINE OUTSIDE WAS ABOUT 45 MINUTES THIS MORNING.

THE COURT: I UNDERSTAND.

***

THE COURT: WELL, ON THIS MATTER, MR. DUNN, YOU HAVE THE LAST WORD; YOU ARE THE MOVANT.

MR. DUNN: YOUR HONOR, I WANT TO UNDERSCORE HOW THE COURT SHOULD BE GREATLY CONCERNED OVER HOW –

THE COURT: I AM. BUT THERE – THERE ARE TWO THINGS THAT I THINK YOU NEED TO ADDRESS: ONE IS MS. WASHINGTON FRANKLIN'S COUNSEL'S SUGGESSTION THAT YOU CAN ACCOMPLISH WHAT YOUR CLIENTS WANT TO ACCOMPLISH WITHOUT INTERVENING IN THIS MATTER, WHICH WAS SENT BACK TO ME FOR A VERY LIMITED PURPOSE, WHICH IS TO MAKE FACTUAL FINDING ON WHETHER OR NOT THERE WAS A TRIGGER FOR THE FEE UNDER THE SETTLEMENT TERMS THAT LED ME TO TURN THAT SETTLEMENT INTO JUDGMENT.

WITHOUT THAT TRIGGER, I.E., WITHOUT MONEY HAVING PASSED INTO THE DEFENDANT'S HANDS, THERE WAS NO REASON – NO BASIS FOR HER TO PAY A FEE TO MS. WASHINGTON FRANKLIN. AND THAT IS THE LIMITED NATURE OF THE INQUIRY ON THIS REMAND ORDER.

AND SO MS. WASHINGTON FRANKLIN'S COUNSEL SUGGESTS THAT BRINGING NEW PARTIES INTO THIS CASE TO EXPLORE QUESTIONS OF FRAUD PERPETRATED ON THEM AND OTHERS, AS WELL AS ON THE COURT, YOU KNOW MAY NOT MAKE – MAY NOT BE A GOOD USE OF THE COURT'S OR ANYBODY ELSE'S TIME. THAT IS ONE THING. THE OTHER THING AS A PROCEDURAL MATTER THAT YOU RECOGNIZE NEEDS TO BE FULFILLED AND THAT COUNSEL HAS RAISED, WHICH IS THAT YOU DON'T – YOU ARE MOVING UNDER A RULE, BUT YOU DIDN'T COMPLY WITH THE RULE BY FILING A COMPLAINT.

COMMENT AND ANALYSIS: #7 JUDGE EKANS ACCUSED ME OF PERPETRATING A FRAUD ON THE COURT, YET HE AVOIDED HIS JUDICIAL RESPONSIBILITY OF TAKING THE NECESSARY STEPS TO HOLD ME ACCOUNTABLE. INSTEAD, HE CHOSE TO USE HIS TIME STRIPPING ME OF THE MILLIONS OF DOLLARS OWED TO ME IN ATTORNEY'S FEES. HE IS THE ONLY JUDGE, AS WELL AS THE ONLY INDIVIDUAL DURING MY ENTIRE LIFETIME, THAT HAS ACCUSED ME OF FRAUD, AND ON A PUBLIC RECORD, IN FURTHERANCE OF SHIELDING HIMSELF AND HIS CORRUPT COLLEAGUES AND JUDICIAL CO-CONSPIRATORS FROM THEIR UNSPEAKABLE CRIMES OF JUDICIAL FRAUD, THEFT, CORRUPTION AND EXTORTION. NEVERTHELESS, MY REPUTATION FOR HONESTY AND INTEGRITY IN WASHINGTON. D.C. AND ACROSS THE NATION CONTINUES UNBESMIRCHED.

THE D.C. COURT OF APPEALS CONFIRMED THAT THE D.C. JUDICIAL FRAUD AND THEFT TO WHICH I WAS RUTHLESSLY SUBJECTED WAS SYSTEMIC WHEN THE D.C. COURT OF APPEALS REMAINED SILENT ON MY LAWSUIT'S DOMINANT ISSUE OF D.C. JUDICIAL AND FBI FRAUD, THEFT, CORRUPTION AND EXTORTION, AND ADDING INSULT TO INJURY, INFORMED JUDGE EKANS HE WOULD BE FREE TO ISSUE A NEW JUDGMENT IF I SHOULD EVER FIND THE SETTLEMENT PROCEEDS THAT I HAD REPEATEDLY ALLEGED TO HAVE BEEN STOLEN BY CORRUPT D.C. COURT JUDGES AND FBI AGENTS WORKING TOGETHER AS JUDICIAL PARTICIPANTS IN A MASSIVE D.C. JUDICIAL AND FBI CRIMINAL ENTERPRISE.

BUT MORE IMPORTANTLY, THE D.C. COURT OF APPEALS OBSCENELY AND EGREGIOUSLY ABDICATED ITS RESPONSIBILITY AS AN APPELLANT TRIBUNAL BY REFUSING TO ADDRESS MY LAWSUIT'S DOMINANT ISSUE OF D.C. JUDICIAL AND FBI FRAUD, THEFT, CORRUPTION AND EXTORTION. THE CHIEF JUDGE SIMPLY PASSED.

BARBARA WASHINGTON FRANKLIN

MR. DUNN: I ASKED FOR 10 MORE DAYS, YOUR HONOR, TO FINISH.

THE COURT: I HEARD THAT. THAT DOESN'T ADDRESS THE POINT WHICH IS RIGHT NOW YOU
                  HAVE GOT AN INCHOATE MOTION PENDING BEFORE THE COURT. SO I GUESS
                  MAYBE WHAT I AM HEARING IS THAT AS TO THE PROCEDURAL MATTER YOU HAVE
                  TOLD ME YOU ALREADY ADDRESSED IT. YOU ARE ASKING FOR LEAVE TO FILE A
                  COMPLAINT. PRESUMABLY, THE MOTION WOULDN'T BE RIPE FOR AN
                  OPPOSITION UNTIL THAT 10 MORE DAYS HAS EXPIRED AND YOU HAVE FILED A
                  COMPLAINT.

                  COMMENT AND ANALYSIS: #8 WHEN I FILED THE MOTION FOR COURT
                  INVESTIGATION OF THE STOLEN SETTLEMENT PROCEEDS, INCLUDING MY
                  ATTORNEY'S FEES, JUDGE EKANS DENIED IT THE VERY SAME DAY. THE
                  DEFENDANT WAS GIVEN NO OPPORTUNITY TO RESPOND AT ALL. THAT IS
                  BECAUSE HIS ABUSES OF DISCRETION CONFIRM THAT HE SAW HIMSELF AS ABOVE
                  THE LAW. HE IS AN AMERICAN COURT JUDGE THAT ANSWERS TO NO ONE BUT
                  HIMSELF. PERIOD. TO EKANS, THE CONCEPT OF JUDICIAL ACCOUNTABILITY IS A
                  NON-SEQUITOR.

MR. DUNN: WE COULD FILE IT SOONER, YOUR HONOR. WE COULD FILE THE 24 (C)
                  COMPLAINT TOMORROW, BUT I URGE THE COURT –

THE COURT: THAT IS WHY IT IS _ PROBABLY MORE IMPORTANT FOR YOU TO ADDRESS THE
                  QUESTION THAT MR. RAMSEY IS RAISING WHICH IS WHAT IS THE BENEFIT TO
                  ANYBODY OF HAVING YOUR CLIENTS INTERVENE IN THIS MATTER, WHEN THEY
                  ARE PERFECTLY CAPABLE, AT LEAST ACCORDING TO YOUR PRESENTATION – AND
                  INDEED I THINK I HEARD YOU SAY THEY INTENDED TO FILE A SEPARATE CLAIM.

MR. DUNN: NO. THEY WERE GOING TO FILE IT IN THIS CASE, YOU HONOR.

THE COURT: WHY? THAT IS HIS QUESTION, WHY?

MR. DUNN: WELL, YOUR HONOR, THERE ARE STATUTE OF LIMITATIONS ISSUES FOR ONE.
                  AND, SECONDLY, YOU'RE THE ONLY JUDICIAL AUTHORITY THAT HAS JURISDICTION
                  OVER MS. FRANKLIN IN THIS MATTER. IT IS A VERY SERIOUS MATTER WHAT SHE
                  DID, SHE ENLISTED THE COURT TO OBTAIN DOCUMENTS TO PAPER OVER A
                  FRAUD. AND THE COURT SHOULD BE – THAT SHOULD BE THE FOREMOST
                  INTEREST OF THE COURT. I PRAY THE COURT NOT DISMISS THE CASE; NOT LET
                  THEM TURN AWAY NOW.

THE COURT: I DIDN'T SAY--- WHOA, WHOA, WHOA. I THINK – WE ARE NOT TALKING ABOUT DISMISSING THE CASE. WE ARE TALKING ABOUT FINDINGS THAT I AM UNDER A REQUIREMENT, UNDER A MANDATE TO MAKE. AND YOU HAVE TOLD ME THAT YOU HAVE PROOF POSITIVE THAT THERE WAS NO SETTLEMENT. MS. WASHINGTON FRANKLIN'S ATTORNEY SAYS THAT – SHE IS PREPARED TO CORROBORATE THAT. I – I DON'T THINK YOU HAVE SPOKEN TO THAT ISSUE YET FOR MS. JONES. **BUT AT ANY RATE, IT SEEMS CLEAR THAT NOW THERE IS SOLID EVIDENCE THAT THERE WAS NO BASIS FOR THIS JUDGMENT THAT I ENTERED.**

COMMENT AND ANALYSIS: #9 *JUDGE EKANS DEMONSTRATES THAT HE IS COMMITTED TO HIS KEY ROLE IN THIS HISTORIC D.C. JUDICIAL CRIMINAL ENTERPRISE RIGHT UP TO THE VERY END. HE WILL DO ANYTHING AND SAY ANYTHING AS LONG AS IT IS IN FURTHERANCE OF THE HISTORIC D.C. JUDICIAL AND FBI CRIMINAL ENTERPRISE TO DEFRAUD ME OF THE MILLIONS OF DOLLARS OWED TO ME IN ATTORNEY'S FEES.*

THE COURT: NOW, THAT DOESN'T NECESSARILY MEAN THAT I AM PREPARED TO DISMISS THE CASE. IT MEANS THAT THERE ARE REASONS TO CONSIDER WHETHER OR NOT WE SHOULD KEEP IT OPEN FOR INTERVENTION FROM SOME OTHER PARTIES. NOW, YOU HAVE TOLD ME TWICE THAT THERE IS STATUTE OF LIMITATIONS ISSUES. DO YOU WANT TO BE CLEARER ABOUT THAT? BECAUSE YOU HAVE ALSO SAID IN THE SAME BREATH THAT CLEARLY THERE ARE NO STATUTE OF LIMITATIONS ISSUES AFFECTING **THE FRAUD THAT WAS PREPETRATED IN THIS COURT.** SO IS THERE OR ISN'T THERE?

COMMENT AND ANALYSIS: THE FRAUD THAT WAS PERPETRATED IN MY LAWSUIT WAS DESIGNED, ENGINEERED AND ORCHESTRATED BY JUDGE EKANS AND HIS JUDICIAL CO-CONSPIRATORS IDENTIFIED AND PROFILED IN THIS SPIRITUAL MEMOIR AND JUDICIAL EXPOSE'.

***

MR. RAMSEY: IF THERE ARE STATUTE OF LIMITATIONS ISSUES HERE OR IF THERE ARE NOT STATUTE OF LIMITATIONS ISSUES HERE DOES NOT TURN ON WHETHER THE COMPLAINT IS FILED AS INTERVENTION OR WHETHER IT IS INDEPENDENTLY FILED, IF THERE ARE CLAIMS THAT CAN BE PURSUED, THEY CAN BE PURSUED; IF THEY CANNOT, THEY CANNOT.

THE COURT: I DON'T KNOW. YOU KNOW, I AM NOT AS COMFORTABLE AS SOME OTHERS MAY BE SPEAKING DEFINITIVELY ON MATTERS THAT I HAVEN'T HAD A CHANCE TO RESEARCH. SO I DON'T KNOW. BUT I DO KNOW THAT THIS MOTION AS IT STANDS RIGHT NOW THEY CAN EITHER BE DENIED WITHOUT PREJUDICE OR I CAN GRANT HIM LEAVE TO FILE THE COMPLAINT AND COMPLY WITH THE RULE. YOU KNOW, I GUESS I AM A BIT CURIOUS. *I AM SURE IF I ASKED YOU WHY YOUR CLIENT ISN'T HERE YOU WOULD PROBABLY RESPOND THAT YOU DIDN'T KNOW SHE HAD TO BE HERE.* IT WOULD BE – I REMARKED I THINK BEFORE YOU WALKED IN –

BY THE WAY, YOU SHOULD KNOW, IF YOU GET A TRANSCRIPT OF THIS PROCEEDING YOU WILL SEE THAT WE HAD BARELY BEGUN THE PRESENTATION, WE BARELY OPENED THE HEARING WITH MR. DUNN'S PRESENTATION WHEN YOU WALKED IN THE DOOR, SO YOU REALLY --- THE ONLY THING THAT YOU MISSED WAS US TRYING TO REACH OUT AND FIND YOU. THAT IS THE ONLY THING THAT YOU MISSED. WE DID CALL YOUR OFFICE AND WE ASKED ONE OF THE PEOPLE WHO WORK IN YOUR OFFICE TO SEE IF THEY COULD LOCATE YOU ON THE PHONE. WE SUSPECTED YOU WERE IN THE SECURITY LINE. SO I SAY THAT TO SAY THAT YOU DIDN'T MISS ANYTHING. WHEN YOU WALKED IN, YOU WERE WALKING IN AS HE WAS STILL IN HIS FIRST SENTENCE.

MR. DUNN: I MEAN, OUR –

THE COURT: *AND BABARA WASHINGTON FRANKLIN HAS NEVER FAILED TO BE HERE BEFORE. SHE HAS BEEN HERE AT EVERY HEARING. AND, IN FACT, WAS THE CHEERLEADER FOR THESE PEOPLE SITTING IN THE FRONT ROW, AS WELL AS TWO OR THREE OTHER FOLKS WHO USED TO ATTEND ALL OF THE HEARINGS. SO THIS IS THE VERY FIRST TIME THAT WE HAVEN'T SEEN HER.*

COMMENT AND ANALYSIS: *MY ATTENDNCE AT THE OUT-OF-TOWN FUNERAL SERVICES FOR AN IMMEDIATE FAMILY MEMBER TOOK PRECEDENCE OVER ATTENDANCE AT A RIGGED COURT HEARING IN FURTHERANCE OF THE RIGGED DISMISSAL OF MY CASE AND THE OVERALL ULTIMATE SUCCESS OF THE D.C JUDICIAL AND FBI CONSPIRACY AND CRIMINAL ENTERPRISE UNDERWAY IN EKANS' COURTROOM AND FOR WHICH HE SERVED AS GRAND MARSHALL.*

MR. RAMSEY: WELL, I SUGGEST, YOUR HONOR, THERE IS NOTHING TO READ INTO IT RELATING TO THE FILING OF THE MOTION TO INTERVENE.

COMMENT AND ANALYSIS: I SHALL NEVER KNOW WHY COUNSEL CHOSE NOT TO DISCLOSE THE REASON FOR MY NON-ATTENDANCE AT THE HEARING.

THE COURT: I AM GLAD TO HEAR THAT. BUT I THINK THAT THERE ARE SOME INTRIGUING QUESTIONS GOING FORWARD. I HAVEN'T LOOKED AT THESE PAPERS THAT MR. DUNN HAS FILED. I DIDN'T WANT TO LOOK AT THEM BEFORE WE HAD THIS HEARING TODAY, BUT AS SOON AS THEY GET COMPLETE, I AM GOING TO LOOK AT THEM. *I AM GOING TO GRANT YOU LEAVE TO FILE YOUR COMPLAINT. AND THEN WE'LL HAVE WHATEVER POSITIONS THAT MS. WASHINGTON FRANKLIN OR MS. JONES WANT TO TAKE.*

ARE YOU STANDING IN THIS CASE?

MR. RAND: YOUR HONOR, THERE IS A MOTION –

THE COURT: I GOT WIND OF SUCH A MOTION. DO YOU WANT THAT HEARD OR WHAT IS GOING TO HAPPEN WITH THAT?

MR. RAND: WE WOULD LIKE TO DISCUSS THAT IN COURT TODAY IF YOU HAVE TIME.

THE COURT: I HAVE TIME. I AM JUST TRYING TO FIGURE OUT, YOU KNOW, IT IS – I ALWAYS SAID THAT IT IS AN ADVANTAGE TO HAVE COUNSEL IN THE CASE. BUT CERTAINLY THIS HAS BEEN A CASE THAT HAS BEEN MOST CHALLENGING FOR THE COURT AND I WOULD IMAGINE FOR COUNSEL AS WELL. THIS IS – THIS HAS BEEN A VERY UNUSUAL CASE. WHEN I CAME IN THIS CASE, IT WAS PRESENTED TO ME THAT THERE HAD BEEN A SETTLEMENT WORKED OUT WITH THE JUDGE WHO WAS A PREDECESSOR ON CALENDAR 7. I AM NO LONGER ON THAT CALENDAR. MY LAW CLERK, WHO HERSELF IS A LAWYER, TOLD ME THAT I WAS AN IDIOT FOR TAKING THIS CASE ON THE CALENDAR THAT I AM ON NOW, BECAUSE WE COULD HAVE LEFT THIS FOR SOME OTHER UNSUSPECTING JUDGE TO TRY TO WORK THROUGH. BUT WHEN I TOOK CALENDAR 7, THE CIVIL II CALENDAR, THIS CASE HAD BEEN QUOTE/UNQUOTE SETTLED WITH THIS AGREEMENT. AND SO IT CAME TO ME IN THE POSTURE OF MOTION BY MS. WASHINGTON FRANKLIN THEN FOR SETTLEMENT.

AND, ULTIMATELY, I BECAME VERY FRUSTRATED WITH MS. JONES' RESPONSE OR FAILURE TO RESPOND, MORE APPROPRIATELY, TO SUBPOENAS TO PRODUCE DOCUMENT. I MEAN, SHE JUST PRESENTED HERSELF AS A MYSTERY WOMAN, A WOMAN WITH MEANS BUT NO EVIDENCE OF THOSE MEANS. AND SO MS. WASHINGTON FRANKLIN – AND I AM SURE YOU KNOW IF YOU HAVE READ THE TRANSCRIPTS FROM PRIOR HEARINGS, SHE ASKED ME TO ENLIST THE FBI INVOLVED IN THE CASE AND SHE WANTED ME TO DO ALL SORTS OF THINGS TO FIND THIS MONEY. AND I SAID, WHY DON'T YOU DO THAT? WELL, I CAN'T DO IT.

SO I DID SOME LIMITED RESEARCH AND DETERMINED THAT THE WAY FOR A PLAINTIFF TO FIND A JUDGMENT/DEBTOR'S ASSETS WAS TO HAVE A JUDGMENT. AND SO, YOU KNOW, IN HINDSIGHT ONE MIGHT SAY THAT WAS A BIT RASH ON MY PART. I SAID, IF YOU ARE GOING TO KEEP COMING HERE AND TELLING ME, PUT THIS DEFENDANT AT THE DC JAIL FOR A WEEK TO SEE IF THAT WOULD MOTIVATE HER TO BRING THESE DOCUMENTS THAT WE REQUESTED, TO LITTLE AVAIL, SO YOU ARE GOING TO KEEP COMING BACK HERE ASKING ME TO DO INVESTIGATIONS TO FIND THE MONEY, LET ME GIVE YOU THE TOOL TO DO IT.

AND SO WE CHANGED THE SETTLEMENT INTO A JUDGMENT. AND TOOK IT UP TO THE COURT OF APPEALS AND THE COURT OF APPEALS SAID, WELL, EKANS, YOU MISSED A STEP. YOU HAVE GOT TO FIRST FIND THAT THERE WAS A REASON, A BASIS FOR JONES TO PAY FRANKLIN A FEE. DID SHE EVER COME INTO THE POSSESSION OF THE MONEY? WELL, THESE PEOPLE APPARENTLY DID SOMETHING THEY SHOULD HAVE DONE A DECADE AGO. **WELL, YOU KNOW, FRANKLIN HAS ENGINEERED THIS WHOLE THING, WHERE IS THE PROOF OF A SETTLEMENT?** AND NOW, AFTER ALL OF THIS TIME, SOMEBODY COMES UP WITH A RECORD FROM THE COURT DOWN IN – WHERE IS IT DOWN IN FLORIDA?

COMMENT AND ANALYSIS: *THE PROOF OF A SETTLEMENT IS IN THE SWORN TESTIMONY OF BRIANNA JONES BEFORE BOTH JUDGE STARR AND JUDGE EKANS.*

THE PROOF OF A SETTLEMENT IS ALSO IN THE FINDINGS OF D.C. BAR COUNSEL, THE DISCIPLINARY ARM OF THE D.C COURT OF APPEALS, OF WHICH EKANS HAD BEEN INFORMED DURING COURT HEARINGS AND WAS FULLY AWARE OF THESE FINDINGS. HOWEVER, WHEN A D.C. COURT JUDGE IS COMMITTED TO FRAUD, THEFT AND CORRUPTION AND NOT THE RULE OF LAW, HE CHERRY PICKS CRITICAL EVIDENCE, FACTS AND TESTIMONY THAT HE WILL BE GUIDED AND RESTRAINED BY, OR IN KEEPING WITH THE REQUIREMENTS OF THE CRIMINAL ENTERPRISE UNDERWAY, HE WILL SIMPLY IGNORE.

CONSISTENT WITH HIS PROMINENT AND CRITICAL ROLE AS A KEY JUDICIAL CO-CONSPIRATOR, EKANS COULD CARE LESS ABOUT THE FINDINGS OF THE D.C. BAR COUNSEL BECAUSE HE KNEW THAT THE CURRENT POLICY, PRACTICE AND CULTURE OF THE D.C. COURT SYSTEM PROTECTED HIM FROM EVER HAVING TO ACCOUNT TO ANYONE FOR HIS JUDICIAL MISCONDUCT IN ANY DEGREE. THE UNSPOKEN RULE AMONG D.C. COURT JUDGES IS THAT NO D.C. COURT JUDGE WILL EVER REPORT ON THE MISCONDUCT OF ANOTHER JUDGE, NO MATTER HOW EGREGIOUS OR CRIMINAL IN NATURE THE JUDGE'S CONDUCT. JUDICIAL ETHICS MUST TIE ITS HANDS BEHIND ITS BACK, AND THEN TAKE A BACK SEAT DURING ALL COURT PROCEEDINGS.

THE ODYSSEY OF JUDICIAL CORRUPTION

D.C. COURT JUDGES ARE THE LAW AND THUS, ABOVE THE LAW.

I, ON THE OTHER HAND, HAD SPENT A LIFETIME PLAYING BY THE RULES, SERVING IN EVERY RESPECT AS A LAW-ABIDING CITIZEN. MOREOVER, I HAD BEEN A DISTINGUISHED AND PROMINENT MEMBER OF THE NEW YORK BAR AND DISTRICT OF COLUMBIA BAR FOR 35 YEARS WHEN I FIRST APPEARED IN EKANS' COURTROOM ON JANUARY 21, 2011.

THIS BROADBRUSH OF MY PROFESSIONAL BACKGROUND AS A TRIAL ATTORNEY DIDN'T MEAN A HILL OF BEANS TO EKANS. HE, ALONG WITH HIS JUDICIAL CO-CONSPIRATOR COLLEAGUES SAW ME AS NO MORE THAN A BLACK FEMALE SLAVE STANDING BEFORE THE COURT AND AT THE COUNSEL TABLE TO BE STRIPPED, ROBBED, RIPPED AND RAPED OF THE MILLIONS OF DOLLARS OWED TO ME AS A RESULT OF THE CONTINGENCY FEE AGREEMENT WITH THE CLIENT AND THE SETTLEMENT OF THE $100 MILLION LAWSUIT THAT I HAD CRAFTED AND FILED AND THAT HAD SETTLED IN 1996/1997 FOR $34 MILLION AS VERIFIED BY THE COURT RECORD, SPECIFICALLY THE SWORN TESTIMONY OF BRIANNA JONES AND THE FINDINGS OF THE OFFICE OF D.C. BAR COUNSEL.

HOWEVER, WHEN YOU ARE UNDER THE JURISDICTION OF A CORRUPT JUDGE COMMITTED, NOT TO JUSTICE AND THE RULE OF LAW, BUT TO THE ONGOING CRIMINAL ENTERPRISE FROM WHICH HE WILL BE HANDSOMELY AND FINANCIALLY COMPENSATED AND REWARDED FOR HIS KEY ROLE AS THE PRESIDING JUDGE WHO REPEATEDLY ABUSED HIS POWER OF ABSOLUTE JUDICIAL DISCRETION TO RIG MY CASE FOR ITS ULTIMATE DISMISSAL IN JANUARY 2015, THE COURT ENGAGES IN CASE ADJUDICATION AS A "KANGAROO COURT" AND ANY SEMBLANCE OF JUSTICE, TRUTH AND FAIR PLAY WILL BE NECESSARILY STOMPED ON FOR THE FAR MORE SINISTER PURPOSE OF D.C. CO-CONSPIRATOR JUDGES FILLING THEIR POCKETS WITH STOLEN CASE SETTLEMENT PROCEEDS.

MR. DUNN: BROWARD COUNTY, FLORIDA, YOUR HONOR.

THE COURT: BROWARD COUNTY. VERY WEALTHY COUNTY, AS I RECALL. TOO BAD WE COULDN'T HAVE HAD THAT A FEW YEARS AGO.

COMMENT AND ANALYSIS: *A FEW YEARS AGO, JUDGE EKANS WAS TOO BUSY RIGGING MY CASE FOR ITS ULTIMATE DISMISSAL AND THE ULTIMATE RECEIPT OF HIS FAIR SHARE OF THE MILLIONS OF DOLLARS IN MY STOLEN ATTORNEY'S FEES PLANNED, EXECUTED AND ORCHESTRATED BY THE JUDICIAL AND FBI PARTICIPANTS IN THIS LEGENDARY CRIMINAL ENTERPRISE WHOSE MISSION ACCOMPLISHED WAS TO DEFRAUD ME OF AN ESTIMATED $50 MILLION IN ATTORNEY'S FEES.*   ***

***

THE COURT:	LET ME QUOTE THE LAST PARAGRAPH OF THE COURT – OF THE COURT OF APPEALS ORDER. IT READS, "WE REVERSE AND REMAND THE CASE TO THE TRIAL COURT FOR FURTHER FINDINGS ON WHETHER MS. JONES ACTUALLY POSSESSED OR HAD CONTROL OVER MONEY FROM THE RIDGEWAY SETTLEMENT."
	AND IT SAYS, "WE DO NOT FORECLOSE ANY REASONABLE INFERENCES OF POSSESSION OR CONTROL DERIVED FROM MS. JONES' TESTIMONY AND BEHAVIOR IN THE CASE."
	I THINK IN THE CIRSUMSTANCES THAT IT IS APPROPRIATE FOR ME TO AUTHORIZE THE SUBPOENA.
	ALL RIGHT. LET'S GET ANOTHER HEARING DATE. I GUESS IT COMES DOWN TO WHETHER YOU WANT TO DO IT IN DECEMBER OR JANUARY.
	COMMENT AND ANALYSIS: *THE D.C. COURT OF APPEALS ABDICATED ITS ROLE OF APPELLATE REVIEW WHEN IT REMAINED SILENT ON THE DOMINANT ISSUE IN MY LAWSUIT WHICH WAS THAT OF MASSIVE D.C. JUDICIAL AND FBI FRAUD, THEFT, CORRUPTION AND EXTORTION.*
	THE D.C. COURT OF APPEALS WAS AND IS LACKING IN CREDIBILITY AS AN IMPARTIAL JUDICIAL TRIBUNAL. ITS COMPLICITY IN THE MASSIVE FRAUD AND THEFT IS OBVIOUS.
MR. DUNN:	WELL, YOUR HONOR, I BELIEVE I CAN OBTAIN THE RECORDS QUICKLY. I WOULD LIKE AT LEAST 30 DAYS JUST TO MAKE SURE. AND THAT PUTS US REALLY INTO – ALMOST INTO CHRISTMAS AT THAT POINT.
THE COURT:	SO I THINK I HEAR JANUARY.
MR. DUNN:	IS THERE A PARTICULAR DATE BEST FOR THE COURT?
THE COURT:	I THINK DO WE HAVE –
THE LAW CLERK:	JANUARY 13TH, 14TH, 15TH OR 16TH.
THE COURT:	WHAT DAYS OF THE WEEK ARE THOSE, TUESDAY, WEDNESDAY, THURSDAY, FRIDAY?
THE LAW CLERK:	YES, SIR.

THE ODYSSEY OF JUDICIAL CORRUPTION

THE COURT:	SO CHOOSING TUESDAY, WEDNESDAY, THURSDAY OR FRIDAY. YOU WANT TO BE HEARD ON YOUR MOTION; I UNDERSTAND THAT. BUT IN THE MEANTIME, YOU WANT TO CONSULT YOUR CALENDAR.
MR. DUNN:	YOUR HONOR, I HAVE A --- I HAVE A COOPERATING DEFENDANT TESTIFYING IN FEDERAL COURT IN ALEXANDRIA THAT WEEK. I DON'T KNOW WHAT DAY, BUT I'M PRETTY SURE THE JUDGE DOESN'T SIT ON FRIDAY. SO IF YOU SET THIS MATTER FOR FRIDAY, THAT WORKS BEST FOR ME.
THE LAW CLERK:	JANUARY 16TH.
THE COURT:	ALL RIGHT. JANUARY 16TH.
THE LAW CLERK:	AT 10:00 A.M., YOUR HONOR.
THE COURT:	I THINK THAT BRINGS US TO YOUR MOTION.
MR. RAND:	YES, YOUR HONOR. I HAVE A COPY HERE, IF YOU HAVEN'T HAD AN OPPORTUNITY TO REVIEW ONE YET.
THE COURT:	WHAT DOES IT SAY?
MR. RAND:	IT IS SIMPLY A MOTION FOR LEAVE TO WITHDRAW BASED ON THE DEFENDANT'S WISH TO PROCEED PRO SE. AND AS YOU CAN SEE, DEFENDANT MS. JONES IS HERE AND IS ABLE TO ADDRESS QUESTIONS THAT YOUR HONOR MAY HAVE.
THE COURT:	WHY DO YOU WANT TO PROCEED PRO SE?
MS. JONES:	WELL, FIRST OF ALL, THERE IS DIFFICULTY – THIS HAS BEEN A TREMENDOUS EXPERIENCE. AND SO WITH REGARD TO THIS WHOLE – AS I SAID PREVIOUSLY THE VERY FIRST DAY IN THIS PROCEEDINGS, THAT THIS WAS A MASSIVE ---
THE COURT:	COULD YOU ADDRESS THIS MATTER OF REGARDING YOUR DESIRE TO HAVE COUNSEL, NOT HAVE COUNSEL.
MS. JONES:	IT COMES DOWN TO THE ISSUE OF – WITH REGARD TO FINANCES. AND SO, THAT IS THE REASON. MR. RAND HAS BEEN A WONDERFUL ADVOCATE. I JUST WANT TO MAKE SURE THAT IS CLEARLY UNDERSTOOD. II DO PLAN AT SOME POINT TO SEEK COUNSEL, AT SOME POINT.
THE COURT:	YOU KNOW, I MEAN, THERE IS REALLY NO – NO LEGAL REASON FOR ME TO DENY YOUR MOTION SO I GUESS I WILL HAVE TO GRANT IT. MY HEAD IS SPINNING TRYING TO THINK OF SOME LEGITIMATE BASIS FOR SAYING NO, BUT NOTHING OCCURS TO ME.

MR. RAND:	WELL, AS YOUR HONOR KNOWS, THERE IS A GENERAL REASON IN THE INTEREST OF JUSTICE. AND IF YOUR HONOR WOULD LIKE 30 DAYS TO CONSIDER THAT –
THE COURT:	WELL, I DON'T NEED TO CONSIDER. I KNOW THAT SHE HAS NOT DONE PARTICULARLY WELL WITHOUT COUNSEL IN THE CASE. BUT I ALSO KNOW THAT IN OUR LEGAL SYSTEM, PEOPLE HAVE THE RIGHT – CONSTITUTIONAL RIGHT TO REPRESENT THEMSELVES AND LAWYERS HAVE A RIGHT TO EXPECT TO BE PAID FOR THEIR SERVICES. IF WE WERE, YOU KNOW, LOOKING AT A TRIAL LETTING YOU OUT OF THE CASE WOULD UNDUE DELAY OR UNNECESSARY DELAY, I THINK THAT WOULD BE A GOOD REASON NOT TO LET YOU OUT OF THE CASE.

COMMENT AND ANALYSIS: *BRIANNA JONES AND I, BOTH PRO SE BEFORE JUDGE KATE STARR, REACHED AN AMICABLE SETTLEMENT WITH MINIMAL TIME AND CONFLICT. AND OF COURSE, WITHOUT THE POISONOUS SCOURGE OF D.C. JUDICIAL FRAUD, THEFT, CORRUPTION AND EXTORTION.*

THE COURT:	BUT HERE WHERE YOUR CLIENT HAS I THINK – I THINK I—THINK I AM RIGHT ABOUT THIS, WHERE SHE HAS STEADFASTLY MAINTAINED THAT SHE HAS NO IDEA WHAT THE SOURCE OF HER – THE SOURCE OTHER THAN MYSTERIOUS PEOPLE WHO GIVE FINANCIAL RESOURCES TO HER FROM TIME TO TIME – I MEAN, I DON'T THINK SHE HAS CHANGED THAT STORY FROM THE TIME THAT I FIRST SAW HER IN THIS COURTROOM.

IT SEEMS TO ME THAT NOW IT IS PROBABLY MUCH MORE IMPORTANT THAT MS. WASHINGTON FRANKLIN HAVE COUNSEL. ALTHOUGH THE COURT OF APPEALS DID SAY – AND I AM SURE YOU ARE AWARE THAT I SHOULD CONSIDER A JUDGMENT IN ANY EVENT FOR FINANCIAL BURDENS THAT MS. JONES CAUSED WASHINGTON FRANKLIN TRYING TO ENFORCE THE SETTLEMENT. BECAUSE THAT COULD GET SPUN AROUND ON ITS HEAD IF MR. DUNN'S THEORY OF WHAT HAPPENED HERE IS BORN OUT BY HIS EFFORTS.

COMMENT AND ANALYSIS: *AT NO TIME DID BRIANNA JONES TESTIFY THAT MYSTERIOUS PEOPLE GAVE HER FINANCIAL RESOURCES FROM TIME TO TIME. SO JUDGE EKANS OBVIOUSLY OBTAINED THIS INFORMATION FROM SOME OTHER SOURCES SUCH AS HIS CO-CONSPIRATOR COLLEAGUES.*

BRIANNA JONES DID, HOWEVER, TESTIFY THAT SHE WAS SUMMONED TO MEET PERIODICALLY WITH "OFFICIALS" IN VARIOUS HOTEL SUITES WITHIN THE WASHINGTON REGION, WHO JUDGE EKANS, DURING COURT PROCEEDINGS AND FOR SOME UNKNOWN REASON, CHOSE TO REFER TO AS ***PHANTOM PEOPLE.***

THE COURT:	SO IT CERTAINLY IS THE CASE WHERE I WOULD BENEFIT FROM HAVING THE PARTIES REPRESENTED. BUT I DON'T KNOW THAT I HAVE A SOLID BASIS IN LAW FOR DENYING YOUR MOTION. IT IS ALSO NOT CLEAR TO ME WHAT KEEPING YOU FOR ANOTHER 30 DAYS WOULD DO, OTHER THAN GIVE HER THE BENEFIT OF PRO BONO COUNSEL. I MEAN, THAT – I SUPPOSE IF YOU AND MS. JONES WORK SOME ARRANGEMENT OUT – I MEAN, SHE IS SITTING HERE SAYING THAT SHE INTENDS AT SOME POINT TO SEEK COUNSEL. I DON'T KNOW WHAT TO MAKE OF THAT. BUT, HONESTLY, I DON'T KNOW WHAT TO MAKE OF A LOT OF WHAT SHE SAYS. SO IF YOU WORK SOMETHING OUT AND YOU WANT TO COME BACK IN THE CASE, I WOULD WELCOME YOU BACK IN THE CASE.
	COMMENT AND ANALYSIS: JUDGE EKANS WOULD WELCOME RAND BACK INTO THE CASE BECAUSE HE HAD CONTRIBUTED TO RIGGING THE DISMISSAL OF MY CASE, AND IN SO DOING, HAD SERVED THE ULTIMATE GOAL OF THE D.C. JUDICIAL CRIMINAL ENTERPRISE TO DEFRAUD AND STRIP ME OF AN ESTIMATED $50 MILLION IN ATTORNEY'S FEES.
MR. RAND:	THANK YOU, YOUR HONOR.
THE COURT:	ALL RIGHT. WE HAVE GOT OUR MARCHING ORDERS AND OUR NEXT DAY. AND YOU HAVE GOT SUBPONAS THAT YOU WANT ME TO LOOK AT. ALL RIGHT. LET'S DO THAT.
MR. DUNN:	MAY I BRING THEM UP?
THE COURT:	YES. ALL RIGHT. I HAVE AUTHORIZED THESE SUBPOENAS.
MR. RAMSEY:	THANK YOU, YOUR HONOR.
THE COURT:	THE PARTIES ARE EXCUSED.
MR. DUNN:	THANK YOU, YOUR HONOR.
MR. RAND:	THANK YOU, YOUR HONOR.
THE COURT:	HAVE A GOOD DAY.

(PROCEEDINGS ADJOURNED.)

BARBARA WASHINGTON FRANKLIN

SUPERIOR COURT OF THE DISTRICT OF COLUMBIA
CIVIL DIVISION
WASHINGTON, D.C.

THE HONORABLE MATTHEW D. EKANS, ASSOCIATE JUDGE, PRESIDING

THE FOLLOWING ARE EXCERPTS OF THE OFFICIAL COURT TRANSCRIPT OF THE
JANUARY 16, 2015 COURT PROCEEDING
ANNOTATED BY THE AUTHOR'S PERTINENT COMMENTARY AND ANALYSIS

JANUARY 16, 2015

PROCEEDING

COMMENT AND ANALYSIS: #1 DURING MY LAST PRO FORMA HEARING BEFORE
EKANS ON JANUARY 16, 2015, SCHEDULED FOR THE PURPOSE OF ANNOUNCING
THE DECISION OF THE DC COURT OF APPEALS AND CONCLUDING THE CASE, I WAS
GREATLY DISAPPOINTED IN THE UNJUST OUTCOME OF MY LAWSUIT.

I KNEW ALL TOO WELL THAT THE DECISIONS OF BOTH EKANS AND DAEMON HAD
BEEN BASED, NOT ON THE FACTS, EVIDENCE AND CIRCUMSTANCES OF THE CASE
BUT RATHER ON THE REQUIREMENTS OF THE CRIMINAL ENTERPRISE THAT MY
CASE BE RIGGED THROUGH THE ABUSIVE AND CORRUPT EXERCISE OF ABSOLUTE
JUDICIAL DISCRETION BY THE PRESIDING JUDGE IN THE IMPORTANT DECISIONS
MADE DURING THE PENDENCY OF MY LAWSUIT.

I WOULD BE REMISS IF I DID NOT SAY THAT, BUT FOR MY GIFT OF FAITH IN THE
GOD OF THE UNIVERSE WHO, THROUGH HIS DIVINE SOVEREIGNTY, RULES AND
OVERRULES IN ALL OF THE AFFAIRS OF MEN AND WOMEN ON EARTH, AND DOES
SO WITHOUT EXCEPTION, I WOULD NOT HAVE BEEN ABLE TO MAINTAIN MY
SANITY AND UNYIELDING EXPECTATION THAT THE EXPOSURE AND PRESENTATION
OF MY STORY TO THE COURT OF PUBLIC OPINION THROUGH THE PUBLICATION
OF A JUDICIAL EXPOSE' WILL USHUR IN THE JUST, SOMEHOW, SOME WAY
IMPARTIAL, FAIR AND EQUAL JUSTICE THAT HAS FOR ALL THESE MANY YEARS
BEEN DENIED ME FOR NO OTHER REASON THAN THE EXTRAORDINARY
ECONOMIC ADVANTAGE AND UNJUST ENRICHMENT OF THOSE IN POSITIONS OF
POWER AND AUTHORITY, NAMELY THE UNAPOLIGETICALLY CORRUPT D.C. COURT
JUDGES AND FBI AGENTS.

THE ODYSSEY OF JUDICIAL CORRUPTION

AT THE END OF THE DAY, MY STORY AND UNVARNISHED TESTIMONY SET FORTH IN MY JUDICIAL EXPOSE' ENTITLED *THE ODYSSEY OF JUDICIAL CORRUPTION* IS THE STORY OF MODERN-DAY SLAVERY IN AMERICA THAT IS FLAGRANTLY PRACTICED IN THE D.C. COURT SYSTEM IN BROAD DAYLIGHT. SPECIFICALLY, IT IS THE STORY OF MY JUDICIAL AND FBI ENSLAVEMENT AS A BLACK FEMALE TRIAL ATTORNEY WHO ASSUMED THE GREAT RISK OF REPRESENTING, ON A CONTINGENCY FEE BASIS, A BLACK , HOMELESS AND EMOTIONALLY ILL BLACK FEMALE CLIENT, WHEN NO OTHER ATTORNEY WOULD TAKE SUCH RISK.

THEREAFTER, USING MY OWN LEGAL KNOWLEDGE, EXPERIENCE, CREATIVITY, FINANCIAL RESOURCES, TIME AND EXPENSE, I CRAFTED AND FILED A $100 MILLION LAWSUIT IN THE STATE OF FLORIDA WHICH REQUIRED THAT AS A WASHINGTON, D.C. ATTORNEY I TAKE THE NECESSARY STEPS TO BE ADMITTED TO PRACTICE LAW IN THE STATE OF FLORIDA FOR THE LIMITED PURPOSE OF REPRESENTING BRIANNA JONES. I WAS ALSO REQUIRED TO IDENTIFY AND RETAIN A FLORIDA LAW FIRM TO SPONSOR MY ADMISSION TO THE FLORIDA COURT, ALL OF WHICH WAS DONE AT MY EXPENSE AND FOR WHICH I WAS NEVER COMPENSATED IN ANY AMOUNT.

THE $100 MILLION LAWSUIT THAT I FILED WAS SETTLED BY THE CLIENT, BRIANNA JONES, FOR $34 MILLION WITH THE OPPOSING ESTATE ATTORNEYS WITH NO PAYMENT WHATSOEVER TO ME AS PLAINTIFF'S COUNSEL. THAT, BY ANY DEFINITION, IS ECONOMIC AND FINANCIAL ENSLAVEMENT, DESIGNED AND ORCHESTRATED BY A TEAM OF D.C. COURT JUDGES AND FBI AGENTS.

IN JULY 2014, THE D.C. COURT OF APPEALS, UNDER THE LEADERSHIP OF CHIEF JUDGE MYRON DAEMON, OVERTURNED THE $13.6 MILLION "PAPER" MONEY JUDGMENT THAT HAD BEEN ISSUED TO ME BY JUDGE MATTHEW EKANS, A KEY JUDICIAL CO-CONSPIRATOR IN THE CRIMINAL ENTERPRISE TO DEFRAUD ME OF AN ESTIMATED $50 MILLION IN ATTORNEY'S FEES. THE UNDERLYING APPEAL HAD BEEN FILED BY BRIANNA JONES IN 2011.

WHILE JUDGE DAEMON'S NAME WAS NOT INCLUDED IN THE LIST OF THE THREE APPELLATE JUDGES DECIDING THE CASE, THE CHIEF JUDGE HAD THE PRE-EMPTIVE POWER TO CHANGE THE FINAL DECISION OF THE JUDGES' ASSIGNED TO THE CASE. REPORTEDLY, THAT IS TRADITIONAL D.C. APPELLATE COURT PRACTICE. IT WAS CERTAINLY D.C. APPELLATE COURT PRACTICE IN MY CASE. IT WAS ALSO COLD-BLOODED APPELLATE COURT POLITICS WHEN MASSIVE FRAUD AND CORRUPTION PERMEATE AND DOMINATE THE ATMOSPHERE AND ENVIRONMENT OF THE COURTHOUSE, AND MORE SPECIFICALLY, ITS JUDGES' CHAMBERS AND COURTROOMS.

JUDGE DAEMON, AS CHIEF JUDGE OF THE D.C. COURT OF APPEALS, PLAYED A MAJOR ROLE IN THE MASSIVE FRAUD, THEFT, CORRUPTION AND EXTORTION CONSPIRACY AND CRIMINAL ENTERPRISE. HIS ROLE WAS COMPARABLE TO THAT OF THE MAJOR ROLE PLAYED BY JUDGE GEORGE SKINNER, CHIEF JUDGE OF THE D.C. SUPERIOR COURT. THE MAJOR DIFFERENCE IN THE CO-CONSPIRATOR ROLES PLAYED BY CHIEF JUDGES DAEMON AND SKINNER IS THAT DAEMON PLAYED HIS MAJOR CO-CONSPIRATOR ROLE BEHIND-THE-SCENES; WHILE SKINNER AUDACIOUSLY PLAYED HIS ROLE IN THE COURT HALLWAY, IN BROAD DAYLIGHT AND IN THE FACES OF ME AND BRIANNA JONES, THE FORMER CLIENT AND NOW DEFENDANT IN MY LAWSUIT.

CHIEF JUDGE SKINNER'S HUTZPAH CAME WITH NO APOLOGIES AND STRAIGHT OUT OF THE PLAYBOOK OF THE CLASSIC MOVIE, "THE GODFATHER," THE STORY OF A MAFIA FAMILY AND ITS RULE OF ITS NEW YORK EMPIRE.

SIGNIFICANTLY, WITHIN THE SAME DAY OF THE ISSUANCE OF THE JULY 2014 D.C. COURT OF APPEALS' OPINION IN MY CASE, MY KITCHEN HOME PHONE RANG AND JUDGE DAEMON'S FULL NAME, I.E., MYRON DAEMON, APPEARED ON THE TELEPHONE SCREEN. WHEN I ANSWERED, THE CALLER REMAINED SILENT. I INTERPRETED THIS STRANGE CALL TO HAVE BEEN MADE BY THE SLEUTH CO-CONSPIRATORS TO INFORM ME THAT JUDGE DAEMON HAD BEEN RESPONSIBLE FOR THE REVERSAL OF THE $13.6 MILLION "PAPER" MONEY JUDGMENT PREVIOUSLY ISSUED TO ME BY JUDGE EKANS.

I FURTHER INTERPRETED THE CALL TO MEAN THAT WHETHER DAEMON'S NAME APPEARED ON THE COURT JUDGMENT OR NOT, HE HAD WEIGHED IN ON THE FINAL DECISION. THE CRYPTIC CALL ALSO CONFIRMED MY BELIEF FROM THE MOMENT I STEPPED INTO JUDGE EKANS' COURTROOM IN JANUARY 2011 THAT MY CASE HAD BEEN RIGGED FOR DISMISSAL, AND FOR THE FRAUDULENT CONFISCATION OF MY ATTORNEY'S FEES FROM THE MOMENT MY CASE WAS TRANSFERRED FROM JUDGE KATE STARR TO THE DOCKET OF JUDGE MATTHEW EKANS.

A FURTHER CONFIRMATION THAT THE D.C. COURT OF APPEALS, STILL UNDER THE LEADERSHIP OF CHIEF JUDGE MYRON DAEMON, WAS A KEY D.C. JUDICIAL CO-CONSPIRATOR IN THE CRIMINAL ENTERPRISE, AND WAS THEREFORE, KNOWINGLY, INTENTIONALLY AND PURPOSEFULLY COMPLICIT IN THE D.C. JUDICIAL AND FBI FRAUD AND THEFT OF MY FEES WAS ITS OPINION ISSUED IN AUGUST 2017 IN RESPONSE TO AN APPEAL FILED BY THE SIMPSONS, FORMER LAW CLIENTS, AND NOW CURRENT CREDITORS OF BRIANNA JONES.

THE ODYSSEY OF JUDICIAL CORRUPTION

THE SIMPSONS, *ENCOURAGED* BY JUDGE EKANS IN OPEN COURT TO GO AFTER ME FOR REPAYMENT OF THEIR $50 THOUSAND LOAN MADE TO BRIANNA JONES, THEREAFTER, AND PURSUANT TO JUDGE EKANS' ADMONITION, SUED ME. THEIR SUIT WAS DISMISSED BY JUDGE RENNER, *A NON-CORRUPT D.C. COURT JUDGE,* BUT REVERSED ON APPEAL UNDER THE LEADERSHIP OF CHIEF JUDGE DAEMON, A KEY CO-CONSPIRATOR OF THE D.C. JUDICIAL CRIMINAL ENTERPRISE.

IN NOVEMBER 2016, AND IN RESPONSE TO THE SIMPSONS' APPEAL, I FILED AN EXHAUSTIVE BRIEF CONSISTING OF 174 PAGES, PLUS AN APPENDIX DETAILING THE EVIDENCE OF THE DOMINANT ISSUES OF D.C. JUDICIAL AND FBI FRAUD AND CORRUPTION. THE D.C. COURT OF APPEALS INVOKED THE CODE OF SILENCE AND DECIDED THE APPEAL JUST AS IF I HAD NEVER FILED A BRIEF. THE D.C. COURT OF APPEALS CONCLUDED ITS DECISION BY REMANDING THE CASE TO THE LOWER COURT FOR FURTHER PROCEEDINGS JUST AS IT HAD DONE IN THE APPEAL FILED BY BRIANNA JONES IN 2011.

IN FERUARY 2017, SIX MONTHS PRIOR TO THE ISSUANCE OF THE SECOND RELATED OPINION TO MY CASE, THE WASHINGTON POST NEWSPAPER REPORTED THAT CHIEF JUDGE MYRON DAEMON HAD STEPPED DOWN FROM HIS POSITION AS CHIEF JUDGE OF THE D.C. COURT OF APPEALS. HIS REASON FOR STEPPING DOWN WAS NOT REPORTED TO THE PUBLIC.

I BELIEVE THIS MOVE BY CHIEF JUDGE DAEMON NOW ALLOWED HIM TO CONTINUE TO WORK BEHIND THE SCENES AND ON BEHALF OF THE FBI AND D.C. JUDICIAL CO-CONSPIRATORS. THUS, THE SECOND APPELLATE OPINION THAT MADE ABSOLUTELY NO REFERENCE TO MY CASE'S DOMINANT ISSUES OF FBI AND D.C. JUDICIAL FRAUD, THEFT, CORRUPTION AND EXTORTION IS REFLECTIVE OF THE FACT THAT CHIEF JUDGE DAEMON AND ALL THE OTHER CORRUPT JUDGES ON BOTH COURTS ARE ACCUSTOMED TO EXERCISING *THEIR PLAYBOOK AND TRUMP CARD OF ABSOLUTE JUDICIAL DISCRETION* FROM A PERSPECTIVE OF WHAT IS POLITICALLY EXPEDIENT AND ECONOMICALLY BENEFICIAL TO THEM, THEIR FAMILIES, FRIENDS AND COLLEAGUES. IN OTHER WORDS, AS FAR AS THESE COURT JUDGES ARE CONCERNED, AND TO PARAPHRASE THE LATE TINA TURNER, "WHAT HAS JUSTICE GOT TO DO WITH IT?"

WHILE CHIEF JUDGE DAEMON'S NAME DOES NOT APPEAR ON THE JULY 2014 COURT OF APPEALS DECISION OVERTURNING THE $13.6 "PAPER" MONEY JUDGMENT, HIS HANDPRINTS AS CHIEF JUDGE ARE ALL OVER THE CONTENTS OF THE DECISION. MY FIRM BELIEF THAT CHIEF JUDGE DAEMON WAS A KEY PLAYER AND JUDICIAL CO-CONSPIRATOR IN THE HISTORIC CASE OF D.C. JUDICIAL FRAUD, THEFT, CORRUPTION AND EXTORTION IS SUPPORTED BY TWO INCIDENTS OF MY ON-THE-STREET-ENCOUNTERS WITH CHIEF JUDGE DAEMON.

BARBARA WASHINGTON FRANKLIN

SINCE MY OFFICE BUILDING WAS THE LAST STOP IN D.C. ON THE METRO BEFORE CROSSING INTO CHEVY CHASE, MARYLAND, I USUALLY TOOK THE METRO TO AND FROM THE COURTHOUSE WHEN I HAD TO ATTEND COURT HEARINGS, FILE NEW CASES, OR FILE VARIOUS PLEADINGS IN PENDING CASES. ONE DAY AFTER MY VISIT TO THE COURTHOUSE, AND WHILE WAITING ON THE STATION PLATFORM FOR MY TRAIN TO ARRIVE TO RETURN TO MY LAW OFFICE LOCATED IN THE CHEVY CHASE PAVILION, I CASUALLY TURNED TO MY LEFT AND THERE WALKING TOWARDS ME SOMEWHAT HURRIEDLY WAS CHIEF JUDGE DAEMON.

AS SOON AS THE JUDGE RECOGNIZED ME, HE QUICKLY TURNED AND WALKED IN THE OTHER DIRECTION SO QUICKLY HE ALMOST APPEARED TO BE RUNNING ON THE PLAFORM, HOWEVER CAUTIOUSLY. MY COMMON SENSE AND INTUITION TOLD ME DAEMON'S REACTION IN RESPONSE TO SEEING ME WAS EVIDENCE OF A GUILTY CONSCIENCE DUE TO HIS PARTICIPATION AS A KEY D.C. JUDICIAL CO-CONSPIRATOR IN THE MASSIVE D.C. JUDICIAL CONSPIRACY AND CRIMINAL ENTERPRISE TO DEFRAUD ME OF MY ATTORNEY'S FEES.

THE SECOND INCIDENT OF A FACE-TO-FACE ENCOUNTER WITH THE D.C. COURT OF APPEALS CHIEF JUDGE OCCURRED IN FRONT OF THE COURTHOUSE OF D.C. SUPERIOR COURT. I WAS APPROACHING THE BUILDING IN ORDER TO ENTER. SURPRISINGLY, STANDING ON THE SIDEWALK WITH ANOTHER PERSON WAS CHIEF JUDGE DAEMON. WHEN HE SAW ME CROSSING THE STREET AND WALKING IN HIS DIRECTION, HE BEGAN TO JUMP UP AND DOWN AS IF HE WERE ON A TRAMPOLINE. HE APPEARED TO BE TRYING TO GET AS FAR AWAY FROM ME AS HE COULD, WHILE KEEPING HIS EYES FIXED ON ME IN A GLARING, AND EVEN FREAKED-OUT FASHION.

I, ON THE OTHER HAND, CALMLY CONTINUED TO WALK PAST HIM ON MY WAY TO THE ENTRANCE OF THE COURTHOUSE LOCATED ON INDIANA AVENUE, N.W. IN DOWNTOWN WASHINGTON, D.C. AS I ENTERED THE COURTHOUSE AND HEADED TOWARDS THE CLERK'S OFFICE, I REMEMBER SAYING TO MYSELF, QUITE MATTER-OF-FACTLY, AND IN RESPONSE TO MY OBSERVATION OF DAEMON'S STRANGE BEHAVIOR, "HE'S CORRUPT."

IN JUNE 1995, MY HUSBAND AND I RECEIVED IN THE MAIL JUDGE DAEMON'S CORDIAL INVITATION TO ATTEND JUDGE DAEMON'S INVESTITURE AS ASSOCIATE JUDGE OF THE SUPERIOR COURT OF THE DISTRICT OF COLUMBIA ON THE FOURTEENTH OF JULY, NINETEEN HUNDRED AND NINETY-FIVE, AT HALF PAST FOUR O'CLOCK IN THE AFTERNOON, IN THE THIRD FLOOR ATRIUM OF THE H. CARL MOULTRIE 1 COURTHOUSE, 500 INDIANA AVENUE, NORTHWEST, WASHINGTON, D.C., RECEPTION IMMEDIATELY FOLLOWING.

THE ODYSSEY OF JUDICIAL CORRUPTION

I WOULD NEVER HAVE BELIEVED THAT NINETEEN YEARS LATER I WOULD UNEQUIVOCALLY INCLUDE JUDGE DAEMON IN THE PANTHEON OF D.C. JUDGES THAT KNOWINGLY AND WILLINGLY PARTICIPATED IN THE HISTORIC CRIMINAL ENTERPRISE THAT DEFRAUDED ME OF AN ESTIMATED $50 MILLION IN ATTORNEY'S FEES. IN JUNE 2014, I HAD BECOME TIRED OF WAITING ON THE D.C. COURT OF APPEALS TO RENDER A DECISION IN BRIANNA JONES' APPEAL SEEKING THE OVERTURN AND NULLIFICATION OF THE $13.6 MILLION "PAPER" MONEY JUDGMENT ISSUED TO ME BY JUDGE EKANS IN OCTOBER 2011.

ACCORDING TO MY NOTES RECORDED IN MY CASE FILES, ON MAY 5, 2014, I CONTACTED THE WASHINGTON POST'S ADVERTISING DEPARTMENT REGARDING MY INTEREST IN TAKING OUT AN ADVOCACY ADVERTISEMENT REGARDING WHAT I CONSIDERED TO BE THE D.C. COURT OF APPEALS' ABUSE OF POWER DEMONSTRATED IN THE EXCESSIVE AMOUNT OF TIME IN RENDERING AN OPINION IN THE JONES' APPEAL. OF COURSE, I CONSIDERED THE APPELLATE COURT'S DELAY INTENTIONAL AND PURPOSEFUL, AND PURSUANT TO ITS KEY ROLE IN THE CRIMINAL ENTERPRISE INVOLVING BOTH COURTS AND THEIR FRAUDULENT AND ILLEGAL CONFISCATION OF MY ATTORNEY'S FEES.

IN RESPONSE TO MY INQUIRY, THE WASHINGTON POST REQUESTED THAT I SUBMIT A CASE SUMMARY AND COPY OF MY PROPOSED ADVOCACY AD. MY AD WAS THEN REVEIWED AND CLEARED BY THE POST'S LEGAL DEPARTMENT FOR PUBLICATION IN ITS SUNDAY OUTLOOK SECTION.

AFTER REVIEWING THE PRICING OPTIONS FOR MY AD, I DECIDED NOT TO PURSUE THIS COURSE. THE VERY NEXT MONTH, JULY 2014, THE D.C. COURT OF APPEALS RENDERED ITS DECISION, OVERTURNING THE $13.6 MILLION "PAPER" MONEY JUDGMENT THAT HAD BEEN ISSUED TO ME BY JUDGE EKANS. I SHALL ALWAYS BELIEVE THAT THE D.C. COURT OF APPEALS WOULD NOT HAVE RENDERED ITS OPINION SO QUICKLY AFTER MY CONTACT WITH THE WASHINGTON POST HAD I NOT MADE INQUIRY OF THE POST REGARDING MY INTEREST IN RUNNING AN ADVOCACY AD IN THE NEWSPAPER REGARDING WHAT I CONSIDERED TO BE AN ABUSE OF JUDICIAL POWER BEING EXERCISED BY THE D.C. COURT OF APPEALS, GIVEN THE ONGOING CRIMINAL ENTERPRISE REGARDING THE D.C. JUDICIAL AND FBI THEFT OF MY ATTORNEY'S FEES.

COMMENT AND ANALYSIS: #1(a) FROM MY EARLIEST CHILDHOOD, I HAD HEARD AND BEEN TAUGHT THAT TRUTH HAS A FUNNY WAY OF SHOWING UP, AND IN SURPRISING WAYS. MY FATHER, ROBERT BENJAMIN WASHINGTON'S MEMORABLE EXPRSSION WAS "TRUTH CRUSHED TO THE GROUND SHALL RISE AGAIN." YOU WERE RIGHT DADDY.

NOTHING COULD HAVE BEEN MORE TRUTHFUL THAN EKANS' USE OF THE TERM "GADGETS" IN REFERRING TO THE JUDICIAL TOOLS HE WAS ABOUT TO USE IN HIS *RIGGED* ADJUDICATION OF MY LAWSUIT AND ITS ULTIMATE *RIGGED* DISMISSAL. ONE OF JUDGE EKANS' GADGETS WAS THE GADGET OF *JUDGMENT CREDITOR* THAT HE LABELED ME WITH IN ORDER TO PUT THE LEGAL RESPONSIBILITY OF FINDING THE ALLEGED STOLEN SETTLEMENT PROCEEDS ON ME. EKANS ALSO USED THE JUDGMENT CREDITOR LABEL AS JUSTIFICATION OF HIS ADAMANT REFUSAL OF MY REQUEST FOR AN INDEPENDENT INVESTIGATION OF THE WHEREABOUTS OF THE $34 MILLION IN SETTLEMENT PROCEEDS. AND LASTLY, EKANS USED THE JUDGMENT CREDITOR THEORY TO SUPPORT HIS *RIGGED* DISMISSAL OF MY LAWSUIT ON JANUARY 16, 2015.

MY ABILITY AND REASON FOR WISHING JUDGE EKANS A HAPPY NEW YEAR WAS TO REMIND MYSELF OF WHO I WAS AND WHOSE I WAS. I WAS A DAUGHTER OF THE GOD OF THE UNIVERSE. MORE IMPORTANTLY, I WAS A DAUGHTER OF THE KING OF KINGS AND LORD OF LORDS AND HIS HOLY SPIRIT DWELT INSIDE ME.

THIS HEARING WAS MERELY A STEP ALONG MY JOURNEY TO JUSTICE. JUDGE EKANS AND NO OTHER MAN OR WOMAN WOULD HAVE THE FINAL SAY AS I PROCEEDED TOWARD THE FULLNESS OF MY DESTINY AND GOD'S CALL ON MY LIFE. BASED ON THE LEVEL OF MY ANOINTING, I RESOLVED TO GO INTO THE ENEMY'S CAMP, I.E., THE D.C. COURT SYSTEM, AND TAKE BACK WHAT WAS STOLEN FROM ME AND MY FAMILY. TO NOT DO SO WOULD BE TO ABORT THE FULLFILLMENT OF GOD'S WILL, PLAN AND PURPOSE FOR MY LIFE.

I HAVE NEVER DOUBTED DURING ALL THESE MANY YEARS PAST THAT MY PURSUIT OF JUSTICE WOULD ONE DAY BE FULFILLED AND THAT RESTITUTION WOULD BE MADE TO ME IN THE FORM OF THE PAYMENT OF THE ATTORNEY'S FEES OWED TO ME SINCE DECEMBER 1996. THIS WAS A PROPHECY I LOOKED FORWARD TO MANIFESTING IN MY LIFE NO MATTER HOW INCREDIBLE IT MIGHT APPEAR TO THE WATCHING WORLD. I ACKNOWLEDGED THAT I WAS A WOMAN OF FAITH LIVING IN A FAITHLESS WORLD. WHILE I WAS BEING SPIRIT-LED, THE WORLD WAS TURNING UP-SIDE DOWN.

WHEN I FIRST APPEARED BEFORE JUDGE EKANS ON JANARY 21, 2011, HE INTENTIONALLY, PURPOSEFULLY AND WITH DEMONIC PREMEDITATION, LAUNCHED HIS CAMPAIGN TO CATAGORIZE AND DEFINE ME AS A *JUDGMENT CREDITOR.* AS THE CASE MOVED FORWARD, I ALSO FOUND IT NECESSARY TO ADJUST MY VISION TO BEGIN SEEING HIM AS *THE JUDICIAL GASLIGHTER THAT HE WAS* IN MORE THAN ONE INSTANCE DURING THE LITIGATION OF MY CASE WHICH I HAVE CITED ELSEWHERE IN THE CONTENTS OF THIS JUDICIAL EXPOSE'.

THE ODYSSEY OF JUDICIAL CORRUPTION

NO MATTER HOW MANY TIMES I POINTED OUT TO EKANS THAT **I WAS NOT A JUDGMENT CREDITOR**, HE SIMPLY IGNORED ME. HIS EGREGIOUS AND REPEATED ABUSE OF HIS *POWER OF ABSOLUTE JUDICIAL DISCRETION* COMBINED WITH THE ABSENCE OF ACCOUNTABILITY ALLOWED HIM TO DO SO.

EKANS WOULD NOW SHOCKINGLY CONCLUDE THE FINAL HEARING IN MY CASE BY STATING AT THE CLOSE OF THE HEARING THAT MY LAWSUIT HAD BEEN ASSIGNED TO HIM IN MY STATUS AS A *JUDGMENT CREDITOR*. THIS IS AN ILLUSTRATION OF THE EGREGIOUS AND UNCONSCIONABLE ABUSE OF ABSOLUTE JUDICIAL DISCRETION ON STEROIDS.

IN A WELL-KNOWN LITERARY CLASSIC, ONE OF THE CHARACTERS REMARKED THAT HE HAD THE POWER TO DEFINE. WHEN HE SAID SOMETHNG WAS SO, IT WAS SO. PERIOD. JUDGE EKANS MUST HAVE READ THIS LITERARY CLASSIC MORE THAN ONCE AND DECIDED HE WOULD ABUSE HIS POWER OVER AND OVER AGAIN IN THE ADJUDICATION OF MY CASE BY FALSELY DECLARING ME A *JUDGMENT CREDITOR* IN CONTRADICTION OF THE SPECIFIC FACTS AND IN THE FULFILLMENT OF HIS ROLE AS A KEY JUDICIAL CO-CONSPIRATOR IN THIS MASSIVE D.C. JUDICIAL CRIMINAL ENTERPRISE.

EKANS WOULD END MY CASE JUST AS HE HAD BEGUN IT 4 YEARS EARLIER BY FALSELY DECLARING THAT I WAS A *JUDGMENT CREDITOR* AND THERE WOULD BE NOTHING I COULD DO ABOUT IT. YEARS LATER, HE WOULD FIND OUT THAT HE WAS WAY OFF BASE ON THIS POINT. WHEN YOU ARE ENGAGED IN JUDICIAL CORRUPTION, IT BLINDS AND BLURS YOUR VISION TO THE TRUTH OF A SITUATION. AND EKANS WAS CLEARLY ALL-IN FOR PURPOSES OF THE D.C. JUDICIAL CRIMINAL ENTERPRISE THAT STRIPPED ME OF THE MILLIONS OF DOLLARS OWED TO ME IN ATTORNEY'S FEES RESULTING FROM THE SETTLEMENT OF THE $100 MILLION LAWSUIT I HAD CRAFTED AND FILED ON BEHALF OF BRIANNA JONES IN MAY 1996.

JUDGE EKANS HAD ESTABLISHED THAT HE WAS ABOVE THE LAW AND SO WERE THE REST OF HIS D.C. JUDICIAL CO-CONSPIRATOR COLLEAGUES. WHILE I MAINTAINED MY COMPOSURE FOR THE DURATION OF THE HEARING AND CONDUCTED MYSELF, AS ALWAYS, PROFESSIONALLY, RESPECTFULLY AND CONFIDENTLY, I NEVERTHELESS REGARDED MYSELF AS BEING REPEATEDLY ABUSED BY A KANGAROO PRESIDING COURT JUDGE WHOSE EGREGIOUS JUDICIAL MISCONDUCT WAS SUPPORTED BY OTHER KANGAROO D.C. COURT JUDGES.

WHILE EKANS SAW HIS READING OF THE RIGGED MANDATE OF THE D.C. COURT OF APPEALS AS THE END OF MY STORY AND THE CONCLUSION OF MY PURSUIT OF JUSTICE SET FORTH IN MY LAWSUIT, I SAW IT AS JUST THE BEGINNING. IN DEALING WITH EKANS, THE HOLY SPIRIT WOULD PERIODICALLY REMIND ME THAT I WAS DEALING WITH A GODLESS MAN THAT FEARED NEITHER GOD NOR MAN, AND NEITHER DID HIS COMPLICIT D.C. JUDICIAL COLLEAGUES.

NEVERTHELESS, I COULD BE ASSURED THAT ONE DAY HE WOULD HAVE TO GIVE AN ACCOUNT FOR HIS CRIMINAL AND DEADLY PARTICIPATION IN THE HISTORIC CRIMINAL ENTERPRISE THAT STRIPPED ME OF MY FEES AND BEFORE THAT, CRIMINALLY PROSECUTED MY LATE HUSBAND, IN SUBSTANTIAL PART, DUE TO MY REFUSAL TO WITHDRAW MY LEGAL REPRESENTATION OF BRIANNA JONES AND, THEREAFTER, VOLUNTARILY FORFEIT MY ATTORNEY'S FEES.

NOTHING IS MORE INDICATIVE AND EVIDENT OF THE FRAUD, THEFT, CORRUPTION AND EXTORTION THAT DOMINATES THE D.C COURT SYSTEM THAN THE COMPLIMENTARY REFUSAL OF BOTH THE D.C. SUPERIOR COURT, REPRESENTED BY PRESIDING JUDGE EKANS AND THE D.C. COURT OF APPEALS, REPRESENTED BY CHIEF JUDGE DAEMON, IN PROHIBITING THE INTRODUCTION OF ANY AND ALL EVIDENCE AND TESTIMONY ON MY LAWSUIT'S DOMINANT ISSUES OF D.C. JUDICIAL FRAUD, THEFT, CORRUPTION AND EXTORTION.

PARAMOUNT IN MY ABILITY, UNDERGIRDED BY MY RESILIENCE, TO WITHSTAND THE TEAM OF POWERFUL, ALBEIT CORRUPT, D.C. COURT JUDGES AND FBI AGENTS WAS A MIND-SET THAT NEVER ALLOWED ME TO SEE OR RELATE TO THEM AS ALL POWERFUL. IN ADDITION, I KNEW THEY HAD THEIR LIMITS. THEY COULD NOT HARM ME BEYOND WHAT THE HOLY SPIRIT PERMITTED AND I LEANED ON THAT KNOWLEDGE. IN THIS REGARD,I HAD LEARNED MANY YEARS EARLIER THAT SATAN IS UNDER ORDERS, TOO. HE AND HIS DESIGNEES WOULD HAVE TO GET THE GREEN LIGHT FROM THE GOD OF THE UNIVERSE BEFORE THEY COULD HARM ME IN ANY WAY, AND THAT INCLUDED EKANS' FINAL AND RIGGED DISMISSAL OF MY LAWSUIT.

IF GOD ALLOWED EKANS TO DISMISS MY CASE, IT WAS BECAUSE HE HAD A PLAN AND THE DISMISSAL WOULD ONE DAY SOON SERVE HIS DIVINE PURPOSE AND MY ULTIMATE GOOD. ALL I HAD TO DO WAS TO TRUST GOD AND NOT BE MOVED BY WHAT I SAW, WHAT I HEARD OR WHAT I EXPERIENCED AT THE HANDS OF THE CORRUPT AND AMORAL D.C. COURT JUDGES. I WOULD REMEMBER MY BROTHER JOB AND AN ALL-ENCOMPASSING PEACE WOULD POSSESS MY SPIRIT, SOUL AND MIND.

THE ODYSSEY OF JUDICIAL CORRUPTION

AS I LEFT THE COURTHOUSE FOLLOWING THE DISMISSAL OF MY CASE, AND AS I MADE MY WAY TO THE PARKING GARAGE ON THAT BRIGHT, SUNNY, BUT COLD JANUARY MORNING, I ASKED THE LORD "WHAT SHOULD I DO?" EKANS HAD, WITH CERTAIN PREMEDITATED DEMON POMPOSITY, AND IN CONSULTATION WITH HIS CO-CONSPIRATOR COLLEAGUES, CORRUPTLY DISMISSED MY CASE.

UNDAUNTED, I WOULD RETURN HOME DISAPPOINTED, BUT NOT IN DESPAIR. DENIED, BUT NOT DISCOURAGED. DISMISSED, BUT NOT DESTROYED. FIVE DAYS LATER ON JANUARY 21, 2015, IN THE WEE HOURS OF THE MORNING, THE HOLY SPIRIT WOULD BRING TO ME A DREAM THAT REVEALED TO ME THAT I WOULD PREVAIL IN MY PURSUIT OF JUSTICE, IF I DID NOT GIVE UP, GIVE OUT OR GIVE IN. FOUR DAYS LATER, THE HOLY SPIRIT GAVE ME A SECOND DREAM WHOSE SYMBOLS REVEALED THAT I WOULD PREVAIL IN MY PURSUIT OF JUSTICE, AGAIN, IF I DID NOT GIVE UP, GIVE IN OR GIVE OUT.

THE HOLY SPIRIT ASSURED ME THAT BOTH DREAMS WERE PROPHETIC. EKANS' DISMISSAL WAS JUST A DIP IN MY PATHWAY TO VICTORY. GIVEN THESE TWO BACK-TO-BACK DREAMS WITHIN DAYS OF JUDGE EKANS' RIGGED DISMISSAL OF MY CASE, I WAS STRENGTHENED TO PREPARE AND FILE A MOTION FOR RECONSIDERATION OF EKANS' JUDGMENT OF DISMISSAL. THE MOTION CONSISTED OF A DETAILED DESCRIPTION OF THE COMPONENT PARTS OF THE MASSIVE D.C. JUDICIAL AND FBI FRAUD, THEFT, CORRUPTION AND EXTORTION CONSPIRACY AND CRIMINAL ENTERPRISE.

IT WAS MY INTENTION TO MAKE A DOCUMENTED RECORD OF THE CRIMINAL ENTERPRISE THAT HAD BEEN DESIGNED, ORCHESTRATED AND EXECUTED TO DEFRAUD ME OF THE ESTIMATED $50 MILLION OWED TO ME IN ATTORNEY'S FEES. THE MOTION FOR RECONSIDERATION WAS FILED IN MARCH 2015 AND THEREAFTER IN MARCH 2015, JUDGE EKANS ISSUED A *JUDGMENT OF DISMISSAL WITH PREJUDICE* WHICH MEANT I COULD NEVER BRING MY CASE BACK TO COURT AGAIN.

I WAS NOT AT ALL SURPRISED. NEVERTHELESS, I ASKED THE LORD, "WHAT SHOULD I DO? THE LORD ANSWERED "PURSUE." THE HOLY SPIRIT THEN BROUGHT TO MY REMEMBRANCE THE STORY OF DAVID UPON HIS RETURN HOME TO ZIKLAG (1 SAMUEL 30:8-15). HE FOUND HIS HOME AND VILLAGE COMPLETELY DESTROYED AND THE WOMEN AND CHILDREN ABDUCTED BY HIS ENEMIES. DISTRAUGHT AND NOT KNOWING WHAT TO DO, DAVID SOUGHT THE LORD. "AND DAVID INQUIRED OF THE LORD, SAYING, SHALL I PURSUE AFTER THIS TROOP? SHALL I OVERTAKE THEM? AND HE ANSWERED HIM, PURSUE: FOR THOU SHALT SURELY OVERTAKE THEM, AND WITHOUT FAIL RECOVER ALL." (1 SAMUEL 30:8-15 KJV)

REMEMBERING THAT STORY OF DAVID AND ZIKLAG, I, TOO, ASKED THE LORD "SHALL I PURSUE?" AND THE LORD ANSWERED ME AS HE HAD ANSWERED DAVID THOUSANDS OF YEARS AGO: "PURSUE AND YOU SHALL RECOVER ALL." AND SO IT WAS THAT BIBLICAL ADMONITION THAT I MEDITATED ON IN THE DAYS, WEEKS AND MONTHS FOLLOWING EKANS' RIGGED DISMISSAL OF MY LAWSUIT ON JANUARY 16, 2015.

SINCE EKANS DISMISSED MY CASE WITH PREJUDICE, HE HAD SEEN TO IT THAT I WAS FOREVER BARRED FROM SEEKING JUSTICE VIA THE COURT ROUTE. AND SO, I AGAIN INQUIRED OF THE LORD, "WHAT DO I DO? HOW DO I PURSUE?" THE ANSWER THAT ROSE FROM MY SPIRIT AND IN CONSTANT CONVERSATION WITH THE HOLY SPIRIT WAS THAT I WOULD TAKE MY CASE TO THE COURT OF PUBLIC OPINION FOR THE REDRESS OF THE JUSTICE THAT HAD BEEN DENIED ME BY A SYSTEMICALLY CORRUPT, DEMONICALLY INFLUENCED AND ABSOLUTELY AMORAL D.C. COURT SYSTEM.

AND HOW WOULD I DO THAT? I WOULD DO IT WITH MY WORDS, WITH MY GOD-GIVEN GIFT OF THE WRITING SKILLS OF A WORDSMITH, WITH MY KNOWLEDGE OF SCRIPTURE, WITH MY UNIQUE PERSONAL AND PROFESSIONAL BACKGROUND AND EXPERIENCE AND, MOST OF ALL, WITH THE HELP, POWER, STRATEGIES, IDEAS AND PARTNERSHIP WITH THE HOLY SPIRIT.

AND IT WAS THAT THINKING, PRAYER, MEDITATION, OUTLINING OF THE STORY OF THE MEMOIR AND EXPOSE', ORGANIZING AND FORMATING OF SO, SO MANY COURT TRANSCRIPTS, FILE NOTES, COURT DOCUMENTS AND DAILY PRAYER JOURNAL ENTRIES THAT COMPRISED THE JOURNEY THAT LED TO THE FINAL CRAFTING AND COMPOSITION OF THE SPIRITUAL MEMOIR AND JUDICIAL EXPOSE' THAT YOU NOW HOLD IN YOUR HAND.

THE COURT:	GOOD MORNING.
	LET ME GET ALL MY GADGETS GOING HERE.
THE CLERK:	YOUR HONOR, BEFORE THE COURT FOR HEARING IN THE MATTER OF BARBARA WASHINGTON FRANKLIN VERSUS BRIANNA JONES AND OTHERS, CASE NUMBER 2009 CA 4417.
	WILL COUNSEL AND PARTIES PLEASE STEP FORWARD TO COUNSEL TABLE AND STATE YOUR NAMES FOR THE RECORD.
MS. WASHINGTON-FRANKLIN:	GOOD MORNING, YOUR HONOR. BARBARA WASHINGTON FRANKLIN, YOUR HONOR. HAPPY NEW YEAR, YOUR HONOR.
THE COURT:	HAPPY NEW YEAR.

MS. WASHINGTON FRANKLIN:	PRO SE AGAIN.
MR. KEVIN DUNN:	GOOD MORNING, YOUR HONOR. MAY IT PLEASE THE COURT, KEVIN DUNN FOR THE INTERVENOR PLAINTIFFS, DONALD AND DORETHA SIMPSON, AND THEY'RE HERE WITH ME IN COURT TODAY.

COMMENT AND ANALYSIS: #2 THE SIMPSONS WERE THE CREDITORS OF BRIANNA JONES. BECAUSE I HAD ASSISTED IN THE ARRANGEMENTS OF LOANS MADE TO BRIANNA JONES, THEY WERE NOW PURSUING ME FOR REPAYMENT OF THE LOANS MADE TO JONES AND USED EXCLUSIVELY BY AND FOR JONES.

THE COURT:	GOOD MORNING.
MS. SIMPSON:	GOOD MORNING, YOUR HONOR.
THE COURT:	GOOD MORNING. YOU CAN FEEL FREE TO KEEP YOUR SEATS THROUGHOUT THIS HEARING.
THE COURT:	JUST A BRIEF HISTORY. THE COURT OF APPEALS ISSUED ITS MANDATE IN THIS CASE ON THE 20TH OF OCTOBER, 2014, ENTERED ON THE DOCKET HERE IN THE SUPERIOR COURT ON THE 22ND OF OCTOBER, 2014. THE MEMORANDUM OPINION AND ORDER OF JUDGMENT CONCLUDES BY SAYING, AND I'M QUOTING, WE REVERSE AND REMAND THE CASE TO THE TRIAL COURT FOR FURTHER FINDINGS ON WHETHER MS. JONES ACTUALLY POSSESSED OR HAD CONTROL OVER MONEY FROM THE RIDGEWAY SETTLEMENT. WE DO NOT FORECLOSE ANY REASONABLE INFERENCES OF POSSESSION OR CONTROL DERIVED FROM MS. JONES' TESTIMONY AND BEHAVIOR IN THIS CASE, AND IF THE TRIAL COURT SO FINDS, IT MAY ENTER A JUDGMENT AGAINST HER IN SUCH AMOUNT AS IT DEEMS APPROPRIATE. ADDITIONALLY, THE TRIAL COURT MAY WISH TO CONSIDER WHETHER IT WOULD BE APPROPRIATE TO ENTER A JUDGMENT IN AN AMOUNT PROPORTIONAL TO THE COSTS OF MS. JONES' FAILURE TO PROVIDE MS. WASHINGTON FRANKLIN WITH HER FINANCIAL RECORD, ITSELF A BREACH OF THE 2010 SETTLEMENT AGREEMENT. AND IT CONCLUDES WITH, SO ORDERED.

COMMENT AND ANALYSIS: #3 NOTHING IS MORE UNCONSCIONABLE OR MORE EVIDENT OF THE DEPTH AND BREADTH OF THE FRAUD, THEFT, CORRUPTION AND EXTORTION THAT DOMINATED THE D.C. COURT SYSTEM THAN THE SCHEME AND PLAN JUDGE EKANS AND HIS CORRUPT COMRADES ON THE D.C. COURT OF APPEALS CAME UP WITH IN ORDER TO EXECUTE THE MISSION OF THEIR HISTORIC CRIMINAL ENTERPRISE TO DEFRAUD ME OF THE MILLIONS OF DOLLARS OWED TO ME IN ATTORNEYS' FEES.

THEIR PLAN WAS NOT CREATIVE, NOR WAS IT COMPLEX NOR COMPLICATED. JUDGE EKANS' EGREGIOUS ABUSE OF HIS ABSOLUTE JUDICIAL DISCRETION FUELED BY HIS WANTON DEMONIC POMPOSITY, ALLOWED HIM TO RULE IN ANY WAY HE CARED TO, IRRESPECTIVE OF THE LAW, FACTS, CIRCUMSTANCES AND EVIDENCE IN MY CASE.

JUDGE EKANS ADAMANTLY PROHIBITED ANY AND ALL EVIDENCE AND TESTIMONY ADDRESSING MY LAWSUIT'S DOMINANT ISSUES OF D.C JUDICIAL AND FBI FRAUD, THEFT, CORRUPTION AND EXTORTION IN THE IDES OF MARCH 18, 2011 COURT HEARING. JUDGE EKANS ALSO ANNOUNCED A CONTRIVED COURT RECESS, WITHOUT FEAR OF ADMONITION OR PUNISHMENT, OPENLY AND WITH CONSPIRATORIAL PREMEDITATION, AIDED AND ABETTED FORMER CHIEF JUDGE GEORGE SKINNER IN THE INTIMIDATION OF BRIANNA JONES THROUGH SKINNER'S COURT HALLWAY CONFRONTATION, SHAKE DOWN AND INTIMIDATION OF BRIANNA JONES. I STOOD AND PERSONALLY WITNESSED THE JUDICIAL OBSTRUCTION OF JUSTICE BEING COMMITTED BY TWO D.C. COURT JUDGES IN BROAD DAYLIGHT. IN DOING SO, JUDGE EKANS COMMITTED PREMEDITATED OBSTRUCTION OF JUSTICE IN HIS POSITION AS A SITTING D.C. COURT JUDGE SWORN TO UPHOLD THE LAW AND CONSTITUTION AND TO ADJUDICATE CASES FAIRLY AND IMPARTIALLY. HOWEVER, NEITHER COURT JUDGE HAD TO ACCOUNT TO ANYONE FOR THEIR OUTRAGEOUS JUDICIAL MISCONDUCT THAT WAS IN ALL WAYS UNCONSCIONABLE AND CRIMINAL.

THE D.C. COURT OF APPEALS UNCONSCIONABLY ABDICATED ITS SPECIFIC ROLE OF APPELLATE REVIEW AND ITS LEADERSHIP ROLE AS AN APPELLATE TRIBUNAL IN COURT ADJUDICATION WHEN IT FOLLOWED IN JUDGE EKANS' FRAUDULENT FOOTSTEPS AND REMAINED SILENT ON MY LAWSUIT'S DOMINANT ISSUES OF D.C. JUDICIAL AND FBI FRAUD, THEFT, CORRUPTION AND EXTORTION.

THE ODYSSEY OF JUDICIAL CORRUPTION

WHEN CORRUPT D.C. COURT JUDGES ARE STEEPED IN MASSIVE FRAUD, THEFT, CORRUPTION AND EXTORTION, IT IS BECAUSE THEY HAVE PERFORMED THEIR DUE DILIGENCE, SURVEILED THE SOCIETAL, CULTURAL AND POLITICAL LANDSCAPE AND THEREAFTER, CONCLUDED THAT THEY ARE ABOVE ACCOUNTABILITY, ABOVE ADMONITION, ABOVE DISCIPLINE, ABOVE PENALTY, AND MOST ASSUREDLY ABOVE INDICTMENT, PROSECUTION, CONVICTION, HOUSE ARREST AND INCARCERATION.

THIS SET OF CIRCUMSTANCES LEAVES THESE ROGUE, RUTHLESS AND MYSOGYNISTIC D.C. COURT JUDGES FREE TO SIT AND WAIT ONCE-IN-A-JUDICIAL-LIFETIME FOR A CASE SUCH AS MINE TO COME ALONG, WHICH THEY EVALUATE AS A SLAM-DUNK SUCCESSFUL CRIMINAL ENTERPRISE THAT IS GUARANTEED TO ENRICH THE D.C. JUDICIAL AND FBI CO-CONSPIRATORS WITH THE SWINDLE OF AN ESTIMATED $50 MILLION IN ATTORNEY'S FEES THAT WERE MINE AND EARNED BY ME FROM MY LEGAL REPRESENTATION OF BRIANNA JONES.

THE COURT:

NOW UPON RECEIVING THAT JUDGMENT AND MANDATE FROM THE COURT OF APPEALS, WE SCHEDULED A STATUS HEARING IN THIS MATTER, AND THERE WAS AN APPEARANCE ENTERED IN THIS CASE ON BEHALF OF ATTORNEY BARBARA WASHINGTON FRANKLIN BY THE LAW FIRM OF MARTY BEN JASON, A LAWYER BY THE NAME OF PAUL RAMSEY, R-A-M-S-E-Y. PRIOR TO THE HEARING, THE SCHEDULED STATUS HEARING, THE ATTORNEY THAT PURSUED THIS MATTER ON APPEAL FOR MS. JONES, MR. SIMEON RAND, R-A-N-D, MOVED TO WITHDRAW HIS APPEARANCE. AND ON THE 18TH OF NOVEMBER, 2014, DONALD AND DORETHA SIMPSON, BY COUNSEL, FILED A RULE 24 MOTION TO INTERVENE, WITH A CLAIM OF FRAUD, MISREPRESENTATION AND BREACH OF CONTRACT AGAINST BARBARA WASHINGTON FRANKLIN.

WE CONDUCTED A STATUS HEARING ON THE 19TH OF NOVEMBER, AND AT THAT TIME DIRECTED THAT THE PARTIES SHOULD GATHER WHATEVER EVIDENCE THEY COULD GATHER TO PRESENT TO THIS COURT IN ACCORDANCE WITH THIS ORDER FROM THE D.C. COURT OF APPEALS THAT THE COURT DETERMINE FACTUALLY WHETHER MS. JONES ACTUALLY POSSESSED OR HAD CONTROL OVER MONEY FROM THE RIDGEWAY SETTLEMENT.

COMMENT AND ANALYSIS: #4 NOTHING WAS DASTARDLIER DEMONIC OR PATENTLY PATHETIC THAN THE CORE DIRECTIVE OF THE APPELLATE MANDATE DELIVERED TO EKANS AND EKANS' REPEATED RECITATION OF THE DIRECTIVE THROUGHOUT THE FINAL HEARING, TO WIT: **"DETERMINE FACTUALLY WHETHER MS. JONES ACTUALLY POSSESSED OR HAD CONTROL OVER MONEY FROM THE RIDGEWAY SETTLEMENT."**

BUT MORE IMPORTANTLY, THE APPELLATE MANDATE WAS AN ILLUSTRATION OF THE ABUSE OF ABSOLUTE DISCRETION EXERCISED BY THE D.C. COURT OF APPEALS AND THEREAFTER EXERCISED BY EKANS AS PRESIDING JUDGE.

POSSESSION OF THE SETTLEMENT PROCEEDS BY BRIANNA JONES WAS NEVER AN ISSUE IN THE CASE. AND BOTH CORRUPT COURTS KNEW IT. THEY JUST CHOSE TO USE THIS REASONING TO STRIP ME OF MY FEES IN ORDER TO FILL THEIR POCKETS WITH STOLEN CASE SETTLEMENT PROCEEDS. THE STELLAR SUCCESS OF THE CRIMINAL ENTERPRISE ENGAGED IN BY BOTH THE TRIAL COURT AND THE APPELLATE COURT WAS ENABLED BY JUDGE EKANS' PREMEDITATED REFUSAL TO ADDRESS MY LAWSUIT'S DOMINANT ISSUES OF FRAUD, THEFT, CORRUPTION AND EXTORTION AND THE PREMEDITATED AND UNCONSCIONABLE SILENCE OF THE COURT OF APPEALS REGARDING THOSE ISSUES.

WHETHER BRIANNA JONES EVER ACTUALLY HAD CONTROL OR POSSESSED MONEY FROM THE RIDGEWAY ESTATE WAS A *NON-SEQUITUR*. MOREOVER, IT WAS SIMPLY THE DECEPITON PRESIDING JUDGE EKANS AND CHIEF JUDGE DAEMON USED TO STRIP ME OF THE ATTORNEY'S FEES BRIANNA JONES OWED ME.

BRIANNA JONES WAS UNDER JUDGE KATE STARR'S ORDER TO PRODUCE BANK OF AMERICA BANK STATEMENTS WHICH JUDGE EKANS CAREFULLY AVOIDED IN KEEPING WITH HIS OBLIGATIONS AS A CO-CONSPIRATOR OF THE D.C. JUDICIAL AND FBI CRIMINAL ENTERPRISE.

THE COURT: THE COURT ALSO ISSUED AN ORAL RULING GRANTING MR. RAND'S MOTION TO WITHDRAW AS COUNSEL FOR MS. JONES, EVEN THOUGH I BELIEVE THAT ATTORNEY SAID TO ME AT THE TIME -- -- IT DOESN'T APPEAR IN THE DOCKET ENTRY   BUT I BELIEVE THAT ATTORNEY SAID TO ME AT THE TIME THAT, EVEN THOUGH HE WAS FORMALLY WITHDRAWING -- -- HE MADE NO DEFINITE COMMITMENT - -- BUT I THINK HE SAID HE MIGHT SEE IF HE COULD BE OF SOME ASSISTANCE TO MS. JONES, IN FINDING WHATEVER DOCUMENTATION SHE NEEDED.

ON THE 20TH OF NOVEMBER THERE WAS AN AMENDED COMPLAINT FILED BY THE WOULD-BE INTERVENORS. AND THEN ON THE 16TH OF DECEMBER ATTORNEY BARBARA WASHINGTON FRANKLIN FILED HER RESPONSE TO THE MOTION TO INTERVENE. AND, TO CONCLUDE, THE PAPERS THAT HAVE BEEN FILED SINCE THE STATUS HEARING IN NOVEMBER, ON THE 6TH OF JANUARY THE WOULD-BE INTERVENORS FILED A REPLY, AND IT'S CAPTIONED, TO NEW MATTER IN THE FRANKLIN OPPOSITION.

COMMENT AND ANALYSIS: #5 *IN MY RESPONSE TO THE MOTION TO INTERVENE FILED BY THE SIMPSONS, CREDITORS OF BRIANNA JONES, I DETAILED THE COMPONENT PARTS OF THE CRIMINAL ENTERPRISE TO DEFRAUD ME OF MY ATTORNEY'S FEES. I IDENTIFIED BY NAME SPECIFIC D.C. COURT JUDGES WHO HAD PLAYED KEY CRIMINAL ROLES IN THE D.C. JUDICIAL ENTERPRISE TO DEFRAUD ME OF AN ESTIMATED $50 MILLION IN ATTORNEY'S FEES. THEREAFTER, UNEXPRESSED FURY DIRECTED AT ME BY JUDGE EKANS DURING THE REMAINING COURT HEARINGS WAS CLEAR AND DISCERNABLE, ENOUGH SO THAT EVEN RAY CHARLES COULD HAVE SEEN IT.*

THE COURT: OH, I DON'T WANT TO OVERLOOK THIS. THERE IS THIS LAST PAPER FILED ON THE 8TH OF JANUARY OF THIS YEAR, PRAECIPE TO WITHDRAW APPEARANCE OF MARTY BEN JASON AND PAUL RAMSEY, ON BEHALF OF PLAINTIFF, BARABARA WASHINGTON FRANKLIN. THAT WAS FILED WITH A SIGNATURE THAT IS ASSERTED TO BE WASHINGTON FRANKLIN'S SIGNATURE, CONSENTING TO WITHDRAWAL, AND I SEE THAT THE ATTORNEYS AREN'T HERE TODAY. BUT I CONCLUDE FROM THEIR FAILURE TO BE HERE THAT THEY MADE AN ASSUMPTION THAT THE COURT WOULD GRANT THAT MOTION.

COMMENT AND ANALYSIS: #6 ONCE MY ATTORNEYS RECOGNIZED THE DEPTH AND EXTENT OF THE D.C. JUDICIAL AND FBI CRIMINAL ENTERPRISE THAT CIRCUMSCRIBED MY LAWSUIT, THEY REQUESTED, AND I GRANTED, MY CONSENT TO THEIR WITHDRAWAL

THE COURT: SO THAT'S THE HISTORICAL RECORD SINCE THE STATUS HEARING, AND I THINK I SHOULD BEGIN WITH ATTORNEY WASHINGTON FRANKLIN. IF YOU HAVE EVIDENCE THAT YOU INTEND TO PRESENT TODAY TO ALLOW THE COURT TO MAKE THESE FACTUAL FINDINGS, THIS WOULD BE THE TIME TO PRESENT IT.

MS. WASHINGTON FRANKLIN: YOUR HONOR, I'M NOT SURE FACTUAL FINDINGS WITH REGARD TO THE MOTION TO INTERVENE?

THE COURT:	I THINK THAT THE FIRST ORDER OF BUSINESS IS TO COMPLY WITH THE COURT OF APPEALS MANDATE; THAT IS, FOR ME TO DETERMINE WHETHER OR NOT THERE ARE FACTS THAT WOULD ALLOW -- ---
MS. WASHINGTON FRANKLIN:	OH, OKAY, YOUR HONOR.
THE COURT:	TO BE CLEAR, THE COURT OF APPEALS REVERSED THE JUDGMENT THAT I HAD ENTERED IN YOUR FAVOR.
MS. WASHINGTON FRANKLIN:	THAT IS CORRECT.
THE COURT:	THAT'S NO LONGER ON THE TABLE.
MS. WASHINGTON FRANKLIN:	I UNDERSTAND YOUR HONOR.

COMMENT AND ANALYSIS: #7 THIS WAS AT LEAST THE 3RD OR 4TH TIME THAT EKANS STATED THAT THE MONEY JUDGMENT HAD BEEN OVERTURNED. WHAT EKANS DIDN'T UNDERSTAND WAS THAT I NEVER SAW THE MONEY JUDGMENT AS NO MORE THAN A PIECE OF PAPER OR RATHER ONE OF THE "GADGETS" THAT HE HAD USED TO DEFRAUD ME OF MY ATTORNEY'S FEES. FROM THE VERY FIRST HEARING ON JANUARY 21, 2011, I HAD SEEN JUDGE EKANS AS THE KEY JUDICIAL CO-CONSPIRATOR THAT HE WAS AND THAT HE WOULD REMAIN FOR THE DURATION OF THE COURT ADJUDICATION OF MY LAWSUIT. I SAW EKANS FOR WHO HE ACTUALLY WAS AND NOT WHO HE WAS PRETENDING TO BE. HIS ENDURING GASLIGHTING OF ME HAD NOT WORKED AND NEVER WOULD.

THE COURT:	SO WHERE WE ARE NOW, THE COURT OF APPEALS HAS DIRECTED ME TO DETERMINE FROM FACTS AND REASONABLE INFERENCES TO BE DRAWN FROM THE FACTS WHETHER ANY MONEY EVER CAME INTO THE POSSESSION AND CONTROL OF MS. JONES, WHO IS WALKING IN THE COURTROOM NOW, IN HER TYPICAL FASHION; LATE.

COMMENT AND ANALSIS: #8 THIS WAS MERELY A STATEMENT OF THE TRICK AND DECEPTION THE TWO D.C. COURTS HAD COME UP WITH TO ENRICH THE CO-CONSPIRATORS WITH THE STOLEN SETTLEMENT PROCEEDS, INCLUDING THE ESTIMATED $50 MILLION IN ATTORNEY'S FEES OWED TO ME, WITHOUT FEARING PROSECUTION, PENALTY, PUNISHMENT OR INCARCERATION WHERE WARRANTED.

THEY RELIED ON THE FACT THAT THEY WERE EXEMPT FROM EXPOSURE BY CAMERS IN THE COURTROOM, MEDIA INVESTIGATION OF ANY KIND AND LAST BUT LEAST, THE PUBLICATION OF A JUDICIAL EXPOSE' BY AN AGGRIEVED AND VICTIMIZED PARTY SUCH AS THE AUTHOR.

MS. WASHINGTON FRANKLIN: YOUR HONOR, IN RESPONSE TO THE COURT'S INQUIRY, I HAD COUNSEL TO DO JUST AS THE COURT OF APPEALS HAD INDICATED WITH REGARD TO SEARCHING FOR ASSETS. I DID NOT RETAIN THEM TO ENGAGE IN LITIGATION ON MY BEHALF. SO WE AGREED, ONCE THEY HAD MADE THEIR SEARCH AND MADE THEIR INVESTIGATION, THEY WERE NOT ABLE TO IDENTIFY ASSETS IN THE DEFENDANT'S NAME. AND ONCE THEY LEARNED AT THAT HEARING -- -- BECAUSE I WAS NOT PRESENT   THAT IN FACT THERE WAS GOING TO BE LITIGATION IN TERMS OF THIS RULE 24 MOTION FILED BY THE INTERVENORS, THEN WE AGREED THAT I WOULD PICK UP THE CASE AGAIN FOR PURPOSES OF LITIGATION.

COMMENT AND ANALYSIS: #9 HERE I LOOKED INTO THE FACE OF JUDGE EKANS, A KEY CO-CONSPIRATOR OF THE HISTORIC D.C. JUDICIAL AND FBI CRIMINAL ENTERPRISE, AND SAID IN MY OWN WORDS, "I KNOW YOU STOLE MY MONEY, BUT I'M NOT THROUGH WITH YOU AND THE CALVARY OF CORRUPT D.C. COURT JUDGES. WITH HELP OF THE HOLY SPIRIT, I SHALL YET PREVAIL, ACHIEVE VICTORY, RESTITUTION, VINDICATION AND PROMOTION."

THE COURT: I SEE.

MS. WASHINGTON FRANKLIN: SO I HAVE RETAINED COUNSEL, THEY HAVE SPENT SUBSTANTIAL SUMS, AND AT THIS JUNCTURE I'M NOT SAYING WHAT THE FUTURE HOLDS, BUT AT THIS JUNCTURE THE LAW FIRM THAT I RETAINED WAS NOT ABLE TO IDENTIFY ASSETS.

THE COURT: AND THAT'S WHERE WE ARE?

MS. WASHINGTON FRANKLIN: THAT'S THE LONG AND SHORT OF IT; YES.

THE COURT: THEN I THINK THAT IT'S CLEAR THE BURDEN WAS ON THE PLAINTIFF TO IDENTIFY ASSETS, IF SHE'S ABLE TO DO SO. AND THAT BEING THE CASE, I THINK THAT WE, IN COMPLIANCE WITH THIS DIRECTIVE FROM THE COURT'S MANDATE, MUST CONCLUDE THAT THERE IS NO BASIS FOR THE COURT TO ENFORCE THE SETTLEMENT AGREEMENT, BECAUSE THERE WAS NOT A TRIGGER FOR THE ATTORNEY FEE TO BECOME DUE AND PAYABLE.

COMMENT AND ANALYSIS: #10 I HAVE ALWAYS KNOWN THAT THE D.C. COURT ACTION AGAINST ME WAS NOT THE FINAL ACTION IN MY JOURNEY AND PURSUIT OF JUSTICE. AND IF THIS MEANT I WOULD HAVE TO FIND A WAY TO SHARE MY STORY WITH THE WORLD, THEN SHARE MY STORY I WOULD DO.

MS. WASHINGTON-FRANKLIN: WELL, YOUR HONOR, IT WOULD BE REMISS ON MY PART TO NOT, AT THIS TIME AND AT THIS HEARING, INDICATE THAT ------ AND I'VE DISCUSSED THIS AT LENGTH WITH MY ATTORNEYS ----- **THE COURT OF APPEALS VERY CAREFULLY SIDE-STEPPED THE WHOLE ISSUE OF FRAUD IN THIS CASE.**

THIS CASE, IF NO ONE ELSE IS PREPARED TO SAY IT   BECAUSE I KNOW AT SOME POINT IN THE FUTURE I'M GOING TO BE VINDICATED WITH REGARD TO MY POSITION   THIS CASE HAS BEEN, FROM THE VERY BEGINNING, CIRCUMSCRIBED BY FRAUD. SYSTEMIC, BROAD AND WIDE FRAUD. SO WHEN MY ATTORNEYS GOT BACK TO ME TO ADVISE ME THAT THEY WERE NOT ABLE TO IDENTIFY ASSETS, I HAD ALREADY WARNED THEM. I SAID, IF YOU'RE NOT PREPARED TO VIEW THIS CASE AND TO GO FORWARD AND LOOK AT ALL OF THE FACTS THROUGH A LENS OF FRAUD AND CORRUPTION, YOU CAN JUST STOP, BECAUSE YOU'RE WASTING MONEY AND YOU'RE WASTING TIME. SO THAT'S MY POSITION. I DON'T KNOW WHAT ELSE TO ADD TO IT, BECAUSE IT'S SO VERY CLEAR TO ME. AND AS YOUR HONOR KNOWS, THE DEFENDANT MADE REPEATED STATEMENTS WITH REGARD TO HER EXPERIENCES. I'VE HAD MY OWN EXPERIENCES.

COMMENT AND ANALYSIS: #11 *IN AS LADYLIKE FASHION AS POSSIBLE, I LOOKED EKANS IN THE FACE AND SAID THAT ALTHOUGH MY CASE WAS ABOUT DEEP, WIDE AND SYSTEMIC FRAUD, YOU, AS A COURT JUDGE, CHOSE TO ALIGN YOURSELF WITH THE THIEVES AND THUGS WHO LEFT NO STONES UNTURNED IN STRIPPING ME OF MY FEES.*

MS. WASHINGTON FRANKLIN: I WENT INTO SOME VERY SPECIFIC DETAIL IN THIS COURT RECORD. WHY? BECAUSE AFTER REVIEWING THE WHOLE RECORD, AND ESPECIALLY SINCE I HAD RETAINED NEW COUNSEL, I NEEDED TO HAVE A FRESH LOOK AT ALL THE FACTS. AND MY DECISION WAS I COULD NOT BE AT PEACE WITH MYSELF UNLESS I MADE SOME KIND OF RECORD, TO COMPLETE THE RECORD IN THIS COURT, BECAUSE YOUR HONOR HAS NEVER HAD ALL THE FACTS. YOUR HONOR HAS HAD A SCINTILLA OF INFORMATION. BECAUSE WE SETTLED. AS YOUR HONOR KNOWS, YOU SETTLE A CASE, AND THAT SHUTS DOWN ALL THE EVIDENCE COMING IN.

COMMENT AND ANALYSIS: #12 I WAS DETERMINED TO LET EKANS KNOW THAT I WAS NOT AFRAID OF HIM OR HIS CORRUPT COLLEAGUES. NOR HAD HE AND HIS CO-CONSPIRATORS EXTINGUISHED MY RESOLVE TO PURSUE JUSTICE AND THE RESTITUTION OF MY ATTORNEY'S FEES, NO MATTER HOW LONG IT TOOK.

MS. WASHINGTON FRANKLIN: AND I UNDERSTAND WHY YOUR HONOR HAS ALWAYS MANAGED TO MOVE VERY CAREFULLY AND CAUTIOUSLY, BECAUSE YOUR HONOR DID NOT HAVE CERTAIN BASIC INFORMATION. HOWEVER, NOW THAT WE'RE AT THIS JUNCTURE, I CAN LIVE WITH THE FACT THAT I HAVE DOCUMENTED FOR THIS COURT, WHETHER THIS COURT   AND I'M NOT JUST TALKING ABOUT YOUR HONOR; I'M TALKING ABOUT D.C. SUPERIOR COURT AT LARGE -- -- EVER ADDRESSES THE ISSUE OF FRAUD. *I AM SATISFIED WITH THE FACT THAT I HAVE DONE MORE THAN MY SHARE IN TERMS OF DOCUMENTING FOR THIS COURT THAT THERE WAS AND IS AND STILL IS, VERY DEEP, WIDE AND SYSTEMIC FRAUD THAT COMPLETELY CIRCUMSCRIBES THIS CASE.*

COMMENT AND ANALYSIS: #13 I WAS CAREFULLY, BUT POINTEDLY LETTING EKANS KNOW THAT WE BOTH KNEW THAT GIVEN THE FACTS, EVIDENCE AND CIRCUMSTANCES OF MY CASE, SPECIFICALLY REGARDING MILLIONS OF DOLLARS IN SETTLEMENT PROCEEDS, INCLUDING ATTORNEY'S FEES, ALLEGEDLY MISSING, AT A MINIMUM, AN INDEPENDENT INVESTIGATION WOULD HAVE BEEN AN APPROPRIATE, IF NOT MANDATORY, REMEDY, BUT FOR THE RAGING D.C. JUDICIAL AND FBI CRIMINAL ENTERPRISE UNDERWAY.

MS. WASHINGTON FRANKLIN: AND SO I'M NOT PREPARED TO   I MEAN, I'VE DONE MY DUE DILIGENCE. MY ATTORNEYS DID THEIR DUE DILIGENCE. BUT AS I SAID, I WARNED THEM, AND THEY SAID TO ME, BARBARA, YOU WARNED US. YOU CANNOT GO OUT AND PROCEED IN TERMS OF IDENTIFYING ASSETS AS YOU WOULD A NORMAL CASE. THERE'S NOTHING NORMAL ABOUT THIS. IT'S NEVER BEEN NORMAL. AND SO, EVEN IN TERMS OF THEIR RESPONSIBILITY TO COLLECT, THEY WERE ACCUSTOMED TO TAKING CERTAIN STEPS, AND HIRED A BIG INVESTIGATIVE FIRM. BUT IT'S FRAUD. **AND WHEN YOU HAVE FRAUD, YOU'RE NOT SUPPOSED TO BE ABLE TO FIND ASSETS.**

BARBARA WASHINGTON FRANKLIN

COMMENT AND ANALYSIS: **#14** I WOULD NEVER ALLOW CORRUPT AND AMORAL D.C. COURT JUDGES TO DENY ME THE JUSTICE I WAS ENTITLED TO DUE TO THEIR OWN GREED AND DETERMINATION TO, IN EFFECT, TREAT ME AS A SLAVE FOR PURPOSES OF THEIR OWN UNJUST PERSONAL ENRICHMENT. I KNEW SOONER OR LATER I WOULD BE FORCED TO TAKE MY CASE TO THE COURT OF PUBLIC OF OPINION. I JUST DIDN'T KNOW THAT THIS PART OF MY JOURNEY WOULD INCLUDE THE CRAFTING OF THIS LITERARY WORK.

MS. WASHINGTON FRANKLIN: I DON'T KNOW WHAT ELSE TO ADD, BUT, AS I SAID, I'M DISAPPOINTED ONLY BECAUSE I FEEL THAT JUST A BASIC KIND OF JUSTICE AND FAIRNESS TO ME WOULD AT LEAST   BECAUSE I'VE BEEN INVOLVED IN OTHER CASES, FAR LESS CIRCUMSTANCES, FAR LESS ASSETS, I MEAN MAYBE A COUPLE OF HUNDRED THOUSAND DOLLARS, AND THERE'S BEEN INVESTIGATION HERE AND INVESTIGATION THERE. IN THIS CASE? NOTHING. NOTHING.

COMMENT AND ANALYSIS: #15 THE CORRUPT AND AMORAL D.C. COURT SYSTEM HAD MADE VICTIMS OF US ALL.

AS I STOOD BEFORE EKANS, A MAJOR AND RUTHLESS ENEMY, I NEVERTHELESS RECOGNIZED THAT MY ABILITY TO STAND AGAINST THIS KNOWN ENEMY WAS DUE TO THE UNDAUNTING FAITH, BRILLIANCE, WISDOM AND RELENTLESS RESILIENCE I FELT COMING FROM MAMA, MOTHER AND DADDY, EVEN THOUGH THEY WERE ALL NOW ON THE OTHER SIDE.

MS. WASHINGTON FRANKLIN: BUT I AM COMMITTED TO GETTING JUSTICE, AND WHETHER IT'S IN THIS FORUM OR IN ANOTHER FORUM. BECAUSE ALL OF THE FOLKS INVOLVED IN THIS CASE HAVE NOT SPENT YEARS ON END AND SUBSTANTIAL FUNDS, INCLUDING THE INTERVENORS, AND I'M IN SYMPATHY WITH THE INTERVENORS, BECAUSE THE INTERVENORS ARE JUST ONE SET OF INDIVIDUALS WHO GENEROUSLY LOANED MONEY TO THE DEFENDANT, AND NOW THEY'RE OUT OF POCKET.

COMMENT AND ANALYSIS: #16 BUT IN LIVING WITH THE D.C. COURT SYSTEM'S PREMEDITATED REFUSAL TO ADDRESS MY LAWSUIT'S DOMINANT ISSUE OF FRAUD IN ORDER TO ROB ME, I WOULD NEVER GIVE UP MY PURSUIT OF JUSTICE TRANSLATED, IN PART, TO THE PAYMENT OF MY ATTORNEY'S FEES WITH INTEREST.

I WOULD JUST HAVE TO PURSUE JUSTICE OUTSIDE OF THE D.C. COURT SYSTEM, A SYSTEM SATURATED AND HAMSTRUNG BY JUDICIAL FRAUD, THEFT, CORRUPTION AND EXTORTION, AND FRAMED BY A CONTEXT, MOST IMPORTANT OF ALL, BY DEMON POMPOSITY.

MS. WASHINGTON FRANKLIN: THEY'RE NOT THE ONLY VICTIMS. I, TOO, AT A CERTAIN LEVEL, AM A VICTIM. AND SO ARE MANY, MANY OTHER INDIVIDUALS WHO CHOSE NOT TO COME INTO COURT AND BRING SUIT. BUT NEVERTHELESS, THEY'RE OUT OF POCKET ALSO OF SUBSTANTIAL SUMS.

COMMENT AND ANALYSIS: #17 GIVEN THE FACTS, EVIDENCE AND CIRCUMSTANCES OF MY CASE, IT WOULD TAKE A POMPOUS AND CONSCIENCE-FREE D.C. COURT JUDGE TO UTTER SUCH A STATEMENT. NEEDLESS TO SAY, EKANS PROVED OVER AND OVER AGAIN THAT HE WAS ALTOGETHER POMPOUS AND CONSCIENCE-FREE AND TRAFFICKED IN WHATEVER WAS WITHIN HIS POWER AND AUTHORITY TO GUARANTEE PROMOTION OF THE CRIMINAL ENTERPRISE OF WHICH HE WAS A MAJOR PLAYER.

MS. WASHINGTON FRANKLIN: BUT HERE AGAIN, WE HAVE THE ISSUE OF THE SETTLEMENT AGREEMENT. WHERE ARE THEY? WE HAVE THE ISSUE OF NO REFERENCE ON THE DOCKET IN FLORIDA WITH REGARD TO SETTLEMENT. AND IN REVIEWING THE FILE, I REALIZED THAT WHEN MR. WINSLOW, THE ESTATE'S ATTORNEY, FILED A REQUEST TO EXTEND THE FINAL ACCOUNTING TO, I THINK IT WAS, MARCH OF '98   I INCLUDED THAT AS AN EXHIBIT IN MY RESPONSE   HE WAS PERHAPS, OR HE COULD VERY WELL EXPLAIN THE FACT THAT HE DIDN'T REFERENCE SETTLEMENT, BECAUSE THE DEFENDANT'S CASE IN TERMS OF SETTLEMENT WAS-----------THE DEFENDANT, AFTER SETTLEMENT, BECAME A CREDITOR. AND, YOU KNOW, WHEN YOU FILE FOR THE FINAL ACCOUNTING OR YOU ASK FOR AN EXTENSION OF FINAL ACCOUNTING HE INDICATED ON THE FINAL ACCOUNTING THAT ALL CREDITORS HAD BEEN SATISFIED. SO THAT WOULD ALSO COVER THE DEFENDANT'S CASE AS WELL, BECAUSE SHE WAS A CREDITOR AND SHE HAD SETTLED THE CASE WITH THEM.

SO I'M JUST AT A POINT IN TIME WHERE I DON'T KNOW WHAT ELSE TO SAY. I REALLY DON'T. I DON'T KNOW WHAT ELSE TO SAY. BECAUSE, AS I SAID, **THERE HAS BEEN NO ATTENTION TO THE ISSUE OF FRAUD**. AND SO THEREFORE I FEEL I'VE NOT REALLY BEEN DEALT A FAIR HAND HERE, BECAUSE FRAUD IS THE BOTTOM LINE. IT'S ALWAYS BEEN THE BOTTOM LINE. BUT IF THE COURT IS NOT PREPARED OR WILLING TO ADRESS IT FOR WHATEVER REASON, THEN I'M GOING TO HAVE TO LIVE WITH IT.

COMMENT AND ANALYSIS: #18 EKANS AND THE COURT OF APPEALS HAD PUT THEIR HEADS TOGETHER AND COME UP WITH THE STRATEGY AND RATIONALE TO NULLIFY THE SETTLEMENT AGREEMENT BETWEEN ME AND BRIANNA JONES IN ORDER TO FULFILL THEIR RESPECTIVE ROLES AS CO-CONSPIRATORS, AND MORE IMPORTANTLY, TO COMPLETE THE MISSION OF THE CRIMINAL ENTERPRISE WHICH WAS TO DEFRAUD ME OF AN ESTIMATED $50 MILLION OWED TO ME IN ATTORNEY'S FEES.

THE COURT: VERY WELL.

MS. WASHINGTON FRANKLIN: THANK YOU, YOUR HONOR.

THE COURT: YOU'RE WELCOME.

I TRY TO MAKE A PRACTICE OF FOLLOWING THE LAW AND HAVING FAITH THAT, IF I DO THAT, WE'LL ENHANCE OUR LIKELIHOOD OF GETTING A FAIR AND JUST RESULT FOR LITIGANTS IN THIS COURT. ONE OF THE THINGS THAT WE'RE BOUND TO DO, I BELIEVE, IS NOT REACH BEYOND THOSE THINGS THAT ARE BEFORE US TO DECIDE.

SUBSTITUTE: **COMMENT AND ANALYSIS: #19** GIVEN THE FACTS, EVIDENCE AND CIRCUMSTNCES OR MY CASE, IT WOULD TAKE A POMPOUS AND CONSCIENCE-FREE D.C. COURT JUDGE TO UTTER SUCH A STATEMENT. NEEDLESS TO SAY, JUDGE EKANS PROVED OVER AND OVER AGAIN THAT HE WAS ALTOGETHER POMPOUS AND CONSCIENCE-FREE AND TRAFFICKED IN WHATEVER WAS WITHIN HIS POWER AND AUTHORITY TO GUARANTEE PROMOTION OF THE CRIMINAL ENTERPRISE OF WHICH HE WAS A MAJOR PLAYER.

THE COURT: THE MANDATE FROM THE COURT OF APPEALS, I READ WHAT I THINK IS THE OPERATIVE PORTION, BUT JUST SO THAT EVERYBODY IS ON THE SAME PAGE, LET ME READ ONE OTHER PARAGRAPH FROM THIS OPINION. AND I'M QUOTING.

THE COURT:

THE OPINION SAYS AS FOLLOWS: THIS LEAVES US TO CONSIDER A THIRD AND FINAL ARGUMENT MADE BY MS. JONES, AN ARGUMENT SHE ALSO MADE IN HER MOTION TO SET ASIDE THE JUDGMENT, THAT THE TRIAL COURT SHOULD NOT HAVE ENTERED A JUDGMENT AGAINST HER BECAUSE THE SETTLEMENT WITH MS. WASHINGTON FRANKLIN DID NOT ACTUALLY REQUIRE ACTION ON MS. JONES' PART UNLESS AND UNTIL SHE RECEIVED THE PROCEEDS OF THE RIDGEWAY SETTLEMENT. WE CONCLUDE THIS ARGUMENT CORRECTLY IDENTIFIES A DEFICIENCY IN THE TRIAL COURT'S ORDER.

COMMENT AND ANALYSIS: #20 JUDGE EKANS HAD THE JUDICIAL RESPONSIBILITY TO ENFORCE THE OCTOBER 18, 2010 COURT ORDER ISSUED BY JUDGE KATE STARR WHICH DIRECTED BRIANNA JONES TO PRODUCE BANK OF AMERICA BANK STATEMENTS OF THE SETTLEMENT PROCEEDS.

HOWEVER, CONSISTENT WITH HIS PARTICIPATION IN THE CRIMINAL ENTERPRISE, EKANS, WITH JUDICIAL PREMEDITATION, INTENTIONALLY AND PURPOSEFULLY REFUSED TO DO SO BECAUSE THE ENFORCEMENT OF JUDGE STARR'S ORDER WOULD HAVE GIVEN ME ACCESS TO THE SETTLEMENT PROCEEDS.

MY POSSESSION OF THE MILLIONS OF DOLLARS IN ATTORNEY'S FEES OWED TO ME WOULD HAVE PRECLUDED THE THEFT AND ILLEGAL CONFISCATION OF THE SETTLEMENT PROCEEDS BY THE D.C. JUDICIAL AND FBI TEAM OF CO-CONSPIRATORS AND DEPRIVED THEM OF THE UNJUST ENRICHMENT AT MY AND MY FAMILY'S EXPENSE.

THE COURT:

NOW, WHEN YOU PUT THAT PARAGRAPH WITH THE LAST PARAGRAPH THAT I READ EARLIER TODAY, IT'S VERY CLEAR THAT THE COURT OF APPEALS SAID THAT THE JUDGMENT THAT I ENTERED WAS IN ERROR. THEY REVERSED THAT. THEY SENT IT BACK TO SEE IF THE COURT COULD FIND ANY FACTS ON WHICH TO ENTER A JUDGMENT BASED ON THIS TRIGGERING MECHANISM IN THE SETTLEMENT AGREEMENT THAT MS. JONES ACTUALLY CAME INTO POSSESSION OR CONTROL OF SETTLEMENT FUNDS. THERE IS NO EVIDENCE THAT SHE DID.

SO I WILL ENTER THIS MATTER AS A JUDGMENT FOR THE DEFENDANT IN THIS CASE.

COMMENT AND ANALYSIS: #21 IN ENTERING JUDGMENT FOR BRIANNA JONES, EKANS HAD PERFORMED ANOTHER IMPORTANT FUNCTION IN HIS ROLE AS A KEY JUDICIAL CO-CONSPIRATOR. HE WAS CLEARLY SOLD OUT TO THE WORK OF THE ADVESARY IN THE EXECUTION AND ORCHESTRATION OF THE CRIMINAL ENTERPRISE.

THE COURT: NOW, THE OTHER QUESTION THAT THE COURT LEFT OPEN ON THIS REMAND WAS WHETHER OR NOT THE COURT SHOULD ENTER A JUDGMENT IN AN AMOUNT PROPORTIONAL TO THE COST OF MS. JONES' FAILURE TO PROVIDE WASHINGTON FRANKLIN WITH HER FINANCIAL RECORD, ITSELF A BREACH OF THE 2010 AGREEMENT.

I'LL LEAVE THIS RECORD OPEN FOR TEN DAYS. IF, ATTORNEY WASHINGTON FRANKLIN, YOU WISH TO PUT IN AN AFFIDAVIT OF COSTS TO YOU DURING THAT PERIOD OF TIME WHEN THE COURT WAS ATTEMPTING TO GET MS. JONES TO PRESENT HER FINANCIAL RECORDS, WHICH COULD HAVE PRESUMABLY LED TO A MUCH EARLIER RESOLUTION OF THIS MATTER THAN WHAT HAPPENED AFTER THE *COURT HELD A SERIES OF HEARINGS, ULTIMATELY SENDING MS. JONES TO JAIL FOR SOME PERIOD OF TIME, TO TRY TO GET HER TO PRODUCE FINANCIAL RECORDS.*

COMMENT AND ANALYSIS: #22 TO SAY THAT AS A COURT JUDGE, WITH A PANOPLY OF REMEDIES AND POWERS AT YOUR DISPOSAL, YOU WERE UNABLE TO HAVE A DEFENDANT COMPLY WITH A COURT ORDER IS TO INSULT MY INTELLIGENCE AND COMMON SENSE, AS WELL AS THAT OF THE AVERAGE AMERICAN CITIZEN. THIS IS HOW JUDGE EKANS' ABUSE OF ABSOLUTE JUDICIAL DISCRETION IN THE PREMEDITATED D. C. JUDICIAL FRAUD, THEFT, CORRUPTION AND EXTORTION PLAYED OUT IN MY CASE.

THE COURT: ANYWAY, WE'LL ENTER THE JUDGMENT AS A JUDGMENT IN FAVOR OF THE DEFENDANT ON THE LAWSUIT TO ENFORCE THE SETTLEMENT AGREEMENT. WE'LL LEAVE THE RECORD OPEN FOR TEN DAYS FOR ANY AFFIDAVIT THAT MS. WASHINGTON FRANKLIN WANTS TO FILE REGARDING THE COST TO HER OF THE EFFORT TO GET DISCOVERY IN WHAT SHOULD HAVE BEEN A FAIRLY ROUTINE ORAL EXAMINATION BUT TURNED INTO SOMETHING MUCH BROADER.

MS. WASHINGTON FRANKLIN, IF YOU FILE SUCH AN AFFIDAVIT, YOU SHOULD SERVE IT ON MS. JONES, AND I'LL GIVE MS. JONES A REASONABLE TIME, FIVE DAYS OR SO, TO RESPOND BEFORE MAKING A DECISION.

COMMENT AND ANALYSIS: #23. MY PRIME REASON FOR ATTENDING THE FINAL HEARING ON JANUARY 16, 2015 WAS TO PERMIT JUDGE EKANS TO SEE ME IN FULL BLOOM; TO SEE THAT NOTHING THAT HE AND HIS CO-CONSPIRATORS HAD DONE IN THE RIGGED ADJUDICATION OF MY LAWSUIT AND THE THEFT OF MY ATTORNEY'S FEES, NO DEMONIC DECISIONS THEY HAD MADE, NO JUDGMENTS THEY HAD ISSUED, NO ORDERS THEY HAD, WITH CONSIDERED PREMEDITATION, OVERTURNED HAD RATTLED ME, CRUSHED ME, DISCOURAGED ME, DESTROYED ME OR EXTINGUISHED MY RESOLVE TO FIGHT FOR JUSTICE AND THE EXPECTED RESTITUTION OF MY ATTORNEY'S FEES.

I WOULD NEVER GIVE UP MY PURSUIT OF JUSTICE AND FOR CERTAIN, I WOULD NOT TAKE MY STORY TO MY GRAVE. WHILE MY EARS HEARD THE COMMENTS OF JUDGE EKANS, MY MIND AND VISION WERE ON THE STEPS OF MY JOURNEY THAT WERE POST-RIGGED DISMISSAL OF MY CASE.   ***

THE COURT: SO WHAT WE HAVE IS A CASE THAT'S NOW CONCLUDED ON THE LACK OF EVIDENCE OF A SETTLEMENT THAT ACTUALLY PUT MONEY IN THE POSSESSION OR CONTROL OF MS. JONES, THE DEFENDANT IN THIS COMPLAINT, TO ENFORCE A SETTLEMENT AGREEMENT, BECAUSE THE COURT CONCLUDES THAT CASE IN HER FAVOR ON THE FACT THAT THERE'S NO PROOF THAT SHE EVER CAME INTO ANY MONEY. THERE'S NO BASIS FOR THE SIMPSONS TO INTERVENE IN THIS CASE TO TRY AND RECOVER LOSSES THEY SUSTAINED, REGRETTABLY SUSTAINED, THROUGH WHATEVER REPRESENTATIONS WERE MADE BY MS. WASHINGTON FRANKLIN TO THEM.

THAT DOESN'T SEEM TO BE DOUBTED THAT THEY ACTED ON REPRESENTATIONS THAT WASHINGTON FRANKLIN MADE, AND THERE DOESN'T SEEM TO BE ANY DOUBT THAT THOSE REPRESENTATIONS WERE MADE FOR THE BENEFIT, PERHAPS THE MUTUAL BENEFIT, BUT FOR A BENEFIT TO JONES. **ONE CAN ONLY WONDER WHY WASHINGTON FRANKLIN WAS NOT NAMED AS A DEFENDANT IN THE 2010 AND 2011 ACTION. IT CLEARLY WOULD HAVE BEEN AN EASIER PERSON TO ACHIEVE SERVICE ON.**

COMMENT AND ANALYSIS: #24 HERE EKANS, SEEING CLEARLY THAT ALL OF HIS UNETHICAL AND, EVEN CRIMINAL, ACTIONS TAKEN AGAINST ME HAD NOT IN ANY WAY DESTROYED ME OR THE FIGHT IN ME IN MY DETERMINATION TO PURSUE THE JUSTICE THAT HE AND HIS CORRUPT COLLEAGUES HAD STRIPPPED FROM ME, NOW TURNS TO THE WOULD-BE INTERVENORS IN THE CASE, CREDITORS OF BRIANNA JONES AND ENCOURAGES THEM TO GO AFTER ME FOR THE PAYMENT OF LOANS MADE TO BRIANNA JONES. THIS IS A CLASSIC CASE OF DEMON JUDICIAL POMPOSITY AND DISCRETION EXERCISED BY A CORRUPT D.C. COURT JUDGE SWORN TO UPHOLD THE RULE OF LAW AND THE CONSTITUTION.

IT IS ALSO A CLASSIC EXAMPLE OF A D.C. COURT JUDGE WHO CONSIDERS HIMSELF AS ABOVE THE LAW AND UNTOUCHABLE FOR HIS WICKED WAYS CARRIED OUT IN OPEN COURT. FURTHER, IT IS AN ILLUSTRATION OF A D.C. CORRUPT COURT JUDGE WHO NEVER IMAGINES THAT HIS BEHAVIOR, RECORDED IN OFFICIAL COURT TRANSCRIPTS, WILL EVER BECOME EXPOSED AND MADE PUBLIC.
SIGNIFICANTLY, HE IS PROTECTED BY THE ABSENCE OF CAMERAS IN THE COURTROOM.

THE COURT:	BUT AT ANY RATE, I THINK YOU UNDERSTAND WHAT I'M SAYING HERE. THERE'S NOT A LEGAL BASIS THAT I CAN SEE FOR THE COURT TO GRANT A MOTION TO INTERVENE IN THIS MATTER. THIS MATTER IS NOW CLOSED, EXCEPT FOR THIS LIMITED WINDOW OF OPPORTUNITY FOR WASHINGTON FRANKLIN TO SEE IF SHE CAN PERSUADE THE COURT TO ALLOW HER TO RECOVER A JUDGMENT FOR THE MONEY SHE SPENT TRYING TO GET MS. JONES TO COOPERATE WITH THE ORAL EXAMINATION.
	SO THE MOTION TO INTERVENE IS DENIED.
THE COURT:	I THINK THAT BRINGS US TO CONCLUSION OF THIS HEARING. IS THERE ANYTHING ELSE?
	MS. JONES.
MS. JONES:	YES. GOOD MORNING, YOUR HONOR. I'D LIKE TO SAY SOMETHING.
THE COURT:	THIS IS NOT AN OPPORTUNITY FOR -- -- --
MS. JONES:	I UNDERSTAND.

THE COURT:	DO YOU UNDERSTAND -- -- AND I SAW YOU NOD YOUR HEARD, SO I BELIEVE YOU DO THAT THE COURT HAS LEFT OPEN THE RECORD OF THIS MATTER FOR A LIMITED PURPOSE OF DETERMINING WHETHER IT SHOULD ENTER JUDGMENT AGAINST YOU FOR COSTS, ATTORNEY COSTS. AND, OF COURSE, SHE WAS ACTING AS HER OWN COUNSEL DURING THAT TIME, SO THAT'S AN ISSUE. BUT ACTUAL COSTS THAT SHE SUSTAINED IN TRYING TO GET YOU TO COOPERATE IN AN ORAL EXAMINATION, AND THAT, BECAUSE A PART OF THE SETTLEMENT SAID THAT YOU WOULD PAY COSTS IF SHE HAD TO INCUR COSTS TO GET TO YOUR FINANCIAL RECORDS. SO THAT'S THE ONLY THING THAT'S LEFT HERE. SO I AM NOT GOING TO GIVE YOU A FLOOR TO MAKE A SPEECH AFTER I'VE ENTERED JUDGMENT IN YOUR FAVOR.
MS. JONES:	**IT WAS JUST A COMMENT I WANTED TO MAKE WITH REGARD TO THE SETTLEMENT, OR THE ALLEGED SETTLEMENT.** I WANT TO JUST SAY THIS. MY REPUTATION HAS BEEN DEMEANED, DEFAMED. MY CHARACTER . THE PERSON, THE LATE WILLIE LEE RIDGEWAY, HE BRUTALLY RAPED ME IN THE SHADOWS, *THEREFORE, IF HIS REPRESENTATIVES, IT WAS NO SURPRISE TO ME, I WAS NOT TAKEN ABACK THAT HE WOULD NEGOTIATE WITH ME IN THE SHADOWS.*
THE COURT:	MS. JONES, DO YOU WANT TO TELL ME TODAY UNDER OATH THAT YOU DID RECEIVE MONEY?
MS. JONES:	I HAVE NOT RECEIVED ANY MONIES WHATSOEVER FROM THE ESTATE OF WILLIE LEE RIDGEWAY AND/OR HIS REPRESENTATIVES. I HAVE BEEN PROMISED.
	COMMENT AND ANALYSIS: #25 HERE JUDGE EKANS BECOMES FRANTIC AND TRIES TO HIDE IT. WHY? BECAUSE BRIANNA JONES HAS JUST ACKNOWLEDGED THE SETTLEMENT BETWEEN US. SHE HAS ALSO ACKNOWLEDGED THAT SHE NEGOTIATED A SETTLEMENT WITH THE WILLIE LEE RIDGEWAY ESTATE. SHE WAS REPRESENTED IN THE SETTLEMENT NEGOTIATIONS BY HER CLOSE FRIEND AND MENTOR, BETH HOLLISTER, THE ABC NEWS ANCHOR AND A KEY CO-CONSPIRATOR OF THE CRIMINAL ENTERPRISE, AND HOLLISTER'S ATTORNEYS.

JUDGE EKANS' SOLE ATTEMPT TO COVER UP AND SHUT DOWN JONES' TESTIMONY, WHICH UNEQUIVOCALLY ACKNOWLEDGES BOTH THE SETTLEMENT WITH ME AND THE SETTLEMENT WITH THE RIDGEWAY ESTATE IS TO ASK HER WHETHER SHE HAD EVER RECEIVED ANY MONEY.

BRIANNA'S ANSWER IS THAT WHILE SHE HAS NOT RECEIVED ANY MONEY, SHE HAS BEEN PROMISED (MONEY). EKANS' REHEARSAL OF WHAT THE COURT OF APPEALS SAID IS NOTHING MORE THAN A WEAK RETORT AND DOES NOTHING MORE THAN CONFIRM THE ONGOING CRIMINAL ENTERPRISE ENGAGED IN BY BOTH COURTS, WITH EKANS LEADING AS GRAND MARSHALL OF THE D.C. JUDICIAL CORRUPTION PARADE.

THE COURT: THAT'S WHAT THE COURT OF APPEALS SAID THAT THE ONLY THING -- -- THEY RECOGNIZED THAT YOU TOLD ME AT ONE TIME THAT YOU HAD A SETTLEMENT. THEY RECOGNIZED THAT ATTORNEY BARBARA WASHINGTON FRANKLIN SAID AT ONE TIME YOU HAD A SETTLEMENT.

MS. JONES: THAT IS CORRECT.

THE COURT: BUT THEY ALSO SAID THAT JUXTAPOSED AGAINST THAT TESTIMONY WAS OTHER TESTIMONY FROM YOU THAT YOU NEVER RECEIVED A DIME. THAT'S A QUOTE. YOU NEVER RECEIVED A DIME. SO UNLESS YOU'RE PREPARED TO TELL ME TODAY THAT YOU DID RECEIVE A DIME --

MS. JONES: NO, I'VE ALWAYS BEEN CONSISTENT WITH THE ABSOLUTE TRUTH.

AND ONE OTHER THING. I PROVIDED THE PLAINTIFF WITH A VAST POWER OF ATTORNEY, INCLUDING SOCIAL SECURITY NUMBERS, ALL THE NECESSARY TOOLS TO CONFIRM WHETHER OR NOT THE-- -- --

THE COURT: THAT'S CERTAINLY A PART OF MR. DUNN'S CONTENTIONS IN HIS COMPLAINT, IF THE COURT WERE GOING TO ENTERTAIN THAT. HE CERTAINLY HAS JUST A LOT OF EVIDENCE THAT HE COULD PROCEED ON, JUST NOT AS AN INTERVENTION IN THIS CASE. THIS CASE WAS FILED FOR A VERY LIMITED PURPOSE, AND THAT WAS A COMPLAINT THAT ASKED THE COURT TO ENFORCE WHAT BASICALLY WAS A CONTRACT BETWEEN MS. WASHINGTON FRANKLIN AND MS JONES.

THAT'S WHAT A SETTLEMENT IS. IT'S A CONTRACT. AND AS MS. WASHINGTON FRANKLIN SAID EARLIER THIS MORNING, THE COURT NEVER DECIDED ON EVIDENCE THAT JONES OWED FRANKLIN A COMMISSION OR A FEE, BECAUSE THEY SETTLED BEFORE THE COURT HELD A FACT-FINDING HEARING. THEY SETTLED. AND THAT WAS THE UNFORTUNATE CIRCMSTANCE IN WHICH THE CASE FELL TO ME. BECAUSE IT WAS DONE WHEN I TOOK OVER THIS CALENDAR, THE SETTLEMENT, THAT IS. IT WAS IN THE RECORD.

THE COURT: **AND SO WHAT CAME BEFORE ME WAS A FAIRLY ROUTINE FRIDAY AFTERNOON HEARING CALLED AN ORAL EXAMINATION, WHERE A "JUDGMENT CREDITOR" GETS TO PUT A "JUDGMENT DEBTOR" ON THE WITNESS STAND AND DETERMINE WHERE THE ASSETS ARE. THAT WAS THE WAY THIS CASE WAS PRESENTED TO ME.**

AND, WHAT, THREE YEARS LATER WE MADE FINDINGS THAT THE COURT OF APPEALS SAID RIGHT ON THIS, RIGHT ON THAT, BUT WRONG ON THE CENTRAL THING, WHICH IS WHETHER OR NOT WASHINGTON FRANKLIN PROVED THAT SHE WAS DUE A FEE.

COMMENT AND ANALYSIS: #26 *JUDGE EKANS BOLDLY, AND ADMITTEDLY TO MY SURPRISE, ENDED MY LAWSUIT IN THE IDENTICAL MANNER THAT HE HAD BEGUN HIS RIGGED ADJUDICATIN OF MY CASE ON JANUARY 21, 2011 WITH HIS CHARACTERISTIC GASLIGHTER DECEPTION AND FALSE STATEMENT.*

*JUDGE EKANS FALSELY STATED THAT MY CASE HAD BEEN PRESENTED TO HIM AS A "FAIRLY ROUTINE FRIDAY AFTERNOON HEARING, CALLED AN ORAL EXAMINATOIN WHEN A **JUDGMENT CREDITOR GETS TO PUT A JUDGMENT DEBTOR ON THE WITNESS STAND AND DETERMINE WHERE THE ASSETS ARE. THAT WAS THE WAY THIS CASE WAS PRESENTED TO ME."***

*JUDGE EKANS' STATEMENT WAS INTENTIONALLY FALSE AND UNTRUE IN EVERY RESPECT. **IT WAS JUST A REITERATION OF THE BIG LIE AND A FURTHER ILLUSTRATION OF EKANS' CRAFTINESS AND SOPHISTICATED TRICKERY. I WAS NOT A JUDGMENT CREDITOR AND BRIANNA JONES WAS NOT A JUDGMENT DEBTOR.***

*BUT IF THERE IS ONE THING I KNOW FOR SURE FROM MY LIFETIME WALK WITH THE LORD AND MY KNOWLEDGE OF SCRIPTURE, IT IS THAT, ABOVE ALL ELSE, **THE ADVERSARY IS A LIAR.***

THIS IS A CLASSIC EXAMPLE OF HOW A CORRUPT D.C. COURT JUDGE, NOT ACCOUNTABLE TO ANYONE AND TREATED AND REGARDED AS ABOVE THE LAW, IS ABLE TO SIGNIFICANTLY CONTRIBUTE TO A CRIMINAL ENTERPRISE WHOSE MISSION WAS TO DEFRAUD ME, A TRIAL ATTORNEY AND COURT LITIGANT, OF MILLIONS OF DOLLARS IN ATTORNEY'S FEES.

THE COURT: AND SO WHAT WE'VE DONE HERE   AND I'M LOATHE TO REPEAT, BUT I'M REPEATING   WHAT WE'VE DONE HERE IS TO SAY THAT THIS IS THE OPPORTUNITY, BACK FROM NOVEMBER TO NOW, TO BRING IN SOME EVIDENCE. SHE'S HIRED   I THINK THAT WAS A VERY REPUTABLE LAW FIRM, AS FAR AS I KNOW, AND THEY'VE DONE WHAT THEY CAN DO, AND SHE'S REPRESENTED THAT THEY DID NOT PRESENT TO HER ANY EVIDENCE THAT WOULD ALLOW HER TO GO FORWARD.

THEREFORE, JUDGMENT FOR JONES.

THANK YOU VERY MUCH. THE PARTIES ARE EXCUSED.

MS. WASHINGTON FRANKLIN: YOU HONOR, I DO HAVE ONE QUESTION, IF YOUR HONOR WOULD INDULGE ME. MR. DUNN STATED IN HIS RULE 24 MOTION THAT I HAD A CONTRACT WITH THE SIMPSONS AND I HAD BREACHED THE CONTRACT, AND I'M JUST CURIOUS AS TO WHAT CONTRACT I HAD WITH THE SIMPSONS, BECAUSE I'M NOT AWARE OF IT. I JUST WANT TO COMPLETE THE RECORD IN TERMS OF   I MEAN, I'M JUST CURIOUS AS TO WHEN AND HOW DID I BREACH A CONTRACT AND WHAT CONTRACT?

THE COURT: THAT'S SOMETHING THAT COUNSEL CAN CERTAINLY TALK ABOUT IF YOU WANT TO TALK ABOUT THAT.

MS. WASHINGTON FRANKLIN: I WANTED THAT ON THE RECORD, YOUR HONOR, BECAUSE HE MAKES THAT AS A PART OF ONE OF HIS MAJOR ALLEGATIONS IN HIS MOTION.

THE COURT: THE MOTION WAS DENIED. THE MOTION WAS NOT GRANTED.

MS. WASHINGTON FRANKLIN: ALL RIGHT.

THE COURT: THANK YOU VERY MUCH. THE PARTIES ARE EXCUSED.

MS. WASHINGTON FRANKLIN: THANK YOU, YOUR HONOR.

COMMENT AND ANALYSIS: #27 I LEFT THE COURTHOUSE KNOWING THAT BEGINNING IN DECEMBER 1996, A TEAM OF CORRUPT, MONEY-MAD, CONSCIENCE-FREE AND AMORAL D.C. COURT JUDGES AND FBI AGENTS HAD DESIGNED, EXECUTED AND ORCHESTRATED A CRIMINAL ENTERPRISE TO STRIP ME OF AN ESTIMATED $50 MILLION IN ATTORNEY'S FEES.

I RESOLVED THAT MORNING TO NEVER STOP FIGHTING FOR THE RESTITUTION OF MY FEES. I EXPECTED TO PREVAIL EVEN THOUGH I HAD NO IDEA HOW LONG IT WOULD TAKE OR THE STEPS I WOULD HAVE TO TAKE. QUITTING MY PURSUIT OF JUSTICE WAS NOT AN OPTION. NOTWITHSTANDING JUDGE EKANS' RIGGED DISMISSAL OF MY LAWSUIT, MY EXPECTATION, INSPIRED BY THE ANOINTING OF THE HOLY SPIRIT, WAS TO, WITHOUT FAIL, RECOVER ALL.

(PROCEEDINGS CONCLUDED AT 10:50 A.M.)

CONCLUSION

Because of my intimate relationship and amazing partnership with the Holy Spirit, I am able to acknowledge and cherish my ability to have survived the very dark and excruciatingly painful period in my life and that of my family, a season that I now recognize as the dark night of the soul and that is the subject of *"The Odyssey of Judicial Corruption."* Be that as it may, my expectation of the ultimate triumph of law and justice over absolute power and brute force remains unwavering, fixed and deeply rooted in my fidelity to justice.

More specifically, I could not have survived the traumatic adversary-attempted assassination and annihilation of me and my family, but for being Spirit-led at every twist and turn along the treacherous, mine-filled pathway of my journey towards the fulfillment of my God-given destiny.

Nevertheless, I have found ways to truly thrive, at all times knowing that the best is yet to come, "Because we know that God is causing all things to work together for good for those who love Him, and are the called according to His purpose" (Romans 8:28 KJV).

I am one of untold numbers of District of Columbia residents who have been immeasurably abused by the District of Columbia Court System, through the use and abuse of *absolute judicial discretion* by corrupt, money-mad, conscience-free, amoral and unaccountable D.C. Court Judges in demonic alliance with corrupt, conscience-free, money-mad, amoral and unaccountable FBI Agents whose mantra, policy and practice was "Grab what you can, take what you want, and do what you will. We have the power. We are the law. Period." And they saw to it that our universe was traumatically torn to shreds spiritually, emotionally, physically, economically and socially.

I trust that the sharing of my 20-year-odyssey of D.C. Judicial and FBI egregious injustice found within these pages will encourage others to return to their enemy's camp and, based on the level of their anointing, take back what was stolen from them in peace of mind, economic wealth, moral justice, the constitutional right to life, liberty, and the pursuit of happiness, and in so doing, fulfill their God-given purpose in the earth and mightily serve as legacy role models for their respective families and communities and the betterment of all people and for generations to come.

www.ingramcontent.com/pod-product-compliance
Lightning Source LLC
Chambersburg PA
CBHW052107030426

42335CB00025B/2873